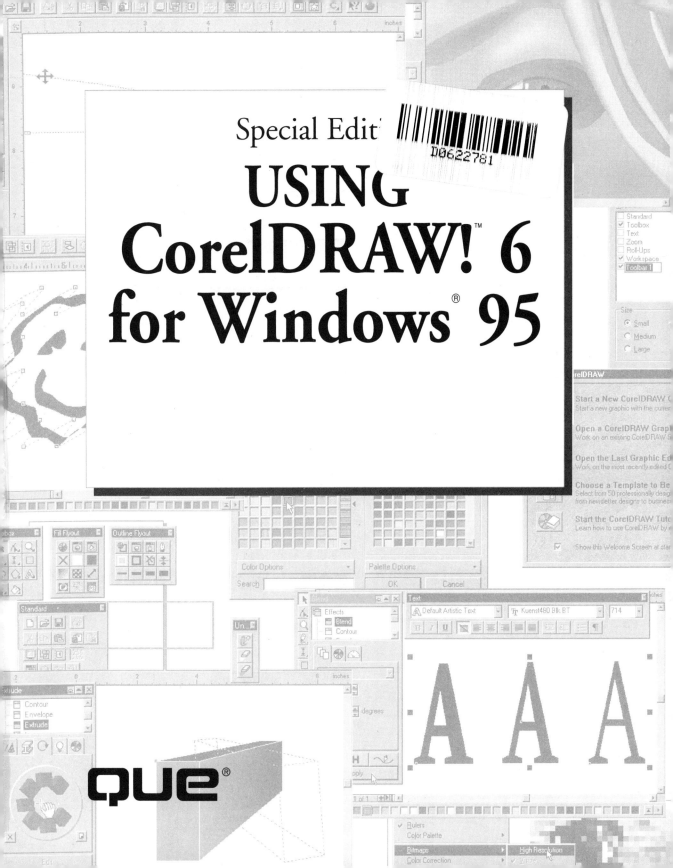

Special Edit⁷

USING
CorelDRAW!™ 6
for Windows® 95

D0622781

que®

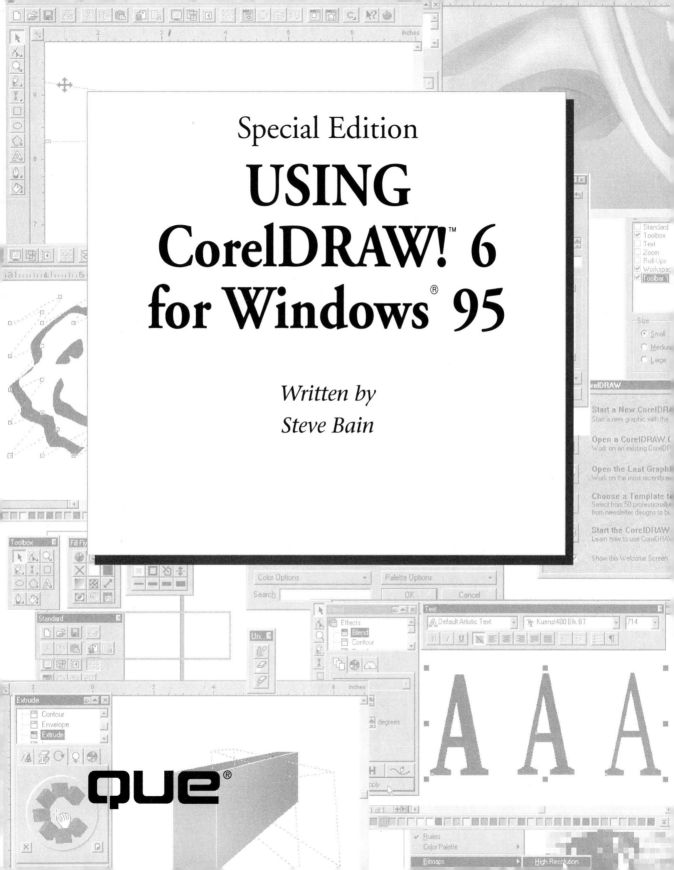

Special Edition

USING
CorelDRAW!™ 6
for Windows® 95

Written by
Steve Bain

que®

Special Edition Using CorelDRAW! 6 for Windows 95

Library of Congress Catalog No.: 95-71436

ISBN: 0-7897-0295-9

97 96   6 5 4 3 2

Interpretation of the printing code: the rightmost double-digit number is the year of the book's printing; the rightmost single-digit number, the number of the book's printing. For example, a printing code of 95-1 shows that the first printing of the book occurred in 1995.

Screen reproductions in this book were created using Collage Plus from Inner Media, Inc., Hollis, NH.

Composed in *Stone Serif* and *MCPdigital* by Que Corporation.

Credits

President
Roland Elgey

Vice President and Publisher
Marie Butler-Knight

Director of Marketing
Lynn E. Zingraf

Editorial Services Director
Elizabeth Keaffaber

Managing Editor
Michael Cunningham

Senior Series Editor
Chris Nelson

Acquistions/Development Editor
Stephanie Gould

Production Editor
Thomas F. Hayes

Editors
Charles K. Bowles II
Julie McNamee
Silvette D. Pope
Christine Prakel
Paige Widder

**Assistant Product
Marketing Manager**
Kim Margolius

Technical Editors
Tony Wasson
John Senez
Kim Connerty
David Farkus

Acquisitions Coordinator
Tracy M. Williams

Operations Coordinator
Patty Brooks

Editorial Assistant
Carmen Phelps

Book Designer
Ruth Harvey

Cover Designer
Dan Armstrong

Production Team
Steve Adams
Claudia Bell
Jason Carr
Juli Cook
Anne Dickerson
Joan Evan
Bryan Flores
Trey Frank
Amy Gornik
George Hanlin
John Hulse
Damon Jordan
Brian Kent-Proffitt
Daryl Kessler
Bob LaRoche
Stephanie Layton
Michelle Lee
Julie Quinn
Kaylene Riemen
Susan Springer
Mike Thomas
Scott Tullis
Kelly Warner
Suzanne Whitmer
Jody York
Karen York

Indexer
Ginny Bess

Dedication

The effort made in the writing of this book is first dedicated in no small part to my son David, who just passed his first birthday. Unfortunately, he will have to wait a decade or so to fully comprehend the subject matter. We can only imagine the wonders of technology children of his age group will see in their lifetimes and use in their careers. The software pioneers of today will become their history legends, and we will have each played some small part in shaping the computer world they will eventually live and work in.

An equal portion of dedication goes to my wife, Wendy, whose enthusiastic encouragement and endless optimism compelled me to complete chapter after chapter of unrelenting detail and discussion. Thanks also goes out to my 71-year-old mother who, during her babysitting shifts, had the habit of hovering around the back of my chair while I was working and muttering "amazing," over and over.

Finally, this book is dedicated to the learning spirit in each of us to conquer our technophobia and explore our own hidden talents as managers, organizers, creators, and survivors.

About the Author

Steve Bain is a freelance illustrator, designer, and writer in Vancouver, Canada. He has been using Corel software since 1990, and has followed in the Corel revolution using many of Corel's software products. Steve was also top-prize winner in Corel's 1993 World Design Contest for technical illustration. Since 1994, Steve has been an active beta version tester for Corel and he serves on Corel's Corporate Advisory Council. In 1995 he served as a finalist judge in Corel's World Design Contest in Ottawa, Canada.

Steve has been involved in the progression of desktop publishing since before its vast popularity began with the Macintosh computer platform. After graduating in commercial art and graphic design, Steve began the first nine years of his career in eastern Canada in 1978, working as a publication designer and technical illustrator. The early part of his career began laboriously hand-illustrating in pen-and-ink for illustration and rendering, and he had the opportunity to use one of the first Macintosh-based illustration and publishing software systems. Steve also claims to be one of those artists who was dragged to the keyboard kicking and screaming because he didn't want to become a computer nerd. He later began his love/hate relationship with DOS and Windows-based PCs and is now amazed at the ease at which this platform dominates the business community.

Following a relocation to the West Coast of Canada in 1987, Steve continued his career by concentrating on graphic design, production, and management in print communications using both Macintosh and Windows publishing systems. In keeping abreast with the technology wave sweeping the communications industry, he recently graduated from an interactive multimedia development and Internet communications school in Canada and continues his focus toward fully digital communication methods regardless of the native platform.

Steve now continues his freelance career writing and illustrating. He has contributed to a small handful of Corel software books. His illustration and writing work can be seen each month in *Corel Magazine*, and occasionally in *The Desktop Journal*.

Acknowledgments

Allow me the liberty of acknowledging the efforts of the software engineers and programmers at Corel Corporation who log largely inhumane workdays to make their software creations fully functional and technically sound. And, failing that, the ability to quickly do it all again a few months later, and once again, the very next year.

I also would like to extend my thanks to Corel's director of sales and marketing Arlen Bartch, who came this close to letting me carry his luggage on one of his trips to Tokyo. To Micheal Bellefeuille and the other staff at Corel product support who spend 90 percent of their days on the road helping people, I thank you. I'd also like to thank Corel's media relations manager Carrie Dopson, for keeping me informed; Corel's product development manager Bill Cullen, for taking the time to answer my probing questions; the entire quality assurance department at Corel; and beta coordinators Kelly Greig and Christel Mack who put up with the evil comments of more than 200 beta testers all summer long.

Allow me also to acknowledge the due diligence of the layout artists, typesetters, designers, illustrators, and prepress professionals who began their careers more than fifteen years ago (as I did) with pre-desktop computers. These professionals have been faced with re-educating themselves to use computers that will someday force a large number of them into early retirement or a completely different career.

Finally, I'd like to acknowledge Stephanie Gould at Que for her direction with this project and Tom Hayes and his group of editors for their attention to detail.

We'd Like to Hear from You!

As part of our continuing effort to produce books of the highest possible quality, Que would like to hear your comments. To stay competitive, we *really* want you, as a computer book reader and user, to let us know what you like or dislike most about this book or other Que products.

You can mail comments, ideas, or suggestions for improving future editions to the address below, or send us a fax at (317) 581-4663. For the online inclined, Macmillan Computer Publishing has a forum on CompuServe (type **GO QUEBOOKS** at any prompt) through which our staff and authors are available for questions and comments. The address of our Internet site is **http://www.mcp.com** (World Wide Web).

In addition to exploring our forum, please feel free to contact me personally to discuss your opinions of this book: I'm **sgould@que.mcp.com** on the Internet.

Thanks in advance—your comments will help us to continue publishing the best books available on computer topics in today's market.

Stephanie Gould
Product Development Specialist
Que Corporation
201 W. 103rd Street
Indianapolis, Indiana 46290
USA

Contents at a Glance

Introduction	1

Building a Solid Foundation   **9**
1 Getting Started   11
2 Managing Your Drawing Files   43
3 Making CorelDRAW! 6 Easy to Use   59
4 What's New in CorelDRAW! 6   85

Creating Text and Drawings   **123**
5 Working with Text   125
6 Working with Objects   177
7 Using Fills and Outlines   229
8 All about Blends   271
9 Arranging, Shaping, and Applying Effects   305
10 Working with Powerlines and Lenses   353
11 Working with Digital Images   387
12 Working with Presets   411
13 Using Color, Wizards, and Applying Color Masks   425
14 Customizing CorelDRAW! 6   459

Sharing and Printing Files   **479**
15 Importing and Exporting Files   481
16 Printing   513

Beyond CorelDRAW!   **553**
17 Creating and Editing Images with PHOTO-PAINT   555
18 Making High-Quality Presentations with Corel PRESENTS   579
19 Creating 3D Illustrations in CorelDREAM 3D   599
20 Using CorelDRAW! 6 Utilities   615

Building a Solid Foundation

Creating Text & Drawings

Sharing & Printing Files

Beyond CorelDRAW!

Appendixes 641

A Glossary of Terms   643

B Keyboard Shortcuts   659

C What's on the *Special Edition
   Using CorelDRAW! 6 For
   Windows 95* CD   669

Index   673

Appendixes

Contents

Introduction   **1**

Why You Should Use This Book 1
Why You Should Use CorelDRAW! 6 2
   CorelDRAW! 6 Is Fully Customizable 3
   Graphic Power for the Everyday User 3
   Drawing Control for the High-End Technical Illustrator 3
   Word-Shaping Utilities for Text Composition 4
How This Book Is Organized 4
Conventions Used in This Book 5

1 Building a Solid Foundation   **9**

1 Getting Started   **11**

Opening Your First New Document 11
Drawing Simple Objects 13
   Creating Your First Line of Text 13
   Creating Your First Simple Objects 15
Getting Help 16
   Using Help Topics 16
   Printing Help Topics 16
   Using Context-Sensitive Help 17
   Using the Tutor Notes 17
   Using the CorelDRAW! 6 Tutorial 17
Selecting, Zooming, and Views 18
   Selecting Multiple Objects 19
   Selecting Guidelines 23
   Selecting and Moving Nodes 24
   Changing Views and Zooming 25
   Editable Preview versus Wireframe 25
   Full-Screen Preview 26
   Preview Selected Only 26
   Using the Zoom Tool 27
   Using the Panning Tool 28
Scaling, Rotating, and Moving Objects 29
   Scaling 29
   Rotating and Skewing 32
   Moving Objects Around 35

Dialog Box Shortcuts 36
    Introduction to Outline and Fill Colors 37
From Here… 40

2 Managing Your Drawing Files   43

Opening New Files 43
Opening Existing Files 44
    Opening Native DRAW 6 Files 44
    Corel's Welcome Screen 46
    Shortcuts to Recently Opened Files 47
    Opening CorelDRAW! Version 3, 4, and 5 Files 48
    Opening Template Files 48
    Drag and Drop Opening 49
    Opening Pattern (.PAT) Files 51
    Opening with Wild Card Characters 51
    File Management from the Open Dialog Box 52
Closing and Saving Files 54
    Saving Backwards: Working with Older Draw Files 54
    Saving Selected Only 55
    Saving Image Header Options 56
    Closing Files 56
Advanced Backup and File-Saving Features 56
    Save All 57
    Saving for Speed or Storage 57
From Here… 57

3 Making CorelDRAW! 6 Easy to Use   59

Page Setting Options 59
    Page Sizes and Other Options 60
    Customizing Labels 62
    Special Purpose Layouts 64
Understanding Tools Options 65
    General Options 66
    Display Options 68
    Advanced Options 71
        File Backup Options 71
        Save and Restore 72
        Pop-Up Menu Customization 72
    Missing Preference Options 72
    Pick Tool Properties 73
    Bezier Tool Options 74
    Edit Resolution 77
Advanced Customizing: Status Bars, Tools, and Toolbars 78
    Toolbar Options 78
    Status Bar Options 80
From Here… 83

4 What's New in CorelDRAW! 6 85

A Fresh New Face for CorelDRAW! 6 85
    Multiple Document Interface (MDI) 86
    Using the Save All Command 86
    Properties for Everything 87
New Toolbox Players 88
    Pick Tool 88
    Shape Tool 89
    Zoom Tools Are Revamped 91
    Dimensioning Tools 94
    Curve, Bezier Tool Properties 95
    Rectangle & Ellipse Tools 96
    Completely New Star & Polygon, Spiral,
        and Grid Tools 97
Significant Menu Differences 99
    The New File Menu 99
    The New Edit Menu 100
    The New View Menu 101
    The New Layout Menu 103
    The New Arrange Menu 107
    The Effects Menu 109
New Text Menu Features 111
    Text Tools 111
    Word-shaping Tools 115
Customization of Toolbars and Menus 116
New Object Properties 117
From Here… 120

II Creating Text and Drawings 123

5 Working with Text 125

Creating and Editing Artistic Text 125
    Creating Artistic Text 126
    Editing Artistic Text 127
Working with Paragraph Text 130
    Creating and Editing Paragraph Text.............................. 131
    Frames and Columns 133
Character Formatting 136
    Formatting Artistic Text 137
    Formatting Paragraph Text 139
Using Indents and Tabs.. 143
Working with Text Styles and Properties 147
Spelling, Grammar, and Proofreading Your Text 148
    Spelling Check 149
    Quick Proofreading 150
    Full Proofreading 151
    Advanced Options 152
    The Rule Manager 153

Using Thesaurus and Type Assist 155
   Thesaurus 155
   Type Assist 156
Other Text Tools: Find and Replace 157
   Using the Replace Command 157
   Using the Change Case Command 158
   Converting Text Objects 158
Fitting and Unfitting Text to a Path 159
Applying Envelopes and Perspective to Text 163
   Applying Envelopes to Artistic Text.............................. 164
   Applying Perspective to Artistic Text 166
   Applying Envelopes to Paragraph Text 168
Setting Text Options 168
Text Display and Editing Controls.. 169
   Formatting 170
Creating Fonts and Symbols 171
   Create a Font 171
   Create a Symbol 173
From Here… 175

6 Working with Objects   177

Creating Curves, Lines, Rectangles, and Ellipses 177
   Creating Curves and Lines 178
   Creating Rectangles 180
   Creating Ellipses 180
Editing Simple Objects: The Shape Tool and the Node
   Edit Roll-Up 181
   Editing Lines and Curves 181
   Editing Rectangles 183
   Editing Ellipses 185
Working with Polygons 186
   Creating Stars 187
   Creating Spirals and Grids 188
   Editing Star, Polygon, Spiral, and Grid Shapes 188
Editing Using the Node Editor 191
Properties.. 194
   Object Properties 194
   Select by Properties Roll-Up 195
Cloning Objects 197
Transforming Objects 199
   Position 199
   Rotation 200
   Scale & Mirror 202
   Size 203
   Skew 203
Using Align and Distribute 204

Grouping and Ungrouping Objects 204
Working with Object Curves 205
  Breaking Apart Curves 205
  Combining Curves 208
Applying Envelopes 211
Working with Extrude 217
  Working with Extrusion Types 217
  About Extrude Vanishing Points 220
  Color Options 221
  Setting Light Sources 222
  Rotating Extrusions 225
  Using the Extrude Wizard 226
From Here… 227

7 Using Fills and Outlines   229

Using the On-screen Color Palette 229
Using Uniform Fills 231
  Color Models 232
  Using Palettes 234
  Palette Commands 235
  Choosing a Palette 235
  Mixing Areas and Custom Colors 235
  Creating Custom Palettes 239
Using Two-Color Bitmap Pattern Fills 242
  Assigning a Two-Color Bitmap Pattern 244
  Creating a Custom Two-Color Bitmap Pattern 245
  Importing Images to Create Two-Color
     Bitmap Patterns 247
Using Vector Pattern Fills 247
Using Full-Color Pattern Fills 249
Using PostScript Fills 250
Using Fountain Fills 250
  About Steps and Edge Pad Options 256
  About Presets 258
Using Texture Fills 258
Using the Special Fill Roll-Up 260
Pen Controls 262
  Applying Line Styles 263
  Corner Controls 264
  Line Cap Controls 265
  Calligraphy 265
  Arrows 266
  Behind Fill and Scale with Image 267
  Outline Flyout 268
  Pen Color 268
  Outlines Roll-Up 269
From Here… 269

8 All about Blends   271

Understanding Blends 271
   The Blend Object Tab...................................... 273
   The Blend Color Tab 273
   The Mapping Options Tab 273
   Other Controls 274
   Before Beginning a Blend 275
Using Blend to Reduce Drawing Time 276
   Blending Simple Objects 279
   Using the Rotation Option 280
   Using the Loop Option 282
   Blending Similar Objects 282
   Assigning a Blend Path 283
   Setting Start and End Objects 286
   Editing a Blend 287
   Copying and Cloning Blends............................ 288
   Splitting a Blend 290
   Building a Compound Blend 292
Weird and Wonderful Blend Effects 295
Blending Text Objects 295
   Creating Blended Highlights............................ 296
   Blending and Powerline 300
From Here… 303

9 Arranging, Shaping, and Applying Effects   305

Shaping Objects 306
   Add Instant 3-D with Extrusions 306
      Using and Creating Extrude Presets....................... 306
      Extrude Depth Tab 308
      Extrude Rotation 309
      Extrude Lighting Controls 311
      Extrude Color Fill Controls 313
   Adding Realism with Perspective 315
   Applying Contours to Objects 318
   The Contour Properties Tab 319
   Contour Color Options Tab 320
Drawing Alignment Tools 322
   Align and Distribute 322
   Using Rulers 326
      Setting Ruler Units 327
      Setting Scale Options 327
   Using Guidelines 329
      Snap to Guidelines Option 333
      Show Snap Locations Marks 333
      Snap to Objects 334

Working with a Drawing Grid 335
Understanding Layers 336
    Creating Layers 337
    Working with Layer Settings 337
Using Weld, Intersection, and Trim 338
    Weld 338
    Trim 341
    Intersection 343
    Object Priorities 346
Using Powerclip Effects 346
From Here… 352

10 Working with Powerlines and Lenses 353

Solving the Mystery of Powerlines 354
Using the Powerline Roll-Up 355
    Pen Options 360
    Ink Options 361
Dissecting Powerlines 367
Creating a Simple Powerline Drawing 370
Editing Powerlines 370
Saving Custom Powerlines 374
Applying Powerlines to Objects 374
Secrets of Lens Effects 374
    Transparency 376
    Magnify 377
    Brighten 377
    Invert 378
    Color Limit 379
    Color Add 379
    Tinted Grayscale 380
    Heat Map 381
    Custom Color Heat Map 382
    Wireframe 383
    Fisheye 383
    Canceling the Lens Effect 384
From Here… 385

11 Working with Digital Images 387

Understanding Bitmaps 388
Defining Bitmap Formats 388
Bitmap Sizes 389
Color and Grayscale Types 392
Resolution 392
Understanding Image Headers 393
Image Sources 395
Displaying Bitmaps 395
    High Resolution Bitmap Display 396
    Visible Bitmap Display 396

Editing Images 397
    Cropping Bitmaps 397
    Rotating and Skewing 400
    Applying Color 402
    Using DRAW!'s AutoTrace Feature 403
    Bitmap Properties 404
    DRAW!'s Text-Wrapping Option 406
Importing Bitmap Images 407
    Using the Import Options 407
From Here… 409

12 Working with Presets   411

Understanding Preset Effects 411
    When Do You Use a Preset? 412
    What Presets Won't Do 413
Working with Presets 413
    The Presets Roll-Up 415
    Planning a Preset Recording 416
    Recording and Saving Presets 417
    Editing Preset Scripts 421
    Merging Two Preset Files 422
    Removing a Preset and Its Effects 423
From Here… 424

13 Using Color, Wizards, and Applying Color Masks 425

Color Calibration Issues 426
Using the CorelDRAW! 6 Color Manager 427
    Creating a Color Profile Using the Color Wizard 428
    Assigning a Color Profile 435
Understanding Color Models 436
    DRAW!'s Color Models Defined 436
Defining Color Palettes 443
    About Pantone Spot and Process Color Palettes 445
    About the Focoltone Color System 447
    About the Trumatch Color System 447
    About the SpectraMaster Color Palette 449
    About DIC Color Guides and the TOYO 88
        Color Finder System 449
    Creating a Custom Palette 449
Using Mixers 452
    Working with the Mixing Area Mixer 452
    Working in the Color Blend Mixer 453
    Sampling Colors from Scanned Images 454
From Here… 457

14 Customizing CorelDRAW! 6   **459**

Customizing Toolbars 460
Custom Keyboard Assignments 462
Customizing Menus 465
Customizing Roll-Ups 468
     Left- and Right-Align Roll-Up Controls 468
     Grouping Roll-Ups Together 469
     Breaking Apart a Roll-Up 470
     Naming a New Roll-Up Group 471
Customizing the Color Palette 471
Using Task Progress 472
More Customizing Tips 474
From Here… 478

III Sharing and Printing Files   **479**

15 Importing and Exporting Files   **481**

The Potential of Importing and Exporting 482
All about Importing 482
     The Import Dilemma: Which Filter? 483
     Corel's Import Filter Collection 485
Common Import Filters Explained 491
     AutoCAD Filters 491
     EPS File Formats 493
     Bitmap Filters 494
     Plotter Formats 494
     PhotoCD 494
Mastering DRAW!'s Export Filters 495
     Frequently Used Exporting Formats 496
     Bitmap Formats 498
     Encapsulated PostScript Formats 499
     Exporting to SCODL Format 500
     Using AutoCAD Formats 501
     Using JPEG Compression 502
         Using HPGL and Plotter Formats 503
         Exporting Fonts 505
         Exporting to Macintosh PICT 506
Object Linking and Embedding 506
     Using the Clipboard 508
     CorelDRAW! 6's Drag-and-Drop Functions 509
From Here… 511

16 Printing 513

Preparing to Print 513
Determining what Your Printing Company Needs 516
Converting Fonts to Curves 516
Deciding Whether to Trap 517
Using the Print Command 517
Setting Printer Properties 519
Paper 520
Graphics 520
Device Options 521
PostScript 521
Setting Print Options 521
Reviewing the Preview Window Controls 522
Viewing the Print Preview Window 523
Using Printer Styles 525
Choosing Printer's Marks 526
Using the Layout Tab 527
Using the Separations Tab 529
Using the Options Tab 533
Print Options, Options Tab, and Special Settings... 534
PostScript Preferences 537
Viewing the CORELPRN Settings 539
Using Print Merge 540
Working with Service Bureaus 543
Reviewing Service Bureau Terminology 544
Understanding Imagesetters 549
Types of Digital Imagesetters 549
Imaging Output Material 550
Preparing a Print File 550
From Here… 552

IV Beyond CorelDRAW! 553

17 Creating and Editing Images with PHOTO-PAINT 555

Taking a Glance at PHOTO-PAINT 556
Creating and Editing an Image 556
Using PHOTO-PAINT's Tools and Controls 558
Using Toolbox Tools 559
Using Roll-Ups in PHOTO-PAINT 565
Reviewing PHOTO-PAINT Toolbars 568
Understanding the Gallery of Filter Effects 569
2D Effects 569
3D Effects 570
Adjust 570

Artistic 571

Blur 572

Color Adjust 572

Transform 573

Noise 574

Render 574

Sharpen 575

Working with Masks 575

From Here... 578

18 Making High-Quality Presentations with Corel PRESENTS   579

Using PRESENTS 6 Views and Tools 580

Creating Presentations 582

Getting Started Using Wizards 582

Typing Text into Outline View 583

Setting the Scene in Background View 584

Adding a Chart or Map to Your Slide 586

Working with Animation Tools 588

Using Audience Handouts and Speaker Notes 589

Organizing Your Presentation in Slide Sorter 590

Adding Sound and Video 591

Using Special Effects 591

Running the Presentation 593

Controlling Time 593

Using the PRESENTS 6 Runtime Player 595

Using the Annotation Feature 596

From Here... 597

19 Creating 3D Illustrations in CorelDREAM 3D   599

Understanding DREAM's Three-Dimensional Concept 600

Using DREAM's Windows and Tools 601

Working with Windows in DREAM 3D 601

Using the Perspective Toolbox 604

Using the Free Form Modeler Toolbox 607

Using DREAM's 3D Clip Art 608

Understanding Rendering 609

Setting Size Options 610

Setting File Format Options 611

Setting Options 612

Importing into DREAM 3D 612

From Here... 614

20 Using CorelDRAW! 6 Utilities   **615**

Using Corel MOTION 3D 615
    MOTION 3D's Animation Concept 616
    Working with MOTION 3D Tools and Windows 616
    Creating a Flying Object Movie 619
    Creating a MOTION 3D Using Stagehands 622
Using Multimedia Manager 625
    What Is Multimedia? 625
    Multimedia Manager's Hierarchy Concept 626
Using Corel CAPTURE 6 626
    Activation 628
    Source 630
    Destination 632
    Image 634
    File 635
    Preferences 638
From Here… 639

V Appendixes   **641**

A Glossary of Terms   **643**

A 643
B 643
C 644
D 645
E 646
F 647
G 648
H 648
I 649
J 650
K 650
L 650
M 651
N 651
O 652
P 652
R 653
S 654
T 656
U 657
V 657
W 657

B Keyboard Shortcuts **659**

General Keyboard Conventions 659
CorelDRAW! 6 Keyboard Shortcuts 660
Hidden Interface Controls 666

C What's on the *Special Edition Using CorelDRAW! 6 for Windows 95* CD **669**

Using the Royalty-Free Images 669
Corel Magazine Sampler 671
Ray Dream Gallery 672
CorelDRAW! 6 Working Model 672

Index **673**

Introduction

Canadian-based Corel began in 1985 as the little company that could and in just over ten years has become the little company that did. CorelDRAW! software sales have outstripped all graphics software competition on the PC platform. Previous versions of CorelDRAW! are available in seventeen languages and are marketed and distributed worldwide. Corel ships its products to more than 60 countries by way of a network of over 150 distributors.

Corel estimates it has captured more than 85 percent of the market share and has won more than 200 international awards from major trade magazines. With the release of CorelDRAW! 6, these figures should continue to climb.

Why You Should Use This Book

This book has been written for the intermediate-to-advanced user in non-technical, everyday language. A special effort has been made to focus on the realistic use of features in the program by the average, everyday user, but also provides coverage for the concerns of the professional electronic artist.

Whether you are just using CorelDRAW! for fancy text headlines, or taking it to its limits with graphic design, or full-blown illustration work, this book will provide you with a realistic view of the capabilities of tools and functions of the program, which you will quickly find out can occasionally be complex and involved. This book will serve as a guide through the hordes of new features that have been piled into CorelDRAW! 6 as well as provide comprehensive instructions on how to use the carryover tools from previous versions of the program.

This book will be a necessary part of the CorelDRAW! toolkit for the following users:

- *Technical illustrators*, who demand the most out of their software and require the greatest degree of control over their digital drawing tools and drawing objects

- *Multimedia artists*, who use digital everything to fill the red-hot graphic needs for such things as home pages on the Internet, electronic-multimedia presentations, and interactive information kiosks

- *Electronic artists*, whose needs range from creating simple logos for handouts and flyers, to full-color brochures

- *Digital publishers*, who know that CorelDRAW! has the capability of talking to nearly any file format and would like the inside reference

- *CorelDRAW! upgraders*, who have been using version 3, 4, or 5 for years and need a comprehensive reference to the new features in CorelDRAW! 6 when they faithfully upgrade

- *Service bureau operators*, who are new to CorelDRAW! and need a reference manual about CorelDRAW! 6 and would like a better understanding of their rapidly growing client base of CorelDRAW! users

- *CorelDRAW! 6 service bureau users*, who send native CorelDRAW! files out for high-resolution imagesetter output and need to know exactly how to use the latest printing features built into CorelDRAW!'s print engine

Why You Should Use CorelDRAW! 6

There are many reasons that CorelDRAW! 6 is much richer in features than previous versions of the program, beginning with the fact that CorelDRAW! 6 was designed to reap the benefits of Microsoft's new 32-bit Windows 95 operating environment. This environment leaves DRAW! with the capability of support for long file names, multi-threading, multi-tasking, and a multiple-document interface (MDI).

CorelDRAW! 6 features extended right mouse button support, which provides easy access to user settings, preferences, and property sheets. Additional features include e-mail and fax support for Windows 95 accessory applications, automated installation, and new uninstall capabililities.

CorelDRAW! 6 pays special attention to color and calibration by featuring an easy-to-use Color Wizard that guides you through the color system setup and developing a custom color profile for the various color systems you may be using.

CorelDRAW! features compatibility with many other applications by including more than 80 importing and exporting filters for standard and non-standard vector, bitmap, and text formats.

CorelDRAW! 6 Is Fully Customizable

CorelDRAW! 6 features controls to display tool properties, tool settings, toolbars, and menu bars to suit the way you use the program in your everyday work. Further and more complex customization is available through setting object and text styles, custom toolbars, hotkey combinations, effects presets, printing presets, and menu bars. By effectively using the elaborate customization features in CorelDRAW! 6, you may increase your overall productivity.

Graphic Power for the Everyday User

The strongest trait for CorelDRAW! has long been ease-of-use by making drawing and graphic design more accessible for the novice user. As an occasional electronic artist doing daily business work, CorelDRAW! 6 will help you:

- Add basic effects to simple shapes to enhance their graphic appeal

- Get quick technical assistance through the elaborate Help features, context-sensitive help, and bubble-hints for nearly all interface parts, features, options, and functions

- Create and save text and object styles to quickly apply a multitude of attributes

- Capitalize on the speed and power of your system by using the Presets for effect, and object for quickly creating dazzling effects

- Access the more than 25,000 clip art images, 1,000 TrueType and Type 1 fonts, 260 video clips, and other multimedia samples available for you to use

Drawing Control for the High-End Technical Illustrator

The demanding work of technical renderers and illustrators requires that CorelDRAW! be flexible and adaptable, and have a high degree of accuracy.

- Customizable scale and grid options for the professional renderer

- Add basic effects to simple shapes to enhance their graphic appeal

- Quick effects through presets for the technical illustrator

- Accuracy to 0.10 microns

- Superior printing controls for offset reproduction

- Layout tools for the Desktop Publisher such as columns, multiple pages, and text wrap functions

Word-Shaping Utilities for Text Composition

CorelDRAW! 6 contains all the tools necessary for composing the content of your work including built-in type assist, thesaurus, and proof-reading utilities. DRAW! 6 also features full text formatting including text styles, automatic customizable bullets, tabs, and indent tools.

How This Book Is Organized

CorelDRAW! 6 is loaded with features and the occasional complex control set. It can be straightforward and easy to learn if approached correctly. This book is organized to help you learn CorelDRAW! 6 quickly and efficiently.

 If you are familiar with CorelDRAW! 6, you should scan the table of contents for new features and look through the book for pages marked with the "new for version 6" icon that marks the new features. Many of the CorelDRAW! 6 commands have been moved so that they are more accessible to the average user and if you are an upgrader, you may not readily find your favorite commands.

This book also contains design and illustration ideas for the novice user or to get you started thinking about new ways in which you can apply what you have learned in the chapters. You also will find a sixteen-page color insert that illustrates specific color-oriented information including color-trapping techniques, color filter effects from Photo-PAINT, and color model theories.

Special Edition Using CorelDRAW! 6 for Windows 95 is organized into the following parts:

Part I: Building a Solid Foundation

This part enables you to build a sound foundation for getting started by learning the tools, managing files, and making CorelDRAW! easy to use.

Part II: Creating Text and Drawings

Chapters 5 through 14 dig deep into the tool capabilities including the use of text and object controls, shaping and effects, and working with color.

Part III: Sharing and Printing Files

This part takes a close look at the multiple document interface and advanced considerations such as learning DRAW!'s new toolbar, hotkey, and menu customization capabilities. This section also takes a thorough journey into the world of Corel's powerful print engine with concentration on using high-end imagesetters.

Part IV: Beyond CorelDRAW!

This part takes a look at the other modules included in the CorelDRAW! 6 suite, including Corel PHOTO-PAINT 6, Corel PRESENTS 6, and Corel DREAM, with a focus on quickly getting started and using these feature-rich programs. It also provides an understanding of the included utilities that support CorelDRAW! 6 such as Corel Motion 3D, Corel CAPTURE, Corel MULTIMEDIA MANAGER, Corel OCR-TRACE, Corel SCRIPT, and Corel DIA-LOGUE EDITOR.

Part V: Appendixes

The appendixes in this book include a glossary of CorelDRAW! terms, a listing of keyboard shortcuts, and a section explaining what's on the CD.

Conventions Used in This Book

Conventions used in this book have been established to help you learn how to use the program quickly and easily. As much as possible, the conventions correspond with those used in the CorelDRAW! 6 documentation.

Two different types of key combinations are used with this program. For combinations joined with a comma (Alt, F), you press and release the first key and then press and release the second key. If a combination is joined with a plus sign (Alt+F), you press and hold the first key while you press the second key.

Que has over a decade of experience writing and developing the most successful computer books available. With that experience, we've learned what special features help readers the most. Look for these special features throughout the book to enhance your learning experience.

Chapter Roadmaps

Near the beginning of each chapter is a list of topics to be covered in the chapter. This list serves as a roadmap to the chapter so you can tell at a glance what is covered. It also provides a useful outline of the key topics you'll be reading about.

Notes

Notes present interesting or useful information that isn't necessarily essential to the discourse. This secondary track of information enhances your understanding of Windows, but you can safely skip notes and not be in danger of missing crucial information. Notes look like this:

Note

Turning off the Automatically Center New Powerclip Contents feature may cause objects to seemingly disappear when using DRAW!'s Powerclip Place Inside Container command. The object that has been placed inside the container object may disappear if it isn't already overlapping the container object. It will only be visible if it is already overlapping. To view the contents object, you must use the Edit Contents command also found in Powerclip under the Effects menu. Then you may reposition the container object to overlap the contents object and become visible.

Tips

Tips present short advice on quick or often overlooked procedures. These include shortcuts that save you time. A tip looks likes this:

Tip

If you select Large Status Bar from the Status Bar pop-up menu, DRAW! will allow two horizontal rows of regions. If you also set your Number of Regions to the maximum of 6 you may set up to twelve regions to display. The Large Color Swatch actually occupies two regions, so it is only available when Large Status Bar is displayed.

Cautions

Cautions serve to warn you about potential problems that a procedure may cause, unexpected results, and mistakes to avoid. Cautions look like this:

Caution

Displaying all or many toolbars at one time significantly reduces the amount of available RAM on your system. One indication of this will be Windows 95 Warning Messages appearing on your screen. If your system has a limited amount of RAM, try opening only the toolbars you use the most frequently. If you are unsure of your available system resources, be sure to save often. It's usually much easier and quicker to save often than it is to start your work over again.

Troubleshooting

No matter how carefully you follow the steps in the book, you eventually come across something that just doesn't work the way you think it should. Troubleshooting sections anticipate these common errors or hidden pitfalls and present solutions. A troubleshooting section looks like this:

Troubleshooting

I have a printer that uses its own color accuracy formula. Every time I print from CorelDRAW! 6, the colors look terrible! Why?

If your printer has its own proprietary color management system built in, you must disable it. If the printer is using a different color management system than CorelDRAW!, it may cause the two profiles to conflict with each other and result in inaccurate results.

Cross References

Throughout the book in the margins, you see references to other sections and pages in the book, like the one next to this paragraph. These cross references point you to related topics and discussions in other parts of the book.

▶ See "Understanding Color Models," p. 436

In addition to all these special features, there are several conventions used in this book to make it easier to read and understand. These conventions include the following:

Underlined Hotkeys or Mnemonics

Hotkeys in this book appear underlined, like they appear on-screen. For example, the F in File is a hotkey, or shortcut for opening the File menu. In Windows, many menus, commands, buttons, and other options have these hotkeys. To use a hotkey shortcut, press Alt and the key for the underlined character. For instance, to choose the Properties button, press Alt and then R.

Shortcut Key Combinations

In this book, shortcut key combinations are joined with plus signs (+). For example, Ctrl+V means hold down the Ctrl key, press the V key, and then release both keys (Ctrl+V is a shortcut for the Paste command).

Menu Commands

Instructions for choosing menu commands have this form:

> Choose File, New.

This example means open the File menu and select New, which in this case opens a new file.

This book also has the following typeface enhancements to indicate special text, as indicated in the following table.

Typeface	Description
Italic	Italics are used to indicate new terms and variables in commands or addresses
Boldface	Bold is used to indicate text you type, and Internet addresses and other locators in the online world
`Computer type`	This typeface is used for on-screen messages and commands (such as DOS copy or UNIX commands)
MYFILE.DOC	File names and directories are set in all caps to distinguish them from regular text, as in MYFILE.DOC

Part I

Building a Solid Foundation

1   Getting Started

2   Managing Your Drawing Files

3   Making CorelDRAW! 6 Easy to Use

4   What's New in CorelDRAW! 6

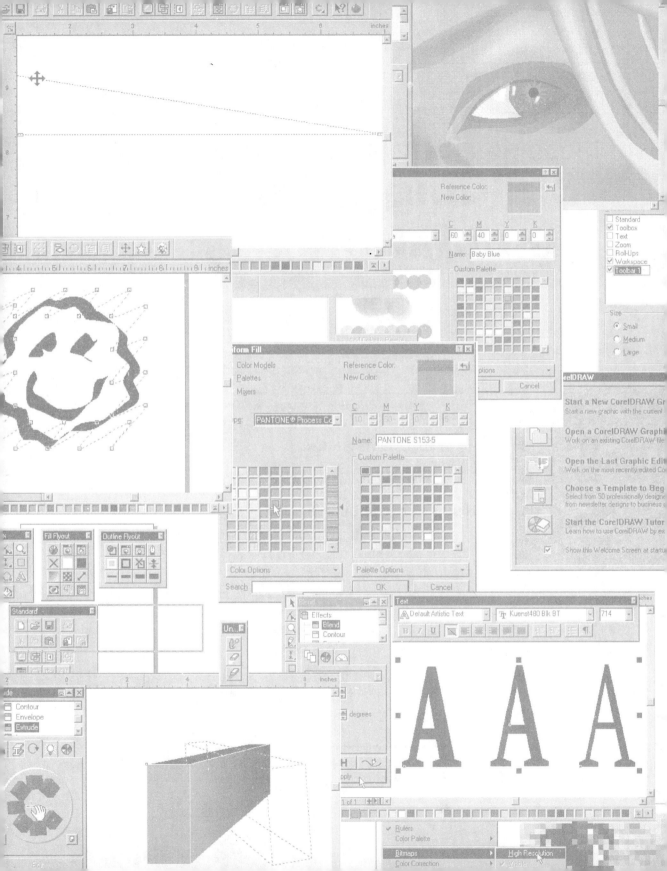

Chapter 1

Getting Started

CorelDRAW! 6 is the flagship program of all the Corel 6 suite of applications. If you are just about to begin your journey exploring Corel's arsenal of programs this is perhaps the best place to start. For some, it may be the only Corel program they ever use. CorelDRAW! 6 is an extremely powerful graphics application capable of fulfilling the needs of beginners and professionals alike. DRAW! 6's features and toolsets measure among the best and most popular in the PC software industry and, some would say, it is the leading software in graphics publishing.

Whether you're intending on using DRAW! 6 for quick, simple drawing and layout work or professional-quality illustrations (or everything in between) you'll find it's a robust, feature-rich drawing program that seems to get more useful with each project you tackle.

The first four chapters of this book offer an introduction to CorelDRAW! and its rich features. If you are familiar with CorelDRAW!, then jump to Chapter 4 to learn what's new in CorelDRAW! 6.

In this chapter, you learn how to

- Open your first file

- Work with menus, status bars, toolbars, and roll-ups

- Use online help, pop-up help, and DRAW!'s tutorial

Opening Your First New Document

When you open CorelDRAW! 6 for the first time you'll likely see a blank, untitled page that DRAW! automatically opens on your behalf (see fig. 1.1) or you may see the CorelDRAW! welcome screen. At the top of the screen, just below the main menu bars, you'll see DRAW!'s Standard toolbar, and in the upper corner you'll notice the Toolbox, the bottom of the screen will display a color palette, and your document window will be surrounded by a ruler bar. DRAW! opens all of these features by default.

Fig. 1.1
Viewing the
CorelDRAW! 6
screen, opened
to an untitled
document.

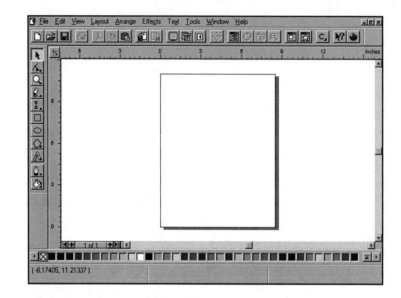

If, for some reason, you don't see an untitled document (see fig. 1.2) you may see a blank gray screen and all but a few of the icons on the top and on the left grayed out and unavailable, and just three menus displayed (File, View, and Help). If this is the case then you have a number of options:

- Open a new file by choosing File, New and Document

- Use the shortcut Control+N

- Press down the right mouse button on the blank gray area once and select New from the menu that appears;

- Click the New Document Button in the Standard toolbar.

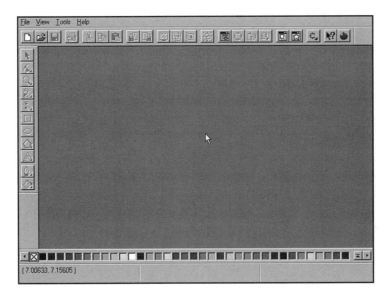

Fig. 1.2
If you see this type of condition, CorelDRAW! 6 is indicating there are no documents currently opened.

Drawing Simple Objects

If you are a new CorelDRAW! user, you may be interested in creating some text or simple objects immediately. If you are trying to decide if CorelDRAW! 6 is all it's cracked up to be, here you'll see some of the ease of use of the program.

Creating Your First Line of Text

To create a simple line of text, follow these steps:

1. Click the Artistic Text tool in the Main toolbar. Your cursor will change to a cross-hair type cursor.

2. With the artistic text cursor as your tool, click a text entry point on your page using the left mouse button, and type a few choice words of wisdom.

3. Once you have finished typing, select the Pick tool from the toolbar to complete creation of the text.

4. If your text isn't quite the correct size on your page, use the Pick tool to grab and drag any of the corner handles to resize the text (see fig. 1.3). Release the mouse button when your text is at the correct size.

Fig. 1.3
To resize your first
line of text, use
the Pick tool to
grab and drag the
corner handles.

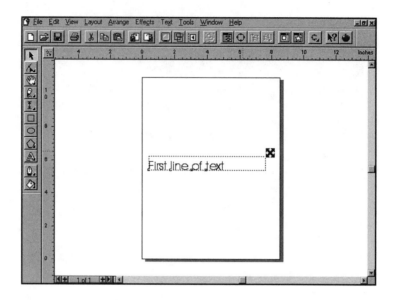

5. To change the font or character, choose Text, Character (Ctrl+T) to
display the Character Attributes dialog box (see fig. 1.4). Text formatting is covered in more detail in Chapter 5, "Working with Text."

Fig. 1.4
Change anything
you wish about
your new text
using the Charac-
ter Attributes
dialog box
controls.

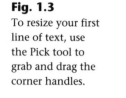

Creating Your First Simple Objects

CorelDRAW! 6 is an extremely powerful drawing package, but that shouldn't prevent you from creating even the simplest of objects; all that power is probably one of the main reasons you became interested in a graphics drawing program in the first place.

To create a simple object, follow these steps:

1. Select the Rectangle tool from the main toolbar. Your cursor will change to a cross-hair type cursor.

2. With the Rectangle cursor as your tool, click and diagonally drag using the left mouse button. A solid-lined box will appear, representing your new rectangle. Release the mouse button when your rectangle is at the size you desire (see fig. 1.5).

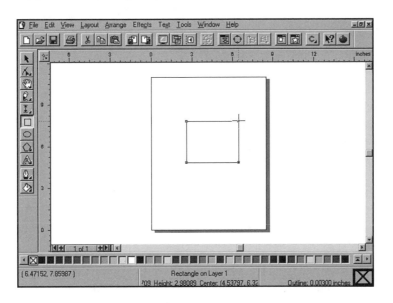

Fig. 1.5
Draw your first rectangle using the Rectangle tool and diagonally click-dragging.

3. To proportionately resize your rectangle, grab and drag any of the corner handles. To change either the width or height, grab and drag any of the side handles (see fig. 1.6).

Fig. 1.6
Resizing your
rectangle propor-
tionately.

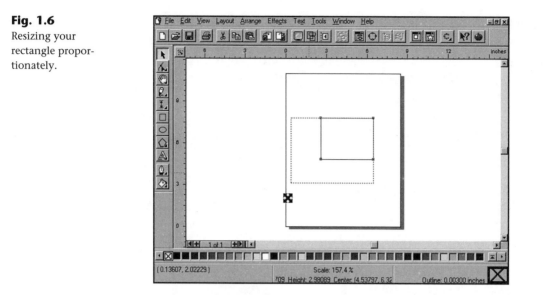

Getting Help

In CorelDRAW! 6, there are a number of ways to get help on either tool
definitions, procedures, or technical notes. You may also use the context-
sensitive help, or the What's This command at the bottom of every right
mouse-click pop-up menu.

Using Help Topics

For getting help on generic definitions and exact procedures, choose Help,
Help Topics (Ctrl+F1) to access the Help Topics: CorelDRAW! Help dialog box
(see fig. 1.7).

The CorelDRAW! Help dialog box is divided into three tabbed areas: Contents, Index, and Find. Selecting Help, Help Topics will take you directly to
the Index tab where you may keyboard any topic you require assistance on
and select the Display button to see either a more narrow list of choices or
the actual topic itself, depending on how extensive your selected topic is.

Printing Help Topics

While in the CorelDRAW! Help dialog box, you have the option of printing
any of the information contained in the specific help page you are viewing
by selecting the Print button at the bottom of the dialog box.

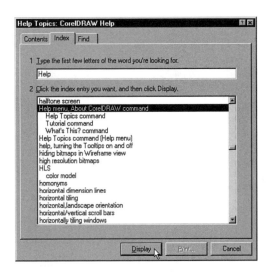

Fig. 1.7
Getting help using
the Help, Help
Topics command.

Using Context-Sensitive Help

Context-sensitive help can be accessed in CorelDRAW! 6 in a number of
ways. Choosing context-sensitive help changes your cursor so that it becomes
a cursor with a question mark beside it. While your cursor is in this state, the
very next thing you click will initiate a dialog box with a definition of that
item. Here are four ways context-sensitive help can be accessed:

- Choosing Help, What's This?

- Pressing Shift+F1

- Choosing the Context Help button in the Standard toolbar

- Choosing What's This? from the bottom of any right mouse click
  pop-up menu

Using the Tutor Notes

To use the CorelDRAW! 6 tutorial, choose Help, Tutor Notes to display the
CorelDRAW! Help Tutor Notes dialog box (see fig. 1.8). The Tutor Notes
give access to a tools-and-procedures-oriented style of help rather than the
definition-focus of the main Help dialog box.

Using the CorelDRAW! 6 Tutorial

To access the CorelDRAW! 6 Tutorial, choose Help, Tutorial to display the
text-based Tutorial Help dialog box (see fig. 1.9).

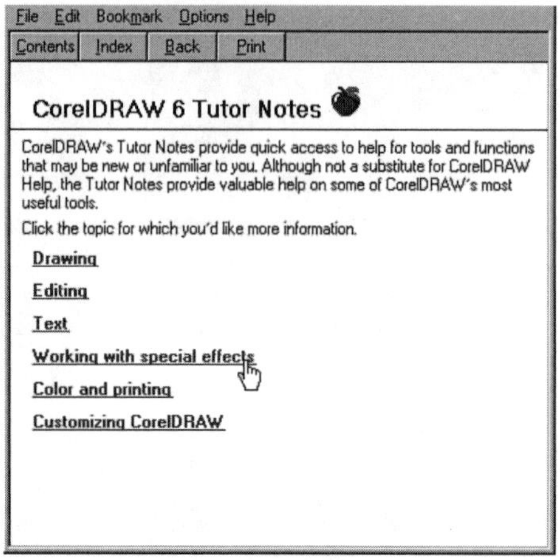

Fig. 1.8

Getting electronic
help using the
CorelDRAW! 6
Tutor Notes.

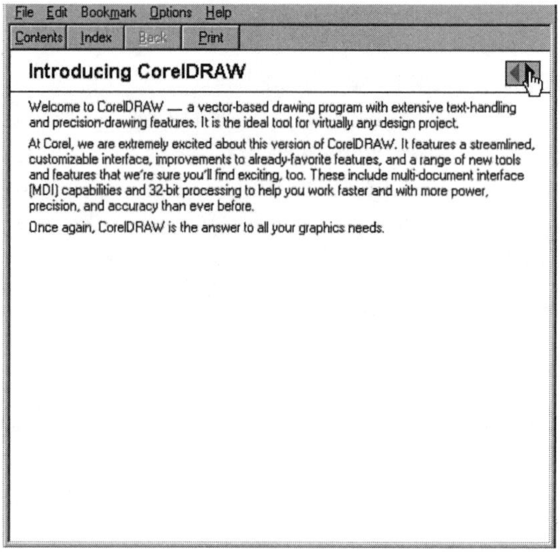

Fig. 1.9

The Tutorial
dialog box con-
trols feature an
option to move
forwards and
backwards
through the pages
in order as you
progress through
the lessons.

Selecting, Zooming, and Views

Selecting, zooming, and view controls are the most important controls you
need to master in order to work effectively in DRAW!. When selecting, there
is no ribbon bar, dialog box, or keyboard shortcut to help you through the
steps or show you the shortcuts you should be aware of.

The Pick tool is your main selection tool. To select an object or objects click this tool and then click the object. You'll notice the object is highlighted by eight black squares or *handles*. In figure 1.10 you'll notice a graphic of two business people shaking hands.

Fig. 1.10
No elements are currently selected in this illustration.

Each of the eight handle bars, when grabbed and moved using the Pick tool, perform different actions. When your Pick tool is positioned directly over one of these handles, your cursor changes from a pointer to a small, cross-hair cursor.

Figure 1.11 shows the handles labeled one through eight. When selected and dragged using the mouse, handles labeled two, four, five, and seven will alter the shape of the object horizontally or vertically. Moving the handle toward the center of the selected object will cause it to shrink in the direction moved and moving the handle away from the center will cause it to expand. Selecting handles one, three, six, and eight will cause the object to shrink or expand vertically and horizontally simultaneously.

▶ See "Pick Tool," p. 88

Selecting Multiple Objects

You also may choose objects by *marquee-selecting* them. The term marquee originates from the effect caused by blinking bulbs on those 1960s movie theater signs.

Fig. 1.11

There are eight handle bars associated with any selected object, as illustrated here.

Marquee-selecting is done by positioning the Pick tool pointer in one of four corners (top right, top left, bottom right, or bottom left) and dragging toward the opposite diagonal corner, essentially surrounding the object. When the mouse is released, the object will again be highlighted. If there is more than one object in the area you have defined using the marquee selector, marquee-selecting constrains the selection area to a perfect square. All objects contained inside the area surrounded by the marquee will be selected.

To select additional objects without having to use the marquee method, you also may use the multiple select method, which is done by holding down the shift key and clicking selected objects. DRAW! also tells you how many objects you have selected in the status bar. Once you have finished selecting all of your objects, you also will see the eight handles displayed, only this time they represent a bounding box that surrounds all your objects.

With one or more objects selected, an additional click (without holding the shift key down) will cause the handles to change to double-headed arrows—curved arrows in the corners and straight arrows at the sides (see fig. 1.12). Now you have changed from a selection mode to a rotation mode and DRAW! is waiting for you to rotate the object. To switch back to your original selection mode, just click the object or objects.

I

> **Caution**
>
> Clicking a blank part of your screen (a part that contains no objects) deselects every-thing, and you're back where you started.

> **Tip**
>
> Using the Alt key in combination with the Pick tool to marquee-select multiple ob-jects causes the marquee to select all objects that come in contact with it.

Fig. 1.12
Clicking on an object a second time invokes the rotate and skew controls for the object.

To select all of the objects on your page you may use one of two methods. First, you may use the marquee method to surround all of the objects. Or, you may choose Edit, Select All, which is the easiest method. DRAW! displays exactly how many objects have been selected in the status bar.

While trying to select a single object in an existing drawing, you may inad-vertently discover that it is a grouped object. Collections of objects may be locked together by choosing Arrange, Group (Ctrl+G). In this case you have two options: You may choose to select Ungroup from the same menu

▶ See "Grouping and Ungroup-ing Objects," p. 204

(Ctrl+U) and continue your selection, or you may hold down Ctrl and click the object you want to select. Watch out though, the object is still part of the group and behaves differently from an independent, ungrouped object.

Whether an object is a vector object (an object drawn using lines and curves) or a bitmap object (an object imported into DRAW! in any of the DRAW!-compatible bitmap formats) you may select it using the Pick tool.

Troubleshooting

I'm having trouble selecting objects in my drawing. What can I do to fix this?

- Try toggling your drawing view between Editable Preview and Wireframe view (Shift+F9). It may be easier to select objects in the Editable Preview mode where you can see the assigned colors and fills.

- Make sure that you haven't selected Full Screen Preview by pressing the keyboard shortcut for that function (F9) once to activate it and again to deactivate it.

- Try activating the option Treat All Objects as Filled in the Advanced tab of your Options (Ctrl+J).

- Check to see that your object isn't grouped to any other objects by zooming out to view the entire page and checking the status bar while clicking on the object.

You also may select single items and groups in your drawing by using the Tab key. Each time Tab is pressed, DRAW! moves to the next object or group in the order they were created. Holding down the Shift key while pressing Tab selects objects in the reverse order from which they were created. Holding down Tab continuously cycles through the objects and holding down Tab together with Shift cycles through your drawing objects in reverse order.

You could encounter the situation where you discover cloned objects in a drawing and you would like to select the master clone. A clone is a copy of an object that references a master object somewhere in your drawing. Finding the master object may be quite time-consuming if it weren't for one precious feature found in the pop-up menu. To find the master clone, click a cloned object identified as a clone in the status bar. Now click and hold down the right mouse button on the object and choose Select Master. DRAW! highlights the master object provided it is on the same page as your clone.

Selecting Guidelines

The capability to select guidelines is a new feature for CorelDRAW! 6. Guidelines now feature handles that appear at each end of the guideline. To select the guidelines, click on the handle, then drag the guideline handle to the desired location (see fig. 1.13)

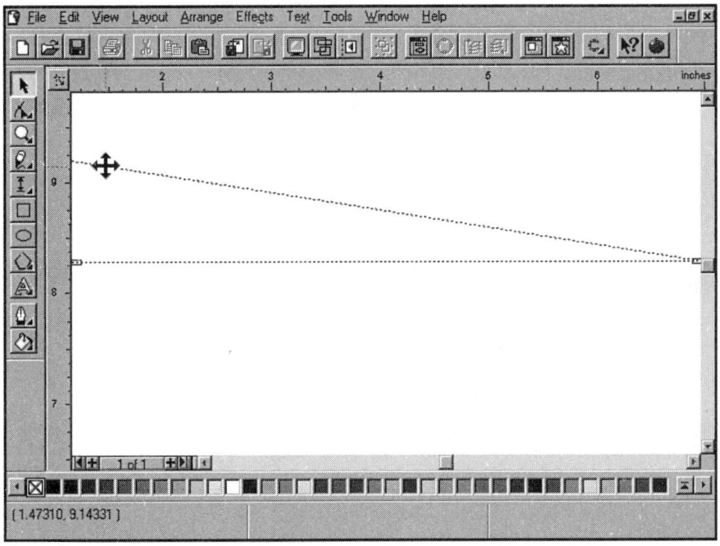

Fig. 1.13
Guidelines may be moved using the mouse by clicking the guideline handle and dragging it.

You may also change the position of a guideline using the Guidelines Setup dialog box (see fig. 1.14). To access the Guidelines Setup dialog box, double-click the guideline with the Pick tool or choose Layout, Guidelines Setup.

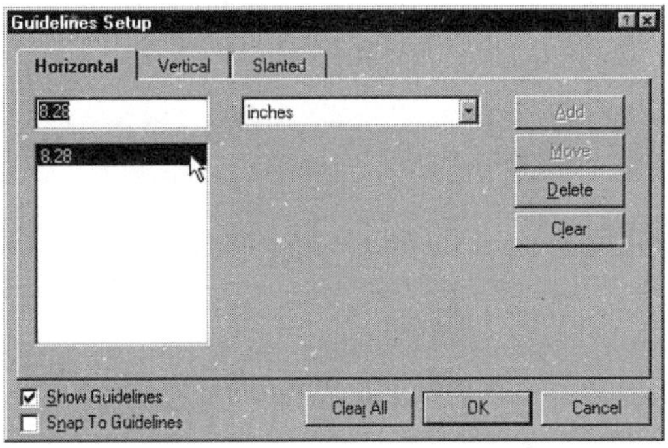

Fig. 1.14
The Guidelines Setup dialog box controls give access to options for setting Horizontal, Vertical, and Slanted guidelines.

Selecting and Moving Nodes

The Pick tool isn't the only tool you can use to make selections. The second item in DRAW!'s Toolbox is called the Shape tool and is used to select nodes on an object or curve. A node controls the characteristics of a line or curve.

Note

Nodes and selection handles operate quite differently from each other. Manipulating nodes changes the composition of the slope and curve of individual lines and curves of an object, while selection handles are used to shape and transform the entire object. For the first-time user, object nodes and selection handles may be easily confused.

Tip

It's a common mistake for new users to confuse the Pick tool with the Shape tool because they look so much alike. If you're having troubles telling the two apart, remember that the Pick tool has straight sides to its shape, and the Shape tool has curves.

With the Shape tool selected (F10), nodes on a curve may be selected using the same conventions as those for the Pick tool. Nodes may be selected by using a single click, multiple shift-clicks, marquee-selection, and tabbing. When the Shape tool is used for selecting and manipulating key points on whole objects such as rectangles, ellipses, polygons, powerlines, and text, it becomes obvious that the Shape tool has seemingly endless capabilities for editing objects. Check out Chapter 6, "Working with Objects," for more information on the Shape tool, along with other tools and ways to edit objects.

Table 1.1   Summary of Selection Shortcuts

Key	Action
Pick tool click	Selects a single object or group of objects
Pick tool click+Shift	Deselects an object
Pick tool dragging	Marquee-selects objects within the area defined by the marquee
Second pointer click	Changes the selection handles to rotation handles
Select All (Ctrl+S)	Selects all of the objects on your page

Key	Action
Shift+click with pointer	Selects multiple objects selectively
Tab key	Selects objects or groups of objects in the order in which they were created
Shift+Tab	Selects objects or groups of objects in the reverse order in which they were created
Ctrl+pointer click	Selects an object within a group
Right mouse pop-up menu, Select Master	Identifies and highlights a master clone from a clone reference

Changing Views and Zooming

A seasoned commercial airline pilot was recently overheard explaining to a cockpit visitor on how technology is reshaping his role in the cockpit: "I pull this backward to make the houses get smaller," he said pointing at the control column, "And I push it forward to make the houses get bigger."

For some, this may be the extent of changing views and zooming from one magnification to another. Moving from one view to another may seem like a fairly simple concept and for the most part it is. But, due to demands of long-time Corel users, a wide selection of controls are now available that include variations on the in and out concept. The capability to use various views and zooming magnifications plays a critical role in helping you to shape your drawings quickly and accurately. From this point on, the term *view* will refer to a method of preview and *zoom view* will refer to magnification of your drawn objects.

Editable Preview versus Wireframe

Perhaps the most useful of views is the Editable Preview view (Shift+F9), which is the default view that DRAW! first opens up to display. What you see in this view is all of your bitmap objects and drawn objects with all the line, fill, transformations, effects, and color attributes applied to them. This view toggles with the Wireframe view (see fig. 1.15) available from the View menu. When the Wireframe selection is unchecked, you will automatically be in Editable Preview (also Shift+F9). The Wireframe view shows only the basic object structure of a drawing without rendering any line or fill colors, effects, or bitmaps. In either view all window controls, ribbon bars, menus, and palettes are visible and all objects are editable.

> **Tip**
>
> The greatest advantage to using Wireframe view is that it takes a fraction of the time to redraw objects on your screen than when using Editable Preview. You won't have the luxury of being able to view all of the fills applied to objects in your drawing or illustration, however you may not always have the *need* to. Setting your view to Wireframe may considerably speed up drawing time for highly complex CorelDRAW! 6 documents.

Fig. 1.15
Working in Wireframe view, illustrated here, may take some getting used to for the first-time user, but it saves considerable drawing time.

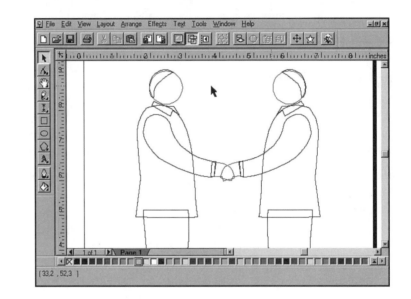

Full-Screen Preview

Selecting Full-Screen Preview (see fig. 1.16) from the View menu (F9) causes all references to the DRAW! window to disappear, including all menu bars, ribbon bars, tools, and palettes. The only image you see will be a full-color, full-screen, uneditable preview of your drawing at whichever magnification view you happen to be in at the time you select this view. To refresh the screen, click once with the pointer anywhere on the screen. To return to your previous view select F9.

Preview Selected Only

Preview Selected Only is invaluable to users who are working in highly complex drawings that contain many objects, fountain fills, or imported bitmaps. You may find that toggling between the Wireframe view and Preview Selected

Only view allows you to not only model the shapes of your objects quickly, but also preview just the objects you are currently working on without having to view the entire drawing.

Fig. 1.16
Full-Screen Preview enables you to view your drawing with all object display characteristics and without the distractions of the CorelDRAW! 6 working window.

Using the Zoom Tool

The Zoom tool, the third Toolbox item from the top in CorelDRAW! 6 has changed significantly as have a few of the tools. It is still accessed by way of a flyout menu from the Toolbox, but no longer includes an individual Zoom Out tool as in the past. Instead, the Zoom tool (resembling a magnifying glass with a bold plus sign in it) works in combination with the right mouse button or by way of the Function keys in order to provide quick functions and less Toolbox menu access.

By selecting the Zoom tool from the toolbox (F2) you can either click once in the center of the area you wish to zoom into for a quick 2X enlargement, or marquee-zoom into objects in any preview by surrounding the area to be magnified holding down the left mouse button. Magnification is limited only by the capabilities of your monitor. Marquee-selecting while holding down the Ctrl key constrains the selected area to a perfect square.

As you zoom in by increments, DRAW! remembers each zoom magnification and view frame you used when you zoomed in. If you use the F3 shortcut to zoom out, DRAW! will step you back out in the reverse order of those previous views.

You also may zoom in and out using the Zoom toolbar. Access the Zoom toolbar by choosing View, Toolbars and selecting Zoom, OK. The Zoom toolbar tools include Zoom In (F2), Zoom Out (F3), Zoom 1:1, Zoom to Selection (Shift+F2), Zoom to All Objects (F4), Zoom to Page (Shift+F4), and Pan One-Shot.

Table 1.2 Summary of Zoom Shortcuts		
Key		**Action**
⊕	F2	To marquee zoom into a specifically defined or pinpointed area in the drawing window
⊖	F3	To zoom out at the same increments used to zoom in
⊕	Shift+F2	To zoom into a selected object or group of selected objects
⊠	F4	To zoom in or out to fit all objects in your objects in the drawing window
▢	Shift+F4	To zoom in or out to fit the entire page in the drawing window

Using the Panning Tool

The Panning tool, shown in figure 1.17, is new for CorelDRAW! 6 and has a similar function of your CorelDRAW! 6 window scroll bars, enabling you to navigate through your drawing in measured steps. Panning has the added advantage of enabling you to scroll in diagonals in a single step, which the scroll bars can't do. The Panning tool is also much more accurate than using the scroll bars because of the small distances it allows you to step through.

To use the Panning tool, follow these steps:

1. Select the Panning tool from the Toolbox. If it is not currently displayed, click and hold on the Zoom tool until the Zoom tool flyout appears and then select it. Your cursor changes to a hand with a crosshair cursor.

2. Click-drag on your page. Notice that while you drag, a line appears to let you know the distance and angle of the pan.

3. Release the mouse button when the panning line indicates the correct amount of panning. Notice that your screen has scrolled the exact amount of pan that you selected.

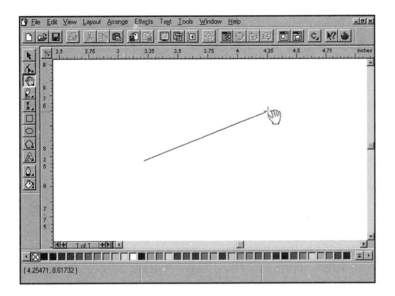

Fig. 1.17
Using the Panning tool to pan through your drawing enables you to move in very small or diagonal steps.

Scaling, Rotating, and Moving Objects

Once you have created your objects, you will likely want to fine-tune them. Using options incorporated into the Pick tool you are able to either scale, transform, or reposition your objects.

Scaling

Scaling objects using the mouse begins by using the Pick tool to either marquee-select or click+select an object or group of objects (see fig. 1.18). After the object is highlighted and the eight handles appear, you may grab onto a handle and drag it to resize the object. Grabbing onto one of the side handles and dragging shrinks or expands the object without changing the scaling in the other direction (see fig. 1.19). For example, if you were to grab and drag the right-middle handle you would be changing the horizontal scaling (known by DRAW! as the Y scale) of the object only. The vertical scaling (known by DRAW! as the X scale) would remain the same and you would have essentially distorted the original object.

Fig. 1.18

Before you may scale an object or collection of objects, you must first select them using the Pick tool to either multiple-select or marquee-select as illustrated here.

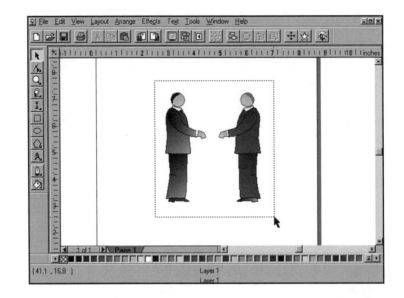

Fig. 1.19

Dragging object handles using the Pick tool enables you to transform proportionately, horizontally, or vertically as illustrated here.

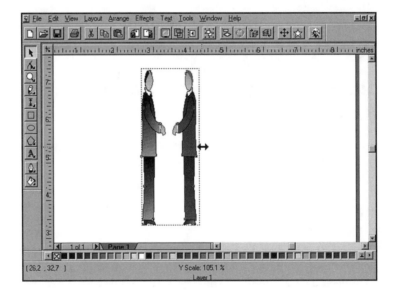

Grabbing and dragging any of the corner handles of an object (see fig. 1.20) will alter both the vertical and horizontal dimensions of the object simultaneously, keeping the original proportions intact. Only the size of the object changes in this case. Holding down the Shift key while dragging on any of the side handles of the object causes it to scale horizontally from the center origin of the object (see fig. 1.21). Holding down the Shift key while dragging on any of the corner handles causes the object to scale proportionately from the center origin.

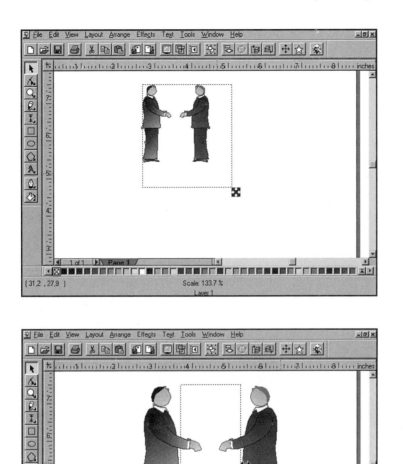

Fig. 1.20
Resizing a group of objects proportionately by click-dragging one of the corner handles with the Pick tool.

Fig. 1.21
By click-dragging on the side handle you are able to resize objects horizontally, as illustrated here. A dotted bounding box line will appear indicating the new size of your objects.

If you watch the status bar while you are dragging a handle, you'll notice that it displays the exact percentage of enlargement or reduction based on calculation changes from the original size. This may be useful if you plan to reduce an object by a certain fixed amount and are skilled enough with the mouse to do it this way. Or, conversely, you may want to quickly find out exactly what percentage of the original size an object must be enlarged or reduced in order to fit a certain space. This would be the quickest way to do that.

Rotating and Skewing

Rotating and skewing is another manipulation method available through dragging objects and uses methods similar to the steps just described. Follow these steps to rotate an object:

1. First you must select an object or group of objects by clicking it once.

2. Click the object again to invoke the rotation handles. Each click will alternate the object or groups between the sizing (or object) handles and rotation handles.

3. Now grab onto one of the corner rotation handles and notice that your cursor changes to an open circle with arrows in it (see fig. 1.22).

4. While still holding down the mouse button, drag the cursor in a circular motion as if drawing an imaginary circle around the center of the object.

5. Release the mouse button and the rotated object is redrawn in its new position.

Fig. 1.22

Rotating an object with an offset center of rotation.

When the rotation and skew handles appear, you'll notice there are four rotation controls in each corner and one extra little handle in the middle resembling a small target. This is known as the center point or rotation origin point. This special handle plays a key role in the rotational behavior of an object. When positioned at the center it feels quite logical to be rotating the object around its center.

But there may be situations where you need to rotate an object on a corner. That's where the rotation origin point comes into play. It moves independently of the other handles. To rotate an object around a corner point follow these steps:

1. Invoke the rotation handles by double-clicking the object.

2. Use the left mouse button to grab and drag the rotation origin handle until it is positioned above one of the corners of your object. If your object has no corners, then position it above any reference point near the outside edge of the object.

3. Grab the rotation handle on the opposite corner (or if not a corner then the opposite side) and watch your cursor change to a circular cursor with arrows.

4. While still holding down the mouse, drag the cursor in a circular motion as if drawing an imaginary circle around the newly positioned origin point.

5. Release the mouse and let the program finish drawing the object in its new location.

If you examine figure 1.23 you'll notice that the angle of rotation is measured by the status bar. If you need an exact rotation degree and are good with the mouse, you could watch this degree measure while rotating to obtain an exact angle. If you hold down the Ctrl key while rotating an object, DRAW! constrains the object to 15 degree increments (the default). You also can set the Constrain Angle in the General tab of the Options dialog box accessed by choosing Tools, Options.

So far, you've learned about the four rotation handles but there are still four other handles left at the sides of the selected object. They are the four skew handles, with double-headed arrows at each end. Skewing distorts the actual shape of an object or group by slanting it (see fig. 1.24). When the skew handles are being moved, your cursor changes to a pair of parallel lines with arrows on each one pointing in opposite directions. To skew an object follow these steps:

1. First select the object by clicking it once, and then invoke the rotation and skew handles by clicking it an additional time using the left mouse button.

2. Use the left mouse button to grab either the left or right skew handle and drag it either up or down.

Fig. 1.23
Watch the status bar while rotating your objects for exact reference to the angle of your rotation action.

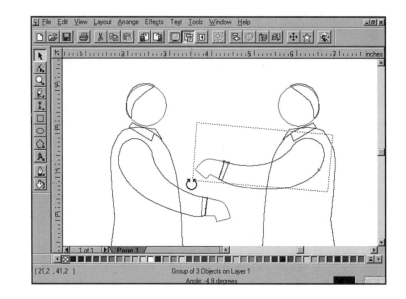

▶ See "Rotation," p. 200

▶ See "Skew," p. 203

3. Notice that your cursor changes to a pair of parallel lines with arrows on each one pointing in opposite directions.

4. Release the mouse and let the program finish drawing the newly slanted object.

Fig. 1.24
Skewing an object using the Pick tool skew controls.

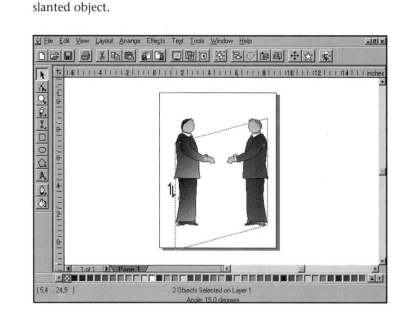

Moving Objects Around

Moving objects from one point to another can be done quickly and easily using the mouse. Clicking once using the left mouse button on an object selects it, while holding and dragging the mouse moves the object until you release the mouse and drop the object. But, what if you want to move the mouse a specific distance? You could stare intently at the status bar as the object moves across the screen and stop when it's in position. Or you could use certain keyboard combinations to make the job a bit easier.

Holding down the Ctrl key while dragging an object constrains it to a straight line either vertically or horizontally. Using the arrow keys to move an object can be effective and productive as well, if your preferences have been set to the proper setting. If you need to move an object a small distance and don't quite trust yourself to use the mouse, you could set your Nudge setting under the General tab of Preferences to that exact amount and use the appropriate arrow key to move the object. In most cases though, the mouse in combination with the Ctrl is extremely effective.

▶ See "Significant Menu Differences," p. 99

Tip

Clicking with the right mouse button while dragging an object makes the object you are dragging a copy and leaves the original in its place.

Moving, Scaling, Mirroring, Rotating, Sizing, and Skewing also can be accomplished using the precision Transform roll-up accessed from the Arrange menu or by selecting one of the keyboard shortcuts in table 1.3.

▶ See "Transforming Objects," p. 199

Table 1.3 Transformation Roll-Up Shortcuts	
Action	**Keyboard Shortcut**
Moving	Alt + F7
Rotating	Alt+F8
Scale and Mirror	Alt+F9
Sizing	Alt+F11
Skew	Alt+F12

Dialog Box Shortcuts

If you're constantly accessing dialog boxes in DRAW! (or any of the Corel programs), you may find it easier to use your keyboard for setting your navigation or selection of some functions and knowing the keyboard equivalent of the mouse may just help. When using any dialog box, study the hidden shortcuts in table 1.4 with an aim toward improving your speed and efficiency.

Table 1.4 Keyboard Shortcuts for Navigating Dialog Boxes	
Keyboard Shortcut	**Dialog Box Function**
Tab	Move to the next dialog box item (such as list box, text box, check box, command button, or group of option buttons)
Shift+Tab	Moves to the previous dialog box item (list box, text box, checkbox, command button, or group of option buttons)
Arrow Keys	Moves and selects within an active group of option buttons
Spacebar	Turns the active check box On or Off or chooses the active command button
Letter Keys	Moves to the next item beginning with that letter in an active list box
Alt+Underlined letter	Selects the item with the corresponding underlined letter
Enter	Chooses the active command button
Esc	Cancels the command and closes the dialog box

Tip

One shortcut not always obvious to newer Corel software users is the capability to change numerical values in dialog boxes by placing the mouse directly between the up and down arrows of a numeric field until your cursor changes to a black bar with two arrows pointing up and down. When this cursor appears, press and hold with your left mouse button and move the mouse either up or down for increasing or decreasing the numerical values respectively. As you move the mouse, the values in the corresponding field change.

Introduction to Outline and Fill Colors

One of the first commands you will want to perform on an object is assigning a fill color to it. For the first-time user, it looks much simpler than it is. Highlighting the object and clicking a color in the color palette at the bottom of the screen is not a complex procedure. You can impress your coworkers by showing off how easy CorelDRAW! 6 is to quickly learn and use. Beyond that the commands tend to get a bit trickier.

What kind of color have you assigned to the object? How do you put a color border around the object? How do you make the border thicker? How do you remove the color completely? All pretty good questions and likely among the first you'll ask.

The first thing you should know about selecting colors directly from the palette displayed at the bottom of your screen is that the left and right mouse buttons control different things. The left mouse button controls the fill color and the right mouse button controls the outline color. With an object selected, clicking any color with the left mouse button turns the fill for the object that color. Clicking any color with the right mouse button turns the outline that color.

There are many different kinds of colors available, and selecting colors depends on how your drawing is going to be reproduced (for the computer screen only, for printing in process or spot color, for exporting into other programs). Assigned colors only appear on-screen if you are viewing your drawing in Editable Preview (Shift+F9) or Full-Screen Preview (F9).

The next thing to be aware of, is the symbol at the far left end of your on-screen color palette (it looks like a black square with a black X inside it). When this symbol is selected using either the left or right mouse button it changes the fill or outline to None, respectively. If you click with both the left and right mouse buttons on this square, and you are viewing your object in either Editable Preview (Shift+F9) or Full-Screen Preview (F9), your object will appear to have become invisible. You likely won't be able to find it or select it again unless you select Wireframe Preview (Shift+F9) to see the outline of the object.

The fact that fill and outline colors are controlled using separate mouse buttons is perhaps a reflection of the entire color-attribute system in DRAW!. Fill colors are set independently of outline colors, and in fact they are treated separately in almost every respect. Each has its own color dialog box, and each has its own flyout controls. As with many of the features in CorelDRAW! 6, color for fills and outlines may be controlled many different ways to the same end.

Starting with the fill controls, the simplest of which is using the on-screen color palette and the left mouse button (see fig. 1.25). This color palette may be navigated left or right by selecting the small arrow buttons at each end of the palette (which can be very easily confused with the scroll bar arrows). By clicking once or pressing down continuously on these arrows using your left mouse button you can scroll the entire palette from one end to the other. You also may choose to display the entire palette as a flyout by selecting the arrow button pointing upward on the far right of the palette.

Fig. 1.25

CorelDRAW! 6's on-screen color palette in the expanded position.

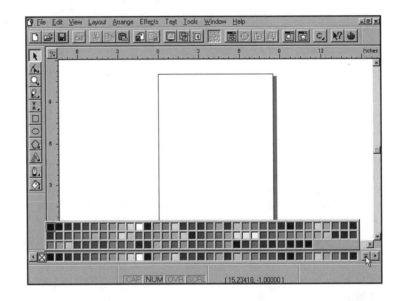

Tip

When navigating through the on-screen color palette using the left- and-right arrow buttons on either side of the palette, clicking down once on an arrow button with the left mouse button moves the palette one color at a time.

Pressing and holding down on the arrow button moves it continuously one color at a time until reaching the end. For speed, try using the right mouse button. Clicking an arrow button with the right mouse button causes the palette to shift over one whole screen's worth of colors, and holding down the right mouse button on the arrow button causes the palette to shift continuously until reaching the end.

The on-screen palette also contains its own pop-up menu that provides access to navigation, color assignment, color definitions, and palette handling including: Set Outline Color and Set Fill Color; Move to Start and Move to End;

Edit Color, Rename Color, and Delete Color; and palette handling commands for New, Open, Save, and Save As.

With an object selected, choose either the Uniform Fill dialog box (Shift+F11) or the Fill roll-up (Shift+F6). Either one of these controls will enable you to set exact colors for your objects (see fig. 1.26). You also may select the Outline Colors dialog box or the Outline roll-up to set color characteristics for the outline of your object (see fig. 1.27).

▶ See "Color Models," p. 232

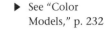

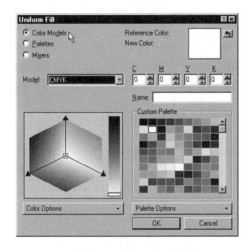

Fig. 1.26
The Fill roll-up and the Uniform Fill dialog box controls enable you to set any uniform color fill available within CorelDRAW! 6.

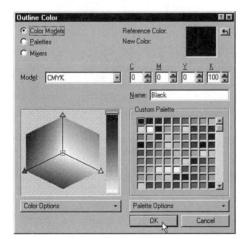

Fig. 1.27
The Pen roll-up and the Outline Color dialog box controls enable you to set any Pen or Outline color available in CorelDRAW! 6.

Tip

For first-time users, a useful habit to develop for quick access to the most commonly used fill and outline controls is to keep the Fill and Outline toolbars within mouse reach (see fig. 1.28).

Fig. 1.28

Keeping the Fill and Outline Color controls on-screen while you are working is a great habit to get into. They take up little screen space and give you nearly full access to color controls.

Note

If there are no objects selected prior to selecting either the Uniform Fill Color or Outline color dialog boxes, a message appears on-screen asking whether you want to assign the new color you are about to define to a Graphic, Artistic Text, or Paragraph Text (see fig. 1.29).

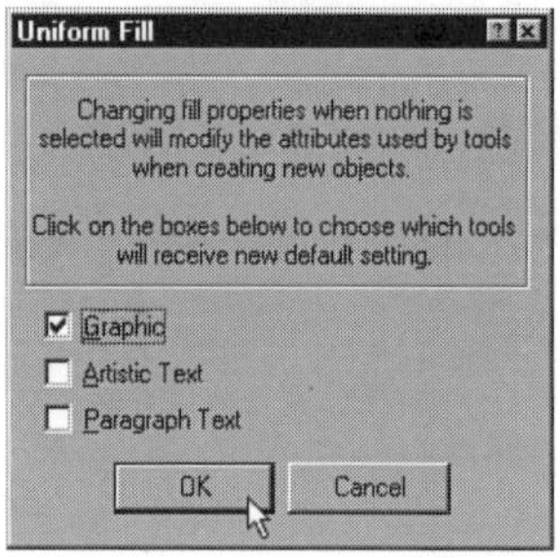

Fig. 1.29

A default attribute dialog box exists for each of the Uniform Fill, Fountain Fill, Outline Color, Outline Pen, and Paragraph Attributes.

From Here...

The thrust of this chapter has been to set a solid understanding of CorelDRAW! 6. Understanding how to use the basic tools before you begin drawing with them is a critical step in remaining efficient. If you study the information contained in this chapter carefully you will gain an excellent understanding of the tools and lay out a very solid learning foundation to using CorelDRAW!.

For related topics discussed in this chapter, see:

- Chapter 6, "Working with Objects."

- Chapter 7, "Using Fills and Outlines."

- Chapter 9,"Arranging, Shaping, and Applying Effects."

Building a Solid Foundation

Chapter 2

Managing Your Drawing Files

The capability to save a file is by far the most important function an application can offer. If you can't save your work for later, what good would the program be to you? Nonetheless, saving your work is all about being organized and orderly. If the first task at hand is to save a file, the second is *how* to save it.

File management operations are a basic, but integral, part of working in CorelDRAW! 6. Learning the Opening, Saving, and Save As commands will bring you closer to becoming more efficient with not just CorelDRAW! 6, but with organizing your files, your work, and possibly your career. The use and re-use of files brings about the potential of performing a task the least number of times as possible, and to no small extent, capitalizing on the real strength of your computer system.

In this chapter, you learn to

- Open, save, and work with CorelDRAW! files and templates

- Set file backup and save preferences

- Save to previous versions of CorelDRAW!

- Use new, open, and save shortcuts

Opening New Files

Before you can do anything at all in CorelDRAW! 6 you must first open a file, and if you haven't yet built up a collection of previously saved files, the file you need to open will be a brand new one. The Corel engineers have made this easy for you by integrating a number of ways for you to do this into the interface.

 First, if you happen to have the Standard toolbar displayed (which displays by default unless you have specified otherwise), you may click the New button. This is the very first button in line on the left of the Standard toolbar, which usually resides directly above your main working window.

Next, if you don't immediately see the Standard toolbar displayed, choose File, New, which displays a menu flyout containing two options: Document and From Template. Choose Document from this flyout menu, and a new document opens up and is assigned the default name Graphic1 until you save it for the first time and give it a specific file name.

To open a new file based on a saved template file, select From Template from the menu flyout. A brand new document will open containing any of the setup parameters built into the template file, but will not contain any objects or text. In this case, CorelDRAW! 6 essentially opens the file format and ignores any of the text or object information in the file. If the template has special type or object styles, columns, or master elements in it, these will be included. The new file will also be named Graphic1 until you first save and name it.

Opening Existing Files

Being able to retrieve files that you (or someone else) previously worked on is another basic, but critical operation. For the expert computer junkie, this may be a bit of review, but for the first-time computer operator, it's one of the first valid questions that needs to be answered.

Opening Native DRAW 6 Files

If you need to open an existing file there are four ways of doing this:

Choose File, Open

Use the keyboard shortcut Ctrl+O

 Press the second button on the Standard toolbar (which looks like an opening folder)

Press and hold down the right mouse button and choose Open from the menu that appears.

The Open Drawing dialog box that appears (see fig. 2.1) on your screen asks the proverbial questions "Where is your file?" and "Which file?" in relation to what you want to open. In the upper left you see Look In:, which displays the folder you are currently being shown in the center of the dialog box.

To the right of Look In: you'll see two buttons—Up One Level (shortcut is your backspace key) and Create New Folder—which represent the basic DOS commands Change Directory and Add New Directory to the directory you currently see. Beside those controls you'll see a pair of adjoining buttons to control file display commands List and Details. Figure 2.1 shows the Details button depressed and a more verbose list of information about file name, type, size, and last modified date. A scroll bar for viewing extended details also appears at the bottom of this text box if needed.

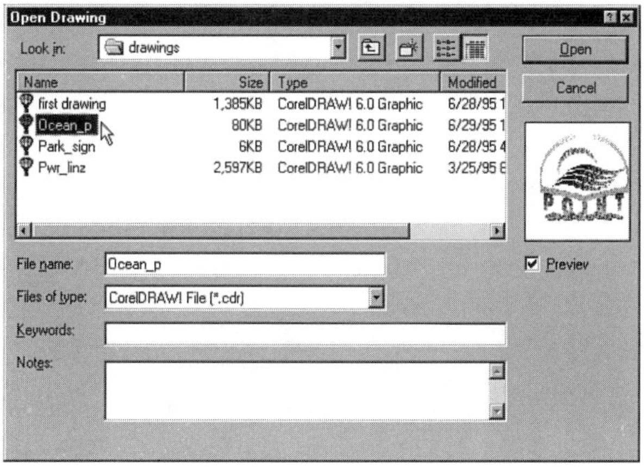

Fig. 2.1
Getting more information about files using the Details button.

The four remaining text boxes in the lower half of the dialog box give options for narrowing your file parameters. The first, File Name, lets you keyboard your file name, or when a file is selected in the main directory using the mouse, the name is automatically entered into this text box. The Files of Type is a drop-down list from which you can specify either a CorelDRAW! file (.CDR), a Pattern file (.PAT), or a CorelDRAW! Template (.CDT). No other file types will be displayed in this window. If your file supports Keywords or Notes, they will be displayed in the remaining text boxes. See "Opening Template Files" later in this chapter for more information on this subject.

A Pattern file (.PAT) is a support file created from within CorelDRAW! that contains bitmap information which can be tiled over a certain defined area. A Template File (.CDT) is a file saved in Corel's template file format.

The last feature you see in the Open Drawing dialog box is the Preview window. Once Preview is activated, it displays a header image (if any exists within the file) after your file is selected and before it is opened. To open the file, either double-click its name in the main file information text box, or click it once and select Open.

A header is a low-resolution image that visually represents the information contained in an electronic file. Header information is usually contained in the preceding part of the data that describes a file.

Tip

If you use the file Details function frequently, you can customize the width of the columns labeled Name, Size, Type, and Modified by click-dragging the seam between the column headings and widening or narrowing them. You will find the file Details button directly to the left of the Open button in the Open Drawing dialog box controls.

Corel's Welcome Screen

The Welcome screen is a new feature for CorelDRAW! 6 and opens automatically when you launch the program (see fig. 2.2).

Fig. 2.2
CorelDRAW! 6's new Welcome Screen greets you when you launch the program.

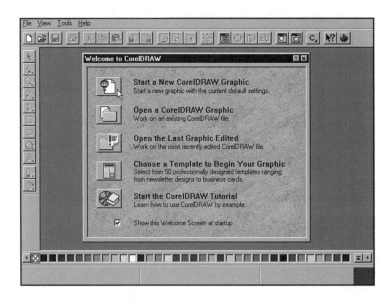

The Welcome screen gives you quick-access buttons for beginning a new file, opening an existing file, opening the last graphic edited, opening a template, or beginning a CorelDRAW! 6 tutorial. An additional option allows you to hide this welcome screen the next time you launch the program. If you wish, you may customize CorelDRAW! 6's launching action by choosing Tools, Options (Control + J) to display the Options dialog box and selecting the General tab. An Application Startup option at the bottom-left of this tab may be set to the same set of actions from the pull-down menu including Welcome Screen, Start a new Document, Open an Existing Document, Open the last Edited Document, Select a Template, or Start Application Tutorial (see fig. 2.3).

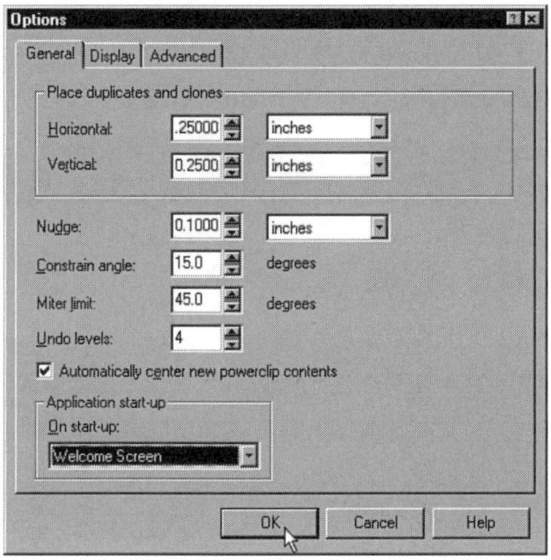

Fig. 2.3
Setting the Application Startup action using the Tools, Options, General tab of the Preferences dialog box.

Shortcuts to Recently Opened Files

One useful shortcut is the ability to open recent files from the File menu. If you have been working on a number of files (or want to see if someone else has been viewing your files) you may want to try selecting File and examining the bottom of the menu. You'll notice a number of file names (not including their paths) preceded by numbers which correspond to the order in which they were last opened. For example, selecting Alt+F+1 automatically opens the last file worked on, and so on. This is a standard Windows-supported feature being engineered into many software programs even back in Windows 3.1. The recent file function will give access to the last four files you have worked on.

> **Note**
>
> If you've been performing some housekeeping duties on your files and have moved any of the files you have been working on to different directories, you have changed their path and the recently opened files shortcut will be unable to locate the file. Don't panic though, your file is still there somewhere, just not where Draw last saw it. If you have really lost the file, try using the tools within the Windows Explorer application to locate it again.

Opening CorelDRAW! Version 3, 4, and 5 Files

To open files created using a previous version of CorelDRAW!, select the open command as you would any Corel 6 created file. CorelDRAW! automatically updates your file to the version 6 format. The new format becomes permanent once the file is saved for the first time using version 6.

> **Troubleshooting**
>
> *Sometimes, when I open earlier file versions of CorelDRAW!, I get a warning about default fonts being used in my files where no fonts even exist.*
>
> This is an idiosyncrasy of older CorelDRAW! files and usually renders no harm to the file or the fonts themselves.

> **Caution**
>
> If you are using more than one version of CorelDRAW! on your system and wish to keep backup versions of your files (always recommended) in the previous version format, the recommended procedure is to save a copy of your older version file to a safe location *before* opening and resaving it in version 6. See "Saving Backwards: Working with Older Draw Files," later in this chapter for information on this subject.

Opening Template Files

CorelDRAW! 6 offers the option to open files already saved as CorelDRAW! templates. There are a number of saved templates included in the Corel60\ Draw\Templates folder, which you can experiment with if you wish, or you may have your own saved templates to work with.

To open a CorelDRAW! 6 template file, follow these steps:

1. Select File, Open, and change the Files of Type option to CorelDRAW! Template (*.CDT) from the pull-down menu (see fig. 2.4).

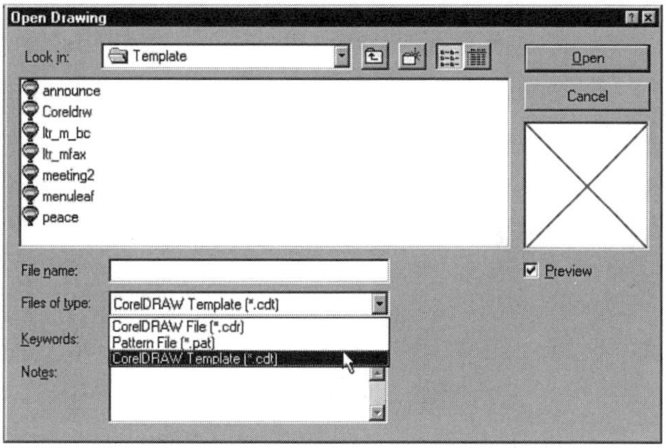

Fig. 2.4

Opening a CorelDRAW! template file using the File, Open dialog box controls.

2. Locate the directory where the template file resides, and click the Open button. The template file opens.

As you are working in a template file, use the File, Save As command to save the file as a regular CorelDRAW! 6 document immediately after making any changes to it. You will need to specify that you would like to save it as a CorelDRAW! 6 file (*.CDR) unless you choose otherwise. If you do not specify for Draw to save the template as a .CDR file, using the Files of Type pull-down menu options, your template file will automatically be saved as a template file again when you select File, Save.

Drag and Drop Opening

There always seems to be a multitude of ways of doing the same thing in Windows 95 and also in CorelDRAW! 6. Drag and drop opening has been available since Windows 3.1 and the last two versions of CorelDRAW!. To open a file by dragging and dropping, follow these steps:

1. Make sure that CorelDRAW! 6 is already open and Windows 95 Explorer also is open.

2. Make sure that the CorelDRAW! 6 window is Maximized, while the Explorer window is smaller than maximized.

3. Position your applications so that you are viewing the CorelDRAW! 6 window in the background and the Explorer window in the foreground (see fig. 2.5).

Fig. 2.5
Getting ready to drag and drop a file.

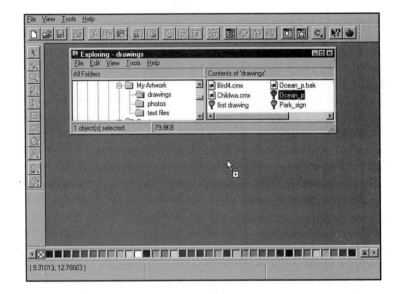

4. Click the file you wish to open and, using the left mouse button, drag it out of the Explorer window and into the CorelDRAW! window and Draw will open the file.

Or,

Now that Draw supports a multiple document interface (MDI) you may click on multiple files in combination with the Ctrl key and Draw will open all files (providing they are compatible to the Draw file format). To change your view to see a particular drawing that has been opened using MDI, select the specific file name from the Window menu (see fig. 2.6).

Tip

You also can use the Drag and Drop method for moving files into new directories within the main file window of the Open Drawing dialog box. The same feature is available in the Save Drawing, Import, and Export dialog boxes.

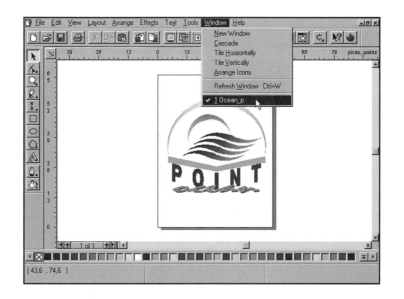

Fig. 2.6
Using the Window menu to change your view to a different opened document.

Caution

When using Drag and Drop, if there are any fonts used in the file you are opening that you don't have loaded on your system, Draw will not warn you. Instead, it will perform its own font substitution on your file without giving you a choice of fonts.

Opening Pattern (.PAT) Files

A pattern file is a file that contains a full-color vector pattern usable with CorelDRAW!'s vector pattern fill option. There is an extensive collection of vector pattern files stored in the Corel60/Custom/Patterns folder.

To open an existing Corel vector pattern file, choose File, Open to display the Open Drawing dialog box and select Pattern File (.PAT) from the Files of Type pull-down menu. CorelDRAW! 6 comes with a collection of pre-saved pattern files (see fig. 2.7) located in the Corel60/Custom/Patterns folder. Pattern files are based on vector formats supported by CorelDRAW! and are used to create vector fill patterns.

▶ See "Using Vector Pattern Fills," p. 247

Opening with Wild Card Characters

You may use the DOS wild card characters * and ? to make it easier for opening files or when you're not quite sure of the exact name. This feature is a valuable tool to become familiar with in any program.

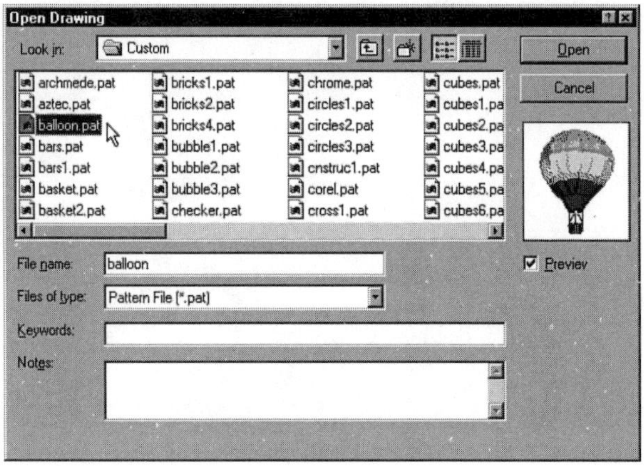

Fig. 2.7
Opening Pattern
(*.PAT) files using
the File, Open
command.

Using figure 2.6 as an example, typing OCEAN*.CDR (one asterisk added to the file name) in the File Name text box and selecting Open lists all CorelDRAW! files in the current folder that begin with OCEAN. Entering OCEAN*.* will locate all of the files that begin with the first letters "OCEAN" followed by any other characters and of any file type.

When using the question mark character (?) and entering OCEAN?.CDR (one question mark added to the file name) and selecting Open lists all CorelDRAW! files that begin with OCEAN and are followed by one more character. Entering OCEAN??.CDR will find all the files that begin with OCEAN followed by two characters, and so on. In this case, the wild card file name OCEAN??.CDR would locate the file OCEAN_P.CDR.

File Management from the Open Dialog Box

In the past with Windows 3.1 you were forced to use the Windows File Manager to delete, copy, or rename individual files. Now, thanks to Windows 95, you may do this directly in the Open Drawing dialog box using right mouse button controls (see fig. 2.8). By right-clicking on the file you now have the option of performing a wide variety of commands including: Select, Open; Print; Import; Quick View; Send to; Cut; Copy; Create Shortcut; Delete; Rename; and Properties.

While many of these file management commands are redundant with many file functions already existing in CorelDRAW!, you may find Cut, Copy, Delete, and Rename useful for performing basic file management without having to open Explorer. Cutting a file copies it to the Windows 95 clipboard where you can Paste it into a different directory.

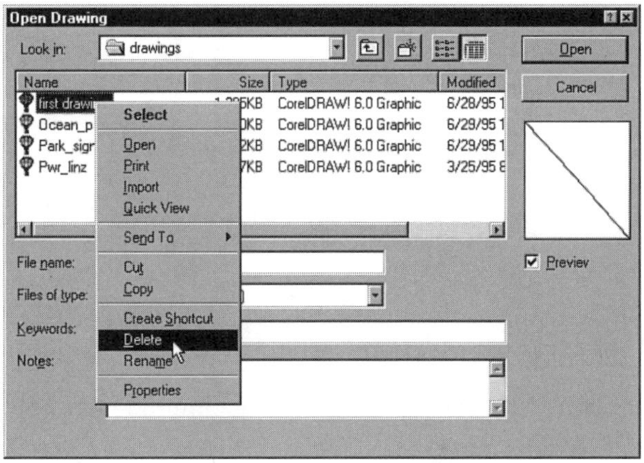

Fig. 2.8
A right mouse button click on a file in the Open dialog box will present a pop-up menu that also gives access to the Open command.

- *Copy.* The Copy command will ask you for both a new name and/or a new path where you would like to store the file.

- *Cut.* The Cut command will remove the file to the clipboard and allow you to do the same, and change the pop-up menu to include a Paste function allowing you to perform that command in a new (or the same) directory by clicking on a blank part of the main file window.

- *Delete.* The Delete command (shortcut is Delete on your keyboard) will move the file you have selected to the Windows Recycle bin. Anytime you select to delete an item, Windows will highlight the file with a blinking text entry point and allow you to give the selected file a new name.

- *Rename.* Renames a file with the new name you keyboard.

During your basic file operations and organization it may be necessary for you to create a new directory to store your file in. By selecting the Create New Folder button in the upper-right area of the Open Drawing dialog box you can instantly create and name a new directory (see fig. 2.9). Selecting this Windows 95 function creates a directory named New Folder, highlighted and waiting for you to keyboard your chosen name.

Tip

Using the backspace key on your keyboard will not delete items from the Open Drawing window. Instead you'll notice your directory will change and you will have inadvertently discovered that the backspace key is the keyboard shortcut for Up One Level, which moves you out of the directory you are currently viewing.

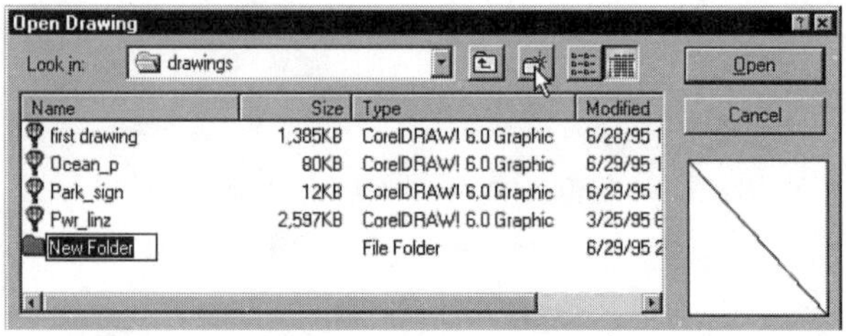

Fig. 2.9
Creating a new folder using the right mouse button controls while in the Open Drawing dialog box.

Closing and Saving Files

Closing and saving files under Draw offers much more than in previous versions. While saving files is a fairly basic operation, CorelDRAW! 6 provides you with quite a number of options.

Saving Backwards: Working with Older Draw Files

Saving is a command you will always use and it helps immensely if you know all that it is capable of doing for you. Saving to previous formats of Draw may be required if you are working on files that you are handing off to others who may not own as recent a version of Draw as you. Draw provides Save As functions which enable you to save as far back as version 3, including versions 4 and 5.

By choosing File, Save As, or holding down the right mouse button and selecting Save As from the menu that appears, a Save Drawing dialog box appears asking you to define a name and path for your new file. You'll see many of the same file management commands you saw in the Open Drawing dialog box (see fig. 2.10). Incidentally, this is the same dialog box you see when you save a new, untitled drawing file for the first time.

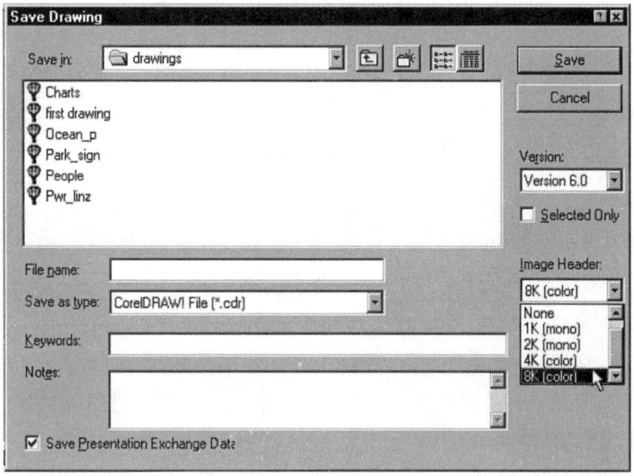

Fig. 2.10
Using the Save As command opens a dialog box identical to the Save Drawing dialog box.

On the far right center of the screen you'll also see the Version option, which incorporates a pull-down menu for specifying which version you would like your drawing to be saved under. After selecting the Save command, Draw saves all changes according to your selections in this dialog box. Finally, at the bottom of this dialog box you see an option to save the Presentation Exchange Data with the file that represents any data stored with objects to be built into your new file.

Troubleshooting

I'm having trouble naming files and saving them in the right format.

If it's your first time or you are unsure of using the Save As command, move ahead gingerly. When using the Save As command, it may be wise to always give your new document a name that is different from the file name you are currently using. Draw files are not differentiated by extension.

Whether it's a version 3, 4, 5, or 6 file you're saving, Draw always names the file with a CDR extension, unlike other programs that will add a numeral to the end of the extension. If you intend on managing more than one version of Draw, develop a convention for identifying your file versions by adding a numeral into the name of the file.

When saving to a previous version of Draw, another reason to save your files under a different name (and not have them overwritten) is because previous versions may not support all of the features and tools that you have used in your version 6 file. Depending on how far back you save to, certain elements created using the latest CorelDRAW! 6 tools may not always save "cleanly" to a previous version and the results may not always be desirable.

When it comes time to name your files, Windows 95 will actually allow you to create a name 255 characters in length. You may use any characters you wish (even characters that used to be illegal under previous Windows versions, such as periods). Keep in mind that the Corel Save command will add the .CDR extension automatically, so there is no need for you to keyboard it.

A potential hazard may exist if your files are used on a previous version of Windows and if you have used extra long file names. The file name characters beyond the eight-character limit, will be replaced by a tilde (~). For example, the file named ILLUSTRATION-95.CDR will be truncated to ILLUST~5.CDR. Try to place the most critical identifier at the beginning of the file's name. That way, if your file is ever used under previous versions of Windows, it will still be identifiable.

Saving Selected Only

The Selected Only option becomes active if you have some or all objects in your drawing selected. This time-saving feature allows you to save portions of your drawing as separate documents.

To select something in your drawing, click the object. To select multiple objects, hold down the Shift key while clicking different objects. To select all of the objects in your current drawing, choose Edit, Select All.

Saving Image Header Options

An Image Header is the information written into your files that briefly describes how your file looks. This header information is stored in bitmap format and is read by any software that supports header display or thumbnail viewing. For example, when you open a file using File, Open and the Open Drawing dialog box displays an image in the Preview window, that little picture is the header information of the file.

Headers can be saved to varying degrees of detail. The more detailed the header is, the easier it is to visually recognize the file. Unfortunately, highly-detailed headers take up more memory on your system and so Draw provides controls to select various header formats (refer to fig. 2.10) including Current, None, 1K (mono), 2K (mono), 4K (color), and 8K (color).

If you select Current header, Draw leaves the header setting unchanged from its last-saved format. Selecting None will erase any header information in the file. Selecting 1K or 2K writes a header equivalent to a 1-bit or 2-bit black-and-white or grayscale image of your file as a header. Selecting 4K or 8K writes the equivalent of a 4-bit or 8-bit color image of your file as a header. Selecting None doesn't increase your file size while selecting 8K (color) increases your file size the most of all of the header selections.

Closing Files

Once again there are a couple of ways to do this. First, and possibly the most common, is to choose File, Close. The second, of which you may want to adopt the habit, is to click the close button in the upper-right corner of your document window. In both cases, Draw prompts you about saving any changes you've made.

Advanced Backup and File-Saving Features

▶ See "Understanding Tools Options," p. 65

Back-up, auto back-up/path, and auto back-up time interval are all features that can be set by selecting the Advanced tab from the Preferences dialog box, which is found by choosing Tools, Options.

Save All

Along with Draw's MDI comes this new Save All command found in the File menu, which allows you to perform a save command on all opened documents.

When this option is active it allows you to stop a Save command in progress by pressing the Escape key (Esc) on your keyboard. The result is that the file is reverted back to its original state immediately before the Save command was given. If you had intended on selecting Save As instead of Save, this feature may just come in handy. You know when your save is still in progress by the hourglass icon that displays beside your cursor. If your computer system is equipped with an "active" indication lamp you also will quickly be able to tell if the save is still in progress, but if you have the latest lightening-speed computer you'll likely have to be lightening-fast to take advantage of Interruptible Save.

Saving for Speed or Storage

CorelDRAW! 6 now has the capability of performing full saves or mini-saves by using either For Storage or For Speed options found in the Optimize section of Save and Restore. Draw's Save and Restore options can be found at the bottom of the Advanced tab of the Preferences dialog box (Tools, Options or Ctrl+J).

The Optimize for Storage option when active allows Draw to compare the bitmap contained in the file, saving it in the smallest format possible.

▶ See "Understanding Tools Options," p. 65

From Here...

In this chapter you have learned how to perform basic but critical Corel-DRAW! 6 file operations. You have also used some of the customization tools available, although there is a large gamut of them in CorelDRAW! 6. This book covers tool preferences and customization features in further chapters, and provides information about the other file functions relating to saving and opening imported and exported files formats.

For related topics discussed in this chapter, see:

- Chapter 15, "Importing and Exporting Files," for information on common import filters.

- Chapter 14, "Customizing CorelDRAW! 6," for more customizing tips.

Chapter 3

Making CorelDRAW! 6 Easy to Use

CorelDRAW! 6 now enables you to do such things as create your own toolbars, compose all of your favorite interface buttons, and display or hide any screen features, including menus. If you don't particularly like Corel's choice of keyboard shortcuts, now you can change them. If you want to maximize your productivity, there are specific customizing features for that too.

In this chapter, you learn to

- Use CorelDRAW! 6 Page Setup options

- Set tools and toolbar options

- Understand CorelDRAW! 6 Options

- Customize the Status Bar

Page Setting Options

The very first options you may want to set when just beginning a new file in CorelDRAW! 6 are the Page Settings (see fig. 3.1). This dialog box may be accessed by either selecting Layout, Page Setup or double-clicking the page frame on your screen. The Page Setup is also sometimes referred to as the printable page, because anything that lies completely or partially on your page will be printed provided you select the correct corresponding page size and provided your printer is ready, willing, and able.

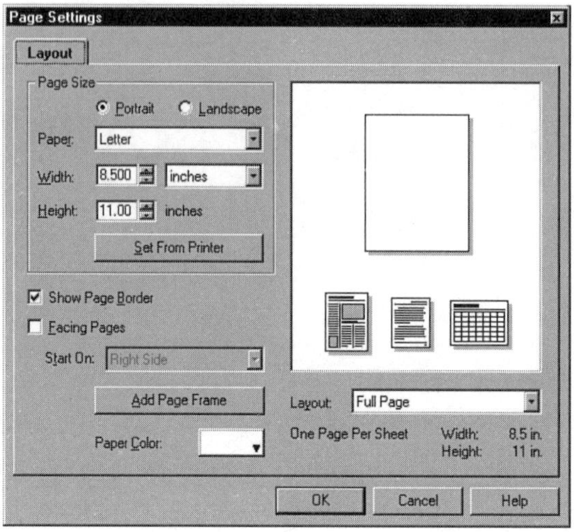

Fig. 3.1
Setting or checking your Page Options should be one of the first tasks at hand when beginning a new file.

Page Sizes and Other Options

Page Size settings are set using the Page Settings dialog box and include Portrait or Landscape orientation, Paper, Width, and Height. For a quick, automatic setup based on the settings for your currently selected printer press the Set From Printer button.

Portrait and Landscape orientation controls allow you to set either a vertical (tall) or horizontal (wide) page. The Paper control provides access to a selection of 40 different preformatted page sizes including page measures for North American and European sizes using both metric and standard measurement systems. Width and Height controls include an option to enter or view the page dimensions in units including inches, millimeters, picas and points, points, ciceros and didots, and didots. Changing Paper size or orientation changes the page representation in the Page Settings preview window at the right of the dialog box, and also changes the status display of Width and Height in the lower-right area.

Tip

Universal measuring conventions dictate that when describing any area always quote the width measure before the depth, height, or length. DRAW! conforms quite nicely to this convention as you'll notice if you repeatedly select Portrait and Landscape while keeping an eye on the Width and Height measurement. For example, choose a letter size page and select Portrait. The Width measure is automatically 8.5 inches and the Height measure is 11 inches. Then select Landscape and watch as the unit measure for Width switches to 11 inches. Understanding this concept will help you in figuring out the difference between Landscape and Portrait orientations.

Editing the dimensions of an existing page will cause DRAW! to automatically enter a Custom page definition in the Paper field. Changing the unit measure will not change the dimensions of your paper, only the units. DRAW!'s maximum Paper size is a staggering 1,800 inches by 1,800 inches. Detailed documents using this maximum Paper size will no doubt require excessive amounts of RAM to perform operations such as saving, printing, and so on.

The Show Page Border checkbox enables you to hide the page frame representation in DRAW!. The Facing Pages option allows you to display your pages in pairs as they face each other, or as single independent pages. Once Facing Pages is active, the Start On option becomes available, enabling you to select a Right or Left side page from the pull-down menu provided.

Pressing the Add Page Frame once will add a thin black open-filled rectangle around your page. Paper Color is also an option allowing you to choose a color for the background of your document. This feature will be useful to users formatting documents that need to simulate a colored paper for offset printing. Paper color only affects the visual appearance of your page layout and will not affect printing. To choose a Paper Color, follow these steps:

1. Select the Paper Color button.

2. Choose from any of the currently displayed colors from the Color palette flyout that appears. The last palette you were using is the palette that is being diplayed. Choose a color by clicking on it and the color palette flyout disappears.

3. If you need access to another color selection, click the More button to bring up DRAW!'s main color Layout controls, which provide access to all color models available in DRAW!. Selecting a color from this dialog box and selecting the OK button returns you to the Page Setup dialog box.

Note

Pressing the Add Page Border button multiple times will add a black page frame each time it is pressed. This may not affect the appearance of your drawing, but can be pretty puzzling when you try to delete your page frame and discover that there is more than one. If this happens to you, delete the extra page frames to reduce the complexity of your file, and reduce confusion.

▶ See "Understanding Color Models," p. 436

Customizing Labels

If you select Labels from the Paper selection, you'll notice that the entire Page Settings preview window changes appearance, splitting into two separate viewing windows (see fig. 3.2). The upper window still serves as a preview window, but the lower window now serves as a mini-Explorer style window allowing you to select from literally hundreds of scripts defining sticky labels, envelopes, Post-It notes, disk labels, badges, name tags, and plastic sleeve inserts, some of which have been formatted to fit specific manufacturer's product dimensions. Each product selected displays a simple representation in the Page Settings preview window.

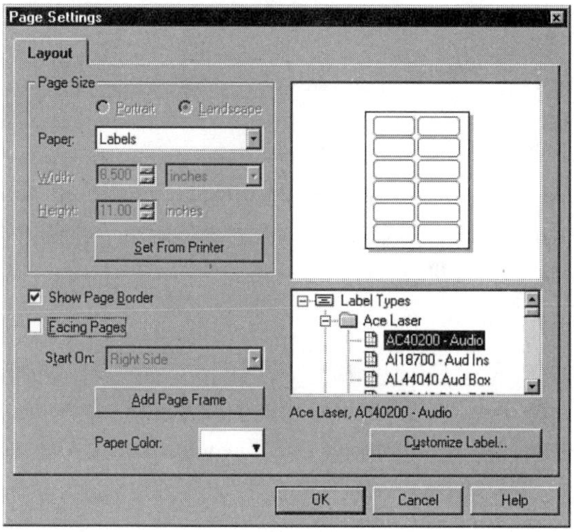

Fig. 3.2
CorelDRAW! 6 comes equipped with a huge selection of specialty label formats.

If you don't find a preformatted page that suits your needs in the Labels Paper selection, try choosing the Customize Label button at the lower right of the dialog box. The Customize Label dialog box that appears (see fig. 3.3) is a tool you may use to format your own specific label, envelope, or insert page. This dialog box features fields for entering measurements for your own Label size, Margins, and Gutters, including a Layout control for the number of Rows and Columns.

Label Size may be defined by Width and Height measurements, and an additional option allows you to provide for Rounded corners. The concept here is that you enter the exact dimensions of a single label on your page so that DRAW! can repeat this single element a number of times in repetition on your page. Entering the Width and Height is the first step to this process.

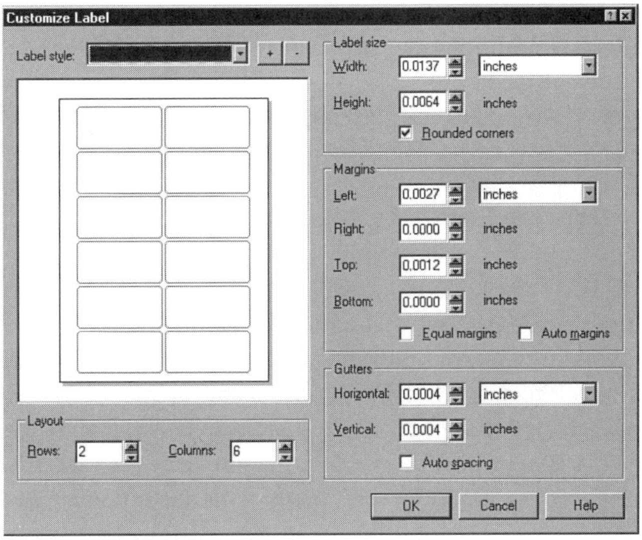

Fig. 3.3
If you don't locate
the label format
you need, or don't
see a compatible
format, use the
Customize Label
dialog box controls
to create and save
your own.

Building a Solid Foundation

Margin measurements define the empty space to the Left, Right, Top, and Bottom of your label or "live" area. This empty space will be considered by DRAW! as unavailable when formatting the remaining dimensions of your custom labels. Selecting the Equal Margins option will cause DRAW! to copy the current measures entered in the Top and Left fields to the Bottom and Right fields, respectively, essentially causing equal space around all labels. Selecting the Auto Margins option causes DRAW! to enter identical measures for Top and Bottom, and Left and Right, respectively, essentially centering your "live" label area on the page. *Margins* are the empty, mostly unused space between the live or usable area and the edges of a page.

Defining the Gutter in Horizontal and Vertical measures determines how far apart your labels are. The *gutter* is the space between the individual elements—in this case, labels. Choosing the Auto Spacing option formats your labels to be evenly spaced horizontally and vertically.

The last options available in the Customize Label dialog box are the Layout controls defined by Rows and Columns. If you imagine for a moment that you are looking at a spreadsheet, your Rows would be the horizontal stripes and your Columns would be your vertical stripes. The numbers entered will determine the total number of labels on your label sheet, and DRAW! will reflect your changes in the Customize Labels preview window.

Once you have entered the specific dimensions for your customized label, DRAW! will display a preview of your measurements in the Custom Label preview window on the left side of the dialog box. Once you are satisfied that you have exactly the correct measurements for your label, you may also save it by entering a name in the Label Style field and pressing the plus (+) button to add the name to the label list. To delete a Label Style, select it from the Label Style pull-down menu and select it, then press the minus (-) button. DRAW! will ask if you are sure you want to delete it.

Special Purpose Layouts

The next significant feature in the Page Settings dialog box is the six different Layout styles: Full Page, Book, Booklet, Tent, Side-fold, and Top-fold. Each time a different layout is selected, a simple representation is displayed in the lower half of the Page Settings preview window. The purpose of having these different layouts is to alleviate some of the headaches associated with last minute layout changes and preformatting of printed hard copies. By integrating these special layouts into DRAW! 6, Corel has made it a lot easier to make major layout changes during the end phases of production of a project.

When you change from Full Page layout to one of DRAW!'s special Layouts, DRAW! makes a calculation to divide your Paper size up into the number of parts needed to format your layout. Then, DRAW! will reflect this change visually, and your screen will display the new, smaller version of your page.

In most cases, once your layout has been set you won't need to change it. But, in some instances you may be able to take advantage of a twist on this feature. For example, say you have just laid out a four-page newsletter that is being proofed on a laser printer, but will eventually print from a high-resolution imagesetter. At the moment, you are at the laser-proof stage and just want to print out a copy of your lastest layout on your tabloid-sized laser printer. Ideally, you'll want to avoid taping or gluing pages together by hand. And after all, this isn't the dark ages. You have expensive equipment at your disposal. Why not use it?

Your newsletter, which has a Paper size of Letter, is currently set to DRAW!'s Full Page layout selection (the default). Full page will work just fine if you're printing to a letter-sized printer. But, if your printer is capable of printing a larger size you may want to try changing the Page Settings and Layout to take advantage of it. First, select Booklet from the Layouts option. You'll see a representation (see fig. 3.4) of two folded, horizontally oriented pages and a diagram of a page layout where pages four and one are paired, and pages two and three are paired. Exactly the way you would need them to be if you were going to print these pages out and fold them in half together to form a book. Page one would have page two on its back and be faced by page three. Page three would have page four on its back and be faced by page one. This process of joining pages together in this way to form a book is called *imposition*.

Fig. 3.4
Viewing the layout of your booklet using the Preview window.

Then, before changing anything else, select Tabloid from the Paper option, and select Landscape for the paper's orientation. Then select OK and, although nothing appears to have changed at all in your layout, you have just set up to print a booklet from your laser printer. To revert the Layout back to its original format, select Layout once again, choose a Letter Paper size, oriented Portrait, and change the Layout back to Full Page. Again, nothing seems to have changed but your layout is back to normal and ready to print normally once again.

The real beauty about this sort of Layout juggling is that you can change the layout of your file whenever you want without changing the arrangement of the pages in your CorelDRAW! file. In other words you could change the Layout of your newsletter back to Full Page later when you need to print to the imagesetter without changing the numbering of your pages.

These special features of Layout, with some experimentation, can prove to be a powerful tool for large-scaled, mass-production type projects where you'd normally be using tape and scissors for hours on end.

Understanding Tools Options

If you are, or plan to be, a regular user of CorelDRAW! then CorelDRAW! 6 Options are another of those master controls that, when finely tuned, can save you literally hundreds of hours of frustration. DRAW!'s Options have gone through many changes since early versions, when the controls consisted of just a few display and editing options. Back then, they fit just nicely onto a single, full-screen dialog box. Now CorelDRAW! 6 Options have been expanded and organized into three tabbed categories—General, Display, and Advanced—and the terminology in the menu bars has been changed to Tools, Options instead of Preference, which may cause some confusion for users who are upgrading.

The significant change in the Options for version 6 though, is that certain options have been shifted to other dialog boxes, including previous View and Curves tab options. Some of these options have been shifted within the CorelDRAW! 6 Options tabs themselves, but others have been moved to the Tool Properties dialog box controls.

General Options

The General tab (see fig. 3.5) provides controls for duplicate and clone placement, nudge, constrain angle, mitre limit, undo levels, automatic placement of Powerclipped contents, and six application start-up options.

The Duplicate command (Ctrl+D) is found under the Edit menu. Duplicate is a command you will likely use often if you need instant copies of single objects or groups. It copies anything you have currently selected and pastes it onto your page to a specific offset according to what position you have set here in the Options dialog box. Entering a positive value in the Horizontal or Vertical places the duplicate, in an offset, above or right of the original, respectively. Vice versa, entering a negative value places the duplicate below or left of the original, respectively.

The Clone command, also found under the Edit menu, works in a similar way by copying and pasting a *clone* of your currently selected object according to the offsets specified here in the Options dialog box. The default value for both duplicates and clones is 0.25 inches.

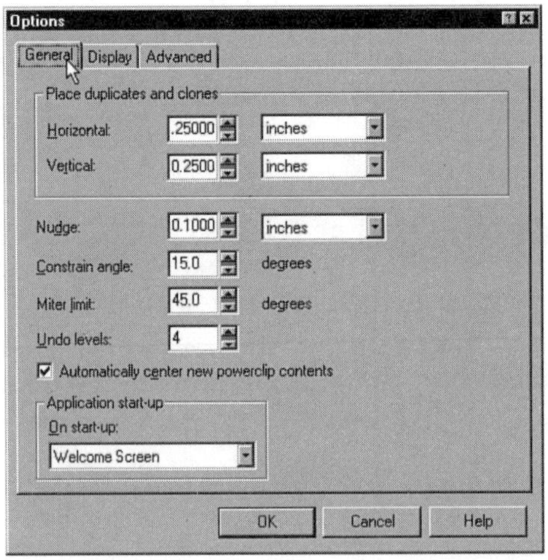

Fig. 3.5

Using the General tab options of the Options dialog box.

The Nudge command is controlled by the Left, Right, Up, and Down arrows on your keyboard. Each time you press an arrow key your object(s) will move according to the value you enter here. Holding down an arrow key will continuously move the selected object(s). DRAW!'s default value for the Nudge command is 0.10 inches.

The Constrain Angle feature controls how mouse transformations behave in combination with the Ctrl key. Constraining works while drawing and rotating objects, moving nodes and control points, and when using Envelope and Perspective tools. In figure 3.5, notice the constrain angle is set to 15 degrees by default.

▶ See "Creating Curves, Lines, Rectangles, and Ellipses," p. 177

To illustrate how helpful this feature is, try to draw a line at exactly 15 degrees using the pencil tool. It's nearly impossible, or at least very time consuming. Using DRAW!'s Constrain feature you need only select the first anchor point, then press and hold down the Ctrl key while circling that first point. Notice that the line angle *jumps* between 15 degree angle increments. Now, try setting the angle to 30 degrees here in the General Options tab and take note of how it reacts.

The next setting under the General heading is Mitre Limit, which can be described as the way in which DRAW! handles vector segment cornering, or in plain English, how it creates a corner that joins two line segments together. Mitre Limit is best left unedited in most cases. Fiddling with it often does more harm than good—especially with text and fonts. The default setting of 45 degrees is the optimum setting. Setting a lower setting causes drawn objects to be more complex and may cause printing errors, and setting a higher setting may cause text to look either spikey at the corners, or dirty.

DRAW!'s multiple Undo Levels may be set to an infinite number, limited only by the resources of your computer system. The default value of 4 undos is the setting you might choose if your system is equipped with up to 4 megabytes of random-access memory (RAM). If you have eight megabytes of RAM it may be worthwhile to set this to eight undos, or if you have 16 megabytes of RAM, try 12 undos. If you set more than 12 levels of undo, you'll likely discover over time that more than 12 levels may unnecessarily tie up system resources.

Automatically Center New Powerclip Contents is an option available when using DRAW!'s Place Inside Container command, part of the Powerclip tool functions accessed from under the Effects menu. Activating this feature (the default) causes DRAW! to place one object inside a designated container object and automatically center it. It is also best to leave this feature active because, occasionally, Powerclipped objects are placed inside container objects and become invisible or otherwise lost, causing you to waste time searching for them again.

Note

▶ See "Using Powerclip Effects," p. 346

Turning off the Automatically Center New Powerclip Contents feature may cause objects to seemingly disappear when using DRAW!'s Powerclip Place Inside Container command. The object which has been placed inside the container object may disappear if it isn't already overlapping the container object. It will only be visible if it is already overlapping. To view the contents object, you must use the Edit Contents command also found in Powerclip under the Effects menu. Then you may reposition the container object to overlap the contents object and become visible.

Display Options

The Display tab (see fig. 3.6) controls all aspects of display including Preview Fountain Steps, Preview dithering, Full-Screen preview, Moving object previews, and a series of display options including screen refresh, color palette appearance, auto-panning, snapping feedback, and tooltips display.

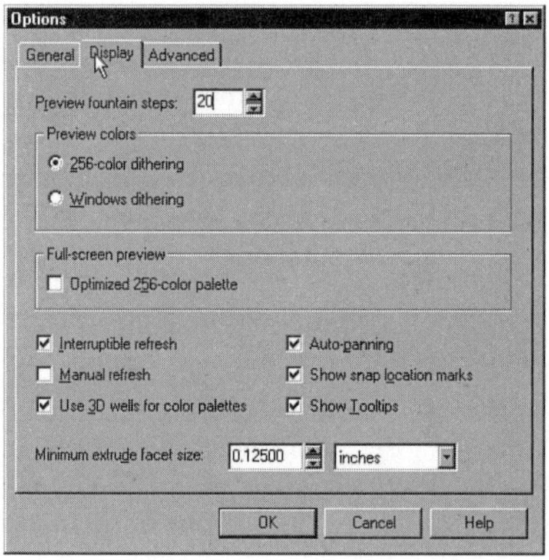

Fig. 3.6
Exploring
CorelDRAW! 6's
display options.

Settings controlling the way in which DRAW! renders color and options controlling display only affect the way in which DRAW! renders your images to the screen, and will not affect printing.

Preview Colors dithering consists of two choices: 256-color dithering or Windows dithering. DRAW! gives you the choice of using the 256-color dithering method your video graphics card is capable of rendering, or using the dithering method Windows uses—whichever looks better or operates faster. Some video cards do not offer support for 256-color dithering. In most cases though, the true-color display or 24-bit color that your graphics card provides will work better and faster than that of Windows dithering.

Using the Optimized 2_5_6-Color Palette option found under Full-Screen Preview is recommended for the fastest redraw time. Turning this option off may increase the time it takes for your screen to render color images.

DRAW!'s Preview Fountain Steps feature is another feature you may find yourself fiddling with often if you work with fountain fills a lot. The measure of fountain steps is dependent on the size of the object you have filled and has nothing to do with screen resolution. When DRAW! is rendering images to your screen and finds an object with a fountain fill of some sort, it simply divides the space occupied by the object into the number of steps set here. It also blends from one shade or color to another using that number of steps.

When set to a low number, this feature causes your fountain fills to draw at lightening speed but also causes them to look crude. When set to higher settings it makes your fountain fills look just great, but unfortunately will take longer to draw. The happy medium is likely the default setting of 20 steps.

The remaining preferences feature controls for visual options including Show Snap L_ocation Marks, Show _Tooltips, Auto-_Panning, Use _3D Wells for Color Palettes, _Interruptible Refresh, and _Manual Refresh.

- *Show Snap L_ocation Marks*. This is a new feature to CorelDRAW! 6 and works in combination with DRAW!'s Guidelines controls activated by selecting Snap to Guidelin_es from the _Layout menu. Snap L_ocation Marks provides a screen indication when objects have reached or snapped to a vertical or horizontal guideline. In figure 3.7 you see that a vertical guide has been set to 4 inches and a horizontal guide to 6 inches. A white square has been positioned to sit above and right of where these two guides intersect and with the Snapping _Feedback active, DRAW! indicates the shape is touching the guides with a blue highlight. Anyone who uses the Guides feature in DRAW! will find this a great time-saver.

- *Auto-_Panning*. DRAW!'s Auto-_Panning feature is another you'll likely want to leave active all the time you're working in CorelDRAW!. As the name suggests, Auto-_Panning kicks in whenever you are dragging an object beyond the boundaries of your screen. DRAW! updates the screen and moves "with the object" as you push the object beyond the screen boundary.

Fig. 3.7
The effects of the
Snap to Location
Marks option
when activated.

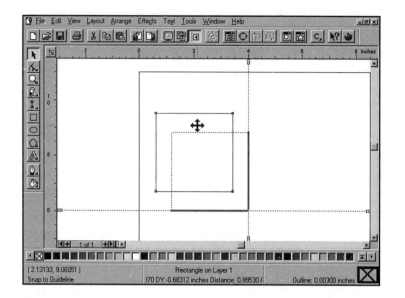

■ *Show Tooltips.* The Display tab is also where you control the appearance of tooltips, which can be compared to using training wheels when you're just learning to ride a bicycle. It can help immensely when you're getting to know the screen elements and controls. Show Tooltips gives you a message identifying a certain feature when you allow your mouse to sit above that screen control or feature. Once you know what all the screen parts are called you'll likely want to turn this useful—but somewhat irritating—feature off.

■ *Interruptible Refresh and Manual Refresh.* These two refresh options are indispensable features that you won't be able to live without. Interruptible Refresh allows you to stop your screen in the middle of a screen redraw without having to wait for it to finish. Manual Refresh, when active, will only refresh your screen when forced to by using the Ctrl+W command. Otherwise it will leave half-drawn objects cluttering your screen. In most cases, you will want to leave this feature active.

■ *Min. Extrude Facet Size.* This option is definitely easier to say than it is to comprehend. It enables you to set the minimum facet depth when creating extrusions using DRAW!'s Extrude feature. *Facet size* is the difference in color shades created in an *extrusion* (a 3D version of a selected object). DRAW!'s default setting is 0.00197 inches, which is significantly lower than an optimum facet size of between 0.01 and 0.05 inches. Higher settings reduce the time it takes DRAW! to render your extruded image, but will appear much better, whereas lower settings will draw faster but look poorer.

- *Use 3D Wells for Color Palettes.* Color wells is the name Corel has given to the squares of color in the on-screen color palette, which, by default, appear as actual depressions containing ink. A three-dimensional inter-face is nice to look at, but not always necessary, especially when you are trying to squeeze the most screen-draw speed out of your system. Although it takes just a fraction of a second for the CorelDRAW! 6 windows and interface parts to refresh, you may choose to select this option off to marginally speed up screen redraw time.

Advanced Options

The Advanced preferences tab (see fig. 3.8) gives access to critical Backup controls, Selection methods, and Save and Restore settings—a must-set for every user.

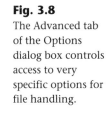

Fig. 3.8
The Advanced tab of the Options dialog box controls access to very specific options for file handling.

File Backup Options

When DRAW! makes backups it doesn't make just one, it makes two: one named with the extension of BAK like most programs do, but also another with an ABK extension. The ABK file is created when you select Auto-Backup active. It renames your old BAK file as an ABK extension and stores it in a designated directory. Then writes the new data to a new BAK file stored in the same directory as your original file. When you close your file or quit DRAW! the ABK file takes the place of your BAK file, which is flushed out of memory.

In cases of system crashes where DRAW! was interrupted between saves, you can usually recover to at least your BAK file by locating the ABK file and re-naming it with a CDR extension. Here in the Advanced tab of Options is where you tell DRAW! where to store your backup copy by using the Select

Directory button and defining a path. Also, it's always a good idea to leave Make Backup on Save active and leave Auto-Backup active and set to a comfortable time interval (the default is 10 minutes).

Save and Restore

Another new feature in CorelDRAW! 6 is the Save and Restore area of the Advanced tab. The name is somewhat deceiving because it implies that you can somehow "restore" files but that's not the purpose at all.

Optimizing your file-saving method For Storage or For Speed gives you control over how DRAW! performs Save commands on your files. Each time you save, DRAW! has the option of saving files one of two ways. The first method is controlled by the For Storage option, and completely rewrites the data describing the entire file—a process that may be time-consuming for large, complex files but tends to compact the file data most efficiently. The second method controlled by For Speed saves the file by making amendments to the end of the data file—a quicker process that usually takes up more space. The more amendments added to the end of the file, the larger the file becomes.

One strategy to use here is to set your save method to For Speed so that you can work most efficiently, and then when necessary, force DRAW! to completely rewrite the file by selecting Save As from the File menu and save using the same file name, replacing the original file. This method will give you total control over your saving methods.

Pop-Up Menu Customization

The Pop-up menu is the menu that appears when you click an object or an interface element using your right mouse button. A menu will appear with options specifically relating to commands or options available to the item you have clicked. A solitary menu command stands separate and above all the rest of these commands and is your new access to those old right mouse click commands.

This menu item may be set according in the Advanced tab of the Options dialog box controls by selecting one of the options from the pull-down menu, including 2x Zooming, Character Attributes, Text Editing, Full-screen Previewing, and Node Editing.

Missing Preference Options

The Options area of CorelDRAW! 6 has changed significantly from version 5. Anyone who has upgraded and just opened the program to set his or her favorite Preferences is in for a slight surprise. What was once five tabs is now three. The following is a reference of what became of those missing features.

Pick Tool Properties

One of the hiding places that a selection of options from the old View tab ended up is the Pick Tool Properties (see fig. 3.9). These tools may be accessed by right mouse clicking on the Pick tool in the main Toolbox, and selecting Properties from the pop-up menu. You may also use the View, Properties, Tools command and select the Pick tool from the list of options that appears. The Pick tool contains the following controls:

Fig. 3.9
The Pick Tool Properties are now home to a few of the old View tab Options of version 5.

- *Missing Right Mouse Button Function.* The Right Mouse Button Function was one of the more useful features first introduced with CorelDRAW! version 4. It allowed you to designate a right mouse button click to cause several actions, including invoking the Object Menu, 2x Zooming, the Character Attributes dialog box, the Text Editor, Full-screen Preview, and the Node Editor.

  The right mouse button functions have now moved to the Advanced tab of the Options dialog box controls under the heading Pop-up Menu Customization. The pop-up menu is the menu that appears when you click on an object or an interface element using your right mouse button. The menu command that sits separate at the top of these commands is your new access to those old right mouse click commands.

  This menu item may be set in the Advanced tab of the Options dialog box controls by selecting one of the options from the pull-down menu, including 2x Zooming, Character Attributes, Text Editing, Full-screen Previewing, and Node Editing.

- *Draw Objects When Moving.* The Draw Objects When Moving option is definitely something to leave active—although you can turn it off if you choose to. When moving oddly shaped objects around your page, it's nearly always useful to see exactly where they are as they are moved into position. DRAW! also features a Delay To Draw When Moving time measured in seconds, which sets a delay time between the time your object stops moving to when it previews on your screen. Meanwhile, all that you will see is a marquee outline of the bounding box that your object occupies. The minimum time delay is 0 seconds (the default) and the maximum is 0.11 seconds.

■ *Cross Hair Cursor.* The Cross Hair Cursor option changes your cursor to vertical and horizontal lines that extend beyond the boundaries of your screen. This would be useful if you need a quick reference for aligning several objects visually and use the mouse to perform your positioning.

■ *Treat All Objects As Filled.* Setting the selection method of objects is a new feature to CorelDRAW! 6 and enables you to tell the program to Treat All Objects as Filled. Without this feature, selecting an object that had a fill setting of None became a bit of a mystery for new users until they discovered that you actually had to click on a visible part of the object—like the outline—to select it. Also, objects that had both fill and line settings of None became virtually unselectable unless you were viewing it in DRAW!'s Wireframe Preview (Shift+F9), and even then you still had to select the actual wireframe of the object to activate it. Selecting the Treat All Objects as Filled feature as active will allow you to choose which way you like to work.

Bezier Tool Options

The Bezier Tool Properties (see fig. 3.10) were once the Curves Preferences tab in previous versions of CorelDRAW! The location and reference may have changed, but the way they work has remained unchanged since CorelDRAW! version 5. These settings control all aspects of mouse drawing and tracing, including Freehand Tracking, Autotrace Tracking, Corner Threshold, Straight Line Threshold, Auto Join, and Auto-Reduce.

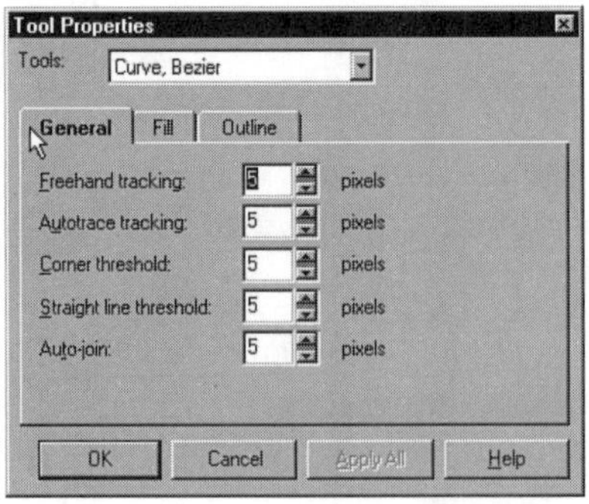

Fig. 3.10
The Bezier Tool Properties are now home to what used to be the Curves tab of the Options dialog box in version 5.

■ *Freehand Tracking.* Your setting for controlling Freehand Tracking is dependent on how good you are at screen-drawing using the mouse. It controls instances where you are using the Bezier or Pencil tools. Holding down the left mouse button while drawing allows DRAW! to drop a drawing node whenever it detects a change in line characteristic. If Freehand Tracking is set too low, objects drawn using this method will become overly complex and likely contain so many nodes that they'll become unmanageable. If you're really good, you might want to leave this setting at the default of five pixels. The average user might be better off changing this setting to 7 or 8.

■ *Autotrace Tracking.* The Autotrace Tracking setting controls how DRAW! traces bitmaps. The Autotrace tool is one of those hidden features in DRAW!, and only becomes active when you import a bitmap image into DRAW! and select the Bezier drawing tool. The purpose of this tool is to trace out portions of your bitmap image automatically. The Autotrace Tracking default setting of 5 pixels is a medium setting. A setting of between 1 and 4 pixels will give a much tighter bitmap tracking, and a setting of between 6 and 9 will provide a very loose tracking result. Each setting has its own unique effect and results may vary depending on bitmap characteristics.

■ *Corner Threshold.* Corner Threshold controls the characteristics of corners drawn using the Freehand drawing tool. Corners drawn at a setting lower than 5 pixels (the default) result in more cusped nodes joined by straight lines, and corners drawn at a higher setting result in more smoothed nodes joined by curves. Cusped nodes are nodes that allow both line segments they control to curve and slope independently of each other.

■ *Straight Line Threshold.* The Straight Line Threshold setting will affect DRAW!'s Autotrace function. Settings above 5 pixels (the default) create straighter and longer lines, while settings below this create shorter lines and more curves.

■ *Auto-Join.* The Auto-Join affects node joining when drawing polygons with the Freehand Drawing tool. Auto-Join affects how beginning and end points of objects behave when placed in close proximity to each other. When beginning points and end points combine, a closed polygon is created. Auto-Join works like a magnet attracting nodes to each other. A setting of 5 pixels (the default) sets the radius of this magnetic effect.

■ *Missing Auto-Reduce.* This is a feature that used to be located in the Curves tab of the Preferences dialog box, but is now found in the Node Edit Tool Properties sheet (see fig. 3.11). You may access the Node Edit Tool Properties by selecting the Shape tool and selecting View, Properties, Tool, Node Edit. The Auto-Reduce setting is of significant value when tracing bitmaps using the Autotrace tool. A nice, tight setting in the Autotrace Tracking creates an abundance of nodes, and, to a large degree, many are unnecessary. Taking precautions to make sure that your traced objects don't contain excessive nodes will pay off when it comes time for you to print—especially when printing to a high-resolution imagesetter.

Auto-Reduce has a default setting of 0.00002 inches, which may not significantly reduce excessive numbers of nodes. A setting of 0.05 inches will work much better without distorting the traced shape of your image.

Fig. 3.11
Auto-reduce is now located in the Node Edit Tool Properties sheet as the single control.

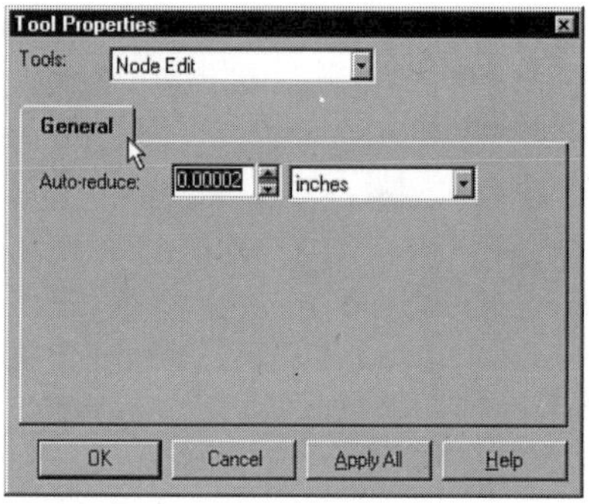

■ *Missing Min. Extrude Facet Size.* Min. Extrude Facet Size in version 5 was previously found in the Curves tab of the Preferences dialog box controls, but you won't find it there anymore. Instead, you'll find it in the Display tab of the Options dialog box controls.

This option is definitely easier to say than it is to comprehend. It enables you to set the minimum facet depth when creating extrusions using DRAW!'s Extrude feature. *Facet size* is the difference in color shades created in an *extrusion* (a 3D version of a selected object). DRAW!'s default setting is 0.00197 inches, which is significantly lower than an optimum facet size of between 0.01 and 0.05 inches. A higher setting will increase the time it takes DRAW! to render your extruded image, but will appear much better. Lower settings will draw faster but look poorer.

Edit Resolution

You used to find this option in the View tab of the Preferences dialog box, but you won't anymore. Instead, it has become part of the Zoom Tool Properties and may be accessed by right-clicking the Zoom tool and selecting Properties from the pop-up menu.

Edit Resolution allows you to match the size of objects viewed on your screen with the size of the physical object. It is primarily used in drawing using the view ratio of 1:1 (see figs. 3.12 and 3.13).

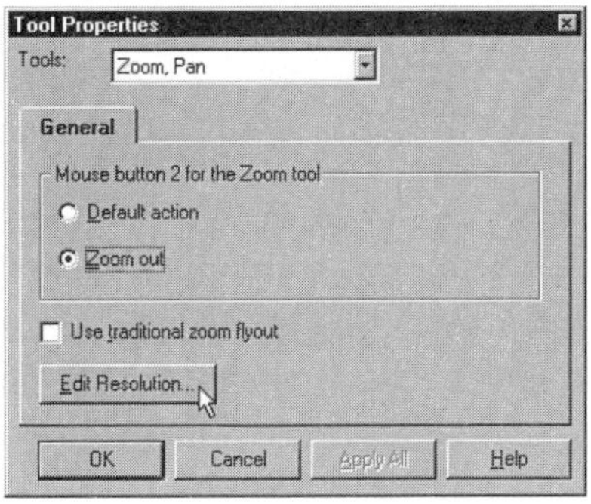

Fig. 3.12
If you're looking for the Edit Resolution button you'll find it here in the Zoom Tool Properties sheet.

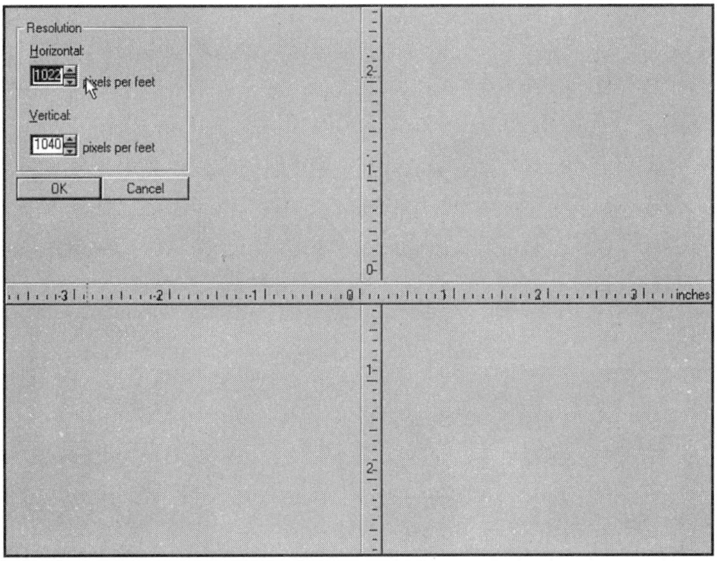

Fig. 3.13
When you select the Edit Resolution button you will be presented with this screen, enabling you to match your screen dimensions with actual 1:1 ratio dimensions.

Advanced Customizing: Status Bars, Tools, and Toolbars

▶ See "More Customizing Tips," p. 474

When Corel said it had introduced a customizable interface, it wasn't kidding. You've already learned about a part of the CorelDRAW! 6 customizable interface in the Options topic earlier in this chapter. But there are some other new and hidden features you should be aware of. The CorelDRAW! 6 interface is extremely customizable and you have the choice of working with the program exactly as you see it, or changing things here or there to suit your own work habits.

Toolbar Options

Toolbars have been introduced to cover nearly all of the functions within CorelDRAW! 6. You may choose to display one or all of the 12 toolbar categories available in DRAW! including Dimensioning Flyout, Fill Flyout, Node Edit Flyout, Curve Flyout, Outline Flyout, Shape Flyout, Text Format, Zoom Flyout, Standard, Text Tools Flyout, Toolbox, and Zoom. For access to these toolbars select View, Toolbars (see fig. 3.14). By using the mouse to select or deselect toolbars you determine which toolbars are displayed. You may also set all toolbars to display in Small, Medium, or Large buttons. Figure 3.14 illustrates how the Standard and Toolbox toolbars are currently selected to display.

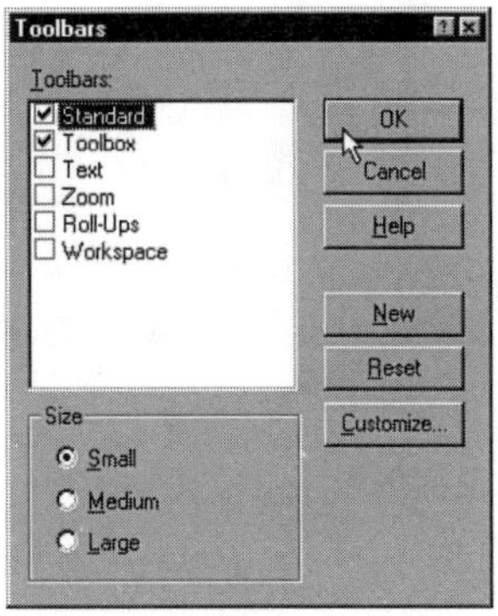

Fig. 3.14
Access the full toobar collection by selecting View, Toolbars.

When double-clicked, toolbars automatically attach themselves to the main DRAW! interface. If you decide that you don't like where they are, you may change the position of each by grabbing onto any blank portion of the toolbar and dragging it to a different position within the DRAW! interface.

Also, if you decide that you would like to have a toolbar float independently of the interface, you may "tear" it off the interface by again grabbing onto a blank portion and dragging it off of the interface and onto the program's drawing area. Figure 3.15 illustrates all of the toolbars available in DRAW! displayed and still attached to the interface. In this illustration the toolbars have been arranged to take up as little space as possible and are displayed in the §mall button size. The shortcut to the Toolbar dialog box is to hold down the right mouse button on a blank portion of any toolbar. All of the toolbars currently available will be listed in the menu that appears. The items with check marks beside them are the toolbars that are currently displayed. You may select or deselect items from this list to change your toolbar display.

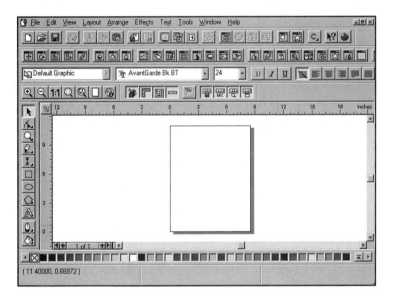

Fig. 3.15
Selecting all of the toolbars to display at the same time will significantly reduce the space you have to work in.

Displaying all of the toolbars significantly reduces the remaining space of your work area. One way around this would be to tear off only the toolbars you would like to float. Return a toolbar back to the interface by double-clicking on its top Title bar. Each toolbar is also equipped with a close button in the upper-right corner of its Title bar.

> **Caution**
>
> Displaying all or many toolbars at one time significantly reduces the amount of available RAM on your system. One indication of this will be Windows 95 Warning Messages appearing on your screen. If your system has a limited amount of RAM, try opening only the toolbars you use the most frequently. If you are unsure of your available system resources, be sure to save often. It's usually much easier and quicker to save often than it is to start your work over again.

Toolbars may also be further customized while they are floating by resizing their width and height. You can do this by grabbing the edge and using the left mouse button (see fig. 3.16). Large and unwieldy toolbars such as the Standard (20 buttons), Outline (16 buttons), and Fill (14 buttons) are quite long and, in their default horizontal shape, may be quite difficult to work with. To resize a toolbar follow these steps:

1. Position the cursor over the bottom or side edge of the toolbar you wish to resize.

2. When you see the cursor change to a left/right or up/down arrow cursor hold down the left mouse button and drag up, down, right, or left.

3. As you drag you will see a gray outline indicating the new shape of the toolbar. Once the gray outline resembles a more desirable shape, release the mouse and the toolbar will redraw in its new shape.

Fig. 3.16
To make your toolbars more managable, you may choose to resize them.

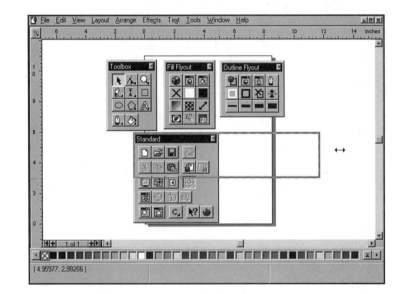

Status Bar Options

Another new feature in CorelDRAW! 6 is the capability to fully customize your Status Bar. The Status Bar provides you with an abundance of information on a wide variety of topics about your drawing items, system, resources, and keyboard states. If it is not already on your screen, you may activate the Status bar by choosing Status Bar from the View menu. The Status Bar is positioned at the bottom of your screen by default.

Options for customizing the Status Bar are accessed by holding down the right mouse button directly on the Status Bar. The menu that appears provides controls for a variety of options (see fig. 3.17), including a Large or Small Status Bar size, and Place At Top or Bottom of the screen. The Status Bar may also be positioned using the left mouse button by grabbing it on a blank portion and dragging it to either the top or bottom of your program window. A gray outline will appear on your screen to hint at the actual position of the bar. Don't be too concerned with lining it up with the rest of the interface though. The Status Bar will snap into its correct position.

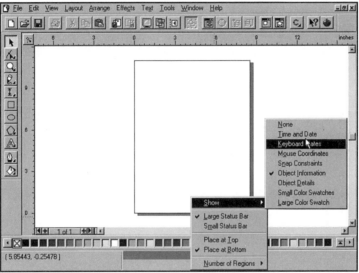

Fig. 3.17
Customizing the
Status Bar.

The new and expanded capabilities of the Status Bar become obvious with the remaining options available from the pop-up menu. The Status Bar may now be chopped up into either three, four, five, or six regions. Each region may provide one of ten displays including Time and Date, Keyboard States, Memory, Mouse Coordinates, Snap Constraints, Object Information, Object Details, Small Color Swatches, Large Color Swatches, or None.

To set the number of divided areas in the Status Bar, select Number of Regions from the pop-up menu accessed by holding the right mouse button down on the Status Bar. Select from either 3, 4, 5, or 6 regions. Once you have set the number of regions, DRAW! will divide the Status Bar. The default setting is 3.

When the regions are first created, they each default to None. To assign a function to a region you must first hold down the right mouse button on the region and assign a function by selecting from the Show flyout. Once an item has been selected DRAW! will mark it with a check mark.

Tip

If you select Large Status Bar from the Status Bar pop-up menu, DRAW! will allow two horizontal rows of regions. If you also set your Number of Regions to the maximum of 6, you may set up to 12 regions to display. The Large Color Swatch actually occupies two regions, so it is only available when Large Status Bar is displayed.

For example, in figure 3.18 you'll see the Large Status Bar is displayed and four regions have been assigned. From the left, the regions each display: Object Details (in inches), Keyboard States, Memory, and Large Color Swatch.

Fig. 3.18
Using the Large
Status Bar option
enlarges the area
that your Status
Bar occupies.

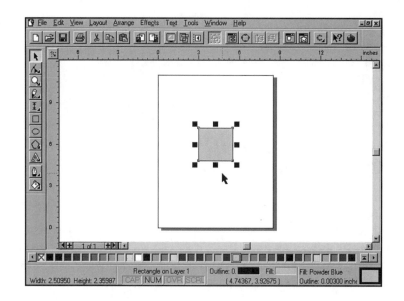

If needed, DRAW! also enables you to change the sizes of the individual display regions by selecting Size Regions from the Status Bar right mouse button.

Table 3.1 Summary of Status Bar Display Functions	
Display Name	**Type of Information Displayed**
Time and Date	Shows current time, day, date, and year
Keyboard States	Displays Caps key lock, NUM key lock, OVR type, and SCRL key lock on or off
Memory	Current system memory free in kilobytes
Mouse Coordinates	Current mouse coordinates measured according to ruler units
Object Information	Displays the type of object and which layer it is on
Object Details	Displays object width and height measure, and center coordinates
Small Color Swatches	Displays object outline thickness, and shows outline and fill colors in separate boxes
Large Color Swatches	Displays object's color name, and outline and fill colors combined in one box

From Here...

This chapter has explained many of the basic options available in CorelDRAW! 6. Some are new, while others have been reorganized into new additions of the tool options. The purpose of these options is to control the behavior of CorelDRAW! 6 itself and make it easier for you to get your work done. While this chapter explains basic controls, don't stop here, review:

■ Chapter 14, "Customizing CorelDRAW! 6," for information on customizing toolbars, customizing keyboard assignments, customizing menus, and other customizing tips.

Chapter 4

What's New in CorelDRAW! 6

CorelDRAW! 6 is more than just a beefed up version 5. At first glance it may look like the same program, but a closer look shows that developments to version 6 have matured the program far beyond any previous release.

This chapter looks at some significant differences between CorelDRAW! 5 and CorelDRAW! 6, with the aim of providing an overview for users upgrading their software, and a quick reference to the how-to sections in this book. The information covered will be of interest to anyone who needs to get up to speed on the new functions, options, tools, and capabilities of this latest feature-rich version.

In this chapter, you will see highlights of what has been added to CorelDRAW! 6 since its last release, including:

- Tool and object properties
- New tools, including Spiral, Grid, Star, and Polygon
- Learn about the new Knife and Eraser tools
- Significant changes to the menu bars
- New roll-ups, including the View Manager and Align & Distribute

A Fresh New Face for CorelDRAW! 6

With the implementation of Windows 95 comes a whole new look for the Corel software lineup. The order of the day here is definitely user customization. Nearly every aspect of the program can be tailored to the user including menus, toolbars, tools, roll-ups, display, and so on. Some features have been a long time coming while others come as a pleasant surprise and are worth checking out.

Multiple Document Interface (MDI)

This is one of those features that CorelDRAW! users have been waiting for—the ability to open more than one file at a time without having to load CorelDRAW! twice as in the past with Windows 3.11 (see fig. 4.1). With this feature comes the ability to open the same document twice using the New Window command from the Window menu. This is excellent for working on the same document in different views simultaneously.

Fig. 4.1

CorelDRAW! 6 now gives you the ability to open multiple files, and multiple views of the same file.

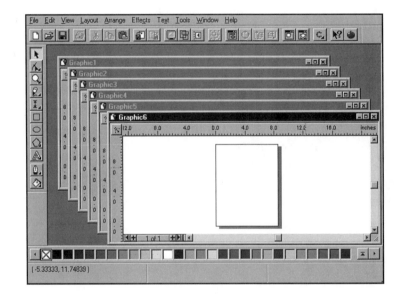

Using the Save All Command

While having multiple documents open and making changes to some or all, you now have the option of saving all of your changes at once by selecting the Save All command from the File menu (see fig. 4.2). This is a great feature for those who work fast and furiously and sometimes forget to save changes. All unnamed files will generate the Save dialog box, which enables saving files with various headers and version formats back to version 5.0 (see fig. 4.3). The Save command also features file and folder management functions and supports Corel's Keywords and Notes options.

Fig. 4.2
The CorelDRAW! 6
File menu and
Save All command.

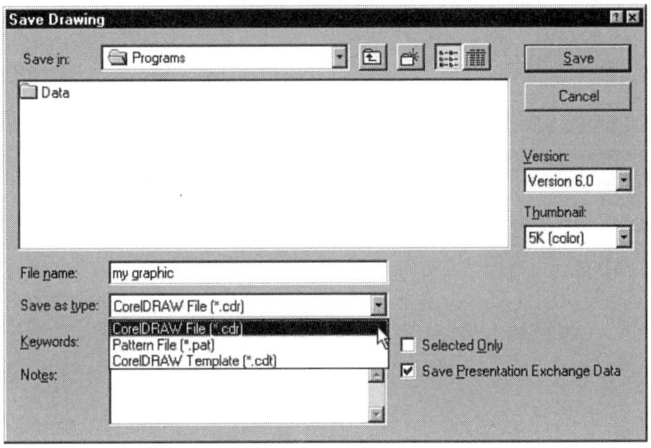

Fig. 4.3
The Save Drawing
dialog box.

Properties for Everything

CorelDRAW! 6 has gone properties-wild. Nearly everything in the program is somehow linked to this feature in one way or another. Properties is a term given to a broad range of attributes from tools and objects, to styles and special effects. There are tool properties, object properties, and style properties. Each may be examined and edited by the user. Properties for most tools and objects may be accessed through the right mouse button. Just click and hold the right mouse button on a toolbar tool or an object, and you have access to a pop-up menu containing several available commands (one of which is access to properties).

Nearly all of the tools may be assigned properties. For more information about object and tool properties see the "New Object Properties" section later in this chapter. The Edit menu also features the Select by Properties command that allows you to use a special interface tool called a Roll-up to set options for searching your CorelDRAW! 6 file for specific types of objects (see fig. 4.4). A roll-up is an interface element that can be temporarily displayed, minimized, or maximized, to give the user access to a collection of specific controls.

Fig. 4.4
The Select by
Properties Roll-up.

New Toolbox Players

At first you'll swear there have been only minor changes to the tools arsenal since version 5, but after digging through the flyouts you'll likely find out there is more than meets the eye here. Using the right mouse button to click on the flyouts will reveal some new players to the CorelDRAW! 6 toolkit. The term *flyout* is used to describe a part of the CorelDRAW! 6 interface that expands beyond a regular menu or toolbar, when clicked or pressed, to reveal more options or choices.

Pick Tool

Clicking on the Pick tool with the right mouse button displays the Tool Properties dialog box. The Pick tool now has options available for treating all objects as filled for those who became frustrated when trying to click on an object they thought was white only to discover that it had no fill (see fig. 4.5). You may also set the Pick tool to display as a cross hair instead of the old standby pointer. This option is easier and more logical to locate in front here. In version 5 of CorelDRAW! it was buried in what used to be called Preferences (Ctrl+J), which is now called Options and located under the Tools menu.

There also is an option to set the drawing of moving objects to a specified time delay.

Fig. 4.5
The Tool Properties dialog box displayed for the Pick tool.

Time delay
option

Shape Tool

Clicking and holding your cursor on the Shape tool reveals a couple of new-comers: a new Knife tool and an Eraser tool. The Knife tool works like a break and combine tool. Clicking once on the edge of an object makes a break point, while clicking a second time on a different point along the object's edge makes another break point splitting the object into two parts and rejoining the broken nodes. The result is an object that appears to have been cut with a knife (see fig. 4.6).

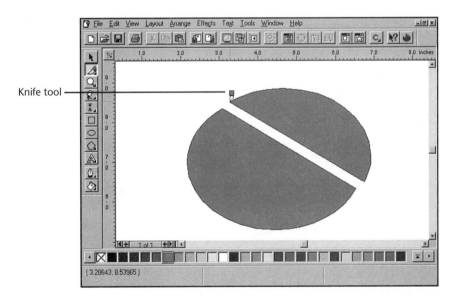

Knife tool

Fig. 4.6
The new Knife tool cuts objects apart along a straight line.

Tip

Double-clicking on the Shape tool in the toolbox displays the Node Edit Roll-up.

The Eraser tool works just as the name implies by erasing the area directly beneath where it is applied. The object must have a fill or an outline of some sort and must be selected prior to applying the Eraser tool. Essentially, this tool creates a new unfilled area beneath where it is applied and recombines this new area with the object that it's being applied to (see fig. 4.7).

Fig. 4.7
How the new Eraser tool affects an object.

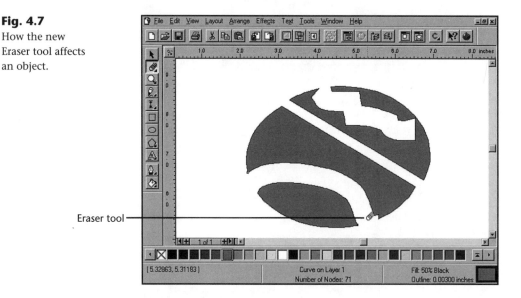

Eraser tool

The Shape tool and each of its new associated tools are controlled by properties set in the same way described earlier in the chapter for the Pick tool. Just click on the tool in the toolbox using the right mouse button. The Shape tool can also be controlled by the Node Edit Properties dialog box (see fig. 4.8) which contains an Auto-reduce control. Auto-reduce is also one of the buttons available in the newly revamped Node Edit Roll-up (see fig. 4.9).

> **Tip**
>
> Double-clicking on either the Eraser tool or the Knife tool displays their respective Tool Properties dialog boxes.

▶ See "Editing Simple Objects: The Shape Tool and the Node Edit Roll-Up," p. 181

The Knife tool is controlled by its Tool Properties dialog box (see fig. 4.10). It consists of options for leaving the cut up object whole, and automatically closing the cut objects after the cutting operation is completed.

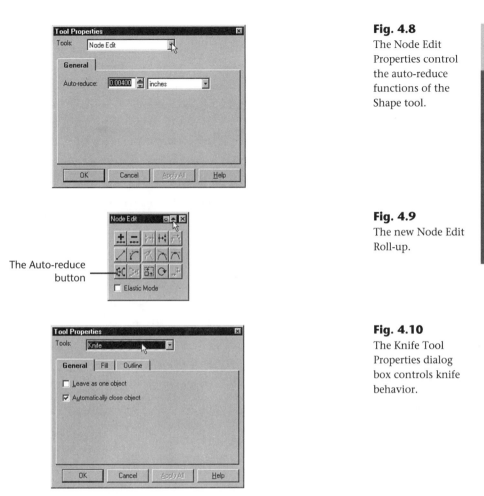

The Auto-reduce
button

Fig. 4.8
The Node Edit
Properties control
the auto-reduce
functions of the
Shape tool.

Fig. 4.9
The new Node Edit
Roll-up.

Fig. 4.10
The Knife Tool
Properties dialog
box controls knife
behavior.

Building a Solid Foundation

The Tool Properties dialog box for the Eraser tool, like the Shape tool, consists of an auto-reduce feature, which affects the number of nodes created when the Eraser tool removes portions of an object (see fig. 4.11). There is also a control to set the thickness of the eraser tip for precise or broadly sweeping elimination of drawing areas.

Zoom Tools Are Revamped

To better see the work you are doing, CorelDRAW! 6 also features better zooming tools than in version 5. The Zoom tool flyout at first looks like it may only contain a single new tool—the Pan tool—but double-clicking on the Zoom tool displays an enormously useful tool: the View Manager (see fig. 4.12). The View Manager is a roll-up which is capable of saving various views of different parts of your drawings at different magnifications. You may also name your views if you wish. The View Manager Roll-up also contains various buttons for selecting the zooming tool, including buttons that activate Zoom In, Zoom Out, Actual Size, Zoom to Selected, Zoom to All Objects, and Zoom to Page. You may also display the Zoom toolbar which contains access to the same tool buttons (see fig. 4.13).

Fig. 4.11
The new Eraser tool dialog box contains a single tool size control and an option for reducing the complexity of erased areas.

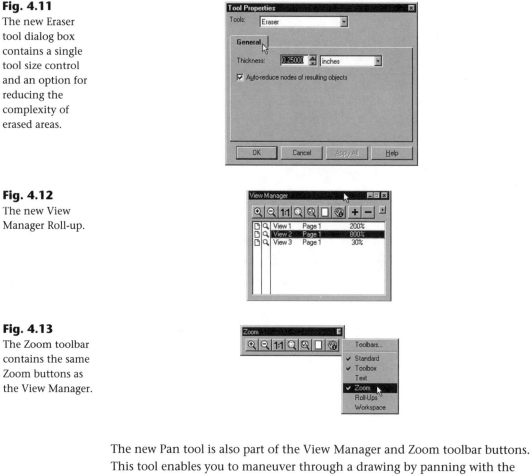

Fig. 4.12
The new View Manager Roll-up.

Fig. 4.13
The Zoom toolbar contains the same Zoom buttons as the View Manager.

The new Pan tool is also part of the View Manager and Zoom toolbar buttons. This tool enables you to maneuver through a drawing by panning with the mouse. The thrust of the Pan tool operation is to move the window view by the amount and direction of your mouse movement. For example, if you wanted to move your view up and to the left of your current view by a distance equal to approximately half of your drawing window, you can select the Pan tool and drag the mouse upwards and to the left a distance of half your screen. When you release the mouse, the view is changed (see fig. 4.14). You may also nudge your view by very small amounts which could only be done by guesswork with the window scroll bars in the past.

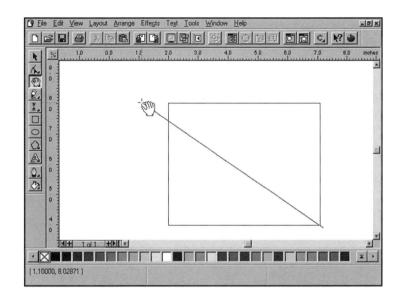

Fig. 4.14
The Pan tool allows you to change your drawing window view quickly and interactively by small amounts or very large amounts depending on your selected view.

Tip

Double-clicking on either the Zoom tool or the Pan tool in the main Toolbox displays the View Manager Roll-up.

The Pan Tool properties are set in the Properties dialog box for the Zoom, Pan tool (see fig. 4.15). In this dialog box you can assign optional Zoom Out functions for the right mouse button, and an option for docking the Zoom toolbar into the Zoom flyout by selecting the use traditional zoom flyout menu. *Docking* is the term given to a toolbar which may attach itself to the application working window.

Fig. 4.15
The new Zoom, Pan Tool Properties dialog box.

Dimensioning Tools

Dimensioning improvements include a double-barrelled Dimensioning Roll-up consisting of separate Angular Dimension and Linear Dimension roll-ups (see fig. 4.16). Both roll-ups feature options for setting the style, precision, and units of dimension marks and offer a sample of the dimensioning style selected. Each roll-up also offers options for choosing dynamic dimensioning as well as text boxes to add your own prefixes and suffixes for customized dimensioning.

Fig. 4.16

The Numeric and Position style tabs of the Linear Dimension roll-up and the Numeric style and prefix and suffix tabs of the Angular Dimension roll-up allow you to fully customize the way you perform dimensioning.

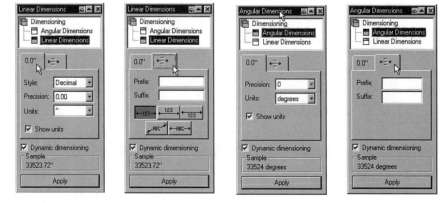

The Dimension toolbar also features options for controlling line sytles and text specifications for dimensioning lines and dimensioning text on Horizontal, Vertical, Slanted, Angular, Callout, and Connector Line tools. Three Property tabs within the Dimensioning Tool Properties dialog box show Text specifications, and offer options for setting text Fill and Outline styles (see fig. 4.17). The Callout tool may now also use curved lines by editing with the Shape tool and the Node Editor.

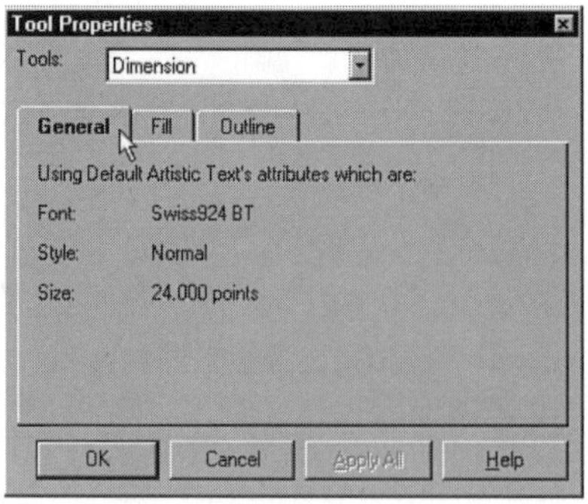

Fig. 4.17

The General tab of the Dimension Tool Properties dialog box provides information about the currently selected font, including its size and style.

> **Tip**
>
> Double-clicking on the Dimension tool displays the roll-up containing Angular and Linear dimension options.

The Connector tool (which is actually a feature borrowed from another Corel program called CorelFLOW) is a newcomer to the Dimensioning tools. This tool enables you to connect a line between two objects using a dynamic link. As you move the objects around the screen, the Connector line continuously links the two objects no matter where they are positioned (see fig. 4.18). The Connector Tool Properties dialog box enables you to set various General, Detail, Pen Outline, and Connector Line options including snapping to the closest node of the control object and locking to the connector node.

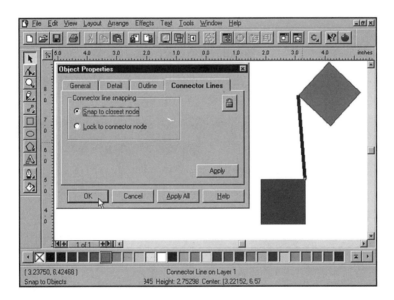

Fig. 4.18
The Connector Line Tool Properties dialog box offers controls for snapping or locking to object nodes.

Curve, Bezier Tool Properties

The Freehand tool, sometimes called the Pencil or Line tool, is still paired in the main toolbox with the Bezier tool, used for drawing curves. The Bezier tool has its own set of properties invoked by right-clicking on the tool in the toolbox (see fig. 4.19). The Curve, Bezier Tool Properties dialog box contains the controls under a General tab for setting Auto-tracing options including Freehand Tracking, Autotrace Tracking, Corner Threshold, Straight-line Threshold, and Auto-join.

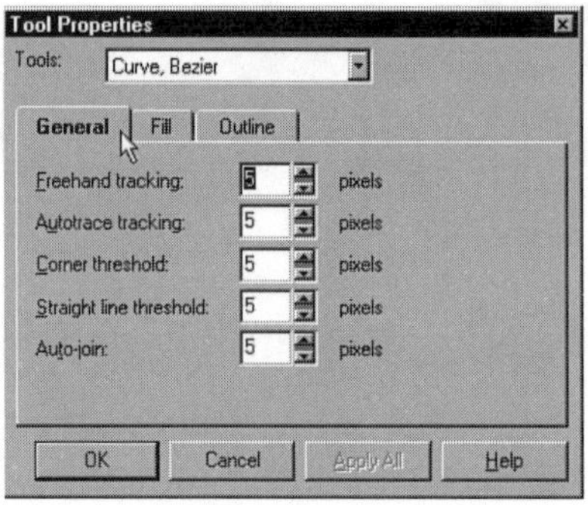

Fig. 4.19

In the Curve, Bezier Tool Properties dialog box you may set the curve behavior, outline, and fill of objects drawn with this tool.

Curved objects have also been assigned their own object properties (see fig. 4.20) that display information about the curve object, including the number of nodes and subpaths, first and last node coordinates, and the open or closed state of the object.

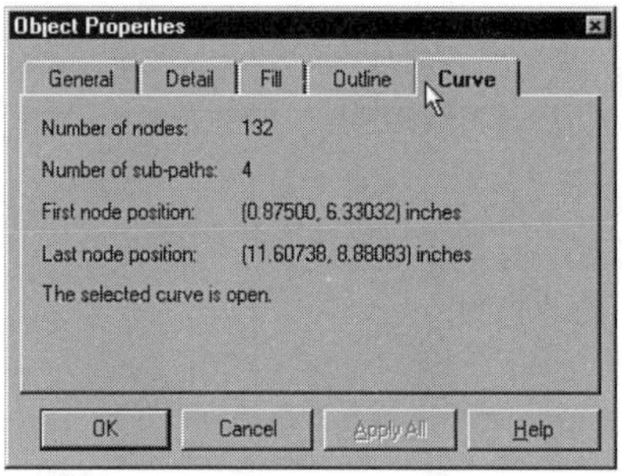

Fig. 4.20

The Curve tab of the Object Properties dialog box provides information about object nodes and path type.

Rectangle & Ellipse Tools

These two solid pillars of the shape tool arsenal have changed little over the years and this holds true for version 6. The only significant change to the Rectangle and Ellipse tools is that each has been assigned a property sheet. The Rectangle Object Properties dialog box contains only two controls for setting the roundness of rectangle corners, and locking the corner settings (see fig. 4.21). The Object Properties dialog box for Ellipse contains a bit more than the Rectangle Object Properties in terms of options (see fig. 4.22). The Object Properties dialog box for Ellipse includes individual settings for ellipse, pie, and arc shapes, starting and ending angles, and options for measuring angle differences clockwise or counterclockwise.

Tip

You may also display the Object Properties dialog box for Ellipse by double-clicking on the Ellipse tool in the main toolbox.

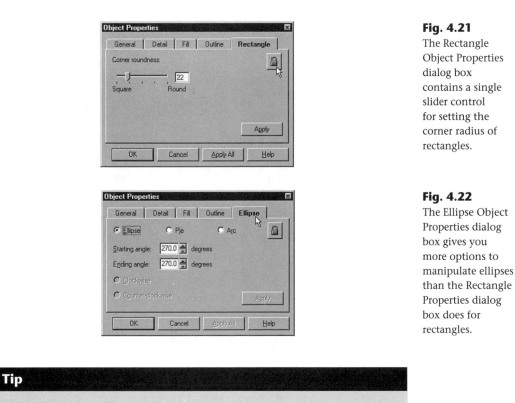

Fig. 4.21
The Rectangle Object Properties dialog box contains a single slider control for setting the corner radius of rectangles.

Fig. 4.22
The Ellipse Object Properties dialog box gives you more options to manipulate ellipses than the Rectangle Properties dialog box does for rectangles.

Tip

Double-clicking on the Rectangle tool adds a page frame around your page.

Completely New Star & Polygon, Spiral, and Grid Tools

Here are three more brand new tools for CorelDRAW! 6—the Star & Polygon, Spiral, and Grid tools which are located in the main toolbox tucked down below the Rectangle and Ellipse tools. These tools all feature their own tool and Object Property sheets as shown in figures 4.23, 4.24, and 4.25.

The Polygon tool can really be considered three tools. The Star part of the tool is used for creating objects having the same number of points as they do sides where the sides may actually intersect each other. The Polygon tool side is used for creating straight-sided objects having the same number of points as they do sides where the sides do not intersect with each other. The third part of the tool is the Polygon as Star option, whereby you are able to set the sides of the polygon to appear as if they eminate from a shape in the center of the object while setting the number of points and sides. The Polygon tool set to the Polygon as Star option creates concentrically oriented objects which contain twice the number of sides as they do points.

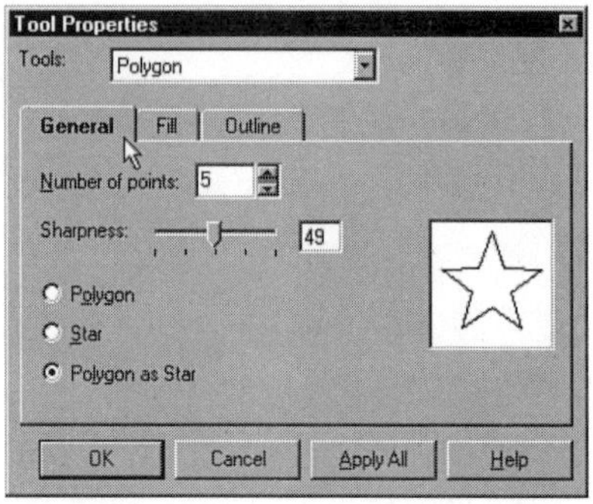

Fig. 4.23
The Polygon Tool Properties dialog box includes controls for setting the Polygon, Star, and Polygon As Star shape options.

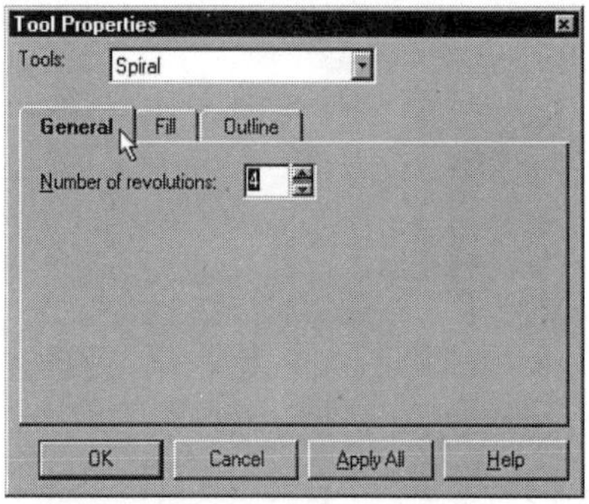

Fig. 4.24
The Spiral Tool Properties dialog box includes a single text box for the number of revolutions it will contain when used.

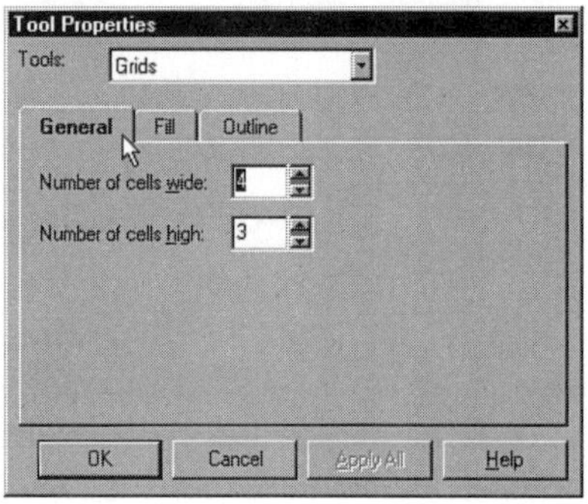

Fig. 4.25
The Grids Tool Properties dialog box enables you to set the width and height of your grid.

The Spiral tool creates objects composed of concentrically reducing curves which appear to stem from a given point, while the Grid tool creates groups of rectangles resembling graph paper.

Tip

Double-clicking on the Polygon, Spiral, or Grid tools displays their respective Tool Properties dialog boxes as well as right-clicking and selecting Properties from the pop-up menu.

Significant Menu Differences

Besides the general differences in the way the CorelDRAW! 6 interface looks, the menus have changed in various ways. Some items have been moved while others seem to have disappeared completely, making way for new program functions whose names may not be self-explanatory. The following is a brief run-through of the menu differences between version 5 and version 6 of CorelDRAW!

The New File Menu

All the basic commands still exist under the File menu and, for the most part, this command list has remained constant throughout the last few versions of CorelDRAW! with these few exceptions (see fig. 4.26).

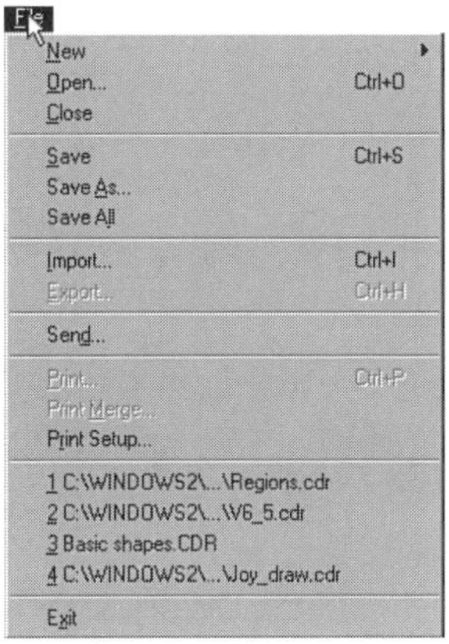

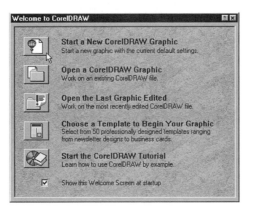

Fig. 4.26
The new File menu has changed little since version 5.

■ *DRAW!'s Friendly New Welcome Screen.* When the program is first launched it's worth mentioning that you now have several options by way of a Welcome dialog box (see fig. 4.27).

Fig. 4.27
The new CorelDRAW! 6 Welcome dialog box adds a friendly greeting to launching the program.

This dialog box allows you to select buttons that include starting a new untitled document, opening an existing document, opening the most recent document, opening a template file, or launching the CorelDRAW! 6 tutorial. You also have the option of getting rid of the Welcome screen for good by deselecting the Show this Welcome Screen At Startup option.

- *New.* This menu command has changed to a flyout which allows you to open a new document or a new template file.

- *Save All.* This feature enables you to save all opened documents with a single command, made possible by the new multiple document inter-face (MDI) that CorelDRAW! 6 is now capable of.

- *Send.* Allows you to transmit drawings through Microsoft Exchange by e-mail. This feature also supports other online services you may choose to install yourself.

The New Edit Menu

It appears that the Edit menu hasn't changed much—until you begin work-ing with the commands (see fig. 4.28). The following list explains the new features.

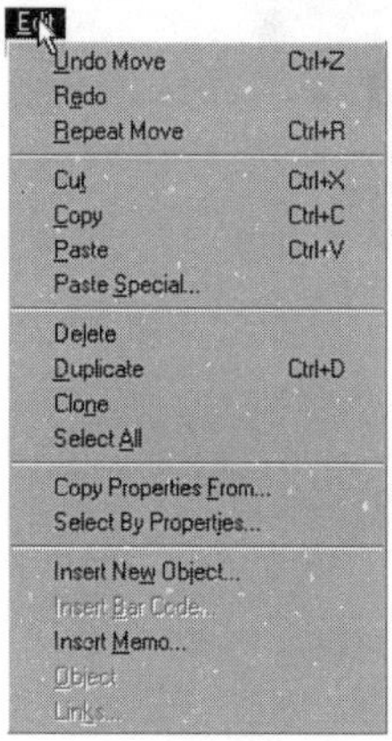

Fig. 4.28
The new Edit menu may not have changed much, but the commands have.

Edit	
<u>U</u>ndo Move	Ctrl+Z
R<u>e</u>do	
<u>R</u>epeat Move	Ctrl+R
Cu<u>t</u>	Ctrl+X
<u>C</u>opy	Ctrl+C
<u>P</u>aste	Ctrl+V
Paste <u>S</u>pecial...	
De<u>l</u>ete	
<u>D</u>uplicate	Ctrl+D
Clo<u>n</u>e	
Select A<u>l</u>l	
Copy Properties <u>F</u>rom...	
Select By Proper<u>t</u>ies...	
Insert Ne<u>w</u> Object...	
Insert Bar Code...	
Insert <u>M</u>emo...	
<u>O</u>bject	
Lin<u>k</u>s...	

- *Undo/Redo.* The Undo Move and Redo commands used for undoing or redoing a specified number of recent commands, now support reversing commands such as Guideline moves. The amount of Undo and Redo commands are limitless and may be set in the General tab of your Tools, Options (Ctrl+J) controls.

- *Cut*. The Cut command (Ctrl+X) now fully supports OLE 2.

- *Copy*. The Copy command (Ctrl+C) now has client/server functionality.

- *Paste*. Now fully supports drag-and-drop functions

- *Paste Special*. Now allows for in-place editing of documents pasted by way of OLE 2 functions.

- *Select by Properties*. One of the more powerful uses of the assignment of property sheets to all objects is the new ability to interrogate your documents and select specific types of objects such as all text objects or all red objects. Choosing Select by Properties displays a roll-up which enables you to search and select any or all object types, fill types, outlines, colors, or special effects, while specifying any object type. For more information on the Select by Properties roll-up see Chapter 6 "Working with Objects."

- *Copy Properties From*. This command displays the Copy Attributes dialog box and allows you to copy Outline Pen, Outline Color, Fill, and/or Text properties from other objects and apply them to new objects.

The New View Menu

The new View menu contains only a few items as in previous versions, but now it has several more flyout menus including Color Palettes, Bitmaps, Color Correction, and Properties menu items (see fig. 4.29). The Color Palettes selection has been expanded to include SpectraMaster, TOYO, and DIC color palettes. The Color Correction options now include Simulate Printer and Gamut Alarm options.

Fig. 4.29
The new View menu has changed very little except for the addition of a Properties flyout menu.

The major changes to the View menu are what you can't see in the menu. Those changes include new toolbars, a fully revamped and customizable status bar, and customizable rulers.

■ *ToolBars*. In CorelDRAW! 6 there are dockable toolbars, meaning you may choose to have the toolbars floating above your page, or attached to the CorelDRAW! window. Toolbars include Standard, Toolbox, Text, Zoom, Roll-ups, and Workspace (see fig. 4.30). Floating toolbars may also be resized to suit your document window size or personal preference. The Roll-ups toolbar alone consists of access buttons to 30 roll-ups.

Fig. 4.30

The new toolbars available in CorelDRAW! 6.

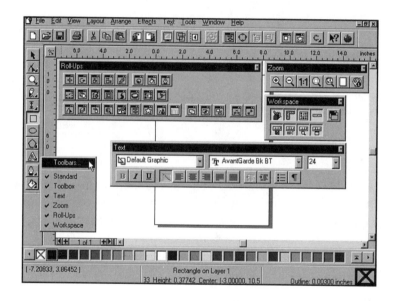

■ <u>Status Bar</u>. The new status bar options are capable of displaying in 12 different sections and will display up to eight different information topics decribing Time, Date, keyboard states, snap constraints, mouse coordinates, object information and details, and large or small color swatch indicators (see fig. 4.31).

> **Tip**
>
> Double-clicking on the scroll bar causes CorelDRAW! 6 to refresh the screen which is the same as the Screen Redraw command (Ctrl+W).

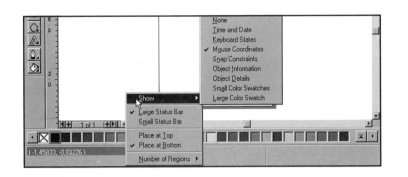

Fig. 4.31
The new Status bar options are accessed through the right mouse button and have changed significantly from version 5.

■ *Workspace.* This is a feature that you will want to have visible all of the time. The brand new Workspace toolbar is an excellent and highly useful innovation that provides access to many brand new features. It enables you to control on-screen display features with the choice of nine buttons, allowing for display of the Toolbox, rulers, color palettes, and display bar, as well as display functions for other toolbars such as the Standard, Text, Zoom, and Roll-ups toolbar. This toolbar will likely prove even more useful than the Standard toolbar. The Workspace toolbar also contains a button for hiding or showing all roll-ups being displayed.

The New Layout Menu
The Layout menu is decidedly different (see fig. 4.32). It now contains several more partitioned areas to define new command functions for the Layers Manager and Styles Manager, and several newcomers such as Snap to Objects, Snap to All, and Snap to None. Other functions not mentioned in this section have either been carried over from version 5 virtually untouched.

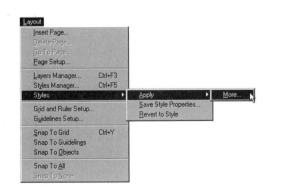

Fig. 4.32
The new Layout menu, including the Styles multiple flyout.

■ *Expanded page setup support.* The first significant change you might notice when setting up for a new document is the Page Setup dialog box changes (see fig. 4.33). Maximum page size may now be set to 150 by 150 feet. That's right, *feet.* There's also a significant difference in the Labels formatting section of the page size selection pull-down menu including label formats for Avery, Ace, MACO, Myers, Nashua, Nebs, Power Up, and UAL.

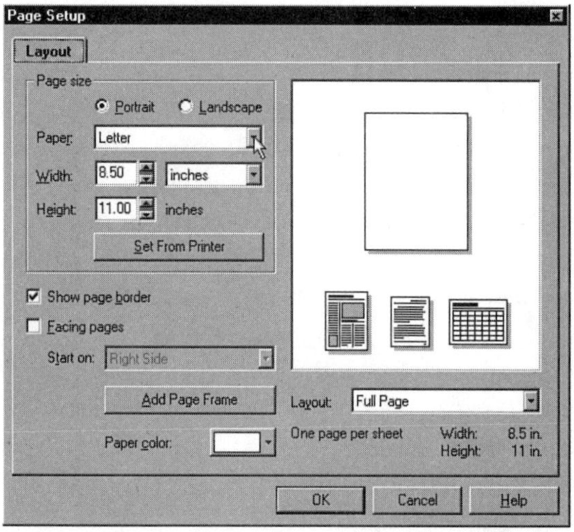

Fig. 4.33
The new Page Setup dialog box has changed significantly in look, but the same basic controls exist.

Tip

Double-clicking on the page border of your document displays the Page Setup dialog box.

■ *Layers Manager.* The Layers Manager command function displays the new Layers Manager Roll-up which contains options for creating, deleting, or editing various layers including the four layers created by default which are the Grid, Guides, Desktop layers, and Layer 1 (see fig. 4.34). The layers may be set to be Visible, Printable, Editable, or a part of the Master Layer either using mouse toggle controls or through the Layers Manager flyout menu under the Settings selection shown in figure 4.34.

■ *Styles Manager.* The Styles Manager is a feature-rich roll-up that contains a flyout menu that gives access to functions for assigning Graphic, Paragraph, and Artistic text styles (see fig. 4.35). Functions also include loading template styles, style show and view controls, hot key assignments, style find, and Properties controls (see fig. 4.36).

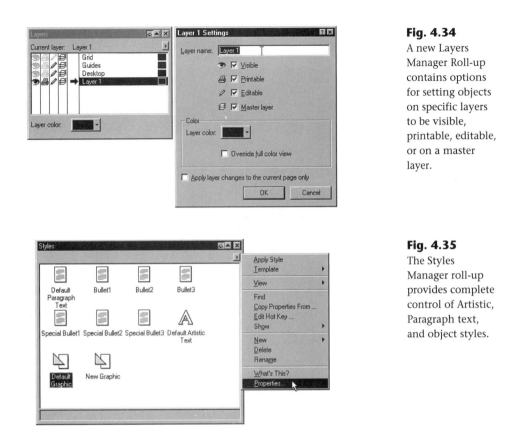

Building a Solid Foundation

Fig. 4.34
A new Layers Manager Roll-up contains options for setting objects on specific layers to be visible, printable, editable, or on a master layer.

Fig. 4.35
The Styles Manager roll-up provides complete control of Artistic, Paragraph text, and object styles.

■ *Styles Flyout.* The Styles flyout in the Layout menu allows more access to style commands including applying, saving, and reverting to previous styles. You may also open the Apply Style dialog box containing all of the available styles in your current document by choosing Layout, Styles, Apply, More (see fig. 4.37).

Fig. 4.36
The Styles Manager Style Properties dialog box allows control and editing of various style attributes.

Fig. 4.37

The Apply Styles dialog box enables you to select from your own list of saved styles without using the Styles Manager.

- *Guidelines Setup.* The guidelines have been beefed up, and now feature their own positioning handles. These handles can be used to move each of the end-points individually, anywhere along the perimeter of your CorelDRAW! 6 document window for slanted guidelines (see fig. 4.38).

- *Show Snap Location Marks.* Snapping feedback has now been implemented with the Snap to Guidelines feature active. When objects come in close contact with the guidelines, the objects snap to the guide and an indicator marking appears on the guide showing the exact contact location (see fig. 4.39). Snapping Feedback may be used while Show Snap Location Marks in the Display tab of the Tools, Options dialog box is selected.

Fig. 4.38

Slanted guidelines are now available in CorelDRAW! 6.

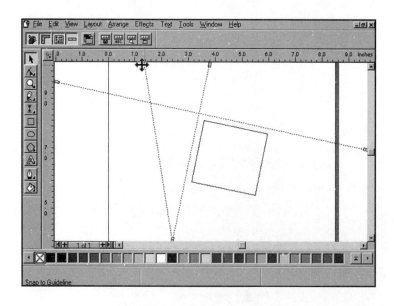

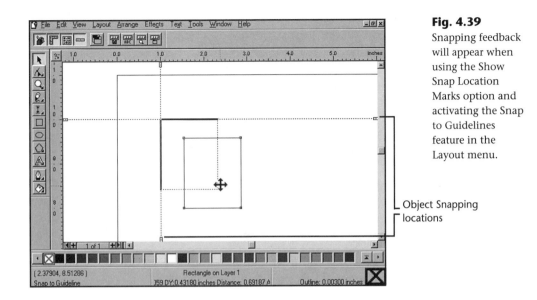

Fig. 4.39
Snapping feedback will appear when using the Show Snap Location Marks option and activating the Snap to Guidelines feature in the Layout menu.

Object Snapping locations

- *Snap To Objects*. This feature causes objects to snap to each other as well as to guides. The snapping points have been set to snap onto object edges, corners, and center points.

- *Snap To All*. This feature automatically selects all Snapping commands to be active, which in turn causes the additional Snap To function of objects snapping to the page border.

- *Snap To None*. This command immediately deactivates all Snapping functions.

The New Arrange Menu

The Arrange menu has gone through few changes, but these small changes are quite significant in terms of tool arrangements. The major change is to the Transform roll-up which is now five separate roll-ups, and a completely refurbished tool in the Align & Distribute roll-up.

- *Split Transform functions*. The single Transform roll-up from version 5 of CorelDRAW! has been redeveloped into five separate roll-ups including Position, Rotation, Scale & Mirror, Size, and Skew (see fig. 4.40). Each of these roll-ups features advanced flyout controls for transformation and the ability of applying transformation to a duplicate instead of your original object.

Fig. 4.40

The new Position, Rotation, Scale & Mirror, Size, and Skew roll-ups offer precise control for nearly any type of object transformation.

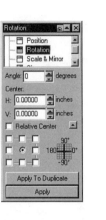

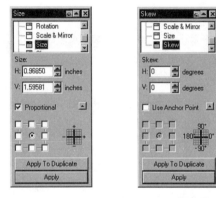

- *Align & Distribute commands in a single roll-up.* This revamped set of controls has been very cleverly designed to allow for a single set of buttons to control two related functions. The Align & Distribute Roll-up consists of vertical and horizontal control buttons, a main preview window, and a full set of align and distribute options (see fig. 4.41).

- *Group nesting maximum raised.* You may now Group-nest up to 99 nested groups from the previous limit of 10 in CorelDRAW! 5.

- *Break Apart/Combine text.* The Break Apart and Combine functions work as before on object commands; however, new Artistic text options have been implemented to allow for breaking apart words in a sentence into individual text objects before converting the words into individual objects. You may also use the Combine command to reassemble the text into a single Artistic text object.

- *Intersection/Trim/Weld in one new roll-up.* These previously separate functions have been grouped together into a single, three-function roll-up (see fig. 4.42). Leave Original Target Object and Other Objects features have been implemented to cover all three parts of this new roll-up.

Fig. 4.41
The new Align &
Distribute Roll-up
now offers you the
capability of even
distribution of
objects.

 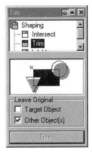 

Fig. 4.42
The revamped
Intersection, Trim,
and Weld Roll-ups
offer new options
for preserving your
original objects.

The Effects Menu

The Effects menu has remained relatively untouched in terms of additional tools; however, some existing tools have been updated to varying degrees. Also, Blend, Contour, Envelope, Extrude, Lens, and Powerline roll-ups have been grouped into a single roll-up.

- *Extrude's arc ball.* The Extrude Roll-up has been completely redesigned and now features tabbed areas for extrude presets, lighting, and color fill controls. A slick, new interactive arc ball has also been implemented, making it easier for setting up and conceptualizing extrude effects before applying them (see fig. 4.43).

- *Contour rainbow effects.* The Contour Roll-up has been revamped to include options for applying contour effects inside, outside, and to the center of objects, as well as now being equipped with options for blending from original objects pen and fill colors to the new colors of the destination contour (see fig. 4.44).

Fig. 4.43
The new Extrude
effect arc ball in
the Extrude Roll-
up is extremely
intuitive.

Fig. 4.44
The Contour pen
and fill color are
two new controls
added to this
feature.

■ *Three new lenses added.* Three new lenses have been added to the Lens
Effect Roll-up including Wireframe, Custom Color Map, and Fish Eye.
Each lens, including the previously existing Transparency, Magnify,
Brighten, Invert, Color Limit, Color Add, Tinted Grayscale, and Heat
Map, each include a Viewpoint and freeze options. Custom Color Map
is similar to the old Heat Map lens but now has controls for controlling
the palette rotation. Wireframe now allows you to reveal the inner
wireframe construction of objects. Fish Eye works in a similar way to a
typical fisheye camera lens distorting and warping the curves of objects.
All three are shown in figure 4.45.

■ *Bitmap Color Mask Roll-up.* The Bitmap Color Mask Roll-up offers controls for creating and applying color masks to imported bitmap objects
(see fig. 4.46). The roll-up also contains a command menu flyout that
offers options for opening previously saved color mask files, or saving
newly created color masks. The roll-up also contains a color picker to
interactively select colors contained in the imported bitmap object.

Fig. 4.45
The Custom Heat Map, Wireframe, and Fish Eye lens Roll-ups.

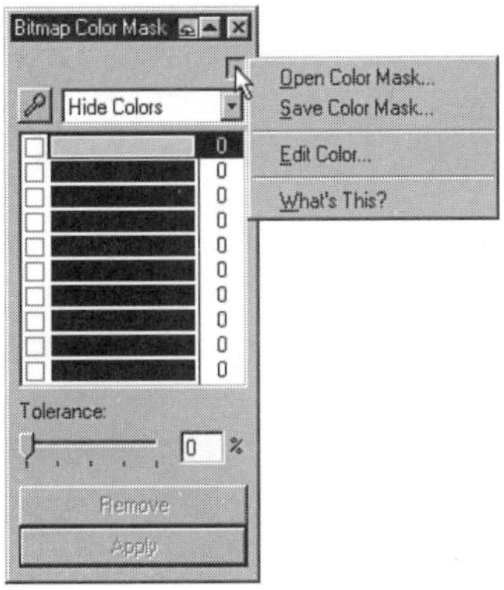

Fig. 4.46
The Bitmap Color Mask Roll-up is CorelDRAW! 6's internal mask control and is identical to the Color Mask Roll-up in PhotoPAINT 6.

New Text Menu Features

The new text controls and features in CorelDRAW! 6 go much deeper than the brief items listed in the Text menu and include a quick-access text toolbar, revamped dialog boxes for text editing and formatting, and spell-check, proofreading, and typing assistance. These changes are quite significant and prove quite different from the previous version 5 set of controls.

Text Tools

The text tools now available have graduated far beyond the Text Roll-up of the previous version 5, and virtually every dialog box for both Artistic and Paragraph text has been revamped. The following is a brief summary of the changes.

- *Text toolbar.* The Text toolbar is the replacement of the previous version 5 text roll-up (see fig. 4.47). It operates on selected text and changes take place immediately.

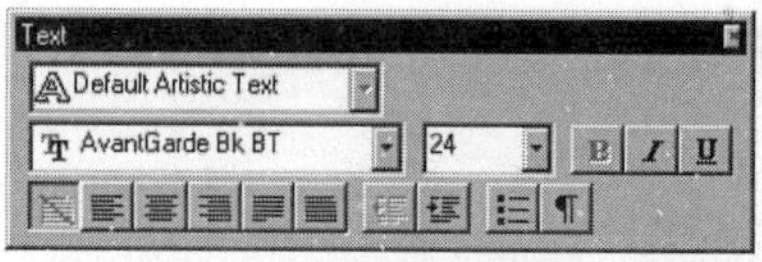

Fig. 4.47
The Text toolbar
contains quick
formatting tools
that cause instant
changes to the
character at-
tributes of your
text.

- *Text options.* Like the main options for the program set through the Tool, Options command, the Text Options dialog box features controls for the overall behavior of text. The text option tabs are divided into text and formatting and include text controls for font display, greeking, clipboard capabilities and Panose Font matching, and formatting options for paragraph frame behavior and non-printing characters.

- *Font Attributes/Alignment tabs.* These are two divisions within the Character Attributes dialog box and control all characteristics of Artistic and Paragraph text such as font, size, spacing, placement, effect, alignment, and style. Strikethrough, Overline, and underline line settings are each editable.

- *Text effects.* Available only to Paragraph text, this is now what Corel refers to as bullets (see fig. 4.48). Bullets may be set to be any symbol currently loaded in any size, and to any indent.

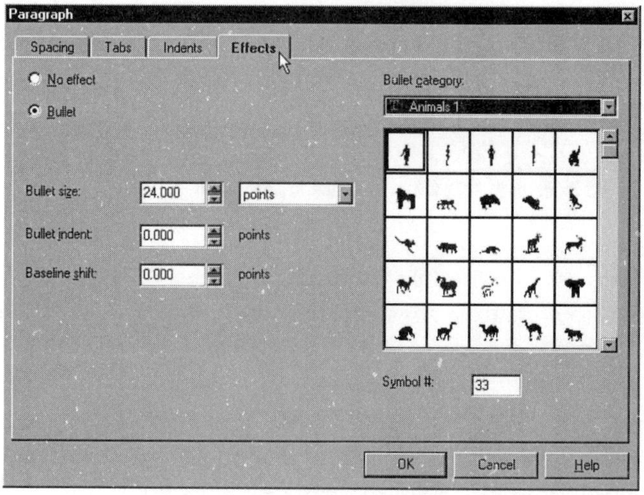

Fig. 4.48
Text effects for
bullet controls
through the
Paragraph text
formatting
command have
been redesigned
and offer bullets
composed of any
symbol font.

- *Columns tab.* A revamped Paragraph Text Columns dialog box now controls how individual paragraph text frames are setup (see fig. 4.49). The controls follow a much more logical sequence and settings structure than previous column controls, including settings for number of columns, width and gutter spacing separately set for each.

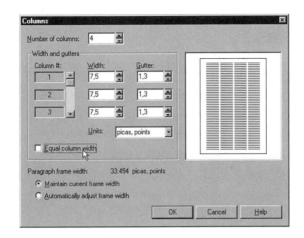

Fig. 4.49
The Paragraph text Columns dialog box is designed much more logically than its predecessors.

Building a Solid Foundation

- *Show non-printing characters*. Text Options are now available to show soft and hard carriage returns, tabs, and spaces in text.

- *Tabs and leaders*. Full control over tabs and leaders is offered through the Paragraph text options only, but to exacting measures and incorporating leaders that may be composed of any keyboard or extended characters (see fig. 4.50).

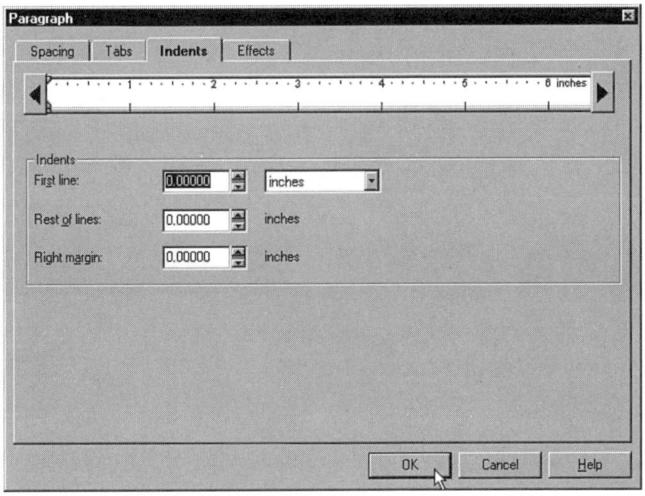

Fig. 4.50
The Indents tab of the Paragraph dialog box now features a separate set of controls from the Tabs controls.

- *Artistic to Paragraph conversions*. CorelDRAW! 6 offers commands for converting Artistic text to Paragraph text, and Paragraph text to Artistic text. Changing the text between types doesn't alter the characteristics of the text.

■ *Full justify and forced justify.* These are two brand new features of the Character Attributes, Alignment tab.

■ *Memo objects.* Memo isn't just a feature, it's actually a mini text editor. It enables you to plant small notes composed of nine short lines of text, and a 20-character heading into icons and drop them into your drawing for future reference. This feature is found under Edit, Insert Memo (see fig. 4.51).

■ *Text Properties.* As with all object types, text has its own Properties sheet, which differs little between Artistic text and Paragraph text. The Property dialog box gives the current attributes applied to text and provides access to basic formatting controls as well as button access to the Character, Paragraph, and Columns tools for further editing.

Fig. 4.51

The Memo utility within Corel-DRAW! 6 enables you to embed various types of notes about your drawing or subject matter.

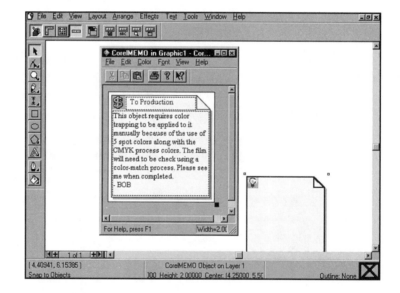

■ *Text Statistics.* This is a new feature which finally gives CorelDRAW! the ability to measure the amount of text being used in a frame. The Statistics dialog box measures the number of paragraphs, lines, words, characters, and the number of each style used (see fig. 4.52).

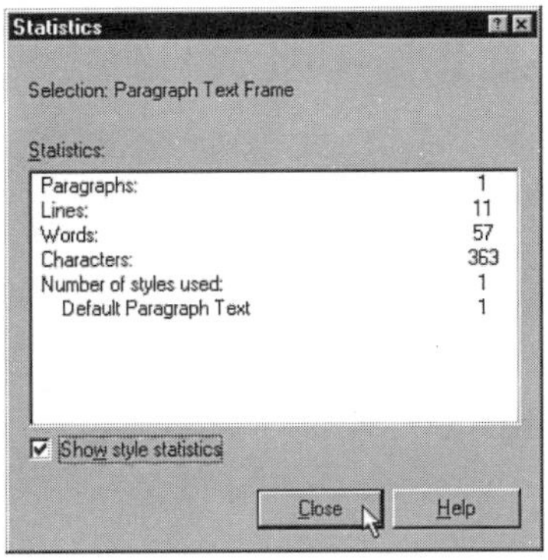

Fig. 4.52
The Text Statistics dialog box provides detailed information about Paragraph or Artistic text objects.

Word-shaping Tools

In version 5 of CorelDRAW! there was a meager thesaurus, and a spell-check utility. Version 6 goes far beyond this level with the introduction of precision grammar tools for spell checking, proofreading on two levels, a thesaurus, and a type assist program.

- *Spell checking.* A spell-check feature checks selected text for errors. The spell check displays the full sentence containing the errors while displaying a full error description (see fig. 4.53).

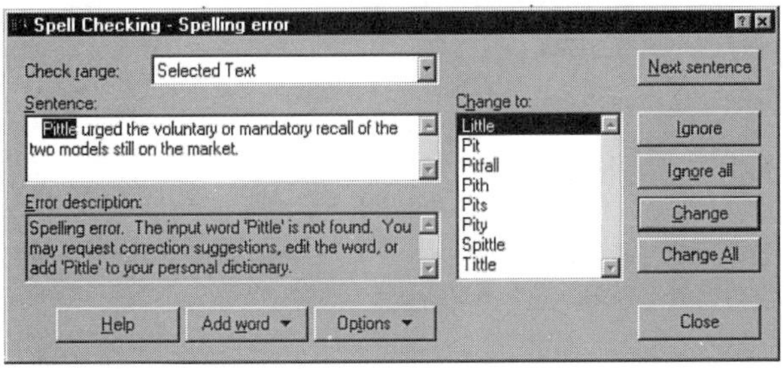

Fig. 4.53
The CorelDRAW! 6 spell checker is a powerful, option-rich spell-check utility.

- *Proofreading, at two levels.* Proofreading may be performed on text at a Quick Proofreading or a Full Proofreading level. As with the spell check command, the Proofreading utility also displays the full sentence containing the errors while displaying a full error description.

- *Thesaurus.* The CorelDRAW! Thesaurus is surprisingly definitive offering a vast array of definitions and replacement words for even the vaguest of terms (see fig. 4.54).

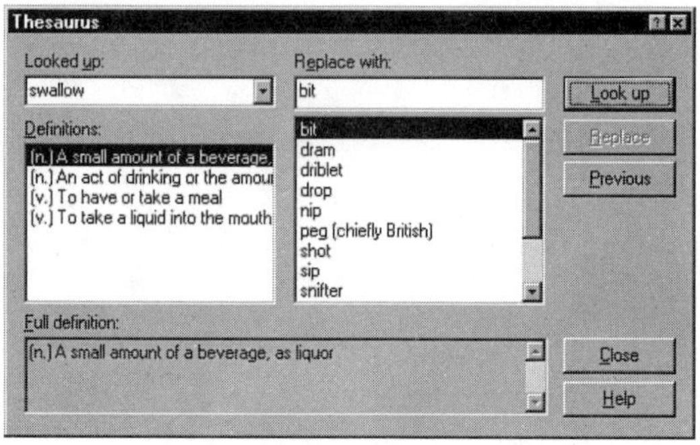

Fig. 4.54
The Thesaurus controls make access to this helpful resource easy.

- *Type Assist.* A basic, but customizable type assist feature is also new to the CorelDRAW! text-editing arsenal. Type Assist is a built-in utility within CorelDRAW! 6 that monitors your keystrokes while you type and makes corrections to your spelling.

Customization of Toolbars and Menus

Customization tools are a powerful feature of CorelDRAW! 6, enabling you to tailor your own personal version of the application, including tools, toolbars, menus, and object properties.

- *Custom toolbars.* The toolbars in general aren't new but a large number of them are and the fact that you can either have them displayed, docked into the interface, or detached and floating makes this feature extremely different. You can now make your own toolbar using any or all of your favorite toolbar buttons.

- *Application launcher.* Normally residing on the Standard toolbar, this button gives quick-access to the rest of the major CorelDRAW! 6 applications (see fig. 4.55).

- *Custom menus.* You may customize any of the menus in CorelDRAW! 6.

- *Page Setup highlights - Label formats.* Overall page maximum size is limited to 150 feet square. Highlights of the Page Setup page sizes include literally hundreds of styles of label formats for printing custom labels from your laser printer.

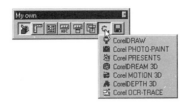

Fig. 4.55
The Application launcher set-up shown here in a floating custom toolbar, contains shortcuts to the other applications in the Corel-DRAW! 6 suite.

New Object Properties

The concept of Properties is featured throughout CorelDRAW! 6. Properties are any collection of data associated with an object within the program. Properties may be created, measured, counted, searched for, or altered.

■ *General properties.* Also sometimes referred to as generic, General properties include information about the currently selected objects, the layer they reside on, type of object, the object's style, and optional Wrap Paragraph text setting to apply to the object (see fig. 4.56). The Wrap Paragraph text is Corel's answer to run-around text options featured in other popular page layout software such as Adobe PageMaker, and Quark XPress. While selected, the Wrap Paragraph Text option causes only paragraph text to be repelled from the object it is applied to.

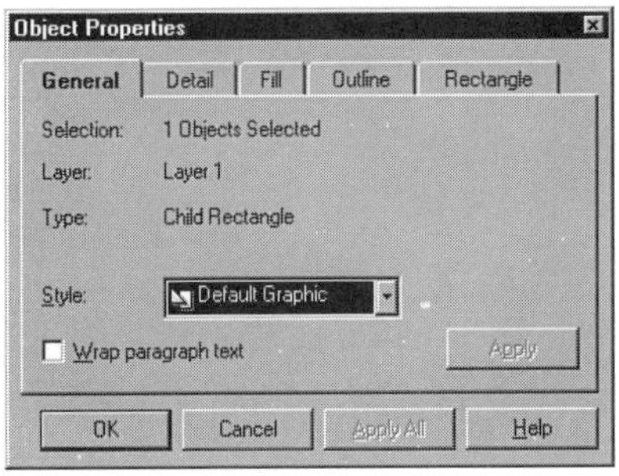

Fig. 4.56
The General page of the Object Properties sheet allows you to understand about your objects in detail.

■ *Detail Properties.* The Detail Properties sheet is one of the few property dialogs that merely displays information rather than allowing you to actually edit settings (see fig. 4.57). This dialog box provides information about the dimensions, center origin on the page, and center of rotation position.

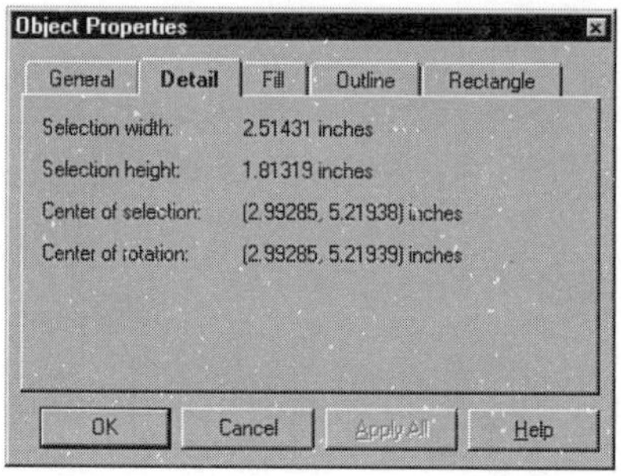

Fig. 4.57
The Detail page
of the Objects
Properties sheet
provided generic
information about
objects such as
height, width,
position, and
center origin.

■ *Fill Properties.* The Fill Properties sheet is packed with both mini-editing controls and has full access to Uniform, Fountain, Two-color, Full-color, Vector, and Texture fill dialog boxes (see fig. 4.58).

■ *Outline Properties.* Outline properties provide displays of current outline settings, access to editing of outline pen width, color, style, and arrowheads, and full access to the Outline Pen dialog controls (see fig. 4.59).

■ *Object, Curve Properties.* The Curve Properties sheet provides information about the number of nodes and sub-paths on a curve, page position of the first and last nodes, and the open or closed condition of the curve (see fig. 4.60).

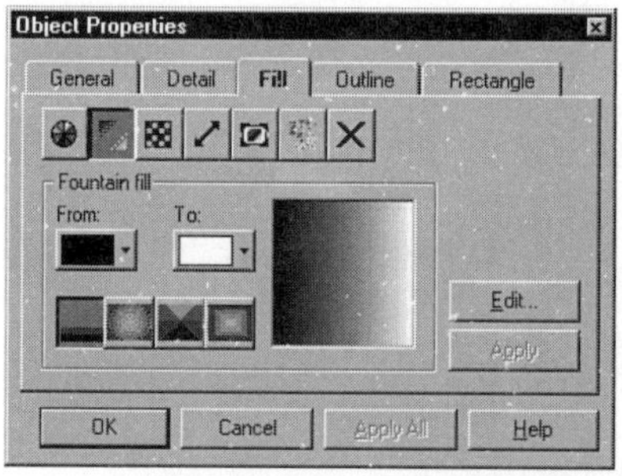

Fig. 4.58
The Fill page of the
Object Properties
sheet has even
more controls to
let you control
your objects.

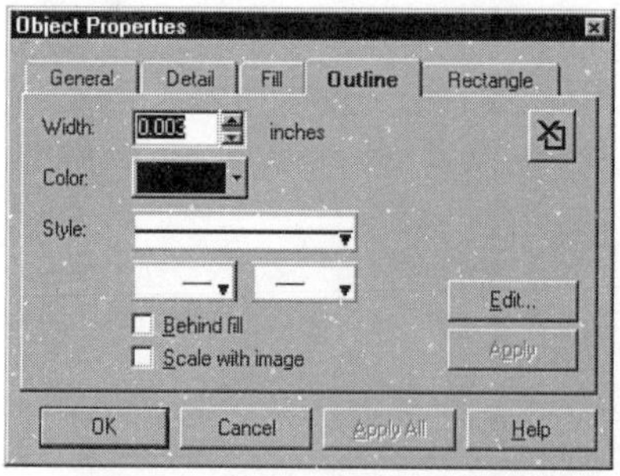

Fig. 4.59
The Outline page
of the Object
Properties sheet
features basic
outline options
and shortcuts to
more detailed
options.

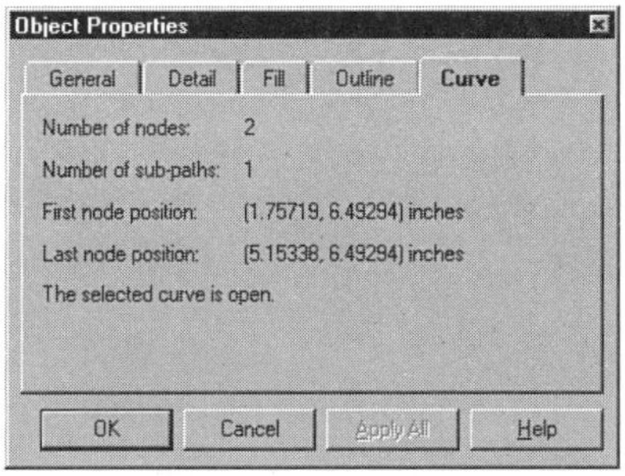

Fig. 4.60
The Curve page
of the Object
Properties sheet
provides data
about curve
objects, including
node, sub-path,
and open/closed
path information.

- *Object, Rectangle Properties.* The rectangle properties contain controls to change roundness of corners via a slider bar, as well as an attributes lock button (see fig. 4.61).

- *Object, Ellipse Properties.* The Ellipse Properties sheet provides controls for setting your ellipse to a Pie or an Arc, and setting the starting and ending angles in a clockwise or counterclockwise direction (see fig. 4.62). An optional attributes lock is also available.

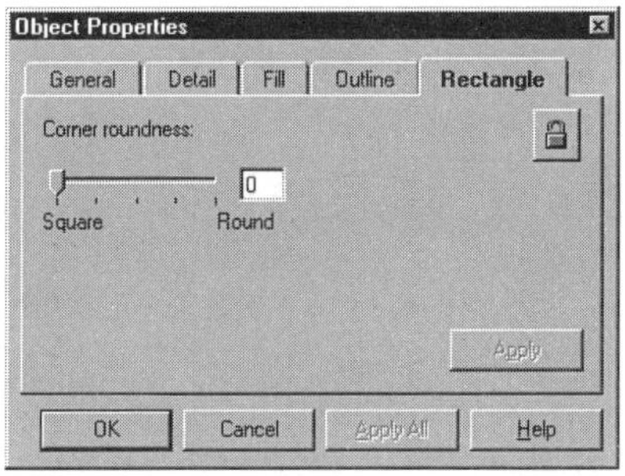

Fig. 4.61
The Rectangle page
of the Object
Properties sheet
lets you control
corner roundness
using two separate
methods.

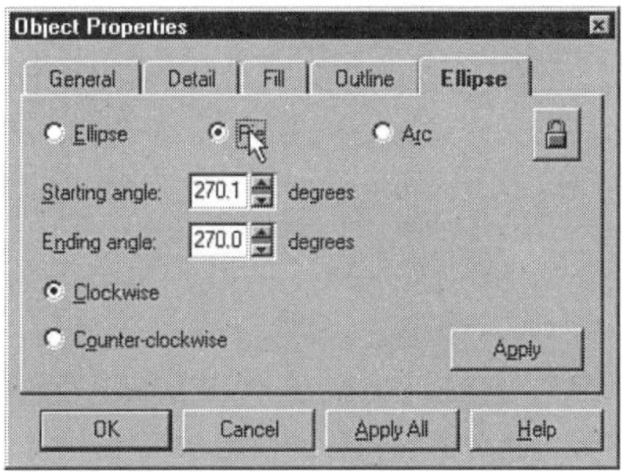

Fig. 4.62
The Ellipse page
of the Object
Properties sheet
features options
for changing
ellipse, pie, and
arc options.

■ *Object, Polygon Properties.* Polygon Properties may be edited through this dialog box including the number of points and/or sides of the shape, sharpness, and polygon to star (or vice versa) settings (see fig. 4.63).

Fig. 4.63
The Polygon page of the Object Properties sheet provides controls for editing existing polygon objects.

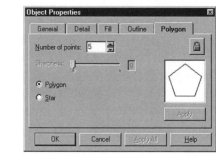

■ *Object, Text Properties.* The Text Properties sheet provides information about the font, size, style, and alignment of the currently selected text with optional editing controls and full access to the Characters Attributes dialog controls (see fig. 4.64).

Fig. 4.64
The Text page of the Object Properties sheet has brief text formatting options and shortcuts to more detailed text controls.

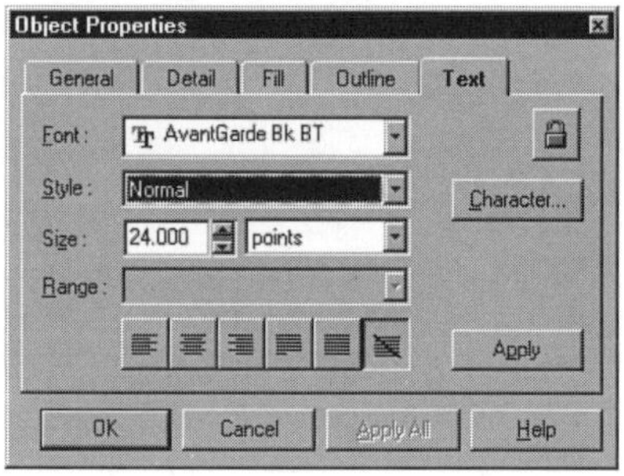

From Here...

Although the basic thrust of the program hasn't changed very much from version to version, CorelDRAW! 6 is significantly improved through the addition and development of features and options. In the past, Corel users have pleaded for the flexibility of more user control and with this version of the software those users who wanted more control, precision, and customization abilities have certainly gotten what they asked for.

For related topics discussed in this chapter, see:

■ Chapter 5, "Working with Text," for information on styles and properties, and pen controls.

■ Chapter 13, "Using Color, Wizards, and Applying Color Masks," for information on the bitmap color mask roll-up.

I

Building a Solid Foundation

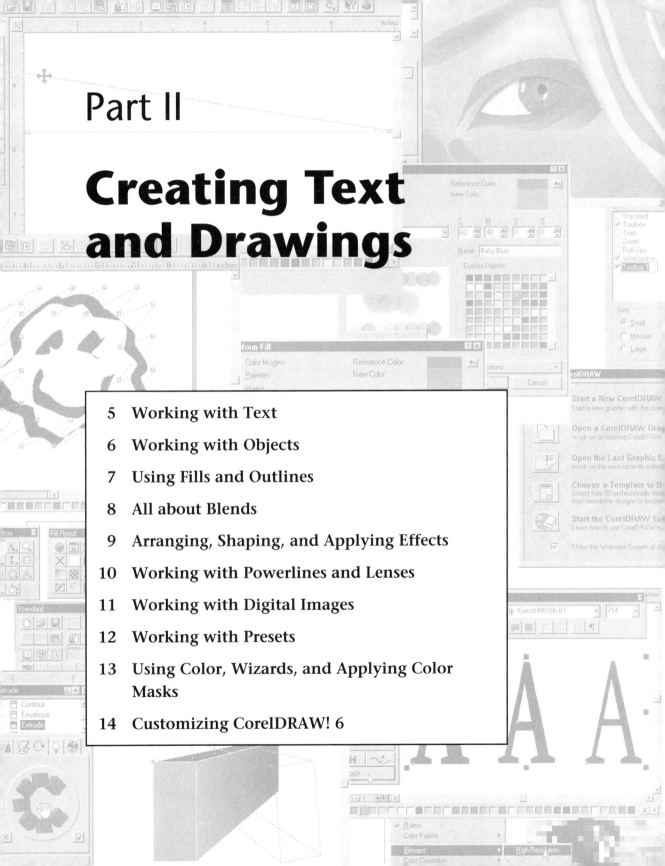

Part II

Creating Text and Drawings

5   Working with Text

6   Working with Objects

7   Using Fills and Outlines

8   All about Blends

9   Arranging, Shaping, and Applying Effects

10 Working with Powerlines and Lenses

11 Working with Digital Images

12 Working with Presets

13 Using Color, Wizards, and Applying Color Masks

14 Customizing CorelDRAW! 6

Chapter 5

Working with Text

The written word is the second-most common way of communicating on paper (the first being pictures). The best drawing programs are those that offer complete and easy-to-use features for manipulating both.

CorelDRAW! 6 is at the top of the list when it comes to controls over text, type, and font manipulation. In this chapter, you learn to

- Create, format, and edit text

- Use CorelDRAW! 6 utilities to check spelling and grammar

- Design and illustrate using text and symbols

- Manage font groups

- Create your own fonts and symbols

Creating and Editing Artistic Text

There are two types of text within CorelDRAW!: Artistic text and Paragraph text (see fig. 5.1). The tools for both are contained in the Text Flyout located third from the end of the Toolbox, or from the Text toolbar if you have it displayed. The Artistic Text tool resembles a capital A. The Paragraph Text tool looks like a white rectangle containing horizontal black lines, the first line shorter than the rest.

Fig. 5.1

Artistic (top) and Paragraph text objects are created using the Artistic and Paragraph text tools.

Artistic Text Tool

Paragraph Text Tool

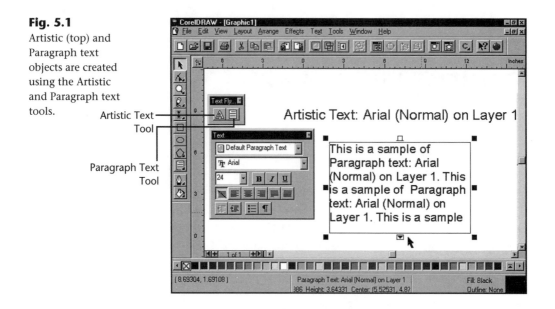

The kinds of text created with these two very different tools have their own characteristics, and each has its own strengths and weaknesses. Choosing which kind of text to use for a specific function is the key, and this question becomes much easier to answer when you know what those strengths and weaknesses are.

Creating Artistic Text

Artistic text is a good format for newsletter headlines, page labels, flow charts, diagrams, or any other situation where you have only a few characters per text string to deal with. Artistic text may be fit to a path, extruded, or given perspective. You may also use Artistic text if your intent is to apply special effects to your text. To create Artistic text for the first time, follow these steps:

1. Select the Artistic Text tool (F8) from the Toolbox, and notice your cursor change to an I-beam.

2. Click a text-entry point where you want your first character to begin. Your cursor will change to a black text-entry point.

3. Type your text before clicking anywhere else. Your text will continue on one line until you press Enter to force a line feed in the text.

4. When you are finished typing your text, click the Pick tool (or any other tool), or click another text-entry point to enter another separate Artistic Text block.

Once you have created your text and re-selected the Pick tool from the Toolbox, your Artistic text is highlighted, and you'll notice that it has eight handles just like any other object highlighted in DRAW!. In fact, it will behave as if it were an object in DRAW!. Using the Pick tool you can apply fills and outlines to it, rotate it, or resize it in the same manner you would any object.

Editing Artistic Text

Once your text has been entered, the characters may be edited a number of ways in CorelDRAW! 6. The simplest, quickest way to edit it is to re-select the Artistic Text tool from the Toolbox and click anywhere in the text block you wish to edit. Once your cursor has changed to an I-beam, it behaves the same way as in any simple word-processing program and you may edit the characters directly on the screen. You may also use the Edit Text dialog box by pressing Ctrl+Shift+T (see fig. 5.2). The Edit Text dialog box enables you to perform character editing on your text, and if necessary, you may also format the character size, style, and font.

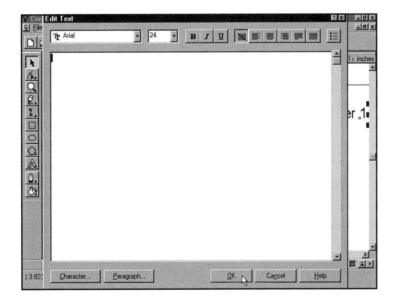

Fig. 5.2
The Edit Text dialog box enables you to edit Artistic and Paragraph text blocks.

To control the format of all the other characteristics of your Artistic Text choose Text, Character (Ctrl+T) which enables you to change character attributes in either Font or Alignment tabbed categories. The Font tab of the Character Attributes dialog box (see fig. 5.3) includes controls for Fonts,

Placement, Effect, Size, Style, Underline, Overline, and Strikeout. The Font tab of the Character Attributes dialog box also displays a sample of the font and style selected, and the Underline, Overline, and Strikeout controls each feature an Edit button. To set more attributes select the Alignment tab which provides controls for type alignment and spacing of Characters, Words, and Lines (see fig. 5.4). The Character Attributes dialog box also applies to type and font characteristics of Paragraph Text.

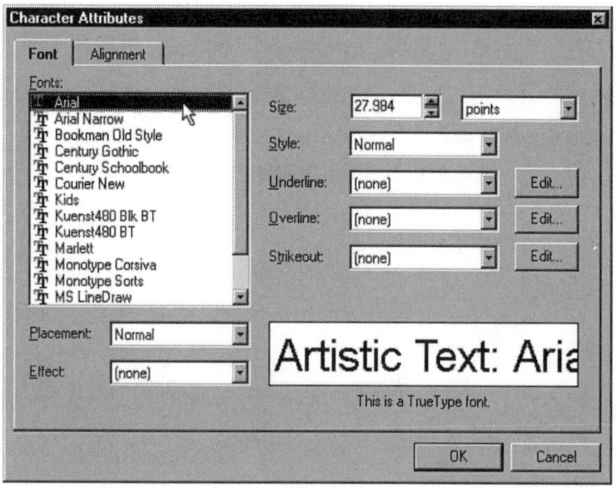

Fig. 5.3
The Font tab of the Character Attributes dialog box includes options for setting all aspects of character attributes.

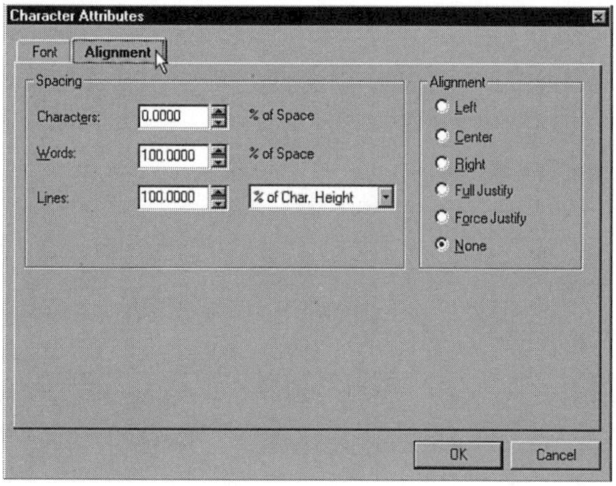

Fig. 5.4
The Alignment tab of the Character Attributes dialog box includes controls for setting all spacing and justification options.

You may also select the Text toolbar for quick formatting, or set the Pop-up Menu First Menu Item under the General tab of Preferences (Ctrl+J) to Edit Text.

When it comes to flexibility though, Artistic text has strengths that far out-
weigh that of the Paragraph text format. Once you have created some Artistic
text containing more than three words you can experiment with the Break
Apart command (Ctrl+K), and the Convert to Curves command (Ctrl+Q) and
alter the shape of text by applying those commands and using the Shape tool
(F10). The following steps explain how to use these features:

1. Using the Shape tool, click on the text once. This time take notice of
   the small marker which precedes the bottom-left corner of each word in
   your text string.

2. Click the right mouse button to open the menu illustrated in figure 5.5.

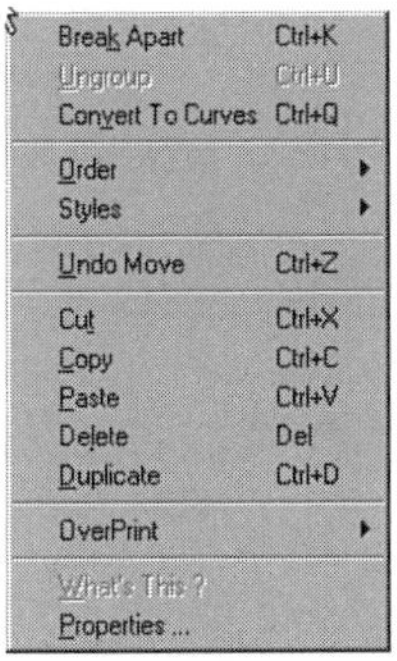

Fig. 5.5
Right-clicking on
the text, opens a
pop-up menu
which includes
specific text
commands.

3. Select the Break Apart command from the menu and watch how
   DRAW! separates the words into separate text blocks without affecting
   any of the character attributes. DRAW! automatically selects the first
   word in the text string.

   Note that DRAW! has placed a small marker at the bottom left of each
   character in the selected word.

4. Now, Zoom In on the first word using the Zoom tool (F2), and select
   the Wireframe view (Shift+F9). If necessary, Zoom In again.

5. Once again select the shortcut menu from the text and select Convert
   to Curves. DRAW! now transforms what was once typed characters into
   one single complicated curve.

6. Click the right mouse button again and select Break Apart again.
   DRAW! changes the single curve into several independent curves (depending on how many characters in your original word).

II

Creating Text & Drawings

7. Select the Shape tool (F10) from the Toolbox and select the first character (curve) in the string. DRAW! highlights the curve and displays the individual nodes of the curve.

8. Click once on one of the nodes and see it change black indicating it's now highlighted. Grab onto it with the left mouse button and drag it. Notice how the curve changes shape (see fig. 5.6).

Fig. 5.6
All text is made up of curves, which, by using the Convert to Curves command, may be altered by dragging the nodes with the Shape tool.

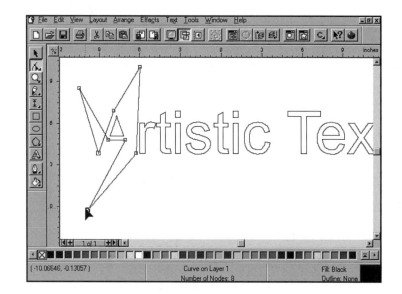

9. Reselect the Pick tool, Zoom Out to your original view, and set the view to Editable Wireframe (Shift+F9).

All text is composed of curves—that's how it's originally designed. You may even study font construction using this same procedure if you want to create your own fonts and symbols.

Working with Paragraph Text

On the other side of the text world is the Paragraph Text tool (Shift+F8) which has strengths of its own. The Paragraph Text tool may be accessed from the Toolbox or the Text toolbar. Figure 5.1 shows samples of both types of text formats, Artistic on the top, Paragraph on the bottom. Notice how the Paragraph text block has a frame around it, a clear tab at the top of the frame, and an arrow tab at the bottom if all the text is not displayed. The frame represents a single column of text. The arrow tab indicates that there is additional text waiting to be displayed. The highlighted handles indicate that you can resize the text frame.

Tip

When comparing Artistic to Paragraph text formats, notice that the resizing handles operate in very different fashions. The resizing handles (corners) on the Artistic text will resize the point size of the text proportionally and the side handles will stretch it horizontally or vertically. The handles on the corners of the Paragraph text frame will only resize the frame proportionally, leaving the point size of the text constant. The side handles of the Paragraph text frame will stretch only the text frame horizontally or vertically.

The same rules apply to rotation and skewing handles on Artistic and Paragraph text. Artistic text rotation and skew handles behave as they would on any object. However, on Paragraph text the skew handles apply to the frame only.

Creating and Editing Paragraph Text

To create a block of Paragraph Text follow these steps:

1. Select the Paragraph Text tool from either the Toolbox or the Text Flyout toolbar if you have it showing. Your cursor changes to a crosshair cursor.

2. Define an area for your Paragraph Text frame by clicking and dragging using the left mouse button. Release the mouse button once you are happy with the frame size and position.

3. Once you release the mouse button, an I-beam cursor will appear in the upper-left corner of the frame, awaiting text to be entered. Enter your new Paragraph text.

4. When finished entering your text, deselect the Paragraph Text tool by clicking on the Pick tool in the Toolbox.

You may reposition your Paragraph text frame by clicking on it with the left mouse button, or you may resize it using the resizing handles.

To edit Paragraph text directly on your screen, select your text frame and choose the Paragraph Text tool from the Toolbox. Your cursor will change to an I-beam cursor. Click an entry point or highlight the text you would like to edit (see fig. 5.7). The Paragraph text editing functions work much the same way as a word-processing program.

Fig. 5.7

Editing Paragraph may be done directly on your screen using the Paragraph text tool.

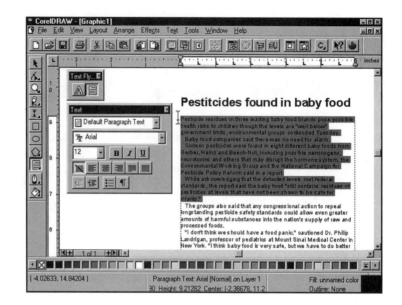

You may also edit Paragraph text in DRAW!'s Edit Text dialog box (see fig. 5.8) by selecting Text, Edit (Ctrl+Shift+T).

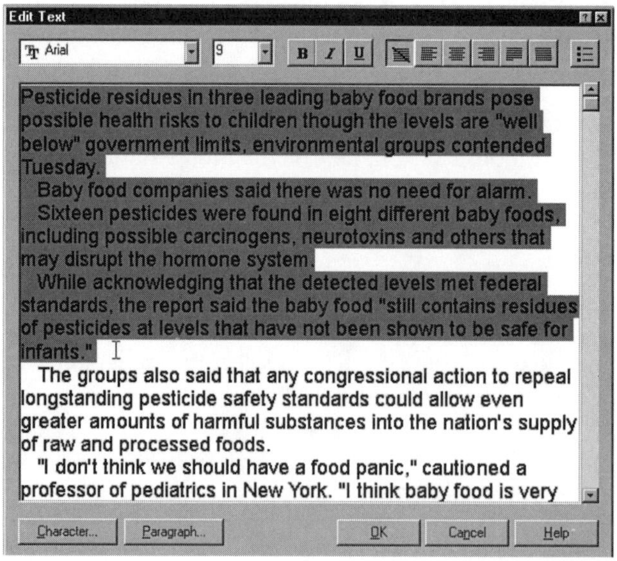

Fig. 5.8

Editing Paragraph text may also be done from within the Edit Text dialog box.

Frames and Columns

If you see the arrow tab at the bottom of a Paragraph text frame you will most likely need to do one of two things. To reveal the text hiding behind that arrow, you'll need to either stretch the frame out to extend beyond the last line of your text, or reposition the additional text in another part of your layout. The arrow tab indicates a warning sign of some sort—that not only is there hidden text in your layout, but that it hasn't been linked to any other Paragraph text frames either.

> **Tip**
>
> To set the default for either or both Artistic text or Paragraph text, select either tool and, without having any objects selected, select the Character Attributes dialog box by selecting Character from the Text menu (Ctrl+T). DRAW! will then display the message There are no objects currently selected. To which types of new objects will the default apply? Select either or both Artistic or Paragraph text, press OK and continue setting the character attributes.

To stretch out the Paragraph text frame, pull downward on the arrow tab or resize the frame to accommodate the extra text. Pulling down on the arrow tab will keep the text frame width and top position constant and is the easiest and quickest way. To reposition the additional text in another part of your layout follow these steps:

1. Select your Paragraph text frame by clicking on it once. Notice the arrow tab at the bottom center of the frame indicating additional text.

2. Click once on the arrow tab with your left mouse button. Observe that your cursor changes to a representation of a frame of text with a line pointing downward and to the right. The tip of this line is the tip of your cursor.

3. Using the tip of the cursor and the left mouse button, define a new Paragraph text frame by clicking and diagonally dragging from top-left to bottom-right to define your paragraph text position and shape.

4. Release the mouse when you have completed defining your frame, and DRAW! will display as much of the hidden text as possible in the new Paragraph text frame (see fig. 5.9). Notice the symbols inside the bottom tab of the first frame and the top tab of the new frame have now both changed.

II

Creating Text & Drawings

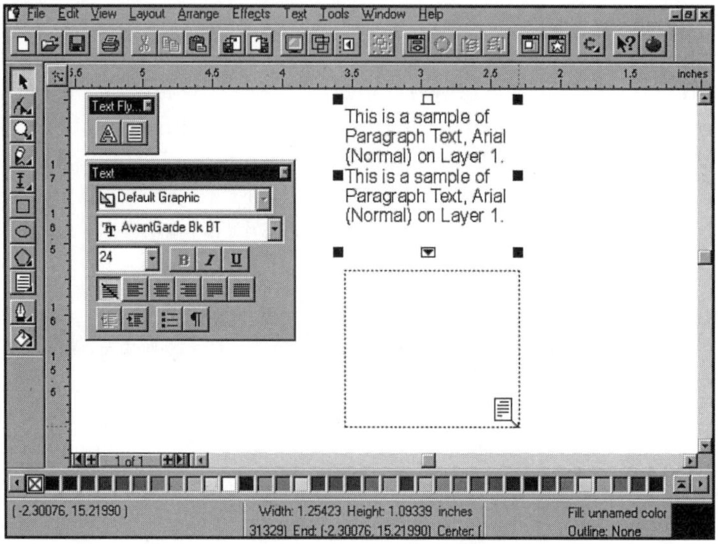

Fig. 5.9

Paragraph text may be flowed from one text block to another, using the text flow tabs at the bottom and top of each text block.

Paragraph frames may be linked from column to column within a page, or may also be linked from page to page. DRAW! 6 also features new controls for column widths within frames (see fig. 5.10). To select the Columns dialog box use your left mouse button to click and highlight a Paragraph text block. Then select Text, Columns. The Columns dialog box will only be available if there is Paragraph text selected in your layout page.

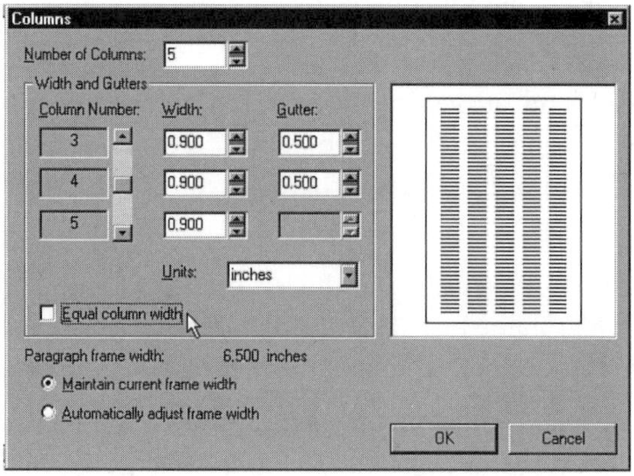

Fig. 5.10

CorelDRAW! 6 now features new column controls to set the number of columns and adjust the spacing between each.

The Columns dialog box features controls for defining the Number of Columns within your Paragraph text frame. Other controls include Width and Gutter measures by Column Number, an Equal Column Width option, and Paragraph Frame Width options.

When you increase or decrease the Number of Columns within your Paragraph text frame, DRAW! automatically provides Width and Gutter measures for each column. By selecting the Equal Column Width option inactive you may edit those measures to format uneven column measures. In fact, each column and each gutter may be formatted to a different measure within one frame. DRAW! also provides a Preview window so that you have an immediate visual reference of your changes (refer to fig. 5.10).

Before moving on, one interesting feature to note at this point is the ability you have to reshape a Paragraph text frame using the Shape tool. The main function of the Shape tool is to alter the shape of individual objects by editing the points that make up the object. By applying an effect called Envelope to a Paragraph text frame, you are able to define the frame as an object. Envelopes are bounding boxes whose shapes may be edited to fit nearly any form. Because DRAW! considers envelopes as objects (in this case, this one just happens to contain text) you are able to use the Shape tool to alter the native rectangular shape of a text frame.

▶ See "Object Linking and Embedding," p. 506

▶ See "Using the Clipboard," p. 508

When using the Envelope effect in this next exercise you will encounter using rollups. A *Roll-up* is an interface element that can be temporarily displayed, minimized or maximized, to give the user access to a collection of specific controls. Termed "rollup," because of the animated action of the display rolling up or down as it minimizes or maximizes.

To reshape a Paragraph text frame to be a non-standard shape follow these steps:

1. Choose Effects, Envelope (Ctrl+F7) which causes the Envelope Roll-up to appear.

2. Select the Shape tool from the Toolbox or from the Text Flyout toolbar if you have it showing.

3. Select Add New from the Roll-up. Notice that the Paragraph text frame now displays eight nodes, one in each corner and one each on the sides of the frame just like any other object. The outline of the frame also changes color indicating that you are now editing an envelope.

4. Grab and drag one or more of the nodes and reshape the frame. Notice that the colored outline changes shape but the shape the text is in remains unaltered (see fig. 5.11).

Fig. 5.11
Using the
Envelope tools
you may reshape
a Paragraph Text
block.

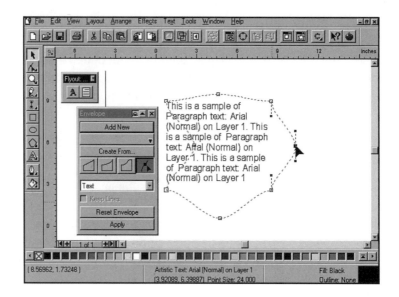

5. If you change your mind about the shape and wish to begin reshaping the envelope again, click on the Reset button.

6. Click Apply on the Envelope Roll-up and the Paragraph text frame takes on the new shape. Click the close box on the Envelope Roll-up.

While the envelope may have a specific shape, the text within the envelope can only approximate its shape. This is a procedure that you will have to try a few times to really perfect. To revert back to the original rectangular shape of the envelope select Clear Transformations from the Arrange menu.

Note

You may also use the Envelope effect on Artistic text.

Character Formatting

Beyond just creating either Artistic or Paragraph text, the next most likely feature you are going to need to use is one that changes the font, style, size, or spacing of the new text. Again, Artistic text and Paragraph text behave differently from each other in this respect.

Formatting different kinds of text in the most efficient manner possible is going to entail several different methods. Artistic text, which is used mostly for headlines, charts, diagrams, and special effects has different formatting needs and priorities than does Paragraph text. Paragraph text is most likely going to be used for handling large quantities of characters such as body text for layouts. So, the emphasis there will be on formatting speed and power.

Formatting Artistic Text

There are several ways to change the font, style, size, and spacing of Artistic text. First, size can be changed directly on your screen by selecting the text and grabbing onto one of the corner handles with the Pick tool and dragging outward or inward while watching your Status bar for the point size reference. To resize your text from the center origin, hold down the Shift key while dragging.

You may also use the Pick tool in combination with the Text toolbar to change Artistic text formatting by selecting the toolbar to display and clicking once on your text to make it active. The Text toolbar will display the current settings of your text. By assigning new styles, fonts, sizes, or alignments in the Text Toolbox you are able to make quick changes to the text formatting.

◀ See "Advanced Customizing: Status Bars, Tools, and Toolbars," p. 78

If you select the Artistic Text tool for editing character formatting, you may cursor-select particular words or characters and change their formatting independently of the rest of the text (see fig. 5.12).

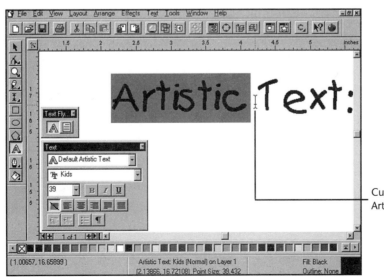

Fig. 5.12
Using the Text tool, you may highlight text to apply text formatting using the Text toolbar.

Cursor-select using Artistic Text tool

II

Creating Text & Drawings

If you select the Shape tool and highlight a block of Artistic text you'll notice that you may also use it to format text. The big difference and advantage in using the Shape tool to format text is that you can format non-sequential characters, or in other words, you get to pick and choose which characters you would like to format. To realign text, you may also use the Align to Baseline command from the pop-up menu by right-clicking on the text.

To format text using the Shape tool, follow these steps:

1. With the Text toolbar displayed, select the Shape tool from the Toolbox and select a block of Artistic text. You'll notice that each character has its own marker or node. The nodes are positioned at the bottom left of each character.

2. Use the marquee-select method to select several character nodes.

3. Make changes to the formatting by assigning a different font, style, and/or size to the text. Changes to the text take place immediately.

4. Click on a blank part of the screen to deselect the text and re-select several characters that do not follow each other in the text string. You will need to hold down the Shift button while doing this in order to select the characters as a group.

5. Assign a different formatting to these characters. Changes are immediate.

6. Grab onto one of the selected characters and drag it away from its original position. The other characters you selected are dragged along with it (see fig. 5.13).

7. Using the right mouse, click on one of the character nodes and select Align to Baseline (Alt+F10). The text snaps back to its original position.

8. With the same characters still selected, double-click on just one of them. This brings up the Character Attributes dialog box where you also have access to a broad range of type controls (including exact type sizes).

Using this type of text selection method to edit text formatting adds a large degree of flexibility to your type controls and opens the door to a lot of creativity. You'll also notice that you can move individual characters or groups of characters away from the original baseline and automatically return them to their original position.

Fig. 5.13
Text may be repositioned away from the baseline by selecting and dragging the text nodes.

It's also worth keeping in mind that any color effects or attributes may be applied using either the Pick tool, Artistic text cursor, or the Shape tool when formatting text.

Formatting Paragraph Text

Paragraph text may be formatted in much the same way as Artistic text. You may also use the Pick, Paragraph, or Shape tools. The Pick tool when used on Paragraph text works like a global formatting tool. Click once on a Paragraph text block to apply character formatting and changes are applied unilaterally to all text in the paragraph frame.

The Paragraph text tool may very well be the best tool to use for formatting text in this Paragraph form. Once you select the Paragraph Text tool you will quickly see that the text formatting functions work much the same as using this tool with Artistic text. Figure 5.14 illustrates editing formatting using the Paragraph Text tool. Notice that when the text is highlighted, the Ruler indicates (to display rulers select View, Ruler) tab markers giving a hint that when using Paragraph text you are able to format not only characters, but also tabs and indents.

II

Creating Text & Drawings

Fig. 5.14
Using the
Paragraph Text
tool, you may
highlight text
for formatting.
If tabbing and
indent formatting
have been applied
to the text,
indicators will
appear in the
Rulers.

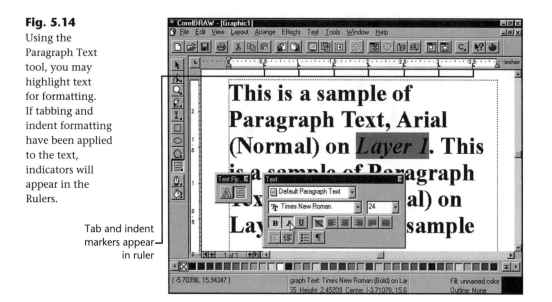

Tab and indent
markers appear—
in ruler

The Shape tool may also be used to format and manipulate Paragraph text in ways unique to this type of tool. While cumbersome to use and memory intensive, the Shape tool is capable of formatting Paragraph text one or several characters at a time. By selecting the Shape tool from the Toolbox and highlighting character nodes in a Paragraph text block, you're able to apply styles and formatting with great flexibility. Procedures for doing this are similar to the ones you have already used for formatting Artistic text, except in instances where text may be moved from its original position.

When using the Shape tool for moving text around, DRAW! actually allows you to move text right out of the Paragraph frame into the open, while still being attached to the original frame (see fig. 5.15). This could be useful in situations where it's necessary to format an initial capital, or drop cap, at the beginning of your Paragraph text frame as in figure 5.15 where the letter 'T' has been resized and repositioned using the Shape tool. The remaining text in this text block has been changed to Times New Roman from Arial (the default), centered in the text block, and then shifted until it overlaps the actual text frame.

When performing any editing, whether it be text editing or character formatting, there are quite a few keyboard shortcuts available. The following table is a list of keyboard shortcuts that may be used in either Artistic text or Paragraph text editing.

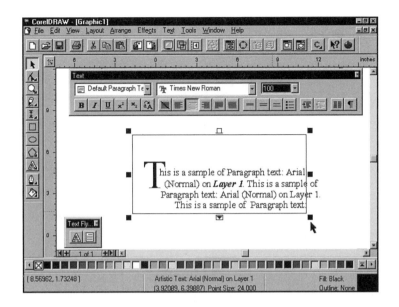

Fig. 5.15
You may drag
Paragraph text
completely out of
the Paragraph text
frame using the
Shape tool.

II

Creating Text & Drawings

Table 5.1   Summary of Text-Editing Keyboard Shortcuts

Use this...	To do this...
Home	Moves the text entry point to start of current line
Ctrl+Home	Moves the text entry point to the beginning of the document
End	Moves the text entry point to the end of the current line
Ctrl+End	Moves the text entry point to end of the document
PgUp or PgDn	Scrolls the Text Editing window in the Text dialog box up or down
Shift+left or right arrow	To select one character at a time in the Text dialog box
Shift+Home	To select all text from the left of the text entry point to the start of the line
Shift+End	To select all the text from the right of the text entry point to the end of the line
Shift+Enter	To begin a new line without beginning a new paragraph
Ctrl+C	To Copy selected text to the clipboard
Ctrl+X	To Cut selected text to the clipboard

(continues)

Table 5.1 Continued	
Use this...	**To do this...**
Ctrl+spacebar	Changes the arrow to the currently selected Text tool
Ctrl+V	To Paste text from the clipboard
Ctrl+left arrow	To move the text entry point from the beginning of a word to the left of text entry point
Ctrl+right arrow	To move the insertion point from the beginning of the word to the right of the text entry point
Ctrl+up arrow	To move the text entry point to the previous paragraph
Ctrl+down arrow	To move the text entry point to the next paragraph
Ctrl+Home	To move the text entry point to the top of the paragraph text frame
Ctrl+End	To move the text entry point to the end of the paragraph text frame
Ctrl+Shift+left arrow	To select the word to the left of the text entry point
Ctrl+Shift+right arrow	To select the word to the right of the text entry point
Shift+up arrow	To select one line up from the text entry point
Shift+down arrow	To select one line down from the text entry point
Ctrl+Shift+up arrow	To select the text left of the text entry point to the previous paragraph
Ctrl+Shift+down arrow	To select the text from the right of the text entry point to the end of paragraph
Ctrl+Shift+Home	To select the text from the left of the text entry point to the start of frame
Ctrl+Shift+End	To select the text from the right of the text entry point to the end of frame
Ctrl+Shift+PgUp	To select the text from the left of the text entry point to the start of the text block
Ctrl+Shift+PgDn	To select the text from the right of the text entry point to the end of the text block
Ctrl+Backspace	To delete a word to the left of the text entry point
Ctrl+Del	To delete a word to the right of the text entry point
Ctrl+numeral key	To apply a paragraph style pre-defined by a numeral key

Using Indents and Tabs

Though you are primarily working in a drawing program, CorelDRAW! 6 has a formidable tabs-and-indents arsenal capable of easily matching the same features in most leading word-processing programs for the PC. You have already seen how DRAW!'s Ruler displays markings and indications when Paragraph text is highlighted on the screen (see fig. 5.16). While text is selected, the Ruler is temporarily transformed into a tab and indent editor, and where the Rulers join in the upper-left corner of the drawing window there is a feature for setting different types of tabs.

Click here to change tab type

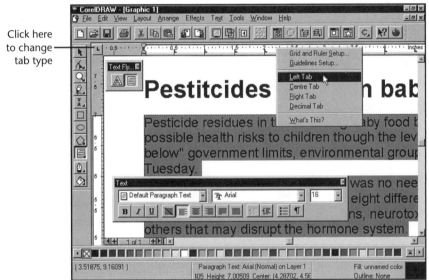

Fig. 5.16
Using the Ruler you can set tabs, indents, and margins.

The next series of steps demonstrates how to format a heading to hang left in the column while formatting the remaining text to be flush left of that heading. To select indenting and tabbing similar to figure 5.16, follow these steps:

1. If you haven't already done so, highlight the Paragraph text. It helps to see the interface better if you Zoom In (F2).

2. Change the indent of your text by grabbing onto the second line indent control while your text is highlighted. The second line indent control is the lower feature of the controls located at the zero mark on the Ruler.

3. Click and drag the second line indent marker to the three-inch mark on the Ruler.

4. Insert your Paragraph text cursor after the colon of your heading and hit your tab key. The default tabbing is automatically set to every half inch.

   The text automatically follows the next available tab. Continue with your formatting, by saving this format as a style.

5. Click the right mouse button to open the text formatting menu or select Layout, Styles and Save (see fig. 5.17).

Fig. 5.17
Using the right mouse button you are able to open the pop-up menu, which gives access to the Styles, Save Properties command.

6. You have activated the Save Style As command. Name your new style and select Save (see fig. 5.18).

By saving your new formatting in a style, you will be able to save time by applying that style to future text. The Save Styles As command will save the properties of the text you have currently selected without you having to define the formatting separately.

Those are DRAW!'s on-screen controls that enable you to perform live-editing of paragraph formats. But there are more precise controls for setting tabs and indents available by selecting Text, Paragraph. The Paragraph dialog box is only available if Paragraph text has been selected and highlighted on your screen using the Paragraph Text tool.

Fig. 5.18
Using the Save,
Style As command,
you are able to
save and name the
currently selected
style.

The Spacing tab (see fig. 5.19) of the Paragraph dialog box includes controls
for Character, Word, Line, Before Paragraph, After Paragraph spacing of your
selected text. It also provides precise controls for Alignment including Left,
Center, and Right alignment, and justification controls for Force Justify and
Full Justify including Minimum and Maximum Word spacing, and Maximum
Character Spacing.

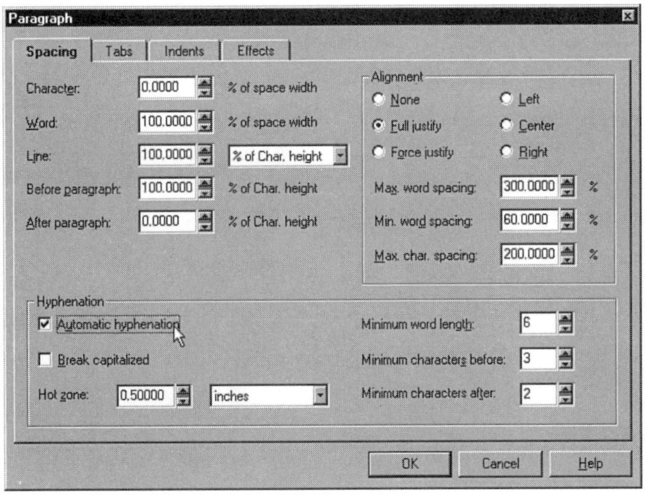

Fig. 5.19
The Spacing tab
of the Paragraph
dialog box features
all controls specific
to paragraph text
options.

The Spacing tab also provides an option for activating powerful Hyphenation
controls including editable user settings for Minimum Word Length, Minimum Characters Before and After hyphenation. The purpose of these elaborate controls is to avoid the danger posed by using large type sizes combined
with text that contains long words in body text. This combination tends to
create spacing nightmares. If you see that your body text spacing is poor and
contains excessive spaces between characters of words (even when using
these optimum spacing settings) try making adjustments here.

Options for activating Automatic Hyphenation and Break Capitalized words (not always desirable) are also available and a control for Hot Zone allows you to tell DRAW! when it's safe to hyphenate, which is determined by the measure you set in the Hot Zone text box. The Hot Zone value you set will set how far your text must be from the right margin before the first word of your next line is hyphenated. A short Hot Zone will cause more words to be hyphenated, but will allow for better word spacing along the right margin. Hot Zone measures are traditionally set in points or picas.

The Tabs tab of the Paragraph dialog box (see fig. 5.20) contains a master ruler for creating and editing Left, Center, Right, and Decimal tab markers. You may also automatically adjust the default tab setting from DRAW!'s default of every half an inch. Tabs can be edited by first selecting the tab position in the vertical field to the left of the dialog box and applying a tab setting such as an alignment style or Leader character. Tabs can be individually deleted or you may delete all of them at once. You may also adjust tab settings by clicking and dragging them in the master ruler.

Fig. 5.20

The Tabs section of the Paragraph dialog box gives full control over tabs and tab leaders.

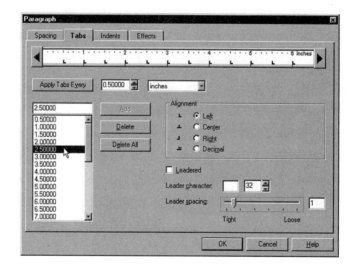

Leader characters may be any character you wish, the default being a period. Leader spacing may also be adjusted from Tight (0) to Loose (10). A list to the left of this dialog box shows each of the tabs currently set up in your Paragraph.

The Indents tab (see fig. 5.21) contains sparse controls First Line, Rest of Lines, and Right Margin; each of which may be interactively adjusted by using your mouse or by entering numeric values.

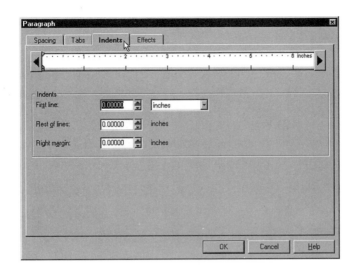

Fig. 5.21
The Indents tab of the Paragraph dialog box consists of detailed controls for formatting first and second line indents.

II

Creating Text & Drawings

The last tab in the Paragraph dialog box (see fig. 5.22) may as well have been called Bullet controls, but is instead called Effects. Options for No Effect or Bullet enable you to add any type of bullet to your paragraph text. Here DRAW! offers you the option of choosing any type of bullet you could possibly imagine. In fact you have the choice of making any symbol font currently loaded on your system available as a bullet. Bullet Size and Indent may be set, and just in case your choice of bullet is too small or too large for your Paragraph text type size, DRAW! provides controls for baseline-shifting the character so that you may center it with your text.

Working with Text Styles and Properties

If you have ever had to endure countless hours or days (or maybe it was your full-time career) repetitively formatting text in either a word-processing program or layout program, you'll love this next feature. Being integrated into a drawing program makes CorelDRAW! 6's styles slightly more complex than either a WP or basic page-layout program. DRAW! is capable of not only remembering the Font, Style and Size of your text, but also the Fill, Outline, Spacing, Justification, Tabs, Indents, Bullet, and Hyphenation settings.

Text Styles are considered only a small part of the types of properties that can be assigned to an object. To access the options for specifically setting up text styles choose View, Properties, and Styles.

Once your Style Properties sheet displays (see fig. 5.22), controls for object and text style formatting include text, fill, and outline attributes. An object must first be selected in order to have three of these property attributes are available, otherwise the attribute will be grayed out. Check marks indicate that an attribute has been set for each option listed, while a blank check box indicates that none has been set. Clicking the plus symbol beside an attribute expands the attribute branch to reveal individual options, while clicking on a minus symbol closes an expanded branch. You may set attributes under tabbed categories including General, Fill, Outline, and text.

To apply a style, select the style name from the Style pull-down menu and click the OK button.

Fig. 5.22
The Style Properties sheet gives access to all text and object styles currently set in your document and provides a quick reference to which attributes have been set.

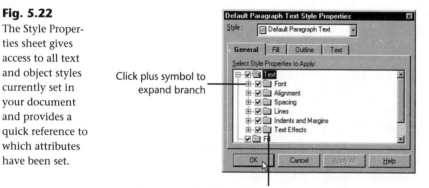

Click plus symbol to expand branch

Grayed-out check box indicates some options are not set

Spelling, Grammar, and Proofreading Your Text

If part of the work that you do involves composing text for correspondence, reports, articles, news stories, or whatever, you'll get perked up by these next features. Controls for Proofreading, Thesaurus, and Type Assist are accessed from the Text menu (see fig. 5.23).

The Proofreading menu choice is sub-divided into a smaller flyout menu containing Spelling (Ctrl+F12), Quick Proofreading, Full Proofreading, and Advanced Options choices.

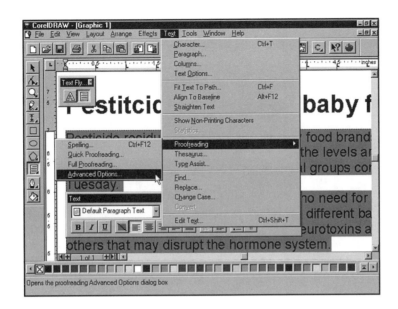

Fig. 5.23
You may access
the Proofreading
tools from the text
menu.

II

Creating Text & Drawings

Spelling Check

The Spelling dialog box (see fig. 5.24) offers controls for Check Range, Sentence, Error Description, and Change To when checking text. There are also control buttons including Add Word, which enables you to add the currently highlighted word to a user dictionary, and an Options button. The Options button includes commands for Undo Edit, Explain Error, Rule Manager, Advanced Options, Formality Level, Personal Dictionary, and Create New Dictionary.

- *Undo Edit.* Undoes the last text edit made to your document.

- *Explain Error.* Displays details of the error caught, if an explanation of the error is not displayed in the Error Discription box.

- *Rule Manager.* Displays the Rule Manager utility, which manages a set of complex rules by which spelling errors are caught. See "Rule Manager," discussed later in this chapter for more information on this command.

- *Advanced Options.* The Advanced Options command enables you to set the specific dictionaries for Language, Rule Language, and Error Language. You may also choose options for Always Providing a Spelling Alternative and to Use Personal Dictionaries. A New button in the Advanced Options enables you to immediately begin a new user dictionary. And from Advanced Options you have another quick-access button to the Rule Manager. See "Advanced Options" later in this chapter for more information on this command.

- *Formality Level.* Three types of formality levels exist in the Formality Level Dictionary including Formal, Standard, and Informal.

- *Personal Dictionary.* The Personal Dictionary command allows you to set a specific dictionary from a list of dictionaries currently saved.

- *Create New Dictionary.* This option enables you to name and save a new dictionary based on your current setting and options.

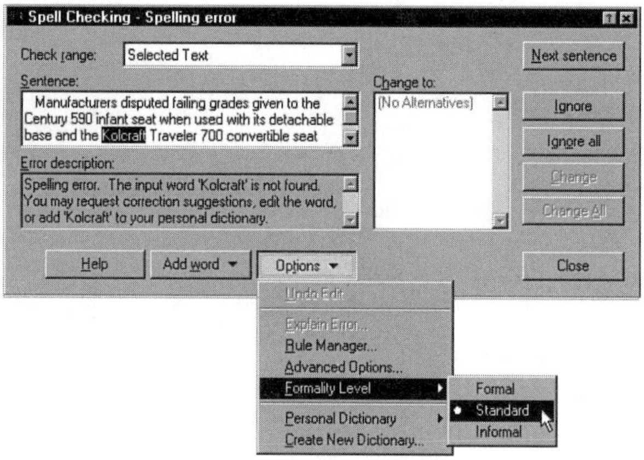

Fig. 5.24
The Spelling dialog box offers a full set of controls for catching spelling errors, offering suggestions for alternatives, and saving and loading other dictionaries.

Quick Proofreading

The Quick Proofreading feature in DRAW! allows you to perform a quick scan of your text to search for the most obvious punctuation, capitalization, and spelling errors. Then it makes suggestions for correcting the problems it finds. The Quick Proofreader feature works on Artistic and Paragraph text.

In each case where DRAW! discovers a problem, it will identify the sentence containing the error and then describe the error in detail. For example, in figure 5.25 Quick Proofreader has discovered the word "stored" should be capitalized. Then it provides an exact reference to the word in the Error Description box and asks you to consider "Stored" instead of "stored." Using the actual word to describe your error speeds your decision time when it comes to changing your word or not. If Quick Proofreader discovers a new word you have used in your document you can also use Add Word to add it to your dictionary.

You may choose to Change this one instance, go ahead and Change All instances of this word, Ignore this time, Ign<u>o</u>re All identical instances or just move on to the <u>N</u>ext Sentence. You may also choose a Check <u>R</u>ange of your Highlighted Text or check all text that exists in your document.

An Options button within Quick Proofreader opens a flyout menu (see fig. 5.25) containing the same controls available in the spell checker including selections for <u>U</u>ndoing Edits made to the document being proofed, <u>E</u>xplain errors, access to the <u>R</u>ule Manager and <u>A</u>dvanced Options, <u>F</u>ormality levels and other custom user dictionary options.

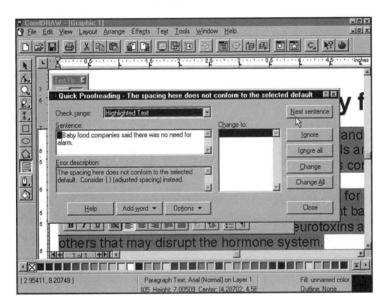

Fig. 5.25
The Quick Proofreader performs a brief grammar and spelling proofread of your selected documents.

Full Proofreading

The Full Proofreader (see fig. 5.26) works exactly the same as the Quick Proofreader. But, instead of just looking for obvious punctuation, capitalization, and spelling errors, this feature goes much deeper. The Full Proofreader checks into issues such as redundant expressions, compounding errors, phrasing, jargon, and wordy expressions. Each time it discovers what it sees as an error, it identifies it, uses it in a sentence, and makes recommendations for changes. Like the other text-checking utilities, the Full Proofreader also features an Options button, which contains access to controls for <u>U</u>ndoing Edits made to the document being proofed, <u>E</u>xplain errors, access to the <u>R</u>ule Manager and <u>A</u>dvanced Options, <u>F</u>ormality levels, and other custom user dictionary options.

Advanced Options

Advanced Options in the Proofreading utilities (see fig. 5.27) enable you to set which language to use when checking text and options for Always Provide Alternative Spelling and Use Personal Dictionaries. Other options are available for setting or creating personal dictionaries and accessing the Rule Manager.

Fig. 5.26

The Full Proofreader command performs a more thorough examination of your document, but it may take a little longer to review all the instances it finds.

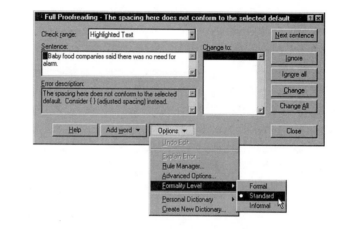

- *Language.* If you have the English language version of CorelDRAW! 6 currently loaded, this option enables you to select from UK English (ise), UK English (ize), or US English. The language selected will be used for both spell-checking and proofreading operations.

- *Rule Language.* Options selected from this pull-down menu will determine which language the Rule Manager uses. If the English language version is installed on your system you may select from UK English (ise), UK English (ize), or US English.

- *Error Language.* Errors will be displayed using whichever language is set from the Error Language pull-down menu. If the English language version is installed on your system you may select from UK English (ise), UK English (ize), or US English.

- *Always Provide a Spelling Alternative.* If the English language version is installed on your system you may choose this option to have CorelDRAW! display the error messages using either UK English (ise), UK English (ize), or US English.

- *Use Personal Dictionaries.* The Use Personal Dictionary option enables you to use saved personal dictionaries. If unselected, the operation will use the default dictionary currently installed in the application.

■ *New*. This button in the Advanced Options dialog box enables you to immediately begin a new user dictionary.

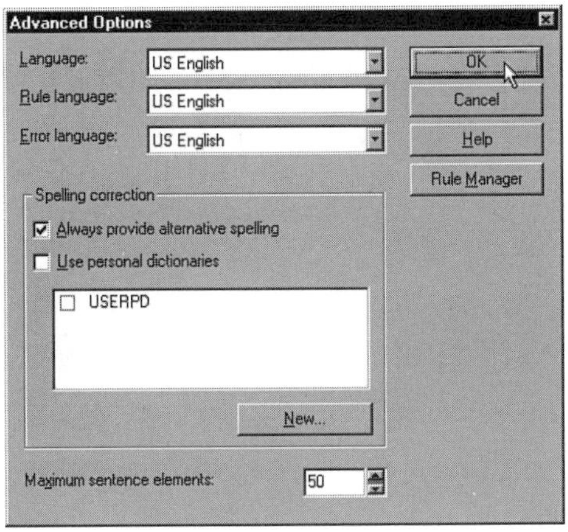

Fig. 5.27
The Advanced Options dialog box controls enable you to set specific language and dictionary options for the Proofreaders and Spell Checker.

The Rule Manager

The Rule Manager (see fig. 5.28) contains 36 types of rules, each of which may be activated temporarily or permanently by selecting Current or Long-Term selectors, respectively, on or off. When a rule is turned off the selector is grayed out. The Rule Manager is also where you tell DRAW! which User Profile you would like to use by selecting from the pull-down list or creating and naming a new one. A Check Mode offers options including Fast Spelling, Spelling, Quick Proofing, and Full Proofing. The Formality level of your proofreader may also be set here to either Formal, Standard, or Informal.

The following is a list of the rule options included in the Rule Manager:

Spelling

Capitalization

Hyphenation

Capitalized Words

Doubled words

A versus An

Compounding errors

Open versus closed errors

Formatting errors

Punctuation errors

Ungrammatical expressions

Misspelled expressions

Missspelled foreign expressions

Inappropriate prepositions

Double negatives

Misused words

Possible word confusions

Homonyms

Wordy expressions

Redundant expressions

Informal expressions

Cliches

Over-used phrases

Stock phrases

Weak modifiers

Vague quantifiers

Unnecessary prepositions

Jargon

Pretentious words

Archaic expressions

Sexist expressions

Gender-specific terms

Contractions

Style settings

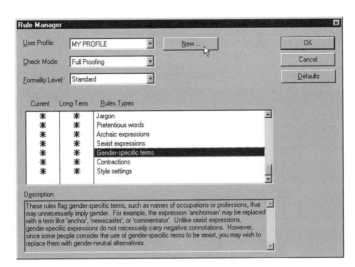

Using Thesaurus and Type Assist

Until now, the text-composing operations have been limited to somewhat limited spell-checking utilites and a thesaurus. CorelDRAW! 6 now offers powerful utilities for the writer, entering text directly into the application. The thesaurus has been beefed up considerably, and Type Assist is completely updated.

Thesaurus

CorelDRAW! 6's thesaurus (see fig. 5.29) is separate from the rest of the text-composing utilities discussed. Thesaurus operates on the basic principle of searching for text and offering a list of alternative definitions, full word definitions, and replacement words. You may access the thesaurus by selecting Text, Thesaurus.

To use the thesaurus, highlight a word in your document, and select Text, Thesaurus. The highlighted word will appear in the Looked Up text box, and the Definitions, Full Definitions, and Replace With text boxes will display synonym information. You may also use the Thesaurus Looked Up text box to enter any word to search for a synonym.

The Thesaurus offers button commands including Look Up, Replace, and Previous. When entering a new word into the Looked Up text box the Look Up button command may be clicked to begin your search for a suitable replacement word. The Replace button becomes available if the word you are currently performing a search with is highlighted in your CorelDRAW! 6 document and allows you to replace it with your search results.

II

Creating Text & Drawings

The <u>P</u>revious button enables you to undo the previous search Look Up command when using repeated searches for a particular word. Select a Definition to see the search results for a particular word meaning.

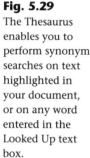

Fig. 5.29

The Thesaurus enables you to perform synonym searches on text highlighted in your document, or on any word entered in the Looked Up text box.

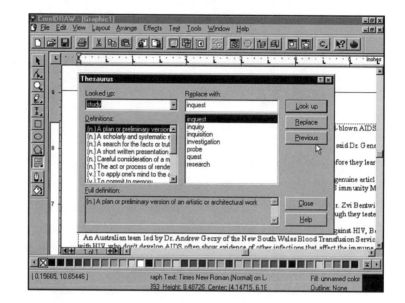

Type Assist

Type Assist (see fig. 5.30) is a feature engineered to save you time when typing. Instead of typing long time-consuming words, Type Assist allows you to define abbreviations for anything you wish. For instance, if you find yourself typing the word 'government' over and over again you may set Type Assist to replace 'gvt.' with 'government' as you are typing. Another example might be using replacements for abbreviations that contain all capitals to avoid having to use the shift key repeatedly for abbreviations such as 'USA'. With a little practice, and if used effectively, Type Assist may significantly reduce the time it takes you to pound out official-type documents on your keyboard.

The Type Assist dialog box also contains five options for automatic typing shortcuts including:

- Capitalize <u>F</u>irst Letters of Sentences

- Change Straight Quotes to <u>T</u>ypographic Quotes

- <u>C</u>orrect Two Initial Consecutive Capitals

- Capitalize <u>N</u>ames of Days

- <u>R</u>eplace Text While Typing

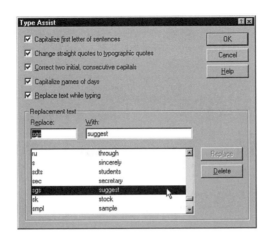

Fig. 5.30
The Type Assist dialog box provides you with tools for abbreviating large, difficult words to type with quick short forms.

Other Text Tools: Find and Replace

The Find command located under the Text menu (see fig. 5.31) is very simple and works like any basic text search command (see fig. 5.32). The only two options available are Find What and Match Case. To perform a search on either Artistic text or Paragraph text, first select the text block using the Pick tool and then choose this option. Enter the text to be found and click Find Next. Once your text is located, DRAW! will display it on your screen behind the Find dialog box. You may continue searching or close the Find command. Find will work on one or more selected text blocks even if Artistic and Paragraph text are both selected.

Fig. 5.31
The Find Text command is a basic, but invaluable tool to use when composing or editing any text.

Using the Replace Command

The Replace command is a powerful tool in any program. To choose the Replace command, select Replace from the Text menu (see fig. 5.32). The Replace command, like Find, is also a simple control offering only a few options save the bare bones. To replace text in any or all of the text in your drawing, enter text in the Find What and Replace With fields, and click either the Find Next, Replace, or Replace All buttons. You also have the option of selecting Match Case.

II

Creating Text & Drawings

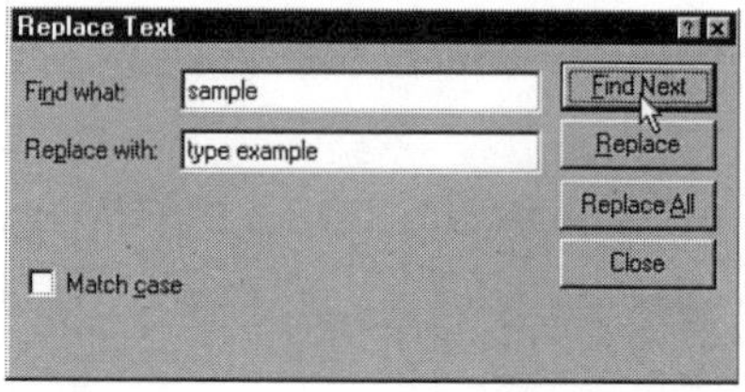

Fig. 5.32
Like the Find command, Replace Text is another of the basic but necessary tools needed for text quick text editing operations.

Using the Change Case Command

The Change Case command can also be a useful tool when changing or converting text from various sources into your drawing (see fig. 5.33). Change Case offers options for changing uppercase characters to lowercase characters (or vice versa), with a few variations to accommodate proper sentence formats and titling. The options for Changing Case include Sentence Case, Lower Case, Upper Case, Title Case, and Toggle Case. To use the Change Case tools, select Text, Change Case.

Fig. 5.33
Options in the Change Case dialog box reflect the changes that will be applied to the selected text.

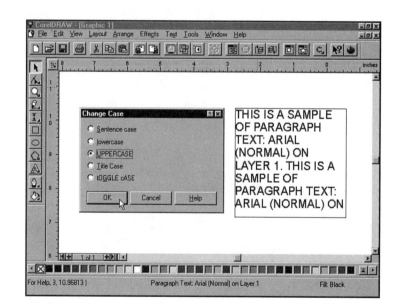

Converting Text Objects

Converting text between Artistic and Paragraph text formats does just that. Selecting Artistic text allows you to convert it to Paragraph text and vice versa. To convert text formats select Convert To Paragraph (Artistic) Text from the Text menu.

Fitting and Unfitting Text to a Path

Fitting text along a path is a feature which has become largely available since the introduction of computer graphics software and is seldom used in illustration or drawing since few really know how to use the effect in a practical way—although admittedly it's a novel feature. Perhaps one of the excuses for not using this feature is that text and characters were designed to be easily read right-side-up and tilting text sideways or upside down only makes it harder to read.

For circumstances where fitting text to a path can be effective, there are a few tricks and time-savers to note. Only Artistic text can be fit to a path. The path itself can be any curve, whether the curve is a simple object such as a rectangle or ellipse, or a simple curve you have drawn using the Freehand tool.

The main control for fitting text to a path is DRAW!'s Fit Text Roll-up which has five basic options (see fig. 5.34). From the top, the features control: text distortion; baseline alignment; flush-left, center, and flush-right alignment; Place on Other Side; and an Edit button for making fine-tuning adjustments to the baseline shift of your text along the path.

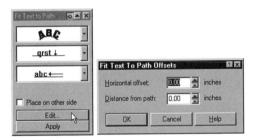

Fig. 5.34
The Fit Text Rollup contains five options for fitting text to a path.

To fit text to a simple curve path follow these steps:

1. Before you begin, select Te**x**t, Fit **T**ext to Path (Ctrl + F). The Fit Text Rollup appears.

2. DRAW! a straight line curve using the Freehand tool. Hold down the Control key to constrain Freehand tool to draw the line straight.

3. Select the Artistic Text tool from the Toolbox and enter a line of text.

4. Resize the text to be about 20 percent shorter than the line you have drawn. At this point the exact point size won't matter, but the size relationship will.

5. Using the Pick tool, Shift-select to select both the line and the text. Notice that features in the Fit Text Rollup now become active.

6. Leaving the Fit Text options just as they are, click Apply. The line and the text become joined according to the settings in the Fit Text rollup.

7. Select the Shape tool and use it to select the line only. Notice the line has only two nodes which become visible after you select it.

8. Double-click on the first node to bring up the Node Edit rollup.

9. Now, using the same tool, click anywhere on the line until you see a black dot appear on the line's path (see fig. 5.35) and select the To Curve button on the Node Edit rollup. The line changes from a straight line to a curved line.

10. Click the close button on the Node Edit rollup.

Fig. 5.35
You may also edit the path that your text has been fit to using the Shape tool and the Node Edit tools.

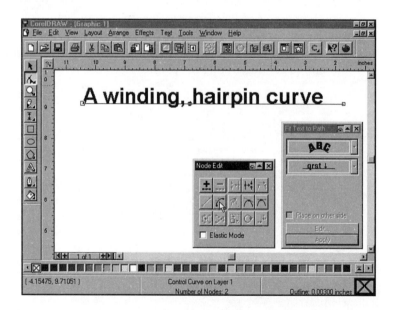

11. Click on the first node of the line once, to activate the node controls which look like little markers. In the case of the line, they will show up at a point directly on the line.

12. Using the left mouse button, click and drag the node control away from the line and notice how the curve changes shape. Release the mouse button. Notice that DRAW! immediately resets the text to the new shape of the curve (see fig. 5.36).

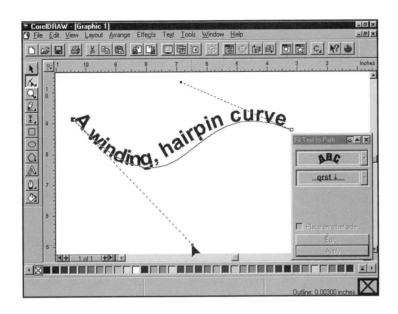

Fig. 5.36
You may edit the
shape of the line
by using the Shape
tool to edit the
position or the
slope and angle of
the curve the node
controls.

At this point you could try out some of the other options in the Fit Text
rollup by setting the alignment to centered and clicking the Place on
Other Side option active. You will need to re-select the Pick tool in
order to regain access to the rollup.

13. After selecting your new options in the Fit Text rollup you will need to
click the Apply button again. Notice how the text changes but the line
doesn't (see fig. 5.37). The text has moved to the other side of the
curve, but the curve has remained stationary.

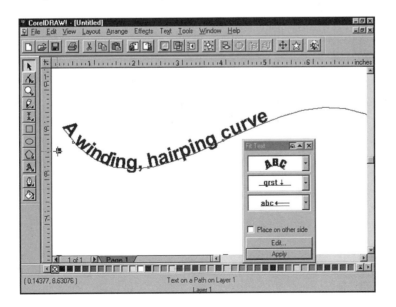

Fig. 5.37
Changes made to
the shape of the
line that your text
has been fit to take
place immediately
after the mouse is
released.

The steps above explain how to join text to a simple curve, using the Shape tool with the Node Editor rollup to reshape the line, and amend the original text fit by editing the options in the Fit Text rollup. Another trick you can use in combination with the Fit Text to Path feature is to make the line invisible by clicking the right mouse button on the None color chip which is located at the farthest left end of the on-screen color palette.

Tip

Text color, style, font, size, and spacing are still editable while remaining joined to a path. When changes to the formatting of the text are made though, DRAW! sometimes will not reshape the text smoothly enough to suit your needs and you may have to redefine and reapply some of the options in the Fit Text rollup.

Also, resizing the objects by dragging one of the resizing handles while both objects are selected resizes both the text and the line. However, you may also resize these two joined objects independently by selecting only one and resizing it. For example, resizing just the curve will cause the remaining unsized text to reshape to the new curve size.

To separate the text from the line again and return it to its original format, follow these steps:

1. Select Separate from the Arrange menu. The text and the line become two separate objects once again.

2. Using the Pick tool again, deselect the objects by clicking anywhere on an empty part of the page.

3. Reselect the text using the Pick tool.

4. From the Text menu, select Straighten Text. The text returns to its upright, straight condition.

Tip

After joining a curve and text together using the Fit Text to Path (Ctrl+F) feature, it's a good idea to leave them joined even if you don't want to have the path showing in your drawing. Leaving them joined together allows you to go back and edit the shape of the curve later on without having to create a new curve. Make the curve invisible instead by assigning a color of None to it.

The next kind of path you have the option of using with the Fit Text to Path feature is a path which follows simple objects such as polygons, rectangles, and ellipses (see fig. 5.38). While fitting text along a simple curve allows you to place the text on one side or the other, fitting text onto objects such as rectangles or ellipses invokes another feature in the Fit Text rollup. The symbol in the center of the Fit Text rollup allows you to place the text on the left, right, top, or bottom of the object. Combining this with the Place on Other Side option allows you to place objects on the inside or outside of rectangles or ellipses.

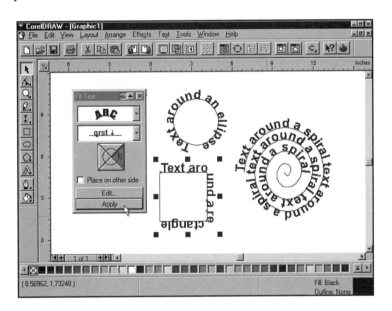

Fig. 5.38
By using the fit text to path on various types of objects some very wild effects may be achieved.

Applying Envelopes and Perspective to Text

Perhaps a bit more useful than the Fit text to Path feature, applying envelopes and perspective effects to text provides you with the option of shaping words into pictures. Again, as in previous examples of text manipulation, creating and editing Artistic and Paragraph text objects are done in different ways.

Also, it's worth mentioning that Envelope controls and Perspective controls are quite different to create and edit, but create similar controllable effects. Applying an envelope to text is sort of like making it fit a mold while still keeping it in a text format you can edit.

Applying Envelopes to Artistic Text

Envelope effects are applied using a rollup (see fig. 5.39). To choose the rollup, select Effects, Envelope (Ctrl+F7). The Envelope rollup features button controls to Add New, [Select from a Preset], or Create From an object that already has an envelope assigned to it. Three more shape buttons also allow you to select envelope types that have only single lines, single arcs, or double arcs. There is also a shortcut button to the Shape tool.

Fig. 5.39

The Envelope rollup allows you to change the features of your envelope effects.

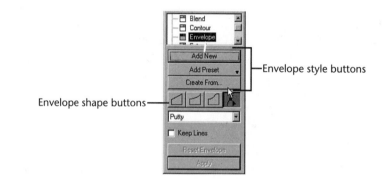

Envelope style buttons

Envelope shape buttons

In addition to these controls there is an additional pull-down menu which allows you to select mapping options including Original, Putty, Vertical, or Horizontal. Mapping is the effect of matching the one shape to another by way of a series of points along the outside or inside of the shape. In this case, mapping applies to the outside nodes of objects mapped to the nodes contained in the envelope shape.

Mapping options enable you to set the behavior of envelope once the envelope is applied. Original maps the corners of the selection, while allowing the sides to be distorted using curves manipulated by using the Shape tool. The Putty mapping option isn't much different from Original except that it maps the object using the corners of the envelope only, while ignoring the effect of curved sides. Vertical allows you to stretch the object vertically to fill the bounding box shape of the selected envelope while Horizontal works the other way.

The Keep Lines option is a seldom-used option in the Envelopes rollup. Its default is set to off. When activated, it stops DRAW! from bending lines within an object into curves when performing reshaping. As a result, objects don't conform very closely to the shape of envelopes applied to them. Because of the fact that text contains straight lines, and you likely would want the lines to become distorted along with the rest of the characters, you may want to leave this option off.

To apply an envelope effect to Artistic text, follow these steps:

1. Create a block of Artistic text and activate the Envelope rollup by selecting Effects, Envelope (Ctrl+F7).

2. Select your Artistic Text object using the Pick tool, and select Add New from the Envelope rollup.

3. Choose a mapping option from either single line, single arc, or double arc, or choose the Shape tool to apply a freehand-shaped envelope.

4. Press the Add New button and notice that a dotted line containing eight node markers appears around the text, and your cursor changes to a Shape tool.

5. To reset the mapping option, press Reset Envelope, choose another mapping option, and press the Add New button once again.

6. Reshape the envelope by grabbing onto one of the nodes and dragging it. Notice how the behavior of the adjoining lines corresponds to the type of mapping option you have chosen. Also, notice that the object doesn't change shape as you drag the node markers around.

7. Once you are finished dragging node markers, click the Apply button on the Envelope rollup and watch how DRAW! applies the envelope shape to the text.

Using the mapping options is a quick way of formatting a shape, but the Shape tool option within the Envelope is perhaps the most useful feature. By using the Shape tool, you are able to manipulate the lines and curves that make up any envelope as you would any curved object. Using the node editor you are able to change the behavior of any line shape in an envelope. Figure 5.40 shows a block of text that has had the top curve manipulated using the Shape tool and the Node Editor rollup.

II

Creating Text & Drawings

Fig. 5.40
You may accomplish some striking effects using the Shape tool on Envelopes applied to shapes. Here the Shape tool is used to reshape an Envelope to the shape that the text describes.

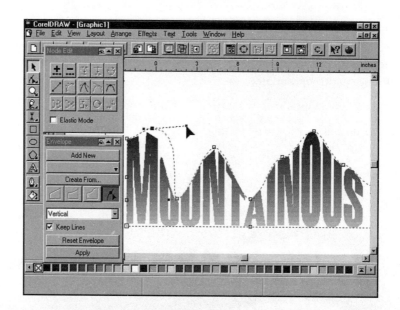

Tip

When using complex envelope effects on text to make slick headings, banners, or design elements, try using all capital letters. It makes it easier to read and your reader doesn't have to distinguish between upper- and lowercase as well as trying to recognize the words. Also, using an easily read font will help make the altered text object just that much easier to read.

Tip

Before you apply an envelope to Artistic text, select the alignment for the text as Centered format by using any of the text formatting methods. This will ensure your text has proper alignment in the envelope.

Applying Perspective to Artistic Text

Creating and editing Perspective controls is a little less complex than working with envelopes. Perspective simulates the distortions caused by the effects of near and far by creating a set of reference points on an object. The corner points may be moved individually, or moved simultaneously as a unit moving the perspective vanishing point. The vanishing point is represented by an 'X' and represents the imaginary point at which all objects eventually shrink to nothing.

To add a perspective effect to text follow these steps:

1. Create a word to which you would like to add perspective. Select a font that is legible even at small and large sizes.

2. Choose Effects, Add Perspective. Notice that the text is surrounded by a dotted-line box which contains four node markers—one in each corner. Your cursor also changes to a Shape tool.

3. Grab onto one of the corner markers and drag it using the left mouse button, noticing that only the dotted line changes shape until the mouse button is released. When the mouse button is released your text will take on the shape of the dotted line.

4. Continue to grab and drag the corner markers until you have your desired shape.

5. To complete your shaping of the Perspective effect click the Pick tool or any other tool.

6. To erase the Perspective effect from the text, first select the text using the Pick tool and then select Clear Perspective from the Effects menu. To remove all transformations from the text, first select it using the Pick tool and then select Clear Transformations from the Arrange menu.

7. Experiment by using the Perspective Effect. Select the text with the Pick tool once again and select Add Perspective from the Effects menu.

8. This time, grab the bottom-right corner marker and hold down the Control key to constrain-drag the marker downwards. Then, constrain-drag the top-right marker upwards. If you drag the markers far enough, the vanishing point marker 'X' will come into view on the left hand side of your screen.

9. Grab hold of the vanishing point marker and constrain-drag it using the Controls key toward the center origin of the text (see fig. 5.41). Each time you release the mouse you will notice that it reshapes the Perspective Effect of the text.

Fig. 5.41
Perspective can have dramatic effect on the simplest of objects. Using fountain fills with Perspective may add a degree of realism to the object's perspective.

> **Tip**
>
> If you wish to further distort the perspective of an object without permanently altering the object shape forever, use the Add Perspective command to add another set of perspective controls over the existing ones. When you're through fiddling you can remove the second set of Perspective controls with the Clear Perspective command.

Applying Envelopes to Paragraph Text

Applying Envelope effects to Paragraph enables you to create shapes using large amounts of paragraph text. Paragraph text may take the form of any existing or preset envelope shape by using the Apply Envelope command in the Envelope Roll-up.

Setting Text Options

The Text Options may be accessed by selecting Text, Text Options to display the Text Options dialog box. These controls consist of options for text on-screen display, editing operations, and clipboard behavior, as well as paragraph text formatting.

Text Display and Editing Controls

The Text Options tab portion of the Text Options dialog box (see fig. 5.42) consists of options which specifically control how text is displayed and edited and a mixed bag of other options.

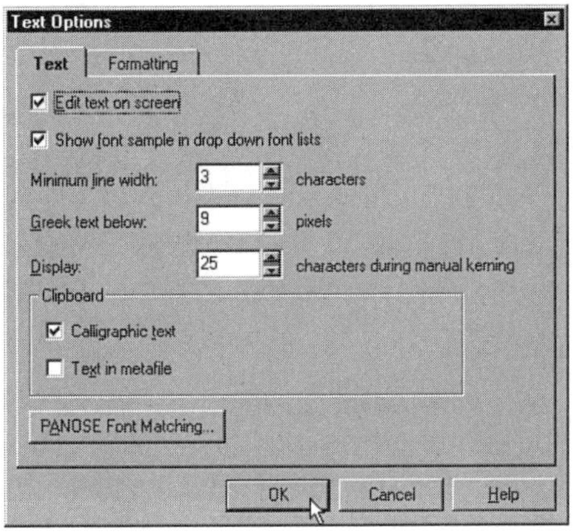

Fig. 5.42

The Text tab of the Text Options dialog box consists of controls for screen display and editing.

Text controls in the Text tab consist of the following features:

- *Edit Text on Screen.* While this option is selected you have the option of editing on your screen directly, without having to open a text-editing dialog box. This option applies particularly to Paragraph text. Disabling this option will make on-screen editing of text unavailable.

- *Show Font Sample in Font Drop-down lists.* Having a sample of the font you are viewing is a useful feature in any program, and with this option selected font samples will appear in such features as the Text toolbar, Character Attributes dialog box, Text Properties, and so on. Turning this feature off may speed operations for those users who have memorized the appearance of fonts currently loaded on their systems.

- *Minimum Line Width.* Minimum line width sets the minimum number of characters that will appear in a single line of text particularly while using Paragraph text. The default setting of three characters is usually sufficient for most editing functions; however, you may increase or decrease this value.

- *Greek Text Below.* The seasoned desktop publisher will quickly agree that choosing Greek text speeds production time immensely. Allowing your screen to laboriously draw each character and word, dramatically increases screen rendering time if your document contains any amount of text smaller than 9 point. The default setting of nine pixels is quite small and it may be wise to increase this if you intend on producing documents using excessive amounts of 9-point text.

■ *Display Chapters During Manual Kerning.* This option enables you to restrict the number of characters displayed on-screen during manual kerning operations. *Kerning* is a method of reducing character spacing between specific character combinations with the aim of improving the readability of text.

■ *Clipboard.* Two options exist for using the clipboard to copy and paste text: Calligraphic text and Text in Metafile. The Calligraphic text option allows text containing calligraphic pen outlines to be transferred to the clipboard or exported using certain filters. Text in Metafile allows you to convert all text transferred to the clipboard to curves.

■ *Panose Font Matching Editing.* The Panose Font matching utility (see fig. 5.43) is nothing new, but having access through the Text Options dialog box is. Panose Font Matching is useful when opening a CorelDRAW! document where the fonts situation is different than when the file was originally created. Using a font matching table, CorelDRAW! may match fonts with similar appearances or names to each other in an effort to smooth out font problems that may occur. The Panose Font Matching utility includes options to allow font matching and display results, tolerance settings, set default font options, and Spelling and Exception tables that may be edited to your own preferences.

Fig. 5.43
Using the Panose Font matching utility you are able to change how CorelDRAW! searches and matches fonts in your document when it is being opened on a system where fonts don't match those used to create the original document.

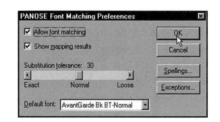

Formatting

The Formatting tab of the Text Options dialog box (see fig. 5.44) consists of features that particularly involve Paragraph text, including options for linking formatting between text frames, isolating formatting to selected frames, or applying formatting to selected and subsequent frames. The Formatting tab also contains options to choose non-printing character display, which includes characters for soft returns, hard returns, tabs, and spaces. Non-printing characters may be displayed using the option button on the Text toolbar (see margin).

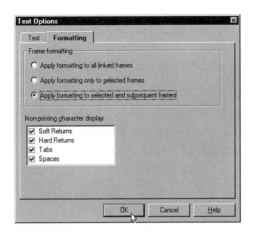

Fig. 5.44
Panose Font
Matching enables
you to recognize
and control when
fonts are being
substituted.

Creating Fonts and Symbols

Creating Fonts is a capability that has been available in previous versions of CorelDRAW! but is seldom used by the beginner or even intermediate user. The creation of symbols is the same as for fonts; however, there are new controls in CorelDRAW! 6 that make symbol creation much easier than before.

Create a Font

Although many font craftsmen and typestyle designers dedicate their careers to developing highly readable and unique typographic designs, it is possible to create your own fonts in CorelDRAW! through the File, Export function. Objects that are to be turned into font characters cannot contain color or any special fill patterns or effects of any kind, and cannot contain fonts themselves. They must be closed curves.

To create a font, follow these steps:

1. Create an object you wish to use as the first character of your collection and select it on your screen (see fig. 5.45) and select File, Export (Ctrl+H).

2. From the Save as Type pull-down menu, select TrueType Font (TTF), and choose the Selected Only option, name your font file, and select OK.

3. An additional Options dialog box appears (see fig. 5.46) asking you to name your font. Enter a name in the Family Name text box, and deselect the Symbol Font option if it is selected. You may also set the style of your new font from the Style pull-down menu including Normal,

Italic, Bold, and Bold Italic. Choose OK when you have completed naming options. There is no need to change the Grid Size or Space Width default values.

Fig. 5.45
Select your object as the first character of your font and use the File, Export command to begin.

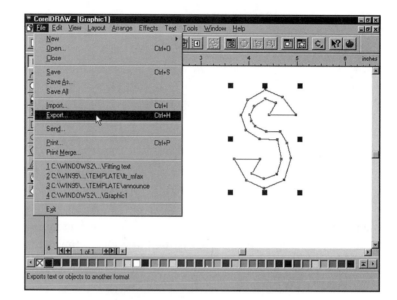

Fig. 5.46
A second dialog box will appear asking you for a font family name as well as other options.

4. After selecting the OK button, CorelDRAW! will ask you if you would like to save the font changes. Click OK to this question, too.

5. The next dialog box to appear will be the True Type Export dialog box (see fig. 5.47) containing controls for setting the character you have created, the spacing you desire, and the Character width. In most cases the default settings will be sufficient; however, you must set the character number by scrolling through the character set listed and clicking on the correct character.

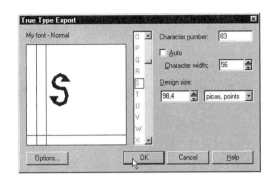

Fig. 5.47
The True Type Export dialog box enables you to begin mapping your objects into a font.

6. Once you have completed selecting the options, select OK to create the character. Your font is started.

This is just the first of 222 possible characters you may load into a TrueType Font file. The more detailed and complex your fonts are the larger your TrueType Font will be and the longer it will take to print.

Create a Symbol

To create a Symbol within CorelDRAW! 6 you may use the same procedure as for creating a TrueType Font, only where you deselected the Symbol Font option—in this case leave it selected and follow the exact same procedures. However, in CorelDRAW! 6 there is an even easier way. The same restrictions apply to symbols as they do to fonts. Objects that are to be turned into symbols, font characters cannot contain color or any special fill patterns or effects of any kind, and cannot contain fonts. They must be closed curves.

To create a Symbol font within CorelDRAW! 6, follow these steps:

1. Begin by creating an object you wish to make into a symbol.

2. Select the Symbols roll-up by clicking on the Symbol button in the Roll-up toolbar.

3. Select your object, and select Tools, Create, Symbol (see fig. 5.48) to display the Create Symbol dialog box (see fig. 5.49).

4. Name your new symbol and select OK.

5. In the Symbols Rollup, select the Symbol font you have just created to make sure your object is correct.

6. To add an additional symbol to the same or any other Symbol font, click the object you wish to add and select Tools, Create, Symbol, select the Symbol font from the list, and click OK.

You may add up to 222 objects to a Symbol Font, the same as for fonts.

Fig. 5.48
To create a symbol font, begin by creating an object, then select Tools, Create, Symbol.

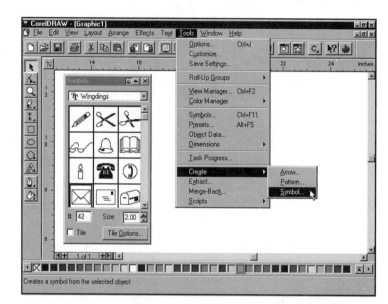

Fig. 5.49
The Create Symbol dialog box enables you to name your new symbol font.

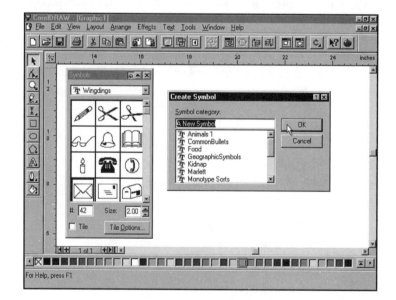

From Here...

This chapter has covered both the basic and complex text controls available in CorelDRAW! 6. While text may not always appear in your drawings, if and when it does, you have all the tools necessary to edit, format, and reshape text to mold it to fit your specific application. CorelDRAW! 6 provides full control over the behavior of text.

While this chapter fleshes out many of the details of text functions, don't stop here. Continue learning CorelDRAW! 6's extended text uses by referencing the following areas:

■ Chapter 14, "Customizing CorelDRAW! 6," for information on exporting fonts.

■ Chapter 6, "Working with Objects," for information on creating curves and lines.

II

Creating Text & Drawings

Chapter 6

Working with Objects

Creation, manipulation, transformation, special effects, and control are each priorities for any successful graphics application, the subject of this chapter. CorelDRAW! 6 provides precision and accuracy in all of these categories when it comes to working with objects.

The previous chapter introduced certain tools used to create and edit text objects. In this chapter you will discover how to use those tools again in working with objects. This is where the real power of CorelDRAW! 6 begins to unfold.

In this chapter, you learn to

- Create, manipulate, and edit simple objects including a few dynamic new tools available only in CorelDRAW! 6

- Use the Node Editor to master object editing

- Use object properties to examine and edit objects

- Build complex objects using simple tools

- Use Envelope, Extrude, and Perspective tools on complex objects

Creating Curves, Lines, Rectangles, and Ellipses

CorelDRAW! 6 object drawing tools haven't changed significantly since previous versions, except a few changes to some controls and features. Rectangles, ellipses, and curves are still created in much the same way using the same tools. It's the properties and editing part of object creation that has changed significantly.

Creating Curves and Lines

Everything you draw—with any drawing program—boils down to curves and lines. Mastering the tool that creates them is perhaps the most important part of learning any graphics program. A curve is defined as any path between two points. Call those points nodes and you're talking about CorelDRAW!. If you've ever asked for highway directions and were told "You can't get there from here" you were probably not talking to someone who has used CorelDRAW!.

To create a simple line in CorelDRAW! 6, follow these steps:

1. Select the Freehand tool (F5) from the Toolbox and click a starting point and an end point for your new line. Notice that when you select the Freehand tool your cursor turns to a crosshair.

2. After you release the mouse from drawing the second point, DRAW! completes the line as an individual object. The next time you click, you begin a new line. This is something to keep in mind for later.

3. Select the Pick tool and click on your new line. When you do this, the eight familiar object handles appear.

4. Grab onto any one of the eight handles and drag it to distort the line. When you do this, the program resizes the object, although it only looks as if the two points get farther apart.

To create a straight line, hold down the Ctrl key in between selecting your first and second points. As you move the cursor around the first point, you will see that DRAW! constrains the angle of the line to 15-degree increments (see fig. 6.1). Before going on, try using a different tool—the Bezier tool.

Also notice the style and color of the lines you have been drawing. If you haven't changed DRAW!'s original default, then the lines are most likely black and solid.

5. Select the Bezier tool from the toolbox Freehand Tool flyout. Access the Freehand Tool flyout by holding the left mouse button down on the Freehand tool until the flyout appears.

6. Using the Bezier tool and the left mouse button, click several points in different areas and end by clicking the Pick tool. Notice how there is a straight line joining each of the points you selected.

The Line tool will only draw two joined points in succession to form a straight line, whereas the Bezier tool continues to join each point drawn, creating a complex object. There is one last point to make concerning the Bezier tool though.

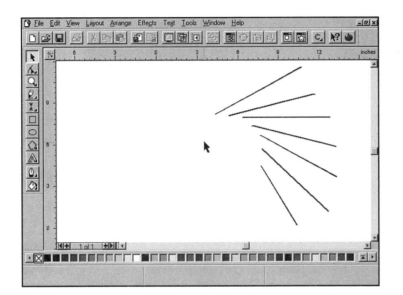

Fig. 6.1
While holding down the Ctrl key you may constrain drawing lines to 15-degree increments.

7. Select the Bezier tool again and draw several points in succession, ending by re-selecting the first point you selected. Notice that DRAW! now considers this a closed object and, if one has been defined, fills the object with the default color fill.

Although the name "Freehand tool" implies that you can pick up and draw with it, the Bezier tool is *really* the tool that enables you to freehand-draw complex objects. The freedom of the Bezier tool to create closed objects makes it infinitely more powerful than the Freehand tool.

Tip

To change the default Outline Pen style and color, deselect all objects by clicking in a blank area of your drawing and select the Outline Pen dialog box (F12). DRAW! displays the Outline Pen message Nothing is currently selected. To which type of new objects will the default apply? followed by three choices for Graphic, Artistic Text, and Paragraph Text (see fig. 6.2). Choose Graphic and continue to set the default color and style of your choice.

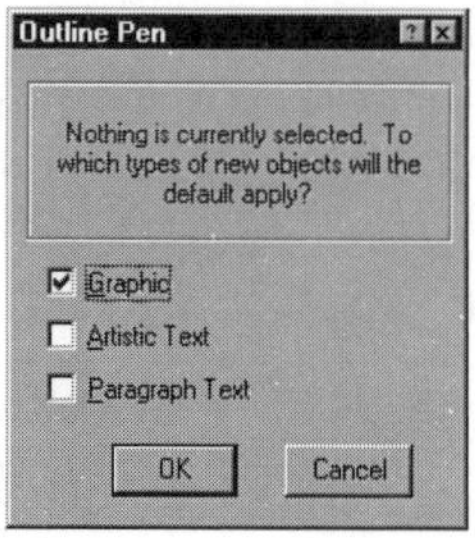

Fig. 6.2
If nothing is currently selected, choosing the Outline Pen dialog controls will display this warning message. Here you may set the Outline Pen defaults for Artistic and Paragraph text and Graphic objects.

Creating Rectangles

Rectangles (see fig. 6.3) are one of the simplest object types to create. To create a rectangle, select the Rectangle tool (F6) from the Toolbox, click in one corner and drag to the next. Drawing a rectangle while holding down the Ctrl key will constrain it to a perfect square. Drawing a rectangle while holding down the Shift key will cause DRAW! to create it from the center outward in the direction you drag the mouse. Holding down the Ctrl key and the Shift key at the same time will cause DRAW! to create a perfect square from the center outward as you drag the mouse.

Creating Ellipses

To create an ellipse select the Ellipse tool (F7) from the Toolbox, click in one corner and drag to the next using the left mouse button. Drawing an ellipse while holding down the Ctrl key will constrain it to a perfect circle. Drawing an ellipse while holding down the Shift key will cause DRAW! to create the ellipse from the center outward in the direction you drag the mouse. Holding down the Ctrl key and the Shift key at the same time will cause DRAW! to create a perfect circle from the center outward as you drag the mouse.

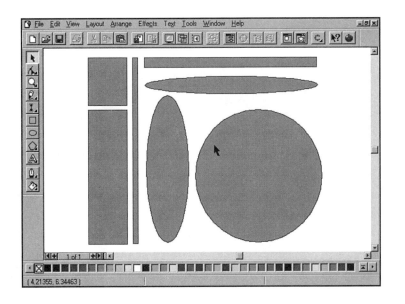

Fig. 6.3
The Rectangle and Ellipse tools are capable of no more than drawing simple rectangles and ellipses.

Editing Simple Objects: The Shape Tool and the Node Edit Roll-Up

Unless the objects you create in your drawings are perfectly shaped every time you create them, there is no doubt that you'll likely have to resize them somehow to fit exactly into your drawing. Editing is the final key to refining your shapes just the way you intended them to appear. Editing isn't just resizing or rotating them but actually manipulating the control points that your shapes are made up of. To do most editing you need to use the Shape tool, which in most cases will be referred to as the Node Editor. The Node Editor features its own special roll-up. The Node Edit roll-up has changed significantly from version 5 of CorelDRAW! and features buttons that perform specific actions on nodes—the points that make up your objects.

As you have seen in previous examples, the Shape tool plays a key role in the CorelDRAW! 6 arsenal of tools. Together, the Shape tool and the Node Edit roll-up (see fig. 6.4) can edit most any object created in the program.

Editing Lines and Curves

Editing lines that contain only two points can be done by selecting the Shape tool, clicking on a node, and dragging it to a new position (see fig. 6.5). If the node is controlling a curve that you have drawn, it will likely change the shape of the curve (see fig. 6.6).

Fig. 6.4

The Shape tool in combination with the Node Edit roll-up is capable of transforming any aspect of a curved line or objects.

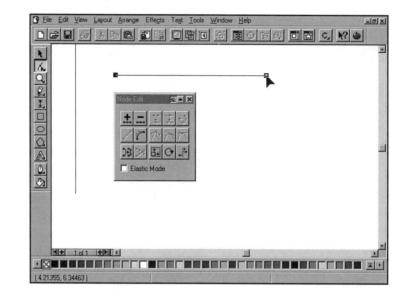

Fig. 6.5

Using the Shape tool you may change the position of individual nodes on a curve or curved object.

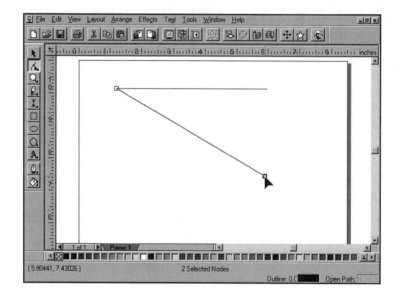

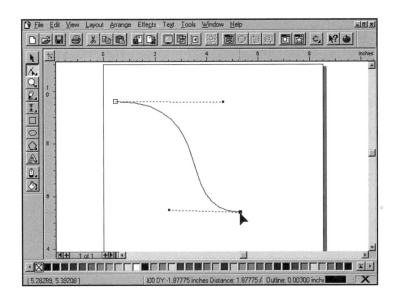

Fig. 6.6
If the Shape tool is used to reposition nodes that control curved lines, the shape of the curve will change as the node is repositioned.

Editing Rectangles

Rectangles are a bit different in that they are not made up of simple curves when drawn in their native form. Instead, a rectangle contains some of the original object data that make it behave like a simple shape instead of an object. The corners of a rectangle are not just nodes but are rectangle corners capable of doing much more than nodes.

To edit a rectangle shape, follow these steps:

1. Select the Shape tool, click any corner of the rectangle with the Shape tool, and drag the corner from its original position (see fig. 6.7). Notice that the corner marker splits apart, creating rounded corners on the rectangle. If you have your status bar displaying object information you'll also notice that it shows the exact radius of the rectangle corner you are reshaping measured in the units you have set in your Tool Options (Ctrl+J).

2. Still using the Shape tool, right-click one of the moved corner markers and select Properties from the menu that appears.

3. The Object Properties dialog box appears. It contains five tabbed areas including Fill, Outline, and Rectangle. Select the Rectangle tab (see fig. 6.8).

Fig. 6.7
Applying the
Shape tool to
native rectangles
enables you to
round the corners
of the object.

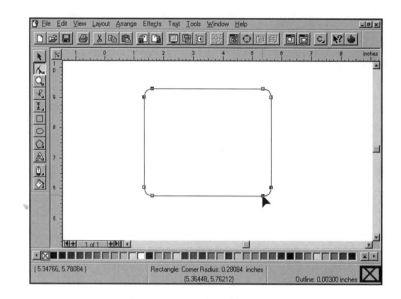

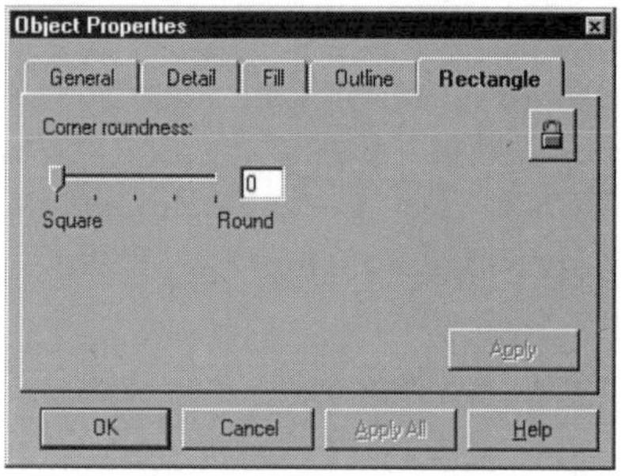

Fig. 6.8
The Rectangle tab
of the Object
Properties dialog
box enables you to
enter exact values
for the roundness
of rectangle
corners.

Object Properties are discussed later in this chapter. But briefly, when you moved the corner markers with the Shape tool, what you were doing was interactively changing the radius of the rectangle's corners. The Properties dialog box allows you more precision when changing this measure.

The value of editing a rectangle's corners in this way capitalizes on the strengths of the program by shaping all four corners simultaneously and identically. Later, if you need to edit the curved corners you may select only one to edit all four. To change the rectangle's corners to be straight again, use the Shape tool to grab and drag any one of the four corner markers back to its original position.

> **Note**
>
> If you edit a rectangle's corners to be rounded using the Shape tool and subsequently resize the rectangle either vertically or horizontally, you will distort the symmetrical effect of the rounded corners. To avoid this distortion, create your rectangle exactly in the shape you need it first, then edit the corners to be round.

Editing Ellipses

Editing ellipses is done in a similar way to editing rectangles—with the Shape tool. Ellipses don't have corners, but what they do have makes up for the lack of corner controls. Circular objects are made up of a curve joined by a line that has a beginning point and an end point, shaped evenly around a center point. In this same vein, ellipses in CorelDRAW! have two points and a center origin. To change these points follow these steps:

1. Select the Shape tool and notice that the Ellipse is now showing a single marker at a point somewhere along its path (likely on the top, bottom, or sides depending on how you created the ellipse).

2. Still using the Shape tool, grab onto the marker and drag in a circular motion around the middle of the ellipse. Keep your cursor positioned outside of the perimeter of the shape. If the ellipse had a fill color, notice now that it has disappeared.

3. Release the mouse button and notice that you end up with what appears to be a simple curve, but it's not. It's still the original ellipse.

4. Now, grab and drag that same marker, only this time keep your cursor inside the perimeter of the shape. Notice that your ellipse now takes on the appearance of a wedge. You'll also notice that you can now identify where the center point is. If the ellipse you created had a fill color, notice also that is has reappeared to fill the shape.

5. Right-click on one of the ellipse markers. The Object Properties dialog box appears again, only this time it includes an Ellipse tab. Click that tab (see fig. 6.9).

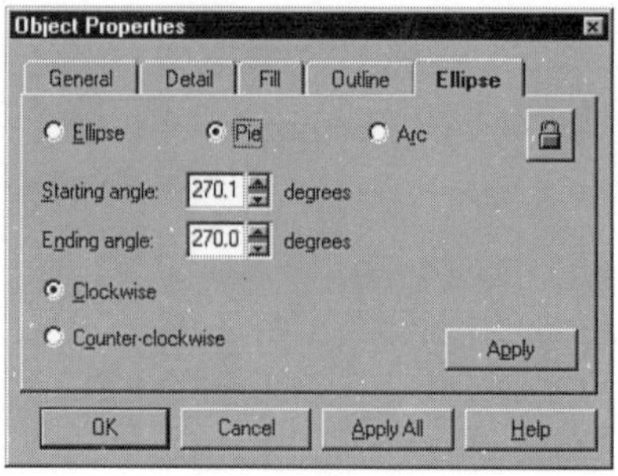

Fig. 6.9
The Ellipse tab of the Object Properties dialog box enables you to set your ellipse to either Ellipse, Pie, or Arc and enter the degree of the start and end points clockwise or counterclockwise.

If your status bar is set to display Object Details, you may have noticed that while you were moving the markers of the ellipse, the status bar displayed details of the number of degree change and total angle of the ellipse. The Ellipse tab of the Object Properties dialog box allows control for exact positioning of Starting Angle and Ending Angle of the Pie or Arc you are editing, and whether the orientation of the shape is Clockwise or Counterclockwise. When your editing is complete select Apply or OK.

Working with Polygons

Polygons are objects that have any number of points or sides. The Polygon tool in CorelDRAW! 6 is new and so its real power is yet to be fully exploited. The Polygon tool is grouped in the Toolbox and the Shape flyout with two other tools, including the Spiral tool and the Grid tool (see fig. 6.10).

Fig. 6.10
Using these three new tools you may create instant grids, stars (and other polygons), and spirals.

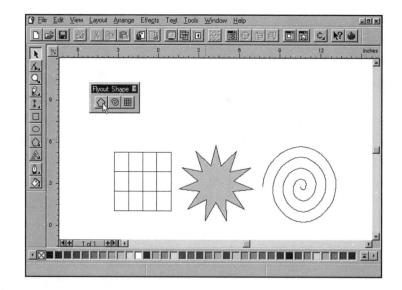

These tools are controlled in different ways. Some can be edited after being created, others can't. The first tool, the Star tool, may be edited after the star is created. The composition of the shapes created by the Spiral and Grid tools may not be edited afterwards, but instead must be preset to draw a certain set of variables.

Creating Stars

The Star tool is actually a part of the Polygon tool. To access the Star tool, double-click the Polygon tool and select Star. A Star object may be controlled or edited by either one of three ways:

- Through the Tool Properties dialog box by selecting, View, Properties, Tool.

- By right-clicking a star shape already created and selecting Properties from the menu that appears.

- By rapidly double-clicking the Star tool button in the toolbox or the Shape flyout. This is the fastest of the three ways.

The Polygon Tool Properties sheet (see fig. 6.11) can be set to draw any number of points as a Polygon, Star, or Polygon as Star. The Polygon option sets the Number of Points to equal the number of sides and joins each point one to the next. The Star option sets the Number of Points and sides to equal each other, but joins the points every two, three, four, or five points, and so on, depending on the setting. Star shapes include the interior structure of the star as well as the exterior curves. Polygon as Star is a cross between these two.

Creating a star, polygon, or polygon as star using these tools is identical to creating a rectangle or ellipse. To create any of these shapes select the corresponding tool from the Toolbox or the flyout, click in one corner and drag to the next.

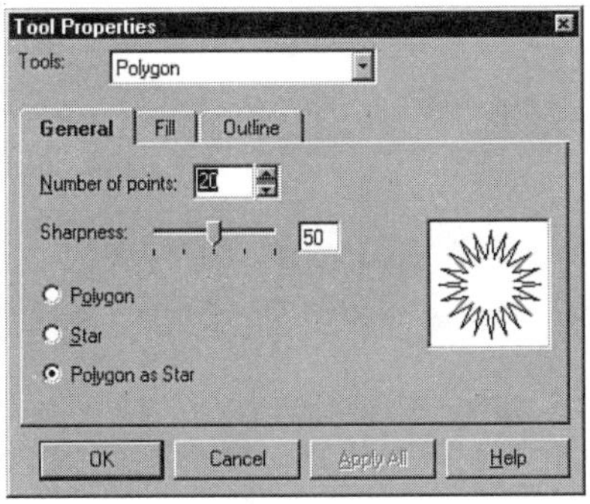

Fig. 6.11

You may use the Polygon Tool Properties sheet to control the various drawing modes of the Polygon tool including Polygon, Star, and Polygon as Star.

Creating Text & Drawings

II

Setting the Number of Points also displays a representation of the new shape in the preview window at the right of the dialog box. When setting the shape type to Star, the Sharpness setting also becomes available, enabling you to increase or decrease the length of the pointed sides of your star. Sharpness values may be set to between 0 and 100, while the maximum number of points may be set to 500.

Once the Apply All button is selected, the tool then draws all subsequent shapes to those settings until changed again.

> ### Tip
>
> Holding down the Ctrl key while drawing any polygon shape constrains the new shape to a perfect circle or square shape. Holding down the Shift key draws the new shape from the center origin outwards. Holding down both the Ctrl and Shift keys while drawing constrains the shape to a circle or square, and draws the new shape from the center origin outward.

Creating Spirals and Grids

The Spiral and Grid tools have few actual functions excepting the fact that you may set the number of revolutions in a spiral, or the number of squares in a grid. To set the number of spiral revolutions, double-click the Spiral tool in the toolbox or the Shape Flyout tool. A Spiral Tool Properties dialog box appears, allowing you to enter a number in the revolutions field. This value has virtually no limit except your system resources.

To set the number of squares in a grid, double-click the Grid tool in the Toolbox or the Shape Flyout tool. A Grid Box Tool Properties dialog box appears, allowing you to enter the Number of Cells Wide and the Number of Cells High fields. These values also have virtually no limit except your system resources.

To create either Spirals or Grids, select the corresponding tool, click on your page, and drag. A shape appears under your cursor. The number of units that make up spirals and grids cannot be edited after the shape has been created.

Editing Star, Polygon, Spiral, and Grid Shapes

For a different type of editing, the Node Edit roll-up comes into play when editing star, polygon, spiral, and grid shapes. Resizing any of these tools is a basic function. Resizing is performed in the usual way by selecting the Pick tool from the Toolbox and grabbing and dragging on any of the object handles. Corners resize proportionately while side handles resize either vertically or horizontally.

Unlike editing simple shapes such as curves, rectangles, or ellipses, these unusual shapes behave in a very different fashion when reshaped using the Shape tool.

To reshape a star, follow these steps:

1. Select the Shape tool from the toolbox and click the Star shape. Notice that the star immediately displays a number of marker points.

2. Double-click any of the marker points in the star shape as a shortcut to the Node Edit roll-up. Notice that only the Add Node, Remove Node, and To Curve buttons are active. That's because DRAW! creates the star shape using only straight lines by default.

3. Select any node, and click and drag it away from its original position. Notice that half the other nodes move at the same time, changing position in relation to the center origin of the shape.

> **Note**
>
> The star shape is created with a series of inner points and another series of outer points. When you select an outer point and reposition it, all outer points change position at the same time. When you select an inner point, all inner points change as well.

4. Experiment with moving the nodes to affect the shape of the star for a moment by repositioning various outer points and inner points to learn how they differ in changing the original shape of the star.

5. Now, select one of the points on the star and click on the To Curve button on the Node Edit roll-up. Notice that all of the lines associated with that outer or inner point change to curves and control points appear for the curve. Notice also that another button has now become active on the Node Edit roll-up—the Smooth Node button.

   After pressing the To Curve button, move that same node by clicking and dragging on it. Notice how the star shape now takes on a completely different shape, unlike a star.

6. Grab onto one of the control points of the curve you have selected and drag it around, noticing how all of the associated curves in the shape change at the same time (see fig. 6.12).

II

Creating Text & Drawings

Fig. 6.12

To edit the shape of a star, use the Shape tool to grab and drag the individual nodes or multiple nodes.

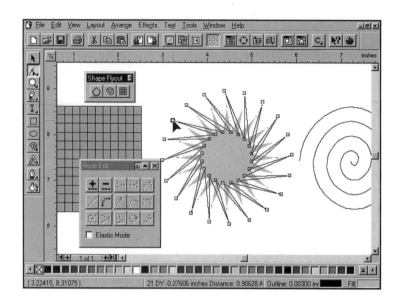

7. With the node still selected, click the Add Node button on the Node Edit roll-up. Notice that one node is added to each associated line in the shape.

8. Grab one of the control points for the node you have selected and drag it to a new position. Notice how each associated curve changes shape at the same time.

Spiral shapes also may be edited using the Shape tool, but after being created, a spiral becomes a simple object made up of curves and smooth nodes. You may edit a spiral shape as you would any curve (see fig. 6.13).

Grid shapes, on the other hand, can't be edited using the Shape editor. In order to edit a grid shape you must use the Pick tool in combination with the Ctrl key. The only type of object editing that may be done to a grid shape is changing the position of its individual grid boxes.

When a grid shape is created, DRAW! treats it like a series of rectangles that have been grouped together. In fact, each of the rectangles in a grid are "child" rectangles (child means part of a group) because the grid shape is actually just a series of grouped rectangles—that is, a group of perfectly aligned rectangles. To edit just one rectangle, hold down the Ctrl key while clicking on one rectangle with the Pick tool. Watch as the status bar displays the details of the objects selected. To ungroup the grid shape, select Arrange, (Ctrl+G). The grid shape changes to a group of rectangles. It's worth noting that these are still rectangles and not just rectangular closed objects. They may still be edited just as rectangles (see fig. 6.14).

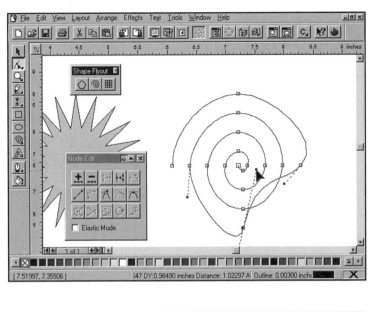

Fig. 6.13
Spiral shapes may be edited in the same way you would edit any curve object using the Shape tool. Spiral objects contain no internal dynamic links.

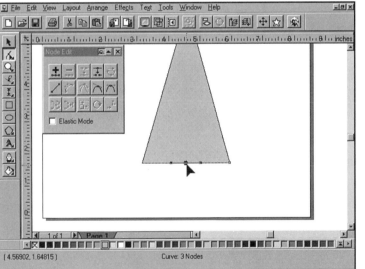

Fig. 6.14
Like Spiral objects, Grid objects don't contain any dynamic links either and may be treated like grouped rect-angles. After ungrouping, the Grid object is simply a series of rectangles.

Creating Text & Drawings

Editing Using the Node Editor

Nodes that separate curves (or straight lines joined to curves) contain control points. A node that separates a line and a curve contains one control point and a node that separates two curved lines contains two control points. The position of the control point determines the behavior of the curve. The Node Edit roll-up consists of fifteen different buttons that perform various com-mands to nodes and curves in editing (see table 6.1).

Table 6.1 Summary of Node Edit Buttons and Their Functions

Node Name	Function
Add nodes	Click to add one node between each selected node (symbolized by a plus sign).
Remove nodes	Click to remove selected nodes (symbolized by a minus sign).
Join node	Joins two unjoined nodes on a curve.
Break node	Breaks one node into two unjoined nodes.
Add line	Adds a line to join two separate unjoined nodes.
To line	Changes a curve to a straight line.
To curve	Changes a straight line to a curved line.
Cusp node	Changes a node to control points to be moved independently of each other. A cusped node allows the curves preceding and following to make abrupt changes in direction from the node.
Smooth node	Changes a node so that the control points belonging to it are locked in a straight line causing the curve to be smooth while it passes the node.
Symmetrical node	Changes a node so that the control points are locked in a straight line and equidistant from the node itself.
Auto-Reduce nodes	Used primarily for reducing the number of nodes in traced objects. Automatically deletes nodes leaving an approximated curve in their place.
Break Apart	Enables you to break off a single or multiple segments of a curve to create a new path.
Stretch	Allows the position of selected nodes to be resized relative to the object.
Rotate	Allows selected nodes of a complex object to be rotated around a center point.
Align	Aligns selected nodes and their control points.

The Node Edit roll-up also contains a single option for Elastic Mode. This feature, when activated, causes nodes to affect curve behavior differently than usual. Elastic Mode only works when more than one node is selected. Instead of moving the nodes and retaining their original control point positions, the control points change to exaggerate the shape of the curves they control.

There are two ways to edit a curve:

■ By editing the control points belonging to the nodes on either end of the line. This method is the most time-consuming, but also gives you the most control over the curve's shape.

■ By selecting the curve by clicking anywhere along its path. You will know when a curve has been selected by the highlight marker that appears on the line. Once the line is selected (see fig. 6.15) you may grab and drag on it to change its shape. Using the Ctrl key in combination with moving the curves shape may also allow you to constrain the curve shape to remain even and symmetrical (see fig. 6.16).

By selecting and moving the actual curve—instead of the nodes that control the curve—you are able to manipulate its shape without having to manipulate the control points of the nodes on each end of it. This way is faster than manipulating the two nodes individually.

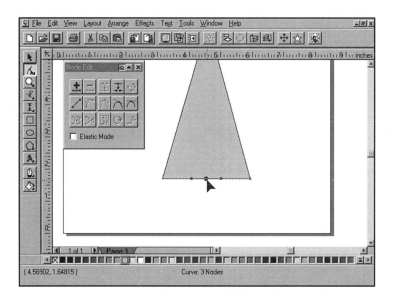

Fig. 6.15
To edit the shape of a line using the Shape tool, begin by clicking on the line once until you see a black marker appear.

II

Creating Text & Drawings

Fig. 6.16
Then, drag the marker in the direction you would like the line to curve to, and the line will change shape as you drag.

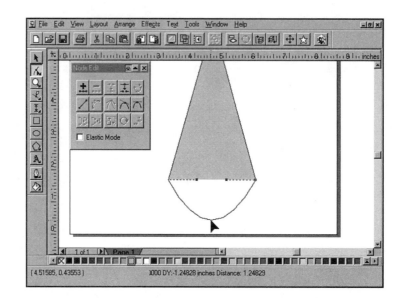

Properties

Every person has his or her own special gift, and every object in CorelDRAW! 6 has its own set of properties that make it different and unique in your drawing. At least that's the theory. By assigning and recording all the properties or data of an object, you are able to perform various commands associated with that data. For example, all data can be stored in a database, and then like any database, it may be sifted and sorted into search results. In other words, objects that have their data recorded can be searched for by property.

Object Properties

Object Properties include any attribute that can be assigned by CorelDRAW! 6 to an object. Table 6.2 identifies each of the property parts and their associated variables.

Table 6.2 Summary of Object Properties				
Object Type	**Fill**	**Color**	**Outline**	**Effect**
Rectangle	None	CMYK	None	Blend
Ellipse	Uniform	RGB	Solid	Extrude
Curve	Bitmap	HSB	Dashed	Contour

Object Type	Fill	Color	Outline	Effect
Artistic text	Fountain	LAB	Thickness	Fit text
Paragraph text	Vector	Grayscale	End caps	Perspective
Dimension	Texture	Spot	Line joins	Powerline
Bitmap	PostScript	Process	Calligraphy	Powerclip
OLE		Trumatch	Lens	Clone

To access or edit the specific properties of an object, select the object with the Pick tool and choose View, Properties and Object, or right-click the object and choose Properties from the menu that appears. Each different type of object that you select has its own Object Properties dialog box: Rectangle, Ellipse, Curve, Artistic text, Paragraph text, Shape, Dimension, Bitmap, and OLE.

Select by Properties Roll-Up

The Select by Properties roll-up is a very powerful new feature for CorelDRAW! 6. Select by Properties enables you to search your drawing for specific types of objects according to the attributes that have been assigned to them. Search parameters include: object, fill, outline, color, and effects. Variations of each of these parameters include:

- ■ *Object Types*. Search parameters for object type may include any or all of Rectangle, Ellipse, Polygon, Curve, Artistic Text, Paragraph Text, Dimension, Bitmap, and OLE object attributes.

- ■ *Fill Types*. Search parameters for fill type may include any or all of No Fill, Uniform Fill, Fountain Fill, Two-Color Bitmap Fill, Full-Color Bitmap Fill, Vector Fill, Texture Fill, and PostScript Fill attributes.

- ■ *Outlines*. Search parameters for outline type may include any or all of No Outline, Solid, Dashed, and Calligraphy outline attributes.

- ■ *Colors*. Search parameters for color type may include any or all of CMYK, RGB, HSB, L*A*B, Grayscale, HLS, YIQ, PANTONE Spot, PANTONE Process, TRUMATCH, FOCOLTONE, Spectramaster, DIC, and TOYO color attributes.

- ■ *Special Effects*. Search parameters for special effect type may include any or all of Blend, Extrude, Contour, Text on a Path, Perspective, Envelope, Powerline, Powerclip, Lens, and Clone effect attributes.

After locating the objects, the search feature automatically selects them for you. After they are selected you may continue searching your drawing and add to, subtract from, or select from the search findings using one of the four selection buttons included in the Select by Properties roll-up. The selection button functions do the following:

■ *New Selection Button.* Begins a new search, enabling you to start the Select by Properties command for specific variables by clicking on the Select button at the bottom of the roll-up.

■ *Add to Selection Button.* Enables you to search for additional objects and add them to your current selection by choosing additional (or different) properties and clicking on the Add to Selection button at the bottom of the roll-up.

■ *Remove From Selection Button.* Enables you to narrow your current selection by eliminating search parameters and clicking on the Unselect button at the bottom of the roll-up.

■ *Select From Selection Button.* Enables you to narrow your selection by selecting new or different parameters and clicking on the Edit Selection button at the bottom of the roll-up.

■ *Clear All.* Unselects any objects currently selected.

To begin a new search using the Select by Properties roll-up, follow these steps:

1. Choose Edit, Select by Properties to display the Select by Properties roll-up (as seen in fig. 6.17).

2. On the Select by Properties roll-up, click the New Selection button and define the variables of the objects you would like to have selected. For example, select Object Types from the General pull-down menu and select the check box named Artistic Text from the Detail list.

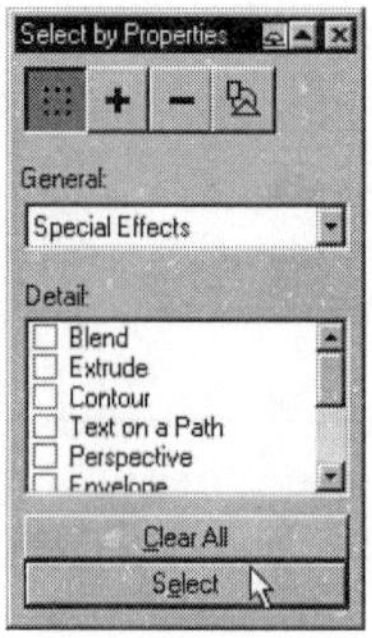

Fig. 6.17
The Select by Properties roll-up enables you to search your drawing for specific types of objects.

3. Click the New Selection button at the bottom of the roll-up. Notice that your objects are selected immediately while the number of objects is displayed in your status bar.

4. To add specific objects to your selection, click on the Add to Selection button, and increase the number of variables in your search. For example, if you had selected your Object Type as Artistic Text, you may choose to widen your selection by selecting Paragraph Text as well.

5. With your search parameters added to, click the Add to Selection button at the bottom of the roll-up. Your current selection will be added to using the new parameters.

The operations to Remove from Selection and Select from Selection may be carried out in the same way as Add to selection mentioned in these steps.

Cloning Objects

Cloning is another powerful tool you may use when composing drawings that contain multiple copies of the same object. There are a number of added advantages to using cloned objects rather than just making copies of the original. The first and most important reason is the immense editing potential of using clones. Any change made to the original cloned object will instantly be reflected in the clone. Even grouped objects may be cloned, giving the added benefit of being able to make changes to highly detailed drawings very quickly. The editing commands on the original cloned object will even apply if the clone has been transformed.

When a clone of an object is made, the original is then referred to as the master, or control object—master being the name that the commands apply to, while control is the name CorelDRAW! 6 identifies the object as in the status bar. The cloned objects are simply referred to as clones.

To clone an object or group of objects, select Edit, Clone (see fig. 6.18). An exact clone of your original object will be placed as a specific offset as determined by the Tools Options, General tab settings. You may also make copies of clones and the same effect will apply.

◀ See "Understanding Tool Options," p. 65

If you have taken full advantage of the cloning feature in CorelDRAW! 6, you may find that locating the master clone is difficult with so many identical-looking objects sitting in your drawing. To locate a master clone in CorelDRAW! 6, right-click one of the clones and select Select Master from the pop-up menu. The master object will be selected immediately.

II

Creating Text & Drawings

Fig. 6.18
By cloning an
object, you may
easily make
changes to the
master object in
order to edit the
clones. In this
example, a female
figure was cloned
several times and
the hair color on
the master was
changed, causing
the clones to
change automati-
cally.

In the reverse of this situation, if you had created several objects while some
were clones and others weren't, you may choose to locate the clones by right-
clicking on the master object and choosing Select Clones from the pop-up
menu.

If you have cloned an object and have made transformations to the clone
itself, you also have the option of removing the transformations from the
clone. To remove a clone's transformations, right-click the clone and select
Revert to Master from the pop-up menu.

Troubleshooting

*I was using the clone command and had to make editing changes to a master file that
spanned a number of pages, but the changes aren't being made in all the pages.*

You've encountered one of the limitations of the Clone command. The editing
changes do not span multiple-page documents. In other words, editing changes
made to a master object on page 1 will not change the clones on any subsequent
pages if you had placed any there. Nor will the Select Master, Select Clones, or Revert to Master commands have any effect. Try to keep a master object for each page
or pair of facing pages.

When I added a special effect to my master object, the effect wasn't applied to the clones.

The Clone command does not support special effects such as Perspective, Lens,
Envelope, Extrude, Contour, Powerline, and so on. The Clone command will, however, support the effect if the effect has been applied before the object was cloned.

Transforming Objects

Transformation controls in CorelDRAW! 6 have changed significantly since the previous version, and for the better. They have improved immensely and offer better control and precision over the manipulation of objects. You have already performed manual manipulation of various kinds using the mouse in combination with keyboard controls in previous chapters. But, as always in CorelDRAW! 6, there is more than one way to skin a cat. Transformation is controlled completely by the Transform roll-up, which has been subdivided into the five categories of transformation: Position (Alt+F7), Rotation (Alt+F8), Scale & Mirror (Alt+F9), Size (Alt+F10), and Skew (Alt+F11).

The roll-up itself is structured in an unusual way. The top of the Transform roll-up features a listing of the various transformation methods, and only displays each of them once they are selected. The very first selection, Transform, isn't really a transformation method, but rather serves as the name of this roll-up group. Clicking it has no effect and applying a transformation to an object with it selected simply applies transformation based on the last selection.

The remainder of the roll-up consists of various options that change with each transformation type selected. The origin position diagram is common to each transformation. This position diagram consists of eight option buttons, which represent the corner, side, or center of your object.

Also, within each of the transformations methods you have the option of applying your transformations to your original object or a duplicate.

Position

The Position roll-up (Alt+F7) may be set to move an object to a certain coordinate on your page (see fig. 6.19). The Relative Position option in the roll-up provides a reference point for the position change of the selected objects.

To move an object to a specific point on your page, select an origin button on the diagram in the lower half of the roll-up and enter the exact page position you wish to move the object to. Selecting Apply moves that origin point to those coordinates.

For example, to move an object to various corners of your page follow these steps:

1. In the Position transformation roll-up, select the top-left-corner origin of your object by clicking on the corresponding origin marker.

2. Assuming that your page size was letter, portrait, enter a horizontal measure of zero inches and a vertical measure of eleven inches.

6

3. Click the Apply button. Your object moves snugly into the upper-left corner of the page.

4. On the same roll-up, select the bottom-right origin marker, and, using the same page setup, enter a horizontal measure of 8.5 inches and a vertical measure of 0 inches.

5. Click the Apply button. Your object moves snugly into the bottom corner of your page.

6. Select the center origin marker, and enter a horizontal measure of 4.25 inches and a vertical measure of 5.5 inches.

7. Click Apply. Your object moves to the dead center of the page.

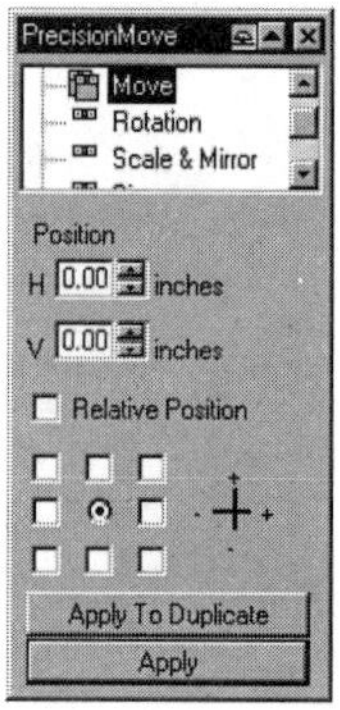

Fig. 6.19

The Position roll-up is capable of moving your object in increments or to certain positions on your page relative to the page coordinates or its current position.

By entering negative values you also may position objects left or below your page, and by entering values that exceed the vertical and horizontal dimensions of your page you may position them above and right of your page.

Rotation

The Rotation roll-up (see fig. 6.20) controls enable you to perform rotation with great accuracy, far exceeding whatever you could attempt to do with your mouse and a steady hand. Rotation controls work only on two variables: angle of rotation and origin of rotation. Imagine for a moment you are using the mouse to rotate an object. Click once to select it, and click a second time to invoke the manual rotation controls. By default, the rotation origin is in the center of the object. But, what if you needed to rotate the object around a certain point somewhere away from the center? You would need to have a steady hand and a keen eye to find the exact position.

The Rotation transformation alleviates this problem by allowing you to select the exact angle and rotation point to an accuracy of a tenth of a micron. Or, you may select the rotation point automatically by using the origin buttons. For example, to rotate an object, follow these steps:

1. Select an object to rotate, and select the Rotation transformation roll-up.

2. Select the lower-right corner and enter an angle of rotation of 45 degrees.

3. Click the Apply button. Notice that the object has rotated on a 45-degree angle counterclockwise around the bottom-right corner.

4. Without changing the angle of rotation, click the Apply button again. Notice that the object rotates counterclockwise, another 45 degrees and around the same point.

5. Change the value in the angle of rotation to -45 degrees while leaving the rotation point the same and double-click the Apply button. Notice that the object rotated back to its original position.

Fig. 6.20
The Rotation roll-up is capable of rotating objects in exact degree measures around its current center or a center position of your choice.

Rotating the object using a positive angle of rotation measure rotated it counterclockwise while negative numbers rotate it clockwise. Each time the Apply button is pressed the transformation is applied, and so transformation may be applied in stepped increments.

Tip

The trick to knowing how the Rotation transformation roll-up works is by watching how the origin point is moved by using numerical values. One way to get a handle on this is to view the changes in the rotation origin point as it is repositioned. To do this, follow these steps:

1. Select the object by clicking it once with the Pick tool. Then click it again to invoke the manual rotation controls. Notice that the rotation origin is in the center by default.

(continues)

(continued)

2. Select the Rotation roll-up and change the rotation origin on the roll-up to the upper-right corner. Make sure the angle of rotation is set to zero degrees.

3. Click the Apply button. Notice that only the origin point has moved.

4. Enter arbitrary values in the horizontal and vertical center of rotation measures, while still leaving the angle of rotation at zero.

5. Click Apply. Try this several times or until you have a grasp on how entering values corresponds to the location of the rotation origin marker.

Scale & Mirror

The Scale & Mirror roll-up (see fig. 6.21) works much the same way as rotate, by applying transformation to objects repeated each time the Apply button is pressed. To scale an object, enter the values of scaling in the horizontal and vertical scale percentage fields. Keep in mind that percentages work on the principle that anything more than 100 percent is an enlargement and anything less is a reduction. An even 100 percent value is no change at all.

The Mirror function of the roll-up is controlled by buttons located to the right of the horizontal and vertical scale controls. Clicking the mirror buttons sets the object to be flipped either horizontally or vertically. The origin marker diagram in the lower half of the roll-up applies to Mirror transformation only. Setting the origin marker to a certain side or corner sets the object to mirror around that point.

Fig. 6.21
The Scale & Mirror roll-up is capable of resizing or flipping your object horizontally and/or vertically, either to a copy or the original.

Size

This feature, which is new for CorelDRAW! 6, has been long awaited since being introduced as a function into the most popular competitors' page layout programs a few versions ago. Both Quark XPress and Adobe PageMaker have this same feature in their tool arsenal.

The Size roll-up (see fig. 6.22) works much like the scale part of Scale & Mirror, only backwards. Instead of entering a percentage value to transform your object, you merely enter the dimensions that you would like your object to become. The origin markers in this case work like anchors. The corresponding origin marker you select causes DRAW! to keep that marker in its original position, building the newly sized object up from that point. Clicking the center origin builds the object from the center.

Fig. 6.22

The Size roll-up enables you to enter exact measurements for your object to be resized to, while sizing proportionately, or by changing vertical and horizontal measures independently.

Skew

The Skew roll-up (see fig. 6.23) controls are the most basic of all controls, yet still allow you to enter measures numerically. To Skew an object select it and enter a value in either or both of the vertical or horizontal measures. In the case of Skew transformation, the origin marker diagram is inactive.

Fig. 6.23

The Skew roll-up enables you to set a vertical or horizontal skew for your currently selected object, and features an anchor point option to serve as a reference for the skew movement.

Using Align and Distribute

▶ See "Align &
Distribute,"
p. 322

This revamped set of controls has been cleverly designed to allow for a single set of buttons to control two related functions. The Align & Distribute roll-up consists of vertical and horizontal control buttons, a main preview window, and a full set of align and distribute options.

Grouping and Ungrouping Objects

There will often be times when it would be convenient to lock collections of objects together. It could be that you want to cement the arrangement together so that object arrangements don't move around on you, or it could be you merely want to organize things into packages. This is when the Group command becomes useful. You may select any objects at all and Group them. If you select an object that is already grouped with other objects, and your status bar is set to display Object Details, you'll see whether your object is grouped and how many items are in that group.

To group a selection of objects in your drawing, choose Arrange, Group (Ctrl+G). To ungroup a group of objects, choose Arrange, Ungroup (Ctrl+U).

To select a single grouped object for editing, hold down the Ctrl key and click on the object with the Pick tool. It will then be highlighted with a set of round-dot handles indicating it is a *child object* (belongs to a group). If you're attempting to select an object that's grouped and you discover that the item you're after is still grouped, continue holding down the Ctrl key while clicking on the object until you have isolated it by itself. Complex drawings may contain several layers of groups.

Tip

To find out exactly how many objects are contained in your drawing choose About CorelDRAW! from the Help menu. DRAW! will display information about your program, including a mention of how many single objects are contained in your drawing and how many groups there are.

CorelDRAW! does not allow you to apply the Group command to objects on different pages. You may, however, group objects inside your page with objects placed outside your page dimensions.

Working with Object Curves

All vector objects are made up of curves. Keeping that in mind, the Convert to Curves command (Ctrl+Q), available from the bottom of the Arrange menu, lets you view the composition of objects. Breaking down objects to their native shapes and curves will often provide you with tips on how to create your own drawing elements.

Once you begin using the Convert to Curves command, it will likely become one of your favorite features. Text, for example, can be broken down into curves. Objects that have had effects applied to them such as Extrude, Envelope, and Perspective may be converted to curves as well.

Breaking Apart Curves

The Break Apart command is found under the Arrange menu (Ctrl+K). To examine the Break Apart command, first take a look at how a native object may be broken down into basic elements. Artistic text is the perfect specimen for this. Text may be broken into individual words using the Break Apart command, or it may also first be converted to curves.

To examine how text may be broken apart, follow these steps:

1. Create a short line of text using the Artistic Text tool.

2. Using the Pick tool, select the text by clicking once on it.

3. Change to Wireframe view (Shift+F9) to view the outline of the text, and select your status bar to display object details.

4. Select Arrange, Convert to Curves command (Ctrl+Q). Notice that each character is now composed of a series of objects highlighted by markers, and your status bar now tells you that you have selected a curve on Layer 1 (see fig. 6.24).

5. Select the Shape tool from the Toolbox (F10) and click once on what used to be text. Notice that your text is now practically covered in nodes and your status bar tells you that the object is now a series of nodes (likely in the hundreds) on a certain number of subpaths.

6. Now, with the object still selected, choose Arrange, Break Apart (Ctrl+K) (see fig. 6.25). Notice that your cursor automatically changed to the Pick tool, your page now appears to contain a series of objects, and your status bar is telling you that you have a number of objects selected. You have just broken apart your text into a series of separate objects.

Fig. 6.24
Artistic text may be changed to a single curved object using the Convert to Curves command. Here a line of text is made up of curves.

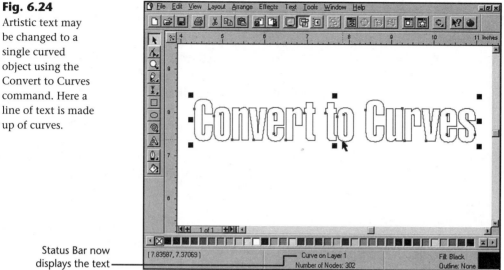

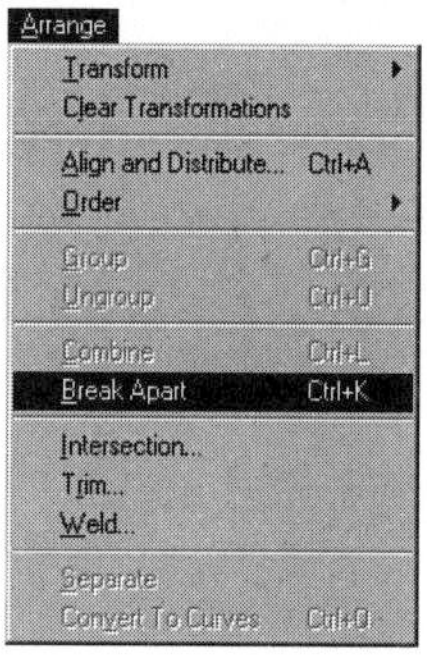

Status Bar now displays the text as a curved object

Fig. 6.25
While your Shape tool is selected, the nodes on your curve appear. You may split up an object containing multiple sub-paths by using the Break Apart command.

7. Turn Wireframe view off (Shift+F9) and view your objects, which likely don't quite resemble your original text anymore.

This example illustrates how text is really just composed of a series of curves. The same commands can be performed on other types of native CorelDRAW! objects such as simple shapes or symbols.

To examine breaking apart other object types, follow these steps:

1. Change your view to Wireframe once again (Shift+F9).

2. From your Symbols roll-up (Ctrl+F11) select a symbol from the WingDings collection by grabbing and dragging them out onto your page. Notice that your status bar describes the objects simply as Curve on Layer 1.

In figure 6.26 a pair of scissors, a hand, a telephone, and an oriental symbol have been selected.

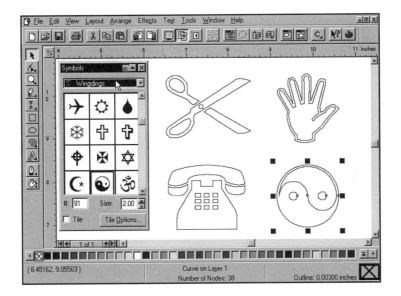

Fig. 6.26

All objects are composed of paths and subpaths containing curves. These four symbols each contain paths and subpaths that have been combined to create complex objects.

3. Select each object individually and choose <u>A</u>rrange, Brea<u>k</u> Apart (Ctrl+K). Notice that the scissors are composed of six objects, the hand two, the phone thirteen, and the last symbol four.

4. Now draw a star, a rectangle, and an ellipse.

5. Using the Shape tool, you change the shape of the star, make the rectangle have rounded corners, or make the ellipse a pie with a missing piece (see fig. 6.27).

6. Convert each object to curves (Ctrl+Q), one by one. Notice that each object is made up of curves containing nodes.

7. Select the Shape tool and marquee-select all the nodes in each object and use the Node Edit roll-up to break all the nodes apart. The shortcut command for selecting all nodes in an object is to hold down Ctrl+Shift and click on any node in the object.

8. Finally, use the Brea<u>k</u> Apart command (Ctrl+K) to separate the curves of each object. Take note of how each object is structured with combinations of straight lines and curves joined together by cusp, smooth, and symmetry nodes and shaped by control points.

Fig. 6.27

Using the Shape tool, you are able to edit simple shapes by manipulating and combining their nodes

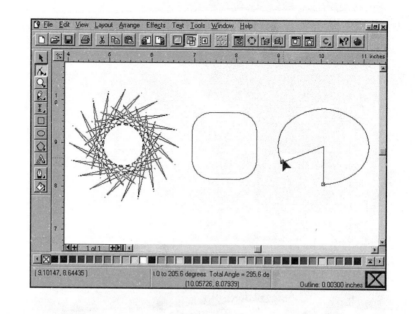

Tip

To use the shortcut command for selecting all nodes in an object, hold down Ctrl+Shift and click on any node in the object.

The example just given shows how every object can be broken down into curves no matter how it was created. In breaking objects down, you will come to understand how they may be put together again. These same rules apply when building objects up from curves. Learning to draw with curves forms the basis of most types of graphic software drawing techniques.

Combining Curves

To join one curve to another, select both curves using the Pick tool and select Arrange, Combine (Ctrl+L). You may also use the Combine command to join multiple curves. Once combined, the nodes of the curves may be joined together to form a complex or even closed object. Once closed, an object may have fills applied to it. Several curves joined together using the Combine command may be manipulated together as a single curve, making this an extremely powerful tool.

To join two curvestogether, follow these steps:

1. Draw a curve using the Freehand tool as in figure 6.28.

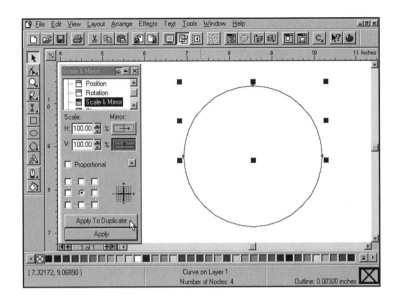

Fig. 6.28
To begin joining
two curves, create
a simple curve as
your first object,
make a copy, and
flip the copy
horizontally.

2. Use the Scale & Mirror roll-up to flip the curve and make a copy by
selecting the Apply to Duplicate button. Use the upper-middle origin
marker to flip the curve in relation to that point.

3. Select both curves by multiple-selecting them and choose Arrange,
Combine (Ctrl+L).

4. Select the Shape tool, and marquee-select the unjoined nodes and join
them using the Node Edit Join Nodes button.

5. When you have finished joining the second set of nodes, select the Pick
tool, and notice that the status bar tells you that you have selected one
curve on Layer 1 (see fig. 6.29).

To combine several complex curves together, follow these steps:

1. Draw a 20-pointed star by choosing the Polygon tool from the Shape
Tool flyout, and setting its tool properties to Polygon as Star, and the
Number of Points to 20.

2. Draw a perfectly round circle by holding down the Ctrl key and drawing an ellipse. Make the circle small enough so that it fits into the
middle of the star shape without touching the inside points.

3. Select each object and use the Convert to Curves command.

Fig. 6.29
By combining two open curves and joining the end-point nodes, you create a single, closed object.

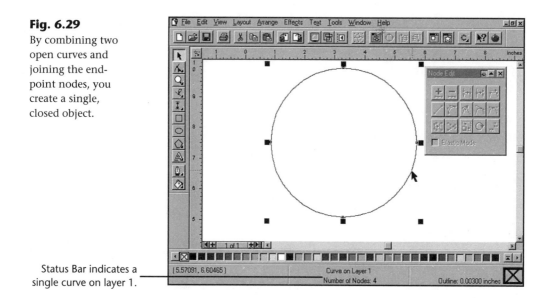

Status Bar indicates a single curve on layer 1.

4. Hold down the Shift key while selecting both objects and then choose Align to Center of Page using the Align roll-up (see fig. 6.30). The objects align to the center of the page and each other.

Fig. 6.30
Using the centering buttons on the Align & Distribute roll-up, center both objects on the page.

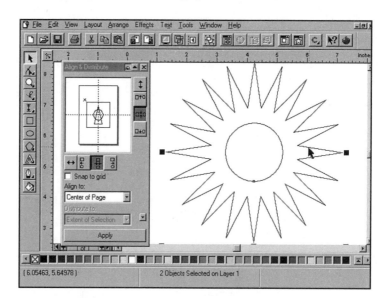

5. Choose <u>A</u>rrange, <u>C</u>ombine (Ctrl+L) and join the two objects together. The object becomes a single curve containing 45 nodes on Layer 1.

6. For effect, you can select the outline as none, and select a Radial Fill (F11) of yellow in the center to orange on the outside (see fig. 6.31).

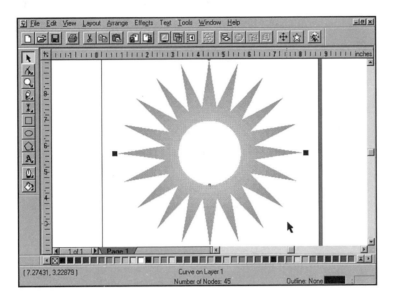

Fig. 6.31

After the star and the ellipse objects are combined using the Combine command, they become a single curve with two subpaths, forming a single object.

These steps explain how to create a complex object by combining two complex curves into one curve and assigning a fill. If you experiment with joining different curves to each other you will get to know how these tools all work in conjunction with each other.

Keep in mind that in order for objects to be combined they must first be reduced to curves if they aren't already. Editing nodes is nearly always involved in the process, as is the positioning of individual objects prior to being combined.

Applying Envelopes

The last chapter covered how to apply envelopes to Artistic text and Paragraph text. Envelopes also may be applied to any object in CorelDRAW! 6. The real advantage to using envelopes is their capability to transform objects without actually changing any of the object's characteristics. The Envelope roll-up (see fig. 6.32) contains four main types of native envelope types: single line, single curve, double-arc, and freehand.

■ *Add Presets.* The Add Presets button gives you access to a small library of basic shapes from which you may choose an envelope shape.

■ *Create From.* The Create From button enables you to create a new envelope from a basic shape existing on your page. Clicking the Create From button changes your cursor to a black arrow that allows you to designate a shape for your new envelope.

Fig. 6.32
The Envelope roll-up contains controls to enable you to create envelopes from existing objects, saved Presets, or to create them yourself.

■ *Single line.* This Envelope style button gives a slanted shape to objects. Single line envelopes contain only lines.

■ *Single arc.* This Envelope style button works the same as single line, except the envelopes use curves instead. The curve shape for each curved line has the same shape.

■ *Double-arc.* This Envelope style button allows objects to have two curves per side split by a symmetrical curve point in the middle.

■ *Freehand.* This Envelope style button allows you to edit any part of the envelope using a Shape tool. Any side or corner may be changed, making it the most versatile envelope type. Ctrl points in freehand mode may also be altered by using the Node Edit roll-up tools with the Shape tool.

To apply a simple envelope, follow these steps:

1. Select an object you would like to apply an envelope to using the Pick tool.

2. Select the Envelope roll-up by choosing Effe<u>c</u>ts, <u>E</u>nvelope (Ctrl+F7).

3. Choose the first envelope type in the roll-up, the single straight line envelope button, and set the mapping to Original.

4. Select Add New. Your cursor changes to a Shape tool and a dotted border line appears in place of the bounding box of your object.

5. Click and drag one of the envelope corner points to change the original shape. You may continue to change the position of several of the envelope points until you are finished (see fig. 6.33).

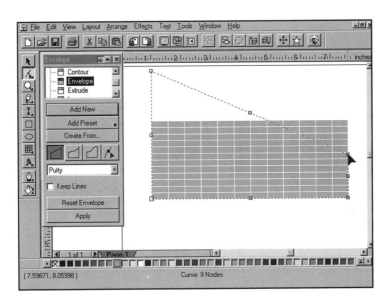

Fig. 6.33
To apply an envelope of your own creation to an object, select a style using one of the style buttons and select New Envelope to begin shaping your envelope.

II

Creating Text & Drawings

6. Once you are finished, click the Apply button on the roll-up. The object changes shape and adapts to the shape of the envelope (see fig. 6.34).

Tip

Holding down the Ctrl key while moving a handle causes the opposite handle to move at the same time in the same direction. For example, if you were to select the single line envelope type, and grab and drag on the top-middle handle to move it upward, the handle on the middle-lower side would move also. Holding down the Shift key while moving a handle moves the opposite handle in the opposite direction. For example, dragging the handle on top of the envelope upwards with the Shift held down causes the handle on the bottom to move downwards, and so on.

To create an envelope using the freehand shape tool, follow these steps:

1. Select the object you will apply the envelope to by clicking on it with the Pick tool.

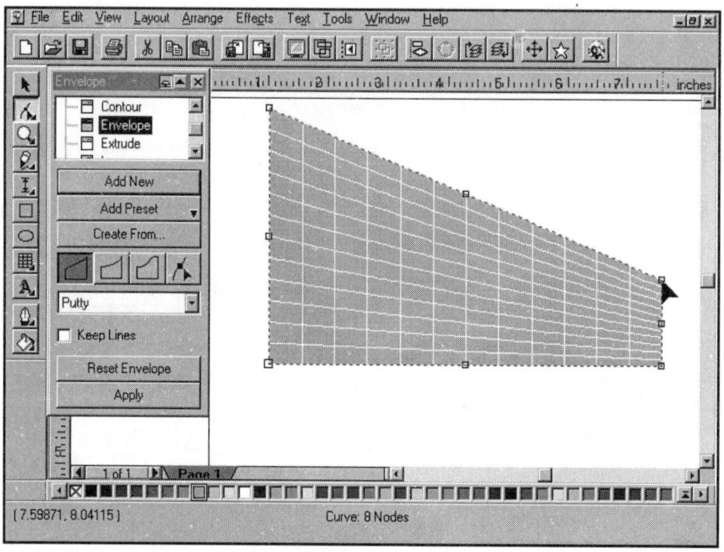

Fig. 6.34
Once you have completed editing the shape of your envelope, click the Apply button to have the effect take place. Shapes will not be transformed to the Envelope shape unless the Apply button is pressed.

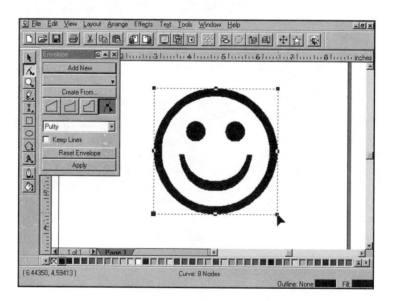

2. Select Effects, Envelope (Ctrl+F7).

3. Click the freehand envelope button and click Add New. A dotted border line appears in place of the bounding box of your object and your cursor changes to a Shape tool (see fig. 6.35).

Fig. 6.35
While reshaping your envelope with the freehand, your cursor changes to a Shape tool, with all of the same editing properties of the Shape tool, of course.

4. Using the Shape tool from the roll-up, double-click on one of the handles of the envelope outline. The Node Edit roll-up appears.

5. Marquee-select all of the handles on the envelope outline and click on the Add Nodes button (plus sign) twice. Notice that three additional nodes are added between each selected handle. Adding more nodes allows more of an interesting shape (see fig. 6.36).

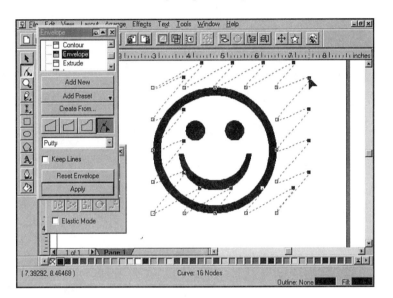

Fig. 6.36
To add additional nodes to your freehand envelope, click on the plus sign button.

6. Manipulate the handles of the envelope to the shape you need and select the Apply button. The object conforms to the shape of the envelope (see fig. 6.37).

The Envelope roll-up also features four mapping options, each of which plays a major role in the way objects behave within envelopes. Figure 6.38 shows the results of all Mapping options applied to an object.

- *Original* is an option that has been in existence since version 3 of CorelDRAW!. This mapping option tries to match the corners of the bounding box of the envelope and maps any internal nodes with bezier curves.

- *Putty* is similar to Original and maps as closely as possible to the corners of the envelope bounding box. For the most part, interior nodes are ignored.

Creating Text & Drawings

Fig. 6.37
Whichever shape
you define for
your envelope,
clicking the apply
button will cause
your envelope to
conform to that
shape.

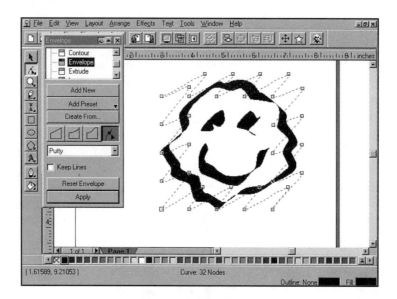

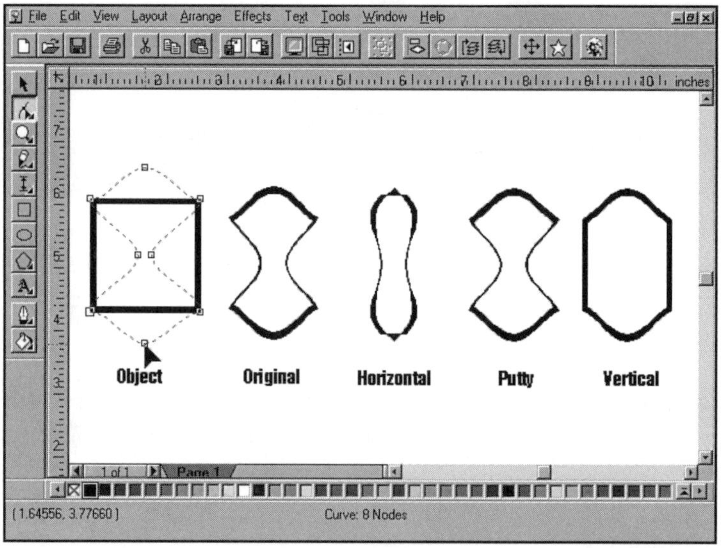

Fig. 6.38
When Mapping
options are used,
they affect the
line behavior of
envelope in
different ways, as
illustrated here.

- *Horizontal* mapping stretches the object to match the corners of the bounding box, and stretches all horizontal lines to fit the width of the envelope.

- *Vertical* mapping works the same as horizontal mapping, by stretching the object to match the envelope corners and then stretches the object to fit the depth of the envelope.

- *Keep Lines* is an optional function that maps any straight line curves in your object to fit the envelope by converting them to bezier curves. The Keep Lines function, when enabled, will match as closely as possible while rendering this mapping effect, but will usually not match the envelope shape exactly.

To clear an envelope effect choose Effects, Clear Envelope while the object with the envelope effect is selected.

Working with Extrude

Extrude is used to give a sense of depth to objects. Any object created in CorelDRAW! (except for Paragraph Text) may have an extrude effect applied to it.

The Extrude controls (Ctrl+E) in CorelDRAW! 6 have been redesigned to some degree but still operate to a large extent in the same manner as previous versions. Applying an extrude to an object actually creates a type of grouped object composed of your original object, which has a live link to the extruded shape attached to it. Altering the properties of your original object will cause the extrusion to change as well.

Extruded objects tend to be extremely complex in nature and some of the rendering that takes place may take a long time to execute depending on your system resources.

Working with Extrusion Types

There are six extrusion types in CorelDRAW! 6 from which you may choose. The names of the extrusions are aimed at reflecting the effect that is created:

- *Small Back.* This option places a smaller extrude behind your original object (see fig. 6.39).

- *Small Front.* This option places a smaller extrude in front of your original object (see fig. 6.40).

- *Big Back.* This option places a larger extrude behind your original object (see fig. 6.41).

II

Creating Text & Drawings

Fig. 6.39
The Small Back extrusion creates a realistic perspective extrusion with the back of the extrusion fading in the distance.

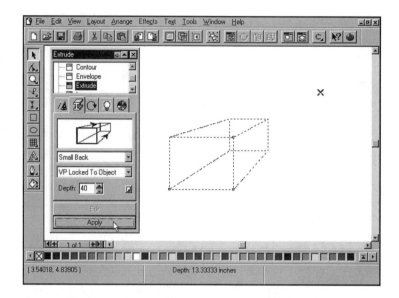

Fig. 6.40
The Extrude Small Front option enables you to create an extrude in front of your original object, smaller than your original.

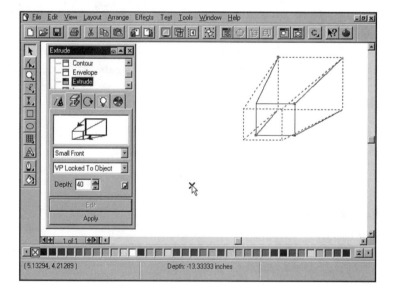

- *Big Front.* This option places a larger extrude in front of your original object (see fig. 6.42).

- *Back Parallel.* This option places the extrude behind your original object (see fig. 6.43).

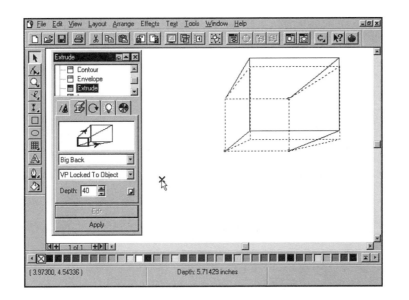

Fig. 6.41
The Extrude Big Back option, opposite of Small Front option, enables you to create a larger extrude behind your original object.

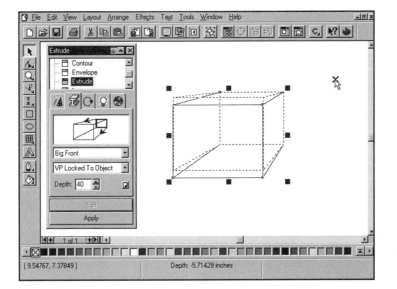

Fig. 6.42
The Extrude Big Front option enables you to create an extrude, larger than your original, in front of your original object.

■ *Front Parallel.* This option places the extrude in front of your original object (see fig. 6.44).

Fig. 6.43
Back Parallel
extrude option sets
a parallel extrude
behind your
original object
with no allowance
for perspective.
Vanishing points
merely set the
position of the
object.

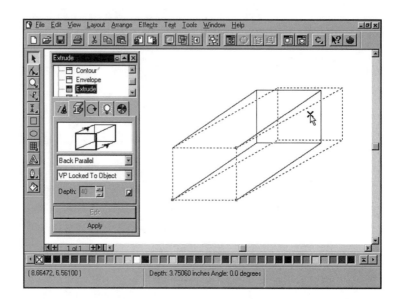

Fig. 6.44
The Front Parallel
option sets a
parallel extrude
in front of your
original object
with no pers-
pective effect.
Vanishing points
merely set the
position of the
object.

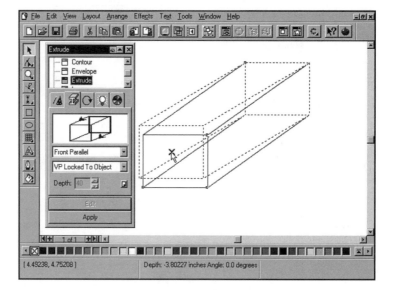

About Extrude Vanishing Points

A vanishing point, in reality, is the point to which all objects converge while
diminishing by distance. And, in reality, when viewing any scene, all objects
share the same vanishing point.

Vanishing points are naturally positioned at a point on the horizon of any scene, and usually perpendicular to the viewing plane and so create a perspective by which the eye may measure distance. Single point perspectives usually have their vanishing points positioned in the center of the scene, while two-point perspectives usually position the vanishing points parallel to the horizon.

Keeping this in mind, vanishing points in CorelDRAW! 6 simulate depth or perspective so that the person viewing the scene may imagine the relative size of the objects in the drawing. Vanishing point options in the Extrude roll-up may be manipulated and repositioned using controls attached to extruded objects. In order for multiple extruded objects in a scene to look like they belong in the same scene, they must be able to share the same vanishing point. Hence, the option of Shared Vanishing Point.

You may wish to set the vanishing points in your drawing before you begin to position your objects, and so the Extrude roll-up provides a Lock Vanishing Point (VP) to Page option. You may also choose to set your vanishing point one time and have it never change no matter where your drawn object appears. The Extrude roll-up offers the Lock VP to Object option. You may also wish to assign the same vanishing point coordinates relative to the object, and so in the Extrude roll-up you may use the Copy VP From option to copy vanishing points from other objects.

Page origin or object center. Clicking on the small page icon in the bottom right of the roll-up reveals the page origin control, which allows you to set the vanishing point to either a position relative on your page or a position relative to your original object.

Color Options

When using the Color options tab of the Extrude roll-up, you aren't restricted to using the coloring that appears in the extrude portion of your object. You may want to change it to something that fits the color scheme of the drawing you are composing. A number of options exist in the Color options tab (see fig. 6.45).

- ■ *Use Object Fill.* Use Object Fill is the default option that sets the extrude shape to the colors of your original object. The single option of Drape Fills exists and applies when the original object is filled with a bitmap, texture, or pattern fill. Drape Fills has the effect of applying the bitmap, texture, or pattern fill over the extrusion having the unique effect of making the object appear as if carved out of the fill material.

Fig. 6.45
The Color tab of the Extrude roll-up enables you to set bitmap, texture, uniform, or shaded fills for your extrusion, adding more realism to the shape.

■ *Solid Fill.* Solid Fill sets the extrude color to a uniform fill color selected by clicking on the color flyout menu and choosing a color.

■ *Shade Fill.* Shade Fill essentially sets the extrude fill to a fountain fill that extends the length of the extruded surfaces. Two color menus become available when this option is selected, enabling you to set a From color and a To color. From is the color closest to your original object while To is the color into which the first color will blend.

Setting Light Sources

You may set light sources for your extruded objects using the Lighting tab on the Extrude Roll-up (see fig. 6.46) using up to three light sources. Each light may be set to a different intensity and position around the extrusion, and may use full or limited color ranges to render the shading.

Troubleshooting

I can't see the effects of the light sources on my objects.

In order to see the effects of the light sources, you must first be using the Shade Fill color option set using the Color tab controls in the Extrude roll-up.

To set a light source for your extrusion, follow these steps:

1. Create an extrusion by selecting an object and an extrusion type in the Depth tab, and apply it. Apply a fill color of 30-percent black.

2. Select the Color tab and apply the Shade Fill, setting your From color to 30-percent black and your To color to solid black.

Fig. 6.46
The Lighting tab of the Extrude roll-up enables you to set up to three light sources for your extrusion adding more depth to the shape.

3. Select one of the three lighting source buttons by clicking it. Notice that by default, the lighting source is positioned in the front-upper-right corner around the extrusion preview in the Lighting tab.

4. Move the light source to the front-upper-left corner of the extrusion preview by grabbing directly on it and dragging it around the preview frame.

5. Set the intensity of your light source to 80 percent and click the Apply button. Notice that the side facing away from the lighting source is in complete darkness (see fig. 6.47).

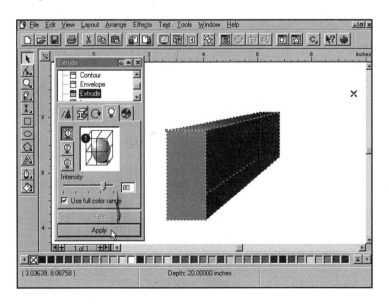

Fig. 6.47
Controls in the Lighting tab allow you to position your light sources and change the intensity for dramatic effects.

II

Creating Text & Drawings

6. Set the position of your light source to the front-lower-right corner of the extrusion preview window. Click the Apply button. Notice that the side that was in darkness is now shaded with the light source (see fig. 6.48).

Fig. 6.48
By repositioning light sources in the Lighting tab of the Extrude roll-up, you may change the shading effects on your extruded objects.

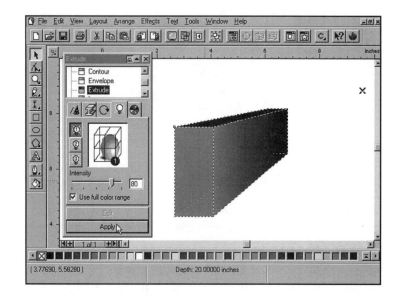

You may add a second and third light source to your extrusion if you wish by clicking the other lighting source buttons down and dragging the light source on the preview frame to position it. To remove a light source, click on its control button in the Lighting tab and it will be removed. While a lighting source is selected it displays black, and while unselected it is grayed out.

Troubleshooting

I chose multiple light sources, but I'm still getting all my light from the front-upper-right corner of the window.

If you click on more than one light source in succession without repositioning them in between selections, you may find out that the default position for all light sources when first installed into the preview window is the front-upper-right corner. As a result, the light sources tend to pile up on each other. To separate them again, try turning them off (by clicking again on the lighting buttons) or grabbing and moving them one-by-one to different positions.

Selecting the Full Color Range option enables you to get the best light rendering possible, but this also makes the extruded object more complex for operations such as printing and exporting. If you are using only black and percentages of black you may turn this feature off, as it will have no effect on this kind of shading.

Rotating Extrusions

The Rotate tab of the Extrude roll-up is the most interesting to manipulate of all the roll-up controls in CorelDRAW! 6 (see fig. 6.49).

Fig. 6.49
The Rotate tab of the Extrude roll-up enables you to rotate your extruded object in three dimensions.

To change the rotation position of the extruded object, click and drag your cursor inside the rotation area of the Rotate tab. As you drag in this window you will notice a bright yellow line appear, temporarily showing your rotation path. When you release the mouse button, the rotation will stop, and a dotted preview line will appear around your actual object indicating the rotation results (see fig. 6.50).

Two control buttons appear at the bottom-left and bottom-right of the roll-up. The left button is a reset control to set your rotate controls to their original position and will only work if the Apply button has not yet been pressed. The right button changes the roll-up appearance to three text fields for entering exact measures of rotation values.

Tip

Holding down the Ctrl key while using the rotation controls in the Rotate tab of the Extrude roll-up constrains the movement of the rotation path to vertical, horizontal, or 45-degree increments.

Fig. 6.50
The Rotate tab controls display a live animation of the rotation effects you are applying to your object and display an actual representation of the rotation effects on your extruded object.

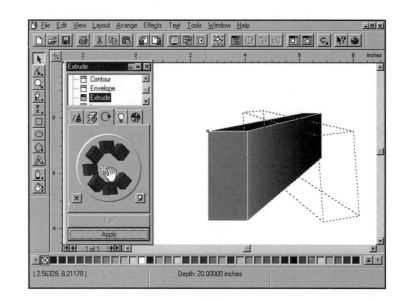

Using the Extrude Wizard

The Wizard portion of the Extrude roll-up (see fig. 6.51) enables you to do basically two operations: choosing from 50 saved extrude formats supplied by Corel, and Extrude-saving functions that enable you to save your own preset collections.

Fig. 6.51
The Extrude Wizard tab allows you access to 50 preset extrusions.

To apply a Preset Extrusion, select the object to apply the extrude to and select a Preset from the pull-down list at the bottom of the roll-up. After selecting, but before applying the extrude, view the effect of the Preset in the Extrude Preset preview window and read any textual instructions or description supplied with the Preset. Some Presets will only work on certain types of objects while others require that certain typefaces be loaded on your system.

The Extrude flyout menu enables you to save and manage your own Preset collection and includes options for New, Open, Save As, and Merge With. New, Open, and Save As compose the file management functions of the preset files, while the Merge With command allows you to combine Preset collections.

▶ See "Using and Creating Extrude Presets," p. 306

From Here...

Knowing object creation and manipulation operations in CorelDRAW! 6 is no small feat. There are a vast number of controls and features to become familiar with. If you are a first-time user of CorelDRAW!, all these controls may seem overwhelming for you. To alleviate this pressure, take your drawing one step at a time, keeping in mind that if you find yourself struggling through laborious drawing tasks, there is likely a pre-existing, better way to do it. All you need do is find it—having read this chapter will help immensely.

This chapter has covered node editing, drawing tools, properties, and effects. Drawing objects is what CorelDRAW! 6 is all about. But, while this chapter covers drawing techniques and effects, don't stop here. Continue learning CorelDRAW! 6 by referencing the following areas:

- Chapter 7, "Using Fills and Outlines."

- Chapter 10, "Working with Powerlines and Lenses."

II

Creating Text & Drawings

Chapter 7

Using Fills and Outlines

While building objects from scratch is the essential basis for any drawing, creating fills and outlines allows you to add depth and effects that make your objects come to life. The fill controls add depth, and the outline controls add definition and separation.

The proper use of fills and lines is an integral part of creating an effective drawing. Using these features together, and truly mastering them, plays a key role in opening the door to your own creativity.

In this chapter you will learn to

- Employ fill roll-ups, fill flyouts, and fill dialog boxes
- Make use of DRAW!'s spot and process color palettes
- Create and edit fountain fills
- Build and edit texture fills
- Assign and edit outline properties
- Specify and edit outline color
- Use pen controls to create and set line options

Using the On-screen Color Palette

Your color palette is perhaps the most accessible of all the color tools in CorelDRAW! 6. Creating objects is usually your first step, immediately following which you will no doubt want to specify a fill or outline, even if the color is None.

The default fill color that is assigned by DRAW! is black and, for the most part, won't be your desired color for all objects. You may find that white or clear is your most useful color when first creating objects. Choosing a default color will keep you from always having to change the color of new objects, since the object will have the default color when it is created.

To set the fill color default, follow these steps:

1. Deselect all objects by clicking on a blank part of your page or screen.

2. Press Shift+F11 to open the Uniform Fill dialog box. DRAW! displays a warning message (see fig. 7.1), which states that you have nothing selected, and which asks which type of object you would like the defaults to apply to.

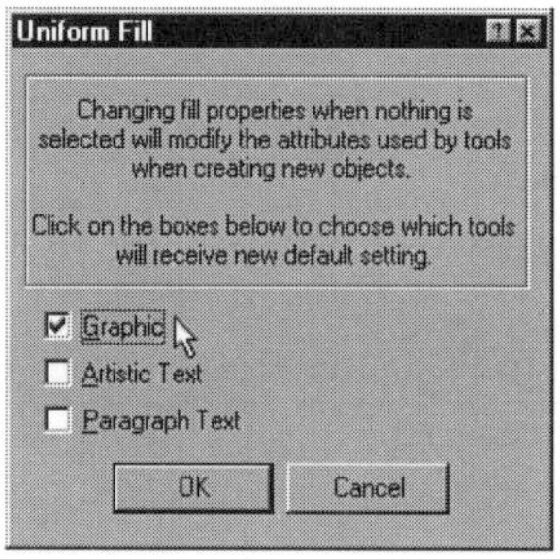

Fig. 7.1

The Uniform Fill default may be set by pressing Shift+F11 to display this default dialog box.

3. Select the object type: Graphic, Artistic Text, or Paragraph Text and click OK.

   DRAW! displays the next Uniform Fill dialog box (see fig. 7.2) from which you may select your default fill color.

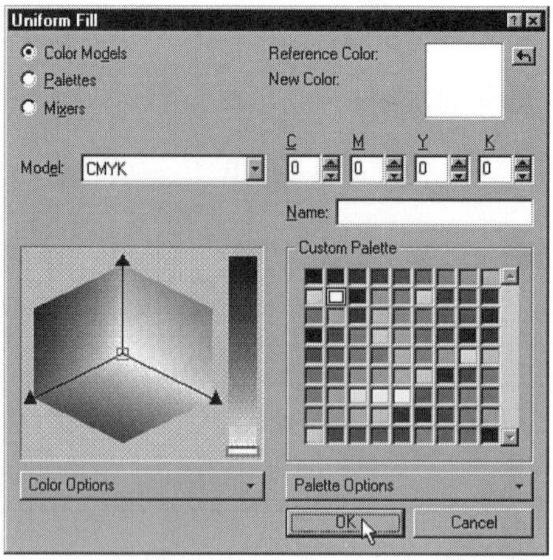

Fig. 7.2

The Uniform Fill dialog box is the main feature for setting, creating, and customizing fill options.

4. When you've finished selecting your color, click OK.

For easy access to any of the Fill dialog boxes, you can also select the Fill flyout (see fig. 7.3) by choosing Toolbars from the View menu, or you can right-click on the empty portion of any toolbar currently displayed and select Fill Flyout from the menu that appears.

Now that you've set your most commonly used color as the default color, you won't have to reset incorrect colors for the majority of objects you create.

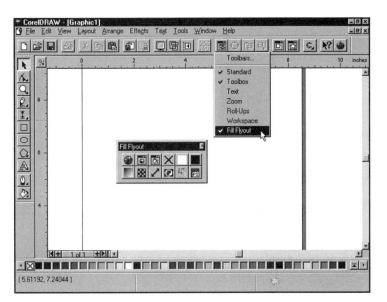

Fig. 7.3
Choose the Fill Flyout to display by right-clicking on the edge of any toolbar to display the pop-up menu and selecting Fill Flyout.

Using Uniform Fills

Uniform fills are even-colored or even-toned fills that may be applied to any closed-path object. Access to the Uniform Fill dialog box may be gained a number of ways, the most convenient of which is by using the keyboard shortcut Shift+F11. You may also access it through the Fill Flyout in the Toolbox.

The third way involves accessing the pop-up menu displayed using the right mouse button. To use this method, follow these steps:

1. Right-click on the object you wish to apply the fill to. A pop-up menu will appear.

2. Select Properties from this pop-up menu to display the Object Properties dialog box, which contains access to all of the object properties controls.

3. Select the Fill tab from the Object Properties dialog box.

The Fill tab displays the current fill applied to the object and enables you to assign another color and Apply it (see fig. 7.4).

The Fill Properties tab also gives you full access to the Uniform Fill dialog box by selecting the Edit button. Under the Uniform Fill dialog box, controls have been divided up into the three main areas of Color Models, Palettes, and Mixers.

Fig. 7.4
The Fill tab of the
Object Properties
dialog box also
enables you
to change fill
attributes.

Color Models

Your eyes are able to detect a huge range of colors; however, your monitor and printer are only capable of reproducing a fraction of that range. Color models are mathematical definitions of color properties, and vary in theory from model to model. Ultimately though, you will be viewing all of your images—at least initially—by way of your monitor, which renders only in RGB anyway. And so, any of the color models you choose will become RGB interpretations of those colors. The RGB color model stands for red, green, blue, and is the method in which all color is rendered by your color monitor.

▶ See "Under-
standing Color
Models,"
p. 436

There are ten color models included in CorelDRAW! 6, most of which have been designed for specific purposes or particular ink types. You will also find that once you have settled on a color palette, the others will be seldom used. They include CMY, CMYK, CMYK 255, RGB, HSB, HLS, L*A*B, YIQ, Grayscale, and Registration Color. The uses for these vary and overlap. In most cases you will either work in RGB (for screen display) or CMYK (for print).

If you are preparing drawings for the print industry you will likely use either CMY, CMYK, or CMYK255, each of which is a variation on the cyan, magenta, yellow, and black ink combinations used in creating full-color (CMYK) or fake full-color (CMY) printing processes. CMY and CMYK255 models are each measured in color units ranging between 0 (white) and 255 (full intensity). CMY is very limited in the colors it will reproduce and DRAW! indicates this by showing an additional color sample below Reference Color and New Color as the Printable Color.

If you are creating images for display only, you might choose to use either RGB (red, green, blue), HSB (hue, saturation, brightness), or HLS (hue, lightness, saturation), which are variations of on-screen display color models.

L*A*B color is defined by Luminance, and chromatic components A and B or color ranges from red to green (A) and blue to yellow (B). L*A*B color is a standard that first originated with the Commision Internationale d'Eclairage (CIE) in 1931, and is a model designed to render accurate color independent of the device outputting the image (monitor, printer, scanner).

The Grayscale color model represents the full range of shades available from using different screen values of black. The Registration color is new to version 6 but has been seen in other types of programs such as Adobe PageMaker. Setting an object in Registration color causes the object to appear visible in all color plates when printing. Use a Registration when printing separations to an output device that will not allow you enough room around the borders of your page to print registration marks, and so using the objects themselves as the registration marks. This is a tricky tool to use since there is no special screen color assigned to the registration color. Trying to locate the object you assigned as the register mark may be difficult.

To choose a color model and assign a color from that model, follow these steps:

1. Select the object you wish to assign a color to and press Shift+F11 to display the Uniform Fill dialog box.

2. If it isn't already selected, click on the Color Models choice in the upper-left corner of the Uniform Fill dialog box.

3. Choose a color model from the pull-down menu.

4. Select a color by either using the interactive color selector that appears on the left, or from the custom palette on the right. You may also enter color values into the text boxes above the custom palette display.

5. Choose OK. The color is applied to the object.

Troubleshooting

I keep trying to apply a color fill to the freehand object I just filled, but nothing happens. What's wrong?

▶ See "Under-
standing Color
Models,"
p. 436

Only objects that have a closed path may be filled. If your object doesn't fill with the color you have selected, make sure that all of the nodes in the object are joined together to form a closed path. Do this by selecting the Shape tool and clicking on the object. If the object is not a closed path, beginning and end nodes will appear, and will look larger than the other nodes

Using Palettes

CorelDRAW! 6 comes with eight different palettes including Uniform, FOCOLTONE, Pantone Spot, Pantone Process, TRUMATCH, DuPont, Toyo, and DIC. Which palette you use depends on how your drawing will eventually be reproduced. Using the Uniform Color palette restricts you to only the color models mentioned in the preceding section. However, setting your palette to any of the other palettes gives you access to specific process color systems such as FOCOLTONE, TRUMATCH, and Pantone, or to specific ink manufacturer spot color palettes such as Pantone, DuPont, Toyo, or DIC.

When working in color, avoid putting all your trust in the colors on your screen for accuracy. Any number of factors can affect the way your colors appear or even how your eyes are reacting to light and color on a given day.

When working extensively in color, use a proper color-matching guide or color swatch. A color swatch will show you exactly how a color will look when it's printed You will notice as you look through the palette selection that each of the palettes represents a color matching system vendor. These companies have each developed their own color matching system and all vie for your business claiming their system is the best.

The FOCOLTONE palette is a process color system that has been set up to reduce the amount of color trapping necessary and ensure the best looking results in process color printing. *Trapping* is the process of overlapping ink colors in an effort to reduce the chances of poor press registration. FOCOLTONE screen percentages are organized in increments of 10 percent with the aim of having common percentages of CMYK values. The FOCOLTONE palette is geared toward process color values only.

The TRUMATCH color palette is designed for optimum screen quality on digital film-output devices. Screen percentages are limited to only the printable screen percentages a printing press will reproduce, and to percentages that combine to form the most attractive screen appearances, avoiding moiré patterns. A *moiré pattern* is caused when overlapping CMYK screens are out of sync or alignment. This optimum screening feature alone makes the TRUMATCH process color palette one of the more attractive palettes to use. The TRUMATCH palette is also geared toward process color values only.

Toyo, DuPont, and DIC are spot color palettes designed by specific ink manufacturers. When using any of these color palettes you should equip yourself with the color swatch from the manufacturer for an exact color reference.

▶ See "About Pantone Spot and Process Color Palettes," p. 445

Palette Commands

Below the Custom Palette display in the Uniform Fill dialog box there's a menu containing a number of palette commands including Rename Color, Delete Color, New Palette, Open Palette, Save Palette, and Save As. The Rename and Delete commands apply to the currently selected custom color, while the New, Open, and Save Commands behave in the same way as file commands. All custom palettes have the extension .CPL and are stored in the COREL60\CUSTOM folder by default.

Choosing a Palette

CorelDRAW! 6, as in previous versions, allows you to choose which color palette will display in your DRAW! window. The on-screen color palette you choose may be any of the color palettes available in the Uniform Fill dialog box, or a custom palette you have created yourself. Palette files are stored in the CUSTOM folder in your COREL60 folder and have a .CPL extension. The default palette when you open DRAW! for the first time is the CMYK color palette called CORELDRW.CPL and is a very basic color selection.

To have DRAW! display a different color palette than the default, choose a palette from the Color Palette flyout under the View menu. After the palette has been chosen, DRAW! will indicate it as the palette being displayed by placing a black bullet indicator beside the name in the View, Color Palette menu flyout.

Mixing Areas and Custom Colors

The Mixers option is located in the upper-left corner of the Uniform Fill dialog box (press Ctrl+F11). New for version 6, this feature allows you to add and define palette colors by two different methods: Color Blend or Mixing area, both available from the Mode pull-down menu.

Color Blend is displayed by selecting Color Blend from the Mode pull-down menu. The Color Blend tools enable you to choose colors and have DRAW! blend between them (see fig. 7.5).

Once colors are blended you may select which ones to add to a new or existing palette. The Color Options button contains several significant features that control how the Color Blend feature behaves and displays. Each of the four corners of the Color Blend display window is a button controlling a color assignment. Clicking on these buttons causes a color flyout to appear, enabling you to select a color to assign to that corner.

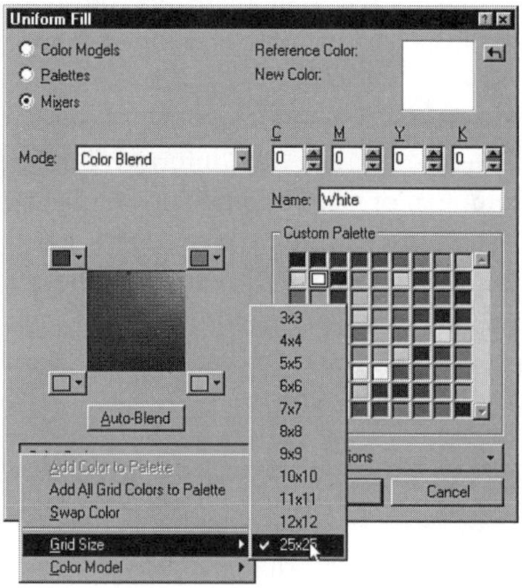

Fig. 7.5
The Color Blend feature contains a grid control that may be set to a variety of grid measures.

The Auto-Blend button toggles on or off to control whether or not the blending of your selected colors takes place immediately. When the Auto-Blend button is depressed, the four corner colors are blended together.

The number of colors contained in the blend grid may be set to one of eleven different sizes. The grid that is set to appear in the display determines how many colors will result from the blend. To set the grid size higher or lower, select Grid Size from the Color Options button. Grid sizes range from 3×3 to 25×25 enabling you to set from 9 to 625 different variations from your blended corner colors. The higher the grid setting the longer the Color Blend window will take to display the blend.

Operation of the Auto-Blend button is different from most interface features. This button doesn't bounce back, but stays down after being pressed. Only by pressing it again will it become unpressed and turned off. The advantage of turning this feature off is that it enables you to halt the display of the blend each time the Uniform Fill is selected.

Add Colors allows you to add the color currently selected to your custom palette, while Add Grid Colors to Palette adds all of them to the custom palette (the amount depends on your Grid Size setting). Swap Color transposes your reference color with your New Color and Color Model sets the color model that the Color Blend feature uses to either RGB (red, green, blue), CMYK (cyan, magenta, yellow, black) or HSB (hue, saturation, brightness).

The other Mixer—and much more interactive—feature is the Mixing Area color picker (see fig. 7.6), which is also a new feature for this version of DRAW! This feature allows you to manufacture your own colors as you would if you were physically mixing colors on a traditional painting palette. It features an Eyedropper tool for pinpoint-selection of colors from the mixing area, and a Paint Brush tool for adding new colors.

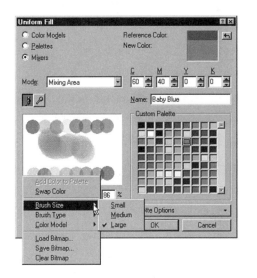

Fig. 7.6
The Mixing area mixer enables you to mix colors much the way an artist would using a traditional-style painters palette.

The Paint Brush tool is also controlled by a blend setting capable of 0 to 100 percent of transparency blend. By making adjustments to the blend control you are able to control how two or more colors behave when one is painted onto another. Setting the blend to 0 causes the brush strokes to be completely opaque, while setting it to 100 causes it to be completely transparent. By selecting a color from the palette being displayed you may begin painting on the palette window to create your new colors. When you are finished blending your colors, select the Eyedropper tool to sample the color, registering it in the New Color window.

Below the New Color window, you will often see an additional window appear labeled Printable Color. If you have used your Color Manager to set a color profile for your system, this will be the closest color your printer is capable of reproducing. If you are still using the default color profile that came with the program originally, this color won't apply to you.

With the Mixing Area feature selected, the Color Option commands change to allow the intriguing options Add Color to Palette, Swap Color, Brush Size, Brush Type, Color Model, Load Bitmap, Save Bitmap, and Clear Bitmap. Add Color to Palette, Swap Color, and Color Model each perform the same way as for the Color Blend feature. The Brush Size options enable you to paint on the color-mixing window either in Small, Medium, or Large brush sizes while the Brush Type sets the brush stroke colors to either Soft, Medium, or Hard.

To create, select, and save your new color from within the Mixing Area window, follow these steps:

1. If you haven't already done so, select the Brush tool and use it to mix your new color in the Mixing Area. Adjust the blend setting and size and type of brush as needed, and use the palette display as the beginnings of your colors.

2. Using the Eyedropper tool, click in the Mixing Area palette directly on the color you have created watching the New Color window to make sure you have the correct color selected.

3. From the Color Options button menu, select Add Color to Palette. A new color is added to the color palette.

    Notice that the Add Color to Palette option is only available when the color you have chosen is a new color and not a color that already exists in the custom palette.

4. This next step is tricky. To name your new color, click on it in the custom palette display and notice that a blinking text cursor appears in the Name field.

5. Type in your new name in the Name field. Then, click on the Palette Options button and select Rename Color. Your color name will be saved for future reference. This is also the same procedure you would use to change the name of a color in your custom palette.

6. To save your custom palette, select Palette Options, Save Palette. To save your palette as a new palette, select Palette Options, Save Palette As, and name your file.

Tip

You may further customize your palettes by moving the position and arrangement of the color indicators within the palette. By grabbing and dragging the colored squares in your custom palette display to a new position in your palette, you are able to re-order more commonly used colors to the front of the palette making them more accessible.

Note

For a shortcut in accessing the Color Options button menu for the Uniform Fill Mixers, try using the right mouse button and clicking on the color mixing areas in either Color Blend or Mixing Area.

To add a new color from the Color Blend display, follow these steps:

1. In the Uniform Fill dialog box, set the controls to display Mixers if you haven't already done so.

2. Set the Mode to display the Color Blend mixing controls by selecting it from the pull-down menu.

3. Define your selected blend colors by clicking on the corner buttons and selecting a color for each corner of the display.

4. Click on the Auto Blend button so that it is depressed. The four colors are blended in a grid according to what your grid size has been set to in the Color Options menu.

5. Select a color from your new range in the Color Blend mixer window.

6. From the Color Options button menu, select Add Color to Palette. The color is added to the custom palette you have displayed.

7. Save your new palette by selecting Save Palette from the Palette Options button, or select Save Palette As to save it as a new palette.

Creating Custom Palettes

If your drawings use many of the same colors over and over again, you should create your own palettes rather than taking the time to scroll through the default that DRAW! uses or define colors each and every time. DRAW!

enables you to not only make up your own custom colors and add them to the existing custom palettes, but it also lets you make up your own custom palettes. For example, if you were working as a publisher and needed to have specific colors quickly available for client logos, you could benefit from this feature.

To create a custom color, using the CMYK color model as an example, follow these steps:

To display a custom palette in the Uniform Fill dialog box, follow these steps:

1. If it isn't already, open the Uniform Fill dialog box by pressing Shift+F11.

2. Select Open Palette from the Palette button in the lower-right corner of the dialog box.

3. Use the Open Palette file finder that appears to locate the palette you wish to open. DRAW! stores a number of different palettes in the CUS-TOM folder. The palette you select will be loaded as the Custom Palette. Only one custom palette may be opened at a time.

> ### Tip
>
> The custom palette currently loaded will be the one you see on your screen when you select the Custom from View, Color Palette. When chosen, DRAW! will indicate this by placing a bullet indicator beside the name.

The last three items, Load Bitmap, Save Bitmap, and Clear Bitmap, may seem at first to be little more than a novelty. But, the capability to load a bitmap image into your color picker has far-reaching possibilities. You may want to save particular mixing areas that contain colors you are currently working on, or you may just want to clear the mixing area to begin a new work area.

To save a mixing area that you are currently working on, select Save Bitmap from the Color Options button menu and name your file. The file will be saved into the COREL60\CUSTOM folder by default as a windows bitmap file format with a .BMP extension. To reload that (or any other file) into the mixing area, choose Load Bitmap from the same menu. DRAW! will ask you to locate the file always defaulting to the COREL60\CUSTOM folder to start with.

For a second example (and the real strength of this feature), consider if you were working on a drawing where you needed to define colors of specific things like the color of skin tone, hair color, or eye color, and you already had a scanned image on hand for reference, you could load this image into the mixing area and pick up the colors from it.

Figure 7.7 shows a Windows Bitmap file of a mother and her child that has been loaded into the mixing area. It was saved as 72 DPI, at a size of 158 by 115 pixels in RGB color. Then the file was loaded into the mixing area by selecting Load Bitmap from the Color Options menu.

Using the Eyedropper tool, the colors of the various skin tone shadows, skin highlights, hair, cheeks, lips, sky color, and trees were loaded and saved to the custom palette being displayed. The first row of colors defined in the custom palette were named to specific parts of the picture. After the comprehensive collection of colors collected from the digital photo were added to the custom palette, it was saved for later reference. This custom palette is now a ready reference for coloring a drawing that could contain the same sorts of color definition, saving you the time of having to visually interpret the colors of your drawing or illustration.

Fig. 7.7
Using the mixing area Load Bitmap option you are able to place bitmap images directly into your mixing area for color sampling.

The Mixing Area is compatible only with the Windows Bitmap format. If you want to load a bitmap image into the Mixing Area you first need to save it as a bitmap image at a resolution of no more than 72 dots per inch (DPI) and a size of no more than approximately 170 pixels wide and 120 pixels high.

This method of sampling colors from digital images may be further enhanced by using the Color Blend option. Figure 7.8 shows how the full range of colors for specific color areas may automatically be added to your new custom palette. By defining the colors available in your custom palette and using the

Auto Blend button to blend the colors you have already defined, you can create up to 625 new colors in your palette automatically. Figure 7.8 illustrates four skin tone colors already defined in the custom palette blended to create 49 new colors with the grid size set to 7×7, using the Add All Grid Colors to Palette command.

Fig. 7.8

Auto-Blend features tools that enable you to create new colors based on sample colors from your bitmap images.

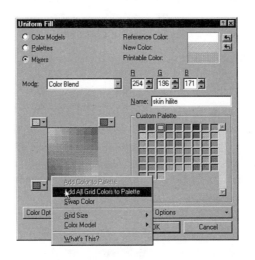

Using Two-Color Bitmap Pattern Fills

Color Bitmap patterns don't function like simply importing a bitmap image into your drawing. They may be assigned to fill any object and will retain their pattern size and proportions no matter how the object is manipulated, sized, or transformed. The use of two-color bitmap patterns will be interesting to someone drawing embellishments for desktop layouts, design drawings, or anywhere you need to define an area to visually represent something without actually having to label it. These patterns may be defined using any of the color models from any of the palettes available in the Uniform Fill dialog box including RGB for display, and CMYK or spot colors for print.

Patterns assigned using this fill method are 1-bit—or black-and-white—bitmap images in which DRAW! can assign the area defined by the black-and-white areas. The images can also be scaled to a certain size, and repeated as many times as necessary to fill the area defined by your object.

The Two-Color Bitmap Pattern dialog box may be accessed in various ways (see fig. 7.9). First, if you have the Fills toolbar displayed, click on the button that looks like a checkerboard pattern, or it may also be accessed through the Fill flyout on the toolbar. It contains options for selecting existing patterns that CorelDRAW! already comes equipped with, creating your own bitmap patterns, or importing your own existing 1-bit bitmap. Figure 7.9 shows the full controls available after selecting the Tiling button at the bottom-left of the first brief dialog box that DRAW! displays.

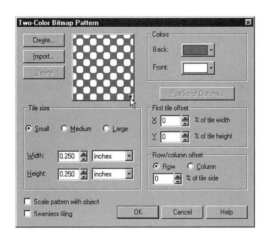

Fig. 7.9
The Two-Color Bitmap Pattern dialog box offers a set of advanced controls visible after selecting the Tiling options button.

Controls for these patterns include customizable tile sizes, custom tiling offset controls, PostScript options, and scaling options. The Tile size can be set to either Small, Medium, or Large, or to a specific Width and Height dimension.

Colors of the two-color patterns may be set independently as Front and Back. Setting either the Front or Back color of the pattern actually sets either the black (positive) or white (negative) space of the bitmap image. The color buttons give access to a range of colors determined by whichever palette is currently in use by the Uniform Fill dialog box. It may also be set to any of the color models or palettes available from those options by selecting the Others button at the bottom of the color flyout. The color flyout appears when you select either the Front or Back color button.

By using the First Tile Offset controls you are able to set exactly where the patterns begin and subsequently affect the rest of the pattern. For example, if your pattern is made up of circles as shown previously in figure 7.9, the first circle can be positioned to begin at any point in the upper-right of the fill. The pattern display window reflects the changes of any offset. Horizontal and Vertical offsets may be set independently of each other enabling you to set the exact beginning point of the fill pattern in percentages of 0 to 100 of the tiled image.

The Row/Column control sets exactly how each of the tiles align. While either the R̲ow or C̲olumn buttons are selected, you are able to shift the tiles vertically or horizontally from 0 to 100 percent of the tile side.

If you choose the option Scale Pattern with Object, the pattern will behave as any bitmap image would and will resize with the object you have filled. With this option selected you may also set the size of the tile by percentage increments of the object in reverse of setting the actual dimension measure in units.

Assigning a Two-Color Bitmap Pattern

To assign a two-color bitmap pattern fill, you need to keep a few details about your drawing in mind. Which color model do you need to use (for example, RGB, CYMK, or HSB)? Will your filled object be resized after the fill is created and will you want the fill to resize with the object? Do you need to set any special PostScript options for PostScript printing? Knowing the answers to these questions will eliminate printing problems or having to reassign the fill pattern.

To add a two-color bitmap pattern to an object, follow these steps:

1. Select the object you wish to fill by clicking on it with the Pick tool.

2. Access the Two-Color Bitmap Pattern dialog box from the Fill flyout or Fill toolbar.

3. With the Two-Color Bitmap Pattern dialog box open, click on the arrow in the pattern display window. Notice that a selection of patterns opens up in a large flyout format equipped with a File menu, and OK and Cancel buttons.

4. Select your pattern choice by clicking on it. Notice that the pattern you select will be indicated by a highlight box, but the flyout box doesn't disappear.

5. To confirm your selection, click on the OK button at the top of the flyout. To cancel your pattern selection and return to the dialog box controls, click on Cancel or press Esc on your keyboard.

6. To change the size, tiling, position, color, or pattern alignment of your fill, use the two-color bitmap fill options. The pattern display window will reflect any changes you make.

7. Select the OK button in the Two-Color Bitmap Pattern dialog box. Your object is filled with the pattern.

8. Before moving on, try rotating or resizing your filled object (see fig. 7.10). Notice that even though the object changes, the pattern remains constant.

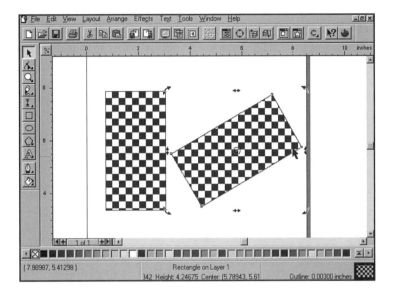

Fig. 7.10
Two-Color Pattern Fills are unaffected by resizing or rotating the object they fill.

Creating a Custom Two-Color Bitmap Pattern

There are controls available in the two-color bitmap pattern fill controls that enable you to create your own two-color bitmap patterns. These controls are accessed by selecting the Create button from the Two-Color Bitmap Pattern Editor dialog box (see fig. 7.11), which give access to the bitmap pattern Editor.

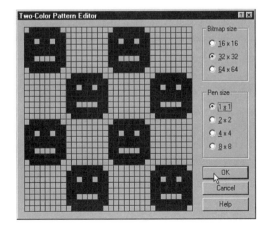

Fig. 7.11
Using the Two-Color Pattern Editor, you may create your own patterns and save them to the pattern collection.

In the Pattern Editor you can create your own patterns using the pixel-pushing method. In other words, you can create or edit a pattern that can be tiled at the pixel level. Clicking on the editor grid boxes fills the square, while right-clicking on a filled grid box clears it. There are three resolutions to create patterns with using either the 16×16, 32×32, or 64×64 bitmap sizes, and you may also set your cursor pen size to the smallest 1×1 size or the largest 8×8 size.

Once your pattern is completed, click the OK button and your pattern is added to the end of the list in DRAW!s current collection of patterns (see fig. 7.12).

Fig. 7.12

By using the mouse as an editing tool you are able to create your own patterns in the Pattern Editor.

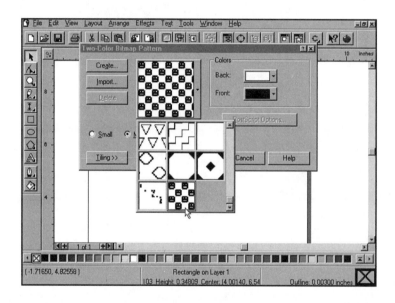

Tip

If you need to re-edit a pattern you created yourself in the Two-Color Bitmap Pattern Editor, first select the pattern to show in the pattern display window, and click the Create button again to invoke the Bitmap Editor. Or, if you would like to make changes to an existing DRAW! pattern, select the pattern to show in the pattern display window and click on Create to edit. Any changes made to the pattern are automatically saved as a new pattern.

Caution

If you're creating a custom two-color bitmap pattern fill using the editor and are using a certain resolution, don't attempt to switch resolutions halfway through your creation. If you do, your current, unfinished pattern will be flushed from the editor without warning. Instead, be sure that the resolution you begin with is the correct resolution.

Importing Images to Create Two-Color Bitmap Patterns

You may want to import images into the Two-Color Bitmap Pattern dialog box to quickly create bitmap patterns. To do this, either click the Import button in the main Two-Color Bitmap Pattern dialog box, or select the flyout arrow from the pattern display window and select File, Import Pattern. You can create patterns from any of the import file formats available in DRAW!. For example, if you needed to create a pattern that contained a company logo you may import that file into the Pattern Editor. The file will then be converted to a 1-bit black-and-white format compatible with the Bitmap Editor. Once you have finished creating your new pattern from the imported image, it will automatically be saved to the DRAW! pattern library.

▶ See "Corel's Import Filter Collection," p. 485

II

Creating Text & Drawings

Using Vector Pattern Fills

Procedures for using vector pattern fills are similar to the two-color bitmap pattern fills discussed previously. The major difference is that these patterns may be created in the full color range and may contain up to any number of colors.

To assign a vector pattern fill access, the Vector Pattern dialog box (see fig. 7.13) by selecting the double-headed arrow button from either the Fill flyout in the toolbox, or by selecting the same button from the Fill flyout toolbar if you have it displayed.

The controls for tiling size and offsets available in the Vector Pattern dialog box are the same as those available in the Two-Color Bitmap Pattern dialog box, however, there are no color controls. Also, there are no color controls to select. You may select a pattern from the vector fill collection by clicking on the arrow button in the lower-right corner of the pattern display window to activate the Fill flyout.

Fig. 7.13
The Vector Pattern
collection in
CorelDRAW! 6
contains over 70
different full-color
patterns.

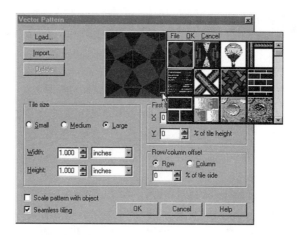

You may also load a prepared vector pattern fill by clicking on the Load button. DRAW! then searches for a pattern file with the extension PAT. A large selection of vector Corel patterns is stored in your COREL60\CUSTOM folder in case you don't have the time to experiment with creating your own (see fig. 7.14).

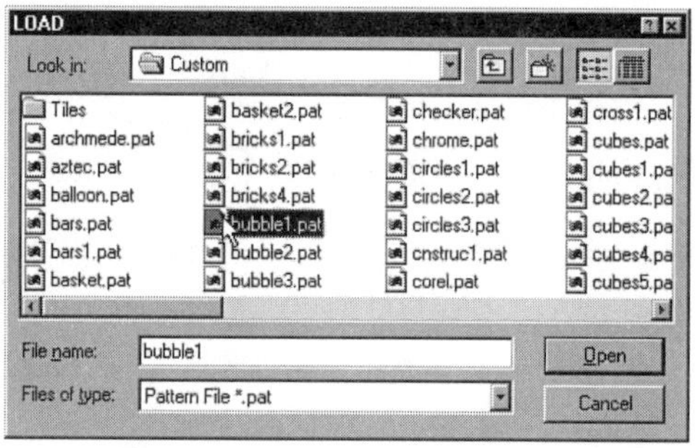

Fig. 7.14
The Load button
enables you to
choose from over
80 Corel-supplied
pattern files.

You are also able to create a vector pattern fill by importing any image type Corel is capable of importing. To do this, click the Import button from the Vector Pattern dialog box and locate the file you wish to make into a pattern. Figure 7.15 illustrates how a CMX file was imported using the Vector Pattern import. Adjustments may be made using the scale pattern with image controls to obtain a perfect fit in the tile size selected.

Once your tile sizing and offset have been set, click the OK button to assign the imported tile to your object as a vector pattern fill.

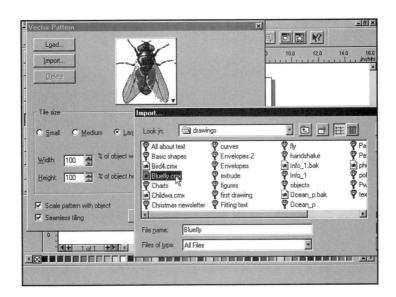

Fig. 7.15
The Vector Pattern Import command is compatible with all images available to CorelDRAW! 6. Once imported, the images may be fine-tuned in terms of size and pattern alignment.

Using Full-Color Pattern Fills

The full-color bitmap pattern fills (see fig. 7.16) work in much the same way as two-color and vector pattern fills. However, like the vector pattern fills, there are no color controls. Unlike the basic uniform colors available in the vector patterns, full-color patterns may contain graduated fills created in any of the color models available in DRAW!.

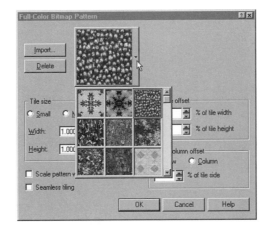

Fig. 7.16
The Full-Color Bitmap Pattern dialog box controls give access to a collection of ten Corel-supplied bitmap patterns. More may be imported into the full-color pattern fill by using the Import command.

II

Creating Text & Drawings

Using PostScript Fills

PostScript fills are created by CorelDRAW! using PostScript programming language. The advantage to using PostScript fills is that the user can set various fixed and random PostScript effects *exactly* for each fill pattern including size of the pattern, frequency, line width, spacing, random effects, and so on. The disadvantages to using PostScript patterns are that most of them only reproduce in black and white, and they can't be previewed on your screen while previewing your drawing. You can however, preview the PostScript fills in the PostScript Texture dialog box (see fig. 7.17).

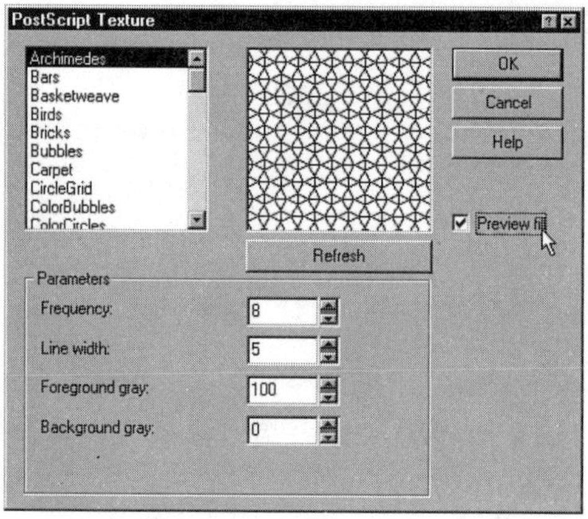

Fig. 7.17
PostScript textures may be previewed in the PostScript Texture dialog box.

To access the PostScript Pattern dialog box, click on the button containing the small PS symbol from the Fill flyout in the Toolbox, or from the Fill toolbar if it is displayed.

Using Fountain Fills

Adding fountain fill effects to drawings can add depth and color to an otherwise drab picture. DRAW!'s fountain fills are easily applied and controlled. Mastering this feature will put you a drawing level above the average person. Fountain fills are designed to mimic what the traditional airbrush artists are capable of doing with paint and air pressure. While there are some things the airbrush artist is capable of doing with an airbrush, there is much more you can do with CorelDRAW!'s fountain fills. All it takes is an idea and a few spare seconds.

To access the Fountain Fill dialog box, select the object you want to apply the fountain fill to and press F11, or select the Fountain Fill button from the Fill toolbar or Fill flyout. It's the button that looks like it has shading in two corners. This will bring up the Fountain Fill dialog box (see fig. 7.18).

It's worth mentioning, before you go any further, that even though fountains are fun to use and create excellent special effects for your drawings, there are some hazards to watch out for. While any type of fountain fill can be rendered by DRAW! to your screen, not every fountain fill is friendly to your printer, and if you intend on imaging your drawing to a high-resolution imagesetter for film output, be careful to avoid applying features and controls that might make your drawing impossible to output.

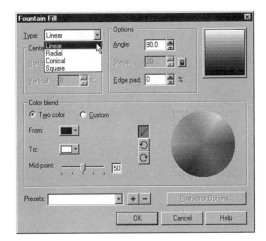

Fig. 7.18
There are four styles of fountain fills available, as seen here in the Fountain Fill dialog box pull-down menu.

Creating Text & Drawings

There are four different types and two variations for each of those types giving you eight different styles of fountain fill to choose from, including linear, radial, conical, and square types; two-color and custom (see fig. 7.19).

■ *Linear Fountain Fills.* These are the simplest of all fountain fills and will simply fill from one color to another in any set direction. This type of fill is also the default fountain fill that DRAW! will apply when the Fountain Fill dialog box is first opened. Linear fountain fills are excellent for simulating distance for backgrounds or realistic shadows on objects.

Fig. 7.19
There are four
basic fountain fill
styles to choose
from, each of
which may be set
to two-color or
custom.

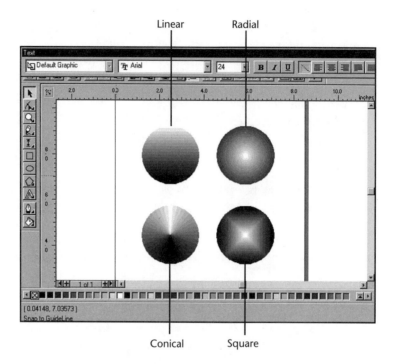

Linear   Radial

Conical   Square

- *Radial Fountain Fills.* Apply this type of fill to round or circular type objects to simulate a sphere or ball with a single highlighted point. The radial fountain fill will blend from one color to another color from the inside to the outside of the object. The center point of the inside color may also be moved by using the Horizontal and Vertical Center Offset controls in the Fountain Fill dialog box.

- *Conical Fountain Fills.* This type of fill is perfect for simulating the look of three-dimensional objects viewed from above, or objects that are highly reflective. This fill builds a fountain fill from a spire radiating from the center to the outside of the object you are filling. It will then build the fill from the first color to the last color in both clockwise and counterclockwise directions until reaching the second color on the other side of the object. The angle of the spire can be controlled through adjustments to the Angle amount, while the Horizontal and Vertical Center Offset controls set the center point.

■ *Square Fountain Fills.* You may not think of any fabulous applications for this fill type right away, but the way it works is impressive. This fill divides your object into four sectors from the center point outwards. Colors then blend in a linear direction from the center to the outside of the object creating a simulation of the object having four distinct sides. The center and angle can be adjusted just like the conical fill.

> **Note**
>
> You may interactively set the angle of linear fountain fills or the center point of radial, conical, or square fountain fills by clicking in the preview window with the Pick tool and dragging the angle or center point. Holding down the Ctrl key while doing this also constrains linear angles in 15-degree increments, or radial, conical, and square centers to 10-percent increments of change.

■ *Two-Color Fountains.* This is the first and most basic blend style, and as the name implies, it will blend from one color to another using any of the blend types (see fig. 7.20). From and To colors may be selected from the color flyouts, and if you need more you can access the complete range of models and palettes in the Uniform Fill dialog box by clicking on the Others button at the bottom of the flyout. Be sure to stick to the same color model and palette for both of your blend colors.

There are also three little buttons to the right of the two-color blend controls that set the direction of your color blend. The two-color controls blend defaults to a straight, linear blend. You may also blend across colors as indicated in the color wheel to the right of these controls. A color swing of clockwise or counterclockwise will include the spectrum of colors in between those two colors in your blend. The position of the colors you selected on the color wheel determine how many colors it will transition through to complete the blend. A mid-point control slider allows you to set the speed at which your colors blend to one another. A lower setting blends quickly between the From and To colors while a higher setting blends more slowly. The preview window reflects any blend changes you have made.

II

Creating Text & Drawings

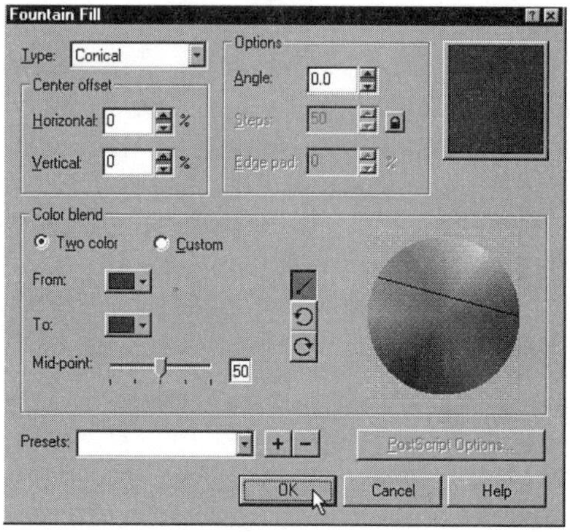

Fig. 7.20
The two color fill options in the Fountain Fills dialog box may be applied to any of the blend styles.

Caution

When using the color wheel to blend colors either in a clockwise or counter-clockwise direction, watch out for the spot-color hazards that can occur. Although DRAW! lets you blend from one spot color to another in a linear fashion, and around the color wheel, you won't want to use these options. If you are using only two colors of ink to print your drawing, none of those other colors will be available to you. Play it safe and avoid using this feature with spot colors of ink.

■ *Custom Fountains.* These fill styles create fountain fill effects that would otherwise be impossible to reproduce by hand using an airbrush or similar traditional tool. Custom fountain fills enable you to blend any of the fountain fill types using up to 99 different colors at a time provided, once again, they are all from the same color model palette. Figure 7.21 illustrates the controls available to you when using a custom fountain fill. The controls include a main slider to set the position of each color selected from the color palette display window. A Position field enables you to enter the exact position of your color by clicking above the slider and adding a new marker. Another control displays the current color you are adding to the fountain and gives you access to the Uniform Fill controls to select any of the palettes or color models available in DRAW!. Any color settings are reflected in the main fountain display window in the upper-right of the dialog box.

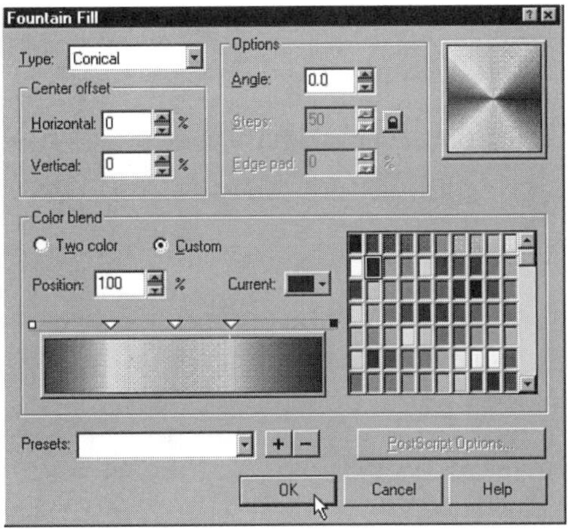

Fig. 7.21
Custom fountain fills seen here may include up to 99 different intermediate colors.

Troubleshooting

Why do my fountain fills take so long to print or not print at all?

One reason may be that fountain fills are set to fill between two colors; however, the two colors are not from the same color model. For example, if the first color you are blending from is a CMYK color, the other color(s) should be from the CMYK model as well. If your first color is a Pantone Spot Color, your following colors should be as well, and so on. Attempting to blend colors from one color model to another may cause your printer to choke when it comes time to print your drawing.

Note

Fountain fills may take extra time to screen draw, especially when working with drawings containing multiple fountain fills. Fills that contain different colors or multiple colors may take several sweeps of the fountain fill in order to render accurately. In order to cut down on screen draw time, you may do one of two things. First, reduce the number of fountain steps that DRAW! assigns to objects. Set your fountain steps display to a lower setting by choosing Tools, Options, Display. The Default setting is 20 steps, but if you want screen draw speed with a color reference, try setting it to 10 steps. This way DRAW! will render much quicker fountain fills and you can change it back to a higher setting when you fine-tune your drawing.

If your drawing contains a large number of fills, the second way to reduce screen draw time is to work in Editable Wireframe mode (Shift+F9 to toggle on and off). Draw in this view mode until you have finished creating and fine-tuning all of the shapes in your drawing.

To assign a fountain fill to an object, follow these steps.

1. First, click on the object you wish to fill.

2. Press F11 to bring up the fountain fill controls.

3. Select a fill type (linear, radial, conical, or square).

4. Select a fill style of either two-color or custom.

5. Set the To and From colors if you are using the two-color fill style, or choose to add colors by clicking in the area above the main color slider control above the slider in the custom style.

6. Once you have finished adjusting the other options and features, click OK and your fountain will be applied.

About Steps and Edge Pad Options

The Steps and Edge Pad options allow you to make adjustments to your fountain steps. This fine-tuning capability comes with a price though, and can add considerable time to how long your drawing takes to print.

■ *Steps.* When DRAW! calculates a fountain fill, it basically divides the space it has to blend by the number of fountain steps. Your fountain steps may be set in the Options Display tab controls located under the Tools menu. Overall, this may work out fine for most of your drawing projects. But, what about when you have several very small objects and one or two very large objects to fountain fill. By default, DRAW! displays each of these objects with the same number of fountain steps making the small object fills seem more detailed than the larger ones. This is where the unlock steps feature comes in handy. The Steps option in the Fountain Fill dialog box may be unlocked to override the Options master setting. This way larger objects, for example, may be set to display at a higher number of steps to make them seem as if they are displaying at a more detailed fountain fill (see fig. 7.22). But what happens to these fountain steps when you print your drawing? The answer is, the number of fountain steps that your printer will print is set by your Print command. Print settings are controlled by the fountain steps. The maximum number of steps that may be set is 256.

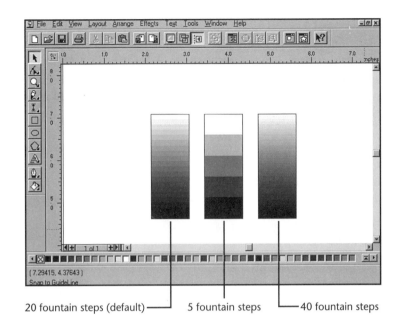

20 fountain steps (default) ——————   5 fountain steps   ——40 fountain steps

► See "Set-
ting Print
Options,"
p. 521

Fig. 7.22
Setting the
number of
fountain steps to
print, dramatically
changes the way
your fountain
filled objects.

- *Edge Pad.* This is the speed at which your fountain fill spreads from one color to the other. When left at the zero setting, the fountain fill is spread evenly between colors. When <u>E</u>dge Pad is set higher it will cause the fountain to transition more quickly (see fig. 7.23). The maximum <u>E</u>dge Pad setting is 45 percent.

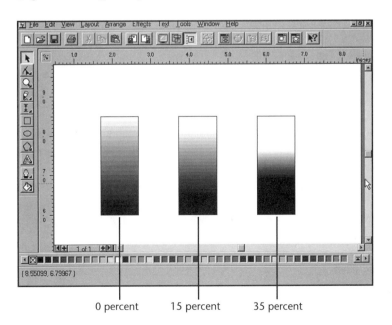

0 percent   15 percent   35 percent

Fig. 7.23
Edge Pad settings
control how
quickly your
fountain fill
changes from one
color to another.

II

Creating Text & Drawings

About Presets

The Presets controls at the bottom of the Fountain Fill dialog box allow you to apply existing Corel-created formulated fountain fills, or save fills you created yourself. To apply a preset fountain fill, select a name from the pull-down menu, while watching the preview window to see what each one looks like. This is also a great way to check out how these other fountain fills were created as the settings are displayed.

To save your own preset fountain fill to the list, follow these steps:

1. Once you have finished formulating your fill type, colors, and so on, click your cursor in the Presets field and name your new fill.

2. Click the plus sign button. Your new fountain fill name is added to the list of presets.

3. To remove a preset from the list, first select it from the pull-down list, and click on the minus sign. The preset is deselected.

4. Select OK to accept your fountain fill changes.

Using Texture Fills

These next fills are one of the more inspiring features of the program. They're called texture fills because they have the capability of simulating different surface textures (see fig. 7.24). But, texture fills can do much more than that. CorelDRAW!'s texture fills will simulate anything from crystal-clear satellite views of the earth, to rusty mineral deposits, or a cloudy sky on a hot day to a cool, blue swimming pool. Basically, any pattern imaginable can be simulated using this fill type. The patterns themselves can use as many as five colors or as few as two, any of which may be user-set to a different color set from the colors and palettes available from the Uniform Fill dialog box.

They're sometimes referred to as fractal fills, a name taken from the technology that produces them. Texture fills are full-color, fully customizable bitmap fills that are seemingly random in pattern and may be applied to any object as a fill. In creating a texture fill within an object, CorelDRAW! is essentially manufacturing an editable bitmap image. As far as printing goes, the texture inside the filled object is printed like any bitmap.

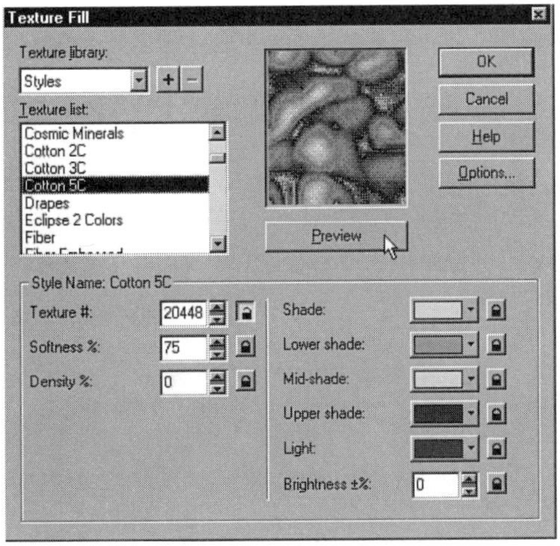

Fig. 7.24

The Texture Fill dialog box contains controls for selecting existing textures or manufacturing your own.

Features and controls for texture fills may include various settings depending on which texture fill you have selected in the Texture List list. They include the style parameters such as colors, minimum and maximum drop width, brightness, phase offset, ripple density, lighting, and so on. Each texture is assigned a texture number as well. To see more variations using the same texture settings, click again on the Preview button.

The Texture Library consists of three categories including Samples, Samples 5, and Styles, each of which gives access to a large number of individual pre-formatted styles. You'll have to explore and experiment to get the hang of adjusting the parameters. Each texture has its own setting names and values relating to the texture itself.

To apply a texture fill to an object, follow these steps:

1. Select the object you wish to fill, and open the Texture Fill dialog box by clicking on the Fill Flyout toolbar button or the Fill flyout from the Toolbox. The button has a spattering of color pattern on it.

2. Select a category from the Texture Library pull down list.

3. Make a selection from the Texture List list, and adjust the parameters to suit your needs. Take time for some exploration at this point to familiarize yourself with changing the variables. Any changes you make may be previewed by selecting the Preview button.

4. Click the OK button to assign the texture fill.

The options available by clicking on the Options button in the Texture Fill dialog box enable you to set the bitmap resolution that your texture will be created at (see fig. 7.25). The default setting for all textures is preset at a resolution of 120 dots per inch (DPI) to a minimum of 75 DPI and a maximum of 400 DPI. A control for setting the tile size of the bitmap also allows you to select the size in pixels of each tile of the bitmap. Here, the larger the tile size is set, the fewer tiles will be used to create your texture fill and the larger the bitmap image that is created will be.

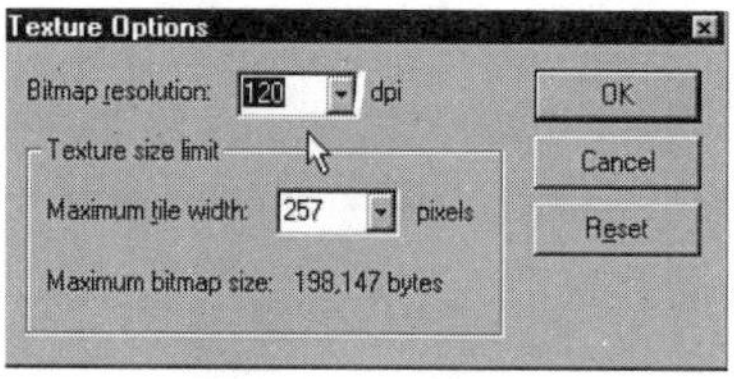

Fig. 7.25
Control your texture's characteristics by adjusting resolution and tile size to your liking.

Texture Options

Bitmap resolution: 120 ▼ dpi

Texture size limit
Maximum tile width: 257 ▼ pixels

Maximum bitmap size: 198,147 bytes

OK
Cancel
Reset

Troubleshooting

I've used large texture fills in my drawing and now it takes ages to print. Why?

Although texture fills create some interesting and unusual effects, system-wise they can become large and cumbersome to work with if you have chosen to set the texture fill options at a setting higher than the default. Memory size and available RAM will play major roles in determining how large and detailed DRAW! will be able to make your texture bitmaps.

You can create your own recipes for texture fills using this feature. To add your special texture creation to the texture list, click on the plus sign button. DRAW! asks for a name and which Texture Library you want to save the new texture to. Click OK and your new texture is added to the list.

Using the Special Fill Roll-Up

Having ready access to the Special Fill roll-up is perhaps even more useful than applying or editing using keyboard shortcuts, toolbars, or the Toolbox flyouts. The Special Fill roll-up allows you to set any color fill specifications for any object (see fig. 7.26). It's perhaps the most versatile of all the color fill tools found in DRAW!. By using the Special Fill roll-up you have access to Uniform, Fountain, Two-Color, Vector, Full-Color, PostScript Pattern, and Texture fill types. You may also set new objects to be filled from fills assigned to other objects by using the Update From feature or you may also edit from an existing object to apply a new fill. It's an ingenious feature and one that you will likely stick with once you become familiar with its operation.

Fig. 7.26
The Special Fill roll-up enables you to set any of your color fill specifications.

To apply a fill to a new object from an existing one, follow these steps:

1. Select the new object to fill by clicking on it with the Pick tool.

2. Select the Special Fill roll-up to display by clicking on the button that looks like a pouring paint can from the Fill flyout on the Toolbox, or from the Fill flyout toolbar.

3. Click on the Update From button on the Special Fill roll-up. Notice that your cursor changes to a large black arrow pointing right (see fig. 7.27).

4. Click on the object you would like to copy the fill from. Notice that the Special Fill roll-up displays the fill specifications of the object you are copying the fill from in the fill preview window.

5. If you would like to accept the fill exactly as it appears, select the Apply button. Otherwise select the Edit button and the dialog box that controls the specifications for that particular type of fill appears.

6. Make your editing changes in the dialog box, and select the OK button from there. The Special Fill roll-up will reflect the changes in the Fill Preview window.

7. Click the Apply button to assign the new fill.

II

Creating Text & Drawings

Fig. 7.27
The Update From
feature enables
you to copy
attributes from
any other object
in your drawing.

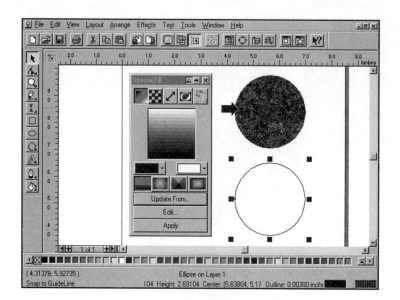

The Special Fill roll-up may be used globally to apply fills to any number of objects.

Pen Controls

The pen controls are important for anyone creating diagrams that have a heavy emphasis on line style flexibility and controls, or those creating schematics, engineering-related, and diagram-type drawings (see fig. 7.28). Like the fill controls, nearly every aspect of lines may be tailored to fit exact needs. DRAW! includes a variety of dotted and dashed line styles that may be dressed up with arrowheads, color, weight, and a few other options few might think of. The keyboard shortcut to the Outline Pen dialog box is F12.

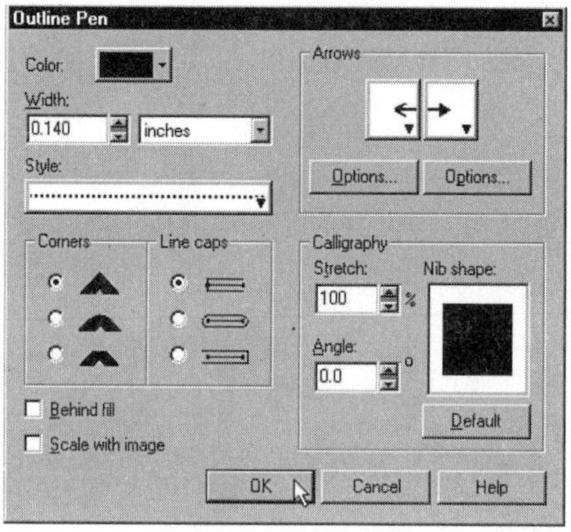

Fig. 7.28
The Pen controls
enable you to
apply different
patterned outlines.

It's worth keeping in mind that the Pen Outline controls will build the thickness, end shape, and any other line effects around the center axis of the line or curve you have drawn. In other words, when you assign an outline to an object, the outline will straddle the actual outline of the object, building the thickness of the Outline Pen attributes on either side.

Troubleshooting

Why is it all text I create ends up having an outline on it?

One of the most common mistakes first-time users make when using CorelDRAW! is leaving their outline default for text set on. This can do a number of really bad things to the appearance of type. You can always tell if DRAW! is rendering a drawing that contains type that has an outline around it. You'll notice that DRAW! will quickly render the text and then it will go back and laboriously draw the outline around it immediately afterward. Type will look dirty at smaller sizes and will take longer to print.

Do yourself a favor and make sure that your outline default on text is set to none. To do this follow these quick steps:

1. Select nothing by clicking the Pick tool on a blank part of your page and press F12.

   DRAW! gives the following message: `Changing the outline attributes while nothing is selected will modify the attributes used by tools when creating new objects, click on the tools below to choose which tools will receive the new default setting.`

2. Click the Text tool option only and click OK.

   The Outline Pen dialog box appears.

3. Set the line width to 0 and select OK.

(This doesn't apply, of course, to situations where you need the outline around the text such as color-trapping operations. Trapping is the process of overlapping ink colors in an effort to reduce the chances of poor press registration.)

Applying Line Styles

There are more than 20 styles to choose from, ranging from solid or unbroken to various states of broken lines—some with large dashes, others with several intervals of small dashes added in an effort to make different types available. Applying a line style does not change the shape of the line or the amount of space it occupies; however, you are able to select the thickness of a line from 0 (none) to a maximum of 4 inches. Line weight may also be set to inches, millimeters, picas and/or points, and ciceros and/or didots.

Troubleshooting

I am trying to apply a fill to an object in a drawing I didn't create, but nothing happens when I try to assign a fill to it. What's wrong?

With a maximum width of four inches it's possible to make a line so thick that it resembles an object like a rectangle while in preview mode. To see whether an object is a line or a shape either click on it with the Pick tool and read the Status bar display, or view your drawing in Wireframe or Editable Wireframe view. In cases where a line is used instead of an object, the effects applied affect it as if it were a line and not a shape. For example, using Weld, Trim, or Intersection on a line with another shape will treat the line as a line and not a shape. The same applies to Perspective, Extrude, and Envelope effects.

Corner Controls

Corners of lines or curves may be set to either square, round, or mitre in shape. Setting corner styles can greatly affect the appearance of objects, especially if the object has a particularly thick line weight and/or the object is particularly small (see fig. 7.29).

Fig. 7.29

Setting the corners of lines or curves to specific shapes is one of the more advanced options for controlling pen controls.

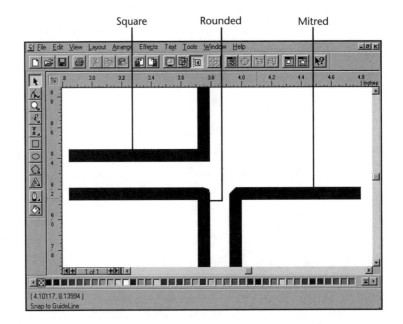

Line Cap Controls

The Line Caps setting determines how the shape of the line is built around the end of the line. Line caps of lines or curves may be set to squared, rounded, or extended.

- Square line cap style builds the end of the line only on either side of the line without adding to the shape of the end, giving it a square look. This is the most common and default line style for DRAW!.

- Rounded line caps build a rounded end onto the ends of lines by a factor determined by the line's thickness.

- Extended line cap style builds a square end to the line equal to the width of the line.

Figure 7.30 illustrates the effects of line caps on a straight line.

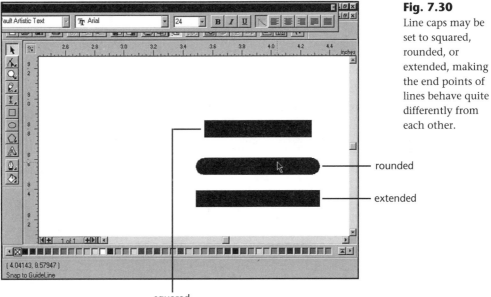

Fig. 7.30
Line caps may be set to squared, rounded, or extended, making the end points of lines behave quite differently from each other.

rounded

extended

squared

Calligraphy

Aptly named, Calligraphy settings for lines make continuous lines or curves appear as if they were skillfully drawn with a calligraphy pen. The Calligraphy controls include a Stretch control, which sets the width of the line anywhere from 0 to 100 percent, and an Angle setting capable of complete 360-degree rotation. Try setting these controls both at the same time by placing your cursor inside the Calligraphy preview window and dragging around on the black square you see there. The animated effects are quite impressive, although they have nothing to do with drawing lines. To reset the calligraphy controls to the normal 100 percent Stretch and a 0 degree Angle, click once on the default button.

Figure 7.31 illustrates the effects of altered calligraphic settings on a spiral shape.

Fig. 7.31
By altering the calligraphic settings on objects you may create a variety of effects.

No calligraphy

Calligraphy:
10 percent,
–45 degrees

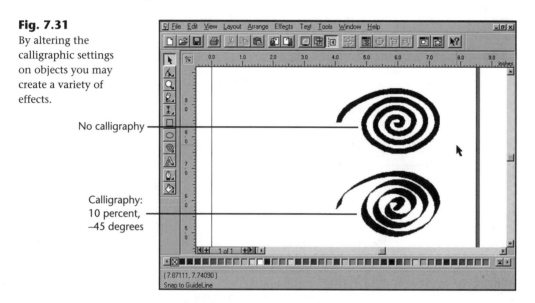

Arrows

The arrow controls will save you from hours of tedious arrow drawing to embellish the ends of your lines or at least give them some direction. Corel has made this feature quite flexible and user-friendly compared to other programs and previous versions. You are able to select an arrowhead from a small library of styles, and apply them individually to the beginning and ending points of lines.

If you find that none of the arrow styles in the collection are suitable, you can always make up your own, or just edit one of the existing styles by choosing Options, Edit and manipulating the shape of the arrow in the Arrowhead Editor (see fig. 7.32). Each of the left and right arrow menus are identical so editing an arrowhead on one side will cause the other side to change as well.

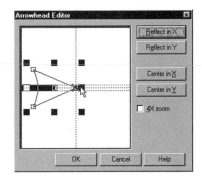

Fig. 7.32
Using the Arrowhead Editor you are able to create your own arrow styles.

Tip

If you do decide to edit an existing arrowhead, make sure it's one you'll never use again. Editing changes made to an arrowhead in the existing CorelDRAW! 6 arrow library are permanent.

Behind Fill and Scale with Image

Selecting the Behind Fill option in the Outline Pen dialog box will build the outline up on the back of the object you are assigning the outline to. The most obvious result will be that you will only see half of the outline if the object is filled.

Scale with Image sets the line attributes so if the image is resized the line attributes will be resized as well. It may be best to leave this feature on with all of the new objects you create.

Figure 7.33 illustrates the effects of Behind Fill and Scale with Image on objects.

Fig. 7.33

The options for Behind Fill and Scale with Image enable you to control how outlines behave when the object they outline is resized.

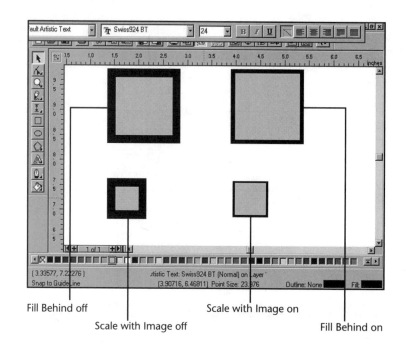

Fill Behind off

Scale with Image off

Scale with Image on

Fill Behind on

Outline Flyout

You may also apply outline attributes using the Outline flyout found in the toolbar. There are, by no means, the tools available to you by using the Pen Outline dialog box controls, but it certainly provides a quick way to change the line attributes from thin to thick. The Outline flyout also provides for setting the line to white by clicking on the white outlined box, or None by clicking on the button containing a big black X. One line thickness worth noting is the button containing a symbol that resembles two vertical arrows pointing toward each other with a line positioned in between. This button sets the line to print at the thinnest possible setting when printing to your printer. In the case of a 300-DPI printer this would make the line approximately one-quarter-point of thickness, or in the case of a high resolution printer it would end up being a hairline of thickness.

Pen Color

Besides all these effects you can apply to the line to make it patterned or calligraphic, you can also color your outlines. In the Pen Outline dialog box there is a button labeled Color that gives you access to a color flyout from which you may select an outline color. If you don't see anything there that you need, click on the Others button at the bottom of that flyout to invoke

DRAW!'s entire realm of color controls in the Outline Color dialog box. This dialog box is similar to the Uniform Fill dialog box giving access to all of the color models and palettes available within the program.

Outlines Roll-Up

Like most of the roll-ups in CorelDRAW! 6, the Outlines roll-up contains access to all of the Pen Outline controls and features available in the program (see fig. 7.34). As in the case of the Fill roll-up, you are also able to copy the line attributes set from any other object to a new object or edit the attributes from another object to suit your new object. Controls in the Outlines roll-up include a thickness, arrowhead, line style, and color buttons.

Fig. 7.34
The Outlines roll-up will provide you with access to a brief set of outline controls, as well as quick-access to the full set of Pen options.

From Here...

Fill and outline attributes can be just as critical to a drawing as the fill attributes associated with drawn objects. When used properly, they can greatly enhance the effectiveness of a drawing, graphic, or diagram. In this chapter you learned to handle these controls and apply them. The fill and outline capabilities in DRAW! are as simple or as complex a feature as you need them to be, making these tools very robust.

You were also able to gain insights into how printing is affected by certain types of fill effects, and where the hazards are that are involved in asking for more than your system is capable of providing.

- See Chapter 4, "What's New in CorelDRAW! 6," to learn more about display options and Pick tool properties.

- See Chapter 13, "Using Color, Wizards, and Applying Color Masks," where you can learn more about color models.

- See Chapter 19, "Creating 3D Illustrations in CorelDREAM 3D," to learn how to set your print options and customize your Fountain Fill display.

Chapter 8

All about Blends

This is definitely where the *real* fun begins. CorelDRAW! 6's Blend command is one of those features where you let your program do all the work, and what could be better? The Blend command enables you to transform one object into another, and to create seemingly endless rows of perfectly spaced objects in a matter of seconds.

This chapter will be of interest to anyone who wishes to take advantage of some of CorelDRAW! 6's automated drawing tools. Illustrators will find blending an invaluable command for creating smooth, highly detailed drawings quickly, while the beginner will use techniques that previously took ages to master by hand.

In this chapter you will learn to

- Quickly blend from one shape to another
- Use the power of the blend tool for lines and curves
- Use editing tricks on blended objects
- Combine the Blend command with other effects
- Understand how the Blend command affects colors

Understanding Blends

The word "blend" may not adequately describe all of the capabilities of the Blend command, but it's close enough without being too misleading. It may have been nice to call it something like the controlled-object repeater/transformer or something similar, because that's essentially what it does. It allows you to create a certain number of copies of an object while transforming it from one shape, color, or size to another along a defined path. A path may be a line, curve, or shape to which a group of blended objects may follow.

The Blend command will perform anything from simple blends between two ordinary, identical objects, to blends between two different, complex objects that include multiple effects such as perspectives, extrusions, fountain fills, and so on. The first thing you'll likely want to do so you can access all of Blend's power is become familiar with all of the Blend tools. Once you know what it's capable of, you'll think up all kinds of applications for it.

When blending two objects, DRAW!'s Blend command does three main things. First, it determines the shape of the objects it will create and performs the necessary calculations to create those intermediate objects. Then, it makes the blend itself into a group. A *group* is a collection of objects that have been fastened together to behave as a unit. And last, it associates the blend group to the original objects calling them blend control objects. Once your blend has been created, DRAW! still allows you to perform transformations on the original objects while constantly updating the blend group to retain the blend. Knowing that you can still transform the control objects without having to manually re-blend them is one of the big advantages of using the Blend command. Also, knowing how the blend is structured will help you to take it apart or edit it later.

 The Blend commands are completely contained in the Blend roll-up (Ctrl+B), (see fig. 8.1). The Blend roll-up is a set of controls and options that can be displayed to give you access to a collection of specific blend commands. You'll find a shortcut to the Blend roll-up in the roll-up toolbar. You can also select the Blend roll-up by choosing Effects, Blend.

Fig. 8.1
The Blend roll-up is organized into three tabbed sections controlling blend, color, and mapping of objects.

The Blend roll-up contains three tabbed sections: Blend Control, Color, and Mapping Options.

The Blend Object Tab

The Blend Object tab (refer to fig. 8.1) features a pull-down menu that gives you two options when blending objects. The first option lets you set the number of Steps, and the second lets you set a Spacing measurement to be used when blending two objects. The Rotation control in this tab allows you to have your blend objects rotate or turn during the blend sequence. The Loop option, when selected, applies to blends on a path and causes the blend to rotate in a complete circle while following the assigned path.

The Blend Color Tab

The Color tab (see fig. 8.2) allows you to control the colors of the blended objects. For instance, if you are blending two objects, one blue and the other red, you may choose to blend straight across the color wheel by using the first button, clockwise around the color wheel with the second button, or counterclockwise with the third. Blending around the color wheel in either direction will cause each of your blended objects to be created in something like a rainbow effect.

Fig. 8.2
The Color tab enables you to set straight, clockwise, or counterclock-wise blend colors using a color wheel.

The Mapping Options Tab

The last tab, Mapping Options (see fig. 8.3), controls the advanced features of mapping nodes, splitting blend groups along a path, assigning a blend path, or fusing the end point or start point of a blend on a path. These are the controls that allow you to assign complex transformations to the control objects and blend paths to create special movements of the blend.

Fig. 8.3
The Mapping
Options tab of the
Blend roll-up
features specific
controls for
mapping the
nodes of two
blended objects
to each other.

- *Map Nodes* allows you to tell DRAW! exactly which nodes to associate with each other on your two objects. Blending objects that don't contain the same number of nodes can sometimes create a pretty sloppy blend. Mapping certain nodes to each other can solve this problem. Also, editing the actual shape of objects slightly can also smooth out a blend.

- *Split* allows you to divide a blend group. Instead of a smooth, even blend, you are able to use this feature to split the blend at desired points making the blend uneven.

- *Fuse Start* and *Fuse End* buttons.

- The *Blend to Path* button in the bottom right of the roll-up lets you assign a path for your blended objects to follow. You may also choose to Show Path or Detach from Path from the menu that appears when you click this button.

- *Start* Point and *End* Point buttons allow you to redefine where blend paths begin and end. The menu buttons also allow you to display where the Start and End points are.

Other Controls

The other controls that affect blends that you need to be aware of are spread around the menus. They don't deal directly with the Blend commands, but can be used in conjunction with them and include commands such as Separate, Ungroup, Reverse Order, and right-hand mouse-button controls.

The first one of interest to you will likely be the Separate command available from the Arrange menu. Separate causes your blend-associated objects to revert back to separate objects, consisting of two control objects and a blend group. Once you have separated a blend group there is no way to rejoin it unless you use the Undo command or re-blend the two objects using the same settings.

The next important command to keep in mind is Ungroup, which will allow you to take apart the blend group, reducing it to a simple collection of objects.

◄ See "Grouping and Ungrouping Objects," p. 204

Last, you will need to know about the Reverse Order command located at the bottom of the Order flyout in the Arrange menu. This command is used to change the layering order of the blended objects.

> **Tip**
>
> The right mouse button also gives access to the Separate command by way of the pop-up menu. To access the Separate command from the pop-up menu, right-click on the blended objects and select Separate.

Before Beginning a Blend

When DRAW! creates a blend, it uses particular information about the original objects, such as their shape, size, color, and position, as guides. There are a few things to keep in mind before applying a blend, such as:

- Blending between two control objects that contain no fill will produce blends that contain no fill.

- Blending two open curve objects will create blend objects that are open. The reverse is true as well—blending two closed objects will create closed objects.

- Blending a closed curve with an open curve causes all blend objects to be open.

- Blending between two objects that are whole, simple shapes, will create a blend containing only curves.

- When blending between two identical objects, DRAW! will look for the first nodes of the objects and map them to each other.

Creating Text & Drawings

Using Blend to Reduce Drawing Time

Now that you've had a chance to view and understand the Blend controls, it's time to get your hands dirty. If you've never created a blend before, now's a good time. To blend two simple objects, follow these steps:

1. Create two objects if you haven't already, and select both of them using the Pick tool.

2. With both objects selected, press Ctrl+B to display the Blend roll-up controls.

3. Set the number of steps in your blend in the Steps field.

4. Select Apply. Your blend is created.

5. Select only one of the objects by clicking a blank part of your page and clicking the object with the Pick tool. Notice the status bar is telling you that your object is a Control object.

6. Select the blend objects by clicking them once. Notice the status bar is telling you that this is now a Blend Group.

7. Select one of the Control objects again and change its position, rotation, color, or size. Notice that the blend is immediately updated using the new information about the object.

◀ See "Grouping and Ungrouping Objects," p. 204

Figure 8.4 illustrates the effect of blending lines and shapes. When blended, the blend objects reflect only the change in shape as they transition from one shape to the other without changing any of the other attributes of the shapes such as rotation or size.

A quick and easy example of how the Blend tool can be useful is to have it divide up a space for you. Suppose you need to make a simple chart to plot company revenue over the past six years. First, you will need a scale of some sort. Use the Blend tool to create the scale.

◀ See "Pen Controls," p. 262

1. Draw a line four-fifths of the width of your chart or diagram. Make it a 1-point line. Use the Pen roll-up to set the line thickness.

2. Place a copy of your new line below the current one by clicking, and control-dragging, and then clicking the right mouse button before releasing the left button. Control-dragging will place a copy of your new line below the current one by clicking the current line and, while keeping your Ctrl key pressed, drag your mouse pointer to the position where you want your new line. A copy will be made and placed in your new position.

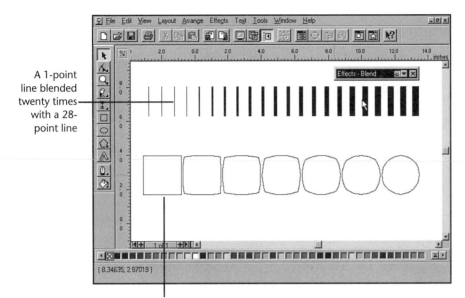

A 1-point line blended twenty times with a 28-point line

Fig. 8.4
The simplest of blend commands involves blending lines to lines, or shapes to shapes as illustrated here using lines, a rectangle, and a circle.

A rectangle blended five times with a circle

3. Select both of the lines using the Pick tool and select the Blend roll-up (Ctrl+B).

4. Decide on the number of lines you need in your scale, and subtract two to allow for the control lines already there, and enter the number in the Steps field.

5. Click Apply to create the blend (see fig. 8.5).

   To finish the chart, you'll need some bars to represent the six years. Blend to create those as well.

6. Draw a rectangle to represent the first bar in the chart and position it on the left-hand side, aligned so it rests on top of the bottom line of your scale. Then, convert the rectangle to curves (Ctrl+Q). It'll help if you give the bar some sort of fill so that it isn't transparent.

7. Place a copy of the object on the other side of the axis lines you created, by using control-drag, while right-clicking to make a copy.

8. Select both of the rectangles by multiple-selecting with the Pick tool.

II

Creating Text & Drawings

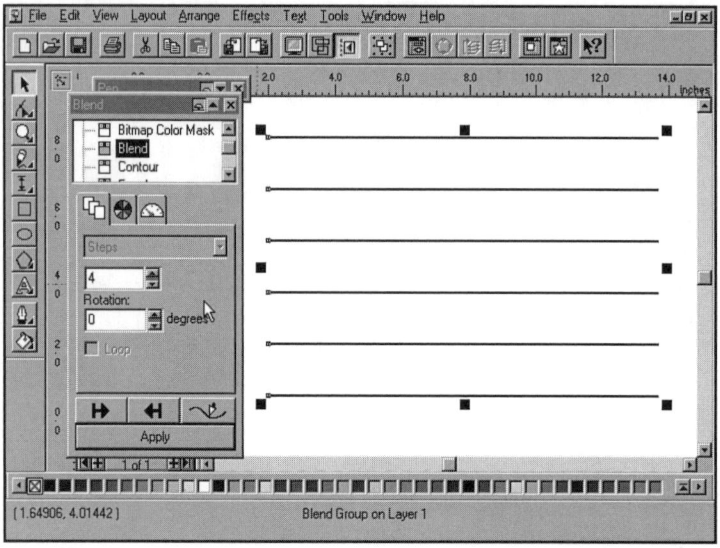

Fig. 8.5
You may use the
Blend tools to
blend identical
objects for such
things as chart axis
lines as illustrated
here.

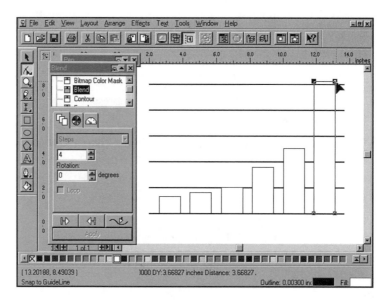

9. Enter the number of Steps to be made in the Blend roll-up as four—six
   minus the two control bars you created (see fig. 8.6).

10. Click Apply.

Fig. 8.6
After blending,
you may separate
and ungroup the
blended objects,
and edit them as
you would any
curve using the
Node Editor and
the Shape tool.

11. Next, you'll need to adjust the size of the bars to match your data, but you won't be able to do this in the state they're in now.

12. Using your right mouse button, select the blended bars and choose Separate from the Pop-up menu.

13. Deselect all the objects by clicking a blank part of your page and use the right mouse button to select the blend group that composes the four blend objects.

14. This time, select Ungroup (Ctrl+J) from the menu that appears. All the objects are then separate.

15. Use the Node Editor to control-drag the top nodes of each bar to suit the data of your chart (refer to fig. 8.6). Add the labels and it's done (see fig. 8.7).

◀ See "Editing Simple Objects: The Shape Tool and the Node Edit Roll-Up," p. 181

Notice that the blends can be taken apart to enable you to work with the individual objects of the blend. This isn't the only way to create quick drawings, but it is one of the strengths of the Blend command.

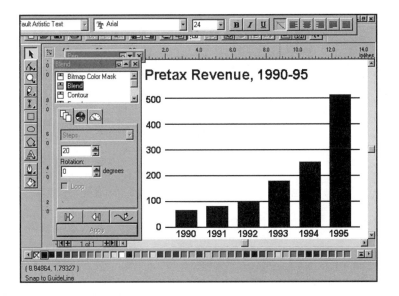

Fig. 8.7
This chart was drawn using the power of the Blend tool rather than a charting program. In many situations charts may be drawn quicker using CorelDRAW! than using special charting programs and importing the chart into DRAW!.

II

Creating Text & Drawings

Blending Simple Objects

On the first try at blending two objects, nearly every first-time user will choose simple objects such as a square and a circle to blend between. Blending even the simplest of objects can produce dramatic effects.

But, no matter how simple a blend may seem, there are always drawbacks and stumbling blocks along the way. When DRAW! blends even the simplest of objects, it first examines the position of all nodes. The first node of any object is the critical node, and when blending, DRAW! uses it to try to align objects. If the first node on the first blend object is in a completely opposite position to the first node on the second object the results can be tragic. To make a successful blend of simple objects, make sure the first node of both objects have been aligned to each other (see fig. 8.8).

Fig. 8.8
Blending to objects that have had their nodes aligned is critical to achieving a perfect blend as illustrated here using rectangles and circles.

A square blended in eight steps to a circle, non-aligned first nodes.

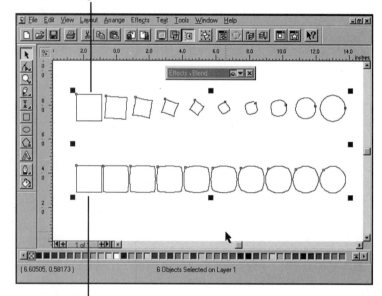

The same square blended with the first nodes aligned.

Using the Rotation Option

The Rotation control causes objects to rotate in a counterclockwise rotation as they are blended based on the 360 degrees in a circle. Entering a negative value causes the blended objects to rotate in a clockwise direction. Leaving the rotation value set to zero causes no rotation to occur during your blend.

To use the Rotation control, select two objects, enter a value in the Rotation box and click the Apply button. You will notice that the blend objects rotate until the last blend object has been rotated to the degree of rotation entered in the Rotation box (see fig. 8.9). Notice also that the blend is performed from the first object created to the next object. In figure 8.9 the objects are blended from left to right because the object on the left was created first.

Switching positions of these objects will cause the blend to occur in the opposite direction (see fig. 8.10). The final blend object continues to be rotated 60 degrees counterclockwise.

Rotation of sixty degrees to final blend object

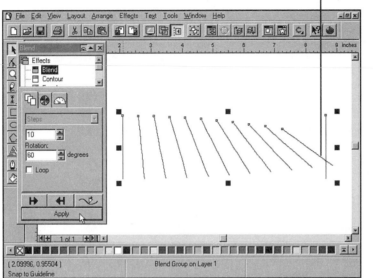

Fig. 8.9
The Rotation control will blend objects counterclockwise or clockwise, with the final blend object having the rotation value entered in Rotation box. As illustrated here, the final blend object has been rotated 60 degrees as requested in the Blend roll-up.

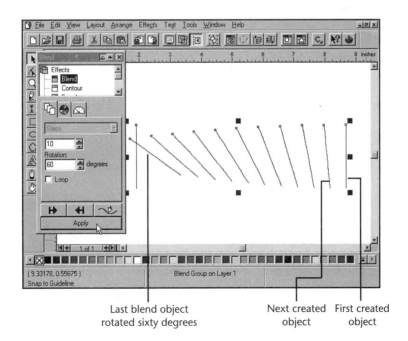

Fig. 8.10
Objects blend from the first created object to the next available object. By switching the position of these objects you are able to control the direction of the blend as illustrated here where the objects are blending from right to left, instead of left to right as in figure 8.9.

Last blend object rotated sixty degrees

Next created object

First created object

Using the Loop Option

The Blend roll-ups Loop option works in combination with the Rotation controls and will only become available when a degree of rotation is selected in the Rotation box. Selecting the Loop option in the Blend Objects tab causes the blended objects to rotate around the center origins of the original objects. Normally, while this option is unselected, the blend objects rotate around their own centers of origin.

Looping the blend of two objects while rotating causes the blend objects to create a fan effect, spreading the blend away from the center of origin of the original objects (see fig. 8.11). Entering a positive rotation value in the Rotation box causes the objects to loop upward or to the right depending on the orientation of your objects, while entering a negative value causes the loop to occur downwards or to the left.

Fig. 8.11
Looping with positive Rotation causes the loop to occur upward or to the right, while looping with negative values causes the loop to occur downwards or to the left.

Loop option selected with rotation of 60 degrees

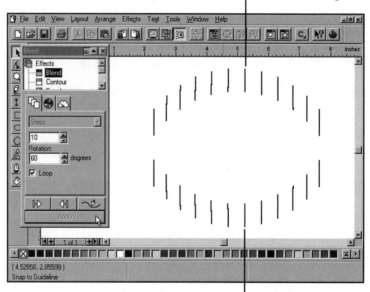

Loop option selected with rotation of -60 degrees

Blending Similar Objects

Blending simple, similar objects can not only create dramatic effects but can save hours of drawing time. Consider for a moment how long it would take to draw a series of evenly spaced lines, curves, rectangles, or ellipses to be exact replicas of each other. Hours or perhaps days of laborious drawing may be saved by using the Blend command for this purpose. Because the blended objects are dynamically linked to the original control objects you are also able to edit the originals and have changes to the blended objects take place almost instantly.

The Blend command may be used to blend objects to copies of themselves no matter which position they are placed in relative to the original. For example, an oddly shaped, closed-path curve may be copied and the copy blended with the original to create a contour effect (see fig. 8.12).

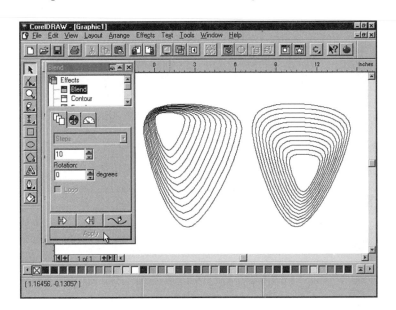

Fig. 8.12
This closed-path curve was blended to a transformed copy of itself. Illustrated here is an example showing the difference in the effect of moving one of the control objects after the blend is applied. This is the basis for creating blend highlights using the Blend command.

II

Creating Text & Drawings

Troubleshooting

One of my blend objects contains a Lens effect and I'm trying to blend it with another object. When I select both objects the Blend tools are unavailable. Why?

Although it is a powerful feature it does have limitations and will not work on all types of objects. Paragraph Text objects and objects that contain Powerline, Powerclip, Extrude, Contour, and Lens effects can't be blended to or from.

Assigning a Blend Path

Another important feature of the Blend command is the option of assigning a path to blend objects. A path may be any curve, line, or shape. Blend paths are assigned using the Blend Path menu available by selecting your blended objects and clicking the Blend Path button (see fig. 8.13). The Blend Path menu contains commands for assigning a <u>N</u>ew Path, identifying an existing path using <u>S</u>how Path, and removing a blend from a path using <u>d</u>etach from Path.

■ *New Path.* When New Path is selected, your cursor will be transformed to a large curved arrow that is used for selecting the path to which you would like your blended objects to follow. After selecting the path and clicking the Apply button your blended objects will become attached to the path (see fig. 8.14).

■ *Show Path.* Choosing this command while your objects blended along a path are selected, identifies the path that has been assigned to the blend.

■ *Detach From Path.* Choosing this command while your objects blended along a path are selected, detaches the blend group from the path.

Fig. 8.13
The Blend Path menu contains path-handling commands and is selected by clicking on the Blend Path button on the Blend roll-up as illustrated here.

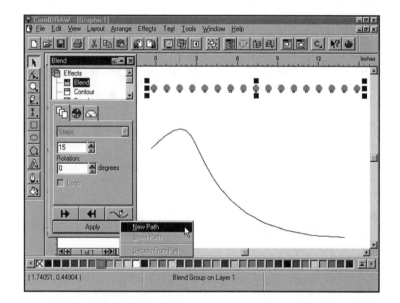

Once the Blend Path has been assigned, you will notice that additional options for blending objects to the Full Path and Rotate All objects of the blend. These options only appear once a blend path has been assigned, but may be selected before first applying the path using the Apply button.

■ *Full Path.* Selecting this option will cause the blended objects to follow the assigned path completely from beginning to end (see fig. 8.15).

If your path happens to be a closed path such as a rectangle or an ellipse, your blended objects will be placed evenly throughout the path (see fig. 8.16).

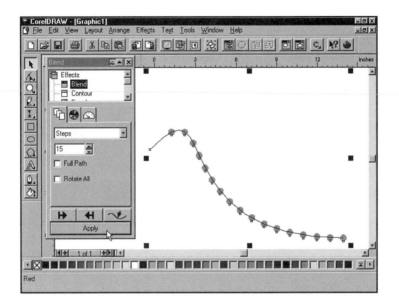

Fig. 8.14
Blend objects may be assigned to a path using the New Path command from the Blend Path menu.

■ *Rotate All.* This option will cause the objects in your blend to be rotated relative to the orientation of the path they follow (see fig. 8.17).

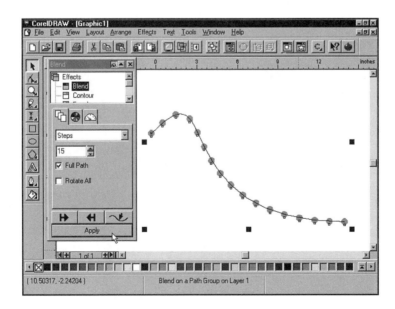

Fig. 8.15
While objects are blended to a path you may select the Full Path option illustrated here with a series of ellipses blended to a simple curve.

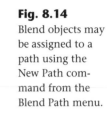

II

Creating Text & Drawings

Fig. 8.16
If your blend path is a closed object such as the ellipse illustrated here, selecting the Full Path option will cause your blend to occur over the full extent of the object.

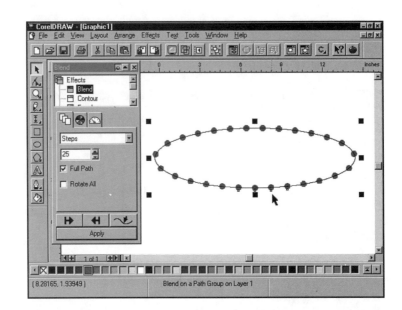

Fig. 8.17
Your blend objects may also be rotated to the shape of the curve by selecting the Rotate All option as illustrated here with a blend using two lines as control objects.

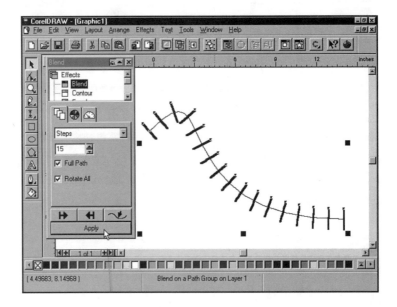

Setting Start and End Objects

Two additional buttons come into play when blending objects, including the Start Path and End Path buttons. These two buttons each give access to their own menus enabling you to Show or set New start and end points for your blend.

- *New Start.* The New Start command enables you to set a new object to begin your blend from. To do this select your blend group, click the New Start command from the Start button, and select the new object you would like to begin your blend from.

- *Show Start.* The Show Start command enables you to select the first object of your blend. To do this, select your blend group, then select the Show Start command from the Start button. The object starting your blend will become selected.

- *New End.* The New End command enables you to set a new object to end your blend. To do this select your blend group, click the New End command from the End point button, and select the new object you would like to end your blend with.

- *Show End.* The Show End command enables you to select the last object in your blend. To do this, select your blend group, then select the Show End command from the End point button. The last object in your blend will be selected.

> ### Troubleshooting
>
> *I have assigned a blend path to an ellipse and would like to set a new start object for my blend. Every time I select the blend and choose New Start I get a strange message from CorelDRAW!. Why can't I set a new start object?*
>
> If your blend is attached to a path it has already created a dynamic link with another object and has set positions for the first and last blend objects on that path. You will not be able to set a new start or new end object unless you first break the dynamic link to the close path object. To do this, select the blend group, click the Blend Path button, and select Detach from Path. You will then be able to set a new Start object.

Editing a Blend

The capability to edit a blend is perhaps half of the power of this effect. Editing a blend may be useful for such drawing techniques as illustration highlighting, diagram drawings illustrating construction elements, or flow charts containing multiple symbols. Using any of the three tabbed areas in the Blend roll-up, you are able to edit any aspect of a blend, including the number steps and spacing, color, and mapping options. Also, you are able to edit any attribute of the control objects and have the blend group be instantly updated. Editing may be performed either before or after the blend is applied.

To edit a blend, follow these steps:

1. Click on the blend group and select the Blend roll-up to display (Ctrl+B). Notice that while your blend group is selected all the currently applied settings are displayed in the roll-up.

2. Click on the tab which contains the blend group attribute you wish to make your editing change and click the Apply button. Your blend edit is completed.

3. To edit either of the control objects in your blend select only on the control object you wish to edit. Clicking on the blend group will not allow you to edit either control object.

To remove a Blend, follow these steps:

1. Select the blend group of your blend by clicking on any of the blended objects.

2. Select Effects, Clear Blend.

Troubleshooting

I have assigned a blend to two objects and want to edit the blend, but I can't seem to find the Object Properties dialog box for the blend group. Where is it?

Stop searching. There isn't any Object Properties dialog box to control your blend groups. If you wish to edit a blend, you must use the Blend roll-up (Ctrl+B).

Copying and Cloning Blends

Like many of the other effects in CorelDRAW! 6, the Blend Effects you assign to a blend group may be copied from or cloned from one group to another. Copying a blend merely copies all of the blend group attributes from an existing blend and applies them to your new blend objects. Copying a blend would be useful for situations where you had spent extra time perfecting the number of steps and color gradations between two objects and simply want to copy the blend attributes to a new blend.

Cloning a blend creates a dynamic link between the master blend and the cloned blend. Each time the master blend is adjusted or edited, the clone is automatically updated. Blending a clone is a highly sophisticated type of drawing technique, not commonly useful for basic types of graphic drawings, but would be immensely useful in drawings such as engineering-type drawings or renderings where using master clone blends could speed editing changes to repetitively drawn objects such as beams, struts, and construction supports.

To copy a blend from one blend group to another, follow these steps:

1. Ensure that you have a blend group in your existing drawing that you would like to copy a blend effect from and create or select two new objects to blend. You do not need to have the Blend roll-up displayed to perform this command.

2. With your new objects selected, select Effects, Copy, Blend From. Your cursor will change to a large black arrow icon.

3. Using the black arrow icon, locate the blend group you would like to copy the blend from and click on it. Be sure to click on the blend group itself and not the control objects. If you miss the blend group or click on an invalid object, DRAW! will give you an error message and ask you if you would like to try again.

4. After clicking the blend group to copy from, your copied blend will take place instantly.

If you would like to copy blend attributes to apply to an existing blend, select the blend group and follow steps 2 through 4 again.

To clone a blend from one blend group to another, follow these steps:

1. Ensure that you have a blend group in your existing drawing that you would like to use as a master blend and create or select two new objects to blend. As with the Copy Blend command you do not need to have the Blend roll-up displayed to perform this command.

2. With your new objects selected, select Effects, Clone, Blend From. Your cursor will change to a large black arrow icon.

3. Using the black arrow icon, locate the blend group you would like to clone the blend from and click on it. Always be sure to click on the blend group itself and not the control objects.

4. After clicking the blend group to clone from, your cloned blend will take place instantly.

5. To ensure a proper master clone relationship exists between your blended objects, click on the master blend group and select the Blend roll-up (Ctrl+B).

6. With the master blend still selected, make an editing change to the blend using roll-up options, such as changing the number of steps or the rotation angle if applicable.

7. Click the Apply button. Your blend clone should be updated instantly to any changes made to your master clone.

◀ See "Cloning Objects," p. 197

An additional command available when using the Clone Blend command is the capability to locate a master clone. While the cloned blend object is selected, right-click it and choose Select Master from the pop-up menu. Your master blend will be selected instantly.

Troubleshooting

I have cloned a blend and I need to edit just this clone itself, but when I select the Blend roll-up and make editing changes to the cloned blend, the Apply button remains unavailable. What's going on?

You are trying to edit a blend that already has a dynamic link to a master blend group. You will not be able to edit the clone using the Blend roll-up. You need to either edit the master to cause the changes, or you need to clear the blend from the cloned objects using the Effects, Clear Blend command and assign an entirely new blend.

Splitting a Blend

There may be times when you would like to create a blend that isn't a linear blend. Most simple blends are linear in that they transform steadily from one object to another. But perhaps you need to fit a series of objects around a curve. You could make two blends and group them together but that involves an extra, unnecessary step. In CorelDRAW! 6 there is a way around this using the Split button command in the Mapping options tab.

Splitting a blend essentially designates one of the objects created in your blend group as a control object. Because the object is a control object you are able to edit the object's attributes, which will in turn dynamically affect the blend groups on either side of it.

To Split a blend and assign an additional control object to your blend group, follow these steps:

1. If you haven't already done so, create a blend group by blending two objects using the Blend roll-up (Ctrl+B). Select at least 5 steps as the number of steps in your blend in the Blend tab.

2. Click on the blended objects in your blend group and select the Mapping options tab in the Blend roll-up.

3. Click the Split button in the Mapping options tab. Your cursor will change to a curved black arrow icon (see fig. 8.18).

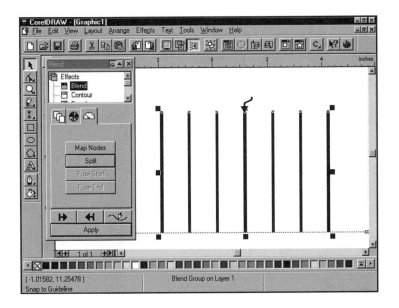

Fig. 8.18
The Split button in the Mapping options tab enables you to designate one of your current blend objects to be a control object as illustrated here.

4. Select the center object of your blend group by clicking on it. Your center object will change to a control object and now your blend will be treated as two dynamically linked blends.

5. Edit the shape of your new intermediate control object and observe as both of the blends on either side of this object change to reflect the editing changes (see fig. 8.19). This blend within a blend is called a compound blend.

6. Edit one side of the blend by holding down the Ctrl key, clicking the blend group, and using the Blend roll-up to make changes to the blend group (see fig. 8.20). You may also edit any of the three control objects that compose your blend by clicking on them and changing their attributes.

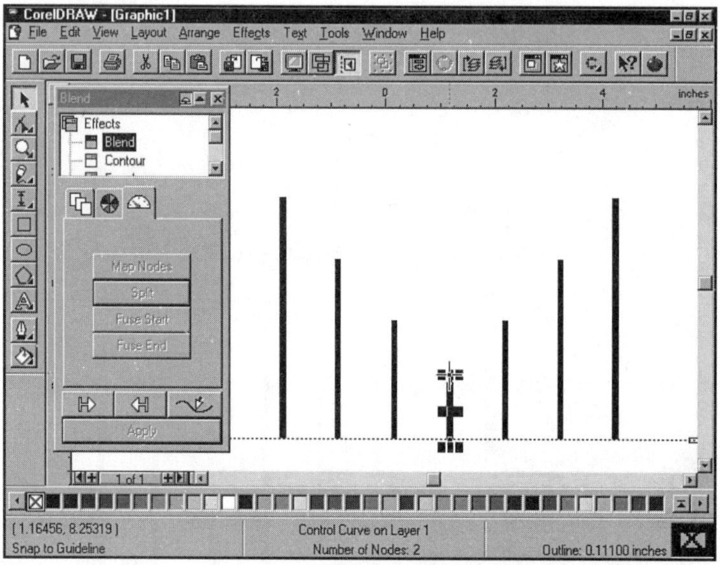

Fig. 8.19
Changing the
attributes of an
intermediate
object changes the
blended objects on
both sides of the
blend.

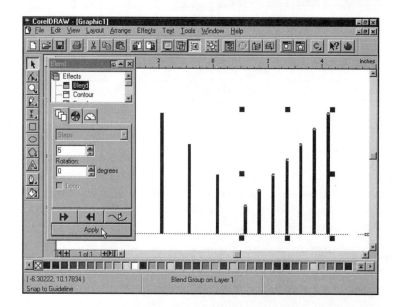

Fig. 8.20
Holding down
the Ctrl key and
clicking on a part
of the blend
enables you to
isolate the
compound blend
within a blend.

Building a Compound Blend

A compound blend is created when you assign more than two control objects
to your blend as when you use the Split Blend command. A compound blend
may contain multiple control objects dynamically linked by blend groups.
This sort of effect may also be used in highly sophisticated drawings where

the movement of one object may affect multiple objects and eliminated time spent repositioning objects created manually.

To create a simple compound blend using similar objects, follow these steps:

1. Create two similar objects and choose the Blend roll-up (Ctrl+B).

2. Create a blend of the two objects using at least 5 blend steps.

3. Create another object similar to the first two you created for your blend, click on one of the first control objects in your blend and the new object.

4. With these two objects selected click the Apply button on the Blend roll-up to create a blend between them (see fig. 8.21). You will now have two blends created between three control objects.

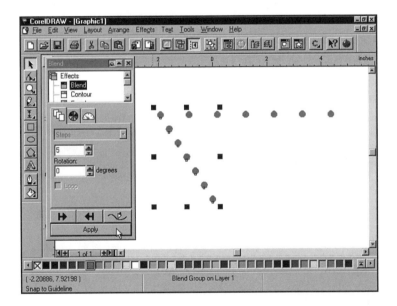

Fig. 8.21
Blending control objects with new objects will create a compound blend containing two blends between three control objects as illustrated here.

5. Create a fourth object similar to the first three, select this new object and the second control object you originally blended with. Blend these objects the same way you did the first two (see fig. 8.22). You will now have a compound blend shape resembling a U-shaped structure.

6. Select the remaining two control objects that have only one blend group attached to them and blend them using the Blend command. You should now have a closed-path structure made up entirely of blended objects.

Fig. 8.22
You may continue making your compound object more complex by blending your control objects with additional new objects.

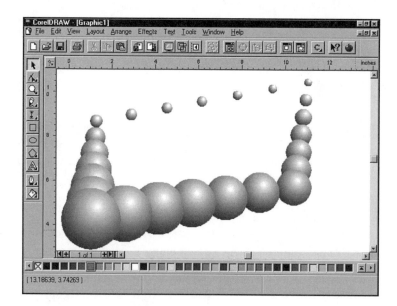

7. Explore the compound blend effects of making editing changes to any of the four control objects that compose your new compound blend. Try adding special fills to create a sense of depth (see fig. 8.23).

Fig. 8.23
The effects can be quite dramatic when editing your control objects to create a sense of depth.

8. To make blending edits to the blend groups of each part of the compound blend, hold down your Ctrl key while selecting the blend group.

Weird and Wonderful Blend Effects

The Blend command is a very important function for CorelDRAW! and may save hours of manual drawing and editing if used wisely. But, the Blend command when used for illustrating is a critical feature enabling you to create effects that would otherwise be impractical or impossible to create on your own. You may use the Blend command for exploring such things as creating your own fonts from existing fonts on your system, creating highlighting for illustration work or combine Blend with other effects such as Powerline for some very interesting and even outrageous creations you may never have imagined before.

Blending Text Objects

The Blend command may even be used on objects as unlikely as Artistic text objects for creating new fonts. By blending a bold font style with a light font style you may use the blended objects to create new font styles in combination with the File, Export command by exporting using the TrueType font filter.

To create new font styles using the Blend command, follow these steps:

1. Select an existing font style installed on your system that includes a bold style and a light or normal style. For example, Kuenstler 480 Heavy and Kuenstler 480 normal.

2. Begin by creating using the Artistic text tool to create an Artistic text object.

3. Assign your selected bold font style to this text object. For speed, use the Text toolbar selected by right-clicking on any displayed toolbar and selecting Text from the pop-up menu.

4. Create an aligned copy of your text object by holding down the Ctrl key, dragging the object horizontally and right-clicking to make a copy.

5. Assign your selected normal font style to this new text object.

6. Select both text objects and select the Blend roll-up (Ctrl+B). Create a blend of 1 step between the two objects (fig. 8.24). A new character is created between the two existing characters and is exactly half the boldness of the bold character you originally blended it from.

Fig. 8.24
The Blend
command may be
used to create new
font styles by
blending two
existing font styles
as illustrated here.

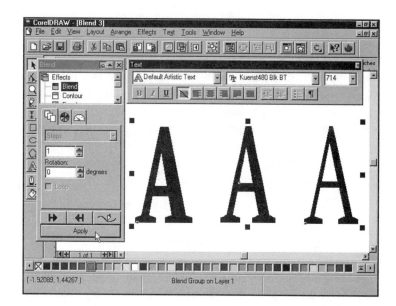

7. Separate the blend by selecting the blend object and choosing Arrange,
Separate. You are now ready to export the new object as a TrueType
font by using the File, Export command.

Creating Blended Highlights

Highlighting using the Blend command has been one of the more important
techniques used by professional illustrators, and provides much more control
than simply using the Fountain Fill options available in CorelDRAW!. Highlighting may be used to create shiny points on a simulated three-dimensional
object or may be used to create depressions or holes in a drawing. Either way,
the Blend command provides an effective tool for creating depth where the
Fountain Fill feature can't (see figs. 8.25 and 8.26).

Highlighting blends are best created by editing two copies of the same object.
While creating two completely separate objects is possible, it may be time-
consuming and may not produce the quickest, most satisfactory results. Using two similar objects is a fast way of ensuring a successful blend. To create a
highlight blend using similar objects, follow these steps:

1. Create a simple, closed-path object composed of lines or curves.
For now, set the object to have no fill, and a thin black outline.

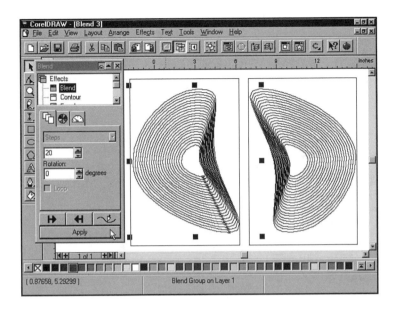

Fig. 8.25
The Blend option provides depth.

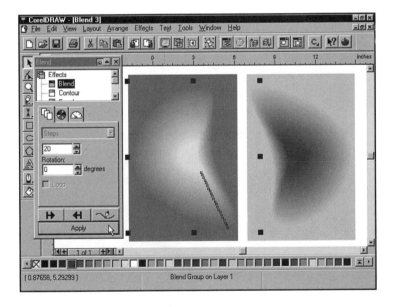

Fig. 8.26
The Blend option also provides depth in your background.

2. Create a smaller, centered copy of this object by holding the Shift key down and reducing the original then right-clicking to make the copy (see fig. 8.27).

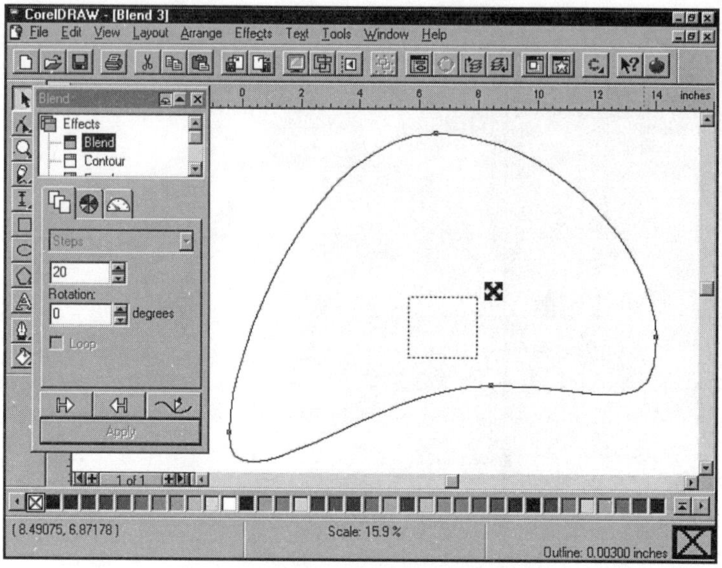

Fig. 8.27
You may make a smaller, centered copy of your original object by click-dragging with the right mouse button while holding down the Shift key as illustrated here.

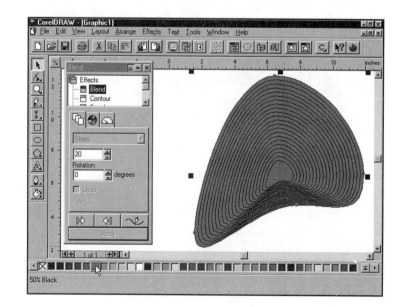

3. Select both objects and select the Blend roll-up (Ctrl+B).

4. Create a blend by using the default twenty steps and clicking the Apply button. Your blend will be created.

5. Click on the larger outside object and set the fill to any dark color such as 50 percent black (see fig. 8.28).

Fig. 8.28
To begin creating a highlight blend, make the larger outside object a dark color.

6. Click on the smaller copy and fill it with a lighter color such as white. Your highlight will begin to take shape.

7. Remove the black outline by clicking on the blend group you created and selecting an outline of none.

8. Place a backdrop in the background of your highlight blend by creating an object larger than the entire blend, assigning it a fill of 50 percent and sending it to the background (Shift+Page Down) (see fig. 8.29). Your highlight is created.

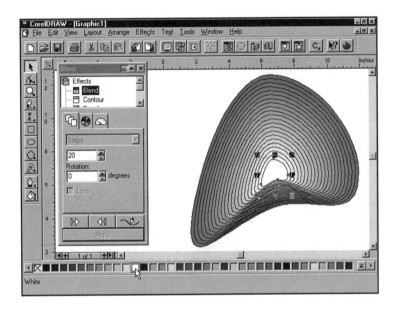

Fig. 8.29
To complete the highlight blend, make the smaller, inside object a lighter color and remove the outline.

To reverse the highlight and make your blend represent a depression, shadow, or hole make the smaller, inside object darker than the larger outside object (see fig. 8.30). By repositioning the center object you will redefine the highest or lowest point of depth.

By using repeated blends for highlights and shadowing full illustration effects may be achieved. While your blend effects may look quite complex and cumbersome to work with (see fig. 8.31) the final effect can be quite striking and dramatic (see fig. 8.32). The higher the number of blends assigned to a highlight, the smoother the transition of shade and color. The more attention to detail that is spent on your illustrations, the higher the degree of realism.

◀ See "Editing Simple Objects," p. 181

◀ See "Using Fills and Outlines," p. 229

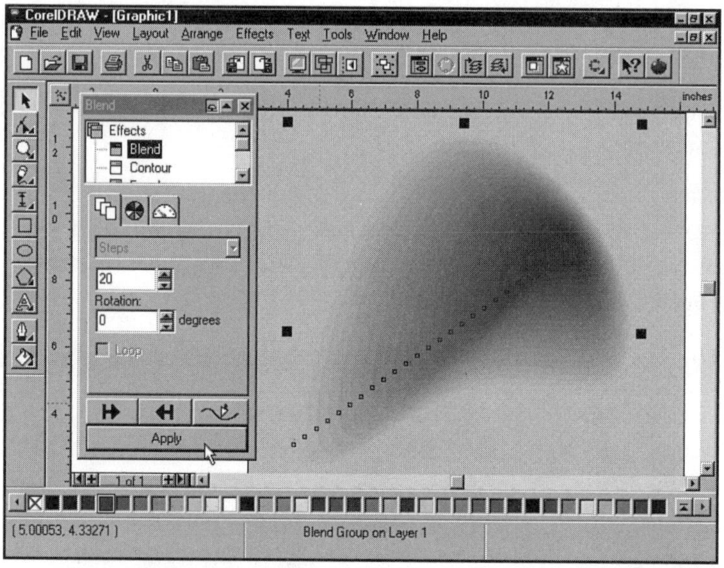

Fig. 8.30
Once your highlight blend is completed you may easily change it to represent a shadow or depression by reversing the light and dark colors of your blend.

Fig. 8.31
Building the highlights of an illustration may appear overly complex and confusing to the eye.

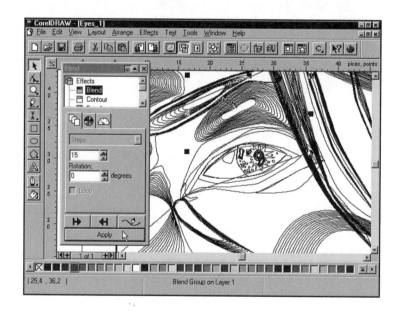

Blending and Powerline

▶ See "Working with Power- lines and Lenses," p. 353

Applying Powerline effects to blended objects can have striking results while being completely exploratory. By blending objects and using the various Powerline styles you may quickly create embellishments or design elements for things such as holiday greetings, formal certificates and so on. Indulge yourself into combining these effects and learning more about the Blend and Powerline commands by following these steps:

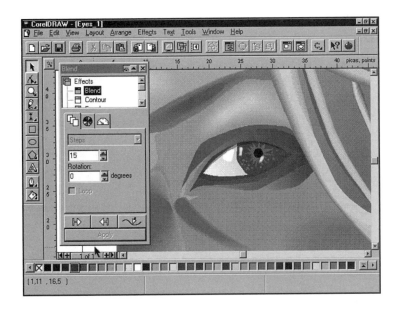

Fig. 8.32
Once your highlight shades and colors are applied to your drawing, the blends you assigned will help create realism.

1. Create a horizontal straight line using the Freehand tool. Make a horizontally aligned copy of it by dragging while holding down the Ctrl key and right-clicking.

2. Select the copy and flip it horizontally using the Scale & Mirror roll-up (Alt+F9).

3. Select both the lines, choose the Blend roll-up (Ctrl+B), and blend the two lines using a step of 20 steps and a Rotation of –170 degrees with the Loop option selected.

4. Select the Blend and choose Arrange, Separate to break apart the blend.

5. Select the blend group and choose Ctrl+U to ungroup it, making it twenty individual objects (see fig. 8.33).

6. Select the entire collection of objects by marquee-selecting them, and choose Ctrl+F8 to display the Powerline roll-up.

7. Choose the Trumpet 2 style from the Powerline roll-up, set a maximum width of 0.30 inches, and click the Apply button. Your lines will become a fan shape.

8. With all 22 of the objects still selected, choose the Fountain Fill dialog box (F11), and set the fountain fill Type to Radial, the Color blend to Two-color, the From color to a dark color, the To color to a light color, and select OK. A radial fill will be applied to your blended Powerline effect with the radial fill emanating from the center of the collection of objects (see fig. 8.34).

Fig. 8.33

After creating your objects, applying a blend, use the Separate and Ungroup commands to dismantle your blend as seen here.

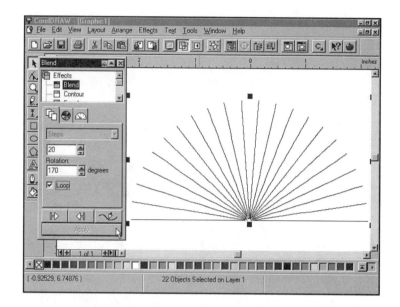

Fig. 8.34

Strange and interesting effects may be achieved by combining different effects and changing the attributes of the final products. Exploring in this way will help you gain an understanding of how certain effects will work with each other to produce your desired results.

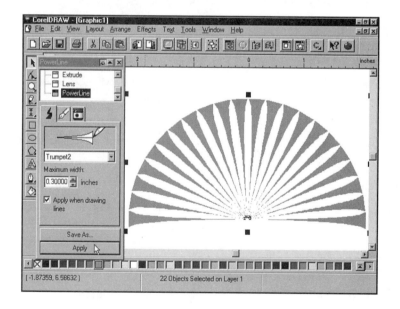

From Here...

There are many different types of effects that may be achieved using the Blend command. Some are quite basic, while others may be quite complicated and require hours of practice using the command. The Blend roll-up in itself is a feature-rich set of controls and options. Learning to use these controls will not only greatly expand your understanding of the relationships between dynamically linked objects, but will provide you with the necessary experience to save you hours of drawing time.

For related information on the topics covered in this chapter, see the following sections:

■ See Chapter 6, "Working with Objects."

■ See Chapter 7, "Using Fills and Outlines."

■ See Chapter 10, "Working with Powerlines and Lenses."

■ See Chapter 15, "Importing and Exporting Files."

II

Creating Text & Drawings

Chapter 9

Arranging, Shaping, and Applying Effects

The expression "can't fit a square peg into a round hole" won't apply in this next chapter, because now you can. In fact you can even fit the round hole inside the square peg if that's what you need to do.

Creating perfect drawings is likely the aim of any budding illustrator, designer, or electronic artist. Producing perfect drawings has a lot to do with manipulating the parts with a keen eye, and expert-precision. In this chapter you'll supply the keen eyes, while CorelDRAW! 6 supplies the arranging, shape, and effects tools.

This chapter will be of interest to anyone wishing to alter objects beyond their originally created appearance.

In this chapter, you learn to

- Become an Expert at Extruding Objects
- Arrange and order objects in complex drawings
- Organize with Align and Distribute, Guides and Rulers
- Use Weld, Intersection, and Trim to create new objects
- Use Contour effects
- Create Effects using Powerclip

Shaping Objects

Shaping objects to add depth and realism to your overall drawings is one of the features that sets DRAW! apart from a CAD or basic drafting program. Shaping objects to simulate a third dimension will allow the audience viewing your drawing to become more interested. For instance, you might use a cube shape to illustrate a package design, or design a dimensional tube for pipes and machinery. Using tools such as those in Extrude, Perspective, and Contours helps you create and control that simulated third dimension.

Add Instant 3-D with Extrusions

◀ See "Bezier Tool Options," p. 74

Extruding is another feature that will stir excitement for those accustomed to the limitations of two dimensions. Extrusion adds a thickness or depth to text and objects. This chapter takes a close look at what the Extrude tools can do to other objects.

Tip
Before performing extrusions, you might want to know how to remove them—just in case. To remove any extrusion, click the extrude part of the object and select Clear Extrude from the Effects menu. Also, it's always a good habit to save your file before performing any extrude effects.

Using and Creating Extrude Presets

The first button in the Extrude roll-up (see fig. 9.1) includes a Presets tab that lets you select from a variety of pre-designed extrusion effects. The rest of the roll-up includes a Depth tab, a Rotation tab, a Lighting Controls tab, and a Color Fill tab. You can access the Extrude roll-up (Ctrl+E) from the Effects menu.

Select an effect from the drop-down list in the Presets tab and click on Apply to apply the effect to the selected object. You may also delete presets that have already been saved. Like many of the Effects features in CorelDRAW! 6 there's a large selection of pre-defined extrusions to choose from.

Each Preset displays a low-resolution preview of the extrusion with information about the extrusion effect. If you are applying the extrusion to text, the message also specifies which font was used to create the effect. The Presets are stored in a file called CORELDRW.PST in your COREL60/DRAW folder. You may create and save your own extrusions by selecting the Extrusion flyout menu from the Presets tab, which contains options for New, Open Save As, and Merge With. By selecting Save As (see fig. 9.2) you may create a completely new Presets file that will store all of your new extrudes.

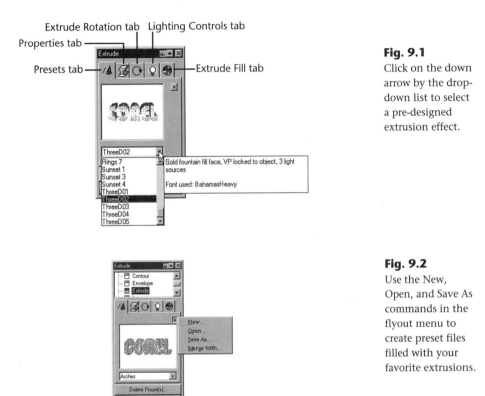

Fig. 9.1
Click on the down arrow by the drop-down list to select a pre-designed extrusion effect.

Fig. 9.2
Use the New, Open, and Save As commands in the flyout menu to create preset files filled with your favorite extrusions.

II

Creating Text & Drawings

Tip

For best results, use the font that the Preset specifies. Otherwise, the results may not be all that great. You need to make sure that you have that particular font loaded into your Windows 95 system folder. If not, you can load from the CorelDRAW! 6 disks.

To save a new extrusion effect in an Extrude Presets file, select the extrusion you created and click the Save As button at the bottom of the Extrude roll-up. The Save Extrude Preset dialog box appears (see fig. 9.3), asking you to name the new extrusion. For quick reference, name the extrusion based on how it makes your objects look rather than just naming them extrusion 1, extrusion

2 and so on. Also, this dialog allows you to enter notes about the extrusion. This is where you enter your brief description about colors, fills, and dimensional measures. It's difficult enough just to imagine what will happen to your object after the extrusion is applied; this brief description will help describe the extrusion in more detail. It will also display as the flyout description when you have the Preset highlighted in the Preset pull-down menu.

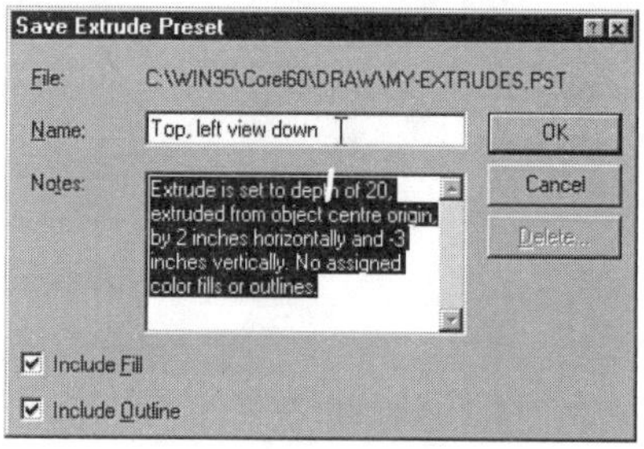

Fig. 9.3

Take time to enter a description when saving a Preset extrusion— the description will display in the flyout when you select the Preset in the roll-up.

Tip

Extrude has one other control which is sort of hidden from the main stream of the extrude options. In the Options dialog under the Display Tab, there is a control for setting the Minimum Extrude Facet Size, the default of which is set to 0.12500 inches. For some unknown reason, this control is lumped in with a hodge-podge of other unrelated options. This feature controls the thinnest setting that DRAW! will make—a three-dimensional object using the Extrude tools. You may set this as low as 0.0100 inches, which is nearly invisible to the human eye when viewed at actual size.

Extrude Depth Tab

The Depth tab (see fig. 9.4) contains controls to change the style, vanishing point, and depth of your extrusion. The vanishing point applies to three-dimensional objects and refers to the point all objects diminish to; the depth of the objects is the point at which the objects stop diminishing. The first set of controls allow you to set depth and vanishing point positions using the mouse, while the second set of controls, accessed by clicking the small page icon button, allow you to keyboard the exact measures.

Styles feature a pull-down menu including Small Back, Small Front, Big Back, Big Front, Back Parallel, and Front Parallel which best describe the shape that your extrusion will take when applied. A preview window reflects how each extrusion style will look. The preview is in three dimensions with your original object outlined with a heavy black line.

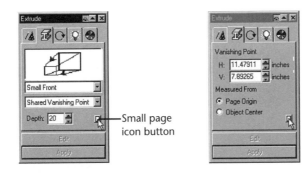

Small page icon button

Fig. 9.4
Use the settings in the Properties tab of the Extrude roll-up to select the style and depth of the extrusion.

The vanishing point, or VP as it's referred to in the DRAW! interface, also features a pull-down menu including options to set the vanishing point to VP Locked to Object, VP Locked to Page, Copy VP from, and Shared Vanishing Point.

The vanishing point of the object you are about to extrude displays as a large black X. It shows up after you select an extrude style and click the Apply button at the bottom of the roll-up. This vanishing point control may be positioned away from the object using your Pick tool while DRAW! updates the results of the changed vanishing point as it moves.

The first two options from the vanishing point pull-down menu allow the extrude controls to anchor the vanishing point to either the object itself or the page. When using these two controls, subsequently moving the object will cause the vanishing point to remain either with the object or stationary on the page, respectively.

The remaining two options also operate in similar ways. Choosing the option Copy VP From allows you to select a different extruded object in your drawing. Selecting this option will change your cursor to a Pick tool, accompanied by a black X (see fig. 9.5) and a question mark. You may then click the object you wish to copy the VP from. DRAW! will then apply the same VP settings to your currently selected object. Shared Vanishing Point allows you to set your object to have the same vanishing point as another object and, in turn, causes both objects to appear as if they share the same dimensional space. Moving either object will cause the extrusion to be updated to conform to the shared vanishing point.

Extrude Rotation

The Rotation controls in CorelDRAW! 6 are extremely interactive, not to mention fun to play with. By placing your cursor inside the interactive rotation control preview window (see fig. 9.6), you are able to manipulate the

II

Creating Text & Drawings

rotation of the object in three dimensions. The object in the Rotation preview window, which is actually the Corel logo, moves fluidly in three-dimensional rotation, the backside of which is displayed as a blue color. When you first place your cursor inside the Rotation preview window, it changes to a hand accompanied by a cross-hair cursor. Click and drag with the left mouse button and notice that the origin mouse-down and mouse-position points are tracked by a bright yellow bezier curve, indicating how much your object will be rotated.

Fig. 9.5

You can copy vanishing points from extruded objects and apply them to other objects.

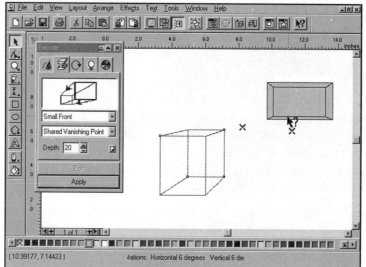

Fig. 9.6

Drag your mouse on the logo to apply three-dimensional rotation to your extruded object.

X button ——— Page Icon

The second set of controls is invoked (see fig. 9.7), once again, by clicking the small page icon button. The Rotation controls may then be keyboarded into the fields labeled Angle, Phi, and Theta representing angle rotation in three dimensions. (You can also think of these as X, Y, and Z dimensions.)

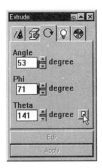

Fig. 9.7
Click the small page icon to enter exact settings for rotating extruded objects.

To reset the three-dimensional rotation controls to 0, 0, and 0 degrees, click the small X button to the lower left of the Rotation preview window (refer to fig. 9.6).

> **Tip**
>
> When using the interactive portion of the extrude Rotation controls, holding down the Control key will constrain rotational angle Phi and Theta movement in 15-degree increments.

After you have settled on the exact measure of extrude rotation, click the Apply button to cause DRAW! to update your extrusion.

Extrude Lighting Controls

The lighting controls in the Extrude roll-up let you add more realism to your extruded object. You may set up to three light sources at various intensities ranging from 0 (no light) to 100 (maximum light). The light sources may be positioned anywhere around the object on a three-dimensional plane. It's important to note that lighting will affect the colors in the extruded object. Take time to experiment with the intensity to achieve the effect you want.

To set lighting sources up for your extrusion, follow these steps:

1. If you haven't already, create a simple object and apply any extrusion style, depth, or rotation to it.

2. Select the object and choose the Extrude Lighting tab from the Extrude roll-up (see fig. 9.8).

3. Click the first lighting button labeled with the numeral 1. This is your first lighting source. Notice that a 1, surrounded by a small black circle, has appeared on the grid to the upper right of the Extrude Lighting

preview window, and the Intensity slider bar below the preview window has become active.

Fig. 9.8

Fig. 9.8
Click the Extrude Lighting tab to display tools for adding up to three light sources to extruded objects.

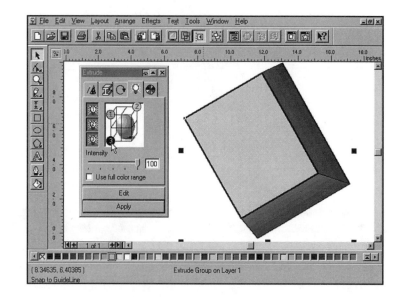

4. Grab onto the small black circle and drag it to a new location on the grid. Use the Intensity slider to set this first lighting source to a value other than 100.

5. Click the second lighting source button labeled with the numeral 2. Again, a black circle labeled 2 appears.

6. Grab that circle and drag it to a new location on the grid, away from circle 1. With the second lighting source still active, set its intensity using the slider control.

7. Click the third lighting button labeled with the numeral 3; drag it to yet another location on the grid, away from circles 1 and 2. Adjust the intensity.

8. Click the Apply button at the bottom of the roll-up.

> **Note**
>
> If you use a bitmap fill for your object, combined with the Drape Fill option, the Extrude Lighting portion of the Extrude roll-up won't be available to you. DRAW! can't adjust the lighting on bitmapped fills. Conversely, if you select to apply lighting sources to an object that already has the Drape Fill option in use, it will revert back to the Shade option when the apply button is selected.

The light sources may not be positioned away from the grid lines set in the preview, and can't be set to a position at some point behind the object. Don't frustrate yourself trying to do this. Trying to position a light source behind the object or off the grid will cause it to either snap back to the default position to the upper-right corner of the extrusion, or to snap back to the closest part of the grid.

Extrude Color Fill Controls

The Extrude Color Fill tab controls color options for the extrude portion of your extruded object only, not the actual object itself. The Color Fill tab features options for filling your extrusion with Use Object Fill, Solid Fill, and Shade.

- *Use Object Fill.* Applies the same fill that has been assigned to the selected object to the extrusion. The fill is applied evenly over all visible sides. The Drape Fill option causes the object sides to be rendered with a realistic distortion (see fig. 9.9 and fig. 9.10).

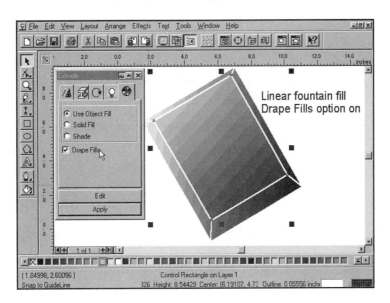

Fig. 9.9
When using fountain fills as the object fill, Drape Fill adds to the three-dimensional look of the extrusion.

Fig. 9.10

When a texture fill is used as the object fill, and the Drape Fills option is applied, the texture applies to the sides with no visible rotation or distortion to account for the three-dimensional depth.

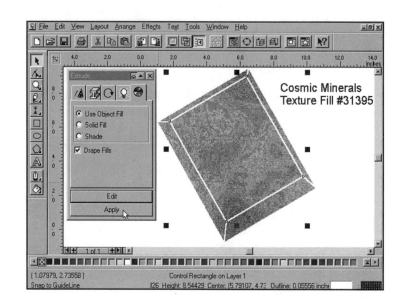

- *Use Solid Fill.* Allows you to fill the extrusion with an even Uniform Fill color by displaying a color flyout from the "Using" button. This option will only set the color to an even Uniform Fill.

- *Shade.* Allows you to use linear fountain fills to apply automatic shading to your extrusion. Fountain fills are set to fill in a linear style from the front of the extrusion to the back, angled from the center of the extruded object. The From color sets the front color of the extrusion, while the To color sets the back color.

Tip

After applying the Shade color option in the Extrude Color tab of the Extrude roll-up, you may adjust the angle or fountain fill type by using the Special Fill. Select the Special Fill roll-up from either the Roll-Up toolbar or the Fill Flyout from the toolbar. Use Ctrl+click to select the individual sides of your extrusion, and the Update From option to sample the actual Linear Fountain Fill setup of each extruded side (see fig. 9.11).

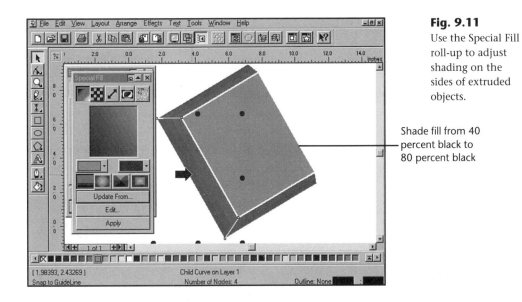

II

Creating Text & Drawings

Fig. 9.11
Use the Special Fill
roll-up to adjust
shading on the
sides of extruded
objects.

Shade fill from 40
percent black to
80 percent black

Tip

You may also copy or clone extrusions from other objects. Selecting Effects, Copy or Clone, Extrude From changes your cursor into a selecting arrow for you to designate the object to Copy or Clone from. Copying an extrusion from another object copies only the extrusion information and applies it to the object you currently have selected.

Cloning an extrusion from another object only clones the extrusion, leaving the extrusion information in the original "master" extrusion object. When using the cloning feature, you won't be able to edit the cloned extrusion. Instead, you will have to edit the master extrusion contained in the object you cloned the extrusion from.

Adding Realism with Perspective

Compared to the Extrude controls, Perspective controls are quite basic. You learned in Chapter 3 how to apply Perspective transformation to Artistic Text and Paragraph text. Now, it's time to learn about Perspective controls applied to simple and complex objects. Unlike the Extrude command, the Add Perspective command, found under the Effects menu, alters flat, two-dimensional objects to simulate a third dimension without actually building any other information into the object.

◀ See "Cloning
Objects," p. 197

When applying perspective to an object, you're working with vanishing points again. When you first apply the Perspective command, your objects will appear with either one or two vanishing points to the left or right and above or below the object. One vanishing point controls the horizontal perspective, while the other controls the vertical perspective. In order to maintain a constant perspective when working with multiple objects in the same drawing, both the horizontal and vertical vanishing points should be common, or the objects will seem mismatched. Also, keep in mind where your horizon line is (even if it's invisible) and keep your vanishing points positioned directly on it.

A one-point perspective uses only one of the vanishing points, while a two-point perspective uses both.

To Add Perspective to an object, follow these steps:

1. Select an object with your Pick tool and choose Effects, Add Perspective. Notice that at least one vanishing point control marker appears. If it doesn't, your view may be too close. Press F3 to zoom out. Notice also that your object is now surrounded by a dotted bounding box with positioning handles in each corner.

2. Grab onto the upper-left-corner handle and drag it (to the right) toward the center of the object until you see the horizontal vanishing point appear in your screen from the left.

3. Grab onto the vanishing point itself and position it on a point on your imaginary horizon. Notice that when you move the horizontal vanishing point toward the object, the top and bottom of the bounding box continue to point toward it, while the closest side becomes smaller and the furthest side remains the same. The closer the vanishing point is to the object, the smaller the closest side will become.

4. Click the Pick tool to finish the Perspective command.

Continue with the next steps to apply the same perspective to additional objects.

1. Create another object on part of the page and choose Add Perspective from the Effects menu again. The same markers and bounding box appear around the new object.

2. Select the horizontal vanishing point for this new object and position it in the same spot as the first object. You may position horizontal and vertical guidelines to intersect this point; turn on Snap to Guidelines under the Arrange menu to make it easier to select pinpoint.

3. End your Perspective command by clicking the Pick tool in the toolbar.

4. Create a third object anywhere on your page and choose Perspective From in the Copy flyout from under the Effects menu. Your cursor will then change to an arrow, allowing you to select from which other object you would like to copy the perspective.

5. Click one of the other objects. DRAW! applies the same perspective (see fig. 9.12).

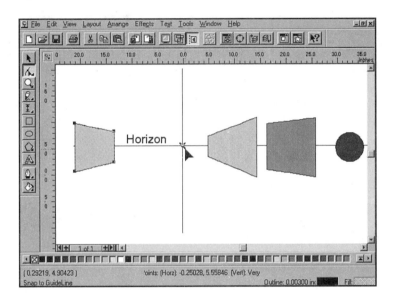

Fig. 9.12
Use the Copy Perspective From command to apply the same perspective to multiple objects.

To clear the perspective from an object, choose Effects, Clear Perspective. To Edit an object that contains a perspective effect, select the Shape tool from the Toolbox and click the object you wish to edit. The same Perspective controls appear, allowing you to make adjustments to the effect.

> **Note**
>
> When first applying perspective to an object, you may not see the vanishing points immediately. Try zooming out (F3) to see more of the page.

Tip

When manipulating corner handles during the creation or editing of an object, hold down the Ctrl key to constrain the movement of the handle to either vertical or horizontal movement. This makes the vanishing point move toward or away from the opposite corner on the same side. You can also hold the Shift key to keep the percent of change constant for the horizontal and vertical sides.

Tip

To create a quick three-dimensional object in perspective, make a rectangle and Add Perspective to it. Make sure that the horizontal vanishing point is about level to the center of the object. After applying the perspective, grab either side of the object and drag it toward the other side of the object. While dragging, right-click to make a copy. Then, make the copy a lighter or darker color/shade than the original. Doing this, you can quickly create a two-second, three-dimensional object (see fig. 9.13).

Fig. 9.13
Make one side of the extruded object lighter or darker to create a quick three-dimensional object.

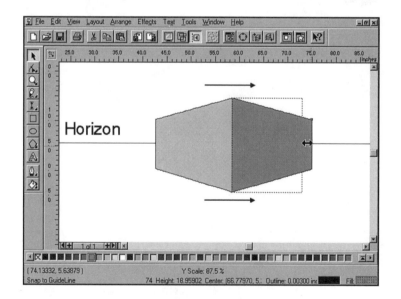

Applying Contours to Objects

Contours are a little like Blends. The Contour command (Ctrl+F9) creates a series of similarly shaped objects based on the object that you have currently selected and joined to it using a dynamic link. The original object is left intact and a dynamically linked contour group is added according to the parameters entered in the roll-up.

The counter group is created concentrically, or around the center of the selected object on the inside or the outside (see fig 9.14). This creates an effect like the elevation lines on a topographical map, or wood grain patterns in a good piece of oak. Contours may also change color or fill pattern as they transition from the original object by way of color controls.

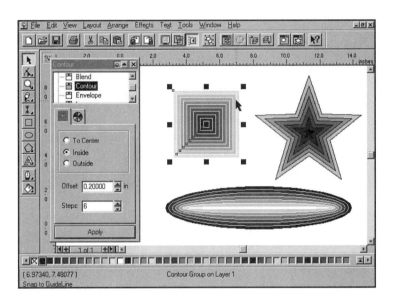

Fig. 9.14
Contours may be applied to any rectangle, ellipse, or open curve. Color controls enable a number of different effects to be applied.

II

Creating Text & Drawings

The Contour controls are all contained in the Contours roll-up, which is another of those multi-purpose roll-ups you've become familiar with in CorelDRAW! 6. The controls in the roll-up are split into two tabbed sections: the contour properties and the color options (see fig. 9.15). Properties include applying Contours to the Center, Inside, or Outside of your object, a contour offset control, and a step control. Color options feature outline and fill controls and color-wheel rotation.

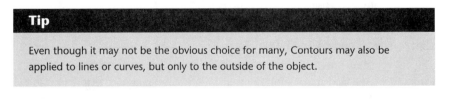

Tip

Even though it may not be the obvious choice for many, Contours may also be applied to lines or curves, but only to the outside of the object.

The Contour Properties Tab

These main controls determine the number of steps or contours and how they will be created.

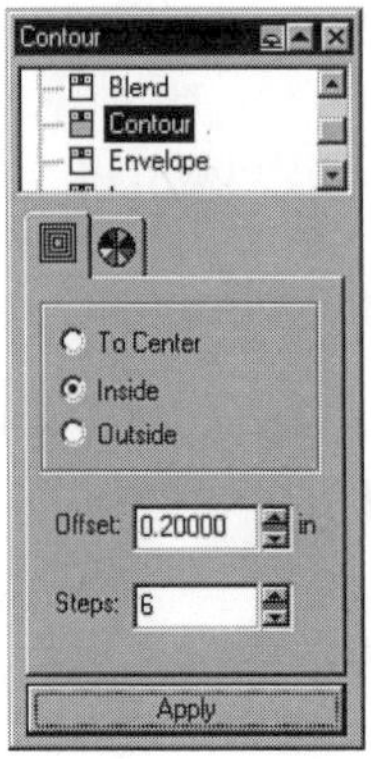

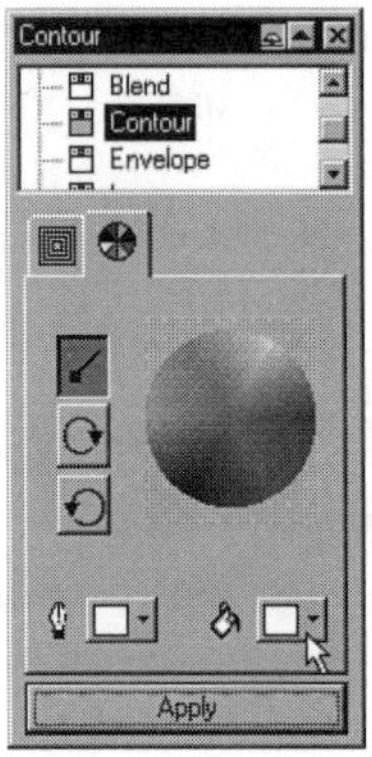

Fig. 9.15
Use the Contour
Properties roll-up
and Contour Color
Options tabs to
format objects
used in a contour
effect.

- *To Center.* Allows you to set the contours to be built toward the center of the object by using the Offset control. Setting To Center with a number entered in the Offset field will create the given number of steps toward the center of the object.

- *To Inside.* When this option is selected, both the Offset and Steps controls become available, enabling you to set the offset spacing and the number of steps. The given number of steps will be built toward the inside of the object and spaced according to the offset measure.

- *To Outside.* Opposite to the To inside controls, when this option is selected both the Offset and Steps controls are available, enabling you to set the offset spacing and the number of steps. The given number of steps will be built on the outside of the object and spaced according to the offset measure.

- *Offset.* The amount entered in this field determines the spacing of each of the steps.

- *Steps.* The number entered in this field determines the number of contour steps that DRAW! will create.

Contour Color Options Tab
The color options include Outline and Fill controls that affect only the contour effect itself and not the object that is being contoured. Outline and Fill

color settings control the parameters of the final contour, allowing DRAW! to blend the various pen and fill colors for each contour between the original object and the last contour. Color blends may also be set, which apply to both outline and fill colors.

- *Straight color blend.* Use this option to blend straight through the color wheel, directly from one color to another.

- *Clockwise color blend.* Blends from one color to another clockwise around the color wheel.

- *Counter-clockwise color blend.* Blends from one color to another counter-clockwise around the color wheel.

With each of these color options, the color wheel display indicates which colors will be transitioned over the contour.

To remove a Contour from an object, select Effects, Clear Contour. To convert the contour to individual objects, select <u>A</u>rrange, <u>S</u>eparate to separate the contour group from the original object, then select Ungroup to ungroup the contour group itself.

◀ See "Cloning Objects," p. 197

Tip

You may also Copy or Clone a Contour from one object to another. To Copy a Contour, select Contour From by selecting Copy from the Effects menu. To Clone a Contour, select Contour From by selecting Clone from the Effects menu. To edit the copied Contour, click the contour group and display the Contour roll-up to display the current settings for the contour group. To edit a cloned contour, you must edit the master contour that controls the particular clone.

Tip

You may also contour from an object filled with a fountain fill. If the Contour roll-up detects an object with a fountain fill, the Fill control splits up to show the To and From colors to control the fountain fill for the final contour (see fig. 9.16).

Fig. 9.16
You can create contours from objects filled with fountain fills for an interesting effect.

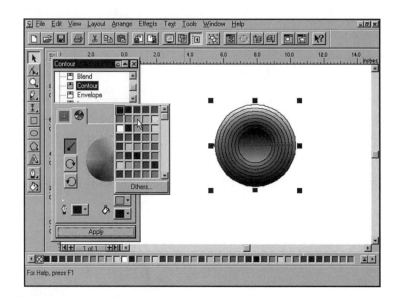

Drawing Alignment Tools

A messy drawing will detract from the information you are trying to convey. CorelDRAW! 6 features an abundance of tools that enable you to organize your visual elements into packages that make them easier to work with, and give your drawings clarity and focus. A new Align and Distribute roll-up leads the way in these tools as the new addition to version 6, but is also accompanied by rulers, guidelines, guides, snap-to functions, and layering controls.

Align and Distribute

In previous versions, the align function allowed full control over vertical and horizontal object alignment. This tool has been enhanced in version 6 to allow for the added dimension of Distributing objects as well.

The Align and Distribute roll-up (see fig. 9.17) is available from under the Arrange menu (Ctrl+A). It's pretty menacing at first glance, but may be dissected down to a few basic controls and options. Dominating the roll-up is the main preview window, which serves as the key to determining what all the options and buttons do. At the bottom of the roll-up are two pull-down menus which control Alignment preferences and Distribute preferences. These are critical for controlling what will serve as reference for alignment and distribution of your objects.

Around the preview window are a series of buttons containing symbols and arrows. The Vertical alignment buttons are along the right side and the Horizontal alignment buttons are along the bottom of the preview window.

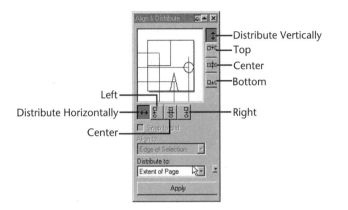

Fig. 9.17
New to version 6, the Align and Distrbute roll-up provides tools for object alignment and spacing.

At the bottom-right of the roll-up is a small down-arrow button which, when pressed, will reveal Distribution options (see fig. 9.18) to control vertical and horizontal distribution preferences. Here you may set the controls to distribute the objects based on specific parts of the objects or the space between them. When extended fully and revealing the Distribution options, the Apply button is also covered up, forcing you to make your Distribution Option preferences before continuing.

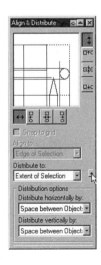

Fig. 9.18
Distribution options allow you to specify what side of the object should be used as the guide for spacing the objects.

Back at the alignment buttons around the preview window, you will notice that there are four choices to each set of vertical and horizontal button controls. Looking at the bottom row of buttons from the left, they represent the following:

- *Distribute Horizontally.* Gives access to the Distribute To pull-down menu, which allows you to either distribute your objects to the Extent of the Page or the Extent of the Selection. This means that the distribution of your objects will either be done by spreading them to the outer page dimensions set by your Page Setup, or to a calculated bounding box currently surrounding your object selection.

- *Left.* Aligns objects vertically along their left edges.

- *Center.* Aligns objects vertically with their center origins.

- *Right.* Aligns objects vertically along their right edges.

And to the right of the preview window, from the top:

- *Distribute Vertically.* Again, allows you to do the same function as with Distribute Horizontally, except in a vertical orientation.

- *Top.* Aligns objects horizontally along their top edges.

- *Center.* Aligns objects horizontally along their center origins.

- *Bottom.* Aligns objects horizontally along their bottom edges.

The main thrust of this collection of buttons and controls is that they be used one at a time or in combination to position the objects on your page exactly how you wish—without using your mouse.

After selecting any of the align buttons, the Align to pull-down menu becomes active and enables you to set your alignment preferences to either align to the Center of Page, Edge of Page, or Edge of Selection. You may also select none of the buttons to be depressed by clicking a second time on whichever button is pressed. This causes all of the options and controls in the roll-up to become inactive.

Try the following simple exercise to get familiar with using the Align and Distribute roll-up.

1. Create four simple, but differently sized and oddly shaped objects.

2. Open the Align and Distribute roll-up by choosing, Arrange, Align and Distribute.

3. First, align all the objects horizontally along the center of the page by pressing the Align Center button to the right of the preview button. Make sure that there are no other buttons pressed.

4. Next, make sure that the Align To pull-down menu selection is set to Center of Page.

5. Select all four of your objects and Click the Apply button. Your objects might still be in a jumbled mess, but nonetheless, they are all centered horizontally on your page, and centered with each other as well (see fig. 9.19).

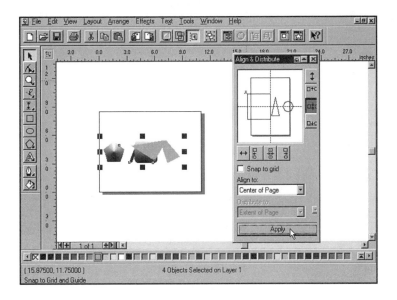

Fig. 9.19

Use the Align and Distribute roll-up to align selected objects to the center of the page.

Continue with the next steps to try another method of alignment.

1. Use your Pick tool to reposition or spread out the objects.

2. Distribute your four objects along the center of the page while still center-aligning them with each other. To do this, click the Align Center button again to the right of the preview window, making sure that the Align To pull-down menu is still set to Center of Page.

3. To distribute the objects to the width of your page, click the Distribute Horizontal button below the preview window. Notice that the Distribute to options becomes available.

4. Select the Extent of Page option; make sure you still have all four objects selected.

5. Click the small down arrow in the lower-right of the roll-up to reveal the Distribute options. Select Space between Objects from the Distribute by pull-down menu. Click the small up arrow to close the Distribute options.

6. Finally, click the Apply button. Your objects are set according to the Align and Distribute options you have selected (see fig. 9.20).

Fig. 9.20
Use the Align & Distribute roll-up to distribute objects evenly across the page.

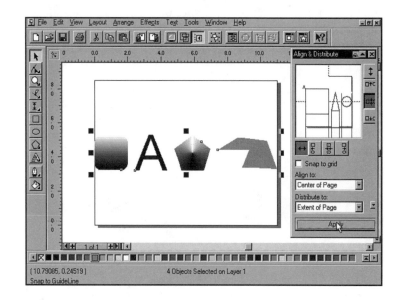

The last feature available in the Align and Distribute roll-up is the Snap to Grid option which may be on or off. When selected on, Snap to Grid causes objects to be positioned to the closest grid coordinate, according to the options set up in your Grid and Ruler Setup controls available under the Layout menu. The Snap to Grid option works independently of the Snap to Grid (Ctrl+Y) control within the program itself.

Using Rulers

Using rulers when composing any drawing that involves either exact spacing or measurements—or when drawing to scale—can make life much easier. The Rulers in CorelDRAW! 6 display either on or off (the default being on). To display the rulers select View, Ruler. Rulers consist of graduated bars positioned on the top and to the left of your document window.

Rulers aid in the visual alignment of objects in your drawing, or for positioning objects. While you move your mouse across the screen, small dotted lines on both the vertical and horizontal ruler bars indicate the exact position of the mouse.

Ruler setups are saved to each file. When no unit measure has been assigned or when a new document is started, the ruler setup of the last open file is used.

Setting Ruler Units

The unit of measurement your ruler uses is set according to the Ruler tab of the Grid and Ruler Setup dialog box (see fig. 9.21). Select Grid Setup from the Layout menu to use this option.

Fig. 9.21
Set the unit of measurement for on-screen rulers with the Grid & Ruler Setup dialog box.

The Ruler tab of the Ruler and Grid dialog box contains settings for Ruler Units in Horizontal and Vertical units that may be entered in inches, millimenters, picas and points, points only, ciceros and didots, or didots only. You may also set the Horizontal and Vertical ruler Origin to the same units. DRAW! uses the bottom-left corner of the page area when setting the origin of the ruler.

Setting Scale Options

The Ruler tab of the Grid & Ruler Setup dialog box also contains settings to set scale preferences in order to compose your measurement system for scale-drawing. Click on the Edit Scale button to display the dialog box for setting the scale (see fig. 9.22). Drawing to scale is a method used for composing scale drawings of either very small or very large representations of objects.

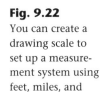

Fig. 9.22
You can create a drawing scale to set up a measure-ment system using feet, miles, and millimeters.

II

Creating Text & Drawings

The scale options include three main features. The first option, Typical Scales, features a pull-down menu containing ratio settings, including a selection ranging from 1:1 to 1:100 for drawing representations of very large drawing elements. For work in very small drawing scales, the ratios include a range from 2:1 to 100:1. The list also includes a selection of preset ratios measuring in feet and inches from 3" =1' to 1/128" = 1'. Setting a ratio from the Typical Scales menu will automatically set the measures for the next two options of Page Distance and World Distance. The thrust of these controls is to allow you to globally set the actual measure of objects on your page to be represented and displayed in dimensions of your choosing.

> **Tip**
>
> To invoke the Grid & Ruler Setup dialog box, click and hold the right mouse button down on either the vertical or horizontal ruler bar and select Grid and Ruler Setup from the menu that appears. You can also double-click on the ruler.

To set your ruler origin, follow these steps:

1. Display the Grid and Ruler Setup by choosing Layout, Grid Setup. Choose your page size and landscape or portrait orientation.

2. Set the unit of measurement for your ruler and the origin for both the horizontal and vertical rulers.

3. Click the OK button.

   Notice the 0.0 markings on the ruler have moved (see fig. 9.23).

Continue with these steps for additional ways to manipulate the ruler settings.

1. Pressing your left mouse button, grab the small square button in the upper-left corner where the horizontal and vertical ruler bars intersect. Drag it out onto your page. Notice that vertical and horizontal dotted lines accompany the cursor while you drag from that point.

2. Release the mouse when your cursor is over a different part of the page. Notice that the ruler's 0.0 marks coincide with the point where you released the mouse. This is the faster, but less accurate, way of setting the zero origin of your rulers.

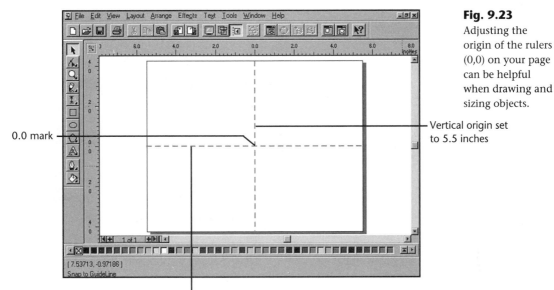

0.0 mark ⎯

Horizontal origin set to 4.25 inches

Fig. 9.23
Adjusting the
origin of the rulers
(0,0) on your page
can be helpful
when drawing and
sizing objects.

⎯ Vertical origin set
to 5.5 inches

3. Before continuing, try one more exercise. Perform the same action by
clicking and dragging the ruler intersection symbol in the upper-left
corner of the ruler bars, but this time, hold down the shift key before
you click the symbol until you release the mouse. Notice that as you
drag the mouse out onto the screen, it's now accompanied by two sets
of dotted lines.

4. Release the mouse at a different part of the page than before. This time
notice that the vertical and horizontal ruler bars have been moved, but
the zero origin for the rulers has remained stationary (see fig. 9.24).

Tip

If you enter zero values in the vertical and horizontal ruler origin fields of the Rulers
tab section of the Grids and Rulers dialog box, the ruler origin will be positioned at
the bottom-left corner of your page.

Using Guidelines

Guidelines are essentially reference or construction lines to help you position
objects in relation to your page or each other. With the added abilities provided by your system and the precision of your computer, placing a guide on
your page will give you not only a visual reference, but may also allow for
speedy organization.

II

Creating Text & Drawings

Fig. 9.24
Hold the Shift key while dragging the ruler intersection symbol to move the ruler bars.

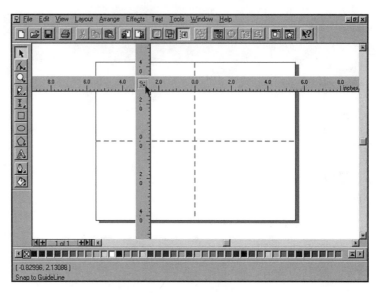

To place a horizontal or vertical guide on your page from either of the ruler bars, use your left mouse button to click and drag as if trying to pull the ruler itself down onto your page. In doing this, as soon as your mouse leaves the ruler bar, you'll notice that you are dragging a dotted line along with your cursor. Once you release your mouse button, the new guideline drops into position.

The guideline itself is represented by a blue dotted line with rectangular markers at either end extending to the edges of your drawing window. You may reposition this line by grabbing on it once again with your left mouse button and dragging it to a new location. By grabbing directly on the blue dotted line, you may drag vertical guidelines up or down, and horizontal guidelines left or right.

The newest guideline feature for version 6 of CorelDRAW! is the ability to slant or angle the guidelines (see fig. 9.25). To do this, grab one of the guideline end markers and drag up or down the edge of the drawing window for vertical guidelines or left or right along the edge of the drawing window for horizontal guidelines.

To manage guidelines or exactly position a single or multiple guidelines, choose Layout, Guidelines Setup to display the Guidelines Setup dialog box. The Guidelines Setup dialog box, like many, is divided into three tabbed sections controlling Horizontal (see fig. 9.26), Vertical (see fig. 9.27), and Slanted guidelines (see fig. 9.28).

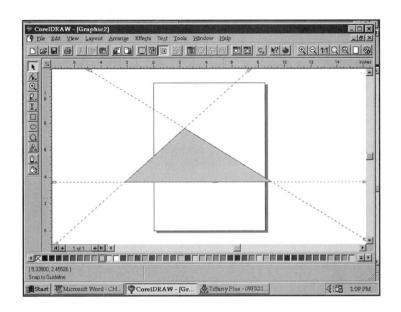

Fig. 9.25
Slanted guidelines
are a new addition
to CorelDRAW! 6.

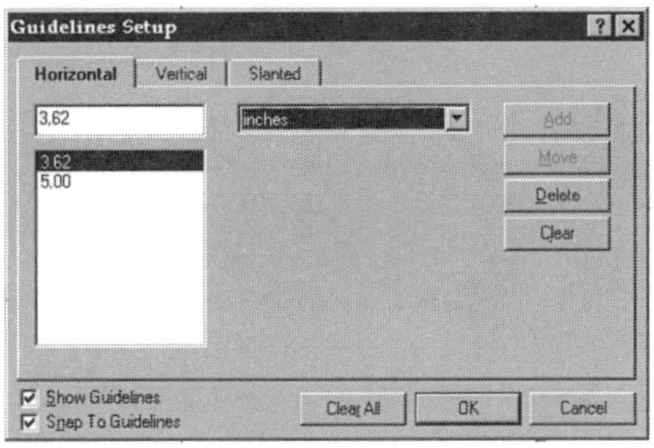

Fig. 9.26
Use the Horizontal
tab to add and
delete horizontal
guidelines.

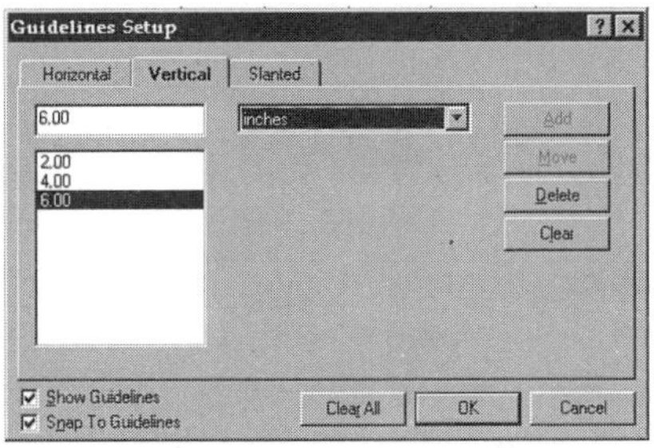

Fig. 9.27
Use the Vertical tab to
add and delete vertical
guidelines.

Fig. 9.28

Use the Slanted tab to add and delete slanted guidelines.

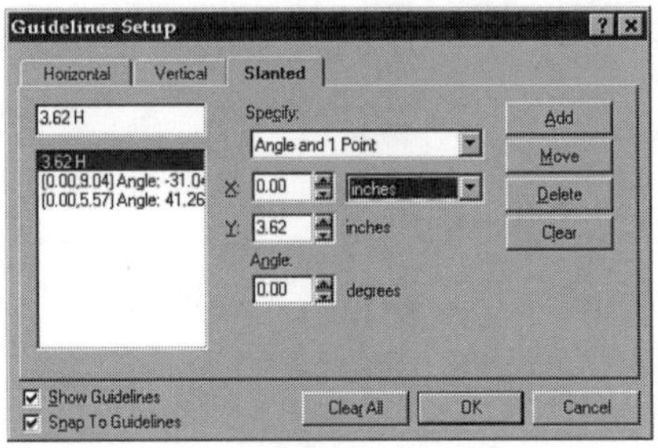

The Horizontal and Vertical tabs are identical except for the guides they control. Each features buttons to either Add, Move, Clear, or Delete a guideline. All tabs include global commands to Clear All, Show Guidelines, or Snap to Guidelines. The latter two are repeats of the options available from the Layout menu.

Guideline fields for the Horizontal and Vertical controls feature a new guideline position field in the upper-left corner of the dialog box, a field below, displaying any guidelines currently positioned on your page, and a guideline and a pull-down menu for setting the measurements of guideline positions.

To add a new guideline, follow these steps:

1. If it isn't already showing on your screen, display the Guidelines Setup dialog box by choosing Layout, Guidelines Setup.

2. Select the Horizontal tab in the dialog box by clicking its tab. In the upper-left corner field, enter the horizontal measure of the guide you wish to add.

   Note that the measurement you enter will be determined by the current position and zero origin of your rulers. The measurement uses defaults to the measure used by your rulers, or you may change to another measure by selecting from the pull-down menu.

3. Once you have entered the position of your new guideline, click the Add button. Your new guideline is added to the guideline inventory field below, where you entered your new guideline position. You can add more guidelines at various page positions. As you click the Add button, the guidelines are added to the guidelines position window.

4. When you've added all your guidelines, click OK.

To delete an existing guideline, click one of the existing guidelines in the page position window; click the Delete button in the Guidelines Setup dialog box. To move a guideline, click an existing guideline in the page position window; enter a new position in the first field and click the Move button. The guide changes according to the new value that you enter. Finally, you can click the Clear button to remove all the guidelines. Notice that any guidelines existing in the Vertical or Slanted guidelines tabs remain unchanged.

The Slanted guidelines tab in the Guidelines Setup dialog box works a bit differently from the other two tabs.

Caution

It may be confusing when using the Guidelines Setup dialog box controls to see two different buttons labeled with nearly the same name—Clear and Clear All. They perform two completely different commands and knowing the difference between the two may save you some re-work. The Clear button in the upper right of the dialog box clears only the guidelines in that tab, while selecting the Clear All button clears ALL of the guidelines in your drawing.

Snap to Guidelines Option

The Snap to Guidelines option causes guidelines to seemingly become magnetic. When objects are positioned within close proximity to the guidelines, they "jump" and stick to the guideline (see fig. 9.29). Objects may easily be separated again by dragging them apart.

When guidelines are used heavily for aligning objects to each other or to specific points, this feature is extremely useful. It may be activated by choosing Layout, Snap to Guidelines. When the feature is active, it is indicated in the menu with a check mark.

Show Snap Locations Marks

This is another somewhat hidden feature that plays a major role in how the guidelines provide object-to-guideline feedback when drawing. Show Snap Location Marks is hidden in the back of the program in Tools, Options, Display tab. When activated, the Show Snap Location Marks feature causes a blue rectangular marker to illuminate the points where your object comes in contact with a guideline, providing you with visual feedback that your object is near the guideline (see fig. 9.30).

Fig. 9.29
Turn on the Snap to feature to add a magnetic pull to guidelines—useful when aligning objects.

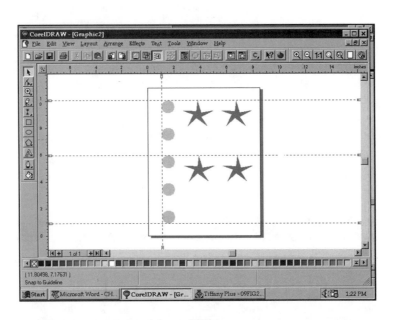

Fig. 9.30
A snap location mark appears when objects are placed near guidelines.

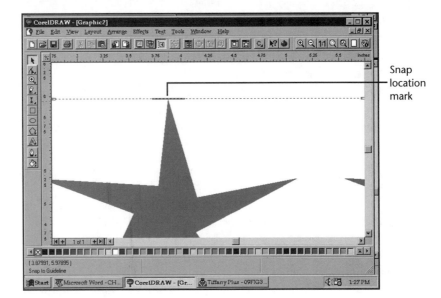

Snap location mark

Snap to Objects

The Snap to Objects feature, when activated, causes objects to appear magnetized when coming near each other. The characteristics of this particular snapping feature are intriguing. Two objects coming close together may snap to each other's edges, corners, or centers. New to version 6 are the reference points represented by blue markers that indicate where objects snap together. Objects can easily be separated again by dragging them apart.

Working with a Drawing Grid

When drawing, you can set up a grid to aid in controlling the size and placement of text and objects. A grid consists of grid markers running horizontally and vertically that cover the entire page. Figure 9.31 shows a grid used to align a group of objects and gauge their sizes. With DRAW!, you specify the amount of space placed between the gridlines. For instance, placing four horizontal and vertical grid markers per inch builds a grid in quarter-inch segments.

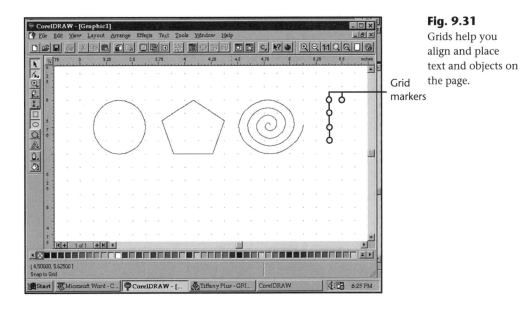

Fig. 9.31
Grids help you align and place text and objects on the page.

Grid markers

To set up a grid, select Layout, Grid and Ruler Setup. Click on the Grid tab and enter the number of markers you want to display per inch in the Frequency section of the dialog box (see fig. 9.32). For instance, enter 2 per inch to create a half-inch grid, enter 8 per inch to create an eighth-inch grid. (As with other dialog boxes, you can change the measurement system if desired.) To display the grid markers, turn on the Show Grid option at the bottom-left of the dialog box. As discussed earlier with guidelines, grid markers can have a "magnetic pull" that forces objects to align to the grid. Turn on the Snap to Grid option to activate the magnetic pull.

II

Creating Text & Drawings

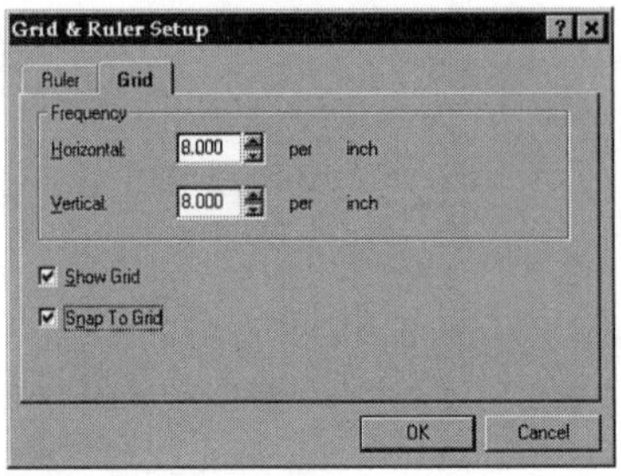

Fig. 9.32
Enter the number
of grid markers
you want to
display per inch.

Understanding Layers

Layers are used to organize and manage text and objects in complex draw-ings. Think of layers as transparent sheets of paper placed on top of each other. As an example, when creating a catalog, you might place the back-ground on one layer, graphics on another, and text on yet another. When working with the text layer, you could hide the background layer and speed up screen redraw time. When working with the graphics layer, you could lock the text layer—preventing you from accidentally moving or editing the text.

Select Layout, Layers Manager (Ctrl+F3) to open the roll-up for working with layers. As displayed in figure 9.33, four layers are automatically included in every document.

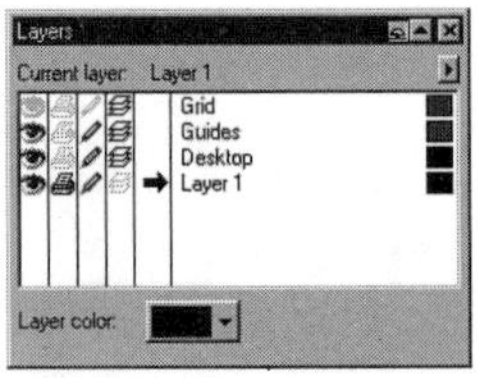

Fig. 9.33
With the Layers
Manager you can
create new layers
and hide and lock
specific layers.

The following bullets discuss the contents of each layer:

■ The Grid Layer contains the grid set up in your document.

■ The Guides layer contains the guidelines set up in your document.

■ The Desktop layer contains any objects placed outside of the printable page area.

■ Layer 1 contains all objects drawn on the page, unless a new layer was specified.

Creating Layers

To add a new layer, click on the flyout menu (see fig. 9.34) in the Layers
Manager and select New. A new layer is added to the roll-up. You can enter a
new name for layer if desired.

Fig. 9.34
The Layers
Manager displays
the layers in your
drawing.

To place an object on a new layer, make sure the layer is selected before creating the object. You can also use the Move To and Copy To commands to
move and copy selected objects between layers.

Note

You can create a large number of layers. However, the number of layers is restricted
by the amount of system resources you have available.

Working with Layer Settings

Each layer contains controls for hiding, printing, and editing the objects on
that layer. Click on the layer name in the Layer Manager and select Settings
from the flyout menu (see fig. 9.35). Turn off the Visible option to hide objects on the selected layer. Turn off the Printable option to not print objects
on the layer. Turn off the Editable option to "lock" objects on the layers—
they cannot be edited.

Fig. 9.35
Use the Settings
dialog box to hide,
print, and edit
layers.

II

Creating Text & Drawings

To repeat the objects on a layer on all pages in the document, turn on the Master Layer option. To display just the outlines of objects on a layer (similar to working in wireframe mode) turn on the Override full color view option. Use the color button to select another color for the outlines. Turn on the Apply layer changes to current page only, when you want to affect only the current page.

Using Weld, Intersection, and Trim

Weld, Intersection, and Trim are features that have remained virtually unchanged from version 5, except for the fact that they have been combined into a single roll-up while remaining as three different effect tools under the Arrange menu. They are considered arranging tools, but when you see how they work, you will likely want to use them to transform simple objects into highly complex objects—using only a few commands.

Weld

The Weld commands are controlled using the Weld roll-up (see fig. 9.36) displayed by selecting Arrange, Weld. The Weld command combines two or more objects to form one completely enclosed object, which is a conglomeration of the first two objects. For example, welding together a circle and a square—positioned so that they slightly overlap each other—will produce a new, single object resembling a circle and square attached as one object.

Fig. 9.36
Welding creates one curve object out of several objects, removing any unnecessary lines.

In essence, the Weld command (or what you would have to do manually to reproduce the same results) takes the objects selected to be welded and converts them to curves, breaks the nodes at points where their edges touch, breaks apart and discards the unneeded shapes, combines the objects to form one curve, and rejoins the broken nodes where the edges of the two objects originally met. All these functions are performed with one single command!

Even though the Weld command may be used with either whole objects or objects converted to curves, or simply closed curved objects created with the Freehand Drawing tool, the result will be the same—a curved object. Multiple objects may also be selected to Weld to an object.

The other options available within the Weld roll-up include:

- *Leave Original Target Objects.* When selected, this option allows the *original* object(s) to remain while DRAW! creates the Weld shape.

- *Leave Original Other Objects.* This option allows the *other* object to be left intact while creating the Weld shape.

> **Note**
>
> When both Leave Original options of Target and Other Objects are selected, and the Weld command is performed, all of the original objects remain intact and unchanged while the Weld shape is created. It may be best, in most cases, to leave both of these options selected unless you make copies of all objects before applying any transformations or effects. Also, watch the effect that is reflected in the preview window of the Weld roll-up while these options are turned on and off. In an effort to show how the options will perform, small shadows appear beneath the objects in the preview.

To Weld an object to another object, follow these steps:

1. Open the Weld roll-up by selecting Arrange, Weld.

2. Position two objects so that they overlap, without allowing one to completely overlap the other.

3. Select both the Leave Original options Target Object and Other Object(s).

4. Click one of the objects and click the Weld To button. Your cursor turns to a large black arrow (see fig. 9.37).

5. Select the object you wish to Weld To the currently selected object to complete the weld command.

6. DRAW! leaves the Weld shape behind the original (and other) object(s) and finishes the weld command by selecting the Weld shape.

7. Drag the Weld shape out from behind the originals and notice how the Weld is an exact outlined-copy of the overlapped originals. Notice also that the fill of the weld is the same as the object that was welded "to" (see fig. 9.38).

Fig. 9.37
Click the black
arrow on the
object you want
to weld to the
selected object.

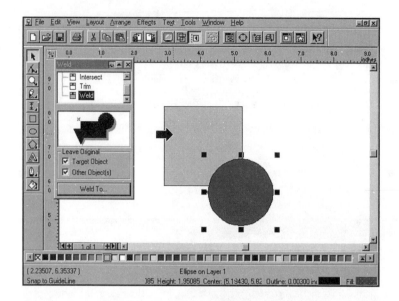

Fig. 9.38
Welding creates an
outline of the
overlapping
objects.

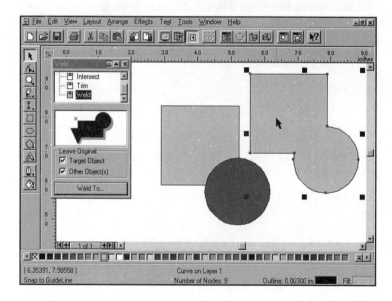

Continue with these steps to weld multiple objects:

1. Delete the first weld now, and prepare for another by positioning two
   of the objects so that they overlap the other. Multiple-select those two
   objects using the Pick tool by shift-clicking them.

2. Click the Weld To button. Your cursor again changes to a large black
   arrow.

3. Click the third object to complete the Weld command. The new Weld shape is left behind the original's. Drag it out to examine its shape (see fig. 9.39).

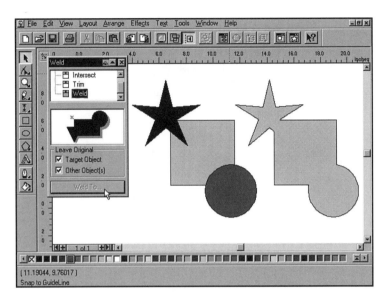

Fig. 9.39
You can weld multiple shapes by selecting several objects, and then clicking the black arrow on the last object to be welded.

> **Note**
>
> The Weld command may not be used with objects that contain previously applied effects such as Blend, Contour, Powerline, and Extrude. Also, you may not use objects created using the Graph Paper tool for welding. You may however, use the Weld command on Text objects, Spiral, Polygon, Perspective, Envelope, and texture and bitmap-filled objects.

Trim

The Trim roll-up (see fig. 9.40) is also contained within the same roll-up as Weld accessed by choosing Arrange, Trim. The Trim command is like the cookie-cutter of CorelDRAW! 6, because that's exactly what it does. You can turn any object into a cookie cutter-template by using it as your trim object. When two objects overlap, you may use one to cut its overlapping shape out of the other.

The main thrust of the Trim command is to remove the overlapping shape of one object from another. In a single command, the Trim command pinpoints the exact common edges of the two objects, removes the overlapping portion, and re-creates a new, trimmed object.

II

Creating Text & Drawings

■ Leave Original Target Objects: When selected, this option allows the original object (or objects) that will be Trimmed to remain intact while DRAW! creates the Trim shape.

■ Leave Original Other Objects: This option allows the other objects to be left intact while creating the Trim shape.

Fig. 9.40

Use the Trim roll-up to cut an overlapping shape out of an underlying Shape roll-up.

To turn an object into a cookie-cutter with the trim command, follow these steps:

1. Open the Trim roll-up by choosing Trim from the Arrange menu.

2. Position one of your objects overlapping the other, and leave it as the only object selected.

3. Click the Trim button at the bottom of the Trim roll-up. Your cursor changes to a large black arrow.

4. Select the object to be trimmed by clicking it, to complete the Trim command. Notice that the first object you selected is still intact while the second object has a portion removed where the two objects overlapped.

5. If you select the trimmed object you just created, and choose the Shape tool from the main Toolbox, notice how the trimmed shape now contains nodes which exactly reproduce the missing image portion (see fig. 9.41). These nodes may be edited using the Shape tool and the Node Edit roll-up.

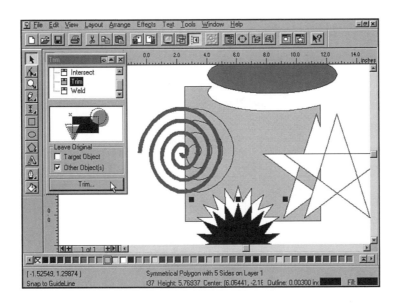

Fig. 9.41
This object was trimmed using various types of objects as the cookie-cutters. The trimmed object can be edited with the Shape tool.

Note

When both Leave Original options of Target and Other Object(s) are selected, and the Trim command is performed, all of the original objects remain intact and un-changed while the Trim shape is created. As with the Weld command, it may be best in most cases to leave both of these options selected unless you always make copies of your objects before applying any transformations or effects.

Tip

Like Weld, the Trim command may work with multiple objects without having to group or combine them. To make multiple objects into cookie cutters, first select the objects to use for the Trim, then click the Trim button and select the object to be trimmed.

Intersection

The Intersection commands are contained in the same roll-up as the Weld and Trim commands and accessed by selecting Arrange, Intersection. The Intersect roll-up (see fig. 9.42) features options identical to the Weld and Trim commands.

■ *Leave Original Target Objects.* This option lets the original object(s) that will be intersected to be left intact while DRAW! creates the intersection shape.

■ *Leave Original Other Objects.* This option allows the other objects to be left intact while creating the Intersection shape.

Fig. 9.42
Use the Intersect roll-up to create a new object over where the selected objects overlap.

> **Note**
>
> When both Leave Original options of Target and Other Object(s) are selected, and the Intersection command is performed, all of the original objects remain intact and unchanged while the Intersection shape is created. As with the Weld command, it may be best in most cases to leave both of these options selected unless you always make copies of your objects before applying any transformations or effects.

The main purpose of the intersect command is to create a new object which matches where two objects overlap. The newly created shape becomes a closed curve created in the same color as the object you intersected from. Essentially, DRAW!, in one command, converts both objects to curves, combines them to form a single curve, and deletes the nodes representing the excess portions outside the intersected area.

To use the Intersection command, follow these steps:

1. Open the Intersection roll-up by choosing <u>A</u>rrange, <u>I</u>ntersection.

2. Position one object overlapping another; leave it as the only object selected.

3. Click the Intersect With button at the bottom of the Intersection roll-up. Your cursor changes to a large black arrow.

4. To complete the Intersection command, click the object to be intersected. Notice that both of the objects you used for the Intersection are
   still intact, while a third object has been created where the two objects
   overlapped.

5. If you select the newly created intersection object and choose the Shape
   tool from the main Toolbox, notice how the intersection shape contains nodes which exactly reproduce the overlapped objects (see fig.
   9.43). These nodes may be edited using the Shape tool and the Node
   Edit roll-up.

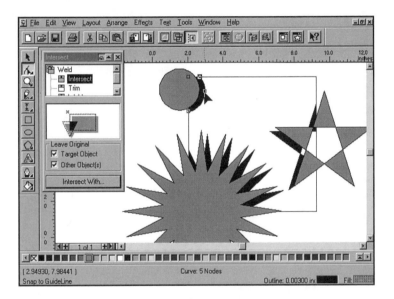

Fig. 9.43
New objects
created with the
Intersection
command can be
edited with the
Shape tool.

Note

The Trim and Intersection commands may not be used with objects that contain
previously applied effects such as Blend, Contour, Powerline, and Extrude, for use as
the cookie-cutter or the target object. Also, you may not use objects created using
the Graph Paper tool when trimming or intersecting. Grouped objects may not be
used either. To use a group of objects with the Trim or Intersection commands,
you will need to perform a series of commands including Ungrouping the objects
(Ctrl+U), converting them to curves (Ctrl+Q), and Combining them into one curved
object (Ctrl+L). Then you will be able to use them with the Trim or Intersection
command. This may not be suitable for all groups of objects, but it is a reasonable
workaround for simple objects.

You may, however, use the Trim and Intersection commands on Text objects, Spiral,
Polygon, Perspective, Envelope, and texture and bitmap-filled objects.

> **Tip**
>
> Like Weld and Trim, the Intersection command may work with multiple objects without having to group or combine them. To make multiple objects into cookie cutters, first select the objects to use for the Intersection, then click the Intersection button and select the object to be Intersectioned.

Object Priorities

During Weld, Intersection, and Trim commands, certain objects take priority over others. Priority depends on their ranking, when they were created, and their relative position to the objects being transformed or otherwise affected.

■ *Weld Priorities.* Object priorities—when working with the Weld command—are fairly inconsequential, considering that the result is a combination of all objects involved.

■ *Trim Priorities.* The trim priorities are determined by the order in which objects are selected, especially when trimming using multiple objects. The object selected first is always the cookie-cutter object, while the object that will be trimmed will always be the second object selected.

■ *Intersection Priorities.* The Intersection priorities are determined by the order in which objects are selected, especially when Intersecting using multiple objects. As with Weld, the results will always be the overlap of all objects involved.

Using Powerclip Effects

Powerclipping is one of the more useful and practical effects available in CorelDRAW! 6 and has changed little since the previous version of the program. The Powerclip command involves clipping objects and container objects. The clipped objects are placed inside the container objects and the combination is considered afterward as one single object. Any overlapping information contained outside the container object is retained, but invisible. After being placed inside the container, the clipped object becomes the contents of the container. The concept may seem tricky at first, but once you have the remaining functions, it becomes quite logical. Container contents may be extracted later, or edited because the information associated with them remains intact. Any transformations applied to the Powerclip container are automatically applied to its contents. This is the real strength of powerclipping.

> **Note**
>
> You may find powerclipping similar to adding bitmapped fills to text and objects.

All Powerclip functions are accessed through the Effects menu (see fig. 9.44) and include commands to Place Inside Container, Extract Contents, Edit Contents, and Finish Editing This Level. Any object that can either be created or imported into CorelDRAW! 6 may be used as a clipped object or container.

◀ See "Using Two-Color Bitmap Pattern Fills," p. 242

The container of the clipped image may be any closed object or group of vector objects. You may use text, bitmap, or vector objects to apply the Powerclip command; the combinations are limited only by your imagination.

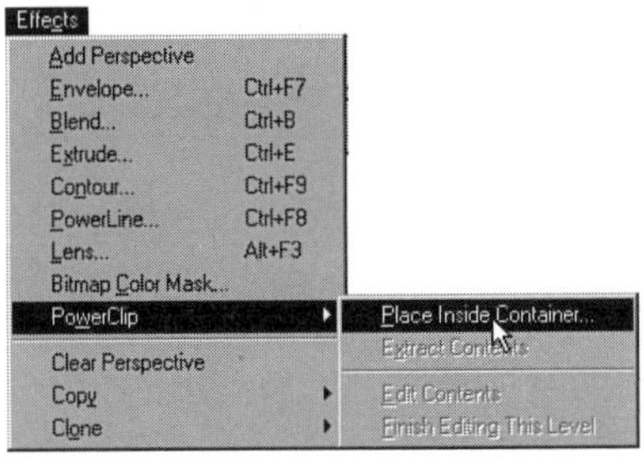

◀ See "Using Full-Color Pattern Fills," p. 249

Fig. 9.44
The Powerclip menu commands are all contained under the Effects menu shown here.

To apply the Powerclip command, follow these steps:

1. Import any bitmapped image onto your page using the File, Import command. If you don't have a bitmap, create a texture fill inside a rectangle.

2. Create another object—either another bitmap or a drawn object—using any of the drawing or shaping tools from the Toolbox.

3. Select the objects you wish to clip (place inside a container) using the Pick tool and choose Effects, Powerclip, Place Inside Container. Your cursor changes to a large, black pointing arrow (see fig. 9.45).

4. Select the object you wish to hold the first object(s) chosen to complete the Powerclip command. Notice that the contents are placed directly in the center of the container object. Notice also that any part of the clipped object that doesn't fit inside the container is not visible beyond the edges of the container. Your clipped object is not likely to be in the exact position you would like it to be. You will need to reposition it.

II

Creating Text & Drawings

Fig. 9.45
The Powerclip command in progress. To select the container to place your contents inside of, click an object with the large black arrow that your cursor has changed to.

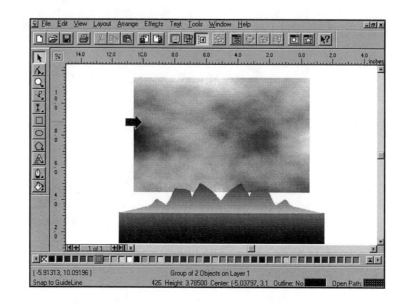

5. Select the menu item Edit Contents from the Powerclip flyout menu again. Your objects separate once again, only this time the contents of the Powerclip can be selected. Notice also that the entire contents are visible.

6. Reposition your clipped object to the exact spot you wish to place it and select Finishing Editing This Level from the Powerclip flyout menu to complete the editing command. Your object contents and the container it is in will once again become a single object on your screen (see fig. 9.46).

7. To take apart the powerclipped objects, select Extract Contents from the Powerclip flyout menu once again. Your objects will be separated.

Tip

There is buried control that significantly affects the operation of the Powerclipping command. It resides in the Tools, Options dialog box (Ctrl+J). The option Automatically Center New Powerclip Contents is available and may be turned off if you wish. It may be wise to leave it on if your Powerclipped images don't already overlap when they are created. If this feature is turned off, any powerclipped objects that do not already overlap your container will disappear completely and may be difficult to locate again.

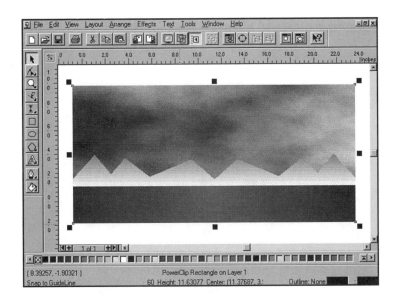

Fig. 9.46
After editing, the excess contents become invisible once again.

One of the more popular effects used with the Powerclipping feature is the application of a bitmap image to Artistic text. To use the Powerclipping effect on an Artistic Text object, follow these steps:

1. Create a string of text with the Artistic Text tool. Try to select a beefy font so the pattern will show through well. At this point, the color of the text won't matter because it will be replaced by the fill associated with the clipped object.

2. Using the Rectangle tool (or any other basic shape tool), create a shape larger than the text itself and fill it with a Texture Fill by selecting the Texture fill dialog box from the Fill flyout in the Toolbox. Or, import a bitmap image larger than the size of the Artistic Text you have created using the File, Import command (see fig. 9.47).

3. Select the texture-filled object with the Pick tool and choose Place Inside Container from the Effects, Powerclip flyout. Your cursor will once again change to a large, black pointing arrow.

4. Using the black arrow cursor, click the text object to complete the Powerclip command. Your texture will automatically be placed, by default, into the center of the text (see fig. 9.48).

5. To reposition the texture that fills your text, choose Effects, Powerclip, Edit Contents, and as before, your two objects will temporarily separate

II

Creating Text & Drawings

with only the texture-filled object available for editing. Reposition it as necessary and, when you're finished, choose Finish Editing This Level to complete the command.

Fig. 9.47
One popular effect is to contain a bitmap fill inside a text string as is about to happen here.

Fig. 9.48
Texture fills or bitmaps may be contained inside Artistic text strings to add punch to your drawings and illustrations.

Tip

You may also "nest" powerclipped objects using the Powerclip command. Nested powerclipped objects are powerclipped objects inside containers that have been placed inside other containers.

Note

Open paths such as lines or curves may also be used as containers for Powerclipping. However, the contents will not be visible until the path has been closed. Likewise, breaking an object that has been used to contain a clipped object will cause the contents to become invisible. The contents are still there, but won't become visible until the path has once again been closed.

Caution

Although nested Powerclips are an interesting feature to work with, the programming code to produce such an object can be extremely complex—even to render your image to the screen. Printing your nested Powerclips is another matter entirely. If at all possible, nesting should be avoided for documents that will eventually be printed to a machine such as a high-resolution imagesetter. One workaround to the problem might be to first export the nested Powerclip to a bitmap format such as BMP, TIF, or PCX. Then, re-import it into your CorelDRAW! document. This step will eliminate any of the clipping path information that makes the image so complex.

Tip

While Powerclipping may be used to place Groups of objects inside containers, interesting effects may also be achieved by Ungrouping the objects of the Powerclip. The result is that each ungrouped item will become its own little Powerclipped object capable of being transformed independently of the other objects.

II

Creating Text & Drawings

From Here...

In this chapter, you were able to take a close look at many of the newer features in CorelDRAW! 6 including the Extrude command, DRAW! 6's new Align and Distribute roll-up, Guides, Rulers, Weld, Trim, Intersection, and Powerclipping. It may be a lot of information to absorb at one sitting; it's always wise to review some of the sections later to refresh your memory. The organizational tools available in CorelDRAW! 6 enable you to organize your documents more accurately than ever before, and the arranging and effects tools covered in this chapter will, at the very least, open the doors of your imagination to all of the various and endless possibilities at your fingertips.

For more information see:

- Chapter 3, "Making CorelDRAW! 6 Easy to Use."
- Chapter 6, "Working with Objects."
- Chapter 7, "Using Fills and Outlines."

Chapter 10

Working with Powerlines and Lenses

While learning how to use the basic drawing tools in CorelDRAW! 6 is quick and easy, Powerlines are much more complex and harder to learn. They require an understanding of not only basic drawing tool functions, but the added complexity of essentially drawing with an effect tool. Powerlines are one of those tools that most users drop like a hot potato after spending their first 15 minutes of exploration in complete bafflement. This chapter will reveal the strengths in using Powerlines and show you how to use the feature as an effect in combination with other effects.

Lens effects have been a long time in coming to vector drawing programs. The capability to apply lens effects to vector and bitmap objects alike is a feature that was first introduced in CorelDRAW! 5, and has had over a year to mature into a well-used feature. This chapter covers uses of Lens effects, with some past years' experience thrown in for good measure.

In this chapter, you learn to

- Create using Powerlines

- Maximize Powerline effects

- Edit Powerlines using the Shape tool

- Dismantle a Powerline object

- Use Transparency Lens effects

- Learn about the new Transparency Lenses and roll-up features

Solving the Mystery of Powerlines

Taking one good look at the controls is enough to make you want to close up the Powerlines roll-up in CorelDRAW! 6. It's a difficult feature to use, even for an expert. If you don't quite grasp the concept, you may just consider them a waste of your effort.

Essentially, *Powerlines* are a type of effect applied to lines, making them behave more like closed-path objects. Powerline effects involve a pre-defined, two-dimensional shape dynamically connected to the shape of a line. A Powerline effect applied to a line will enable the user to apply fill and outline attributes to the effect, while still being able to manipulate the shape of the original line. Changing the shape of the line dynamically affects the shape of the Powerline effect.

In reality, drawing with Powerlines has very little to do with drawing with a pen or brush, but everything to do with applying an effect after drawing a line or curve with the Pencil tool or Freehand Drawing tool. You may even apply a Powerline effect to a simple shape for that matter. But how exactly do Powerlines work and why should you be trying to use them?

Powerline Controls are combined together in a roll-up with Color Bitmap, Blend, Contour, Envelope, and Lens roll-ups in anticipation of each of these features being used in combination with each other. The Powerline roll-up (Ctrl+F8) resides under the Effects menu and is divided up into three tabbed areas (see fig. 10.1): Powerline Styles, Pen Options, and Ink Options.

Fig. 10.1

The Powerline Styles, Pen, and Ink Options tabs.

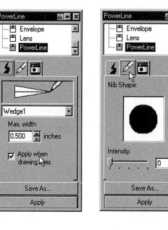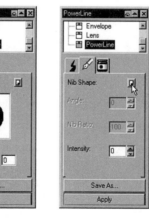

Using the Powerline Roll-Up

All the features and options that control Powerlines are contained in the Powerline roll-up. Styles is the first tab and includes the Wedge, Woodcut, Trumpet, Bullet, Teardrop, Pressure, Nib, Speed, Maximum Width, Custom, and None styles.

Of the styles just listed, the first five each consist of four numbered styles named Wedge 1, Wedge 2, Wedge 3, Wedge 4, Woodcut 1, Woodcut 2, Woodcut 3, and so on. For each of the styles the following applies:

- *Style 1.* Indicates a right-pointing Powerline

- *Style 2.* Indicates a left-pointing Powerline

- *Style 3.* Indicates a double-pointed Powerline pointing outward and away from the midpoint of the line

- *Style 4.* Indicates a double-pointed Powerline pointing inward and toward the midpoint of the line

The remaining styles (Pressure, Nib, Speed, and Maximum Width) are special function Powerline styles designed to work with a pressure-sensitive stylus, which is great if you have one. If you don't happen to have one, there's a keyboard workaround. Custom is the Powerline-assigned style name for a style that has been edited, and None is the option used to remove a Powerline style from a line.

- *Wedge style.* Wedge (see fig. 10.2) is a style involving straight sides that join the narrow endpoint to the wide endpoint of the line.

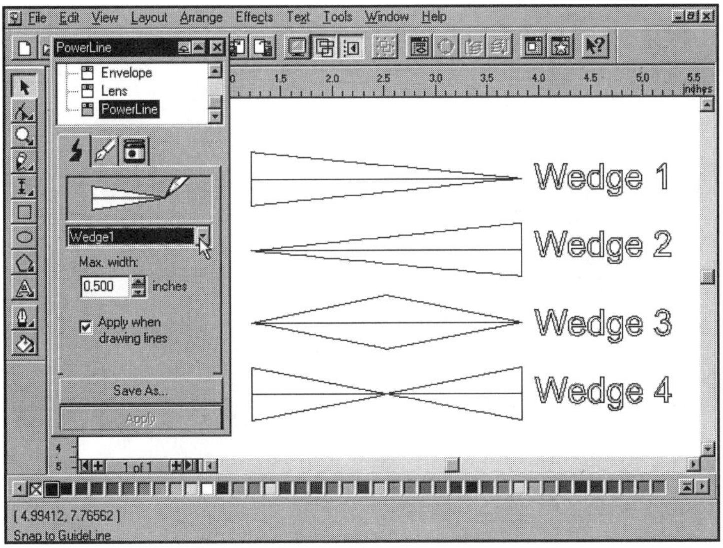

II

Creating Text & Drawings

Fig. 10.2
The Powerline Wedge style.

■ *Woodcut style.* Woodcut (see fig. 10.3) is a style involving smoothly curved sides.

Fig. 10.3
The Powerline
Woodcut style.

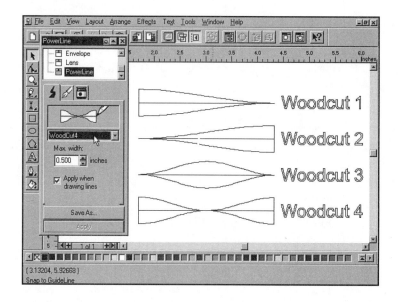

■ *Trumpet style.* Trumpet (see fig. 10.4) is a concave-sided style involving inwardly curved sides.

Fig. 10.4
The Powerline
Trumpet style.

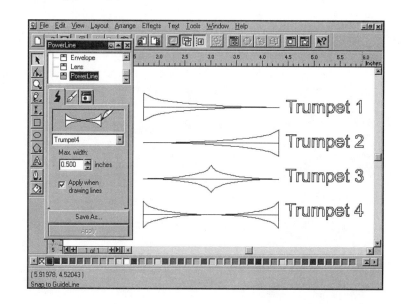

■ *Bullet style.* Bullet (see fig. 10.5) is a convex-sided style involving outwardly curved sides.

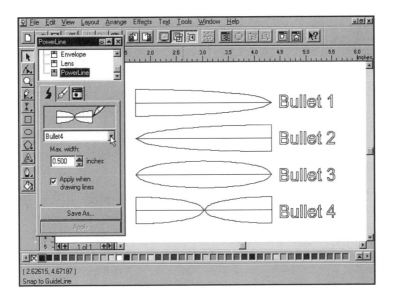

Fig. 10.5
The Powerline Bullet style.

■ *Teardrop style.* Teardrop (see fig. 10.6) is shaped more like the cross-section of an airplane wing than an actual teardrop, and involves smoothly curved sides.

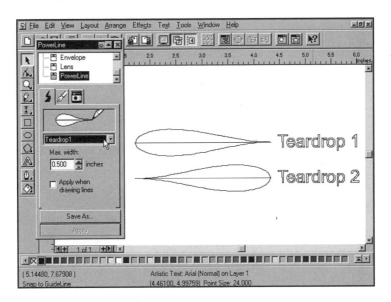

Fig. 10.6
The Powerline Teardrop style.

II

Creating Text & Drawings

■ *Pressure style.* Pressure is geared toward using a pressure-sensitive stylus, but can also be used with the up- and down-arrow keys as a workaround. While drawing a Pressure-style Powerline you may hold down the up-arrow key to increase pressure, or the down-arrow key to decrease pressure. More pressure increases the width of the Powerline effect while less pressure decreases the width (see fig. 10.7).

Fig. 10.7
The Powerline
Pressure style.

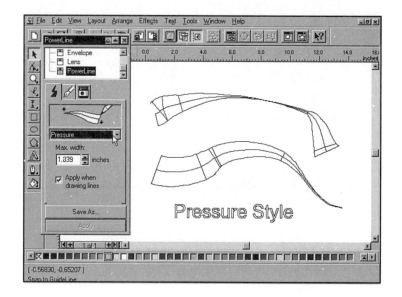

■ *Speed style.* Speed is geared toward using a pressure-sensitive stylus also, and it too may be used with the up and down keys. While drawing a Speed style Powerline, hold down the up-arrow key to increase pressure, or the down-arrow key to decrease pressure. More pressure increases the width of the Powerline effect while less pressure decreases the width (see fig. 10.8). Speed also creates some interesting results when used with the Freehand Drawing tool instead of the regular Pencil tool. Nodes placed close together are considered a slow stylus and allow the Powerline effect to widen, while nodes drawn further apart are considered a faster drawn line and allow the Powerline effect to narrow. Speed Powerlines are also affected by the characteristics of the curve handles of the nodes they contain. The more curvaceous the line, the wider the curved portions will be.

■ *Maximum Width style.* Maximum Width causes the Powerline effect to result in a uniformly straight line having a width set by the measure entered in the Max. Width field on the Powerline roll-up (see fig. 10.9).

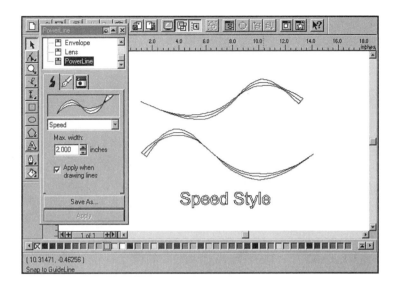

Fig. 10.8
The Powerline
Speed style.

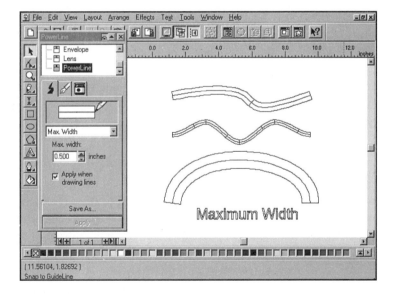

Fig. 10.9
The Powerline
Maximum Width
style.

■ *Nib style.* Nib causes the Powerline effect to create a line that resembles a calligraphy pen or a ribbon effect (see fig. 10.10). The angle of the calligraphy pen tip or ribbon is set by the Nib control in the Pen Options tab of the Powerline roll-up. The Nib style of Powerline may also be better used with the Freehand drawing tool rather than the pen stylus or the Pencil tool and the keyboard pressure controls. The Nib style may also be used with the Bezier tool. The Bezier tool is one of the drawing tools available from the main Toolbox and is used for drawing freehand curves.

Fig. 10.10
The Powerline Nib style created with both the Freehand Drawing tool and the Pencil tool.

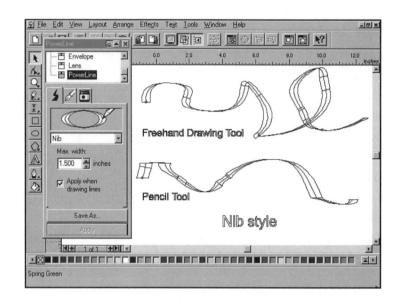

Pen Options

The Pen Options tab of the Powerline roll-up is subdivided into two control areas. The first uses the mouse controls and the second relies on keyboarded entries for building Pen characteristics into the line. The controls feature options for Nib Shape, Nib Intensity (slider), Nib Angle (numeric), Intensity (numeric), and Nib Ratio (numeric).

■ *Nib Shape.* The Nib Shape may be set interactively by placing and dragging your mouse in the Nib Shape preview window. The Nib Shape may be set to narrow or wide, and angled or straight. Both settings may be constrained in increments by holding down the Ctrl key while changing its shape. The Nib Shape setting affects Powerlines in various ways, sometimes with seemingly little consistency. Experimenting with the effects of pre- or post-creation changes will provide the best feedback to learning how this control affects your Powerlines.

■ *Nib Intensity (slider).* The intensity slider is like a volume control for your Powerline effect. When the intensity is set to 100 percent, the volume that the line takes up is at its fullest. Where your Powerline effect is wide it's the widest, where it's narrow it's the narrowest. When set to a lesser intensity, such as 50 percent, it tones down the volume, allowing spacing between your widest and narrowest points to be closer.

■ *Nib Angle (numeric).* The numeric measures for the Nib Angle become available when you select the Small Page icon in the upper-right-hand corner of the Pen Options tab. The Nib Angle may be controlled here independently of the Nib Width. It's measured in rotational degrees whereby a setting of 0 or 180 degrees sets the orientation of the nib to vertical, and a setting of 90 or 270 degrees sets the orientation to horizontal. A popular setting is 45, causing a dramatic calligraphy pen effect.

■ *Intensity (numeric).* The numeric measures for the Intensity setting become available when you select the Small Page icon in the upper-right-hand corner of the Pen Options tab. This feature works the same as the slider control in that it only allows you to keyboard the percentage of volume for your Powerline effect.

■ *Nib Ratio (numeric).* The numeric measures for the Nib Ratio become available when you select the Small Page icon in the upper-right-hand corner of the Pen Options tab. The Nib ratio sets the width-to-height shape of the nib in percentage measures. A setting of 100 percent is a full circular nib, while a setting of 20 percent is a flattened circle.

Ink Options

The Ink Options tab of the Powerline roll-up consists of three slider controls for Pen Leakiness, Ink Spread, and Ink Flow, and a Scale with Image option. Some of these options seem repetitive, and though their effects may seem only marginally different, they can each affect the appearance of your Powerline significantly and uniquely. In the exercise to follow, you'll see how these affect the appearance of your Powerlines.

■ *Pen Leakiness.* Controls the amount of ink that flows from your nib.

■ *Ink Spread.* Ink Spread only becomes available after the Pen Leakiness has been set to a percentage higher than 0. Ink Spread essentially affects the thinnest portions of your Powerline. A higher setting causes a thicker width, most noticeable in the thinnest portions.

■ *Ink Flow.* This option should normally be set to 100 percent so that you may get the full volume of ink flow to your effects. Lowering this setting will restrict significantly the flow of ink to your Powerlines.

■ *Scale with Image.* The Scale with Image option enables you to preserve the proportions of your Powerline effect when resizing.

Applying a Powerline effect to a drawn line or object is easier and takes much less practice than attempting to draw a live Powerline effect in progress, for the simple reason that you don't see the live effect until after the line is completed. This next exercise uses the precision and control of the Bezier tool to create a live Powerline effect. If you need to familiarize yourself with the Freehand Drawing tool first, see Chapter 2, "Managing Your Drawing Files." To begin, follow these steps:

1. Display your Powerline roll-up by selecting Effect, Powerline; or by pressing Ctrl+F8.

2. On your Powerline roll-up, select the Nib style from the pull-down menu and set your Max. Width setting to a setting that will allow you to see easily the effects, such as one inch.

3. Under the first tab, turn on the Apply When Drawing Lines option in order to actively apply the effects as soon as you complete the drawing of each segment of your Powerline.

4. Choose View, Editable Wireframe (or Shift+F9). This will speed up the screen-draw time as you are drawing.

 5. Select the Bezier tool from the Freehand tool flyout in the main Toolbox. A *Flyout* is an expanded menu that reveals additional options, which "flies out" from a menu or toolbar item when selected.

6. With the Bezier tool, click your page to start your line and then add subsequent curve points to your line by clicking and dragging the Bezier tool. Notice the Bezier tool plants a node and alters the curve handles of the line as you drag the mouse along the curve (see figs. 10.11 and 10.12).

7. Complete your Powerline by clicking the Pick tool in the main Toolbox.

8. Before going any further, click the Pen Options tab of the Powerline roll-up and interactively set the Nib Shape by clicking and dragging your mouse in the Nib Shape preview window upwards and to the right (see fig. 10.13).

9. Click the Apply button to have the new Nib Shape take effect. Notice how the new Nib Shape affects the Powerline appearance by changing the Ribbon Shape (see fig. 10.14).

10. Change the Intensity setting to 100 percent (the default is 50), and click the Apply button again. Notice how the width of the wider sections of your Powerline become bloated (see fig. 10.15).

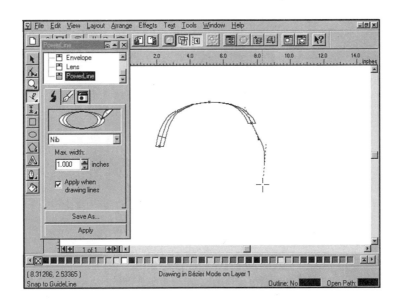

Fig. 10.11
The beginning of a Nib style Powerline drawn using the Bezier tool.

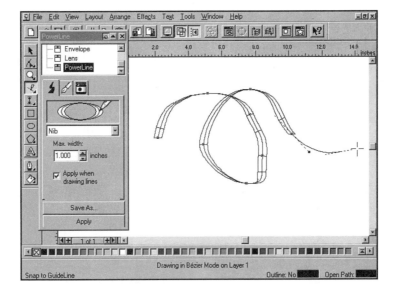

Fig. 10.12
Complete your Nib style Powerline using the Bezier tool.

II

Creating Text & Drawings

Fig. 10.13
Apply the Nib
Shape interac-
tively.

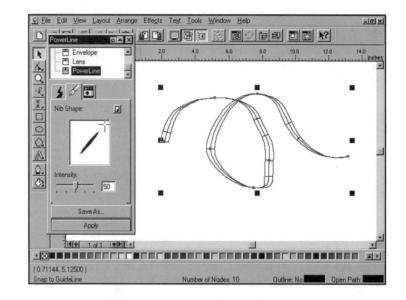

Fig. 10.14
The effect of the
new angled Nib
Shape.

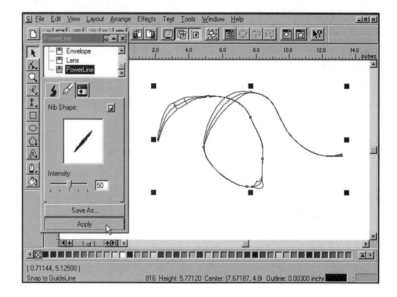

11. Return the Intensity setting to 50 now, click the Ink Options tab in the
Powerline roll-up, and select the Pen Leakiness setting (default is 0) to
50 percent and click the Apply button. Notice the subtle change in the
appearance of the Powerline (see fig. 10.16).

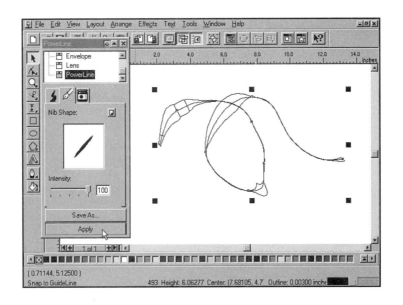

Fig. 10.15
The effect of setting your Intensity to 100 percent.

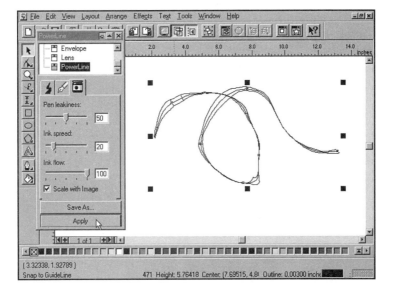

Fig. 10.16
The effect of setting the Pen Leakiness to 50 percent.

II

Creating Text & Drawings

12. While still in the Ink Options tab, set the Ink Flow to 50 percent (the default is 100) and click the Apply button. Notice how severely limited the wider portions of the Powerline become (see fig. 10.17).

Fig. 10.17
The effect of
limiting your Ink
Flow to 50
percent.

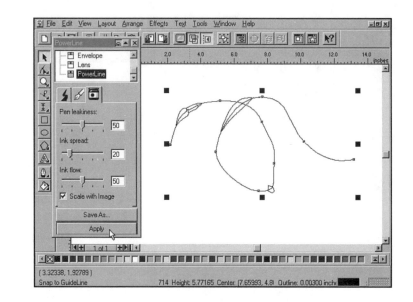

13. Finally, you noticed in step 11 that while the Pen Leakiness setting is
set to more than zero, the Ink Spread option becomes available. But
before you do anything to the Ink Spread option, set the Ink Flow setting back to 100 percent. Now, set the Ink Spread option to 75 percent
(the default is 20) and click the Apply button. Notice that the thinnest
parts of your Powerline became slightly thicker (see fig. 10.18).

Fig. 10.18
The effect of Ink
Spread set to 75
percent.

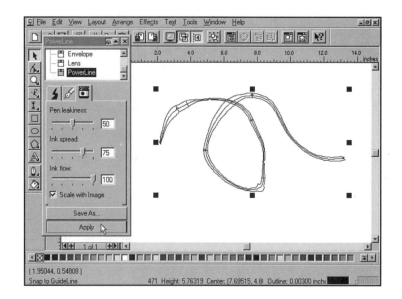

Dissecting Powerlines

While the practice of drawing with the Powerline feature actively applied to the lines and curves that you draw takes just that—practice—applying preset styles to existing lines takes little time and offers a more stable environment for the beginner. To apply one of the preset styles from the Powerline roll-up, follow these steps:

1. Draw a line or curve on your page and, if it isn't displaying already, choose Effects, Powerline roll-up (or press Ctrl+F8).

2. Making sure that your line or curve is selected, choose the very first style in the pull-down menu, Wedge 1, set the Max. Width to a large setting such as 2 inches, and click the Apply button. The Powerline style takes effect. Notice that the Powerline remembers which end of your line or curve was drawn as the first point and builds the Powerline accordingly.

3. With the newly created Powerline still selected, change the Max. Width to 4 inches and click the Apply button. Notice how the shape is affected. Change it back to 2 inches and click the Apply button or select Edit, Undo (or Ctrl+Z).

4. If your line isn't a curve already, change it to one by selecting the Shape tool, selecting the line, double-clicking one of the end nodes to invoke the Node Edit roll-up, and clicking the To Curve button. Notice at this point that the Node Edit roll-up has a new button labeled Edit Width. You will be using that button later in this chapter to edit the Powerline shape.

5. Grab onto one of the end nodes using your Shape tool, and drag it away from its current position (see fig. 10.19). Notice how the line changes shape and as soon as your mouse button is released, the Powerline shape is updated. This is the dynamic link action of the Powerline effect.

6. Now, with the Powerline still selected, choose Arrange, Separate; or use the right mouse button menu (see fig. 10.20). To do this using the right mouse button, click directly on the Powerline effect itself rather than the line it is applied to, making the Separate command active.

Fig. 10.19
Change the curve of a line by using the Shape tool to apply the Wedge 1 style.

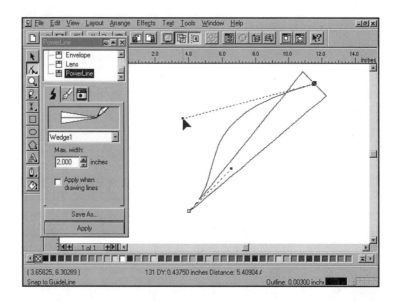

Fig. 10.20
Taking apart a Powerline using the Separate and Ungroup commands.

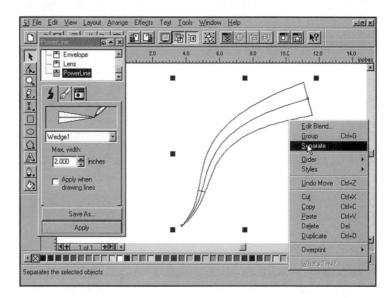

7. Move the original curve away from the Powerline remains, and choose Arrange, Ungroup (or Ctrl+U) or use the right mouse button menu (see fig. 10.21).

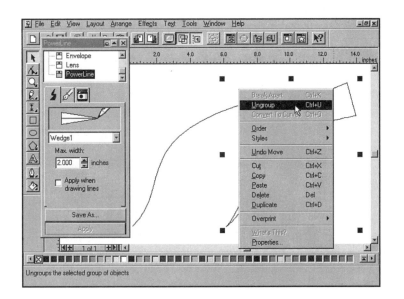

Fig. 10.21
Ungrouping the dynamically linked parts of a Powerline.

8. Move the individual parts away from each other and you will notice that the guts of the Powerline consist of outline objects and fill sections that had originally been dynamically linked to each other. This is how the Powerline effect is constructed. Applying a fill shade or color to a Powerline only affects the fill portion, while applying an outline color only affects the outline portions (see fig. 10.22).

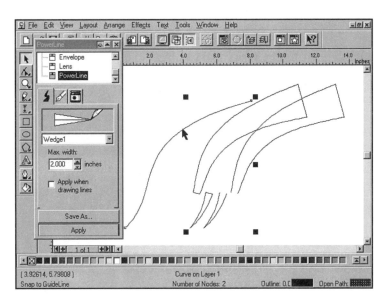

Fig. 10.22
The remains of a dismantled Powerline.

After a Powerline has been created, it will behave just as any other vector or drawn object would. Transformations, effects, Pen Outlines, Fills, and so on, may be applied to the Powerline object as they would normally.

Creating a Simple Powerline Drawing

Now, what about the practical uses of Powerlines? They're a bit more intensive to work with than regular shapes are, so what are the advantages? That's one you'll have to decide for yourself—everybody likes and dislikes Powerlines for different reasons. So let's take a practical look at how to apply them in real life. Powerlines work best in the production of things like stylized drawings, design elements that represent flowing objects such as wind, water, smoke, or anything that could be interpreted as abstract or flowing.

Editing Powerlines

As you have seen already, you may edit the Powerlines by updating styles and options already contained in the Powerline roll-up, and you may also alter the shapes of lines and curves using the Shape tool and the Node Editor. But Powerlines have an editing function all their own in CorelDRAW! 6. By using this editing function you are able to alter not just the shape of the native curve that the Powerline is applied to, but the actual Powerline shape itself.

This editing function works with any of the Powerline styles available in the Powerline roll-up. The way it works is that while the Powerline is selected, you can use the Shape tool to widen or narrow the end points of the Powerline to measures between their maximum width and their minimum width (which is no width). You may also add your own new points along the Powerline that remain hidden and invisible after the editing is completed.

To edit a Powerline, follow these steps:

1. Create a simple shape and apply a Powerline style to it with a maximum width of 1 inch. For this example a circle was converted into a curve by using the Node Editor to unlink a small portion of the circle, and the stray piece was deleted using the Break Apart command (or Ctrl+K).

2. Apply the Powerline style by selecting the Apply button, leave the Powerline object selected, and choose the Shape tool from the main Toolbox.

3. Display the Node Edit roll-up by choosing it from the roll-up toolbar, or by double-clicking either end of the Powerline shape (see fig. 10.23).

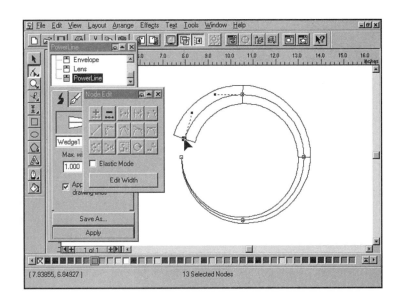

Fig. 10.23
Preparing to edit a
Powerline using
the Shape tool.

4. Select one of the end points of the Powerline by clicking it once with
   the Shape tool. Notice that a new button appears at the bottom of the
   Node Edit roll-up labeled Edit Width.

5. Click the Edit Width button on the Node Edit roll-up and watch as the
   Node Editor completely changes interface and an entirely new set of
   buttons appears (see fig. 10.24). These buttons are new to version 6.
   Notice also that the beginning and endpoints on the Powerline show
   blue axis lines and each of the axis lines contains two control markers
   that control the width of one or both sides of the Powerline.

6. Click one of the markers of an axis and drag it along the axis either
   outward or inward. Notice that both sides of the Powerline Shape are
   altered to match the change.

7. Using the Shape tool, click an empty part of the Powerline and click the
   Node Edit roll-up button labeled with the plus sign to add a marker.
   Notice that another marker appears, featuring a blue axis line and two
   control markers.

8. Click one of the markers on the axis and slide it outward and away
   from the center of the Powerline Shape. Notice that four more of the
   buttons on the Node Edit roll-up have become active. One contains a
   minus sign to delete a marker. The bottom row of buttons features controls to change the behavior of the Powerline outlines (as opposed to
   the actual line the Powerline effect is applied to).

Fig. 10.24
Transforming the
Node Edit roll-up
into the Powerline
editor.

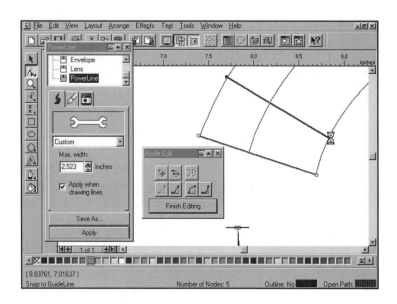

9. Click one of the control markers controlling a node edit marker again, and select Delete on your keyboard. You have just deleted one side of the marker. The remaining marker may be manipulated to change only one side of the Powerline Shape (see fig. 10.25).

Fig. 10.25
By deleting
one half of the
Powerline control
marker you are
able to make
adjustments to
only one side of
the Powerline
Shape without
altering the
adjacent side.

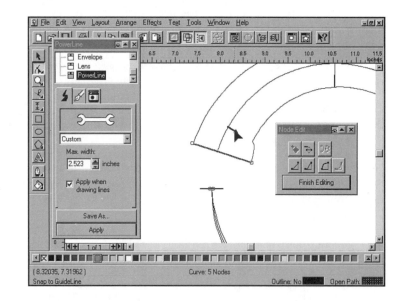

10. To complete the editing of your Powerline Shape click the Finish Editing button at the bottom of the Node Edit roll-up. By adding, deleting, and changing the curve characteristics of Powerline Shapes using the Shape tool you are able to significantly alter its shape (see fig. 10.26).

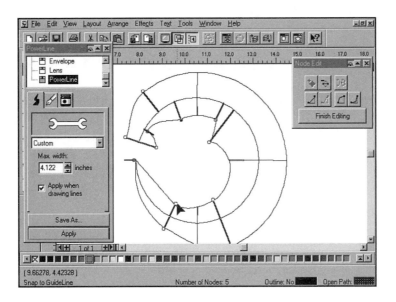

Fig. 10.26
You are able to significantly alter a Powerline Shape using the editing tools. The original line or curve that the Powerline effect is applied to will remain unchanged.

The buttons on the Powerline Node Edit roll-up control commands for manipulating the markers and control points on a Powerline Shape include:

- *Add Marker.* Adds a marker containing two control points to the Powerline Shape.

- *Delete Marker.* Deletes the entire selected marker from the Powerline Shape.

- *Auto-Reduce.* Reduces the number of markers in a Powerline Shape without altering the Shape of the Powerline.

- *Normal Curve.* Changes an outline curve of a Powerline to its normal state.

- *Sine Curve.* Causes an outline curve to take on an S shape.

- *Smoothed Curve.* Changes an outline to a smoothed curve.

- *Cusped Curve.* Allows an outline curve to change direction abruptly.

II

Creating Text & Drawings

> **Tip**
>
> While editing a Powerline, when working with control markers to widen or narrow a Powerline Shape, hold down the Shift key while dragging a marker to change only the width of one side of the Powerline Shape at a time.

> **Tip**
>
> While editing a Powerline, when working with control markers to widen or narrow a Powerline Shape, hold down the Ctrl key while dragging a marker to change all of the markers on one side of the Powerline Shape at the same time. Once one of the markers is moved while holding down the Ctrl key, the remaining markers are updated proportionately.

Saving Custom Powerlines

If you have created a Powerline recipe that you would like to save for later use, or to apply to other objects or curves, the Save As button at the bottom of the Powerline roll-up enables you to do this. Click the Powerline Shape that you would like to save and click the Save As button. A dialog box will appear asking you to name your new style (see fig. 10.27).

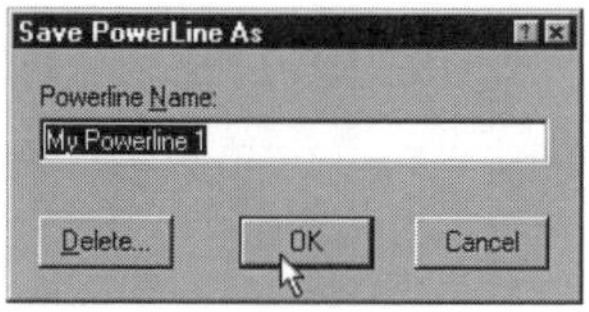

Fig. 10.27
You may create your own Powerline styles to apply by selecting the Save As button at the bottom of the Powerline roll-up. Your new style will then be available in the roll-up pull-down menu.

Applying Powerlines to Objects

Because all objects (except bitmap objects) are made up of lines and curves, a Powerline effect may be applied to any type of object including text, rectangles, ellipses, polygons, spirals, and graph paper.

Secrets of Lens Effects

For years, there have been effects you've likely seen in print advertising and so on that, up until now, have only been available by hiring expert craftsmen who work magic with film or pre-press specialists working with high-end computer systems. They would manually create effects such as headlines in ghosted, transparent-white dropped out of a beautiful photograph in a magazine ad, or a hand-drawn illustration melded with a photographic-quality image.

The tools have been slowly creeping into the digital world over the past decade or so, in the form of photo-manipulating programs such as Adobe PhotoShop, Aldus PhotoStyler, and of course Corel PHOTO-PAINT.

Now, the tools to produce many of the effects you thought were too high-tech for you are available in CorelDRAW! 6 through the use of Lens effects. Lens effects may be applied to any object created in CorelDRAW! and may be applied to any image that you can work with in CorelDRAW!, including imported images such as bitmaps and encapsulated PostScript images. The controls for these Lens effects are accessed through the Lens roll-up (or Alt+F3), which can be found under the Effects menu (see fig. 10.28).

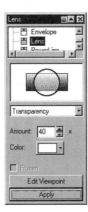

II

Creating Text & Drawings

When a Lens effect is applied to an object while the object is overlapping another object, Draw's special color-filtering method allows the Lens effect to show through in the first object. Lens effects work on an object's fill as well as its outline.

The Lens roll-up, while featuring various changing controls, depending on the Lens selected, also features an Apply button, and an Edit Viewpoint button. The Viewpoint of a Lens may be set regardless of the position of the object the Lens is being applied to. The Viewpoint also works in combination with the Frozen option, which enables you to freeze the viewpoint in one spot while allowing the Lens object to be moved.

Transparency

The Transparency Lens (see fig. 10.29) has the effect of allowing objects behind the transparent object to show through. The illusion is similar to looking through a fogged window, through which you are able to make out the objects in the distance even though they appear muted to a certain extent. This effect may be used quite effectively in layouts where a headline or information box is placed on top of a photograph while still allowing images in the photo to show through. Another obvious application for the transparency Lens would be incorporating objects that are transparent in nature into a drawing or illustration without having to create a series of new objects to manually simulate the incorporated objects.

Fig. 10.29
The Transparency Lens creates the effect of being able to see the images through the transparent object, and is perhaps the most commonly used Lens type.

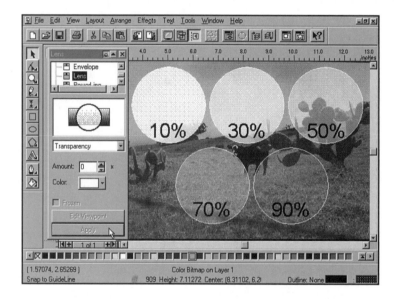

The Transparency Lens effect features a control to set various levels of transparency within a range between 0 and 100 percent. A color flyout also enables you to set the color tint of the transparent object, causing the effect of looking through color-tinted, but foggy, glass.

Magnify

The Magnify Lens (see fig. 10.30) creates the illusion of viewing objects through a magnifying glass, or even a microscope, depending on your magnification setting. The magnify setting may be set between a range of 0.1 to 1000 times an object's actual size. A setting below zero actually has the reverse effect by making objects behind the Lens appear farther away. If you had originally set your Lens object with a color fill, the Magnify Lens effect ignores this color and it will have no effect on the magnified objects seen through it.

Fig. 10.30
The Magnify Lens effect causes all objects seen through it to become enlarged.

II

Creating Text & Drawings

Brighten

The Brighten Lens (see fig. 10.31) has the effect of making objects behind an object with this Lens applied appear brighter. Drawn objects with outlines and fill colors or patterns tend to become uniformly lighter in color. Brighten controls may be set within a range of -100 to 100 times, making this Lens not only a Brighten Lens but also a "darken" Lens. When using a setting below zero, objects behind this Lens effect appear to have a degree of black added to them. If you had originally set your Lens object with a color fill, the Brighten (or darken) effect ignores this color, and it will have no effect.

Fig. 10.31
The Brighten Lens effect automatically changes the brightness setting of objects seen through it.

Invert

Using the Invert (see fig. 10.32) Lens causes objects viewed through it to alter color according to their complimentary RGB colors. If you have ever had the opportunity to view how color negative film appears in comparison to the actual positive image print made from the film, you will have some idea of how the colors will change. Invert contains no other options than inverting the colors of the objects seen through it. If you had originally set your Invert Lens object with a color fill, this color is ignored and it has no effect on the colors of the objects seen through it.

Fig. 10.32
The Invert Lens effect.

Color Limit

Applying a Color Limit Lens effect (see fig. 10.33) to an object has the effect of making it into a camera lens filter. The color of the Color Limit Lens object has a significant effect on the appearance of the colors of objects viewed through it. The Color Limit Lens object works to reduce all colors seen through it, except its assigned color and black, regardless of whether the objects seen are vector or bitmap format. The Color Limit Lens object may be set using the color flyout and the filtering amount may set in the amount control.

Color Limit is a much more difficult Lens effect to contend with than others, but with experimentation, the concept becomes obvious. For example, if the Color Limit lens object has a color of blue, then white color will be tinted blue, and blue and black colored objects will appear relatively unchanged, but all other colors will be muted out according to the Color Limit amount set. The amount set may be within a range of zero and 100, zero being no filtering and 100 filtering out all colors except the color set in the color fill flyout. Color Limit works equally well on vector and bitmap objects.

Fig. 10.33
The Color Limit Lens effect.

Color Add

The Color Add Lens (see fig. 10.34) works on the principle of additive color meaning that when all the colors of the spectrum are combined together, the result is white light. The reverse is also true, when all the colors are removed, the result is no light, or blackness. This is actually the exact opposite of the way printing normally works, and for that reason, most people are confused a little when trying to grasp the function of the Color Add Lens effect.

When adding the color assigned to your Lens object with the color already assigned to the object you are viewing through the Color Add Lens, the result will be a combination of those colors, which usually means a lighter shade. The color of the Color Add Lens may be set by using the color flyout, and the amount of color to be added is set in the Amount field in a range between 0 and 100. The Color Add Lens effect works equally well on vector and bitmap objects.

Fig. 10.34
The Color Add Lens effect.

Tinted Grayscale

The Tinted Grayscale Lens (see fig. 10.35) has the effect of changing the objects viewed through it to strictly a two-tone color image. Grayscale doesn't necessarily mean black and white but it does mean at least white and one other color. The color used may be set by using the color flyout menu. Viewing objects through this Lens will cause the objects to change to your assigned color plus white. The colors you use for the Tinted Grayscale will be determined in large part by the subject matter. For example, viewing a scanned image of people's faces would look terrible in blue or green, but using a brown or sepia color will give the image a rustic appearance. This is definitely one of the more idea-inspiring lenses in the CorelDRAW! 6 collection. Tinted Grayscale Lens effect works equally well on vector and bitmap objects.

Fig. 10.35
The Tinted
Grayscale Lens
effect.

Heat Map

Quite possibly an idea linked to the '60s, the Heat Map Lens (see fig. 10.36) can have the effect of completely altering the color of the objects seen through them, and creates quite dramatic results when applied over bitmap images. The lone control in the Heat Map Lens is a setting for Palette Rotation that may be set to a range between 0 and 100. Changing the Heat Map palette rotation value appears at first to make no sense at all. Even the slightest change in the palette rotation will yield a complete color change of the objects seen through it. But there is actually some sense to it if you imagine a round color wheel with three color areas blended together representing red, green, and blue—the colors that your monitor renders and the colors that the Heat Map filter are based on. As the palette is rotated, so are the colors.

If that slightly vague definition doesn't help much, imagine the Heat Map palette rotation settings divided up into four basic ranges. The first range between 0 and 25 causes greens to shift to purple, reds to shift to blue, and blues to shift to yellow. The second palette rotation range between 25 and 50 causes reds to shift to green, and greens to shift to yellow. The third, between 50 and 70 causes blues to shift to purple, greens to shift to yellow, and darkgreens to shift to blue. And the final range between 75 and 100 causes blues to shift to red, and greens and reds to shift to blue. The accuracy of this color shift will depend on how near the middle of the range you set the palette rotation to, and may in some small way be affected by how well your monitor renders color. Heat Map also works equally well on vector and bitmap objects.

Fig. 10.36

The Heat Map
Lens effect

Custom Color Heat Map

New to the CorelDRAW! 6 Lens effect collection is Custom Color Heat Map (see fig. 10.37) which has a striking similarity to the way Heat Map works. With this Lens though, you have full control over how the colors shift. The controls for Custom Color Map feature a pull-down menu including selections for Direct Palette, Forward Rainbow, or Reverse Rainbow. There are also two color flyouts for assigning the color shifts. The little arrow button between the color flyouts allows you to swap the assigned colors back and forth between selections.

The three color shift options are similar in effect to color changes traveling around or through a color wheel. The Direct palette effect causes direct color shift. In other words, the colors change from one to the other without including any other part of the color spectrum. For example, if one of the color selections was purple and the other green, purple colors would change to green and green colors would change to purple.

The Forward Rainbow option allows colors to shift clockwise around the color wheel and the Reverse Rainbow does the same, only in a counterclockwise direction. Custom Color Map works equally well on vector and bitmap objects.

Fig. 10.37
The Custom Color
Lens effect.

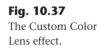

Wireframe

The Wireframe Lens effect consists of only two controls for setting outline
color and fill color by way of color flyouts. As its name suggests, the
Wireframe Lens effect (see fig. 10.38) causes the objects seen through it to
appear identical in color scheme, by changing the outline and fill colors of
objects seen throughout the Lens to the colors specified in the roll-up. For
example, if you were to set the fill color to green and the outline color to red,
all objects seen through this Lens would appear green with red outline. The
Wireframe Lens effect is only effective on drawn vector shapes and has no
effect on bitmap images.

Fisheye

Also new for CorelDRAW! 6, the Fisheye Lens is an intriguing effect (see
fig. 10.39) which works on both bitmap and vector objects. It has the effect
of causing objects viewed through it to look as if they were being viewed
through a 16 millimeter camera lens, making the object's lines and curves
bend outward away from the center or inward toward the center. The only
control on the Fisheye Lens effect is the Amount setting, which may be set to
a range between -1000 and 1000. When the amount is set to a number less
than zero, objects seen through the Lens appear to bend inward toward the
center. When the amount is set to a number greater than zero, objects seen
through the Lens appear to bend outward and away from the center of the
Lens. Any color fills assigned to objects that have the Fisheye Lens effect are
ignored until the effect is removed.

II

Creating Text & Drawings

Fig. 10.38
The Wireframe
Lens effect.

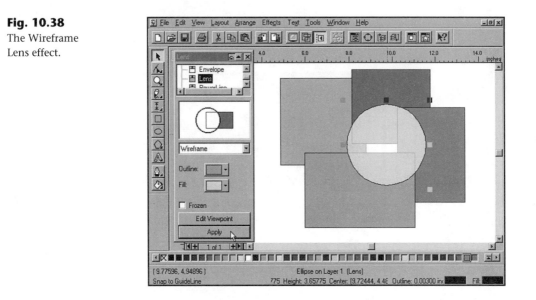

Fig. 10.39
The Fisheye Lens
effect.

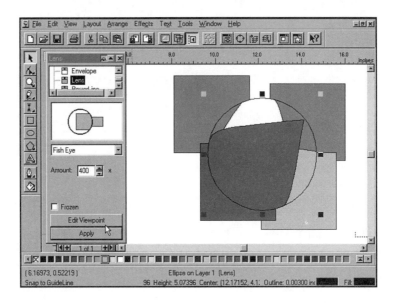

Canceling the Lens Effect

To remove a Lens effect from an object, select None, which is the last option
from the pull-down menu in the Lens roll-up. If you had assigned any color
fills to your object which were ignored during the Lens effect, the fill color
will be returned to the object.

From Here...

Powerlines and Lenses are interesting and creative features but are seldom fully explored by first-time CorelDRAW! users. While Powerlines are a difficult and sometimes cumbersome effect to work with, mastering this effect enables you to produce striking effects not readily possible with conventional drawing tools. Lens effects are also a feature worth exploring for their creativity value, especially beyond the Transparency Lens effect. The added capability of choosing an editable Viewpoint increases the practical applications of Lenses. While this chapter explores the operation of these tools, continue onto these related topics:

- See Chapter 5, "Working with Text," to learn more about Pen controls.

- See Chapter 6, "Working with Objects," to learn how to edit simple objects.

- See Chapter 11, "Working with Digital Images," to understand bitmaps.

- See Chapter 12, "Working with Presets," to learn more about Preset effects.

- See Chapter 13, "Using Color, Wizards, and Applying Color Masks," to learn how to use the Bitmap Color Mask roll-up.

II

Creating Text & Drawings

Chapter 11

Working with Digital Images

There are three basic ways to communicate in print using text, graphics, and photographs. Even though the full CorelDRAW! 6 suite of applications includes Corel PHOTO-PAINT 6 for working with and manipulating digital images, you will no doubt want to reap the benefits of incorporating digital images in your print communication. And, with the increased demand for CorelDRAW! 6 to more fully support all the digital needs of the electronic artist, DRAW! now includes several functions and image-control features to deal with bitmaps.

The ability to work with digital images opens up many doors and allows much more creativity and flexibility in your drawings and electronic layouts. More than ever before, types and variations of bitmaps may be imported into CorelDRAW! 6. There are also more features—some of them buried in the interface—that are available for you to use.

This chapter deals with the tools, features, and options available for working with digital images in CorelDRAW! 6. It will be of interest to anyone who wishes to maximize the use of these powerful features.

In this chapter, you learn to

- Recognize bitmap formats
- Understand resolution and memory space considerations
- Understand the purpose and types of image headers
- Work with cropping tools
- Use CorelDRAW! 6's Wrap Paragraph Text feature
- Use CorelDRAW! 6's AutoTrace features

Understanding Bitmaps

Digital images operate on a completely different level than text or vector objects. Knowing the medium you are working with is critical to using bitmaps effectively and maximizing their use. No matter what the source of your digital images, the various characteristics of bitmaps involve factors such as dimension or physical size, resolution, type of color, and number of colors.

In most cases these factors will affect other more serious issues such as file size or the number of bytes that your image occupies on your system. The size of an image will be of great concern and likely one of the more serious considerations in deciding whether to even use a digital image, or take a more traditional route to reproducing a photograph such as for print repro-duction. There are also various types of bitmap images that can make the issue very confusing for the newcomer to the digital world.

Defining Bitmap Formats

The most common bitmap format you'll likely run into in the digital image realm is the Windows Bitmap (BMP) format. This format is likely the safest and most versatile of all of the formats out there. Tagged Image Format (TIF) is another more common bitmap format. The PC platform has some of its own special formats as well, such as the PC Paintbrush format known as PCX. But, whether your bitmap format is native to the PC platform or coming from a different platform such as Apple's Macintosh's, you can relax, know-ing that CorelDRAW! 6 is capable of importing just about all formats that currently exist. The following table is a reference of all the bitmap formats available for import into DRAW!.

Table 11.1 CorelDRAW! 6 Compatible Bitmap Formats	
Bitmap Type	**Bitmap File Extension**
Adobe PhotoShop	PSD
CALS compressed bitmap	CAL
CompuServe bitmap	GIF
Computer graphics metafile	CGM
GEM paint file	IMG
JPEG bitmap	JPG, JFF, JFT
Kodak PhotoCD bitmap	PCD

Bitmap Type	Bitmap File Extension
MACPaint bitmap	MAC
OS/2 bitmap	BMP
PC Paintbrush bitmap	PCX
Scitex CT bitmap	SCT, CT
Targa bitmap	TGA
TIFF bitmap	TIF
Wavelet Compressed bitmap	WVL
Windows bitmap	BMP
Windows bitmap	DIB/RLE
Corel PHOTO-PAINT	CPT
WordPerfect graphic bitmap	WPG

Bitmap Sizes

The size of a bitmap can refer to either the physical size or dimensions of the actual image, or the file size. The dimensions of a bitmap image may be measured using any number of different unit types including the most common, pixels. *Pixels* are like the native bits of a digital image. Pixels themselves are usually measured by parts per inch (PPI) or bits per inch, which describes how many parts they have been divided into, while a pixel can also be used to measure the actual size of the image.

All digital images are divided into pixel grids or checkerboards with each individual square representing a color or shade. When your computer sees a digital image it looks at each bit of the checkerboard and determines a number of things: first, how big the checkerboard actually is, followed by how big and which type each of the checkers is.

In the case of monotone—strictly black and white—bitmaps, the checkers only contain information that defines them as ON or OFF (see fig. 11.1). A checker or pixel that is ON is assigned a value of 1, while a pixel that is OFF is assigned a value of 0. An ON value turns the pixel on and makes it black, while an OFF value makes it white.

Fig. 11.1
An extremely
close-up view of a
monotone bitmap
imported into
CorelDRAW! 6.

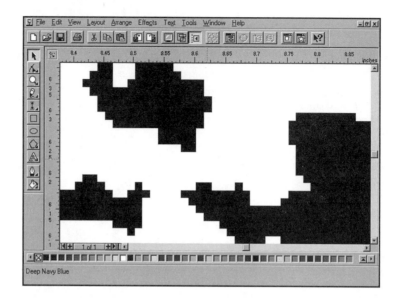

For grayscale images, the pixels are assigned a value in a range between shading black and white depending on the number of divisions the grayscale image has been divided into (see figs. 11.2 and 11.3). A grayscale image can have a range of grayscale from 0 to 16, or 0 to 256 levels. The more levels of gray, the larger the file size.

Fig. 11.2
Close-up view of a
16-level grayscale
image imported
into DRAW!
showing how the
grayscale checker-
board is formed by
the gray pixels.

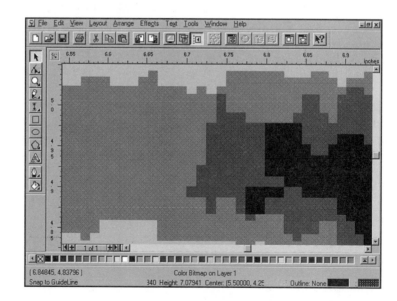

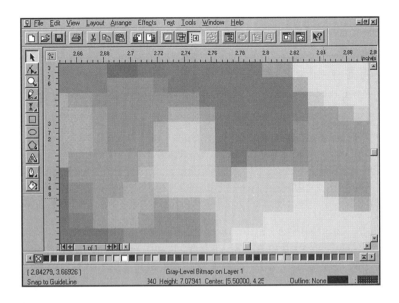

Fig. 11.3
Close-up view of a 256-level grayscale image. Notice the additional colors available with the additional grayscale levels.

A RGB-color image works a bit differently in that each of the pixels is assigned a combination of values of red, green, and blue (see fig. 11.4). Each pixel may have a value from 0 to 16, or 0 to 255 depending on the detail of color that was saved into the file. Once again, the more levels of color, the larger the file. A color image may also be saved as CMYK color, or cyan, magenta, yellow, and black, the four primary colors needed to produce a color photo on a printing press. Color CMYK images contain about 25 percent more information than RGB because of the extra level of digital information.

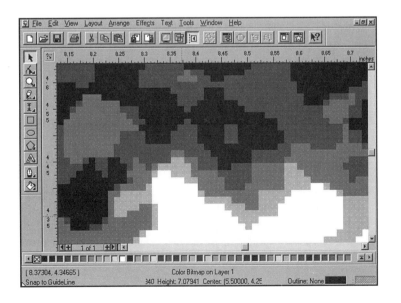

Fig. 11.4
Believe it or not, this is actually a RGB, 256-color digital image imported into DRAW!, viewed extremely close-up, and showing how the color checkerboard is formed by the various pixels.

II

Creating Text & Drawings

Color and Grayscale Types

As mentioned in the previous section, digital images may be imported into CorelDRAW! as monotone (black and white), grayscale, or color. The larger the number of colors in an image, the larger the file size will be, and the longer it will take to perform operations such as importing, saving, and printing.

Most image manipulation programs such as Corel PHOTO-PAINT, and Adobe PhotoShop offer various formats to save digital images including 1-bit black and white, 8-bit grayscale, 16-bit 256-color grayscale, 8-bit color, and 24-bit color having 16.7 million possible colors. A bit is a single unit of computer data.

At best, this bit theory is a little confusing to most beginners. You'll often hear terms thrown around that seem to make no sense, the primary term being "grayscale color." Many people consider gray, like black, to not be a color at all, but rather a lack of color. Some experts in the field interchange the terms "levels of grayscale" with "grayscale colors" to avoid using the word "color" when talking about grays. Remember that no matter how you think of colors, your computer sees black, white, and grays as colors.

To remedy some of the confusion, keep it simple for yourself and use these rules of thumb:

- 1-bit images contain only black or white.

- 2-bit images contain black, white, and two grayscale colors.

- 8-bit images contain black, white, and 256 levels of gray.

- 24-bit images contain black, white, and 16 million colors of gray.

Resolution

Another term easily misunderstood is *resolution*. Digital image resolution is measured in dots per inch (DPI). When trying to understand the resolution of an image, think of the checkerboard concept again. Imagine you were trying to draw a picture by either filling in or leaving blank the squares on a real 64-square checkerboard. You have eight squares across and eight deep to work with. Unless your image is extremely simple (or a picture of some squares) your picture is going to be pretty jaggy looking. If you had more squares to work with, it would probably be much easier to define more detail but it would likely take much longer to draw. That's exactly how resolution works. The more checkerboard squares to work with, the more detail will show through in your final picture, and the larger your file will be.

Measuring the DPI of a digital image is the same as measuring how many checkerboard squares there are per inch. There are some standards to keep in mind as well. A DPI measure of 72 means that the digital image is capable of rendering 72 squares of color per inch. One inch, therefore, will contain 5,184 differently colored dots. If you are working with digital images that are eventually destined for printing on a printing press, your resolution will need to be much higher than that.

Digital image resolution has some other considerations as well, including output resolution. Your screen or monitor will optimally render detail of a 72 DPI because that is nearly the maximum that the screen will reproduce accurately. Your digital images may, however, be able to print much higher than 72 DPI if they were sampled at a higher resolution.

If your digital image is being printed to a typical laser printer, the output will likely be 300 DPI, but don't get the two confused as the same. Just because your printer is capable of printing 300 DPI doesn't mean that it will be able to print a 300 DPI digital image properly. The difference is printer resolution versus image resolution. In order for a digital image to be properly reproduced on a typical printer it first needs to be converted to a series of dot patterns much like the dot patterns you see in your typical newspaper photographs. The dots of these photos are aligned in rows and vary in size to simulate photographic shadows and highlights. Large dots being the shadow areas and small dots being the highlights. These are called *digital halftones*.

The dots of printed photographs are lined up in rows, and the space between those dots is called the line screen. The measure of units for a line screen is lines per inch (LPI). A newspaper photo typically uses a line screen of 65 or 85 LPI while a 300 DPI laser printer may only be capable of printing a line screen of 42 LPI maximum. Those dots are made larger or smaller by being built from dots of resolution. The smaller dots are translated from the resolution of the digital image to the resolution of the printer. Typically, you will need twice the digital image resolution to make a reasonable-quality digital halftone from an imagesetter.

Understanding Image Headers

Image headers are the images you see when you view small representations of your digital images in preview windows such as the one in the Import dialog box (see fig. 11.5). The Import dialog box may be accessed from the File menu. Below the preview window there is also a Preview option to turn the feature ON or OFF. While the preview is being built a progress meter will indicate the progress in the preview window.

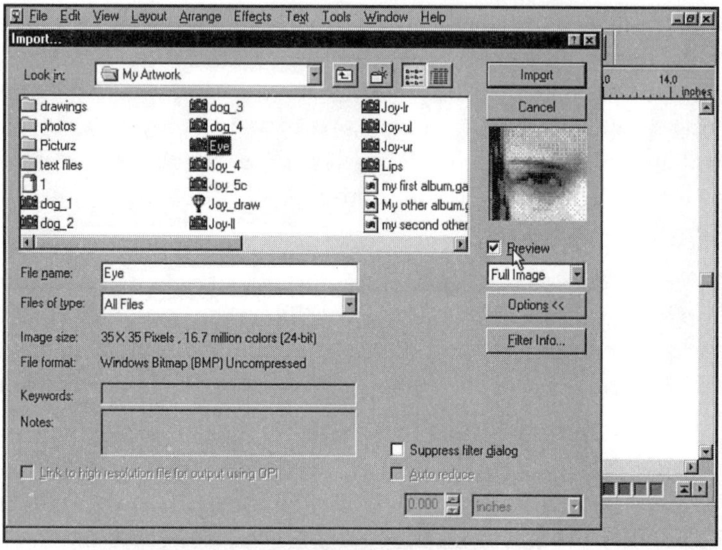

Fig. 11.5
In the upper-right
of the Import
dialog box, the
preview window
displays the
header for the
currently selected
digital image.

Headers are mini snapshots of the images they represent, and are typically stored in the beginning of the file coding that describes the image—hence the name "header." Headers may take a number of formats including 1-bit, 2-bit, 8-bit, color, grayscale, monotone, nonexistent, or any combination of those. The more detailed the header of your image is, the more memory space it will add to your file size. Ideally, the header on the image you are working with will be as detailed as possible and in full color if applicable. Unfortunately, high-resolution headers can add as much as 25 percent of the file size making them a costly little luxury. Time wasted each time the header is read, or each time the file is imported, saved, or printed can add up over the length of a project.

When you import a file into CorelDRAW! 6, the program interrogates the file for header information. If a header exists, it's immediately placed into the preview window. If it doesn't contain a header, DRAW! will manufacture one based on the information contained in the digital image bitmap file. DRAW! has the capability of reading most file types—especially bitmap—and producing some degree of preview representation. The important thing to remember about headers is that you don't always need them. If you're certain you have the right file name, your header information is simply wasted. If you are in a situation where having a small file size is critical, saving your files without the header is always an option. The added benefit of using Windows 95 enables you to use long file names, up to 255 characters. Keep in mind that if your file is moved to a previous Windows platform, these extra characters will be eliminated.

Tip

A good rule of thumb is not to oversample your images destined for importing into your CorelDRAW! 6 file. Follow the "twice the line screen" rule to avoid wasting precious time. For example, if you are producing a layout destined for the print quality of a magazine, you would output at a line screen of 150 LPI. Therefore, the measure of resolution you need for your digital images to be sampled at would be 300 DPI.

Tip

If keeping a small file size is critical when importing digital images into CorelDRAW! and you have the luxury of being able to resample the images you are importing, try saving the files without any image header. For digital images such as CMYK color image files, this could significantly reduce your file size.

Image Sources

Quite a few reliable sources have cropped up in the industry in the past five years including affordable digital cameras, drum scanners, and flatbed scanners. There is also the relatively new Kodak PhotoCD process, which allows you to have your images placed directly onto a computer disc from slide or film negatives, in some cases, for less than a dollar.

Displaying Bitmaps

CorelDRAW! 6 offers two options for viewing imported bitmaps, including High-resolution display and Visible accesses by selecting View, Bitmap. These two commands may be selected, indicated by a check mark beside the menu command, or deselected, indicated by the lack of a check mark..

Note

When working with highly zoomed, high-resolution or multiple images in CorelDRAW! 6, screen redraw time can be maddening if you're in a hurry. Try turning off the Editable Wireframe view (Shift+F9) accessed from the View menu. This will cause DRAW! to leave only a bounding box around the area where your digital image has been placed. Screen redraw time in Wireframe view is significantly faster than in Preview or Editable Wireframe view.

II

Creating Text & Drawings

High Resolution Bitmap Display

In an effort to help speed the time it takes to redraw a CorelDRAW! 6 layout that incorporates digital images, the High Resolution Display option found in the Bitmaps flyout menu under the View menu may be turned off (the default is on, indicated by a menu check mark) (see fig. 11.6). When unselected, the option enables DRAW! to represent digital images on-screen using the header information in the file, or header information that DRAW! has manufactured itself (see fig. 11.7). With such a low-resolution representation of the image being projected to your screen, the screen redraw time is increased at least tenfold. Turning off the high-resolution display does not affect printing of the objects.

Fig. 11.6

Selecting the High Resolution Display option.

Visible Bitmap Display

The Visible bitmap display command comes into effect only while viewing bitmaps in your drawing in Wireframe view (Shift+F9). While in this view, bitmaps are normally displayed by CorelDRAW! in a crude way using a single shade of gray to represent the highlights and shadow areas. If you have ever had the opportunity to work on drawings at a highly zoomed view, you will likely already know how slow these images take to redraw even at this crude display. The Visible command enables you to turn off the display of any detail inside the bounding box of bitmaps while in Wireframe mode, making slow screen redraw time a nonissue.

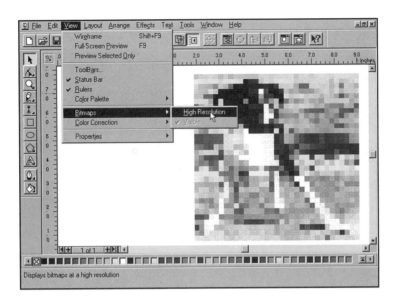

Fig. 11.7
Turning off the
high-resolution
display.

II

Creating Text & Drawings

Editing Images

Bitmap editing capabilities in CorelDRAW! 6 are slim at best; in fact, you can't actually alter your images besides performing commands on them like rotating, resizing, cropping, or applying effects such as those available in the Lens roll-up. The best solution for actually altering the composition of bitmaps would be to use an image-editing program such as Corel PHOTO-PAINT 6 or Adobe PhotoShop.

Cropping Bitmaps

Cropping functions is much more flexible now than in previous versions. After importing a bitmap image into DRAW!, you may find that you don't need or want all of the image to appear in your drawing. You could go to the trouble of resampling the image in the image manipulation program that originated the file, or you could crop it.

Cropping functions work by way of the Shape tool and the Node Edit roll-up (see fig. 11.8). By selecting the Shape tool from the Toolbox and selecting your imported bitmap, a bounding box appears around your digital image. This bounding box may be edited like any other shape in CorelDRAW!. By using the Shape tool you are able to move the position of the corners of the bitmap to suit your cropping needs. You may also add additional points on the middle of lines by clicking any point on a line, and pressing the plus sign on your keyboard. This also works for deleting a point using the minus key.

Fig. 11.8
Fancy cropping
using the Shape
tool and the Node
Edit roll-up on an
imported bitmap.

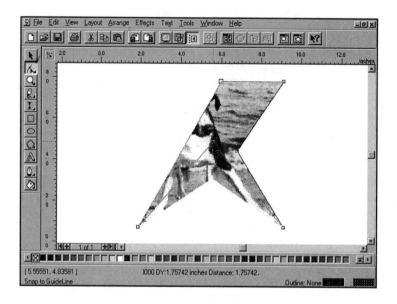

Lines and nodes on the bitmap bounding box may be treated the same as any other shape in terms of changing lines to curves and making nodes cusped, smooth, or symmetrical. For more information on working with curves and the Node Edit roll-up, see Chapter 6, "Working with Objects."

To crop a bitmap in the traditional way, follow these steps:

1. Import a bitmap image into CorelDRAW! 6, and select the Shape tool from the Toolbox.

2. Select the bitmap object by clicking on it. Notice that in each corner there is a node marker.

3. To crop one side, select the two nodes that define it and either press Shift and click, or marquee-select them. Marquee-selecting involves click-dragging to surround all of the objects you wish to select.

4. Holding down the Ctrl key, click on one of the nodes you have selected, and drag it toward the opposite side of the bitmap (see fig. 11.9). Notice that while you are dragging, DRAW! continues to display the bitmap image for reference.

Fig. 11.9
Traditional cropping of a bitmap image using the Shape tool to edit corner markers of a bitmap's bounding box.

5. Release the mouse button when you have reached your chosen cropping point. Notice that only the bitmap's bounding box has changed shape, and the sizing of the bitmap has not changed. Do this to each of the sides until you have finished cropping.

6. Select the Pick tool to complete the cropping.

Note

Making simple cropping adjustments to bounding boxes of bitmaps can add significant time when printing. Making complex bounding box shapes—especially by adding curved lines—using the Shape tool and the Node Edit roll-up can dramatically add time to printing functions especially when outputting your files to a high-resolution imagesetter. In cases where your file is to be output to an imagesetter, keep the fancy cropping to a minimum if possible. Better yet, crop the image before it is imported to save even more imagesetter output time.

Tip

When making straight-sided cropping adjustments to your bitmap images by using the Shape tool to move the node markers defining a side, try holding down the Ctrl key to constrain the dragging of the nodes to a straight vertical or horizontal change.

II

Creating Text & Drawings

Tip

Even though the Shape tool and the Node Edit roll-up are used for fancy bitmap-cropping functions, you won't be able to break a node on a bitmap bounding box.

Rotating and Skewing

Like any object in CorelDRAW!, bitmap images may be rotated and skewed. To use the mouse for rotating or skewing, double-click on the imported bitmap object to invoke the Rotate and Skew controls. To rotate a bitmap (see fig. 11.10), grab onto one of the curved-arrow corner markers using the Pick tool and rotate either clockwise or counterclockwise. A dotted, blue bounding box representation will appear indicating the new rotated position. Release the mouse to redraw the bitmap.

Fig. 11.10

Rotating an imported bitmap using the mouse controls.

To skew a bitmap object, use the Pick tool to grab onto one of the double-headed arrows at the sides of the bitmap object (see fig. 11.11). Again, a dotted blue bounding box will appear to indicate the amount of skew applied. Releasing the mouse will cause DRAW! to redraw the bitmap in it's new form (see fig. 11.12).

Fig. 11.11
Skewing an
imported bitmap
using the mouse.

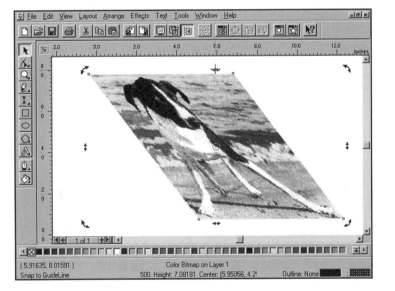

Fig. 11.12
A dramatically
skewed imported
bitmap.

For more accurate rotation or skewing of bitmaps, you may also use the
Rotation roll-up (Alt+F8) or the Skew roll-up (Alt+F12), each of which can
be found by choosing Arrange, Transform.

Tip

As with cropping, when rotating or skewing using the mouse, hold down the Control key to constrain rotation to 15-degree increments, and skewing also to 15-degree increments.

Applying Color

▶ See "Under-
standing Color
Models," p. 436

If you have imported a 1-bit monotone bitmap image into CorelDRAW!, you have the option of coloring it using the outline and fill controls with the mouse. This is one of those idea-inspiring controls that you discover from time to time, that will encourage you to experiment and try new things. It's a relatively simple effect compared to many of the effects available in CorelDRAW! 6. Because you are using a 1-bit image—which only contains black and white to begin with—you are able to treat the black as the outline and the white as the fill using DRAW!'s Outline and Fill controls. Both the outline and fill controls include all of the features available in DRAW! such as Uniform Fills (Shift + F11), Fountain Fills (F11), Two- and Full-Color Patterns, Vector and Texture Fills (see fig. 11.13). See Chapter 7, "Using Fills and Outlines," for more information on this subject.

Fig. 11.13
A Radial Fountain Fill and a black shaded outline applied to an imported, 1-bit monotone bitmap on the left, and the original 24-bit color bitmap on the right.

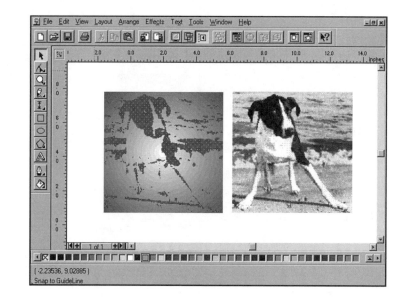

> **Tip**
>
> To apply quick fill and outline assignments to a 1-bit monotone bitmap image, use the left mouse button for a quick uniform fill, and the right mouse button for a uniform Pen outline color.

> **Note**
>
> When assigning colors to a 1-bit monotone bitmap image, you may not apply a fill or an outline of None. The native colors for the object being black for the outline and white for the fill, will take over if either fill or outline of None is selected.

Using DRAW!'s AutoTrace Feature

When working in CorelDRAW! files that contain bitmap images, from time to time you might notice that when a bitmap is selected on your page and the Pencil or Bezier tool is selected, an odd-looking cursor seems to appear. This is DRAW!'s internal bitmap-tracing tool, which works something like a stripped-down version of the utility Corel OCR-TRACE.

When the Auto Trace Tracking tool is clicked in a particular area, it re-creates a vector shape similar in shape to the area it is defining (see fig. 11.14). This vector shape is made up of nodes and is created according to the AutoTrace Tracking, Corner Threshold, and Straightline Threshold options set in the Curves tab in the Options dialog box. (You can get to this dialog box by choosing Tools, Options or pressing Control+J [see fig. 11.15].)

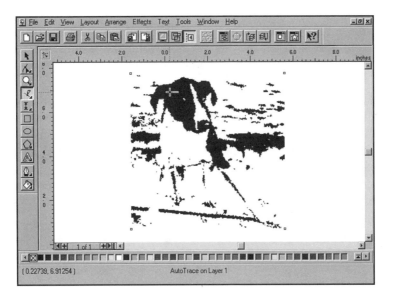

Fig. 11.14

The AutoTrace Tracking tool, DRAW!'s own internal tracing feature, can create simple traced objects from imported bitmaps.

Fig. 11.15

The AutoTrace Tracking options are controlled through the settings here in the General tab of the Curve, Bezier, Tool Properties dialog box.

Tool Properties

Tools: Curve, Bezier

| **General** | Fill | Outline |

Freehand tracking: 5 pixels
Autotrace tracking: 5 pixels
Corner threshold: 5 pixels
Straight line threshold: 5 pixels
Auto-join: 5 pixels

OK | Cancel | Apply All | Help

- *Freehand Tracking.* Not part of the Auto Trace functions, but in essence the feature controls how closely CorelDRAW! follows the motion of the mouse when drawing in Freehand mode using the Bezier tool.

- *Autotrace Tracking.* The Autotrace Tracking setting controls how closely the bitmap is followed using the AutoTrace feature. The lower the number, the closer the tracking to the bitmap shape

- *Corner Threshold.* The Corner Threshold option controls whether the AutoTrace function uses smooth curves or cusped corners to describe the edges of your traced bitmap. A lower setting will use more cusps than smooth corners when tracing.

- *Straight Line Threshold.* This setting controls when AutoTrace draws a straight line and when it draws a curve when tracing your bitmap. A lower setting here will cause the AutoTrace feature to draw more curves than straight lines, while a higher setting will create more straight lines.

- *Auto-Join.* Another feature that does not apply to the AutoTrace function, but in essence sets the distance that beginning and end points of a curve must be before they automatically join. This feature applies to objects drawn using the Freehand or Bezier tools.

This internal Auto Tracing feature may be satisfactory for tracing simple, uncomplicated bitmap objects, but to be honest, these objects require excessive editing and clean-up work, and tend to contain excessive numbers of nodes. Excessive nodes on an object may play havoc with even the most sophisticated printing devices.

Bitmap Properties

With the overall implementation of Properties, you are now able to get information about any imported digital images in DRAW!. The bitmap properties tab of the Object Properties dialog box may be accessed by either selecting View, Object, Properties, or by right-clicking on the bitmap choosing Properties from the pop-up menu (see fig. 11.16).

Fig. 11.16
Right-clicking on a bitmap and selecting Properties from the pop-up menu displays the Object Properties dialog box.

The Bitmap tab of the Object Properties dialog box is automatically displayed and contains information about the size, color, and resolution of the bitmap selected (see fig. 11.17). The remaining tabs of the Object Properties dialog box contain information about Width, Height, Object Center, and Rotational Center in the Details tab, and other general information about the type of object you currently have selected in the General tab (see fig. 11.18).

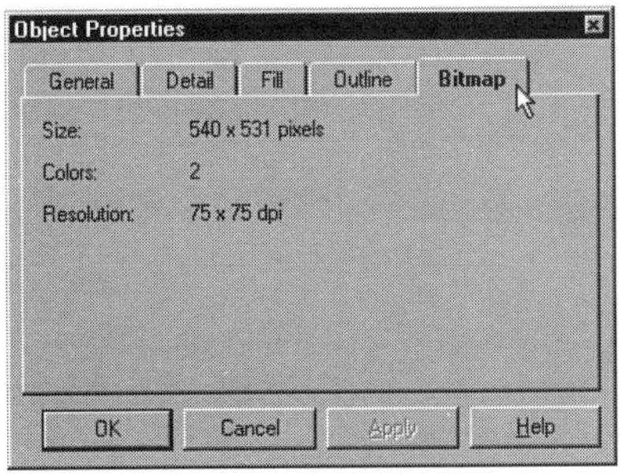

Fig. 11.17
The Object Properties Bitmap tab provides size, color, and resolution information about the bitmap.

Fig. 11.18

The Object Properties General tab provides information about the bitmap type, and any object styles that have been applied.

DRAW!'s Text-Wrapping Option

If you use other page-creation programs for producing publications that incorporate photos into text and layouts, you may be wondering to yourself where the text wrap options are in CorelDRAW!—and you won't be the first. Up until version 6 there was no simple and straightforward method of assigning a text wrap to any type of object.

Now, under the General tab in the Object Properties dialog box there is an option that promises to solve this problem. It's called Wrap Paragraph Text and may be selected ON or OFF. To access the object properties for an object, right-click on the object and select Properties from the pop-up menu.

The Wrap Paragraph text option may be applied to any object including bitmaps. When the "wrap" is applied it causes paragraph text to be pushed away from the bitmap in a shape parallel to the edge of the bounding box of the bitmap (see fig. 11.19).

Fig. 11.19

The Wrap Paragraph Text Option may be applied to any type of object, including bitmaps, making it a long-awaited method for insetting photos into text. Even after effects such as skewing, paragraph text still wraps nicely around bitmap images.

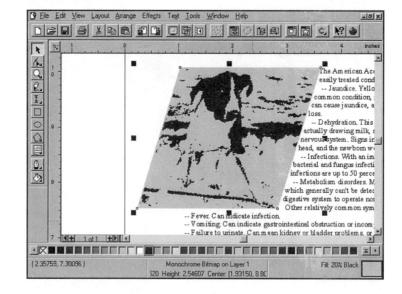

Troubleshooting

I just applied the Wrap Paragraph Text option, but now the space between my bitmap image and my text needs to be adjusted.

You might likely begin searching for a way of adjusting that option. Don't waste your time though—none exists. Instead, try creating another object to contain no fill or outline (an invisible object), placing it directly behind your bitmap, and applying the Wrap Paragraph Text option. This will enable you to resize the "wrap" object and act as a secondary offset control.

Importing Bitmap Images

Importing is a basic function that is largely covered in Chapter 2, "Managing Your Drawing Files." There are some features though that apply specifically to bitmaps that you should familiarize yourself with if you will be using this function.

Using the Import Options

The Options button of the Import dialog box, which can be accessed by choosing File, Import, allows you to obtain more information about the image you are about to import (see fig. 11.20). The Import dialog box also features options for cropping and resampling your images before you actually import them.

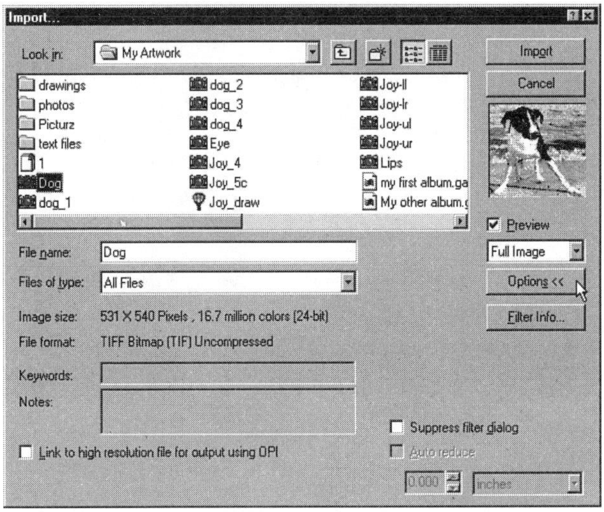

Fig. 11.20
Need to know something about an imported image? Need to make a change to that image? You can do both in the Import dialog box.

- *Cropping.* To use the Cropping controls, first select Crop Image from the pull-down menu just below the preview window on the right side of the dialog box. Then select your file to import and choose the Import button.

  This control allows you to discard some of the image before importing it into your file (see fig. 11.21). Although it might be difficult to visualize exactly how your cropped image will look in your layout, this control provides a general crop for parts of your bitmap image you are certain you won't use. Once the portions of your image have been cropped out of your digital image, they can't be edited back into your image by way of DRAW!'s Shape tool bitmap editing function.

  The Cropping dialog box contains setting options for keyboarding exact reference points and image dimensions as well as a preview window for using mouse controls to move the corner and side markers of the cropping handles.

- *Resampling.* Resampling controls can be activated by selecting Resample from the pull-down menu just below the preview window in the Import dialog box (see fig. 11.22). These controls allow you to keyboard the exact measure of your image in Width and Height, or to set a reduction by percentage. Resolution controls measured in DPI also allow you to raise or lower the actual resolution of your digital images before importing them.

Fig. 11.21
DRAW!'s Cropping controls may be used on a bitmap image before it actually imports into your file.

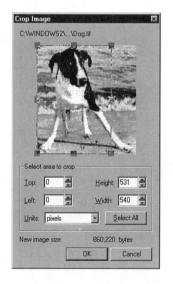

Fig. 11.22
The Resample
Image dialog box
controls also allow
you to change
dimensions and
resolution of your
imported digital
image before
importing
them into your
CorelDRAW! 6 file.

From Here...

Bitmap manipulation operations in CorelDRAW! 6 are limited at best, compared to bitmap editing programs, but that's not what CorelDRAW! was intended for anyway. Through the evolution of software versions, CorelDRAW! has adopted bitmap tools that enable it to treat bitmaps as objects, while still rendering accurate bitmap display.

This chapter has covered key bitmap subjects as they relate to CorelDRAW! 6, including bitmap formats, size, resolution, color, headers, cropping, and Auto Tracing. While this chapter covered these topics, you are encouraged to continue learning about related bitmap issues concerning CorelDRAW! 6 by referencing the following:

- Chapter 10, "Working with Powerlines and Lenses," where you learn about the Bitmap Color Mask roll-up, lenses, and Preset effects.

- Chapter 15, "Importing and Exporting Files," teaches you how to import and export bitmap formats.

II

Creating Text & Drawings

Chapter 12
Working with Presets

If you have ever had the delight of working with a word processing package featuring macros for formatting text, you will appreciate CorelDRAW! 6's Preset commands. Presets are to objects what macros are to text documents. You may record attributes, transformation, and effects being applied to objects, save those commands in a script, and reapply them to new objects, possibly saving yourself hours of unnecessary toiling. For the power-user of CorelDRAW! 6 the Preset controls open a chasm of drawing opportunity that may not have been considered.

The name "presets" has little reflection on the actual function of the commands, and that may be one of the reasons that first-time users take their time in exploring the controls. The concept is relatively easy to understand when explained in plain English and that is exactly what this chapter does.

In this chapter you learn to

- Understand the Preset concept
- Explore the Presets roll-up
- Apply Corel-supplied Presets
- Create and save your own preset effects
- Edit Presets at the Scripting level

Understanding Preset Effects

Presets allow you to harness more of the power of your computer for changing and formatting objects. Think of a Preset as a macro that works on objects, because that's essentially what a Preset is. The function of applying Presets is often confused with the application of object styles. They both apply a set of attributes to an object.

However, Presets are created and applied differently than styles. Styles are basically the static application of attributes to existing text or objects, while Presets actually perform a series of commands that may include assigning color attributes, effects, and transformation in the case of objects. They can even be extended to include the assigning of text attributes such as font, size, style, spacing, and so on. Simply put, a style is a set of attributes applying to a single object, while a Preset may actually create a series of objects each having a different attribute, depending on how the Preset is created and played back.

One of the most confusing issues to understanding Presets is that the term "presets" is used throughout CorelDRAW! 6 and applies to different tools and effects. For example, there are Powerline Presets, Extrude Presets, Envelope Presets in those respective roll-ups, while there also is a Presets roll-up. These Presets have little to do with each other, and it can be pretty confusing when trying to keep them all straight. Try not to confuse the fact that some Presets are native to the tools they apply to, while the main Presets roll-up creates all types of presets. You could even say the Presets roll-up (Alt+F5) is the mother of them all (see fig. 12.1).

Fig. 12.1
The Presets roll-up is the mother of all Presets.

The Presets apply when a single object is selected and do not apply to multiple objects. This object is referred to as a "seed." The seed forms the basis for everything recorded, and is the first object modified in a Preset. CorelDRAW! 6 ships with no less than 130 prepared Presets. Each Preset comes with a brief description of the effects it performs and a thumbnail representation of the effect.

When Do You Use a Preset?

If you find yourself applying the same drop shadow or fill and/or outline colors to different objects over and over again you should be using a Preset.

In fact, if you find yourself doing *any* sort of object manipulation repeatedly, you may want to consider using a Preset.

The following is a list of "transactions" (as Corel refers to them) that Presets may be used for. They may be applied to objects individually or in succession.

- Creating polygons, ellipses, and/or rectangles

- Deleting, repeating, duplicating, and cloning

- Effects such as Perspective, Contour, Envelope, Powerline, and Extrude including creating, copying, cloning, and clearing commands

- Transformation including Rotation, Position, Scale & Mirror, Skewing, and Sizing

- Transformation effects such as Intersection, Weld, and Trim

- Outline and fill attributes, including overprinting attributes for color trapping

- Text attributes including both Artistic and Paragraph text

- Align & Distribute, Convert to Curves, Group and Combine

What Presets Won't Do

There's no question that mastering Presets will open the flood gates to time savings, but before you plan out your Preset strategy, you also need to understand what Presets *can't* do.

- You may not begin creating or applying a Preset to more than one object at a time

- You may not assign two-color and full-color pattern fills

- You may not assign arrowheads and arrow styles to lines

- You may not change font attributes of individual characters in a text string

- You may not compose text

Working with Presets

All of the controls for creating, opening, editing, viewing, and applying Presets are contained in the Presets roll-up (Alt+F5). When you first open the

II

Creating Text & Drawings

roll-up, it displays the list of over 100 prepared Presets that ship with CorelDRAW! 6. The first thing you might consider doing is browsing the list and view the thumbnails associated with each while reading the brief descriptions attached.

To apply a Corel-supplied Preset, follow these steps:

1. Create an object you wish to apply a Preset effect to, something fairly simple such as a rectangle or ellipse.

2. Select the Presets roll-up to display (Alt+F5) by choosing Tools, Presets.

3. Select a prepared Preset by making a choice from the pull-down menu on the roll-up. Notice as you scroll through the list that a brief description of the Preset is displayed as flyout text (see fig. 12.2).

Fig. 12.2

The Preset roll-up enables you to create a simple object and select a Corel-supplied Preset to apply.

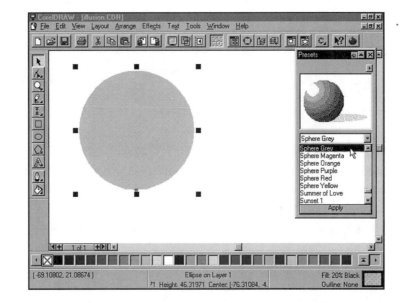

4. With your object selected, click the apply button and the Preset plays out until completed (see fig. 12.3). Some of the more complex Presets may take a few seconds to complete their commands depending on the complexitity of the Preset and the objects they are being applied to.

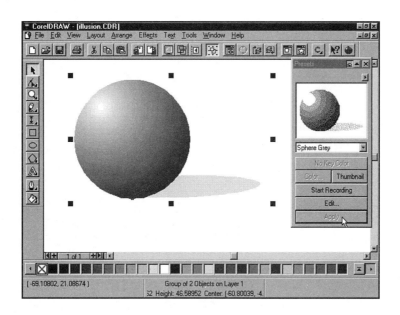

Fig. 12.3
The Grey Sphere
preset is easily
applied to a simple
ellipse.

The Presets Roll-Up

The actual roll-up controls are few. The following is a quick listing of the various controls in the roll-up and their purpose.

- *Preview Window.* This window allows you to view a thumbnail representation of a Preset if one exists. If no thumbnail exists it will simply list the brief text description instead.

- *Preset pull-down.* This is where the various Preset recipies are selected in the roll-up. To select a Preset, use this pull-down menu.

- *Key Color.* This is the color that your Preset objects will be set to. If no key color has been set the key color display states No Key Color Selected. If a color has been assigned it will display here. The key color may be set to fountain fills; however, the key color display does not support fountain fill display and will only display one of the fountain fill colors.

- *Color.* This button on the roll-up enables you to select the key color from an object that already exists in your document. When you select the Color button your cursor will change to a large black arrow cursor allowing you to select the key color from an existing object. Once you do this the color will display in the Key Color display window.

- *Thumbnail.* The Thumbnail button allows you to delete or update the header image that represents the thumbnail of a Preset. Corel-supplied Presets already come with thumbnails. The thumbnail image appears in the preview window of the roll-up.

- *Start Recording/Stop Recording.* To begin recording or stop a current recording press this button.

- *Editing controls.* The Edit button displays the Edit Preset dialog box (see fig. 12.4), which enables you to include notes about your Preset recordings and view and edit the Operations of the Presets. Editable operations appear in bold type, while non-editable operations remain grayed out. Clicking an editable operation will display the edit controls to the right of the Operations window. Scrolling down the list displays the entire list of Preset Operations numbered according to the order they are performed in.

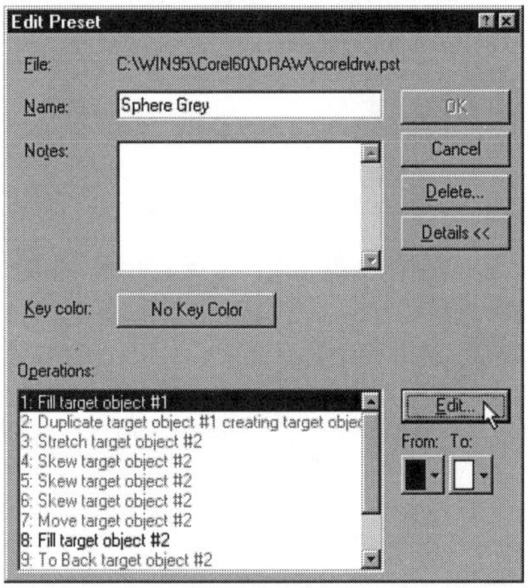

Fig. 12.4

The Edit Preset dialog box contains controls for editing any available object attributes assigned during the originally recorded Preset.

- *The Preset Flyout menu.* The flyout menu contains controls for accessing the Preset New, Open, Save As, and Merge With commands.

Planning a Preset Recording

Rehearsing before beginning to record a series of commands for a Preset is always a good idea. Review the list of allowable and restricted transactions, and try constantly considering that each action you perform is done by way of as few mouse moves as possible. There is no time limit on the recording of your Preset, so don't worry about racing through it. Keep in mind that your attributes, effects, and transformations should remain generic and should be applicable to any type of object (except in the case of text).

Recording and Saving Presets

Think of an effect that you apply most often, even if it is something as simple as adding a black drop shadow to a rectangle. Now imagine if it would work as a Preset. Because applying a drop shadow involves creating an additional object it couldn't possibly be done with a style. And, since it also involves applying a different color to two individual objects and a particular constant offset it would fit in just right with the intended purpose of a Preset.

To apply a shadow effect to an object and save those actions as a Preset, follow these steps:

1. Pull down the Symbols roll-up (Ctrl+F11), select Common Bullets from the list, and choose the airplane (item number 105). Drag the symbol out onto your page and size and position it in preparation for applying some effects (see fig. 12.5). This particular symbol is square, so set the size of the airplane to roughly two inches by two inches.

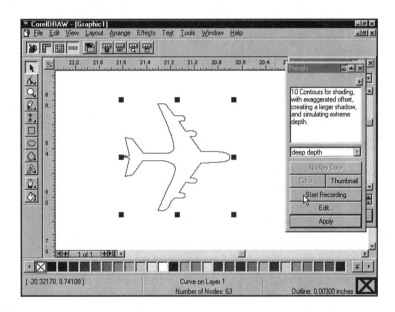

Fig. 12.5

Most Presets may be applied to objects as simple as those contained in the Symbols roll-up.

2. Choose <u>T</u>ools, P<u>r</u>esets (Alt+F5). Press the Start Recording button and select the airplane by clicking it with the Pick tool (see fig. 12.6). Set its outline to none by selecting the No Color box from the on-screen color palette using the right mouse button.

3. Make the fill of the airplane 50 percent black by selecting the airplane, clicking the 50 percent black color in the on-screen palette or by using the Fill Color dialog box (Shift +F11).

Fig. 12.6

Plan your ideas before recording the effect.

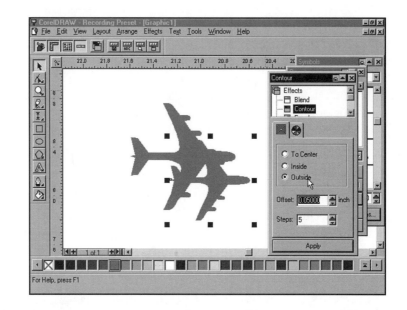

4. Make a copy of the airplane and offset it downward and to the right by an arbitrary amount. Resize the new symbol to be approximately 1.5 inches square, centered on its original position. Center it by holding down the Shift key while click-dragging one of its corners as you watch the status bar while reducing its size.

5. Send the new symbol to the back by selecting it and pressing Shift+Page Down on your keyboard.

6. Select Effects, Contours to display the Contours roll-up (Ctrl+F9) and set the contours tab options to Outside, Offset of 0.0100 inch, and Steps to 5.

7. With the new airplane on the bottom selected, turn to the contour colors tab and select the fill color selector to white and click the Apply button (see fig. 12.7).

8. Select the original airplane on top and set its fill color to solid black by clicking the black color box in the on-screen palette.

9. Click the Stop Recording on the Presets roll-up. An Edit Preset dialog box asks you to name your new Preset effect (see fig. 12.8). Be sure to fill in the field where it asks for Notes about your Preset. Name your Preset something like Small shadow. Also, the notes you added enter in

the Edit Preset dialog box are placed into a flyout accompanying the Preset and a thumbnail representation is added to the preview window (see fig. 12.9).

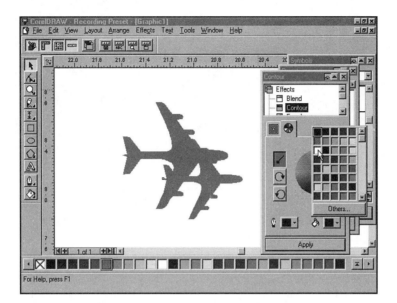

Fig. 12.7
The Presets command supports most effects while in record mode.

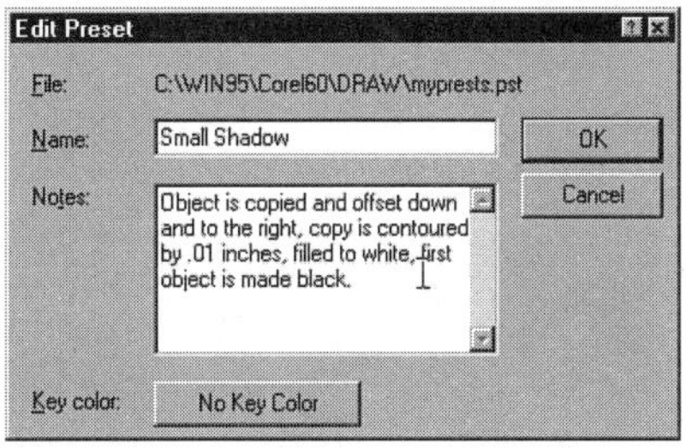

Fig. 12.8
To save your recorded Preset, use the Edit Preset dialog box.

Creating Text & Drawings

10. Select a new and different object and apply your new preset to it. Notice that the same transactions are applied to the new object, and that the newly created objects are automatically grouped together (see fig. 12.10).

Fig. 12.9
Your newly created Preset is added to the list along with a thumbnail and your brief description.

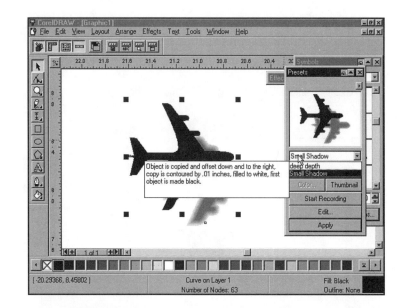

Fig. 12.10
To apply your new Preset to an object, select it from the Preset roll-up list.

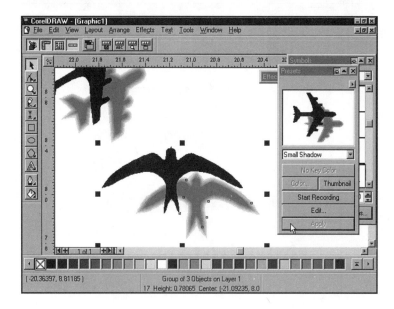

> **Tip**
>
> If during the recording of your Preset you happen to attempt creating an object which the Preset is not compatible with, DRAW! will warn you and simply continue recording. If you begin a recording and then change your mind, click the Stop Recording button. If nothing was recorded DRAW! also warns you of this. If you Stop Recording and do not wish to save your script, click the Cancel button instead of naming your Preset script.

Editing Preset Scripts

When the Preset is recording it essentially captures all of the attribute changes, transformations, and effects that you apply to your seed object. It does not record time or page coordinates unless you have chosen to create a polygon, rectangle, or ellipse—the only three objects the Preset command is capable of recording the creation of. All of these actions are saved to a script file. Certain variables in a script file may be edited depending on the attributes being used.

The Edit Preset dialog (see fig. 12.11) contains controls to either Delete a currently selected Preset script or view more Details about it. Clicking the Details button causes the Edit Preset dialog to expand, revealing the Operations list, which is essentially the captured transactions. The editable transactions are displayed in bold while the non-editable scripts remain grayed out.

Fig. 12.11
To view the transaction details of a Preset, click the Details button to expand the dialog box.

By selecting the editable script lines, brief editing controls appear in the dialog box to the right of the Operations list window. Various attributes such as fill color and outline color may be quickly edited using these tools. For example, in the steps just shown, the seed object was made black as the final operation. This can be changed to any other color or fill type you wish by either selecting the Edit button to gain access to DRAW!'s complete color controls, or by either selecting or clicking on the color button displayed and choosing a new color from the flyout. Editing functions such as this are limited to a certain extent though. For instance, if you had originally set a uniform color as your operation you will not be able to change that color to something like a fountain fill instead.

Merging Two Preset Files

If you find that you become a Presets power-user and use these commands for many different operations, the Presets roll-up offers the option of merging two Preset files together to assist you in organizing your operations. This will work well for someone who has recorded short, quick operations as Presets and wishes to build on his or her Preset collection. One way of saving your Presets might be to divide the operation types into categories such as Transformation Presets, Fill Presets, and Effects Presets.

To merge two Preset files together follow these steps:

1. Open the first Preset file by selecting Open from the Preset roll-up flyout menu (see fig. 12.12). In this case a file containing a text effect was opened first.

Fig. 12.12
To open a Preset file, select Open from the roll-up's flyout menu.

2. Once your first text Preset file is opened select the Merge With command from the Presets roll-up flyout menu and locate the second saved file.

3. Select Merge With from the Preset flyout menu and locate the second file to merge with the current one (see fig. 12.13). In this example a file containing an object effect was merged with the first Preset file. The result is a single Preset file containing both Preset scripts.

Fig. 12.13
To combine more than one Preset collection in a single file, use the Presets roll-up Merge With command.

If you were actually planning a Preset file so that these scripts were going to be used in succession you could also number them by selecting the Edit button and entering a number in front of the name of the Preset (see fig. 12.14) in the Edit Preset dialog box. Numbering the names of the Preset scripts also causes them to display in numerical order.

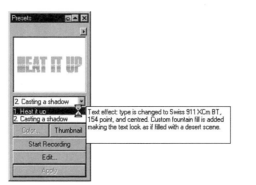

Fig. 12.14
To further organize your Preset into an ordered sequence, rename the scripts with numbers preceding the names.

Removing a Preset and Its Effects

To remove a Preset from the list in the pull-down menu you must first select the Preset so that it is displaying in the pull-down list and select the Edit button to display the Edit Preset dialog box. Once you have the Preset script showing, select the Delete button to display the Delete Preset dialog box. This displays a list of the Preset scripts contained in the currently opened Preset file. To delete one of the scripts showing you must first select it in the window and then press delete (see fig. 12.15). After it disappears from the list you must then select the OK button to save your changes.

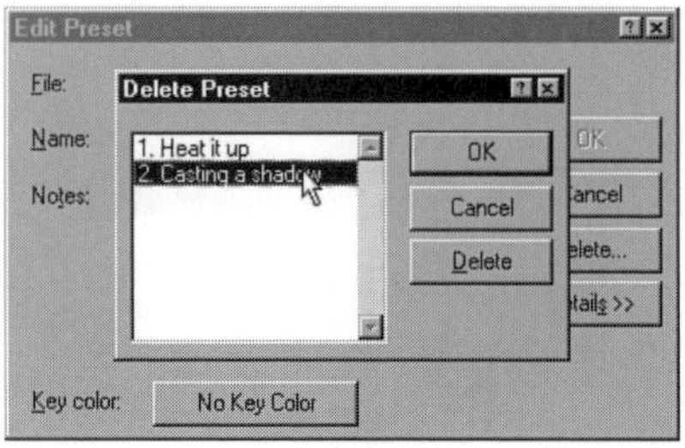

Fig. 12.15
To delete a Preset
script from the
Presets roll-up,
select the Edit
button and the
Delete command.

To remove the effects of a Preset script is not an automatic task. Because Presets are always automatically grouped you must first ungroup the objects. Once they are ungrouped you may then delete the additional objects. Because Presets are a set of actual commands you will not be able to undo them and no remove Preset effect exists in the program.

Note

When applying a Preset to an ineligible object such as a text format edit to a non-textual object, any effects that do not apply will simply be ignored by the script and will not take effect. The remaining script will continue being applied.

From Here...

The Presets roll-up is a powerful tool once you make the effort to overcome its mystery. Once you are familiar with their usefulness, Presets may likely become one of the features you have at your ready during all your drawing chores.

For related information on using CorelDRAW! 6 Presets, see the following chapters:

- Chapter 6, "Working with Objects," to learn how to work with envelopes and extrudes.

- Chapter 10, "Working with Powerlines and Lenses," to learn how to use and create extrude Presets and to understand Preset effects.

Chapter 13

Using Color, Wizards, and Applying Color Masks

The color reproduction process is becoming faster and cheaper with each new software program that hits the publishing and graphics market, and CorelDRAW! 6 is no exception. The key to using color is understanding all of the various permutations of color interpretation. As a creator of color drawings, layouts, and graphic images, much of the added responsibility that comes with progress can sometimes fall right into your lap. If you're caught off guard, the results can be quite costly in terms of time and budget.

With this latest version of CorelDRAW! comes a horde of features that enable you to define and measure the use of color in your documents whether you intend on producing images for the screen, your desktop color printer, or going all the way to print.

In this chapter, you learn to

- Correctly select and work with any one of the army of different color models in CorelDRAW! 6

- Calibrate your color system

- Create and use your own color profile using the Color Wizard

- Work with process and spot colors

- Use the new Color Blend and Color Mixing tools

- Work with DRAW!'s new Bitmap Color Mask Roll-Up

Color Calibration Issues

In the world of digital color production there are, needless to say, almost as many hardware and software variables in the production processes as there are reproducible colors. The key to achieving proper color is controlling these variables, and knowing your digital tools. But with color technology changing so quickly, this is no small feat, and certainly applies to CorelDRAW! software. This latest version does have an advantage over previous versions, though, in that it does provide you with some basic tools to guide you toward color correctness.

Color designs of even the best designers and illustrators can get poor reviews simply because someone, somewhere, missed the mark on color. It's an all-too-familiar story that is often heard in service bureau circles and digital prepress houses. Reasons for poor color can stem from a poorly calibrated monitor or color proofing device, to a sloppy or half-asleep press operator—or any of the many processes in between those two points. The trick to finding out what went wrong and avoiding it the next time around is to understand all of the processes involved.

The desktop color production world, for the most part, consists of a color monitor, your eyes (and the eyes of others), color scanning, and a desktop color proofing device, all connected in one way or another to your computer. The assumption here is that you will eventually need to reproduce your ideas in mass quantity later on, by way of an imagesetter and printing press or equivalent reproduction method. First, you will need a color monitor and a relatively good quality video card capable of at least 256 colors.

Some monitors come with their own calibration software utilities, as do some software packages, CorelDRAW! 6 for instance. There are also a few independent software calibration packages on the market that promise to do the job. Regardless of how you will be calibrating your monitor, there are a few very basic things you must do before you begin. Following these steps will ensure a controlled environment for viewing your colors:

1. First, get your hands on a color swatch of some sort to match your software program. A *color model* is a method in which color is represented including CMYK, RGB, HSB, HLS, and so on. A spot color model is probably the best one to use, but make sure your swatch is recent. Over time, some swatches can fade if left in bright sunlight, or even bright office lighting.

2. Turn on your monitor and let it warm up for at least half an hour to ensure the color has stabilized.

3. Set your work area lighting to your usual working light level. Controlled lighting is ideal; avoid having natural light coming into the room. As the lighting levels change during the day, so does the brightness of your work area and in turn the spectrum of light our eyes let in. This, in turn, affects how the colors on our monitors look to us.

4. Make sure your system is protected from power surges. Power levels can fluctuate during various times of the day, and consequently affect the color generation of your monitor. It's a wise choice to do this anyway, if you value your motherboard or the data stored on your hard drive.

5. Set the brightness and contrast controls on your monitor to comfortable levels. Once you have set these controls, tape them in place. You won't want these settings to move after you have gone to all the effort of calibrating. If you share a machine with other workers, warn them of this.

6. Match your swatch's color model to a color model within CorelDRAW! using either spot color, CMYK color, or a third-party color system available in CorelDRAW! 6.

7. Create a selection of colored objects on a neutral-gray background using the color model you have chosen and compare these colors to your hard copy color swatch. Choose colors that are from a wide variety of the color spectrum and include tertiary, light, and dark colors to enable you to cover the most ground.

Following these steps will at least stabilize the color information your monitor is providing. If the colors on your monitor look fairly close to those in your color swatch, you're in good shape. If they don't, you have some work to do.

Using the CorelDRAW! 6 Color Manager

Part of the purpose of the Color Manager is to enable you to create a color profile to correctly view color throughout your image-creation process using the Color Wizard utility. In order to begin this process, there are a few things you will need to know and do in advance. First, find out the exact make and model of all of your color-related hardware including your color monitor, color printer, and color scanner. If you use multiple hardware configurations, such as several different monitor, scanner, and printer types, you will need to create a profile for each combination. It will help substantially to set your color monitor according to the guidelines listed in the previous section.

Developing a full-color system profile can be time-consuming. As you use the Color Wizard, you'll have choices presented to you and/or decisions to make about developing hardware profiles, referred to specifically as monitor profiles, scanner profiles, and printer profiles. A complete color system profile includes information about all three device types. You may be lucky enough to find the make and model of your particular equipment in the scanner, printer, or monitor selection listed supplied, but the chances are slim at best. It may be safer to obtain the information you need from the manufacturer and use this as a base for developing your profiles.

If your equipment, especially your monitor, is older, you may want to obtain some information from the manufacturer about how the device approaches color rendering. In the case of monitors, you may need to find out the monitor specifications for chromaticity and white point.

You also need what Corel refers to as a *target* original. Ideally, this will be a continuous-tone original that you perform a test scan from and eventually print to your color printer. If you intend on using your own scanned target, you may want to scan it into your system ahead of time. Scan to the most commonly used resolution such as 150 DPI. If you intend on using the scanned target that came with your hardware, you may also want to locate that target ahead of time and copy it to your hard drive.

Creating a Color Profile Using the Color Wizard

The Color Wizard uncomplicates the creation of color profiles. The Color Wizard may be launched independently from the Corel Applications or from within CorelDRAW! 6 itself. To launch the Color Wizard from within CorelDRAW!, choose Tools, Color Manager, Run Color Wizard. The Color Wizard Welcome screen will be the first to appear (see fig. 13.1).

Fig. 13.1
The Color Wizard welcome screen is the first screen you see after launching the application.

A few terms will pop up along the way, and before you begin, you may want to familiarize yourself with their meanings.

- *Automatch.* An option within the Color Wizard for choosing to develop a profile for working with and printing both vector and bitmap-based digital images.

- *Chromaticity.* This mouthful of a term refers to the measure of color that corresponds to the gamut of colors that your monitor is capable of re-producing. Controls exist in the Color Wizard for you to interactively set individual RGB colors of your monitor.

- *Colorimeter.* A device for measuring specific monitor colors, similar in accuracy to the range of color the human eye can perceive.

- *Color Space.* The product of the range of colors and the dynamic range of brightness and darkness that a person, device, or—in this case—color system can accurately render.

- *Color Gamut.* In this case, color gamut is the range of colors that can be seen by a person or a device, whether reflective or illuminated.

- *Color Gamut mapping.* The process of correctly matching the color range of one device to the color range of another.

- *Dynamic Range.* The measure of range between the lightest and the darkest color that can be perceived by a person or device.

- *Saturation mapping.* The mapping technique used for matching vector object colors to the color gamut of the color printing device.

- *GCR.* Stands for *gray component replacement.*

- *K-curve.* A K-curve (K standing for black) defines the range of grayscale in a four-color printing device. A K-curve may be less than or exceed the range of the printer and may be linear, convex, or concave in shape.

- *TAC.* Stands for *total area coverage*, and represents a value between 0 and 100 percent for each of four colors of the total amount of ink that will be transferred to a printed page. A coverage of 400 percent indicates full coverage of each of the four colors of ink.

- *Spectrophotometer.* A device for measuring the reflected or transmitted color of an object dealing with both monitor and printer colors.

- *UCR.* Stands for *under color removal.*

- *White Point.* The temperature of the light at which your monitor renders pure white. In RGB values, pure white color is equal to a full 255 units of red, green, and blue.

Troubleshooting

I have a printer that uses its own color accuracy formula. Every time I print from CorelDRAW! 6, the colors look terrible! Why?

If your printer has its own proprietary color management system built in, you must disable it. If the printer is using a different color management system than CorelDRAW!, it may cause the two profiles to conflict with each other and produce inaccurate results.

The first screen in the Color Manager wizard asks if you would like to Create, Select, or Edit a system profile. To create a new color profile, follow these steps:

1. Select the Create option and select Next.

2. In the next screen, enter a name for your new color profile, and use the area provided to enter particular information about the color profile you are about to create, such as the date, particular hardware information, and by whom the profile was created. Click Next.

3. Choose either Automatch, Photographic, or Saturation color mapping in the next screen (see fig. 13.2). Select Photographic if you are using strictly digital bitmap images, Saturation if you are using strictly vector graphics, or Automatch if your drawings use both bitmap and vector objects. Click Next.

Fig. 13.2

The first decision you must make about your calibration procedure is to elect a color mapping method.

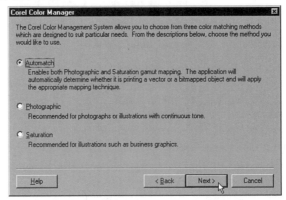

4. The next screen provides you with four choices for setting up a scanner profile (see fig. 13.3). You may check to see if your scanner is available from the list, you may choose to calibrate your scanner immediately, or skip the scanner profile completely. If you were editing an existing color profile, the first option, Use Current Scanner, would be available, but as yet, you haven't set a scanner.

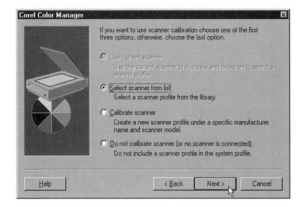

Fig. 13.3
At the beginning of your scanner calibration steps, you have the option of choosing to Select, Calibrate, or skip the scanner profile.

5. If you choose the option Select a Scanner from List, the Color Wizard will immediately present a list of manufacturers, makes, and models for you to choose from. You may also merely go forward to the library screen to check and see if your hardware is listed there. If it isn't, then you may return to the previous screen by choosing the Back button.

6. If your scanner isn't listed, choose the Calibrate Scanner option and the Next button. The Color Wizard will then present a screen for you to enter the make and model of your scanner. After you have made this selection, the Color Wizard will ask you to designate a target file to calibrate from. You may also choose not to calibrate your scanner by selecting Don't Calibrate from the manufacturer's list, or use the Generic Scanner selection.

7. Designate a target file. A target file is supplied with your Corel software in TIF format and the Color Wizard will automatically open to the folder where it is stored. If you choose not to use the Corel-supplied target, you may choose to use your own scanned target file by scanning it before you begin the Color Wizard. The Color Wizard will also provide an opportunity for you to scan your target image from within the Wizard itself by selecting Scan target. You must have your scanner properly connected and installed before selecting this option.

8. Identify the scanned target by clicking on it and selecting Open. Once your target file has been designated, the Color Wizard will ask whether you are using the Corel-supplied target or your own manufacturer's

II

Creating Text & Drawings

target image. If you are using the Corel-supplied target, Color Wizard will use a data file called CORELTGT.REF. If you have supplied your own target, the Wizard will ask you to locate the .REF file supplied by the manufacturer. If no file exists, it may be wise at this point to scan the original continuous-tone color photo supplied with your CorelDRAW! 6 software.

9. Once the target has been designated (see fig. 13.4), click the Calculate button. Color Wizard will then measure the color gamut and the color dynamic of the target scan. Once the Calculation is completed, click Next to continue building your color profile.

Fig. 13.4

Corel supplies a scanning target to use during the scanner calibration process.

10. To calibrate your monitor, click the Calibrate monitor option and the Next button. You will be given the choice of calibrating your monitor to Default characteristics or the Characteristics of another monitor. For example, if you know that your monitor has the exact same characteristics as another manufacturer listed in the monitor library, choose Characteristics of another monitor. If not, click Default and Next. Color Wizard will then generate a color profile of your monitor. If you would like to calibrate manually, select the Calibrate Monitor option and select Next.

11. You will be presented with a screen to name your monitor manufacturer and model number. After you have completed this, click Next. A calibration screen will appear (see fig. 13.5), which will contain all of

the controls for interactively calibrating your monitor. Controls for adjusting Monitor Chromaticity appear initially. After making adjustments to the values to suit your monitor, click the Preview button to verify you have the correct settings. This will likely take several tries to perfect.

II

Creating Text & Drawings

Fig. 13.5
To manually adjust the Chromaticity of your monitor, adjust the RGB settings and click Preview to see the results. This will definitely be a trial-by-error process.

12. To adjust the white point setting of your monitor select the Monitor White Point option. Your controls will change to display a white point slider control (see fig. 13.6). Select the known white point temperature of your monitor, or use the trial-by-error process with the Preview button until the Preview results are satisfactory.

13. Once you have completed your monitor calibration and are satisfied with the results, click Next to move onto the final printer calibration step.

14. As with the scanner and monitor calibration process, to calibrate your printer, choose from the Corel-supplied list, or choose the Calibrate Printer option. You will be presented with a screen to identify the make and model of your printer. You will also be asked if your printer works by CMY (three colors of ink) or CMYK (four colors of ink) or you may choose to print a test sheet by clicking the Classify button. The resulting printout will determine how many ink colors your printer is using. Enter and select your printer details and select Next.

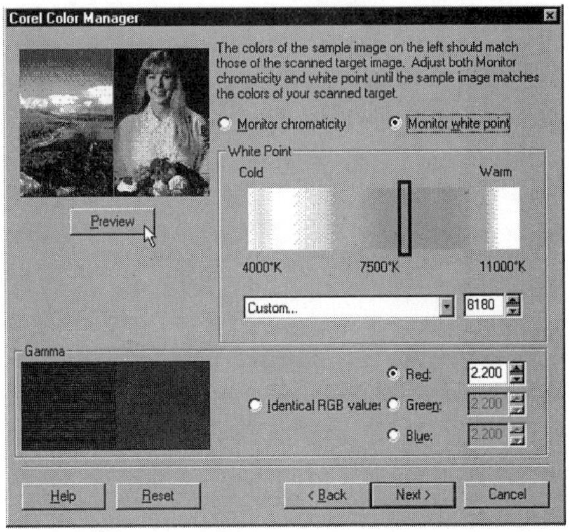

Fig. 13.6

To manually adjust the Monitor White Point settings for your monitor, adjust the white point slider control and click Preview to see the results. Manually setting your white point settings will again be a trial-by-error process.

15. The next screen will ask you to determine whether you would like to use Default Characteristics or Other Characteristics. Choosing the Default Characteristics will apply to most printer types. The Other Characteristics option may be used for specialty type printers such as imagesetters, highly specialized color printers, and so on. Click Next to continue.

16. The next screen to appear will measure the colors your printer is capable of printing. The Color Manager will ask if you would like to use a File or Scanner method for measurement. The File method bases its calculations on an existing color profile and enables you to select a Color Manager File (CMF). The Scanner method enables you to choose a scanned image to calibrate from. In both cases, the Color Manager will provide the screens necessary for choosing these files. In the case of the Scanner method, you may choose to scan a target file immediately from within Color Manager (see fig. 13.7) if no scan target file is available.

17. Once your scan target has been selected, click Next to continue calibrating your printer. Color Manager will automatically name a color measurement file based on the information you have provided and the scan target, and will store this file in your COREL60/COLOR folder with a CMF extension.

18. Once your printer has been measured for color capabilities, your color profile is completed. Click the Finish button to exit the Color Manager.

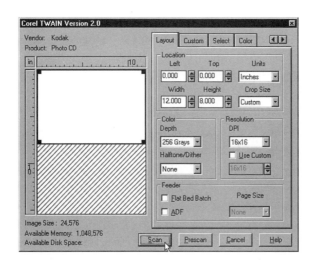

Fig. 13.7
If you choose to
scan an image
immediately to
use as a target file
during printer
calibration, Color
Manager provides
the necessary
scanning tools
seen here.

Assigning a Color Profile

Assigning a color profile is infinitely less time-consuming and complex than
calibrating your entire system. To select an existing color system profile begin
by choosing Tools, Color Manager, Select Color Profile, which will display the
Corel Color Manager. The color profile files are stored by default in your
COREL60/COLOR folder and contain the extension .CCM (which stands for
Corel Color Manager). The Color Manager automatically looks in this folder
for any profiles that exist. If you are moving saved profiles from another
system to your own, you will need to place the files into this folder in order
for the Color Manager to see them (see fig. 13.8).

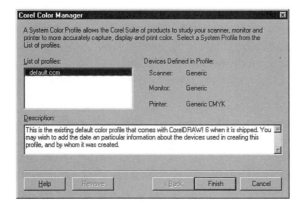

Fig. 13.8
Assign an existing
color profile using
the Color Manager
by selecting Tools,
Color Manager,
Select Color
Profile.

II

Creating Text & Drawings

Once a profile has been highlighted, any information about it that exists will be displayed in the Description window. If you enter any information about the profile itself in the color profile description, this is where it will come in handy. It's always a recommended practice to use these features wherever possible. If you need to make amendments to these descriptions such as additional notes, you may do so here without the need to save changes.

Troubleshooting

I created a color profile and saved the details of the equipment involved in the Color Profile description box. Someone else seems to have changed some of the information in it. Is there any way to prevent this?

If you have created a color profile and would like it to remain intact and unchanged, use the Windows Explorer, Properties option to change the file to a Read Only, Archive file. This way, no one else will be able to alter or edit your profile, including the description you have entered.

Understanding Color Models

Color models are the 31 different flavors of the desktop color production. CorelDRAW! 6 has an extremely intuitive interface for selecting color models and the individual colors within those models. To get the most out of this color model discussion, it would help if you were actually working in DRAW! at the time, due to the lack of color on these pages.

DRAW!'s Color Models Defined

Color Models can be described as mathematical representations of color space or the product of color gamut and color dynamic. Color models are a necessary evil, required by the computer to define color output, and can be very complex and obscure in the way they describe their particular take on color theory.

DRAW!'s color models and interactive color selector can be accessed throughout the Uniform Fill (Ctrl+F11) dialog controls (see fig. 13.9) while an object is currently selected. This dialog opens to the settings determined by your default graphic fill setting. Here, options for displaying the Color Model, Palette, and Mixers are available. While the Color Model option is selected, you are able to select DRAW!'s collection of various color models including CMY, CMYK, CMYK255, RGB, HSB, HLS, L*A*B, YIQ, Grayscale, and Registration color.

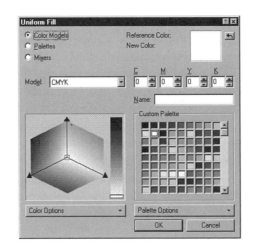

Fig. 13.9
CorelDRAW!'s Uniform Fill dialog gives access to all of the color models available in the program. The default is the CMYK color model.

■ *CMY.* This color model works on the reflective color principle and is composed of the three working primary colors of cyan, magenta, and yellow. Some printers operate on a CMY principle. Color is simulated using these three colors and darkness or shadows are simulated using heavy combinations of all three colors—creating a "fake" black. CMY colors within this model are divided into units ranging from 0 to 255. With the CMY color model selected (see fig. 13.10), the interactive color selector displays a three-axis color graph that may be set by dragging each of the C, M, and Y markers of the color cube to specific positions on their axis. The vertical grayscale to the right of the color graph also controls darkness by equally increasing each of the CMY color values. You may also keyboard values directly into the CMY fields or by using the slider controls beside those fields.

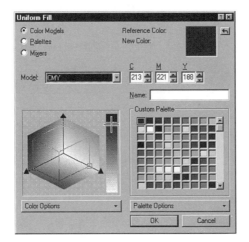

Fig. 13.10
The CMY color model controls use only cyan, magenta, and yellow to reproduce all palette colors.

II

Creating Text & Drawings

■ *CMYK.* CMYK, one of the more popular color models (refer to fig. 13.9), measures color based on the four-color ink printing method used by many color printers, and ultimately included by the traditional four-color process used in offset printing. The four basic colors measured in this color model are cyan, magenta, yellow, and black. Each color is divided into percentages ranging from 0 to 100. Cyan, magenta, and yellow values may be selected by manipulating the corner markers on the color cube graph using your mouse. Black values are controlled by sliding the grayscale marker to the right of the color graph, higher for a darker percentage of black or lower for a lesser percentage. Notice that while using this color model, any combination of cyan, magenta, yellow, and black may be set, regardless of whether your monitor or printer will be able to render the particular color set.

■ *CMYK255.* The CMYK255 color model (see fig. 13.11) is similar to the traditional CMYK color model in that it uses the same four basic colors in combination to render colors, except that in this case, color is divided into values ranging from 0 to 255. To select colors, use the sliding markers of the color graph to set values for cyan, magenta, and yellow and the grayscale slider to set the black value.

Fig. 13.11
The CMYK255 color model controls seen here work with an optimized version of the full CMYK color model.

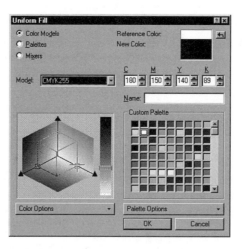

■ *RGB.* As far as your computer monitor is concerned, the RGB color model is the mother of them all. Your monitor renders color using this color method regardless of which model you select. Nearly all monitors use an RGB color gun to project color to your screen, while essentially interpreting the particular color model you have selected to use. RGB color is based on transmitted color, divided into units of red, green, and blue light in values ranging from 0 to 255 (see fig. 13.12). A combination of values where red = 255, green = 255, and blue = 255 will produce pure white, while all values set to zero will render pure black. Color values may be changed interactively using the color markers and the grayscale slider to the right of the graph.

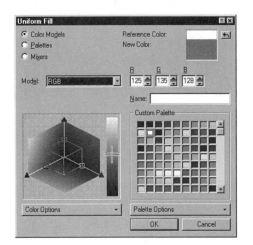

Fig. 13.12

The RGB color model controls seen here work on the same principles as CMY, CMYK255, and CMYK color models, but break down colors into red, green, and blue values.

Creating Text & Drawings

- *HSB.* The HSB color model measures color in terms of the transmitted color values of hue (the actual color), saturation (the amount of color), and brightness (the intensity of color [the amount of white]). Hue is measured in terms of the color's position on the color wheel (see fig. 13.13), which is divided into its 360 degrees, beginning at a value of 0 at the top and increasing clockwise, while saturation and brightness are measured in units ranging from 0 to 100. The hue color wheel is marked by the letters Y, R, M, B, C, and G, which stand for yellow, red, magenta, blue, cyan, and green, respectively. For example, a value of 90 degrees represents a hue of red, while a value of 180 degrees represents cyan. Saturation and brightness values are controlled by a single marker positioned on the triangle shape where the lower-right corner of the triangle sets saturation and brightness to 0,0 and the lower-left corner sets them to 100, 100. Increasing the saturation value causes the color to become more intense while increasing the brightness causes the color to become lighter or whiter.

Fig. 13.13
The HSB color model controls illustrated here are quite different from the rest of the color model controls and involve manipulating a marker on a brightness and saturation scale and controlling another marker on a color wheel.

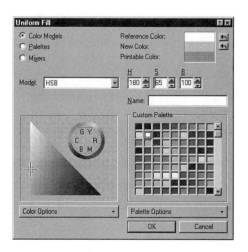

■ *HLS.* The HLS color model (see fig. 13.14) represents color measured in terms of hue, lightness, and saturation, which is a variation on the HSB color model. Color values are controlled by way of a combination of the color wheel and the grayscale slider. As with HSB, hue is measured in terms of degrees around the color wheel, this time 0 being to the center-right side of the wheel (90 degrees). Lightness and saturation are measured in units ranging from 0 to 100, while a lightness setting of 50 sets the color wheel to its widest range of color, and settings of 100 and 0 limit the lightness to lightest and darkest, respectively. Lightness is controlled by moving the vertical slider on the right up and down, while saturation is adjusted in combination with the hue by moving the color-wheel marker toward or away from the center of the wheel.

Fig. 13.14
The HLS color model controls use a single color wheel for both hue and saturation combined with a slider to control lightness.

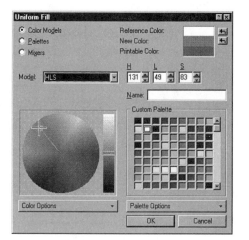

■ *L*A*B.* The L*A*B color model (see fig. 13.15) stems from one of the original color models aimed at describing colors numerically. This color model may appear confusing to use, and rightly so. The interactive selection is tricky to use at best. But, it is critical to the way in which color mode conversions are calculated during display and printing. L*A*B color is represented by a luminance, an 'A' color component on the green-red axis, and a 'B' component on the blue-yellow axis. In the Corel representation of this color model, luminance is divided into values ranging from 0 (darkest) to 100 (lightest), and the A and B components may range in color unit values ranging between -60 and 60. Colors may be selected by moving either the color position marker controlling the A and B components, and by the luminance marker on the vertical sliding scale.

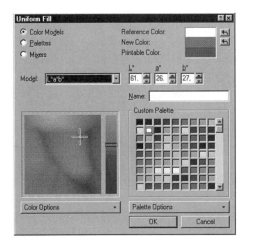

Fig. 13.15
The L*A*B color model controls involve a luminance slider control and the position of a marker controlling A and B components of color.

Creating Text & Drawings

■ *YIQ.* The YIQ model (see fig. 13.16) is the same one used in NTSC North American video standards and television broadcasts. Each of the Y, I, and Q values are measured in a range between 0 and 255. The Y component determines the luminance value, while the I and Q values interconnect to control green, blue, yellow, and magenta colors. An I and Q value set to 0, 0 represents green, and when set to 255, 255 represents magenta. Colors may be adjusted by moving the single IQ marker in the color selector window, while controlling the luminance values using the vertical selector.

Fig. 13.16
The YIQ color model controls work on a principle similar to the L*A*B color model involving a slider control to set luminance and a marker to set I and Q values.

■ *Grayscale.* The grayscale color model (see fig. 13.17) is perhaps the simplest of the CorelDRAW! color models, possibly due to the fact that it deals with only the color black. Values or grayscale shades for this model are divided up into shades ranging between 0 or black, and 255 or white. To set a grayscale color, slide the vertical selector slider bar up or down, or keyboard the value directly into the field.

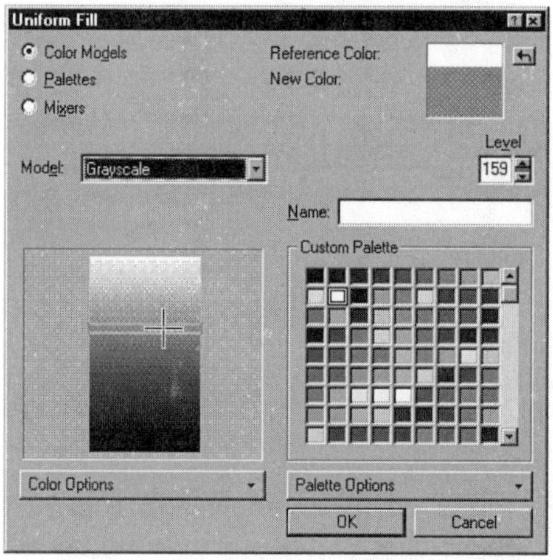

Fig. 13.17
The Grayscale color model controls are simple enough, involving a single slider control, and offer a graduated scale of 255 grayscale colors.

■ *Registration color.* This newcomer to the list isn't really a color model at all (see fig. 13.18). Setting an object in this color will cause it to appear as a solid color on each and every existing color layer in your document. Its purpose is mostly for setting registration alignment when printing to printers that may not accommodate the printer's registration marks to a page. It may also be useful as a security or water-mark color for identifying documents. Notice that its color is divided into cyan, magenta, yellow, and black, with 100 percent values for each. This indicates that it will print as solid CMYK for all process color separations. It will also print as a color on all spot color layers.

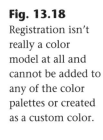

Fig. 13.18
Registration isn't really a color model at all and cannot be added to any of the color palettes or created as a custom color.

Defining Color Palettes

There are color models, color palettes, and color matching systems, and then there are spot color palettes and process color palettes—it can be a daunting maze of terms. By now (hopefully) the confusing terminology has been ironed out somewhat.

Essentially, a model is the method in which a color is visually or physically reproduced. CorelDRAW! 6 has the tools to define color in one of the ten color models mentioned in this chapter. A palette is basically a collection of pre-determined colors. In CorelDRAW! 6, there are seven third-party color palettes including Focoltone, Pantone Spot, Pantone Process, Trumatch, SpectraMaster, TOYO, and DIC. Each has its own characteristics and intended purpose.

With respect to spot and process color palettes, a spot color palette is essentially an RGB, or monitor, color matched to an ink color. When using spot color inks, you are basically selecting a monitor color from your spot color palette with the intent that the ink you are using is that very same color. When you are using process color the plan is a bit different, in that you are mixing screens of three basic colors, possibly with screens of black to reproduce a visible full-color spectrum.

Third-party color matching systems take all of this color theory quite a few steps further. To ensure that the color you select on your monitor is identical to the color of ink that will print on the printing press, most color systems have assigned ink colors a number for tracking. The key to this tracking method is the production of hard copy color swatches, which give a sample of the printed ink, the corresponding ink number, and a recipe for mixing pigments to produce a close likeness to that particular ink color. Cataloging colors puts a thin veneer of civility over the confusing screen percentage system used. Most color matching system vendors will reproduce color swatches for each process and spot color, and sometimes a separate version for printing onto shiny (coated) and non-shiny (uncoated) papers. Printing onto coated or uncoated paper stock can affect how ink colors appear after printing, and so using a color swatch is always a wise choice.

It's important to ensure you are working with at least an accurately calibrated monitor, or you have used the CorelDRAW! 6 Color Manager to develop an accurate color profile. If your monitor is fresh out of the box, drop what you're doing and calibrate it. Most good quality color monitors are tested for color accuracy at the factory, but there will always be variations for room lighting and electrical power sources. Don't stop testing once you have completed your monitor calibration. Continue through your entire system, calibrating through to your scanner and desktop color printer, and digital imagesetter. All of these devices play an integral part of your color production process and each can affect the outcome of your color accuracy in its own unique way.

Deciding which palette will work best for you is the first thing to do before beginning any color project. Once you have made your decision, you will likely want to have quick access to that palette at all times. From the View menu, select the Color Palette flyout and the palette you have chosen to display at the bottom of the CorelDRAW! window. That way you'll reduce the time wasted accessing the Uniform Fill dialog box. Anytime you're using a palette for more than just a few colors, get it on-screen. The less you have to access menus or dialog boxes the better.

The palette you end up using will depend on a number of factors, including your spot or process color needs, the complexity of your layout or illustration, and the amount of color trapping that may be necessary to ensure satisfactory printing results. *Trapping* is a procedure of adding an amount of overlap between adjacent areas of color with the aim of avoiding gaps caused by printing registration errors. Spot color palettes are basically infallible unless, of course, your printer gets the inks mixed incorrectly, but the process color palette is a bit trickier.

About Pantone Spot and Process Color Palettes

The largest and most comprehensive color matching system of them all is offered by Pantone, one of the first internationally recognized color standardization systems to dominate the printing industry. Pantone was on the scene long before digital color fell into the hands of the general public. The electronic palettes found in programs such as CorelDRAW! 6 are supported by a hard-copy collection of high-quality color swatches available in both uncoated and coated paper stock versions. The Pantone electronic process color palette (see fig. 13.19) contains more than 3,000 different colors, all of which claim to fall in the printable screen range. Colors are composed of screen percentages ranging from 0 to 100 in three and five percent increments. While a Pantone process color is selected, the cyan, magenta, yellow, and black color screen values are displayed in the C, M, Y, and K fields. The Pantone electronic spot color palette (see fig. 13.20) contains over 220 different colors. Pantone spot colors also display the approximate process color equivalent in the CMYK fields.

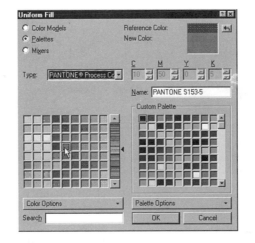

Fig. 13.19
The Pantone Process color palette contains more than 3,000 different printable colors.

Fig. 13.20

The Pantone Spot color palette shown here contains more than 220 different colors.

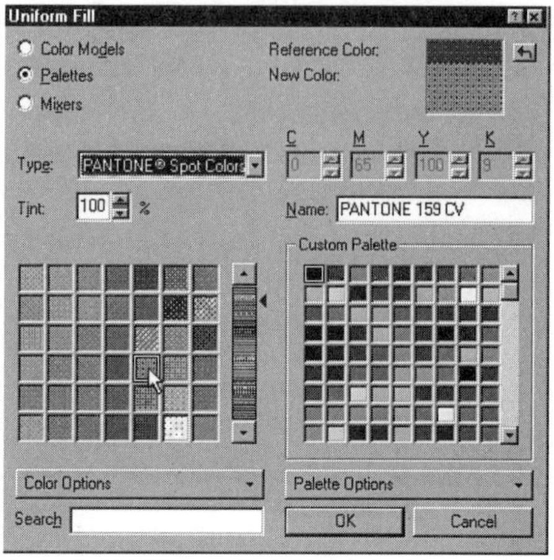

Pantone uses its own numbering system for process colors. Its coding is geared more toward locating the colors on its hard-copy printed swatches. For example, an ink color such as S 97-1 may be recognized first by S, which indicates that SWOP inks were used for print reproduction. The letter is followed by the numeral 97, indicating the page number of the color swatch. The last number, 1, indicates the position counted down from the top of that page. All colors are arranged in chromatic order according to the natural-light spectrum and each page contains nine tints.

The inclusion of Pantone's electronic spot and process color palettes in CorelDRAW! versions 3, 4, 5, and now 6, is just the tip of the iceberg when it comes to the full extent of its entire matching system. The complete Pantone system includes a line of slickly packaged products including color formula guides, color selectors, color specifying chips, color tint selectors, color foil selectors, color papers, markers and inks, transfer systems, and digital color imaging software to name just a few.

Tip

If you would like to contact Pantone for more information about its products, there are three worldwide offices as follows:

- Pantone, Inc., America
  590 Commerce Boulevard
  Carlstadt, New Jersey, 07072-3098
  Tel: (201) 935-5500
  Fax: (201) 896-0242

- Pantone UK, Inc.
  115 Sandgate Road
  Folkstone, Kent, CT20 2BL
  England
  Tel: 44-0303-259959
  Fax: 0303-259830
- Pantone, Asia
  Room 904, New World Tower
  16-18 Queen's Road Central
  Hong Kong
  Tel: (852) 845-8388
  Fax: (852) 845-7841

About the Focoltone Color System

The Focoltone color palette was first introduced in version 5 to DRAW!'s chromatic collection. Focoltone, a European-based company, designed this 750-color palette to reduce the need for tedious color trapping. The Focoltone palette works by standardizing CMYK screen percentages to five percent increments. The thrust of this standardization is to increase the likelihood of common, color screen percentages by reducing the variety of screens used. The Focoltone palette has been arranged in such a way that a full spectrum of colors is displayed on the palette at any given point.

Tip

Focoltone's head offices are located in the United Kingdom. You can reach its Sales offices by phone at 44-0785-712677, or by fax at 44-0785-714587. Its main office number is 44-0222-810940, or fax 44-0222-810962.

About the Trumatch Color System

The Trumatch process color palette is composed of over 2,000 easily printable colors. Trumatch has specifically customized its color matching system to suit the digital color industry, using the Computer Electronic Prepress System (CEPS). The palette is composed of 40 tints and shades of each hue. Black is varied in six percent increments.

Trumatch has developed its own numbering system. For example, a green color that is numbered Trumatch 23-C2 can be tracked by its number. The first number indicates a particular hue value. Hues are numbered sequentially around the color wheel of the visible color spectrum. The following letter indicates the tint of the hue graduated from 'A' or 100 percent to 'H' or 5-percent screens. The number following the letter indicates the percentage of black present. Black is divided up into six percent increments from a zero value, indicated by no number, to 42 percent indicated by the number 7.

The Trumatch numbering system may take some time to get used to, but with practice, the coding will likely become quite familiar. Trumatch has designed and printed process color swatches made up into coated and un-coated versions, printed using a standard set of SWOP (Standard Web Offset Printing) inks using a common screen frequency of 150-line. The printed Trumatch colors are broken down into YMCK colors because that is the way that they have actually been printed. Most other palettes are broken down into CMYK, which implies that the ink colors hit the paper stock in a different order, marginally affecting the final printed color.

Although Trumatch is a relative newcomer to the digital color world and new as far as color matching systems go, its system is quite solid and well-conceived. Trumatch palettes can be seen in other software products such as: QuarkXPress; Adobe Photoshop and Illustrator; Aldus Freehand, PageMaker, and PhotoStyler; Micrografx Designer; and Cachet by EFI. The Trumatch technology has also been adopted by imagesetter manufacturers such as Scitex, Linotype-Hell, and Du Pont.

Tip

Trumatch can be reached at:
    25 West 43rd Street, Suite 802
    New York, NY, 10036-7402
    Tel: (212) 302-9100
    Fax: (212) 302-0890

or, through Hebert Communications:
    233 Harvard Street, Suite 308
    Brookline, MA, 02146-5017
    Tel: (617) 232-1161
    Fax: (617) 232-8939

About the SpectraMaster Color Palette

The SpectraMaster process color palette was developed by DuPont for matching colors used in industrial coatings and colorants. The SpectraMaster color system contains more than 2,400 different colors that have associated CMYK values.

About DIC Color Guides and the TOYO 88 Color Finder System

The TOYO 88 color finder system and the DIC color finder system are widely used in Asia and other Pacific Rim countries, especially Japan. Each contains its own numbering system and collection of different process colors. The TOYO collection of colors has been developed using TOYO's own process ink colors. The DIC color guide has been developed using the DIC brand of process color inks and is divided into three categories of color, including DIC, DIC Traditional, and DIC Part II. When the DIC color palette is viewed by color name (an option available from the Color Options menu) the DIC category is identified. Reproduction and translation to RGB screen color and CMYK color conversion in CorelDRAW! 6 are achieved through L*A*B color space conversion.

Creating a Custom Palette

This is a feature that has been a valuable tool for the serious electronic artist working extensively in color. It enables you to create your own palettes for specific illustration uses. To create a custom palette using DRAW! version 6, follow these steps:

1. Using either the Uniform Fill (Shift+F11) or Outline Color (Shift+F12) dialog boxes, select the CMYK color model palette. You may also note that unless you have an object currently selected on your page, DRAW! will present a dialog box for setting the Uniform Fill or Outline Color default color. You may wish to select an arbitrary object before selecting either dialog box.

2. From the menu button below the Custom Palettes area (see fig. 13.21) select New Palette from the fly-out menu that appears. Select a name for your new palette and CorelDRAW! will add the file extension .CPL, indicating it is a Corel palette (see fig. 13.22). Notice also that the menu you have selected New Palette from contains additional commands to Rename Colors and Delete Colors, Open Palette, Save Palette, and Save As for other color and palette options. By default, DRAW! will store your custom palette in the COREL60/CUSTOM folder. Select the Save button.

Fig. 13.21

The Custom Palette control is found on the right side of the Uniform Fill or Outline Color dialog boxes. Both control the same color features.

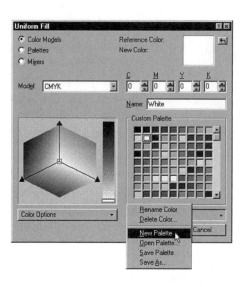

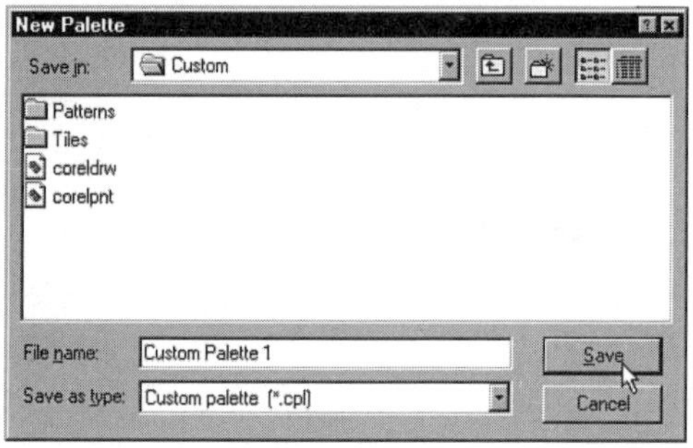

Fig. 13.22

Choosing a name and saving your new Custom Palette.

3. After saving, your custom palette opens to display an empty palette list. You may add colors to your custom palette from a number of sources, including colors already existing in other palettes or your own specified colors. To add a color from the CMYK palette, select the Color Models option in the upper-left of the dialog box and select CMYK from the Model pull-down menu below it.

4. By moving the color selector handles controlling cyan, magenta, yellow, and black, and keeping one eye on the New Color indicator in the upper-right corner of the dialog box and the other eye on the changing C, M, Y, and K percentage values, choose your first color.

5. To add this new color to your new custom palette, click the Color Options button below and select Add Color To Palette (see fig. 13.23). You may also add the color by clicking anywhere in the color selector or on

the New Color indicator with the right mouse button and select the same command. The color is added to the Custom Palette display, but notice it has no name yet.

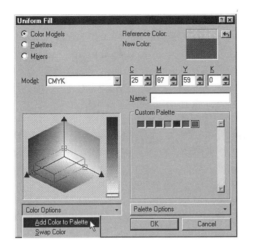

Fig. 13.23
The color controls available include commands to add colors to your custom palette.

6. Name your newly created color by entering a descriptive name in the Name text box. Use a name that is pertinent to the object or area you'll be coloring. Don't call it Red or Green, your monitor will tell you that. Be creative with your names. The Name field will accept names up to 32 characters in length and support upper- and lowercase letters. Once you have entered a name, and before clicking on any other controls, click the Palette Options button and select Rename Color. Your color name is saved.

7. To save the colors you have just added to your palette, select Save Palette from the Palette options button menu.

Tip

Once you have created and saved enough colors to fill the palette display area at the bottom of your CorelDRAW! window, you may want to prioritize them to suit your needs. You may move the colors in your custom palette by clicking and dragging them to a different position in the palette.

Creating Text & Drawings

II

Using Mixers

The Mixers in the Uniform Fill (Shift+F11) and Outline Color (Shift+F12) dialog boxes offer tools for manufacturing new colors based on blended or mixed colors, or by sampling from digital scanned images saved in bitmap format. The Mixers controls are displayed by selecting the Mixers option from the upper-left of the dialog box. There are two mixers available including the Mixing Area and Color Blend available from the Mode pull-down menu. Mixers compose colors based on either the RGB, CMYK, or HSB color models by selecting Color Options, Color Model.

Working with the Mixing Area Mixer

The Mixing Area (see fig. 13.24) works much the same way as an artist's painting palette does, and it first appears in its default format with a series of predrawn primary-colored circles. This feature has been completely revamped for CorelDRAW! 6. There are two main tools available, located to the upper-left of the mixing board: a Digital Brush tool, and a Color Picker or Eyedropper tool.

Fig. 13.24
The Mixing Area mixer enables you to mix color in much the same way a painter would using a traditional-style color palette.

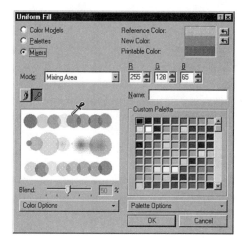

By selecting the Brush tool, you are able to add color to the mixing board. The color currently displayed in the New Color indicator in the upper-right of the dialog box is the color of the digital paint on your brush. You may change this color by clicking any colors displayed in your custom palette. To apply color, click or click-drag the mixing board with your Brush tool. You may also adjust the transparency of color added with the Brush tool by using the Blend slider control below the mixing board. Blend values range from 0 to 100 percent, 0 being completely opaque and 100 being completely transparent.

The size of the Brush tool may be set to Small, Medium, or Large and the type of brush to Hard, Medium, or Soft through the Color Options menu or by right-clicking the mixing board.

Next, to sample colors you have added to your mixing board, select the Eyedropper tool and click the new color. The color will then register in the New Color indicator. To add the color to your palette, select the Color Options button, and Add Color To Palette.

Working in the Color Blend Mixer

The Color Blend Mixer (see fig. 13.25) behaves like a four-way blending tool—smoothly graduating shades of color from four corners of a square display. Each corner may be set to a different color of your current custom color palette in either the CMYK, RGB, or HSB color models. The display area is divided into a grid in which the blended colors fall. The grid may be set to a number of different resolutions using the Color Options button menu, including 3, 4, 5, 6, 7, 8, 9, 10, 11, 12, and 25 units square.

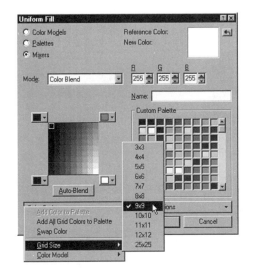

Fig. 13.25
The Color Blend area color mixer Color Options feature a grid flyout menu to set the number of blend colors.

The Color Blend area features an Auto Blend button that toggles ON or OFF. When ON, the Auto Blend feature recalculates all blended colors whenever a corner color changes, or whenever the grid size is changed. To change a corner color, click the closest color button and select a color from the color flyout palette. The palette that displays is the same as the custom palette currently in use.

To add a color to the current custom palette, click the corresponding grid square and select Color Options, Add Color To Palette. You may also Add All Grid Color to Palette (see fig. 13.26), in which case all colors currently displayed in the Color Blend area will be added. In cases where multiple colors are added to the custom palette, it may be wise to periodically rename the colors and save the palette changes.

Fig. 13.26
The Color Blend grid colors may be added to a new custom palette using the Add All Grid Colors to Palette illustrated here.

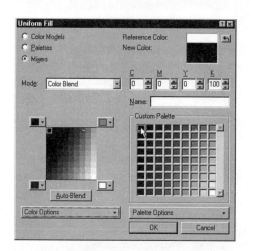

Troubleshooting

I have been working in the Mixing area blending colors and just noticed that my color model controls are set to RGB. Does that mean I have to start over?

No. When using the Mixing Area or Color Blend feature, you may switch at any time between the CMYK, RGB, or HSB color models. When doing this, CorelDRAW! 6 uses the L*A*B color space conversions to translate colors between models.

Sampling Colors from Scanned Images

A newly revamped and slightly hidden feature of CorelDRAW! 6 is the capability of the Mixing Area to import digital color bitmap images.

The Mixing Area Mixer can be used to sample CMYK, RGB, or HSB colors from imported digital bitmap images using the Eyedropper tool. The Color options menu contains three commands for Load Bitmap, Save Bitmap, and Clear Bitmap. When DRAW! is first installed, a Corel-prepared bitmap called PNTAREA.BMP is preloaded into the mixing board and contains enough primary and secondary colors to get you started mixing colors. But this is merely a prepared bitmap and may be substituted with any other bitmap image, as long as it is in .BMP format.

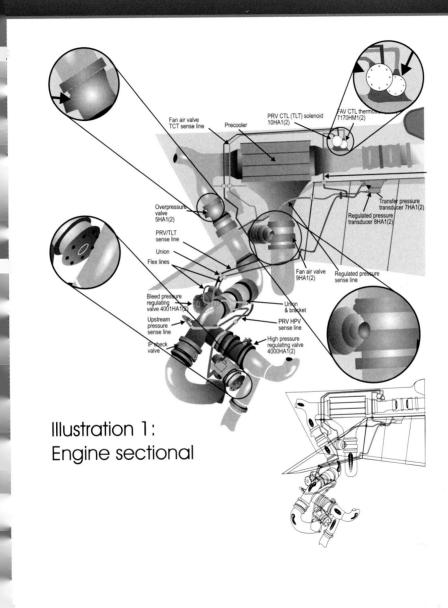

Fan air valve TCT sense line

Precooler

PRV CTL (TLT) solenoid 10HA1(2)

FAV CTL thermostat 7170HM1(2)

Transfer pressure transducer 7HA1(2)

Regulated pressure transducer 8HA1(2)

Overpressure valve 5HA1(2)

PRV/TLT sense line

Union

Flex lines

Fan air valve 9HA1(2)

Regulated pressure sense line

Bleed pressure regulating valve 4001HA1(2)

Upstream pressure sense line

IP check valve

Union & bracket

PRV HPV sense line

High pressure regulating valve 4000HA1(2)

Illustration 1:
Engine sectional

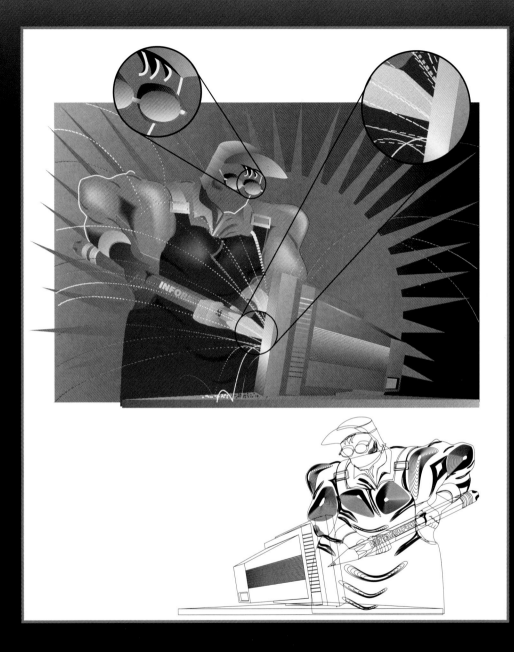

Blacksmith

This highly stylized illustration of a blacksmith thrusting a giant pencil into a
computer monitor was created using mostly blends, fountain fills, and simple
objects. The sparks appearing to shoot from the penetration point were created by blending very short curves and applying them to a blend path. The
wireframe diagram (right) illustrates the concentration of blend objects in the
illustration. Certain areas of detail are highlighted using a Magnify Lens effect.

➤ See "Assigning a
   Blend Path,"
   p. 283

➤ See "Blending
   Similar Objects,"
   p. 282

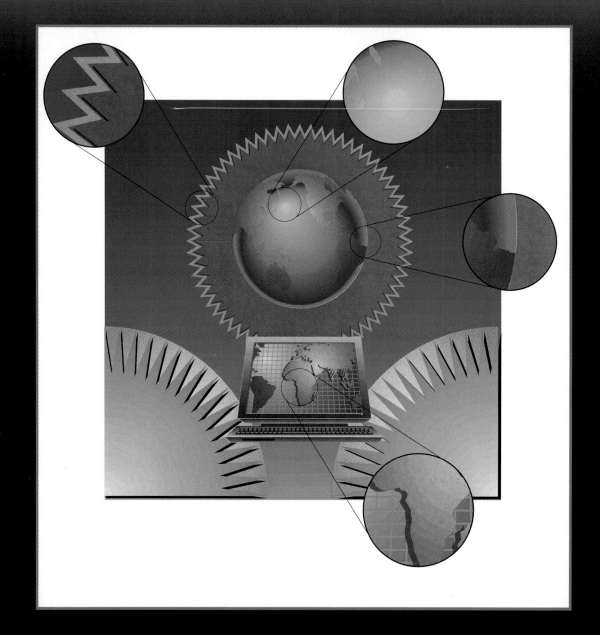

World Communication

This illustration incorporates the concept of computers giving access to world communication. Coloring in the globe was created using a compound blend of ellipses. The backdrop to the globe including the four process colors cyan, magenta, yellow, and black was created using bitmap texture fills. The computer was drawn using basic shapes while the grid was created using the Blend command. The continents were assigned a Transparency Lens effect over the top of a black shadow and the grid. Star shapes in the bottom corners were created using the new Star tool.

➤ See "Using Texture Fills," p. 258

➤ See "Blending Similar Objects," p. 282

➤ See "Secrets of Lens Effects," p. 374

➤ See "Creating Stars," p. 187

Fill Gallery

g seven pages contain highlights of the seldom-used Bitmap incorporated into CorelDRAW! Texture Fills may be created using 27 texture Styles supplied. By changing the various attributes of ncy, density, offsets and so on, of these texture styles you are e different and distintive effects.

➤ See "Usin Fills," p.

Bitmap Texture Fills: Styles

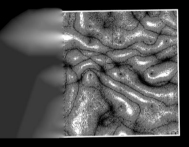

Style name: Biology2 3C
Texture number: 29369

Style name: Blend Colors
Texture: Red, green, blue, black

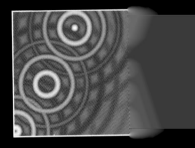

Style name: Rings 3C
Texture number: 841

Style name: Satellite Photography
Texture number: 5846

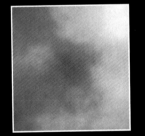

Style name: Fractal Rock Cracked
Texture number: 4291

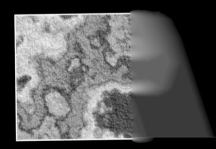

Style name: Sky 3 Colors
Texture number: 16478

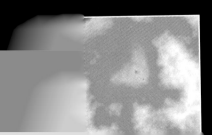

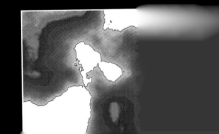

Bitmap Texture Fills: Samples

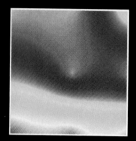

Sample name: Airbrush
Texture number: 25967

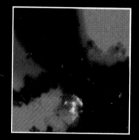

Sample name: Cloudy Nebula
Texture number: 11556

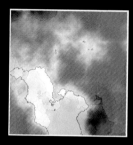

Sample name: Gouache wash
Texture number: 13100

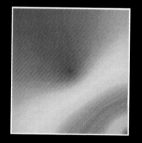

Sample name: Neon slice
Texture number: 26619

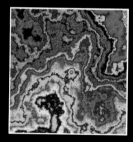

Sample name: Pizzazz mineral
Texture number: 11521

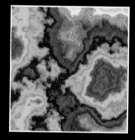

Sample name: Pizzazz mineral 2
Texture number: 16824

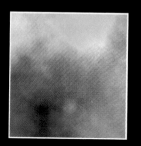

Sample name: Purple haze
Texture number: 14226

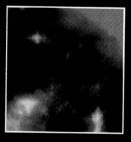

Sample name: Solar flares
Texture number: 28097

Sample name: Vegetation
Texture number: 5467

Bitmap Texture Fills: Samples 5

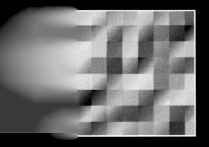

Sample name: Blocks rainbow
Texture number: 32652

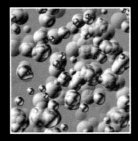

Sample name: Boil
Texture number: 6557

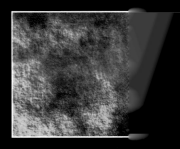

Sample name: Borealix m
Texture number: 16953

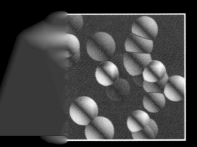

Sample name: Bubble land
Texture number: 28968

Sample name: Crater
Texture number: 18219

Sample name: Curled Dor
Texture number: 2804

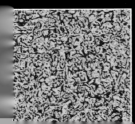

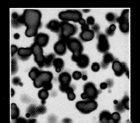

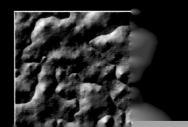

Bitmap Texture Fills: Samples 6

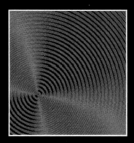

Sample name: Brake light
Texture number: 19818

Sample name: Cotton candy
Texture number: 17382

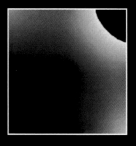

Sample name: Eclipse of the sun
Texture number: 5461

Sample name: Epidermis
Texture number: 1113

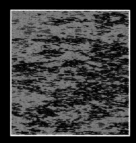

Sample name: Evening ripple
Texture number: 7504

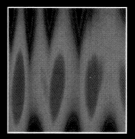

Sample name: Hall of flame
Texture number: 1753

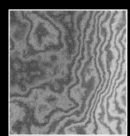

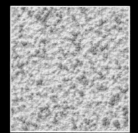

Bitmap Texture Fills: Samples 6 *(continued)*

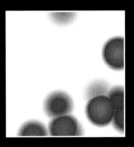

Sample name: Mitosis
Texture number: 19655

Sample name: Moonray
Texture number: 5042

Sample name: Shimmering silk
Texture number: 23333

Sample name: Stormy sky
Texture number: 19439

Sample name: Volcano
Texture number: 14687

Sample name: Waterfall
Texture number: 1501

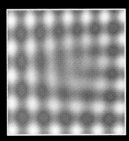

Sample name: Gingham
Texture number: 23334

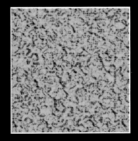

Sample name: Circuit board
Texture number: 1000

Sample name: Cobwebs
Texture number: 4586

Full-Color Bitmap Pattern Fills

CorelDRAW! 6 comes with the tools to apply fully-tiling bitmap pattern fills to any object. You may also assign your own image files to be used as tilable fills. Controls for full-color bitmap pattern fills include options for small, medium, or large tiles, settings for width, height, row and column offsets, and options for seamless tiling.

➤ See "Using Full-Color Pattern Fills," p. 249

Pattern: Star 1

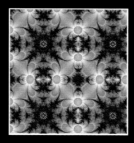

Pattern: Star 2

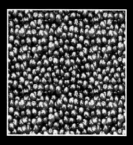

Pattern: Fruit

Pattern: Candies

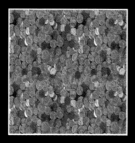

Pattern: Coins

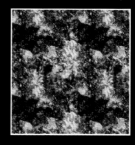

Pattern: Water

Pattern: Flowers

Pattern: Stones

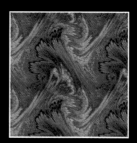

Pattern: Combed ink

Vector Pattern Fills Gallery

CorelDRAW! 6 includes a collection of nearly 70 vector pattern fills. Vector pattern fills are different from bitmap patterns in many ways. Screen redraw time is much faster, and vector fills take much less memory space than bitmap texture fills do. Controls for vector pattern fills include options for small, medium, or large tiles, settings for width, height, row and column offsets, and options for seamless tiling.

➤ *See "Using Vector Pattern Fills," p. 247*

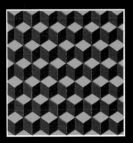

Bubble 1
Tile size: Medium

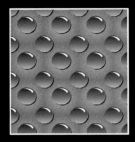

Bubble 2
Tile size: Medium

Bubble 3
Tile size: Medium

Cubes
Tile size: Medium

Cubes 1
Tile size: Large

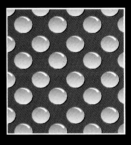

Tile 6
Tile size: Large

Tile 6
Tile size: Large

Tile 2
Tile size: Large

Reptiles
Tile size: Large

PHOTO-PAINT 6 Filter Gallery

The following is a gallery of 24 PHOTO-PAINT 6 filter examples. These digital images were saved at 150 DPI using the CMYK 32-bit color model in TIF format. Each example is identified by the filter name and includes the particular filter variables applied.

➤ *See "Understanding the Gallery of Filter Effects," p. 569*

Hot Air Balloons

Cycling Race

Tropical Beach

Hang glider

Tropical sunset

Pumpkins

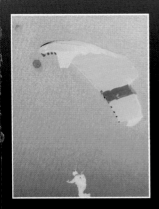

Color Transform, Invert The Color Transform, Invert filter applied to this digital image of a hang glider. Three variables exist named Period, Strength, and Damping. In this case a Period of 28, a Strength of 23, and a Damping of 73 were applied to the image.

Lens Flare The filter applied to this digital image of a hot air balloon ride was Render, Lens Flare. Two variables exist for this filter, including a lens size and a Brightness setting. In this case the lens used was 35 mm prime, while the Brightness was set at 150 percent. The actual hot spot of this filter may be positioned by clicking on the digital preview of the effect while in the Effects dialog.

2D Effects, Wet Paint The 2D Effects, Wet Paint filter applied to this digital image of a hang glider. Two variables exist percent and wetness. In a percent setting of 100 and a wetness setting of 45 was applied to the image.

Artistic, Vignette The Artistic, Vignette filter applied to this digital image of two hot air balloons. The vignette mode may be set to black, white, or Paint Color and offset and fade options may be changed. In this case a mode setting of black was used, while an offset of 0 and a fade of 75 were applied to the image.

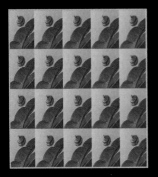

2D Effects, Tile The 2D Effects, Tile filter applied to this digital image of two hot air balloons. Two variables exist to set the number of vertical and horizontal tiles to be created. In this case the vertical number was set to four while the horizontal number was set to five.

Noise, Add Noise The filter applied to this digital image of a hot air balloon ride was Noise, Add Noise. Two variables and two options exist for this filter, including Level and Density settings, and Color Noise and Noise Type options. In this case both Level and Density were set to 50 percent, while the Color Noise option was selected and the Gaussian noise type was used.

2D Effects, Puzzle Filter The 2D Effects, Puzzle filter applied to this digital image of pumpkins. The empty area behind the puzzle parts may be filled with black, white, original image, paint color, or invert, while the block size and offset may be controlled. In this case block size was set to 10, while the empty area was set to invert.

Find Edges The Sharpen, Find Edges filter was applied to this digital image of a hot air balloon ride. Two variables exist for this filter, including Level and Edge type settings. In this case Level was set to 150 while the Edge Type was set to Solid.

...nsform, Bit Planes The Color Transform, Bit Planes ...d to this digital image of a cycling race. The filter may ...ntrol red, green, and blue color planes individually or ... this case all three colors were changed uniformly to ...five while the effect was applied.

Wind The filter applied to this digital image of a cycl... progress was 2D Effects, Wind. Two variables were use... ing an Opacity setting of 90 percent and a Strength se... percent, using close to the maximum settings of both ... characteristics.

...k The Artistic, Glass Block filter was applied to this ...tropical beach. There are two variables that exist for ...cluding Block Width and Block Height. In this case, ...dth and height were set to a square of 50.

3D Effects, ZigZag The 3D Effects, Zigzag filter app... digital image of a tropical beach. Three variables exist ... Period, Strength, and Damping. In this case a Period o... Strength of 23, and a Damping of 73 were applied to ...

...The Color Adjust, Tone Map filter applied to this ...e of a tropical sunset. Multiple variables exist for this ...as a selection of Preset color map curves. In this case ...olarized Response Curve was selected and applied to

2D Effects, Whirlpool The 2D Effects, Whirlpool fil... to this digital image of a tropical beach. Multiple varia... for this filter including Spacing, Smear Length, Twist, ... Detail. In this case however, the Preset style named Su... was selected.

...p The Mesh Warp filter applied to this digital image ...umpkins. The mesh warp grid was divided into 8 and

3D Effects, Page Curl The 3D Effects, Page Curl filt... to this digital image of a sunset. Three variables existir... filter are Horizontal, Vertical, Opaque and Transparent ... a page curl direction option. In this case a horizontal, c...

...he filter applied to this digital image of a tropical ...he incredible Artistic, Alchemy filter. The Alchemy ...r the most option-rich filter of all the PHOTO-PAINT ... are a number of saved filter styles that come with ...NT and the one used in this case was the Vortex ...e.

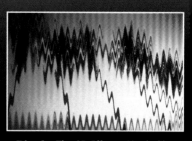

2D Effects, Ripple The 2D Effects, Ripple filter ap... digital image of a tropical sunset. The direction of t... may be set to vertical, horizontal, or Custom angle ... tion option, while the controls for Period, Amplitud... Direction angle may be used. In this case a ripple di... vertical while Period and Amplitude were set to a m...

...he filter applied to this digital image of a tropical ...olor Transform, Halftone. Four variables exist for this ...ng Dot Control and color angle controls for Cyan, ...d Yellow. In this case the default settings of Dot ...van=0, Magenta=30, and Yellow=60 were used.

Adjust, Noise The Adjust, Noise filter was applied ...tal image of a sunrise. Two variables exist for this fil... ing Level and Density settings measured in percenta... case both settings were set at 50 percent, while the ... made was More Uniform.

...Shear The 2D Effects, Shear filter applied to this ...of a sunset. Four areas of adjustment exist including ...rol, undefined fill options, presets, and Shear map ...his case a curve shear map was applied to the image.

3D Rotate The filter applied to this digital image c... was 3D Effects, 3D Rotate. Two slider controls affect ... and horizontal distortion of the image. The horizon... set to -10 while the vertical slider was set to 60. The ... Fit was also activated.

...D Effects, Swirl filter applied to this digital image of ...ngle variable exists named Angle. In this case an...

Impressionist The filter applied to this digital ima... cal sunset was Artistic, Impressionist. Two variables...

series

filter under the Artistic effects filter category in PHOTO-PAINT 6
werhouse of filtering effects in itself and contains a huge variety
rs to choose from. The examples contained here illustrate the
nd in this single filtering tool. These filters were applied as is
ging any of the available variables to produce these effects.

➤ *See
"Understanding
the Gallery of
Filter Effects,"
p. 569*

Filter Preset: Vortex thick style

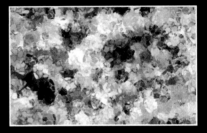

Filter Preset: Ice Cubes

Filter Preset: Diagonal Brick

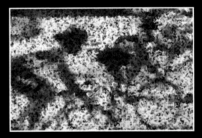

Filter Preset: Cubist

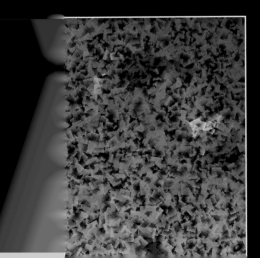

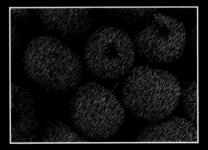

Filter Preset: Sketch Color

If you have access to a color snapshot of your illustration subject (if not the actual subject), and a method of scanning in color and saving in .BMP format, you have all the tools you need to sample and reproduce photographic-like color. PHOTO-PAINT 6 is an excellent tool to use for scanning and saving to this format, but any basic photo-editing package capable of saving files to .BMP format will do.

Troubleshooting

I am trying to load an image into the Mixing Area but when I try to locate it, I can't seem to find it. What's wrong?

The Mixing Area is compatible only with the Windows Bitmap format. If you intend on loading a bitmap image into the Mixing Area you will first need to save it as a BMP format bitmap image at a resolution of at least 72 dots per inch (DPI) and a size of no more than approximately 170 pixels wide and 120 pixels high.

II

Creating Text & Drawings

To prepare and import a digital scanned image into the Mixing Area, follow these steps:

1. Scan the image using either PHOTO-PAINT or your favorite scanning utility. Scan using a resolution of at least 150 DPI in order to capture the most color detail possible. You may scan higher if you wish, however this may cause your file to become quite large and slow down drawing time. Don't worry about color model, you will be able to adjust that in the Mixing Area menus.

2. Open the image into PHOTO-PAINT and make any required color, brightness, contrast, or filter effects needed. If you need to resample or resize your image, do so in PHOTO-PAINT. Make sure that the image size is no more than 170 pixels wide by 120 pixels high. Any image information beyond this area will simply fall outside the mixing board, and no options exist for viewing it. Your image file will automatically be oriented to the bottom-left corner of the mixing area window. If your digital image is larger than 170 by 120 pixels, you may want to consider sectioning it into individual files.

3. For quick-access, save the bitmap image to the COREL60/CUSTOM folder, which is the first folder DRAW! will look in when loading a bitmap.

4. Launch CorelDRAW! 6 and open either Uniform Fill (Shift+F11) or Outline Color (Shift+F12), and select Mixers, and Mixing Area from the pull-down menu to obtain access to the mixing area.

5. Click the Color Options button menu below the mixing board and select Load Bitmap. Locate the directory where your .BMP file is stored, and select it. The image will appear in the mixing board area window (see fig. 13.27).

Fig. 13.27
Loading your prepared bitmap image into the Mixing Area mixer for color sampling enables you to sample directly from the image.

6. Select the Eyedropper tool in the Mixing Area and click an area of your image in the mixing board. If you wish, begin a new color palette specific to your drawing project. To open a new palette click the Palette Options button menu and select New Palette. Name and Save your new palette.

7. Begin sampling particular areas of the bitmap image and adding the colors to your new custom palette in the usual way. For a shortcut, you may drag directly from the bitmap onto your custom palette area using the eyedropper tool. Try to collect as many shadow, midtones, and highlights as possible. Name each color using a reference to the subject matter if possible. You will likely find that while the colors in your image may be well-defined, some colors may actually be quite similar depending on the quality of your scanned image.

The color information you collect from your bitmap image and save into your custom palette may be used in combination with the vector drawing tools found in DRAW, such as Blend and Contour for fills, or for Outline colors. Once you have saved the Corel palette, it may also be used in any of the CorelDRAW! 6 suite of programs including PHOTO-PAINT 6, PRESENTS 6, and DREAM 3D 6.

From Here...

Color issues in CorelDRAW! 6 remain as important as they were in previous versions of the program. The calibration tools have become easier to use, making it all the more imperative to properly calibrate your entire color system including color scanners, monitors, and color printers and proofing devices. There have been few changes to the color models contained in the program. The collection of color models that remains in CorelDRAW! 6 reemphasizes the international status of this application by including color models from a variety of color theories and a palette collection representative of color matching systems used throughout the world.

Color customization tools in CorelDRAW! 6 have improved with procedures for sampling, mixing, saving, and opening custom palettes becoming less cryptic to use. While this chapter focuses on the issues involved in under-standing color theory, you may want to put this knowledge into practice by referring to the following sections:

- See Chapter 7, "Using Fills and Outlines," to learn more about color. You'll also learn how to use palettes, including how to create custom palettes.

- See Chapter 16, "Printing," to learn how to use separation controls.

II

Creating Text & Drawings

Chapter 14

Customizing CorelDRAW! 6

One of the great features of CorelDRAW! 6 is its customization power. The introduction of Windows 95 and its advancements in open interface architecture now allow DRAW! 6 users to customize many aspects of the interface. If you want full control over your digital tools, now you have it. Users have been wanting customization from Corel for several releases and Corel has now granted their wish.

CorelDRAW! 6 enables you to create your own toolbars—composed of all your favorite interface buttons—as well as display or hide any screen features, including menus. If you don't like Corel's choice of keyboard shortcuts, you can change them. If you want to maximize your productivity, there are specific customizing features for that too.

In this chapter, you learn to

- Create your own toolbars

- Custom-build your own menus and flyouts

- Customize keyboard shortcuts

- Access the tools customization

- Tailor your color palette display

- Control display aspects

Customizing Toolbars

The first and most useful customization feature is DRAW!'s capability of enabling you to create your own custom toolbars. The program contains six native toolbars, including Standard, Toolbox, Text, Zoom, Roll-Ups, and Workspace. Add to that the eight tear-off tool flyouts including Node Edit, Zoom, Curve, Dimensions, Shape, Text, Outline, and Fill. You can add to this list of features that can help in customization, a tear-off color palette and all of the commands available in the pull-down menus. Any of these items may be tossed into a new toolbar and saved as your own. There is no limit to the number of custom toolbars you may create.

Creating a new toolbar is a two-step procedure. First you need to create, name, and save the new toolbar. Then, you need to load it up with buttons representing your favorite commands.

To create a new custom toolbar, follow these steps:

1. Choose View, Toolbars to display the Toolbars dialog box (see fig. 14.1), and click the New button. Notice that a new toolbar is added to the list of six existing toolbars.

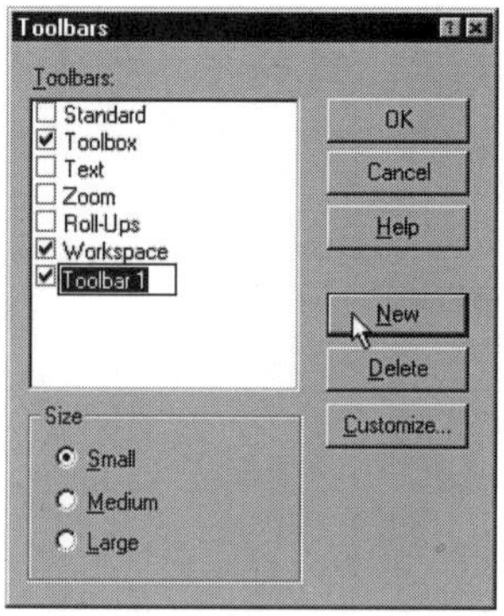

Fig. 14.1
Create a new custom toolbar using the Toolbars dialog box.

2. Name your new toolbar by typing a name. Try to keep your custom toolbar name short so that it displays easily, even if you only add a few tool buttons to the toolbar. Notice that a check mark appears beside the toolbar indicating that it is selected to display.

3. Click the OK button. The Toolbars dialog box leaves the screen and your new toolbar is dropped out onto the screen, naked of buttons. Without any buttons in the toolbar it takes on its smallest shape and you may not be able to read your toolbar's full name until a few toolbar buttons have been added.

4. With the toolbar still displayed, select <u>T</u>ools, <u>C</u>ustomize to display the Customize dialog box controls (see fig. 14.2). You also may access this dialog box by clicking directly on the <u>C</u>ustomize button in the Toolbars dialog box. Once you have the Customize dialog box controls displayed, you may need to reposition the Customize dialog box to see your new toolbar at the same time.

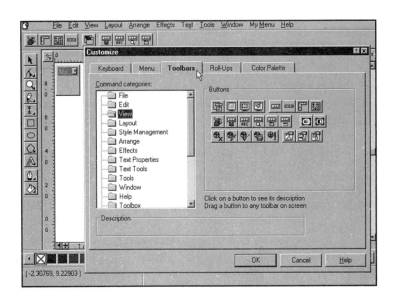

Fig. 14.2
Adding new buttons to your new toolbar.

5. Click the Toolbars tab in the Customize dialog box to display all of the toolbars available in CorelDRAW! 6. Under <u>C</u>ommand Categories you see all of the tools organized into groups. While each category is selected, the buttons area displays the available toolbuttons. Choose the category that contains the command or tool you wish to add to your toolbar.

6. Locate the exact button that represents the tool you wish to add. Use the pop-up help to identify each of the buttons by holding the cursor over the button for approximately two seconds. Or click once on the button and read the text in the description window at the bottom left of the Customize dialog box.

7. Once you have located the correct button, click and drag it onto your new toolbar and release the mouse. The new button is added to your toolbar. Continue adding buttons until you are finished. To reorder the buttons on the toolbar, click and drag them in relation to each other within the toolbar itself.

Creating Text & Drawings

8. Click the OK button to finish adding buttons (see fig. 14.3).

Fig. 14.3
After properly
organizing the
buttons on your
toolbar, finish
creating the
toolbar by
selecting OK.

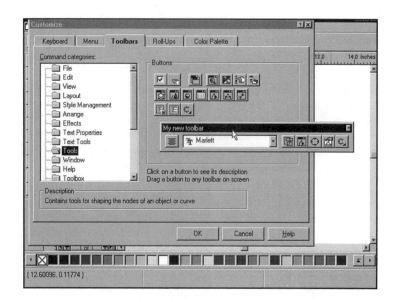

◄ See "Advanced
Customizing:
Status Bars,
Tools, and
Toolbars,"
p. 78

To remove a custom toolbar completely and forever, display the toolbar, and choose View, Toolbars, choose the toolbar from the Toolbars dialog box that displays, and select Delete. To Reset the toolbar, choose Reset from the same dialog box. To close a displayed toolbar, click on the toolbar close button in the upper-right corner of the toolbar.

Custom Keyboard Assignments

Using toolbars instead of menu access is more desirable when using the mouse for most of your routine activities on-screen. But, using keyboard shortcuts is more desirable for productivity when using keyboard-oriented functions such as typing. If you are finding as you work, that the keyboard shortcuts already set up for you in the menus (such as Ctrl+O for File, Open, or Ctrl+N for File, New) are difficult to work with, or you just want to customize for the sake of personalizing your CorelDRAW! 6 setup, you may change or add keyboard shortcuts.

Keyboard shortcuts, sometimes referred to as Accelerator Keys, may be set using up to four different layers or keyboard combinations including the Ctrl key, Function keys, the Alt Key, and up to four native keyboard characters not including Escape, Enter, Return, and the numeric keypad arrow keys.

For example, you may wish to assign a keyboard shortcut of Ctrl+Alt+A,L,L to perform the File, Save All command, or Ctrl+Shift+G,R,I,D to access the Grid and Ruler Setup instead of Layout, Grid & Ruler Setup. In most cases more than one keyboard shortcut may be assigned or has already been assigned.

> **Tip**
>
> Keep in mind that the shortcut you choose should theoretically be easier or faster to access than the shortcut that already exists for the command, or the Alt key combination already built into the interface.

To access the keyboard shortcut controls choose Tools, Customize and select the Keyboard tab (see fig. 14.4).

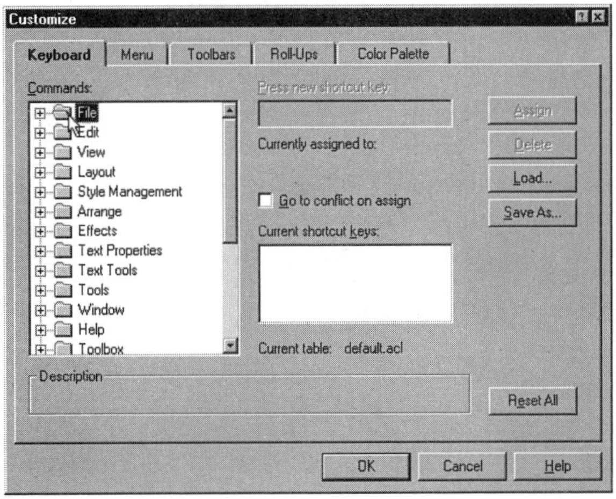

Fig. 14.4
The Keyboard tab of the Customize dialog box contains controls for changing or adding any of the keyboard shortcuts in CorelDRAW! 6.

The Customize, Keyboard tab features several customizing tools including a Commands list window that displays a list of the shortcut-eligible commands in CorelDRAW! 6, as well as fields for Current Shortcut Key and Press New Shortcut Key, and an option to Go To Conflict On Assign.

■ *Current Shortcut Keys.* To see the shortcut key currently assigned to the command you have chosen, look in the Current Shortcut Keys window. If there is more than one shortcut assigned to the command, all keyboard shortcuts will appear in this window.

■ *Press New Shortcut Key.* To enter a new keyboard shortcut, click in the Press New Shortcut Key field and press the new keyboard shortcut.

All keyboard identification will automatically be entered for you in this field.

■ *Go To Conflict On Assign option.* It is impossible to assign the same keyboard shortcut for two different commands. The option Go To Conflict On Assign will activate once a new keyboard shortcut has been entered for a command and the Assign button is pressed. If there is a keyboard shortcut conflict the new shortcut will be assigned to the chosen command, while the command with the conflicting keyboard is highlighted and its keyboard shortcut erased. If a conflict occurs while this option is not selected, entering a keyboard shortcut and pressing the Assign button causes an error message to appear on-screen and the keyboard assignment you had entered will be cleared from the field.

■ *Assign, Delete, Load, and Save As buttons.* The Assign button is pressed once you have entered a keyboard shortcut in the Press New Shortcut Key field. The Assign button causes DRAW! to save your new shortcut association to the command you have chosen unless a conflict has occurred. Once a shortcut is successfully assigned it appears in the menu bar beside the command. To remove a keyboard shortcut from a command, click on the shortcut in the Current Shortcut Keys window and select Delete. To open a previously saved keyboard shortcut setup, select Load, locate the corresponding *.ACL file, and open it. To save a current setup, select Save. To save a changed setup, select Save As.

■ *Reset All.* Pressing the Reset All button causes all command shortcuts that have not been saved to be cleared.

To assign a new keyboard shortcut to a menu or tool (non-menu) command, follow these steps:

1. If you haven't done it already, select Tools, Customize, Keyboard tab, and locate the command you would like to assign a shortcut to in the Commands list window. To see the contents of a folder, double-click the folder or use the right-arrow key on your keyboard.

2. Once you have located the command, click in the Press New Shortcut Key field and proceed to pressing the actual keyboard shortcut you would like to use. You do not need to enter words, commas, plus signs, or spaces.

3. Click the Assign button. If a conflict exists with another command, a warning message appears on-screen. If not, your shortcut is assigned.

4. You will automatically be prompted to save an *ACL file when you select OK.

5. To revert to the original CorelDRAW! 6 keyboard shortcut commands, select the Load button and open the file ARTISTIC.ACL in the COREL60/DRAW folder.

Customizing Menus

You may create custom menus in CorelDRAW! 6 using the Tools, Customize, Menu tab controls (see fig. 14.5). The Menu tab features two main windows listing Commands on the left side and the actual installed Menus on the right side.

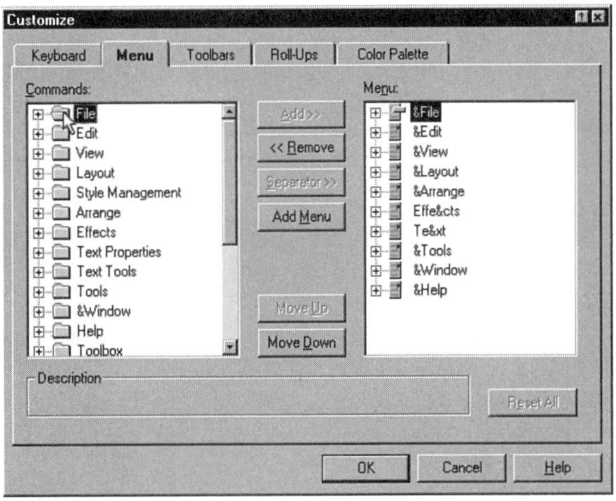

Fig. 14.5
The Menu tab of the Customize dialog box contains controls for changing or adding any of the pull-down menus in DRAW!.

The Commands side lists command group folders and command items, while the Menu side lists menus, submenus and, if applicable, flyout menus currently installed in DRAW!.

- *Add.* Copies a command item selected from the Commands list to the Menu list.

- *Remove.* Removes a Menu item from the installed Menu list.

- *Separator.* Adds a separation line between items in the Menu list at a point just below the currently selected item.

■ *Add Menu.* Adds a new, unnamed menu to the Menu list at a point just below the currently selected item. If your selected item is a menu, a submenu will be added in the form of a menu flyout. Any items added to that flyout will be treated as the menu flyout items. Menus and submenus should be named in a way that describes the items they contain whenever possible.

■ *Reset All.* This erases any current changes between setup saves.

■ *Move Up.* When a Menu list item is selected the Move Up button moves the item upward one level.

■ *Move Down:* When a Menu list item is selected the Move Down button moves the item down one level.

To install a new menu, complete with flyouts and separation lines, follow these steps:

1. If you haven't done it already, choose Tools, Customize, Menu tab, and select a location for your new menu to be installed.

2. Once you have selected a location on the Menu side of the dialog box, select the Menu list item just above that spot (not a submenu, but a main menu item) and click the Add Menu button. A new menu is installed just below the selected menu item. Notice that the new menu has the generic name "Menu."

3. To name your Menu item, click once on it and a blinking cursor appears at the end of the line. Enter a new name. By adding an ampersand to precede a character, an underscore is applied to the character and it becomes an Alt command. This character must be uniquely different from the rest of the main menu items or the Alt command will not apply.

4. Double-click your new menu item to open it. Notice that it opens to reveal the word "Empty," indicating that it contains no items or submenu items.

5. Click on Empty and press the Add Menu button again. Name the new menu item "&Third Flyout." Click on &My Menu again to highlight it and click the Add Menu button a second time. Rename the new item "&Second Flyout" (see fig. 14.6). Repeat this again to add another item, naming it "&First Flyout." This forms a basic structure of the menu bar.

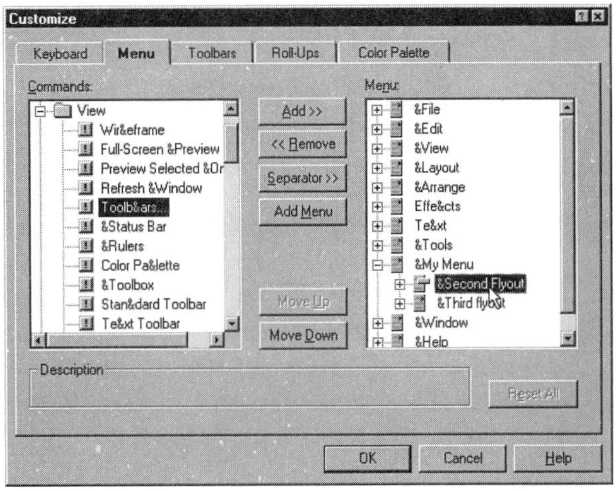

Fig. 14.6
Adding a submenu creates a flyout in the current custom menu.

6. To begin adding <u>C</u>ommands list items to the menu, click on the &My Menu item again and locate a <u>C</u>ommands list item to add to it. Once located, click <u>A</u>dd. Add at least two more items this way.

7. Click the last menu item before the &First Flyout item and click the Separator to add a visual line between the items (see fig. 14.7).

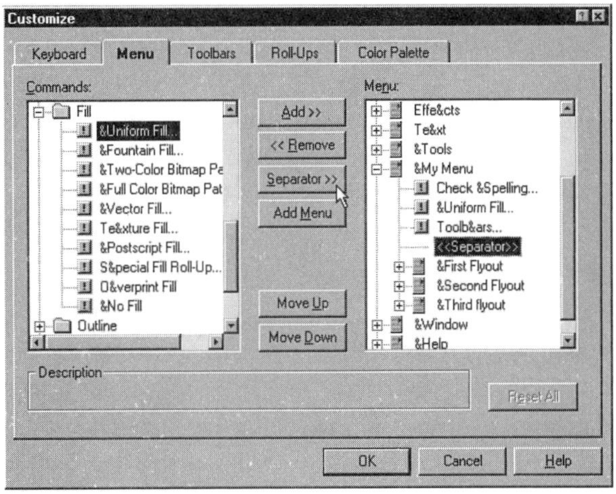

Fig. 14.7
Adding a visual separator line to your menu bar, as illustrated here, helps organize the items—especially if they are complex.

8. Double-click each of the flyout menus to open them, highlight the word "Empty" in each, and add at least three <u>C</u>ommands list items to each using the procedure in step 5.

9. To finish the installation, click OK. Your menu is installed into the CorelDRAW! 6 interface (see fig. 14.8).

Fig. 14.8
The final installed menu item, complete with menu items, Alt-key characters, flyouts, and a separator line.

Customizing Roll-Ups

Roll-ups can be customized to a certain extent. There are more than 30 roll-ups in CorelDRAW! 6. As few as three or four of them on-screen can make your work area pretty crowded, especially if your screen is 640×480 pixels or you are working with a small-sized monitor. The roll-ups are initially set to align with the left side or the right side of your screen.

Like toolbars, roll-ups may be customized into groups so that if you work with certain roll-ups frequently, you may group all of those roll-ups into a single roll-up to keep your screen from getting over-crowded with interface junk.

Left- and Right-Align Roll-Up Controls

Roll-ups may be customized using the Tools, Customize, Roll-Ups tab dialog box (see fig. 14.9). At best, these controls are almost impossible to figure out at your first—or even second—visit to them. Controls consist of two move buttons in between the two lists, one for moving items from the left to the right and another to move them in the opposite direction. The main purpose of these controls is to set your roll-ups to appear on either the left or right side of your screen. Roll-ups in the Left Aligned Roll-Ups window appear on the left when selected, while those in the Right Aligned Roll-Ups window appear on the right.

In the Roll-Ups tab, you will notice that a rough directory tree exists to the left of the roll-up list described by dotted lines. Some of the roll-ups have a plus-sign indicator beside them showing that they contain multiple roll-ups.

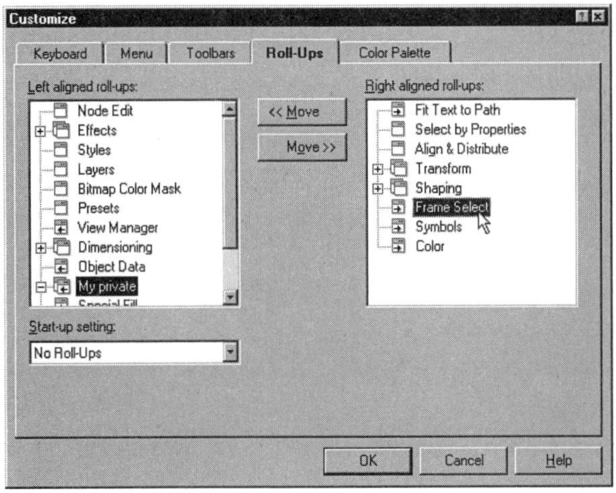

Fig. 14.9
The Roll-Ups tab of the Customize dialog box enables you to set roll-ups to appear on either the left or right side of your working window when selected to display.

Grouping Roll-Ups Together

Roll-ups also may be organized into groups, by holding down the Ctrl key and dragging the main title bar (the top part of the roll-up) onto the surface of another roll-up (see fig. 14.10). If you combine two single-function roll-ups, the result will be a combination roll-up named New Group X, where X represents the next available new group number (see fig. 14.11). To remove a roll-up from a grouped situation, hold down the Ctrl key again and drag the name of the roll-up out onto your page. The roll-ups will split apart and become single roll-ups.

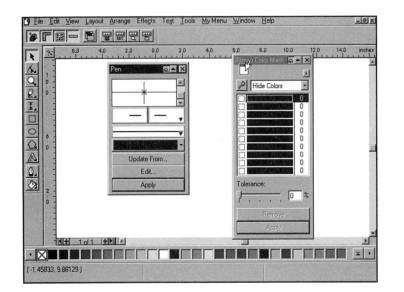

Fig. 14.10
To combine two roll-ups hold the Ctrl key down and drag one on top of the other. The result will be a combination roll-up.

II

Creating Text & Drawings

Fig. 14.11
The Pen roll-up and the Bitmap Color Mask roll-ups combined into a single roll-up.

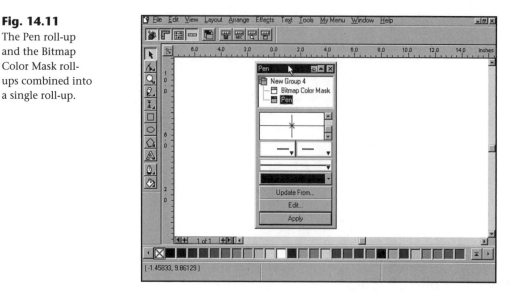

Breaking Apart a Roll-Up

You also may split apart a combination roll-up such as the Transform roll-up that is already organized into five separate roll-ups. To split a combined roll-up apart, grab and drag on the square icon symbol beside the individual roll-ups in the combined roll-up window and drag it out onto your work area. When you release the mouse, a new, single roll-up appears (see fig. 14.12).

Fig. 14.12
Breaking apart the Transform roll-up into five separate roll-ups.

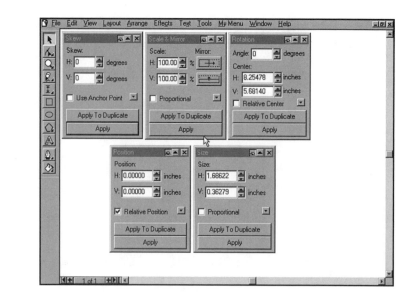

Naming a New Roll-Up Group

To name or rename a newly combined roll-up group, open the Tools, Customize, Roll-Ups tab, and locate and click the roll-up you wish to rename. Click a second time on the roll-up group name until a blinking cursor appears. Backspace and replace the text with your new roll-up group name, or immediately begin typing the new name. The new name is saved when exiting the Customize dialog box.

Customizing the Color Palette

Your on-screen Color Palette may be customized to suit your working needs by accessing either the Tools, Customize, Color Palette tab from the menu bars, or by right-clicking on a blank part of the on-screen color palette and choosing Customize from the menu that appears (see fig. 14.13).

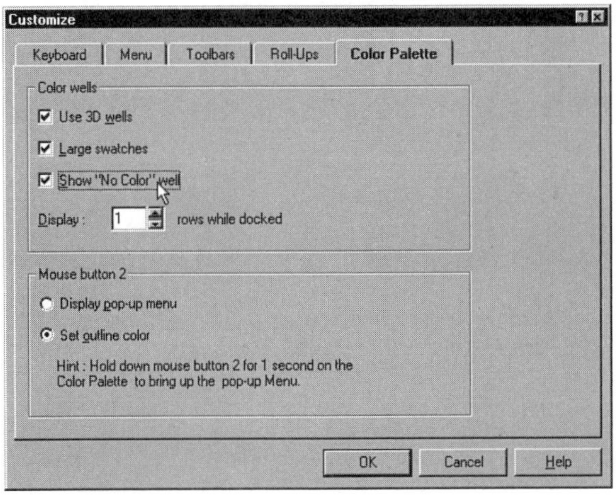

Fig. 14.13

The Color Palette tab of the Customize dialog box contains controls for setting color wells and right mouse button controls.

This Customize tab is separated into Color Wells and options for Mouse Button 2.

- *Use 3D Wells.* Selecting the Use 3D Wells option allows DRAW! to display the color palette wells in a three-dimensional appearance, but doesn't change the way these tools behave. Leaving this option unselected causes the wells to appear as flat, colored squares.

- *Large Swatches.* The Large Swatches option may be useful for handicapped, or infant users who have trouble with either vision or mouse movement. Selecting the Large Swatches option causes DRAW!'s inkwells to display at twice their usual size (see fig. 14.14).

Fig. 14.14
The Color Palette option is Large Swatches available from the Tools, Customize controls may be useful for handicapped or visually-impaired users.

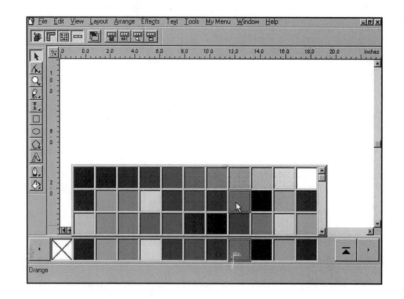

- *Show 'No Color' Well.* If you find that you never use the No Color well, you now have the option of eliminating it completely from your on-screen color palette by deselecting this option.

- *Display Rows.* The Display Rows While Docked option allows you to set the number of rows of color wells that display from a range of 1 to 7 rows.

- *Display Pop-Up Menu.* Using this option, you may set the function of your right mouse button to display the pop-up menu.

- *Set Outline Color.* Using this option, you may set the function of your right mouse button to set the Outline color of objects.

Using Task Progress

Task Progress (see fig. 14.15) is a new feature that enables you to prioritize and monitor your computer's operations while in CorelDRAW! 6. This feature is especially useful when you are printing a large drawing from CorelDRAW! 6 but wish to continue working at the same time without encountering severe interruptions in your CorelDRAW! operations. Task Progress enables you to apply system-intensive operations such as applying effects, opening roll-ups, opening other files, and so on. The Task Progress feature takes advantage of the power of Windows 95 and CorelDRAW! 6's multi-tasking capabilities.

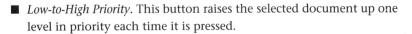

Fig. 14.15
The Task Progress feature enables you to control the priority of document operations such as printing.

To open the Task Progress dialog box controls, select Tools, Task Progress. This feature works much the way a print spooler works by enabling you to control and set priorities. While opened, the Task Progress dialog box still allows you to work on your document page and access menus, although it doesn't have to be open in order to be handling the priorities you have set for your tasks.

By selecting the items in the Document window, you are able to stop the task before it is completed, pause and resume progress, and raise or lower the priority of the task using the following options:

- *End Task*. This button immediately ends the selected task, deleting it from the Document window.

- *Suspend/Resume*. This button temporarily pauses the selected task, immediately making your system resources available for any other tasks in progress. The Suspend/Resume button is a toggle button. In other words, while a document is suspended (paused) the button acts as a Resume button, and once you press the button, resuming action, the button now acts as a Suspend button.

- *Low-to-High Priority*. This button raises the selected document up one level in priority each time it is pressed.

- *High-to-Low Priority*. This button lowers the selected document down one level in priority each time it is pressed.

Even though this feature is useful for tasks such as printing, there are some limitations to its usefulness:

- You cannot close a CorelDRAW! document that is currently printing or paused, no matter what its priority

II

Creating Text & Drawings

- You cannot use Task Progress for importing or exporting operations

- You can, however, close task progress after tasks have been prioritized and the priority you have set will be preserved

---

Troubleshooting

Why is Task Progress grayed out in my Tools menu all the time? Do I have to actually be printing something for it to be available?

Task Progress will only become available once the Enable Multi-Tasking option in the Tools/Options, Advanced tab is selected. Until then, the feature will remain inactive.

More Customizing Tips

The following is a quick-access reference to other customizing features available throughout CorelDRAW! 6:

- *Customizing startup functions.* On program startup, you may set CorelDRAW! 6 to perform a number of immediate tasks, including displaying the Welcome Screen, Start a New Document, Open an Existing Document, Select a Template, or Select An Application Tutorial. The control for setting this function may be found in the Options dialog box found by choose Tools, Options (Ctrl+J) under the General tab, bottom left.

- *Customizing Save and Autobackup.* To customize Back Up, Save, and Restore functions, choose Tools, Options, Advanced tab. Back Up customization tools include options for setting the backup file folder Directory, Make Backup on Save, and an Auto-Backup option with editable time interval. Save and Restore options include Interruptible Saving, and optimizing saves For Speed or For Storage (see fig. 14.16).

- *Customizing pop-up menu first item.* At the top of every pop-up menu there appears a single, separate item. This single item is actually Corel's answer to the previous version's tool-related right mouse button functions that provided functions for accessing the Object Menu, 2× Zoom, Character menu, Text Edit tools, Full-Screen preview, or Node Edit. You can, however, set this first pop-up menu item to be any of those old functions by choosing Tools, Options, Advanced tab and using the First Menu Item pull-down menu (refer to fig. 14.16).

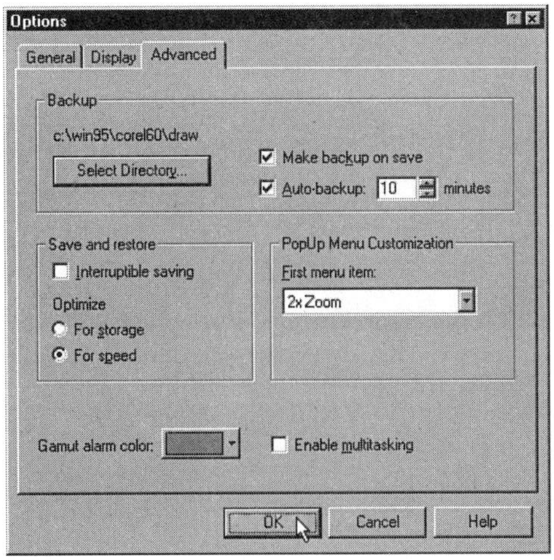

Fig. 14.16
The Advanced tab allow you to set backup and save options.

- *Customizing Duplicate, Clone and Nudge Controls.* The offsets for Duplicated or Cloned objects may be set in the Tools, Options, General tab using the Horizontal and Vertical value fields in the Place Duplicates and Clones area. Nudge values, may be set using the Nudge value field. In most cases, when accuracy counts, setting a small nudge value works best. Nudge is controlled by the up-, down-, left-, and right-arrow keys on your keyboard.

- *Customizing tool behavior.* Setting the particular behavior of a tool can be done by displaying the tool in the Toolbox, right-clicking on it to access the pop-up menu, and then selecting Properties to access the Tool Properties sheet. In some cases, double-clicking will achieve the same results as can be had with the Knife, Eraser, Freehand, Bezier, Ellipse, Polygon, Spiral, and Graph Paper tools. You also may access any of the tools properties by choosing View, Properties, Tool to display the Tool Properties sheet (see fig. 14.17).

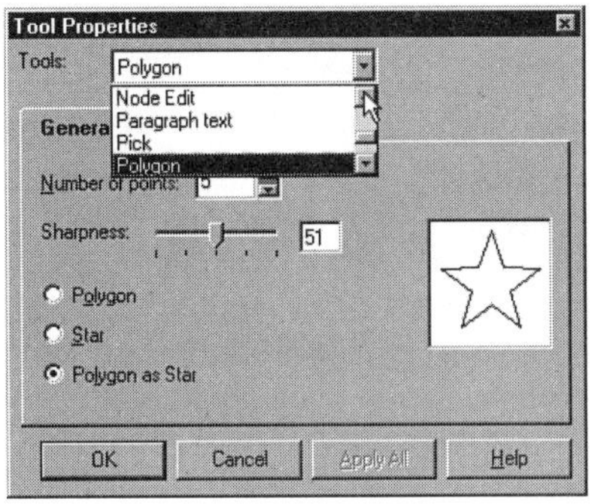

Fig. 14.17
The Tool Properties dialog box is accessed by choosing View, Properties, Tool.

■ *Customizing fountain fill display.* The way in which CorelDRAW! renders its fountain fills to the screen may be customized by choosing <u>T</u>ools, <u>O</u>ptions, Display tab and using the P<u>r</u>eview Fountain Steps option. This control divides each object containing a fountain fill into steps according to the value set. You may set this to a value in a range between 1 and 256.

◄ See "Advanced Customizing: Status Bars, Tools, and Toolbars," p. 78

Troubleshooting

Even though I am increasing the Preview Fountain Steps setting, when I print my drawing the fountain fills always appear the same. Shouldn't they look better?

Print Options are completely separate from Display Options. The Preview Fountain Steps setting terminology is very close to the terminology used in Print Options where you will see the term Fountain Steps used. To improve the appearance of printed fountain fills select <u>F</u>ile, <u>P</u>rint, Op<u>t</u>ions and select the Options tab where you will find the Fountain Steps setting. To increase fountain fill printing, enter a higher setting. The maximum setting for printed Fountain Steps is 250 steps.

■ *Customizing moving objects display.* When objects are click-dragged, a marquee, or dotted bounding box, usually represents the object on-screen. You may change this to a full marquee representation of the object by selecting <u>V</u>iew, Proper<u>t</u>ies, <u>T</u>ool to display the Tool Properties sheet and selecting the Pick tool from the pull-down menu. Select the Draw Objects When Moving option, which also includes a time delay to drawing the selected object representation. The default of 0.50 is usually quite effective.

■ *Customizing Zoom, Pan.* While the Panning tool is selected in the Toolbox, you are able to use the right mouse button for either Zooming Out or the default action which happens to be the pop-up menu most of the time. This choice may be made by choosing <u>V</u>iew, Proper<u>t</u>ies, <u>T</u>ool to display the Tool Properties sheet and selecting Zoom, Pan from the pull-down menu (see fig. 14.18). This dialog box also enables you to change to the traditional Zoom flyout containing all of the zoom controls in the Zoom toolbar.

◄ See "Understanding Tools Options," p. 65

■ *Customizing screen resolution.* Screen resolution also may be customized by choosing <u>V</u>iew, Proper<u>t</u>ies, <u>T</u>ool to display the Tool Properties sheet and using the <u>E</u>dit Resolution button. The resolution editing controls are useful when drawing scale objects in the 1:1 ratio drawing mode. Pressing the Edit Resolution button causes two rulers to display on-screen (see fig. 14.19), which are used to verify the accuracy of your screen by comparing them with an actual physical ruler graduated in the same units. If for some reason your screen ruler doesn't match your physical ruler you may make adjustments to the resolution using the Horizontal and Vertical pixels per foot controls, respectively. Be sure to make adjustments to both vertical and horizontal screen rulers until they both match.

Fig. 14.18
Customizing the Zoom, Pan tools using the Tools Properties sheet.

Creating Text & Drawings

Fig. 14.19
Adjusting the screen resolution using the Edit Resolution controls available in the Zoom, Pan Tool Properties sheet controls.

From Here...

In the future, using someone else's copy of a software program will likely be as difficult as learning the program itself. Customization is definitely the wave of future software applications and Corel seems to have taken a substantial lead with CorelDRAW! 6. By using the customization controls in this program you can change nearly everything except the program itself.

Customizing your application for your own personal use is highly recommended. Everyone has his or her own special and unique way of accomplishing tasks. Now that you have the power to optimize and customize the tools used to accomplish these tasks your productivity is bound to increase dramatically.

For information on related topics:

■ See Chapter 3, "Making CorelDRAW! 6 Easy to Use," to learn more about options, including how to set page options, and advanced customization.

Part III

Sharing and Printing Files

15   Importing and Exporting Files

16   Printing

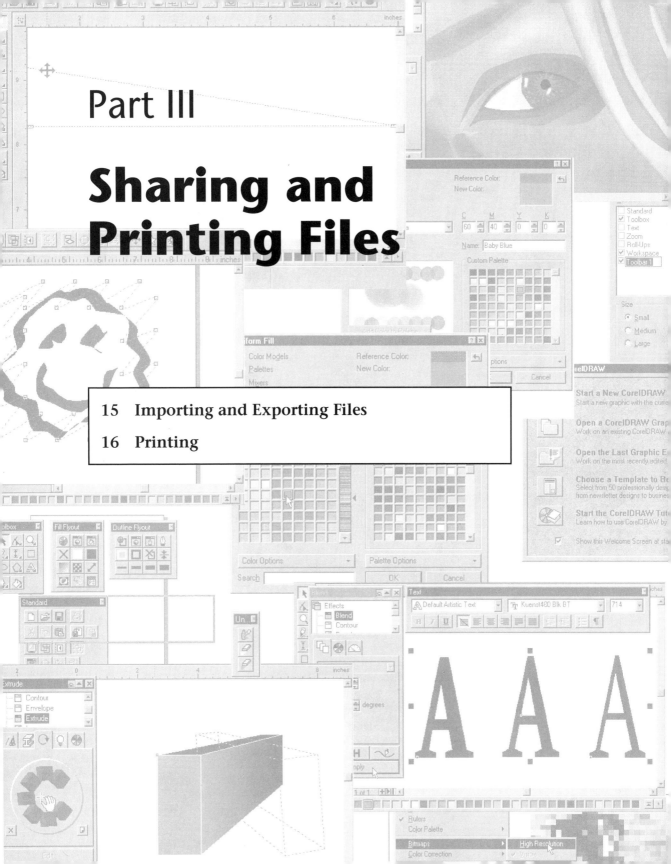

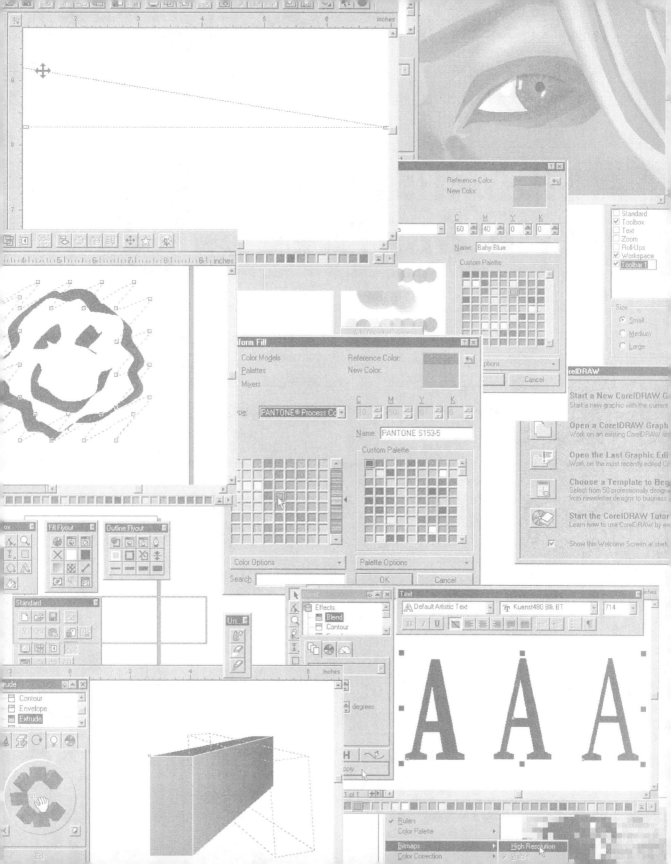

Chapter 15

Importing and Exporting Files

The behind-the-scene technical operations of import and export filters in CorelDRAW! 6 are markedly different than in any previous version. The main difference is that a single filter handles both importing and exporting functions. Therefore, at least theoretically, import issues will be the same as exporting issues. So, at first, the topics of importing, exporting, and using drag-and-drop functions may not appear all that intriguing. But, if you consider them from a business standpoint—and CorelDRAW! is part of your business tool arsenal—they're well worth studying.

If you work in a small or medium-sized business as most CorelDRAW! users do, you may already realize that you need to use specific applications for specific tasks. Somewhere down the line you'll need to either take your documents into another application for further refinement, or you'll need to assemble several elements together in a single application. The key is in preparing your files for the importing or exporting processes and using the correct filter. Whether you use custom fonts or special colors in your documents, or whether you have a specific reproduction method that you're using you'll likely need to tweak or nudge your data in some way to make the task a bit smoother.

In this chapter, you learn to

- Use DRAW!'s vast importing and exporting gateways

- Recognize file formats and file types

- Optimize CorelDRAW! 6 files for exporting

- Prepare files from other applications for importing into CorelDRAW! 6

- Capitalize on drag-and-drop functionality

The Potential of Importing and Exporting

CorelDRAW! 6 is a long way from previous versions where there were only a handful of import or export filters. Version 6 comes equipped with options to install 80 different import and export filters, making CorelDRAW! 6 one of the most compliant programs in the industry.

Import and export filters are like gateways into other worlds. Import filters provide the in door to CorelDRAW! 6 while export filters are the way out.

For example, imagine a small printing business using CorelDRAW! as their choice of software for producing layouts or designs for clients. A single new import filter like the AutoCAD DXF filter could open the door to business opportunities never before thought possible. Architectural or engineering firms who traditionally use this type of program for the bulk of their drawings now have a compatible computer-language translation.

Maybe the architect needs a brochure to advertise housing designs to potential new clients and would like to use the brochure to showcase some of their work without having to manually draw special artwork just for the brochure. Maybe they just need a one-time poster produced to advertise their services. Here's where the import filter (in this case likely the DXF filter) comes in handy. Files may be saved as DXF format from the AutoCAD program and then imported directly into CorelDRAW! 6. It would likely save hours of manual work and the client would end up with a better price for a potentially better-looking brochure.

This chapter gives you an overview of the various import and export filter families, and some idea of which suits your needs in a particular situation. You also may want to keep in mind the potential opportunities that may open up for you as these filters are described.

All about Importing

 The import command in CorelDRAW! 6 (see fig. 15.1) is displayed by choosing File, Import (Ctrl+I). On first opening, the Import dialog box allows you to specify two different variables, including File Name and File of Type, and when the Options button is pressed will expand to display information relating to Image Size, File Format, and any Notes associated with the file (if it supports that feature). The import command also can be accessed through the Standard toolbar, eighth icon from the left.

Further investigation will reveal a Preview option that lets you visually examine your file if there are thumbnail options existing for that particular file type. Also, a Filter Information button provides specific information about the import filter you have selected, and an additional pull-down menu option is available to select either the Full Image, Crop the image, or Resample. These options are available only for bitmap file formats.

Final options in the Import dialog box include an option to Supress Filter Dialog, which allows the Import command to ignore displaying the progress bar and CorelDRAW!'s import messages during importing. Allowing CorelDRAW! to skip displaying the import messages makes importing operations much faster. An Auto Reduce option is also available specifically for vector formats. This enables CorelDRAW! to automatically reduce redundant nodes on vector format files created from scanned documents or traced vector graphics. Reducing the number of object nodes will significantly reduce file size, printing times, and object complexity.

The Import Dilemma: Which Filter?

With 80 import filters to choose from which one should you select? Unfortunately, receiving an exported file does not always come with the luxury of being able to re-import it properly if the filter used isn't compatible or up-to-date. It's important to select the right filter to minimize the amount of unreadable data that comes into your CorelDRAW! 6 file.

III

Sharing & Printing Files

Table 15.1 recommends import filters or methods to try first when importing from specific applications.

Troubleshooting

I just tried to import an old file using the import command and it didn't work. How do I import it?

Some older applications do not automatically add file extensions to the file names, making it almost impossible to tell what the source program was. If you are unfortunate enough to receive one of these files, make your best guess, and then make a copy of the file adding your trial extension and try the import filter. CorelDRAW! 6 tells you whether you have used the wrong filter or not.

Table 15.1   Corel's Recommended File Types and Extensions

Application	Recommended Filter (Extension)
Adobe Illustrator	.AI (EPS filter)
Arts & Letters	.AI (EPS filter) or try clipboard
AutoCAD	.DXF first, or then HPGL (.PLT files)
ASCII text	Use the clipboard with paragraph text tool
CorelDRAW	.CDR, OLE, Drag-and-drop, or clipboard
CorelTRACE	CorelTRACE .EPS or AI
Excel (spreadsheet)	.XLS, or drag-and-drop
Excel (graphs)	Clipboard, or drag-and-drop
GEM Artline	.GEM
GEM Graph	.GEM
GEM DrawPlus	.GEM
Harvard Graphics	.CGM
Lotus 1-2-3	Lotus .CGM or Lotus .PIC
Lotus Freelance Plus	.CGM
Macintosh vector-based	Macintosh PICT .PCT, or .AI
Micrografx Designer	.DRW, .AI (.EPS)

Application	Recommended Filter (Extension)
Graph Plus	.DRW, .AI (.EPS)
Scan Gallery (Scangal)	.TIF
WordPerfect Graphic	.WPG

Corel's Import Filter Collection

Table 15.2 is an excerpt taken straight from CorelDRAW! 6's CORELFLT.INI file. This is what you can expect to be equipped with if you have selected a full install during the installation process.

Table 15.2   Corel's Filter Inventory List
FilterNo1=JPEG,IEJPG60.FLT
FilterNo2=OS2,IEBMP60.FLT
FilterNo3=TGA,IETGA60.FLT
FilterNo4=SCT,IESCT60.FLT
FilterNo5=GIF,IEGIF60.FLT
FilterNo6=ICO,IEICO60.FLT
FilterNo7=CUR,IECUR60.FLT
FilterNo8=BRS,IEBRS60.FLT
FilterNo9=IMG,IEIMG60.FLT
FilterNo10=PCD,IEPCD60.FLT
FilterNo11=PP,IETIF60.FLT
FilterNo12=PSD,IEPSD60.FLT
FilterNo13=MAC,IEMAC60.FLT
FilterNo14=WVL,IEWVL60.FLT
FilterNo15=CALS,IETIF60.FLT
FilterNo16=BMP,IEBMP60.FLT
FilterNo17=CPT,IETIF60.FLT
FilterNo18=TIFF,IETIF60.FLT

III

Sharing & Printing Files

(continues)

Table 15.2   Continued

FilterNo19=PCX,IEPCX60.FLT

FilterNo20=GEM,IEGEM60.FLT

FilterNo21=CGM,IECGM60.FLT

FilterNo22=DXF,IEDXF60.FLT

FilterNo23=PICT,IEPICT60.FLT

FilterNo24=PIF,IEPIF60.FLT

FilterNo25=WPG,IEWPG60.FLT

FilterNo26=CMF,IECMF60.FLT

FilterNo27=HPGL,IEHPGL60.FLT

FilterNo28=EMF,IEWMF60.FLT

FilterNo29=PIC,IEPIC60.FLT

FilterNo30=DRW,IEVCT60.FLT

FilterNo31=MET,IEVCT60.FLT

FilterNo32=NAP,IEVCT60.FLT

FilterNo33=CMX50,IECMX60.FLT

FilterNo34=CMX60,IECMX60.FLT

FilterNo35=CDR,IECDR60.FLT

FilterNo36=WMF,IEWMF60.FLT

FilterNo37=EPS,IEEPS60.FLT

FilterNo38=PS,IEPS60.FLT

FilterNo39=AI,IEAI60.FLT

FilterNo40=TAI,IEAI60.FLT

FilterNo41=CCH,IECCH60.FLT

FilterNo42=QTM,IEQTM60.FLT

FilterNo43=FLIC,IEFLI60.FLT

FilterNo44=MPEG,IEMPEG60.FLT

FilterNo45=PICS,IEPICS60.FLT

FilterNo46=AVI,IEAVI60.FLT

FilterNo47=DOC6,IETXT60.FLT

FilterNo48=DOC1,IETXT60.FLT

FilterNo49=DOC2,IETXT60.FLT

FilterNo50=DOC3,IETXT60.FLT

FilterNo51=DOC4,IETXT60.FLT

FilterNo52=DOC5X,IETXT60.FLT

FilterNo53=DOCM3,IETXT60.FLT

FilterNo54=DOCM4,IETXT60.FLT

FilterNo55=DOCM5,IETXT60.FLT

FilterNo56=WP6,IETXT60.FLT

FilterNo57=WP51,IETXT60.FLT

FilterNo58=WP5,IETXT60.FLT

FilterNo59=WP42,IETXT60.FLT

FilterNo60=WS1,IETXT60.FLT

FilterNo61=WS2,IETXT60.FLT

FilterNo62=WS7,IETXT60.FLT

FilterNo63=WS6,IETXT60.FLT

FilterNo64=WS5,IETXT60.FLT

FilterNo65=WS4,IETXT60.FLT

FilterNo66=WS3X,IETXT60.FLT

FilterNo67=WS3XX,IETXT60.FLT

FilterNo68=WS2000,IETXT60.FLT

FilterNo69=LGC,IETXT60.FLT

FilterNo70=XYWIII,IETXT60.FLT

FilterNo71=XYWIIIPLUS,IETXT60.FLT

FilterNo72=XYWIV,IETXT60.FLT

FilterNo73=XYWW4,IETXT60.FLT

(continues)

Table 15.2   Continued
FilterNo74=SAM1,IETXT60.FLT
FilterNo75=SAM2,IETXT60.FLT
FilterNo76=TXT,IETXT60.FLT
FilterNo77=RTF,IETXT60.FLT
FilterNo78=TTF,IETTF60.FLT
FilterNo79=SCD,IESCD60.FLT
FilterNo80=AT1,IEAT160.FLT

The import/export filters in table 15.2 can be decoded as follows. Take the first filter, for example. The first part,

FILTERNo=1

represents the order that the filter is loaded into CorelDRAW! 6 when it launches. In this case, this filter will be loaded first. The second part of the code,

JPEG

indicates the filter format, or in this case Joint Photographers Expert Group (JPEG) format which represents a standard bitmap compression format. Last, the filter file name itself,

IEJPG60.FLT

which may be broken down and read as "import/export, file extension is JPG, for CorelDRAW! version 6, filter file extension is FLT". If you check the ordering of the import/export filters that load into CorelDRAW! 6 you'll notice that the filters match the order they are numbered in this listing.

Table 15.3 illustrates the CorelFLT.ini information in simpler terms, indicating that the following formats and versions may be imported into CorelDRAW! 6:

Table 15.3   CorelDRAW! 6 Compatible Import/Export Formats

Application/File Type	Version(s)	Extension(s)
Adobe Illustrator	1.1, 88, 3.0	AI
Adobe Photoshop		PSD
Ami Professional	1.1, 1.2	SAM
Ami Professional	2.0, 3.0	SAM
ANSI Text		TXT
AutoCAD DXF		DXF
CALS Compressed Bitmap		CAL
CompuServe Bitmaps		GIF
Computer Graphics Metafile		CGM
Corel Metafile		CMF
CorelPHOTO-PAINT		CPT
Corel Presentation Exchange	5.0	CMX, CDR, PAT
Corel Presentation Exchange	6.0	CMX, CDR, PAT
CorelTRACE		AI
CorelCHART		CCH
CorelDRAW		CDR
CorelMOVE		CMV, MLB
CorelSHOW		SHW
EPS {Encapsulated Placeable}	EPS, DCS	
Enhanced Windows Metafile		EMF
GEM files		GEM
GEM Paint File		IMG
HP Plotter HPGL		PLT
IBM PIF		PIF, PF
JPEG Bitmap		JPG, JFF, JTF
Kodak Photo-CD		PCD

III

Sharing & Printing Files

(continues)

Table 15.3 Continued

Application/File Type	Version(s)	Extension(s)
Legacy 1.0, 2.0		LEG
LOTUS Freelance		PRE
Lotus PIC		PIC
Macintosh PICT		PCT, PIC
MACPaint Bitmap		MAC
MET Metafile		MET
Micrografx	2.x, 3.x	DRW
Microsoft PowerPoint		PPT
Microsoft Word	3.x	DOC
Microsoft Word	4.x	DOC
Microsoft Word	5.0, 5.5	DOC
Microsoft Word for Macintosh 4.0		DOC
Microsoft Word for Macintosh 5.0		DOC
Microsoft Word for Windows	1.x	DOC
Microsoft Word for Windows	2.x & 6.x	DOC
OS/2 Bitmap		BMP
PaintBrush		PCX
Picture Publisher	4	PP4
PostScript Interpreted		PS, EPS, PRN
Microsoft Rich Text Format		RTF
SCITEX		CT, SCT
Targa Bitmaps		TGA, VGA, ICB, VST
TIFF 5.0 Bitmaps		TIF, SEP
Wavelet Compressed Bitmap		WVL
Windows Metafile		WMF
Windows	3.x/NT	CUR, DLL, EXE, ICO

Application/File Type	Version(s)	Extension(s)
Windows	3.0 Bitmaps	BMP, DIB, RLE
WordPerfect	4.2	WP, WP4
WordPerfect	5.0	WP, WP5
WordPerfect	5.1 for Windows	WP, WP5
WordPerfect	6.0 for Windows	WP, WP6
WordStar	2000	WSD
WordStar		WSD
WordPerfect Graphic		WPG
XYWrite		XY

Common Import Filters Explained

As far as filters go there's something for every one when it comes to the number of formats involved. There are many specific application filters newly built into CorelDRAW! 6's import collection, some of which have been improved or updated.

AutoCAD Filters

AutoCAD programs are the favorite of architects and engineers from a wide cross-section of industries. To export a drawing from AutoCAD and into a DXF format that CorelDRAW! 6 filters understand, use DXFOUT, a utility that comes with the AutoCAD application. CorelDRAW! 6 can import from files exported from these applications as long as they are compatible with one of the two common formats: DXF or PLT. Depending on the contents of the DXF file, you may be forced to accept good and evil simultaneously, and be wary of importing files produced by AutoCAD versions 11, 12, and 13 because some of the features available in these versions are not fully supported in CorelDRAW! 6.

If you are the person preparing the files for export or you have some influence over the options selected at the time the file is actually exported from the AutoCAD application you may want to consider these tips:

■ The first thing you may notice on importing a DXF file is that CorelDRAW! 6 tries to enlarge the objects to 18 by 18 inches, although they will be centered on the page. Objects can be scaled after importing.

- If the file you are exporting is being created from a three-dimensional image, be sure the image is being viewed at the desired angle before exporting.

- The best text justification to use is no justification. Multiple variations will not be supported. Non-standard characters will import as a "?" character. Panose font-matching will take place on import. Text size and skewing will be adjusted to conform to the limitations of CorelDRAW! 6.

- Avoid overly-complex files. CorelDRAW! 6's filter (or the available memory on your system) may not be capable of handling excessive import file sizes. If you find your file size is too large, try exporting it from AutoCAD using a HP7475 Plotter and perform a plot-to-file of your drawing; then import the file into CorelDRAW! 6 using the HPGL PLT import filter.

- If you have problems with the dimension entities becoming corrupted, try going back to AutoCAD and exploding the dimension entity before exporting.

- The variable line width available in AutoCAD is not supported in CorelDRAW! 6 and therefore the minimum line width applied to lines will apply as the default.

- Patterned or dashed lines will be assigned similar line styles but may not match exactly.

- Raising curve resolution will substantially increase file size, so hence lowering it will allow the file size to be more manageable.

- Solid and trace entities are filled as long as the view is not set as 3D.

- Points transfer into CorelDRAW! 6 as ellipses at the smallest size possible. Extruded points come in as line segments with two nodes. PDMODE is not supported.

- Files exported as "entities only" may import incorrectly because they contain little or no header information.

- Text anomolies, which include Control characters, overscore, underscore, and non-standard characters are either ignored or are replaced by a question mark character.

EPS File Formats

There are different types of EPS filters that ship with CorelDRAW! 6—Placeable EPS, PostScript (interpreted) EPS and PS, Adobe Illustrator created EPS, and CorelTRACE EPS. Knowing which one to use can be a tricky task, especially if you don't know where the file came from in the first place. To find this out select the All Files *.* selection at the top of the import filter list, click on Options at the bottom right of the dialogue box to expand it, and click on the file you would like information on. At the bottom-left corner you will see all the pertinent information you need to choose the correct filter.

You will not be able to use the All Files selection for importing EPS files due to the fact that more than one EPS filter type exists. CorelDRAW! 6 requires that you manually specify exactly which filter type to use when importing any EPS file. When importing, CorelDRAW! 6 asks which method to use when handling text. If you are not sure whether you have all the fonts needed for the EPS file you may want to import the EPS file using text as curves first to check. Otherwise CorelDRAW! 6 will use the Panose font-matching utility to match any fonts not found installed on your system.

Placeable encapsulated PostScript files contain a small bitmap information called a header representing the imported the image and displays in CorelDRAW! 6. Neither objects nor text contained in the placeable EPS files are editable.

PostScript (interpreted) EPS formats are mostly used for importing PRN or print files. This filter uses the PostScript information describing the page for a digital imagesetter or other PostScript printer to represent the image in CorelDRAW! 6. If there are any fountain fills described in the file you may very quickly run out of memory because of the complex way that these fills are described to the PostScript printer.

CorelDRAW! 6 supports all Adobe Illustrator formats including versions 3.0, 88, and 1.1 created on either Macintosh or PC platforms. Imported AI or EPS files from Adobe Illustrator using this filter will come into CorelDRAW! 6 as groups of objects which can ungrouped and are fully editable.

The CorelTRACE EPS filter is designed to work specifically with files generated solely by CorelTRACE and will not work on any other EPS file type. Objects entering CorelDRAW! 6 through this filter will be grouped objects and fully editable when ungrouped.

III

Sharing & Printing Files

Bitmap Filters

There are fourteen bitmap types that CorelDRAW! 6 supports including BMP, CAL, CPT, CT, SCT, GIF, PCX, TGA, TIF, JPG, JFF, JFT, PCD, IMG, and PP4. They each support black and white, color, and grayscale bitmaps and allow for setting resolution of the imported image before importing. Each bitmap import enables you to crop the image or resample by changing the options in the Import dialog controls.

Windows and OS/2 bitmaps are fully supported as well as CorelPHOTO-PAINT 6, GIF, PCX, Targa (TGA), TIFF, and SCITEC formats. TIFF 6.0 supports the JPEG compression and CMYK data but CorelDRAW! 6 does not support placed objects unless you are using PHOTO-PAINT 6, while SCITEX format supports full 32-bit color images. CorelDRAW! 6 also supports importing of Adobe PhotoShop files while in 1-bit, 2-bit, grayscale, and color up to 32-bit, CMYK.

Plotter Formats

Hewlett-Packard plotter formats are supported as HPGL and HPGL/2 PLT format. The PLT filter allows for scaling and resizing of images. Curve resolution can be set, although the higher the curve resolution the bigger the file size. Corel recommends a curve resolution of 0.004 inches. HPGL does not support color, however on importing the file you have the option to assign a color to each pen number, or CorelDRAW! 6 will assign the colors for you. You are also able to set pen width, velocity, fills, line types, and text.

PhotoCD

The Kodak PhotoCD is fully supported and available for import into CorelDRAW! 6. You have the option of importing from a selection of six sample resolutions including Wallet, Snapshot, Standard, Large, Poster, and Billboard ranging in files sizes from 128 by 192 pixels for Wallet, to over 4096 by 6144 pixels for Billboard.

Troubleshooting

Why won't my PhotoCD images separate properly?

If your PhotoCD images don't print out quite like you expected they would when printing color separations, it may be because the PhotoCD filter only produces RGB images from this format. For offset print reproduction it may be best to use an image-editing package such as CorelPHOTO-PAINT where the color model can be converted to CMYK for offset print reproduction.

Using the PhotoCD filter, you will also have the option of importing in a variety of color ranges including 256 grayscale, or 16 (4-bit), 256 (8-bit), or 16.7 million (24-bit) colors. A Kodak Image Enhancement has also been added to ensure that colors are correct.

Troubleshooting

Why do I have more than one PCDLIB.DLL file on my system?

When installing software, some applications may install an additional copy of Kodak's PCDLIB.DLL file. This file controls all aspects of the PhotoCD format, and may sometimes inadvertently be installed in the Win95 folder instead of the Win95\System folder. This will result in an error message with CorelDRAW! 6. To fix this problem make sure there is only one PCDLIB.DLL file on your system and that the file resides in the Win95/System folder.

Tip

When using the File, Import command (Ctrl+I) to import older CorelDRAW! files, you may notice on some files that contain certain types of font styles that the spacing is slightly off. In most cases, this may not be noticeable. But, in cases where text is wrapped around objects or fit to a path. To correct this, use the Shape tool to adjust spacing between letters, or the spacing command in the Character formatting tools. For text fit to a path, detach the text, straighten it with the Straighten Text command, and refit it to the path.

Mastering DRAW!'s Export Filters

CorelDRAW! 6 is capable of 32 different export file formats, many of them popular bitmap, vector, and page-layout-compatible formats. To use the export functions in CorelDRAW! 6, select File, Export (Ctrl+H) to display the Export dialog box controls (see fig. 15.2). The export function is one of the more critical functions a graphics program can have—especially CorelDRAW! 6. If it doesn't work, some say, the program is worthless. The Corel engineers must have had expert advice on this subject because they really do seem to have covered all bases.

III

Sharing & Printing Files

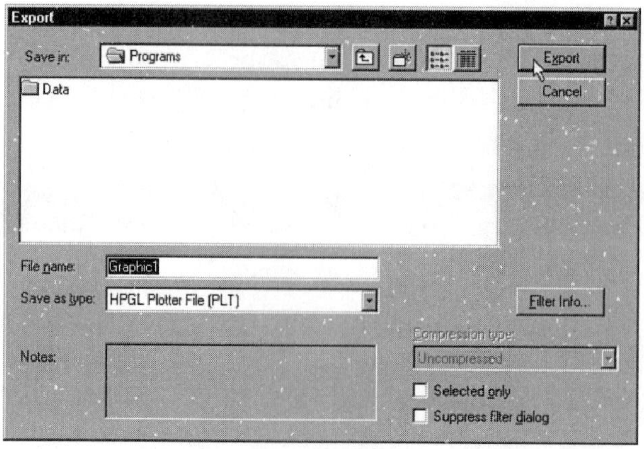

Fig. 15.2

The main Export controls set all export options in CorelDRAW! 6.

Exporting to various file formats allows you to prepare your CorelDRAW! 6 files for use in other programs and platforms. It is critical for preparing graphic files for use in programs such as page-layout and word-processing packages.

One of the best ways to success in preparing files for export is knowing the limitations of your target program. For instance, if you are preparing a multi-color graphic file for use in a program that doesn't support color trapping you shouldn't bother going to the trouble of setting up all sorts of complex and time-consuming overprinting, trapping, or color-object editing.

Frequently Used Exporting Formats

Tables 15.4 shows export formats you may use for specific target applications such as a page-layout or word-processing program. Because of the variety of printer types out there on the market the list is divided up into two basic printer types: PostScript and Non-PostScript unless the format being exported to uses a proprietary printer type.

Table 15.4 Common Export Formats for Graphic Applications

Application	Filter	
	PostScript	Non-PostScript
Ami Professional	EPS	WMF
Delrina Perform	GEM	GEM
PageMaker	EPS	WMF
Corel Ventura	EPS	CMX
WordPerfect	EPS	WPG

For page layout and other programs with graphics-editing capabilities, look at table 15.5:

Table 15.5 Common Export Formats for Page Layout Applications

Application	Filter Type
Adobe Illustrator	AI
Arts & Letters	WMF, EPS (using decipher)
AutoCAD	DXF
GEM Artline	GEM
Macintosh-based vector	Macintosh, PICT, AI
Micrografx Designer	CGM
PC Paintbrush	PCX

III

Sharing & Printing Files

For specific devices, use the following export filter format:

Matrix, Genegraphic, Solataire film recorder: **SCODL**

Computer-driven cutters, machines, or plotters: **HPGL or DXF outlines**

Bitmap Formats

Bitmap exporting filters include Windows BMP, CompuServe GIF, Paintbrush, Targa TGA, and TIFF formats. During exporting bitmaps (see fig. 15.3), you have the options of scaling up or down the image. Watch out when enlarging any bitmap images though. Resolution of the bitmap will decrease when it is scaled up or enlarged at all. If you reduce the size or scale down the bitmap the result is satisfactory.

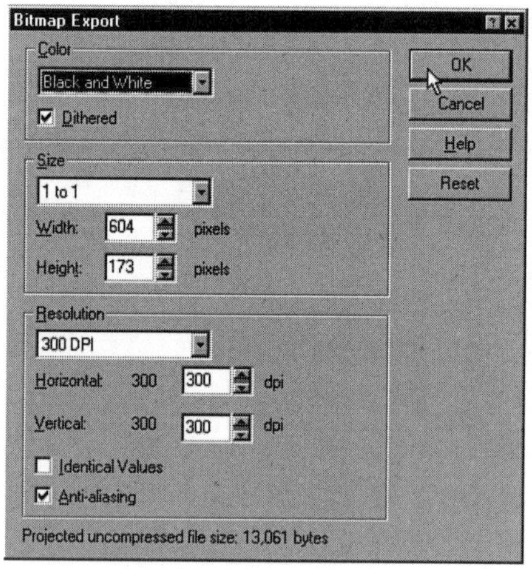

Fig. 15.3
The Bitmap
Export dialog box
controls all bitmap
export options.

If you discover you need to scale by more than 50 percent you may want to consider sampling it at a lower resolution initially because reducing the size of the bitmap image compresses the resolution and may result in wasted information and wasted disk space. A good rule to follow is to always maintain an image resolution twice that of the final line screen resolution of the final output. In other words if you are going to be making digital output from your file at a line screen of 150 lines per inch you need only maintain an image resolution of 300 dots per inch.

CorelDRAW! 6 bitmap formats also support some compression types as follows:

- *Windows Bitmap.* RLE (run-length encoding) for 4- and 8-bit files.

- *MACPaint Bitmap.* RLE.

- *GEM Paint file IMG.* RLE.

- *Paintbrush.* RLE (PCX version 3.0).

- *Compuserve GIF.* LZW, GIF version 87A and 89A.

- *CALS.* CCITT, Group 4.

- *Targa TGA.* Both RLE-compressed color-mapped and RLE RGB are supported. 24-bit color TGA files will automatically be exported as RLE-compressed RGB bitmaps.

- *TIFF.* CorelDRAW! 6 supports TIFF 4.2, 5.0, and 6.0 filter formats. If your objects are CMYK the filter will automatically use version 6.0. For 24-bit color you will get the 5.0 filter, and for 8-bit or 256-color or less you will get the 4.2 version filter.

- *Bitmap.* Bitmap filters also support a number of additional options including colors options, a dithered colors option, compression, resolution, and size. CorelDRAW! 6 will also indicate the projected file size of the exported file. JPEG or Joint Photographers Experts Group compression is also supported.

- *Wavelet Bitmap.* WVL compression.

Encapsulated PostScript Formats

The CorelDRAW! 6 Encapsulated PostScript (EPS) filters (see fig. 15.4) support several formats, and come equipped with options for setting text controls, setting the image header, converting color bitmaps to grayscale, setting fountain stripes options, and open prepress interface options.

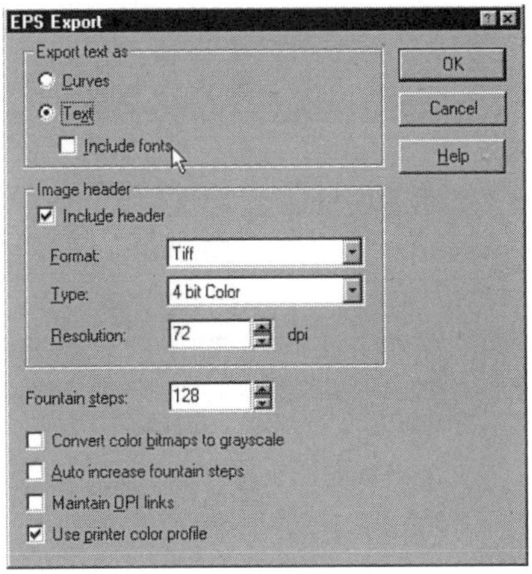

Fig. 15.4
The EPS Export dialog box controls all encapsulated PostScript file export options.

III

Sharing & Printing Files

You may set the header resolution from 1 to 300 DPI. Although a very low resolution header reduces file size it also lessens the user's ability to recognize details of the image on the screen and may sometimes make it difficult to position the image in the target application. Color of the header also reduces the file size and, if you don't mind a black and white representation of your color image, can also greatly reduce the export file size.

In EPS formats texture fills are not supported and will be replaced with solid gray fills. Text should be exported to include font information so that CorelDRAW! 6 may build the font data into the EPS file. Text should also be exported as text not curves unless the number of characters is minimal and will not excessively enlarge the file size. Where text is minimal, choosing the text as Curves will omit the font data leaving the file size small.

The Adobe Illustrator export format (see fig. 15.5) enables you to select a specific version of Illustrator to use during the export process. Either version 1.1, 88, or 3.0 selections are available. You also have the option of exporting text as curves or as text. A Use Macintosh Characters option also becomes available once the Text option is selected. This might come in handy if you had used an extended character set such as a foreign language character or other special characters.

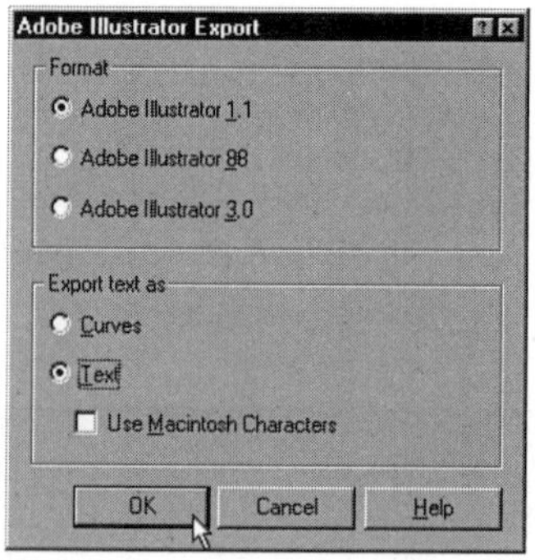

Fig. 15.5
The Adobe Illustrator Export dialog box controls enable you to set which version of Illustrator you are preparing your export file for.

Exporting to SCODL Format

The SCODL format is primarily used for generating slide files on film recorder hardware. Once you select this export filter (see fig. 15.6) you notice very few user options available. If you have placed your own background object in your CorelDRAW! 6 file, either of the Black or White options will be overridden.

Troubleshooting

Why don't my slides scale down to proportionately fit a slide during imaging?

If you're preparing slides from CorelDRAW! 6 you must select the Slide page size as your Page Setup to be sure that your page is set to the proper aspect ratio for slide formatting. Slide proportions follow a 2-by-3 proportion, which doesn't match a regular letter-sized page proportion.

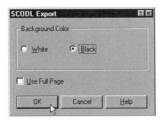

Fig. 15.6
Very few user options may be set in the SCODL Export dialog box controls.

Troubleshooting

Why are my slides imaging with horizontal bands across the center of the slide?

When using the SCODL export filter, do not allow your text or drawn objects to come too close to the frame of your page or you may get an overflow error when imaging the file. The overflow error can usually be recognized by a series of horizontal colored lines across the slide. Also, if you've used calligraphic text and would like to retain that effect, click the Calligraphic TEXT box in Clipboard under Text options in Preferences. Unfortunately, PostScript textures, bitmaps, and two- and four-color patterns are not supported using the SCODL filter.

Using AutoCAD Formats

CorelDRAW! 6 has many incompatible features with basic AutoCAD file formats, and this is reflected in the lack of options when exporting to the AutoCAD DXF format (see fig. 15.7). There are a number of changes that must be made to object attributes prior to moving through this filter.

One of the most critical issues to pay close attention to is that objects without outlines assigned to them in CorelDRAW! 6 are automatically assigned an outline in the DXF format. Text moving through this filter is another issue to consider. All text moving through this filter is converted to curves and will not be editable once imported into the AutoCAD application. It may be more prudent to eliminate text where possible and replace it with the AutoCAD application's own text once the file is imported.

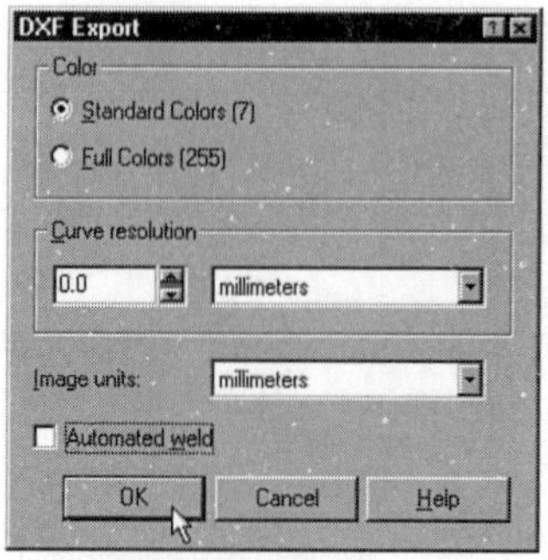

Fig. 15.7

There are disappointingly few DXF Export dialog controls or options. CorelDRAW!'s import filter relies on the DXF file to have been properly exported from it's native CAD application.

Other features not compatible between the two programs include calligraphic pen effects, patterned lines, arrowheads, varying line weights, bitmaps are not supported, and layer information is not matched. Texture fills are not supported and will result in solid gray fills. Color formats when selected as Full Colors may not match exactly to the color scheme you have selected in your CorelDRAW! 6 file. All in all not a pretty sight if you have used any of these features and were expecting them to all filter through to DXF.

Using JPEG Compression

Experts claim that JPEG and MPEG file formats provide superior compression for various image formats. JPEG or Joint Photographer Experts Group compression is compatible with a wide variety of programs and platforms (see fig. 15.8). CorelDRAW! 6 supports a number of JPEG formats including JPEG Interchange format (JFIF), TIFF JPEG (JTIF), and LEAD format (CMP).

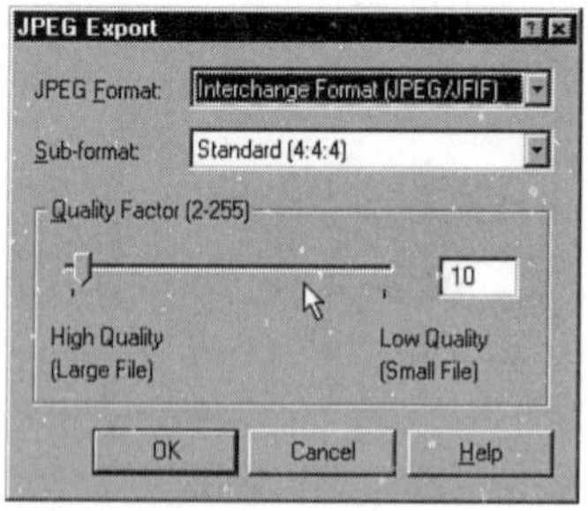

Fig. 15.8

The JPEG Export dialog box controls all options and enables you to choose from a number of JPEG formats. This file format is becoming more accepted in the graphics industry as software developers adopt this filter and capitalize on it's compression capabilities.

The JFIF format is not actually true JPEG but is definitely used more widely than pure JPEG itself. This format is useful for creating compressed files to be used on PC, Macintosh, or UNIX platforms.

TIFF JPEG, or JTIF, uses TIFF 6.0 for JPEG compression supporting the full CMYK color model. These JTIF files cannot be created by a usual TIFF export filter nor can they be imported using an ordinary TIFF filter. The JPEG filter must be used to ensure proper data compression.

LEAD format is the best JPEG compression but tends to be more non-standard than even true JPEG or JTIF. CorelDRAW! 6 supports the LEAD compression standard.

Using HPGL and Plotter Formats

The HPGL (Hewlett-Packard Graphical Language) and Plotter (PLT) export filter (see fig. 15.9) is by far the most option-rich filter of CorelDRAW! 6's collection of export filters. It is designed primarily for adapting files to be used on flatbed plotters, vinyl sign cutters, and automated industrial cutting machines. The HPGL dialog box is sub-divided into three tabbed Options areas—Pen, Page, and Advanced. Before beginning preparation to exporting you should be aware that there are some features that are not supported beyond CorelDRAW! 6 and into the HPGL or PLT file formats. These machines don't operate on the same principles as the average desktop bubble-jet or laser printer and require a different type of instruction from the application.

Fig. 15.9
The HPGL Export, Pen tab options contain a veritable world of options and offer one of the most sophisticated sets of export controls of all of CorelDRAW! 6's filters.

Because the types of printers that reproduce the images use colored pens instead of bubble-jet or laser you will see an abundance of pen controls available in this filter. The Pen tab of the filter allows you to first choose the pen and then its color assignment as well as its width and velocity. The color selection list contains 256 colors as well as a custom color pen setting. You are also able to save any of these Pen settings to a pen library file in order to create a custom library of your own.

The Page tab (see fig. 15.10) lets you scale your exported file to exact enlargement or reduction and included other controls such as Fit to Page, preformatted or custom page sizes, orientation, and Plotter Origin settings. Watch out for this Plotter Origin setting because the origin you set must match the origin setting on the plotter you are using. If your plotter normally starts plotting at the bottom left of the plotter page then set this here. If your

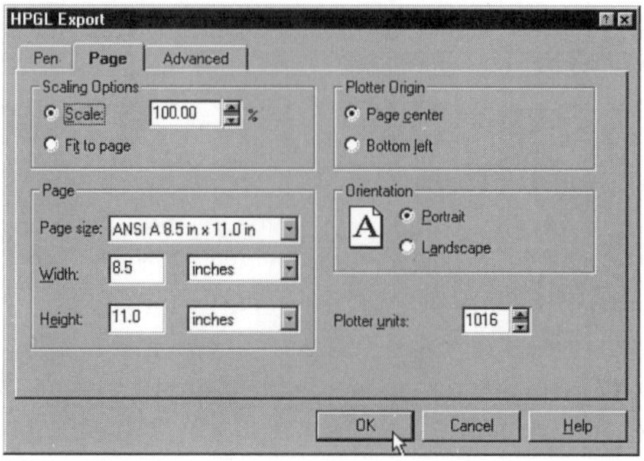

Fig. 15.10
The HPGL Export, Page tab contains specific scaling and page size settings.

Plotter Units setting allows you to adjust the number of plotter units your particular plotter operates on. The norm and default is 1016 units per inch, but check you plotter to make sure, otherwise your images may become distorted.

The Advanced tab of the HPGL export dialog box (see fig. 15.11) includes settings for simulating a fill pattern using pen hatching and cross-hatching marks, the frequency and angle of which are adjustable here. There is also an option to remove hidden lines, which basically tells the plotter to ignore any lines describing objects hidden by other objects. Automatic Weld is a useful function for sign-cutters whereby the objects that overlap each other are allowed to become one outlined object. This feature will only work on single or combined objects, or text objects when Text to Curves is selected. If unsure of whether this feature will work on the objects you have created for export or not, use CorelDRAW! 6 Weld tool before attempting to export the file.

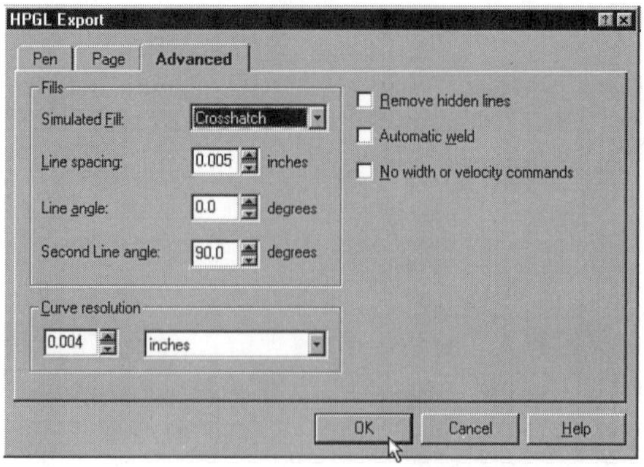

Fig. 15.11
The HPGL Export, Advanced tab contains line, curve, and object controls.

Curve resolution is also controllable in the Advanced tab. As in other filters, the range is between 0.0 and 1.0 inches. The higher the value set here, the smaller the file size will be. The default setting for curve resolution is 0.004 inches.

Exporting Fonts

The TrueType and Adobe Type 1 fonts filters (see fig. 15.12) allow the user to export objects into Type 1 fonts or TrueType compatible characters or symbols. When this export filter is selected the last font name used or exported to is displayed in the Family Name field. Options include assigning a style such as normal, bold , normal italic, or bold italic, and selecting whether it will be a symbol font or not.

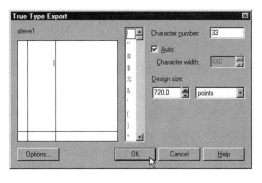

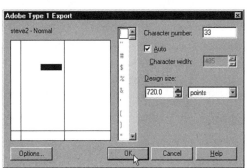

Fig. 15.12
The TrueType Font and Adobe Type 1 Font Export options enable you to create your own fonts or symbols.

Once you have selected the font name and style and selected OK, the filter will take you to another dialog box where you are able to set the size of the character you have created and build a spacing width setting into the font using Space Width. Leave the Design Size setting at the default of 720 points unless you know this won't work for your font. Setting the Character Width at Auto will allow CorelDRAW! 6's filter to automatically calculate the amount of space required between the characters of your font collection.

Below that you will see the Character Number assignment that allows you to assign a keyboard button to the character you are exporting, which follows the Windows 3.1 character map settings. The Options button takes you back again to the first Options dialog box.

Exporting to Macintosh PICT

The Macintosh PICT (PCT) export format (see fig. 15.13) contains few options for the user in this filter except the critical Export text as Curves or Text option and whether or not to use the Macintosh character set, which is slightly different when it comes to special extended character sets such as foreign language or symbol characters.

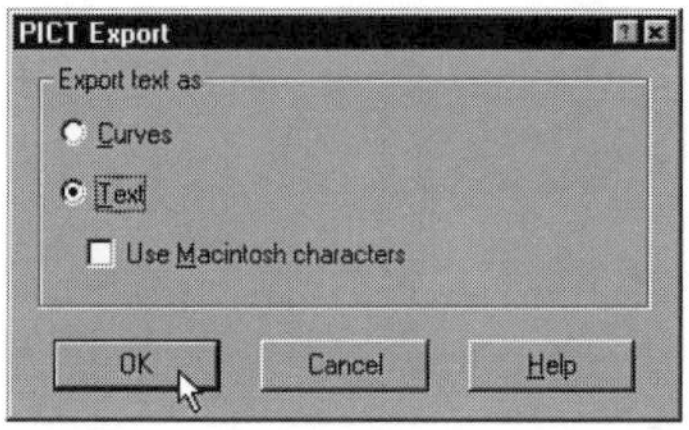

Fig. 15.13
The Macintosh PICT Export options is one of the only formats that links CorelDRAW! 6 to Macintosh applications.

As with many filters, this one also comes with its own set of limitations including unsupported bitmaps, PostScript texture fills, and two- and four-color pattern fills. This filter also converts all objects with both outlines and fills to two separate objects—one for the outline and one for the fill, which may not always be desirable.

Fountain fill steps will be determined by the setting of your Preferences\View dialog box. Color-matching will be made as closely as possible, however the best color model to use is 24-bit, which will translate through the filter virtually identical to CorelDRAW! 6's colors.

Object Linking and Embedding

Object linking and embedding (OLE) has been edging toward popularity since its introduction in CorelDRAW! 4 and other applications. Only software programs that support the OLE technology are able to perform OLE functions. During the installation of CorelDRAW! 6 the files needed to support the OLE functions are installed into your Win95\SYSTEM folder.

To embed a file native to another application, follow these steps:

1. Choose Edit, Insert New Object. The Insert New Object dialog box appears (see fig. 15.14). A listing of Object Types shows all of the OLE-compatible applications registered with Win95.

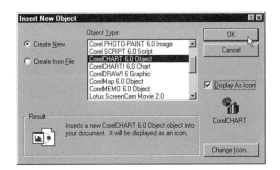

Fig. 15.14
To create a new object using another OLE-compatible application use the Insert New Object, using the Create New option.

2. By default, the Create New option is selected. Choose which type of new OLE object you want to create from the list that displays and choose OK. This list is comprised of programs already installed on your hard drive.

3. The application specific to the object type you have selected is launched opening to a new Untitled document. Create the object to be inserted into CorelDRAW! 6 and save it. Once your file has been saved you will then be returned to CorelDRAW! 6.

   Or

   Select the Create from File option and the Insert New Object dialog box changes from a list of Object Types to a File list and a Browse button equipped with a Link option (see fig. 15.15).

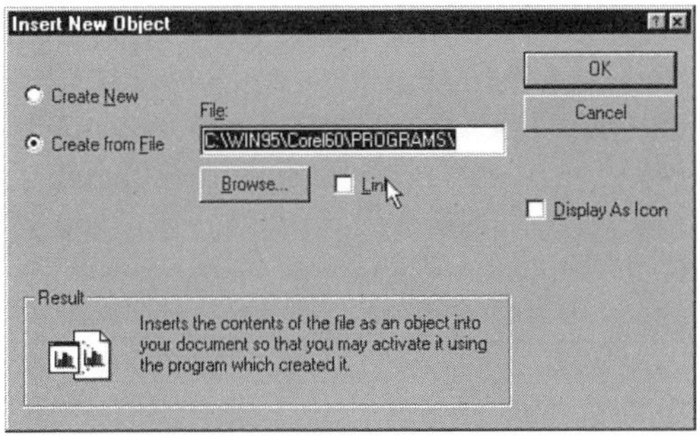

Fig. 15.15
To insert a new object from an existing file, select New Object, using the Create from File option.

4. Selecting the Browse button lets you tell CorelDRAW! 6 where the file you created resides. Selecting the Link option establishes a link only to the file. Any changes made to the original file can be updated in CorelDRAW! 6 by selecting Edit, Link. You have the choice of either Manually or Automatically updating the Linked file (see fig. 15.16).

III

Sharing & Printing Files

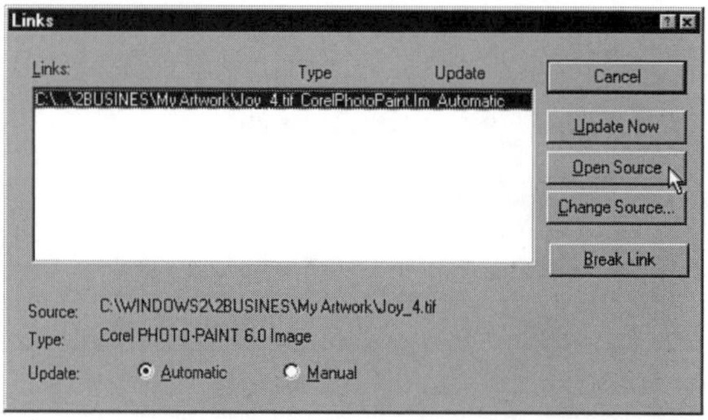

Fig. 15.16
The Links dialog box controls may be used to set options for linked files, following inserting a New Object command, while using the Create From File, Link option.

Troubleshooting

I have just cleaned up my hard drive and now I can't edit some of my linked files. What happened?

Editing of files linked using the object linking and embedding method is totally dependent on the linked file's application being available for editing. If you have just reorganized your hard drive and deleted some of your unused programs, you may have inadvertently deleted a program that is required by linked files for editing. Try reinstalling the program and attempting to re-edit the file.

If you would like to simply insert a file and establish a link, just click on Create from File, select the Link option, and skip steps 2, 3, and 4.

If you choose not to establish a Link with the file but simply place the file as is into CorelDRAW! 6 then do not select the Link option. This is known as "embedding" the file. Any changes made to the original file will not be updated in the Linked CorelDRAW! 6 file. When a graphic file is embedded you may edit any of its object characteristics from within CorelDRAW! 6 as you would any other collection of objects. The objects will be first grouped when they are first inserted. Only Windows applications supporting object embedding will work.

Using the Clipboard

Copying items straight onto the clipboard from other applications supporting OLE gives you an additional way of importing selected file types into CorelDRAW! 6. By opening up the OLE-supporting application and selecting and copying (Ctrl+Insert or Ctrl+C) the object onto the clipboard you are then able to choose Edit, Paste Special.

This brings up the Paste Special dialog box (see fig. 15.17), which enables you to choose exactly how your clipboard pastes its contents onto the clipboard. Remember, the clipboard doesn't just copy certain things from a document. It copies all information. The Paste Special command simply tells the clipboard which information to ignore when pasting, and whether to establish a link or not.

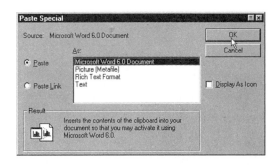

Fig. 15.17
Using the Edit, Paste Special dialog box controls.

Troubleshooting

Why do objects I copy to the clipboard lose some of their attributes after I paste them?

When using clipboard functions, not all operations may go as planned or expected. The clipboard is a convenient, uncomplicated way of getting information from one application to another, but it does have its limitations. Patterned fills and PostScript textures will be lost once the image is copied onto the clipboard. For the Windows Metafile format applications (WMF) the clipboard also doesn't support background colors, pattern fills, clipping regions, flood fills, pixel manipulation, and several other effects including ROP2 mode and "winding" polygons fills (other than "alternate").

When using the clipboard, text-handling is limited to the line- and character-spacing defaults of CorelDRAW! 6 and the amount of memory available on your system at the time the clipboard is used. All in all pretty a pretty risky method of transferring objects and information from one place to another.

CorelDRAW! 6's Drag-and-Drop Functions

This feature enables you to drag foreign files from the Windows Explorer straight into CorelDRAW! 6, or from one application window into the CorelDRAW! 6 window.

To import files using the drag-and-drop feature you may need to do a bit of window juggling:

1. First, while still in CorelDRAW! 6 click once on the center icon (restore) in the upper-right corner of your CorelDRAW! 6 application window. Resize the CorelDRAW! 6 window to half of your screen on the left side.

2. Then, open Windows Explorer and click once on the same icon (restore) and resize the Windows Explorer window to half the screen size on the right side (see fig. 15.18).

Fig. 15.18
To drag-and-drop a file from Windows Explorer directly into CorelDRAW! 6 you must have both program windows open and at least partially visible.

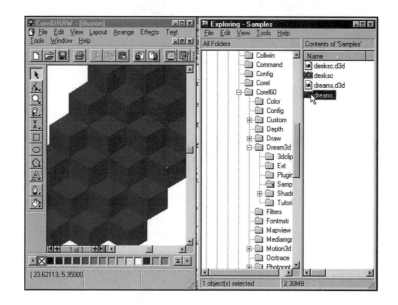

3. If, after reducing the window size of Windows Explorer, the two applications are not appearing on your screen side-by-side then hold down the Alt key and press the Tab key (Windows 95 Fast Switching) until CorelDRAW! 6 appears in the program title bar and release.

4. In Windows Explorer, locate the file you would like to move into CorelDRAW! 6, grab and drag it across the window borders and onto CorelDRAW! 6's document window. It may take a few moments for the OLE features to determine how to import the file into CorelDRAW! 6 but eventually the operation will take place.

There is one drawback with the drag-and-drop function though. Text may not always appear exactly as you had intended it to because CorelDRAW! 6's Panose font matching controls don't operate at all when using this feature.

You may need to re-apply specific letterspacing, wordspacing, and/or kerning after text has been moved using this method.

From Here...

Importing, exporting, OLE functions, and drag-and-drop are critical operations for transferring data and getting CorelDRAW! 6 to interact smoothly with other applications. Knowing these largely undocumented features is worth the effort, as complex as they might seem at first. Take a few moments every now and then to test out the importing and exporting features and get to know how the options affect your data. It may open up doors of opportunity for you in your business or your career.

For related topics, refer to the following:

- Chapter 5, "Working with Text," where text options are covered.

- Chapter 7, "Using Fills and Outlines," where information on how to use Pen controls can be found.

Chapter 16

Printing

Print engine is a good term for this area of CorelDRAW! 6 and the other Corel programs dedicated to crunching out the drawing, layouts, and illustrations you create. This version of CorelDRAW! has the largest number of user-definable features ever. Hundreds of options are available. Some options are easy; others seem like they require a degree in PostScript programming to comprehend them. This chapter helps users better understand those complex options.

This chapter is for everyone who prints their documents on anything from a dot-matrix printer to a high-resolution imagesetter and from Windows 95 to working on a Macintosh platform.

In this chapter you learn to

- Prepare your files for printing
- Set print options correctly
- Use DRAW!'s Print Merge features
- Deal with service bureaus
- Make a proper PRN file
- Print a file

Preparing to Print

If you are printing proofs of your CorelDRAW! 6 file on your desktop printer, you likely know the printer's features better than anyone. What you may not know, though, is that CorelDRAW! has some new tools that offer specific proofing options to customize the way you proof your files.

The first rule to follow when producing output for any project is to leave enough time in your production schedule for proofing. Prepare for at least one imaging hang-up. Ask any seasoned professional and you'll hear it over and over—planning is definitely the key.

It's embarrassing to admit, but about 95 percent of problems encountered when printing are self-inflicted. As a general rule of thumb, keep your documents simple. You may want to tape this list of hazards onto the side of your printer:

- *Font overboard.* Too many fonts are used in the document. DRAW! comes with over 1,000 fonts, which is great. But your printer won't have an appreciation—or the memory—for an excessive number of fonts on a page. Keep your font selection of your design to a tasteful maximum of four to five typefaces, not including light, bold, and italic styles.

- *Overloaded nodes.* One or more of the objects in your drawing is too complex for your printer's available memory. Be sure that no object contains more than 1,500 drawing nodes. You can check the number by selecting the object with the right mouse button, checking its Properties, Curve tab for Number of Nodes. Looking out for excess nodes can become tricky, especially if you have the habit of using tracing programs like Corel OCRTrace or the CorelDRAW! internal AutoTrace function. These images are famous for containing an excessive number of nodes (easily into the thousands!) for superdetailed scanned images. If you do exceed the maximum number of nodes your printer is capable of handling, try using the Node Edit, Reduce Nodes tool on the object. In most cases, this tool reduces the number of nodes without affecting the shape.

- *Texture fill hazards.* You may encounter difficulties when trying to print large, complex, multicolor texture bitmap fills to a non-PostScript color printer.

- *Fit to Page hazard.* Stay sharp when you're using the Fit to Page function, which works great when taken literally. Click Fit to Page, for example, if you want to reduce a tabloid document to automatically fit your letter-size printer. However, Fit to Page does not calculate a percentage of reduction from tabloid to letter. Instead, DRAW! calculates an imaginary box around all the objects and makes sure they all appear within the printable area of your letter-sized page. The trick is to always preview before printing, in case you have any stray objects outside your page borders. These objects are considered part of your document, and DRAW! includes them in the reduction calculation. This feature is useful but potentially hazardous.

- *Auto Increase Flatness.* Flatness affects the number of straight lines used to describe curves in your document. Increase the flatness setting by increments of 4 or 5, for highly complex files. If this doesn't work, select File, Print, Options, choose the Options tab and select the PostScript Preferences button to gain access to the Auto Increase Flatness option. The PostScript Preferences are only available if you are printing to a PostScript printer.

  Use the Auto Increase Flatness option as one of the last resorts. If your document has no curves, you likely won't notice any difference in the printed file, and this could turn out to be a great workaround for you. The Auto Increase Flatness control automatically increases the flatness by increments of 2 until the document prints. If flatness is increased excessively, it has the effect of making curves in your document come out unsmooth. It should only be used as a last resort workaround.

If you eventually will require a high-resolution imagesetter, ask yourself some basic questions. What information is built into your CorelDRAW! 6 file? How many colors have you specified? Have you trapped your colored objects or do you need to? What type of paper will you use? It may be wise to answer these questions before sending your files out for imaging. If you don't think about the answers now, someone definitely will ask for them later. These topics are addressed in the following sections.

Determining what Your Printing Company Needs

Ultimately, you want to deal with a printing company that has some experience using digitally created film. If your first guess is that digitally created film need not be touched by human hands in order to sucessfully reach the printing press, you presume too much. Many pitfalls may exist during the imaging process, and it helps immensely if your printer is capable of recognizing problems and identifying solutions for you as they occur. You need to decide if you are giving the printer finished film or sheets that require assembly (as in process color work). Make sure that the printing company you're working with knows what it will be receiving from you.

In advance of preparing your film, find out exactly what your printing company needs. Which line screen does it need? Does the company require a color proof of your film or will it make its own? Which resolution of film is best to use? You need to answer all these questions before trotting out to image your film.

Converting Fonts to Curves

If you have used any fonts in your file, you need to decide whether to leave them as fonts or convert them to curves. Artistic text in small quantities is sometimes best converted to curves. However, paragraph text is not something you want to convert to curves. Converting paragraph text to curves makes your file so complex that no imagesetter on earth will be able to image it.

If you convert all the text in your file to curves, you may not need to supply a list of fonts used in the file when sending out to a service bureau. However, if you leave the fonts intact, you need to specify which fonts are used in your file so the fonts can be installed on the system driving the imagesetter. If your fonts aren't loaded before you image your file, the imagesetter substitutes its own default font (usually Courier or the Windows Arial font), and the output is ruined.

Deciding Whether to Trap

Trapping describes the overlapping of outlines and fills to avoid press registration problems. You can easily spot a badly registered or untrapped printing job by the slivers of paper that show through between printed inks. If your CorelDRAW! file is being printed and you have used much spot color, you may need to trap the colors to avoid this problem.

Using the Print Command

The CorelDRAW! 6 File, Print command and associated dialog boxes are loaded with nearly every imaginable printing-related feature, and all the control is in the hands of the user (see fig. 16.1). The options available to you depend on which printer you have selected.

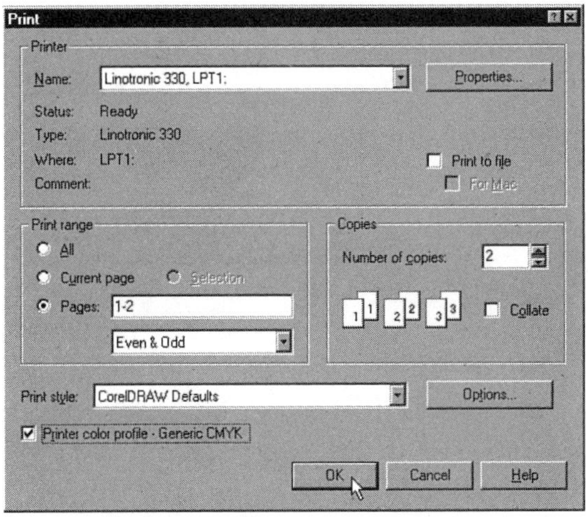

Fig. 16.1
The CorelDRAW! 6 main Print dialog box enables you to instruct your printing device on what and how many copies to print.

The following list describes each part of the main Print dialog box:

- *Name.* This drop-down list box is the key ingredient to which options are set in the rest of your Print dialog boxes. For example, specifying a non-PostScript printer here makes any of the PostScript printer options unavailable. Also, specifying a certain printer here determines what the printer Properties sheet features. If your printer driver is up-to-date with

III

Sharing & Printing Files

Windows 95, you should notice quite a difference from what the previous dialog box looked like in the Windows environment.

■ *Properties*. The type of printer selected in the Name field determines the appearance of the printer Properties sheet (see fig. 16.2). If your printer uses a Windows 95 printer driver, it probably is the PSCRIPT.DRV driver, version 4.00, in combination with a printer definition file. To find out exactly which printer driver version you are using, select the About button in the printer Properties sheet (see fig. 16.3). This driver will likely be updated fast and furiously as Windows 95 goes through its final maturity in general use.

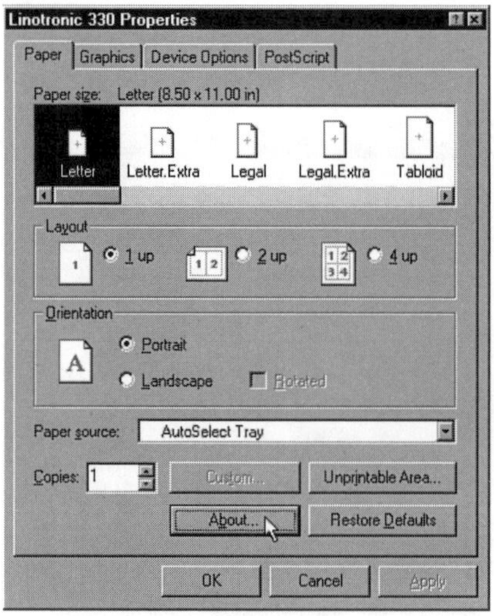

Fig. 16.2
The print Properties sheet enables you to set options specific to your document and your printer type.

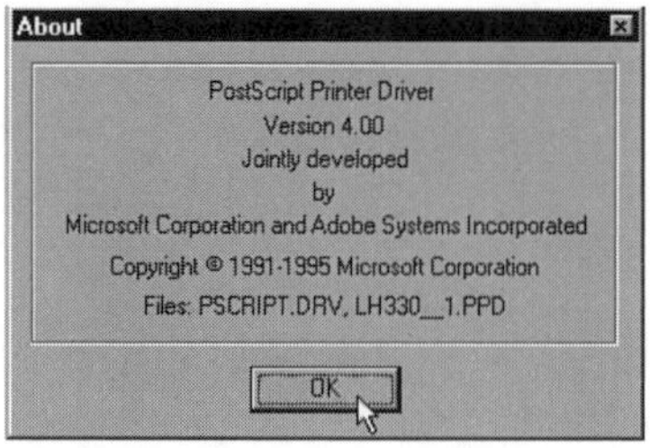

Fig. 16.3
Choose the About button for your printer driver version information.

■ *Print to File, For Mac*. Here are the famous controls for making a print file out of your CorelDRAW! 6 file. The Print to File option is always available, and, when printing to a PostScript printing device, the For Mac option also becomes available.

Troubleshooting

I'm trying to make a Print File that will be imaged from a Macintosh platform, but the For Mac option is unavailable. How do I make it available?

If you will be moving your print file over to the Mac platform for output and need to select the For Mac option, you first need to choose a PostScript-compatible printer. Only then does this option become available. Other types of non-PostScript printing device languages are incompatible with the Macintosh platform.

- *Print Range.* This area enables you to set the number of pages to print to All, Current, Pages, or Selection. Selection becomes available only when objects in your CorelDRAW! file are selected.

- *Number of Copies.* This option enables you to set the number of copies to print. The Collate option becomes available when the number of copies is set to more than one and there's more than one page in the document.

- *Print Style.* New to CorelDRAW! 6, this feature enables you to select from a list of presaved printer styles created using the Save Print Style controls in the Print Options dialog box.

- *Options.* Clicking this button opens the largest selection of printing features you will likely see in any graphics program. These settings control virtually every aspect of printing that the printer Properties dialog box doesn't control.

- *Printer Color Profile.* A single option is displayed here, enabling you to use a prepared color system profile, or leave it unselected. This color profile file is created when you calibrate your color system using the Color Manager's Color Wizard accessed from within CorelDRAW! or from the Corel Applications menu.

Setting Printer Properties

The controls you see in the printer Properties dialog box depend solely on whether you have selected to print using a PostScript printer or non-PostScript printer. If you will eventually be printing to a PostScript printer such as a Linotronic 330, you see a dialog box as in figure 16.2. The printer Properties sheet is divided into four areas including Paper, Graphics, Device Options, and PostScript. Many of the features offered through these tabs are repeated in the CorelDRAW! 6 controls, so you rarely need to access them. But in case you do, the following sections provide a basic review of the features available to a typical PostScript imagesetter.

◀ See "Using Color, Wizards, and Applying Color Masks," p. 425

Paper

Options available through the Paper tab include

- *Paper Size*. Includes nineteen predetermined page sizes ranging from envelope formats to a hardware-determined maximum printer-capable size, in addition to three custom page sizes.

> **Note**
>
> In the Page Size area of the printer Properties dialog box, you sometimes may see a page size that has a red circle with a line through it over the page icon. This symbol means that you need to change a setting in this dialog box or on your printer (such as the paper selection tray) before you can use this paper size.

- *Layout*. The layout section for this particular printer allows 1-up, 2-up, or 4-up printouts, meaning that the printer will print pages in groups of up to four pages at a time.

- *Orientation*. You may choose Portrait or Landscape page orientation. When Landscape is selected, a Rotate option enables you to flip the page upside down when printing.

> **Tip**
>
> To check the printed dimensions of the selected page, including the paper size and unprintable margins, click and hold the left mouse button on the page orientation icon of the Properties dialog box.

- *Paper Source*. This option enables you to select the source of your paper from a pull-down menu. Imagesetters usually operate on a roll-feed or sheet-feed system. However, if you are using a multitray bubble-jet or laser printer, you may see several options available here for selecting a particular paper tray. Selecting a paper size does not automatically select the correct paper tray.

Graphics

These options are available through the Graphics tab:

- *Resolution*. Settings for Resolution include a selection ranging from 635 DPI (dots per inch) to as high as 3386 DPI. Some printers may feature much higher or much lower settings.

- *Halftoning*. This option sets the line frequency of your screening and angle of the rows of screened dots. Accuracy of your screen resolution and screen angle may be set to 0.1 percent. *Screen angle* is the angle at which halftone dots align into rows. Screen angle is critical for achieving proper image reproduction when layering several colors of ink overtop of each other.

- *Special*. These options enable you to set your output to print as Negative image and/or as a Mirror image, essentially controlling the placement of the emulsion side and film options. *Emulsion* is the light-sensitive, silver-coated side of traditional-type film. It can be recognized by its dull finish in comparison to the shiny, uncoated side of the film.

- *Scaling*. The Scaling control is capable of resizing your output and may be set to a value from 1 percent to 100 percent. This control also exists in CorelDRAW's main Print Options dialog box.

> **Tip**
>
> Document scaling options exist in both the printer Properties dialog box and CorelDRAW!'s Print, Options dialog box. Using *both* controls at the same time may result in unsatisfactory scaling of your output. Stick to the CorelDRAW! controls.

Device Options

The options available through the Device Options tab vary substantially from printer to printer, especially when the printer features diagnostic controls and/or programmable options. The Linotronic imagesetter has options for further controlling negative image of your output.

PostScript

PostScript options available through the PostScript tab may include items such as installing Postscript Error Handlers or PostScript Output Formats for optimizing or formatting your PostScript files.

Setting Print Options

The Options area is the heart of the print engine. The Options structure hasn't changed much since CorelDRAW! 5, but many more user-controls have been added to the individual areas. In addition, the Options area has been changed for the introduction of Windows 95. Print Options are

III

Sharing & Printing Files

organized into three tabs including Layout, Separations, and Options, the latter of which can sometimes cause confusion due to the fact that you are already looking at an Options dialog box. Beside the tabbed sections is the print preview window that reflects many of the printing specifications and settings made in the Print Options dialog box.

Reviewing the Preview Window Controls

You access the print preview window by choosing File, Print, then clicking the Options button in the Print dialog box. The preview window is located on the left side and features several new controls for viewing your document, including print styles, layout, file, pages, colors, and printer marks and printer format settings (see fig. 16.4). These controls are described in following sections.

Fig. 16.4
The Print Options dialog box contains the print preview window and its controls.

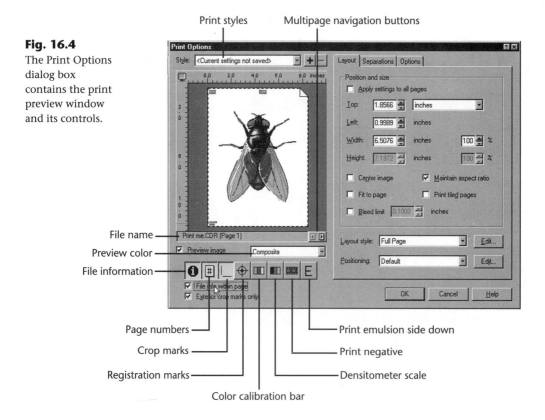

Viewing the Print Preview Window

The print preview window is perhaps the most useful printing tool ever implemented in the Corel print engine. The print preview window contains its own set of hidden features and options that can make proofing your print-out easier and accurate. With CorelDRAW! 6, you are now able to click and drag objects in your print preview window and move them relative to your page borders. (The preview window features two ruler bars used for positioning.)

You may also select viewing options by clicking directly on the preview window with your right mouse button to reveal several viewing options (see fig. 16.5). These options include

■ *Preview Image*. Duplicates the option below the preview window by enabling you to see the detail of the images being printed.

■ *Preview in Color*. When selected, displays the previewed image in full color. When not selected, displays the image in grayscale colors.

■ *Full Image Drag*. Enables you to see the full image when dragging images in the preview window.

■ *Print This Sheet Now*. Immediately prints the image showing in the pre-view window according to the print options selected and the printer currently selected.

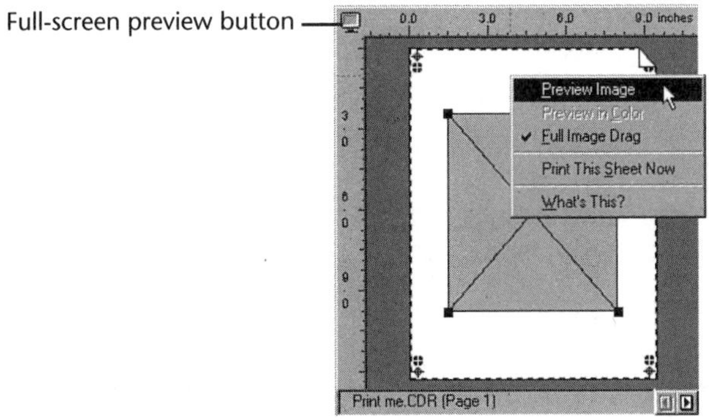

Full-screen preview button ———

Fig. 16.5
Hidden preview window options are available by clicking the preview window with your right mouse button.

Clicking the monitor icon in the upper-left corner of the print preview window where the rulers intersect causes a full-screen preview of the images currently displayed (see fig. 16.6). Even while in full-screen preview, you may drag and position images within or outside the printable page.

Fig. 16.6
Fig. 16.6
Full-screen
preview of the
preview window
and file images.

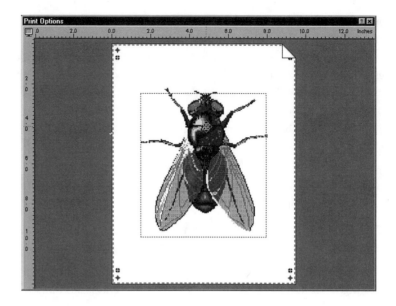

The bottom of the preview window (refer to fig. 16.4) features controls for navigating through your multipage file. You also see the current file name and the page number. To move forward one page, click the right arrow button; to move back one page, click the left arrow button.

Another new feature for CorelDRAW! 6 is the color display pull-down menu. This menu enables you to view a composite of your printed page in whichever display feature you have selected, or to view colors individually. The option to view individually is only available when separations in the Separations Tab have been enabled (see fig. 16.7). For example, if you are printing in four-color process, this feature enables you to view each of the cyan, magenta, yellow, and black plates individually. If you have used spot colors in your drawing and don't quite remember where you left them, this feature helps you view a single spot color at a time. The color display drop-down list box is an excellent feature for complex, multicolor layouts and illustrations.

Note

To use the preview color display list box, you must first enable the Print Separations option in the Separations tab of the Print Options dialog box. Otherwise only the Composite option is available in the color display pull-down menu.

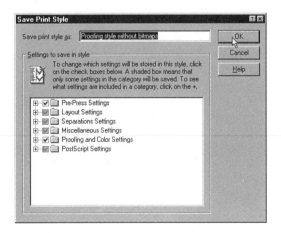

Preview color display drop-down list

Using Printer Styles

A new feature since version 5 of CorelDRAW!, printer style controls enable you to add and delete printer setups. To select a printer style, click the Style list box and choose a style.

To add a style that contains all the print settings you have selected—which includes all settings in the Options dialog box—click the plus-sign button to the right of the Style list box (see fig. 16.8). A dialog box appears, where you can name and save your new style. You may save any number of printer styles for particular proofing preferences, separation layers, layouts, custom screening, and so on.

Fig. 16.7
The color display list box enables you to preview colors individually in the preview window.

Fig. 16.8
To add a printer style, click the plus-sign button to display the Save Print Style dialog box. All aspects of printing may be selected using this control.

III

Sharing & Printing Files

To delete a style, select the name in the Style list box and click the minus-sign button.

Choosing Printer's Marks

Look again at the print preview window in figure 16.4. Below the preview window you see eight buttons that control printer's marks and formatting, plus two options for printing file information and crop mark positions. The buttons represent these elements: printing file information, page numbers, crop marks, register marks, color calibration bar, densitometer scale, negative or positive image, and emulsion up or down. You use these controls most often when you print multiple-page documents and multiple-color projects such as color separations. Clicking any of these buttons one time activates the feature and shows the button depressed; clicking the button a second time deactivates it. The following list describes the preview window buttons:

- *File information.* This option causes specific file information to print at the top of your printout, including file name, and current date and time. If you are printing color separations, color, screen frequency, screen angle, and plate number also print at the bottom of your printout. This option is useful only when printing to a page size larger than your document page size.

- *Page numbers.* Selecting this option prints a page number on your printout. This option is useful only when printing to a page size larger than your document page size.

- *Crop marks.* Crop marks indicate the corners of each page and may be used to trim the excess. This option is useful only when printing to a page size larger than your document page size.

- *Register marks.* This option causes registration marks to print in each corner of your printout. Printers use registration marks to align color separation overlays. This option is useful only when printing to a page size larger than your document page size.

- *Color calibration bar.* Selecting this feature causes a multicolor strip to print beside your page. You use this bar to check the color quality of a color proof or the ink colors on an offset print job.

- *Densitometer scale.* Selecting a densitometer scale to accompany your printout is useful for monitoring the film developing process of film output. You can measure the densitometer scale values with a densitometer and compare them to established values to determine whether film imaging or developing is accurate.

- *Negative or positive image.* Use this button to control printing a negative or positive format of your images. You will likely use this control when printing film for offset printing or plate-making.

- *Emulsion up or down.* When printing film negatives or positives for certain reproduction processes such as silk-screening or offset printing, the emulsion side of the film must be set correctly. This button enables you to set emulsion of your image down by flipping (or mirroring) your printing.

These two check boxes are available below the preview buttons:

- *File info within page.* In most cases, you choose to print file information when printing to a page size larger than your page setup size. Selecting this check box may be useful when printing to a page size equal to the dimensions of your file's page setup size. All printer marks and printer information print inside the dimensions of your page border.

- *Exterior crop marks only.* This option is helpful when printing multiple-page layouts where you don't want crop marks to appear between the actual segments of your layout. When selected, this option prints crop marks only in the exterior margins. Again, this option is most useful when printing to a page size that is larger than your document size.

Using the Layout Tab

The Layout tab of the Print Options dialog box controls all aspects related to the layout of your printed documents. The following list describes the options in the Layout tab:

- *Apply settings to all pages.* This option makes the positioning and scaling values identical for all pages. When left unchecked, you are able to set these values individually for each page printed.

- *Top, Left, Width and Height.* These controls enable you to set the Top and Left corner coordinates of your images on the printed page. The coordinates are set according to the page size you have selected in the printer Properties dialog box. The Width and Height controls enable you to set a scaling measure by selecting exact width and height or by selecting a percentage.

- *Center Image.* Cohesively centers all objects in your document to the center of your printed page size.

- *Fit to Page.* This option makes a calculation to fit all objects in your drawing—even objects outside your page borders—to fit in the page size you have selected.

III

Sharing & Printing Files

■ *Bleed Limit.* This option limits the extent to which bleeding occurs for objects overlapping the border of your document page size.

■ *Maintain Aspect Ratio.* This option locks out the Height measure so your printed objects remain undistorted vertically or horizontally.

■ *Print Tiled Pages.* When selected, the Bleed Limit option becomes unavailable. A new set of controls for Tile Overlap appears, as well as a range for Percentage of Page Width. Tiling pages is useful when the page size of the document you are printing exceeds the maximum page size your printer can handle. You can print your page in sections with slight overlaps for reassembly after printing. This feature has returned after being absent from version 5.

■ *Layout Style.* This drop-down list box consists of various layout styles including Full Page, Book, Booklet, Tent Card, Side-Fold Card, Top-Fold Card, and Tri-Fold Card. The Layout Style controls enable you to divide your printed page into sections and position the pages of your multipage file in specific formats.

The Edit button beside this option gives further customization capabilities by opening the Edit Layout Style dialog box (see fig. 16.9). Here you may set the number of divisions Across and Down, and the Horizontal and Vertical gutter spaces. You also may rearrange the layout of the pages using the Page Number control, set the Angle of individual pages to 0 or 180 degrees, and select a Double Sided Layout with the option to Flip Pages. You may save and reuse your current layout styles by using the Layout Style list box in the upper-left corner of the dialog box. To save new layout settings, click the plus-sign button and name your layout. The name is added to the drop-down list. To delete a style, select the name in the drop-down list and click the minus-sign button.

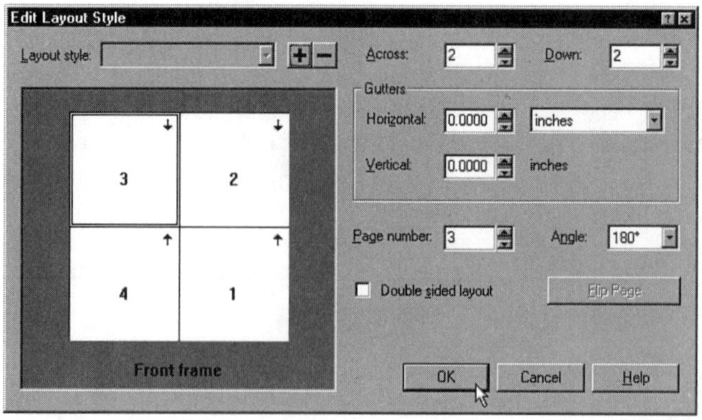

Fig. 16.9
Choosing the Edit button beside the Layout Style list box displays this Edit Layout Style dialog box, enabling you to customize the layout style to suit your needs.

■ *Positioning.* This drop-down list box enables you to select from previously saved Size and Position settings. When you first open CorelDRAW! 6, only the default settings exist. To save your newly set Size and Position measures, choose the Edit button beside the Positioning drop-down list box to display the Edit Positioning dialog box (see fig. 16.10). You can set the number of Rows and Columns, Horizontal and Vertical gutter spacing (or Auto Spacing), Left, Right, Top, and Bottom margins (or Equal Margins or Auto Margins). The Edit Positioning dialog box also contains options to Clone Frame and Maintain Document Page Size.

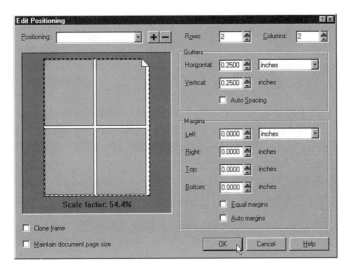

Fig. 16.10
Choosing the Edit button beside the Positioning list box displays this Edit Positioning dialog box.

Using the Separations Tab

For the electronic artist preparing digital illustrations or designs for the print world, or the service bureau operator generating film negatives for a client, knowing about the Separations tab of the Print Options dialog box is critical (see fig. 16.11). The Separations tab contains all the controls for splitting a CorelDRAW! 6 file into its individual color layers and molding those layers into a condition compatible with certain reproduction methods. These controls include CMYK conversion options, screening controls, and auto-trapping options for film output.

III

Sharing & Printing Files

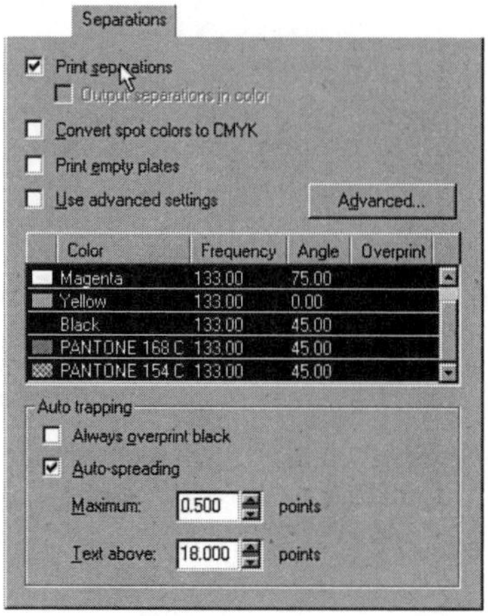

Fig. 16.11
The Separations tab of the Print Options dialog box controls many of the prepress color separation options.

The following list describes the options in the Separations tab.

- *Print Separations.* This option activates all the Separations controls, giving you the choice to separate your file. If you are printing to a color printer, the Output Separations in Color option becomes available. Setting this option prints each of the separations in the color it represents.

- *Convert Spot Colors to CMYK.* This option is an excellent shortcut when portions of your illustration containing spot color have come from other sources and you want to print these portions in CMYK process color only.

- *Print Empty Plates.* This option remains off by default for a good reason, indicating that any pages without objects containing the current color being printed will not be printed. This feature enables you to keep a few extra dollars in your pocket. For example, in past versions, printing a 12-page document where four pages contain CMYK process or spot-colored objects and the remaining pages contain a single color meant having to output the multicolor pages separately from the single-color pages. Otherwise you would end up with a handful of expensive blank film. This new feature avoids that problem.

- *Use Advanced Settings.* This button gives access to the Advanced Separations Settings dialog box, which includes controls for adjusting specific aspects of film output, including custom screen angle and frequency, overprinting by plate color, and specific screening technologies.

■ *The Separation Control window*. This window is the selection control for which colors print and which don't. To select a color of ink to print, click it. To deselect a color, click it again. The Separation Control window also provides information about how the specific color will be output, including the ink name, screen frequency, screen angle, and overprint options for text and objects for each specific color.

■ *Auto Trapping*. Corel's answer to eliminating the tedium of manual trapping, this feature is quite effective for the most common types of process color film output. Auto trapping features an option for overprinting all black objects, where they overlap other process colored objects. The other option, Auto-Spreading, literally builds an extra outline around all filled objects to a specified value. You can build an outline around text above a certain point size, the default of which is 18 points. With this setting, any text below 18 points is unaffected by the Auto-Spreading function.

You still should perform manual trapping on specific objects and in files that contain overlapping spot colors where necessary.

Caution

When using the Auto-Spreading feature, do not attempt to set this value any lower than 18-point type. Setting this value lower causes the type to take on a distorted, blurry appearance.

As mentioned in the preceding list, the Advanced Settings button gives access to the Advanced Separations Settings dialog box (see fig. 16.12). Using the following options, you can adjust specific aspects of film output:

■ *Screening Technology*. The Screening Technology pull-down menu contains scripts for specific technologies including Standard Default, AGFA Balanced Screening, RT Screening, and HQS Screening. In most cases, HQS Screening technology serves the purpose for film output from Linotype imagesetters. You may find some marginal improvement by using these third-party screening technologies, which are dependent on whether the supporting software has been purchased and loaded into the internal memory of the imagesetter.

■ *Resolution*. This setting selects the device output resolutions corresponding to the Screening technology selected above.

■ *Basic Screen*. This setting controls the screen angles for the screening technology and resolution previously described.

■ *Current Selection window controls*. This window is similar to the Separation Control window, with the exception that you may change the settings for screen Frequency and Angle, and select options for Overprinting Color on Graphics and Text. To change the settings for a specific color, click one time on the color and enter values in the Frequency and Angle fields. You may also invoke a blanket overprint command by selecting the Overprint Color option, which in turn enables you to specify both or either of Graphic or Text. While the overprint feature is enabled, small icons representing the Graphics and Text overprint functions appear in the Current Selection window.

■ *Halftone Type*. The Halftone Type pull-down menu contains various settings that control the shape of the actual dots that compose the screens in your output. The list includes such shapes as Dot, Line, Diamond, Elliptical, Euclidean, Lines, Grid, Microwaves, Rhomboid, and Star.

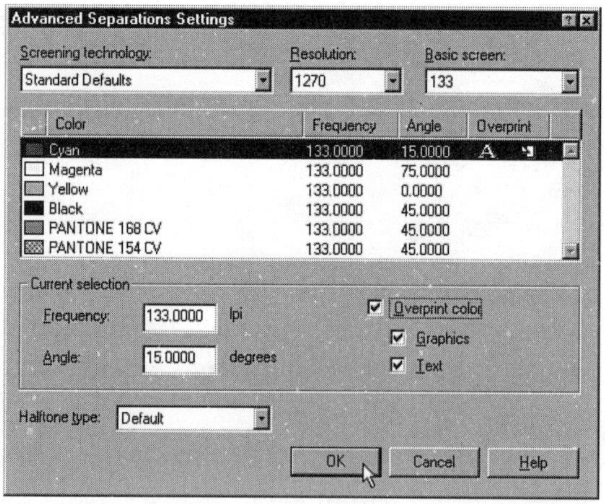

Fig. 16.12
The Advanced Separations Settings dialog box controls specific aspects of film output.

Using the Options Tab

The Print Options tab is comprised of options which will help you customize how you would like your document to be reproduced by your printing device including some of the more advanced printing options available in CorelDRAW! 6. This section explains the specific function of each of these options.

■ *Fountain Steps*. This setting controls the number of overall fountain steps used in printing fountain-filled objects. Fountain steps may be set to a range between 2 and 2,000 steps. A higher setting means a more complex calculation and longer RIP and printing times.

■ *Screen Frequency*. The Screen Frequency control sets the overall number of lines of screen used in producing fill patterns for screens, digital half-tones, bitmap texture fills, and so on. The screen frequency may be set to the default of the imagesetter or printer, a preset incremental range between 60- and 200-line, or a custom measure by typing a value in the Screen Frequency field.

■ *PostScript Preferences*. The PostScript Preferences button gives you access to a battery of PostScript controls now available in CorelDRAW! 6, including flatness, printer warning options, font-handling options, and bitmap printing options.

■ *Proofing options*. Proofing options include settings to optimize printing speed for the purposes of proofing. You can limit the printing of color or text objects, including text proofing controls for printing to color printers. Options for proofing include Print Vectors, Print Bitmaps, Print Text, Full Color, Print All Text In Black, and Fit Printer's Marks and Layout To Page. And, while printing composites, the options All Colors as Black and All Colors as Grayscale also become available.

■ *Print Job Information Sheet*. This option is extremely useful in printing a hard copy of all printing specifications to accompany print files going to a remote site such as a service bureau. The option also may be useful in the offset printing process as information provided to the print supplier. You access the Print Job Information Sheet options by choosing the Info Settings button, which displays the Print Information dialog box (see fig. 16.13). You can set options contained in the information sheet hard copy, plus options for printing information about the Application, Driver, Print Job, Separations, Fonts, and Links. You also can specify whether to print the information to a Text File and/or Send to Printer. The font and linking information should be of paramount interest to anyone proofing the output who is not familiar with the document.

Fig. 16.13
The Print Job
Information dialog
box contains
options for setting
the information
contained in
the hard-copy
printout and quick
access to printing
functions.

Print Job Information: C:\WINDOWS2\2BUSINES\My Artwork\Print me.CDR

Job information:

Bleed Limit:	Disabled
Crop Marks:	Enabled
Crosshairs:	Enabled
File Information:	Enabled
Page Numbers:	Enabled
Densitometer Scale:	Disabled
Calibration Bar:	Disabled
Copies:	1
Level 2 PostScript:	No
Bitmap Color Space:	CMYK

Separation Information:

Angle(degrees)	Frequency(lpi)	Color
15.0000	150.0000	Cyan
75.0000	150.0000	Magenta
0.0000	150.0000	Yellow
45.0000	150.0000	Black
45.0000	150.0000	PANTONE 168 CV
45.0000	150.0000	PANTONE 154 CV

Font(s):	None
Linked Graphics:	None

Information
- ☑ Application
- ☑ Driver
- ☑ Print job
- ☑ Separations
- ☑ Fonts
- ☑ Links

Destination
- ☐ Send to text file
- Select File...
- ☑ Send to printer
- Select Printer...

OK   Cancel   Help

Print Options, Options Tab, and Special Settings

The terminology for this section will confuse some users due to the fact that CorelDRAW! 6 has already used the term "Options" to get to this area. But these settings control the most advanced printing options. In many cases these settings should not be altered from their default settings unless you know exactly what you are doing. Many of the options determine the way the PostScript coding describes your print file and can in some cases play havoc with the printer if not left alone. However, if you are well versed in the behavior of PostScript printing features and are confident that you are making the right choice, you can take advantage of printing control that may well be the most advanced of any current graphics package. Changes are reflected in a file called CORELPRN.INI found in your COREL60/CONFIG folder. You can view this file using the Windows 95 Notepad utility or any word processing program.

The following items exist as options in the Special Settings area of the Options tab and are accessed through the Option drop-down list box.

- *Bitmap Font Limit (PS).* This option limits the number of small-sized fonts that may be converted to bitmaps, a function that DRAW! performs automatically when printing to PostScript printers. Small-sized fonts sometimes appear much better when printed in bitmap format than they appear when printed using their native outline or vector format.

- *Bitmap Font Size Threshold (PS).* Under normal circumstances, CorelDRAW! converts very small sizes of text to bitmap format for printing. The default size is 75 pixels. The threshold limit determines exactly which font sizes are affected. The equivalent font size of 75 pixels when printing to a printer resolution of 300 DPI is approximately 18-point type, and at 600 DPI it is approximately 9-point type, and so on. The higher the resolution, the lower the point size affected. A number of provisions determine whether these controls apply, though, including whether the font has been scaled or skewed, applied Envelope effects, fountain or texture fills, or print scaling options such as Fit to Page. Again, this option applies only to PostScript-compatible printers.

- *Composite Crop Marks (PS).* The Composite Crop Marks option is another useful feature for setting the pen color of crop marks to print black only or full process CMYK colors. This is useful for individuals who output on imaging systems which separate composite files into CMYK colors.

- *Conform to DCS.* This allows users who require PostScript files that strictly conform to the Adobe Document Structuring Convention (DSC). Postscript parsing software such as trapping software or RIP, or Imposition software would fall into this category.

> **Note**
>
> DCS applies only to placer files that have been preseparated to PostScript format, a practice used by high-end power users and previously available only in Adobe PhotoShop versions 2.5 and 3.0.

- *Grayscale Driver Bitmap Output (PS).* This element allows for either of two options including Send Color Bitmaps as Grayscale or Send Color Bitmaps as Color. This feature is available only when printing to PostScript devices.

- *Overprint Black Threshold (PS).* During overprinting functions, CorelDRAW! 6 sets a default value for overprinting black objects only if they contain a uniform fill of 95 percent black or more. You may change the Overprint Black Threshold setting using this option, which enables you to further customize the global overprinting function. You may set the threshold limit to a value from 1 to 100 percent black.

III

Sharing & Printing Files

- *PostScript 2 Stroke Adjust (PS)*. Corel stresses that the PostScript 2 Stroke Adjust option should not be set to On unless you are printing to a level 2 PostScript device. If you are not sure whether your printing device is a level 1 or a level 2 PostScript device, leave this setting Off.

- *Resolve DCS Links (PS)*. This option enables you to Substitute Plates at Print time or Leave DCS Links Unresolved (see Conform to DCS option described earlier). If you are using imported placer files to represent your process color separations using the DCS method, this option enables you to ignore the CMYK files until it is time to finally print film negative color separations from the imagesetter. Resolve DCS Links is available only when using a PostScript-compatible printer.

- *Registration Mark Type (PS)*. If you tire easily from seeing the same old registration marks on your film, or if you are working with over-sensitive registration such as in stamp or currency printing, you are able to change this using the Registration Mark Type option. Here, the norm is printing to 3600 DPI film using a line screen higher than 300 lines per inch; you may find this option of great value. You may change the registration marks that the CorelDRAW! print engine uses by selecting this option and specifying Standard Bullseye, Corel Logo, Elongated Bullseye, Half-inverted Bullseye, Square, or Circle. A preview flyout beside the selection shows the registration mark selected.

- *Bitmap Printing*. You may change this option as a last resort if printing large bitmaps becomes a problem for your printer. You may set this option to Output Entire Bitmap or Output in 64K Chunks. (Chunks isn't necessarily a technical term but it does the job nonetheless.) Outputting in 64K chunks limits the amount of bitmap information being sent to the printer, possibly making the bitmap less complex—but slower—to print.

- *Driver Banding*. This option is applicable only when printing to non-PostScript printers. Under normal circumstances, non-PostScript printers are sent single bands (strips) of data at a time, much like the way traditional-type facsimile machines print. As a last resort, if printing becomes too complex for the printer's memory, you may select Let Driver Handle Banding or Send Bands to Driver.

- *Fill Clipping*. Applied only to non-PostScript printers, this option enables you to select either Printer's Driver for Fill Clipping or Use Software Clipping for Fills. Fill clipping applies to non-rectangular objects, such as ellipses or polygons. The defined shape of the object works as a

clipping path on the fill applied to it. When an object is highly complex, fill clipping calculations may sometimes overcome a printer's
memory or cause printing errors, or both.

■ *Page Orientation Warning.* You may turn the page orientation warning
On or Off using this option.

■ *Preview Image Default.* You may set the Preview Image Default here to
On or Off. This option is essentially a duplication of the Preview control option located below the print preview window.

■ *Print Preview Drag Mode.* The print preview Drag mode option is a duplication of the right mouse button command available by right-clicking
in the preview window. This command enables you to draw images in
the preview window while you drag them using the mouse. This option
may be set to Full Drag or Drag Marquee.

■ *Text Output Method.* Text sent to any printer may be handled one of
two ways. Text will be sent down to the printer driver as text or the text
will be sent down to the printer driver as graphics. This is to resolve
problems when drivers are printing text of poor quality.

PostScript Preferences

The PostScript Preferences button gives you access to the PostScript Preferences dialog box (see fig. 16.14).

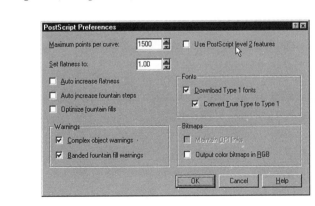

Fig. 16.14
The PostScript
Preferences dialog
box.

III

Sharing & Printing Files

The following list describes the options in the PostScript Preferences dialog box.

- *Maximum Points per Curve*. This option enables you to set a value between 20 and 20,000 nodes per curve. Note that the more nodes you have per curve, the longer your printing will take. This setting by default is fixed at 1500 nodes per curve.

- *Set Auto Flatness*. The Set Auto Flatness setting is enabled by selecting the Auto Increase Flatness option. You can set the flatness limit to a value between 0.20 and 100.0. The Auto Flatness feature has the effect of increasing the flatness of complex objects by a factor of 2 until the object prints. Increased flatness causes the printing of curves to be less smooth.

- *Increase Auto Flatness*. The Increase Auto Flatness option enables DRAW! to simplify the printing of curves by decreasing the number of lines that describe the curve. You may use this option as a last resort when you run into problems printing highly complex shapes in your DRAW! document.

- *Auto Increase Fountain Steps*. In an effort to avoid undesirable banding, this option enables the print engine to examine your document for opportunities to increase the number of fountain steps. Increasing the number of steps that describe a fountain fill increases printing time but achieves better results. If printing time isn't a concern, it may be a good idea to leave this option selected.

- *Optimize Fountain Fills*. This feature works in reverse of the Auto Increase Fountain Steps option by enabling the print engine to decrease the number of fountain steps set for objects in your document to the number of steps your printer is capable of reproducing.

- *Use PostScript Level 2 Features*. This global function tells the print engine that the printer you are printing to is capable of interpreting PostScript Level 2 commands. Don't use this feature unless you are positive that the device you are printing to supports the Level 2 PostScript printing language.

- *Fonts*. Two options are available to control the PostScript handling of fonts in your printed document, including Download Type 1 Fonts and Convert TrueType to Type 1. These options are selected by default and should be left on unless advised otherwise by your imagesetter operator.

■ *Warnings*. If you are sure you will never need a warning that your print file contains overly complex objects exceeding the number of nodes allowable by the Maximum Points per Curve limit, you may turn off the Complex Object Warnings. (However, turning off warnings is generally not a recommended practice.) If you are unconcerned with the appearance of banding in your printed file, you may also elect to turn off the Banded Fountain Fill Warnings option. Both of these warning messages halt the printing process when displayed.

■ *Bitmaps*. During printing, this control enables the print engine to either Maintain OPI (Open PostScript Interface) Links or Output Color Bitmaps in RGB. OPI is the CorelDRAW! 6 print engine alternative to using the DCS (Desktop Color Separation) method of printing. OPI enables PostScript linking to external digital images normally of higher quality than the low-resolution image used to indicate position in your DRAW! file.

Viewing the CORELPRN Settings

Until CorelDRAW! 6, you could control most of the advanced settings for PostScript handling only by using a third-party utility or delving directly into the CORELPRN file found in your COREL60/CONFIG folder. In CorelDRAW! 6 these options now are completely built into the interface. Editing this file is normally a task only for the brave or PostScript-knowledgeable. Although nearly all the options are available, you may still want to view this file out of curiosity.

To view the CORELPRN file, follow these steps:

1. From the Start menu, choose Programs, Accessories, Notepad to launch the Notepad utility.

2. In Notepad, choose File, Open to display the Open dialog box (see fig. 16.15). From the Files of Type list box, select All Files (*.*) and locate the file called CORELPRN in the COREL60/CONFIG folder.

3. Open the file by clicking it and choosing the Open button.

4. View the file. To close the file after viewing, choose File, Exit and choose No when asked to save changes.

III

Sharing & Printing Files

> **Caution**
>
> If you attempt to edit the CORELPRN file and are not exactly sure what you are doing, it may be best to leave it alone. Changing some of these settings may have detrimental effects on your printing operations.

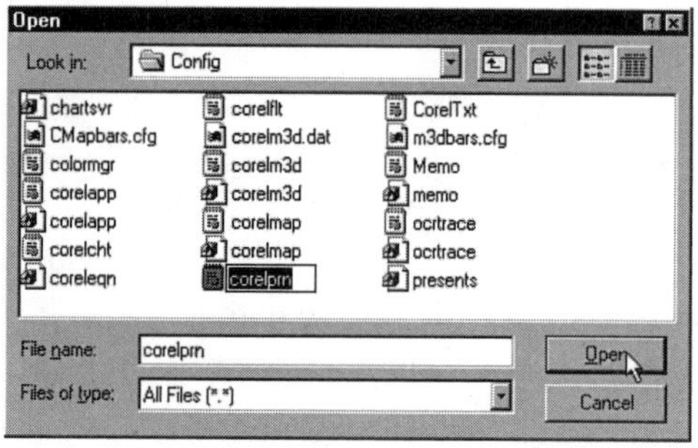

Fig. 16.15

You can open the CORELPRN file using the Open dialog box in the Windows 95 Notepad accessory.

> **Note**
>
> When the CORELPRN file is open, a 0 indicates that the feature is currently turned off, and a 1 indicates the feature is active.

Using Print Merge

The Print Merge feature in CorelDRAW! enables you to do such things as produce personalized correspondence, certificates, envelopes, and so on. These tasks are similar to what you can do in a word processing program, with the added power of having your merged documents be any CorelDRAW! file merged with any simple text document. Providing you have prepared both documents properly using the same codes and symbols, your print merge will happen successfully.

Essentially what you're doing is placing a keyword in your CorelDRAW! file that the Print Merge command searches for, and setting substitute text to replace those keywords. The location of those keywords in relation to your page shape does not matter, as long as they exist and match the substitute text keywords. The keywords also do not need to be in any order, as long as they are somewhere on the page.

When your DRAW! document merges with your substitute text file, DRAW! searches for exact text parameters. Print Merge controls are case sensitive, so be sure to use the same keyword text characters that you use in your substitute text file.

To prepare a CorelDRAW! 6 file for Print Merge, follow these steps:

1. Create your substitute text place holders using the Artistic Text tool in the appropriate places in your CorelDRAW! file.

2. Apply any transformations, envelopes, Lens Effects, or Extrude Effects to your keyword text. Any effects you apply will in turn be applied to your substituted text.

◀ See "Creating and Editing Artistic Text," p. 125

   Plan ahead and leave enough room for the merged text to fit your document space. When your text is substituted, it takes on the same text attributes as your keyword text. Also, try to use a centered format. This format works best for alignment's sake, from a design and layout standpoint.

3. Choose File, Save to save your CorelDRAW! file in the usual way.

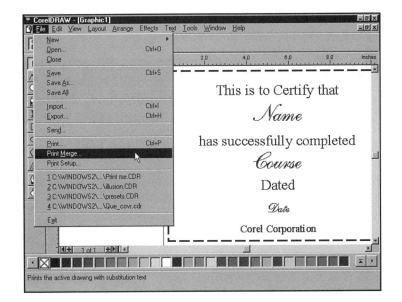

Fig. 16.16
Preparing a CorelDRAW! file for print merging with a text file.

To prepare a text file for merging with your prepared CorelDRAW! file, follow these steps:

1. Using a basic text editor such as the Windows 95 Notepad Editor, begin a new file by choosing File, New.

2. Type a number equal to the number of keywords or parameters you are using, and press Enter.

3. Type ***keyword**\\ (where *keyword* is your first parameter such as Name) and press Enter.

   Remember, Print Merge is case sensitive, so if you entered a *Name* parameter in your CorelDRAW! document, you need to type an uppercase *N* followed by a lowercase *ame*. Do not enter any spaces before or after your keyword.

4. Type your second keyword surrounded by backslashes and press Enter. Continue until you have entered all the keywords. The number of keywords should match the number you entered on the first line of your text file.

5. On the line following your last keyword, begin to enter your substitute text in exactly the same format. Type the text surrounded by backslashes without any extra spaces (for example, \\Bob Smith\\). Continue entering your substitute text until all your information is in the text file.

> **Tip**
>
> To ensure that you have not entered any illegal spaces, use a search command to find backslash+space or space+backslash combinations.

To check your text file for compatibility, count the number of lines of text, subtract one, and divide by the number at the beginning of the file. If you cannot divide the number of lines exactly, an error exists and you need to check your entries.

The following example shows lines from a text document used to create a series of personalized identification cards:

```
7
\name\
\age\
\sex\
\height\
\haircolor\
\eyecolor\
\birthdate\
```

\Tina Kindratsky\
\36\
\Female\
\5 foot, 7 inches\
\blonde\
\blue\
\December 24, 1959\
\Ian McLeod\
\38\
\Male\
\6 foot, 3 inches\
\brown\
\green\
\September 11, 1957\

The preceding example uses seven keyword parameters, so the file begins with the numeral 7. Each of the information groupings contains seven variables surrounded by backslashes. The file has 22 lines, which when subtracted by one and divided by 7, comes out to exactly three variables, indicating a good chance that no errors exist.

After you have saved your file, you are nearly ready for your Print Merge command, except for taking one precaution. In cases where the Print Merge involves producing a large number of merge copies, it may be wise to perform a test of three or so pages first to ensure that everything goes smoothly.

To perform the merge, open the CorelDRAW! 6 file and choose File, Print Merge. DRAW! asks you to locate the text file containing the keyword parameters and then proceeds with the merge without displaying or saving the merge results.

Working with Service Bureaus

Before the advent of desktop publishing, there were (and still are) businesses dedicated solely to word processing, typesetting, and prepress stripping, employing experts in these particular areas. Now, much of that expertise is falling on the shoulders of the composing graphic illustrator using a personal computer and a graphics or layout program. Preparing text, artwork, or photographs for any of these traditional processes was usually a straightforward, logical task. But things have changed since then, and procedures are not exactly what they used to be.

III

Sharing & Printing Files

Using programs like CorelDRAW! 6, anyone can have the tools necessary to create expert layouts and illustrations. With version 6, the tools have been developed to a point where even the most demanding professional can achieve sophisticated results. In this case, artists who may not be familiar with these new procedures of reproduction may find themselves forced into uncertain areas.

If you are using CorelDRAW! 6 to produce artwork that will eventually be reproduced by offset printing, you probably will need to use the services offered by a service bureau dedicated to imaging your electronic files. Film, used to produce offset press printing plates, is a common requirement. You also may need color separations using process color or spot color. With process color, four separate pieces of film are needed to print the cyan, magenta, yellow, and black plates (abbreviated to C, M, Y, and K). Complex illustrations or layouts may require additional spot colors printed together with the process colors. With each additional spot color, you need a separate piece of film.

Service bureaus supply the film for electronically created artwork. A bureau usually is operated by someone who has seen how desktop publishing and computers are changing the needs of the electronic artist. Service bureau operators need to be familiar with the functions of various types of publishing software, sometimes on different platforms. These highly trained output operators can sometimes spend hours troubleshooting client files. Problems caused by incorrectly created files from inexperienced electronic artists can create grief for all involved.

If you are fully prepared for the experience of buying output, you can substantially reduce your chance of having output problems. Whether you are a first time purchaser of output, or a seasoned professional, you'll find that printing your files at a service bureau *can* be a pleasant experience.

Reviewing Service Bureau Terminology

Service bureaus seem to have a language all their own. Operators may ask if your file was uploaded to the BBS, or which RIP you would like to use. Right and wrong reading may even enter into the picture.

The following list describes some of the common terms a service bureau may use. Some terms may be obvious, but take a close look to avoid any confusion:

- *All fonts resident.* No additional font information is needed for the file to print because all fonts you used in your document are already loaded into the memory of the printer you are using.

- *BBS.* Bulletin board service, a service offered by some service bureaus to enable clients to transmit files to the BBS for imaging. Look for this convenience in a service bureau.

- *Bleed.* The area outside your page dimensions where ink will still print. This procedure is used when the excess area of the printed sheet will be trimmed away, leaving the ink to bleed off the edge of the finished page.

- *Composite.* A printout where all colors and overlays are printed.

- *Compression package.* A program that compresses file size, making it easier to do things like transmit files or fit them onto a floppy disk.

- *Crop marks.* Corner marks indicating the edges of a page.

- *Crosshairs.* Used in ink and printing registration, crosshairs describe marks (also known as registration marks) that printers use to line up separate color film overlays.

- *CT scan.* Continuous tone scan.

- *Default.* A preset setting in a software program.

- *Density.* Service bureaus refer to density as the value or measure given to the relative opaqueness of a developed film negative.

- *Dot gain.* This term refers to the phenomena of ink soaking into dry paper (absorption rate). The image becomes slightly larger and may be distorted. You can compensate for the gain at the film stage by adjusting the size of the dots.

- *Download.* The action of transferring a file from a main computer system to a remote computer system.

- *DPI.* Dots per inch, which refers to a measure of dots in scanning resolution. DPI also may refer to the detail an imagesetter renders on a film negative or positive.

- *Driver.* A file composed of machine programming commands that communicates between software and hardware.

- *Drum scanner.* A type of scanner in which the original hardcopy document is mounted on a drum-style holder and spun at high speeds while a laser digitally records the image.

- *DTP.* Service bureau language for desktop publishing.

III

Sharing & Printing Files

- *Emulsion.* A photo-sensitive, silver-based coating applied to one side of a sheet in a polyester carrier. You can recognize the emulsion side of the film by its dull, non-reflective appearance.

- *Extension.* Refers to the three letters at the end of a file's name. The extension sometimes indicates which program the file originated from or which program is capable of editing it. All CorelDRAW! files—regardless of which version they are—have the extension CDR.

- *Flatbed.* A type of scanner in which the original hardcopy document is placed face down on a flat document glass and a reflection-sensitive light bar passes below, recording the image data.

- *Flatness.* Refers to the detail in which curves in your drawing are rendered to the printer or imagesetter.

- *Font conflict.* When one font has the same font identification number as another. This problem is essentially a thing of the past, but font conflict plagued service bureaus in the early days before font identification standards were set.

- *Fonts.* The digital description of a typeface. The term originates from early typesetting systems that used large metal or nylon discs with images of letters cut out of them to represent typefaces.

- *GCR.* Gray Component Replacement, which is the process of replacing RGB (red, green, blue) color with gray values.

- *Gray scale.* A term from the days of camera work, where a small strip of photographic paper graduated in steps of gray was photographed and developed along with artwork, acting as a benchmark for film density and image quality. Digitally speaking, a gray scale describes density values.

- *HQS.* High-quality screening, a screening algorithm developed by Linotype, makers of Linotronic imagesetters. The purpose of HQS-screening technology is to optimize screen angle when imaging process color separations to reduce the frequency of undesirable moires.

- *Imagesetter.* A PostScript or non-PostScript printer that generates a hardcopy printout.

- *Laminate.* Colored layers of a microthin carrier film-bonding process that produces a highly accurate color sample of the finished printed film.

- *Landscape.* Represents page orientation and is set in your page setup dialog box. In CorelDRAW! 6, landscape describes a page that has greater width than height. A feature found in the Special Settings section of the Print Options dialog box enables you to turn on or off DRAW!'s orientation warning when printing. When this feature is on, DRAW! warns you that you may need to turn your paper sideways if your paper is not set to print properly on the device selected.

- *Line art.* Any artwork composed of solid black or solid white image, digital or otherwise.

- *Linen tester.* A small magnifying glass used to closely examine film.

- *Linotronic.* A line of imagesetters manufactured in Germany by Linotype-Hell.

- *Loop.* A small magnifier used to closely examine film.

- *LPI.* Lines per inch, which refers to the number of rows of dots counted in one linear inch of a screen tint or halftone screen.

- *Moiré.* An undesirable effect, pronounced *more-aye*, which appears as a blurry checkboard or tartan style when two or more pieces of screen film are aligned at improper angles.

- *Nested fonts.* Caused by performing unwise procedures such as importing EPS files containing fonts into a drawing in CorelDRAW! and then exporting the file in the same or different file format.

- *Nesting files.* Like nested fonts, this is an unwise practice caused by importing files into a drawing in CorelDRAW! and then exporting the file in the same or different file format.

- *PKZip.* One of the most common file compression programs used. The most current version to date is 6.0. PKZip is available from PKWare, Inc., 7545 N. Port Washington Road, Glemdale, WI 53217-7176, (414) 352-3670.

- *Plate.* A term referring to paper or metal sheets installed onto a printing press. Service bureaus use this term to describe a color separation or film overlay that represents a color of ink.

- *Portrait.* Represents page orientation and is set in your page setup dialog box. In CorelDRAW! 6, portrait describes a page that has greater depth than width. A feature found in the Special Settings section of the Print Options dialog box enables you to turn on or off DRAW!'s orientation warning when printing. When the feature is on, DRAW! warns you that you may need to turn your paper sideways if your paper is not set to print properly on the device selected.

- *Print file.* A PostScript text file created by choosing File, Print, Print to File. You can usually recognize print files by their file extension of PRN. A print file may contain all the information necessary for imaging a file to a particular printer.

- *Processing.* This term means either film processing or image (data) processing. Film processing is the action of developing, fixing, and washing exposed film; data processing refers to computer calculations that the RIP of an imagesetter performs.

- *Processor.* This term refers to either the machine that physically develops, stops, fixes, washes, and dries the actual imagesetter film, or the main computer chip that drives your computer.

- *Raster graphic.* Any type of file that contains bitmapped images such as BMP, TIFF, and PCX.

- *Registration.* The procedure of matching several film overlays by alignment markings imaged onto the film and the images on the film itself.

- *Resident scans.* Digital images stored at the service bureau for the convenience of imaging linked client files.

- *Resolution.* The measure of detail that the imagesetter records on the film. The higher the resolution, the more detail recorded.

- *RIP.* The raster image processor, commonly referred to as a RIP, is a device that converts vector images into raster images before printing to output devices that require it.

- *RRED.* Right reading emulsion down, which describes the condition of imaged film. RRED describes film that, when held up with the emulsion side facing away, the images and type are read from left to right.

- *RREU.* Right reading emulsion up, which describes the condition of imaged film. RREU describes film that, when held up with the emulsion side facing toward you, the images and type are read from left to right.

- *Screen frequency.* Describes the LPI or number of rows of dots in one linear inch.

- *SelectSet.* A line of imagesetters developed by AGFA, Inc.

- *Separations.* A set of film overlays that make up a composite image when combined.

- *Source file*. The original or native file created by a program.

- *Spooler*. A type of software program or dedicated computer that handles the print traffic between one or several computers and one or several imagesetters. Files may be held in the spooler indefinitely, or until it is necessary to image them.

- *System color profile*. The file you create when you calibrate the color-related hardware in your computer system using CorelDRAW! 6 Color Manager and the Color Wizard.

Understanding Imagesetters

This section provides some background on what an imagesetter is and the acrobatics it performs to image your file. Whether you ask for a single page of output or high-resolution film for a 100-page book, your data will likely go through the same channels.

First, your file is downloaded through a raster image processor (RIP) according to the specific directions you have provided. In the case of print files, the files may download directly to the imagesetter. Or if you provided a source file, the file may be imaged directly out of CorelDRAW! 6. In most cases, the service bureau uses a spooler to hold the data until the imagesetter is ready for it. A healthy service bureau business likely has its imagesetters running 24 hours a day and uses dedicated print spoolers to handle the flow of traffic between the operators' computers and the actual imagesetters.

Next, after your data starts feeding to the imagesetter, the image is burned onto a layer of photo-sensitive film. From there, the film is inserted (usually) into an automatic film processor that develops, fixes, washes, and dries the film much the way your local one-hour film processor handles your vacation photos. Then, the finished output is cut into separate film pages and packaged.

Types of Digital Imagesetters

Two principle models of imagesetters are currently used. First, a *capstan* imagesetter uses a 200-foot roll of film that is loaded much like a consumer-type, happy-snap camera. The film enters the imagesetter and is fed by rollers to a laser. The laser mechanism exposes the image onto the film in sections. The film is then fed into a light-tight cassette that can be safely removed from the imagesetter without exposing the contents. The service bureau operator removes the cassette for processing, just like a regular camera.

The *drum model* imagesetter is the other type. In a drum model, the film is cut into large sheets that are vacuum-mounted to the inside a half-barrel shape.

III

Sharing & Printing Files

An imaging laser moves back and forth to expose the film. The exposed film then is track-fed into a take-up cassette, and a new sheet of film is fed into its place.

Imaging Output Material

You likely will order two types of film output from the service bureau: paper and film. These materials may be confusing because both are light-sensitive and considered *film* even though one is paper-based. Film processors automatically process, fix, wash, and dry both types of output. A properly maintained processing system is fed by a filtered, constant water supply that is temperature-controlled. Like imagesetters, processors require regular maintenance to provide constant results. The professional service bureau constantly monitors both imagesetters and processors for such things as dust, dirt, static, and film density.

If you have prepared your files properly and provided the service bureau with everything it needs, you won't have any surprises when your film comes back. If a problem occurs and your output is not exactly what you want, the first thing to do is check your output order form to make sure your output is indeed what you ordered. After that, it is between you and the operators to try to find out why your output is incorrect.

If your files are extremely complex, the service bureau may charge you an extra processing surcharge. Most service bureaus follow the rule of thumb of allowing fifteen minutes to image each letter-sized page. Then you may be charged up to a dollar per minute for the extra time needed to image the page. This practice is not uncommon, but keep in mind that good customers are rarely charged.

Some service bureaus, even though they are equipped with PC-compatible computers and provide output from CorelDRAW!, may penalize you for sending in native CorelDRAW! files. These businesses would rather charge you a 50 percent markup for outputting directly from the CorelDRAW! files. Stay away from these places. They obviously don't need you as a customer.

Preparing a Print File

Creating a print file (sometimes called a PRN file) is not a complicated operation. As long as you have the correct drivers in place and understand the way the target printer operates, you can create a print file.

Printing to file essentially creates a long text file containing a series of PostScript or machine language commands that the target printer interprets. The key element is that you have the correct printer driver installed on your

Windows 95 system before you start. To install a printer driver, obtain the latest version from your hardware manufacturer or service bureau and consult the Windows 95 manual for exact procedures on installing the driver.

After the correct driver is installed, create a print file using these procedures:

1. Open your CorelDRAW! 6 file and choose File, Print. Select the correct printer in the Print dialog box and set your remaining parameters in the usual way or according to your service bureau specifications.

2. In the Print dialog box, select the Print to File option. If your file will be printed through a Mac-based printer, select the For Mac option as well. Doing this deletes the two control characters that your Windows printer driver automatically inserts at the beginning of the file.

3. Choose the OK button. Immediately, a Print to File dialog box appears asking you to enter a file name and destination for your print file (see fig. 16.17). Notice that the file is about to receive the extension PRN.

4. Choose Save, and your print file is created and saved.

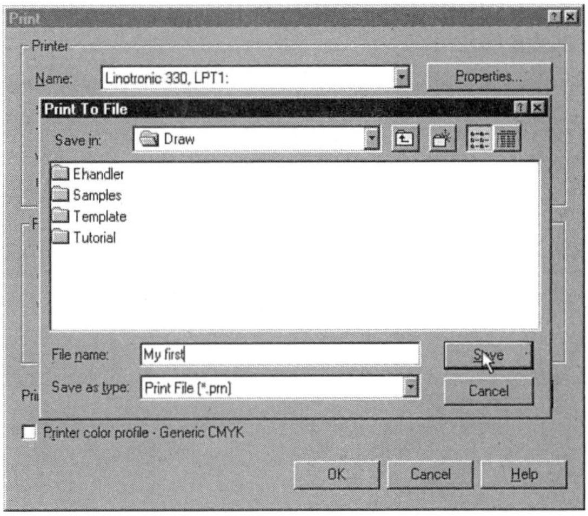

Fig. 16.17
Name and save your print file in the Print to File dialog box.

After your computer has finished writing the file to disk, locate the file and make a note of the file's size. Will the file fit onto a 3.5-inch floppy disk? Probably not, because this file contains every bit of information necessary to output your file. You will likely need to use a file compression package such as PKZip. Windows 95 driver information, font, page size, screen frequency positive or negative, crop marks, and everything else you selected is in the file.

III

Sharing & Printing Files

The service bureau can set up for paper or film as you request. The service bureau now may download the print file directly to the imagesetter.

From Here...

The printing functions in CorelDRAW! 6 may be overwhelming at first, but if you take a step at a time, you can master them. The number of print engine features in CorelDRAW! 6 has grown considerably compared to the features in version 5. Corel has taken some of the most sophisticated and complex options and placed them directly in the hands of the user, right where they should be.

Without proper print controls, drawings produced in any graphics program are completely wasted for the print world—and we are a world married to the printed page (at least for now). Along with the enhancements to this amazing drawing program comes a fully supportive print engine, effectively complementing each of the CorelDRAW! 6 suite of programs.

- See Chapter 3, "Making CorelDRAW! Easy to Use," to learn more about page sizes and other options.

- See Chapter 6, "Working with Objects," to learn how to use Extrude.

- See Chapter 7, "Using Fills and Outlines," to learn about Steps and Edge Pad options and how to use Fountain Fills.

- See Chapter 13, "Using Color, Wizards, and Applying Color Masks," to learn about Color Models.

Part IV

Beyond CorelDRAW!

17 Creating and Editing Images with PHOTO-PAINT

18 Making High-Quality Presentations with Corel PRESENTS

19 Creating 3D Illustrations in CorelDREAM 3D

20 Using CorelDRAW! 6 Utilities

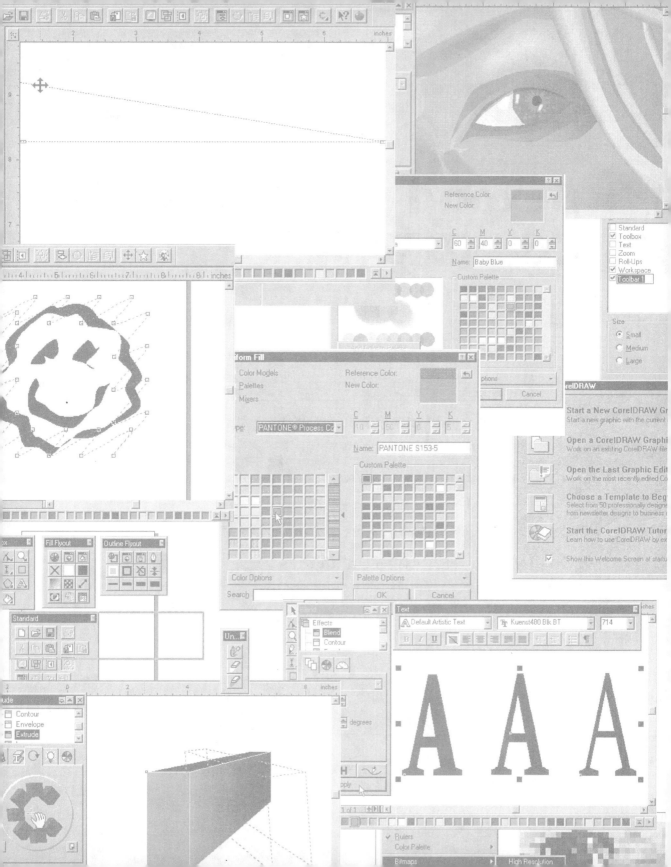

Chapter 17

Creating and Editing Images with PHOTO-PAINT

The Corel pixel partner to CorelDRAW!, PHOTO-PAINT has long been considered the digital image utility of the Corel suite of applications. For some users who still consider Photoshop the absolute leader in digital image handling, PHOTO-PAINT 6 comes as a bit of a surprise with its vast, rich features and horde of filter effects. PHOTO-PAINT performance has also improved to near-professional standards with the added power of Windows 95 32-bit power.

For the loyal Corel user or the recent newcomer, using Corel's PHOTO-PAINT 6 is a cost-effective alternative to purchasing a separate image-editing program. The simple reason is, of course, that you already own a copy. Although an entire manual could be devoted to explaining all the capabilities of PAINT 6, this chapter at least gets you started on the road to discovery.

In this chapter you learn to

- Get to know PHOTO-PAINT 6
- Create and digitally massage an image
- Use PAINT's tools and controls
- Learn about PAINT's new Navigator
- Master filter effects
- Work with masks

Taking a Glance at PHOTO-PAINT

On first opening PHOTO-PAINT 6, you may notice that the look and feel of the interface is much like CorelDRAW! 6. You see the familiar toolbox, although it contains a slightly different toolset, and PAINT's Standard toolbar, color palette, and status bar. Not surprisingly, the specific tools and toolbars are somewhat different than in Draw because PAINT deals with bitmap file formats made up of pixels, rather than Draw's vector objects. To a great extent, many of the tools have nearly similar functions but a different level of importance.

Creating and Editing an Image

One of the strengths you now have in owning a digital manipulation program like PHOTO-PAINT 6 is the ability to create images from scratch, without having to work with an existing image. You can create images for such things as text or multimedia backgrounds, or print backgrounds. After you save your image, you may convert it to any number of color modes for various uses.

To create an image, follow these steps:

1. Choose File, New to display the Create a New image dialog box (see fig. 17.1). Select the options you want to set for your new image file. In this case, select white (RGB: 255, 255, 255) as the background color, a Color Mode of at least 24-bit, an Image Size of at least 640 by 480 pixels, and a Resolution of 72 dpi. When finished setting your options, click OK to create the image.

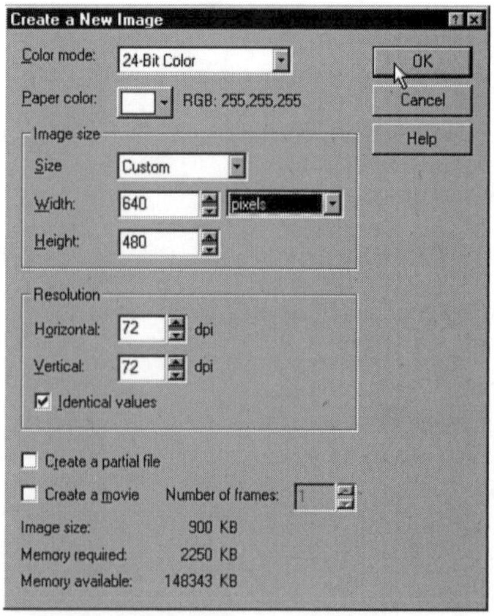

Fig. 17.1

Create a new image using the options in the Create a New Image dialog box.

2. Choose Effects, Noise, Add Noise to display the Add Noise Effect filter controls (see fig. 17.2). Choose a Level of 75, Density of 75, Noise Type of Gaussian, and the option for Color Noise. (The Color Noise option adds CMY color to the filter effect.) Click Preview to see the result. Notice how quickly the Preview is rendered.

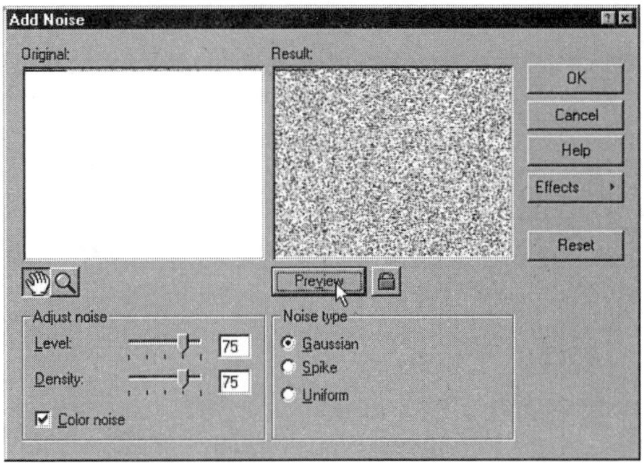

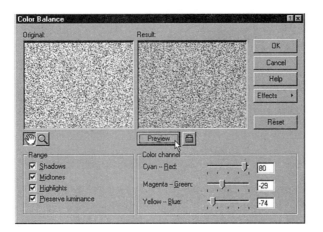

Fig. 17.2
You can add colored noise to an empty image file.

3. Choose OK to accept the effect you have set. Notice how much more time it takes to render the effect than when you used the Preview command. Preview saves you an immense amount of time. You have now created an existing image from scratch.

4. To add a different color tint to your image, choose Effects, Color Adjust, Color Balance (see fig. 17.3). Select all the Range options and set Cyan-Red to 80, Magenta-Green to -29, and Yellow-Blue to -74. Choose Preview to view the effect and then OK to accept the changes. Your image adopts a slightly yellow-red appearance.

Fig. 17.3
You can adjust the color balance of your new image.

5. To further enhance your image, choose Effects, 3D Effects, Emboss to display the Emboss dialog box (see fig. 17.4). Select Emboss Color as Gray, Depth as 3, and Direction as Up.

Fig. 17.4
You can add depth to your image by using the Emboss effect.

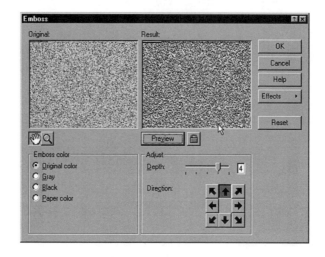

After applying different effects one after another to change your image, you should understand that an *effect* isn't always a single filter applied to an image, but possibly a series of effects that subtly change your image. PAINT's effects offer endless combinations. And when you add the randomness of a scanned or acquired image, the possibilities are truly infinite.

Using PHOTO-PAINT's Tools and Controls

The main focus of PHOTO-PAINT (as with any good image-editing program) is on putting control in the hands of the user. PHOTO-PAINT's controls enable you to perform these functions:

- Open a variety of digital image formats from different sources, including scanned images, Kodak PhotoCD, and other Corel file formats.

- Convert images from one file format to another.

- Assemble and combine portions of different images and sources.

- Apply nearly 80 different digital effects.

- Prepare your digital images for other processes such as digital movies and offset printing.

- Use anti-aliasing features, which are available in the Masking features and brush options in PHOTO-PAINT. *Anti-aliasing* smooths out the jagged edges where two different colors meet. The anti-aliasing process partially fills edge pixels so that they are semi-transparent, allowing certain degrees of each color to show through where the two colors meet. This has the effect of smoothing out the transition from one color to the other.

The tools and controls in PHOTO-PAINT have a heavy focus on area selection and color-handling by incorporating Draw's color management and color palette tools. PAINT also places an emphasis on viewing your work area by providing a large collection of viewing and navigation tools.

Using Toolbox Tools

The appearance of some of the toolbox tools has changed, but for the most part their functions remain the same. PAINT also has enhanced some tools by adding features to the roll-ups and toolbars. The following is a brief overview of PAINT's Toolbox arsenal:

- *Object Picker tool.* The Object Picker looks very similar to the Pick tool in Draw for a good reason. You use this tool to select objects, whether the object is a line of text or a pasted portion of an image from another file. The Object Picker also enables you to resize or reshape objects. Double-clicking the Object Picker displays the Objects roll-up, which provides extra controls for viewing, selecting, and locking individual objects (see fig. 17.5).

Fig. 17.5
The Objects roll-up works in combination with the Object Picker tool to select specific areas or objects.

■ *Rectangle Mask tool*. All Mask tools have one thing in common: they enable you to select different areas of your digital image. These areas may be defined by color, shade, or shape. The Rectangle Mask tool is actually one tool in a series of tools in the Mask tool flyout, which includes Circle, Freehand, Lasso, Magic Wand, Mask Brush, and Mask Transform. Double-clicking the Rectangle Mask tool selects the entire image. You can control each tool in the Mask tool flyout by using the Tool Settings roll-up.

■ *Path Node Edit tool*. The Path Node Edit tool looks similar to the Shape tool from Draw because of the way it works. Double-clicking the Path Node Edit tool displays the Path Node Edit Tool Settings roll-up (see fig. 17.6). You may use the Path Node Edit tool in combination with the roll-up to define paths composed of nodes joining open or closed lines and curves. These paths may also be used for creation of clipping paths for images, or may also be created from other clipping paths.

Fig. 17.6
The Path Node Edit Tool Settings roll-up works in combination with the Path Node Edit tool.

■ *Crop tool*. The purpose of the Crop tool is to quickly eliminate information from the image. Define a rectangular area using the Crop tool and double-click inside that area to delete the information outside of it. Double-clicking the Crop tool button displays the Tool Settings roll-up, which measures or accepts Top, Left, Width, and Height coordinates of your cropping area (see fig. 17.7).

Fig. 17.7
The Crop tool
works in combina-
tion with the Tool
Settings roll-up.

■ *Zoom tool.* One of the more critical controls used in viewing any image is the Zoom tool, which enables you to get a close-up or far-away view. The Zoom tool flyout also contains the Hand tool that enables you to grab and drag to navigate the viewing of your image. Double-clicking the Hand tool displays the Tool Settings for the Zoom tool, which contains a single option for setting the right mouse button to zoom out.

■ *Eyedropper tool.* The Eyedropper tool, as the name implies, enables you to sample foreground colors from your digital image. Holding down the Ctrl key while sampling enables you to set the sampled color as the background color. Double-clicking the Eyedropper tool or pressing Ctrl+F2 displays the Color roll-up (see fig. 17.8).

Fig. 17.8
The Eyedropper
tool works in
combination with
the Color roll-up.

■ *Eraser tool.* The Eraser tool is a straightforward eraser, deleting all image information below it and replacing it with the background color. Double-clicking the Eraser tool clears your entire image area. The Eraser tool is part of the Undo tools flyout, which also contains the Color Replacer tool and the Local Undo tool.

■ *Line tool.* The Line tool is used for drawing lines. You may set the color of the line using the color palette or the color roll-up. The Line tool is accompanied by the Line tool flyout containing the Curve and Pen tools. Double-clicking the Line, Curve, or Pen tool displays the Tool Settings roll-up (see fig. 17.9).

Fig. 17.9
The Line tool works in combination with the Tool Settings roll-up.

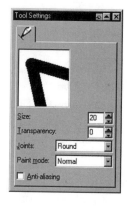

■ *Rectangle tool.* Also accessed by pressing F6, the Rectangle tool draws rectangles and squares. Fill and outline colors that the Rectangle tool uses are determined by the left and right mouse buttons on the color palette, or by the Color roll-up. In the Shape tool flyout, the Rectangle tool is accompanied by the Ellipse (F7) and Polygon tools. Each tool has its own settings, which you access through the Tool Settings roll-up (see fig. 17.10). The keyboard shortcut for opening the Tool Settings dialog controls for the selected tool is Ctrl+F8.

Fig. 17.10
The Rectangle tool is controlled by options set in the Tool Settings dialog box shown here. The Rectangle, Ellipse, and Polygon tools are each controlled by the Tool Settings roll-up.

- *Text tool*. Also accessed by pressing F8, the Text tool enables you to compose Artistic-style text objects. You control the color and outline for text through the color palette or the Color roll-up. You may set text attributes through the Text toolbar. Double-clicking the Text tool displays the Tool Settings roll-up (see fig. 17.11).

Fig. 17.11
The Text tool works in combination with the Tool Settings roll-up.

- *Fill tool*. The Fill tool applies fills to selected areas including masks, text, and objects. PHOTO-PAINT 6 uses the same color engine as DRAW, so you should have no surprises in operating the color controls. Controls for the Fill tool are in the Tool Settings roll-up (see fig. 17.12).

Fig. 17.12
Access the Fill tool color controls through the Tool Settings roll-up.

■ *Paint tool.* The Paint tool works like a paint brush (one that never gets dry). This tool gets most of its flexibility from the Tool Settings roll-up, which you access by double-clicking the Paint tool (see fig. 17.13). Choose from one of the 18 different paint brush styles and 21 different paint types.

Fig. 17.13
Access the Paint tool controls through the Tool Settings roll-up.

■ *Effect tool.* The Effect tool looks like and works like a cotton swab by smudging the image to which you apply the tool. Double-click the Effect tool to display the Tool Settings roll-up (see fig. 17.14). You have access to 18 different effects and 21 different paint types.

Fig. 17.14
The Effects tool works in combination with the Tool Settings roll-up.

- *Clone tool.* This ingenious little tool enables you to copy small or large portions of an image into other areas of your image or areas in other open files. A rich set of controls for the Clone tool are in the Tool Settings roll-up (see fig. 17.15).

IV

Beyond CorelDRAW!

Fig. 17.15
The Clone tool works in combination with the Tool Settings roll-up.

Using Roll-Ups in PHOTO-PAINT

You handle roll-ups in PHOTO-PAINT the same way you do in CorelDRAW! 6, using the same interface controls. Most of the roll-ups in PAINT feature additional flyout menus for opening, saving, and creating user settings. The following are brief descriptions of each roll-up.

- *Channels roll-up.* You use the Channels roll-up for viewing all color channels in an image or a specific color channel (see fig. 17.16). The channels displayed are dependent on the type of color model you are using. For example, if you are working on an image using RGB color, the image channels displayed include four channels: All Colors, Red, Green, and Blue. The same holds true for CMYK or duotoned images. While a single channel is displayed, you may apply changes to that specific color only. Press Ctrl+F9 to display the Channels roll-up. The Channels roll-up also features a flyout menu containing Channel commands.

- *Color Mask roll-up.* If you have used the Color Mask roll-up in Draw, you should find that PAINT's Color Mask roll-up is nearly identical in toolsets and operation (see fig. 17.17). Use the Tolerance and Smoothing slider controls to select and isolate up to 10 image colors. Press Ctrl+F5 to display the Color Mask roll-up.

Fig. 17.16
The Channels roll-up.

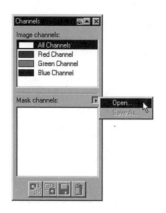

Fig. 17.17
The Color Mask roll-up.

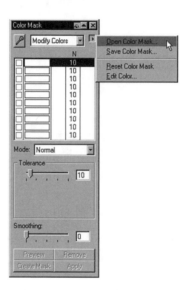

■ *Navigator roll-up.* A new feature for PAINT 6, the Navigator roll-up enables you to view a miniature representation of your image (see fig. 17.18). A bounding box represents the image portion you are currently viewing, while Hand and Zoom tools enable you to change your main screen views quickly. Press Ctrl+F6 to display the Navigator roll-up.

■ *Command Recorder roll-up.* Part of the scripting capabilities of PAINT 6, this roll-up enables you to keep a record of all commands applied to an image. You then can quickly apply those same commands to different images. A series of buttons emulate the controls on a traditional tape recorder including record, play, rewind, and stop (see fig. 17.19). Options also exist to enable you to add or delete commands listed. You may save your recorded list of commands and retrieve it later. Open the command recorder by selecting View, Roll-ups, Recorder (Ctrl+F3).

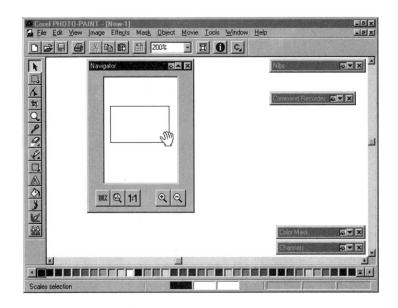

Fig. 17.18
The Navigator roll-up enables you to find your way easily around images when in very close-up views.

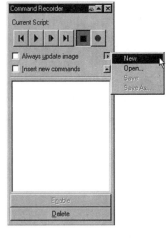

Fig. 17.19
The Command Recorder roll-up.

- *Nibs roll-up.* The Nibs roll-up sets the shape of any paint-type tool in PHOTO-PAINT (see fig. 17.20). Over 100 preset shapes are available plus controls to create and save your own. The shape of a tool may emulate nearly any other object's shape. The Nibs roll-up also features a menu flyout that contains commands for saving and loading user-created nibs. Open the Nibs roll-up by selecting <u>V</u>iew, Roll-<u>u</u>ps, <u>N</u>ibs (Ctrl+F11).

Fig. 17.20
The Nibs roll-up.

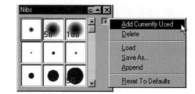

Reviewing PHOTO-PAINT Toolbars

◀ See "Customizing Toolbars," p. 460

Selection and operation of the toolbars in PAINT is identical to that of DRAW!. You may select toolbars by choosing <u>V</u>iew, <u>T</u>oolbars (Ctrl+T) to display a list that includes all six toolbars as well as the five flyout toolbars. Toolbars contain shortcuts to common commands and can be real time-savers as an alternative to groping through menu bars or searching for keyboard shortcuts. Making your own custom toolbar is highly recommended because viewing more than two or three toolbars at a time can significantly overcrowd your screen. You create a custom toolbar through the <u>T</u>ools, <u>C</u>ustomize command as in Draw. Also, toolbars may be torn away from the interface or docked—depending on how you work.

- *Standard toolbar.* You see this toolbar when you first open PAINT. It contains shortcuts for common file, printing, zooming, and file information commands.

- *Mask/Object toolbar.* The Mask/Object toolbar contains shortcuts to commands relating to object and masking functions. The real power of this toolbar is in the mask shortcuts, which are commands found mostly in the Mask menu. These commands include operations for behavior of the Object Picker tool, selection modes, mask painting behavior, and mask and object marquee hide and show options.

- *Movie toolbar.* An exciting newcomer to PAINT, and similar to a feature that appeared in Adobe PhotoShop 3.0, the Movie toolbar features command shortcuts to the Movie Controls menu. Movie controls enable you to import AVI file digital movie files directly into PHOTO-PAINT 6. You may edit frames individually using any of the PHOTO-PAINT tools and save your movie as an AVI file. Using the movie control commands, you can apply paint effects to individual frames of an imported Windows AVI digital movie file. Movie controls also enable you to add, delete, or navigate through frames of a movie. The Movie toolbar includes shortcuts to nearly all these controls that considerably cut menu-access time.

Troubleshooting

I am trying to use the movie controls, but when I see them in the menu they are always unavailable. Why?

Movie controls only become active if you are working in a file that has been created as a movie. You may open new documents as movies using the File, New dialog box and selecting the Create as Movie option. You may also use these controls if the file you opened in PHOTO-PAINT was already a Windows AVI file.

■ *Roll-ups toolbar.* The roll-ups toolbar provides shortcuts to all roll-ups in PAINT, including Channel, Objects, Color, Color Mask, Navigator, Command Recorder, Tool Settings, and Nibs roll-ups.

Understanding the Gallery of Filter Effects

The collection of filter effects now in PHOTO-PAINT 6 is no less than huge. The nearly 80 filter effects have been divided up into categories that you access from the Effects menu by flyouts. Categories include 2D and 3D effects, Adjust, Artistic, Blur, Color Adjust, Color Transform, Noise, Pixelate, Render, and Sharpen.

Although some of these effects are subtle and commonly seen in most image-editing programs, others are quite striking. Ease of use was definitely a priority for the engineers who developed the filter-applying tools; all tools share common application, previewing, and control features. The Filter Effects dialog box contains tools to help you decide about specific variables in the effect you are applying—before applying it. This is a concept other image-editing programs have yet to reach. The Preview button in each of the filters renders the effects you are contemplating surprisingly fast. Hand and Zoom tools also reside in the Filter Effects dialog box, as well as full access to all other effects without closing the dialog box.

2D Effects

Two-dimensional effects in PHOTO-PAINT 6 include Contour, Edge Detect, FFT, Offset, Puzzle, Ripple, Swirl, Tile, User Defined, Wet PAINT, and Wind. Browsing through these filters, you may find exceptional use in the Swirl effect (see fig. 17.21). This filter has the effect of spinning the center of your image in a smooth, directional flow as if it were liquid.

Fig. 17.21
The Swirl filter
controls.

3D Effects

The three-dimensional effects category includes such filter names as Emboss, Map to Object, Page Curl, Pinch/Punch, and Zigzag. The most intriguing appears to be the 3D Rotate filter (see fig. 17.22). This filter enables you to treat your image as if it were a postcard being rendered in full three-dimensional space.

Fig. 17.22
The 3D Rotate
filter controls.

Adjust

The Adjust filter category contains filters for adjusting the overall appearance of your image concerning Blur, Color Hue, Color Tone, Noise, and Sharpness. Operation of each filter set is strikingly similar; however, the Noise filter shown in figure 17.23 may be a bit more sophisticated than the rest. You can apply Noise effects (level and density) to existing images or apply noise to a black image file having no image at all.

Fig. 17.23
The Noise filter
controls.

Artistic

To apply aptly named Artistic effects, choose filters in the Artistic flyout,
which include simulations of Alchemy, Canvas, Glass Block, Impressionist,
Smoked Glass, Terrazzo, and Vignette. Nearly all these filters may be considered power filters and are worth exploring, if only to watch the preview show
as they warp and twist your images into all sorts of shapes and patterns. The
king of them all is probably the Paint Alchemy filter, which features five
tabbed sections for controlling Brush, Color, Size, Angle, and Transparency
settings and full previewing controls (see fig. 17.24).

Fig. 17.24
The Paint Alchemy
filter controls.

Blur

Blurring filters have a disturbing effect on most people. PAINT's collection of Blur filters introduces different ways to create this disturbance by including filter names like Directional Smooth, Gaussian Blur, Jaggy Despeckle, Motion Blur, Smooth, and Soften. Each filter offers a subtly different blur method and subsequent effect. Some of the effects are so subtle, in fact, that you can't tell them apart. Gaussian blur has long been a favorite of digital artists, and Corel hasn't let this crowd down. The Gaussian blur filter effect, shown in figure 17.25, features blurring values ranging from 1 to 50 (focus to no detail whatsoever).

Fig. 17.25
PHOTO-PAINT's
Gaussian Blur
filter controls.

Color Adjust

To apply filters that alter and distort all color aspects of an image, choose the Color Adjust category. This flyout includes filter names such as Brightness-Contrast-Intensity, Color Balance, DeInterlace, DeSaturate, Equalize, Gamma, Hue/Saturation/Lightness, Level Threshold, Replace Colors, and Tone Map. For the color-conscious digital artist, the Tone Map filter offers the most intrigue (see fig. 17.26). Controls in this filter include a shadow/highlight curve that you may edit manually to affect all or individual channels in an image. You also may choose from a collection of nine color-response curves, which are included with this filter and are fully editable. These presets are designed to perform effects such as enhancing, increasing, and decreasing highlights and shadows in images.

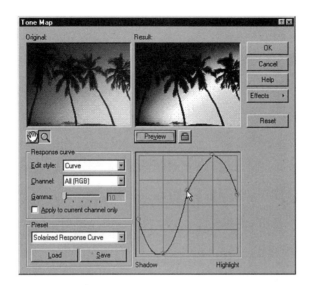

Fig. 17.26
The Tone Map
filter controls.

Transform

Color Transform filters include names such as Bit Planes, Halftone, Invert, Posterize, Psychedelic, and Solarize. Nearly all these color-altering filters apply a single-variable color algorithm to your image, which rotates the color palette of the image or limits the number of colors available to the palette, or both. The exception to this rule is the filter called simply Halftone (see fig. 17.27). This filter transforms your image into what appears to be a badly registered printed color halftone composed of dots and screen angles that you may adjust to the effect you want. This filter emulates stylized color-halftone effects similar to those used commonly in the early 1960s.

Fig. 17.27
The Halftone filter
controls.

Noise

This category of filters manufactures or filters out random, contrasting pixels in an image. The Noise filter collection includes Add Noise, Diffuse, Dust & Scratches, Maximum, Median, Minimum, and Remove Noise. The most dramatic of these filters is the Add Noise filter (see fig. 17.28). This filter has the result of adding speculates to your image, controlled by level and density sliders that set three types of noise: Gaussian, Spike, or Uniform.

Fig. 17.28
The Add Noise filter controls.

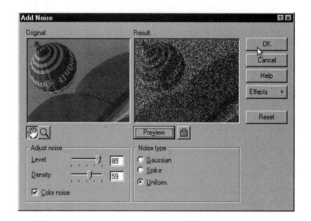

Render

Rendering filters in other programs have become the tool of choice for creating specific types of images from scratch. Filters include 3D Stereo Noise, Lens Flare, and Lighting Effects. Lens Flare creates interesting effects (see fig. 17.29).

Fig. 17.29
The Lens Flare filter controls.

Sharpen

The collection of image-sharpening filters in PAINT includes Adaptive Unsharp, Directional Sharpen, Find Edges, High Pass, Sharpen, and Unsharp Mask. Except for the interface changes and improvements to the image controls, these filters remain largely unchanged from version 5. The Find Edges sharpening filter is capable of producing some interesting effects (see fig. 17.30).

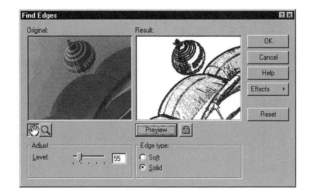

Fig. 17.30
The Find Edges filter controls.

Working with Masks

Using masks in PHOTO-PAINT, you can achieve extremely creative effects, seemingly limited only by your imagination. A mask is a sort of stencil, enabling you to alter specific areas of a digital image without affecting the rest of it. You may define masks by using the shape or color of images. After you have defined a mask, you may save it as an individual mask file, or as a separate channel within the PHOTO-PAINT file.

Three main toolsets work in combination with each other to create masks: Mask tools, the Tool Settings roll-up, and the Mask/Object toolbar. After you have defined a mask, you may Save, Load, or manipulate it using commands in the Mask menu or on the Mask/Object toolbar.

To create and save a mask defined by an area in a digital image, follow these steps:

1. Choose File, Open and select a scanned or imported bitmap image with reasonably well-defined color areas.

> **Tip**
>
> You can experiment using some of the various selection tools. When you are finished, choose the None button on the Mask/Object toolbar.

2. To prepare for the mask creation, get all your tools out on the desktop by selecting the Mask/Object toolbar (Ctrl+T), or by tearing off the Mask tool flyout and displaying the Mask Tool Settings roll-up (Ctrl+F8) as shown in fig. 17.31.

Fig. 17.31

Make a selection using the Mask tool, Mask/Object toolbar, and the Tool Settings roll-up.

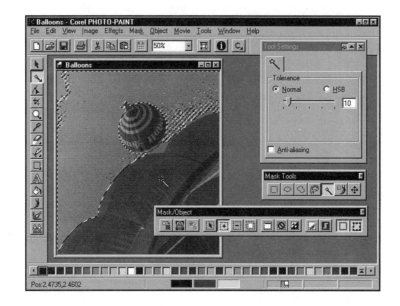

3. Select the Magic Wand tool from the Mask tool flyout and click an area of the image that is fairly uniform in color. You will be isolating this area as a mask.

4. Check the tolerance setting in the Tool Settings roll-up, and select the anti-aliasing option if necessary. Anti-aliasing smooths out the jagged edges where two different colors meet. The anti-aliasing process partially fills edge pixels so that they are semi-transparent, allowing certain degrees of each color to show through where the two colors meet.

5. Click your image in the area you have chosen to isolate as a mask. Notice that the Magic Wand tool selects a color area, bordering its selection at areas of extreme color change. The Magic Wand works on color tolerance settings, so you may need to increase the tolerance and reselect the image area.

6. If your area still isn't completely selected, click the plus-sign button on the Mask/Object toolbar and click the portion of your image area that isn't selected (refer to fig. 17.31). Notice that the area is added to the selection. The minus-sign button behaves in the opposite way.

   After your area is completely selected, your mask is finished. Next, you may want to save your mask before it changes or becomes lost.

7. To save your mask to a channel in the file, choose Mask, Save, Save As Channel, and name your new channel (see fig. 17.32). To save your mask so it's available to other image files, choose Mask, Save, Save To Disk. In this case, save your mask as a channel. Your mask is saved for later retrieval.

Fig. 17.32
You can name your channel anything you like.

8. Test to make sure your mask is saved as a channel in your file by choosing the None button on the Mask/Object toolbar. This step clears the selection. Display the Channels roll-up (Ctrl+F9). Find your mask by looking in the lower part of the roll-up marked Mask Channels.

9. To reload your mask into your image, choose the Channel to Mask button at the bottom of the Channels roll-up. Your mask is loaded back onto your image.

Troubleshooting

I am trying to select an area in my digital photo using the Magic Wand Mask tool, but each time I click on the area it only selects a small portion of my area. How do I select the whole area?

The selection tools, including the Magic Wand Tool, are controlled by the Tool Settings roll-up (Ctrl+F8). Specifically, the Magic Wand Mask tool selects areas based on color or shape and is controlled by the tolerance slider control in the Tool Settings dialog box. If you find that your Magic Wand Mask tool isn't selecting enough of an area, try increasing this setting in increments of five.

From Here...

The features of PHOTO-PAINT 6 are greatly enhanced from version 5 and are near a professional level for image editing. By nearly doubling the filter arsenal and introducing a gamut of new tool controls, Corel has greatly improved the capabilities of PHOTO-PAINT, making it the perfect pixel-handler to accompany Draw 6. For information on related topics, consult the following sections in this book:

- See Chapter 3, "Making CorelDRAW! 6 Easy to Use," to learn how to work with toolbars and how to create your own custom toolbars.

- See Chapter 13, "Using Color, Wizards, and Applying Color Masks," to find more information on color models and the Corel Color Manager.

- See Chapter 15, "Importing and Exporting Files," to learn about Corel's import filter collection, as well some of the most frequently used exporting formats.

Chapter 18

Making High-Quality Presentations with Corel PRESENTS

Created from tools and ideas in previous Corel products, Corel PRESENTS 6 can help you produce high-quality presentations that deliver digital audio and video, graphics, and bitmaps to audiences. PRESENTS is a rejuvenation of the best parts of CorelCHART, CorelSHOW, and CorelMOVE from CorelDRAW! 5. PRESENTS fits the bill for a wide range of professionals from high-end presentation producers to harried business users composing their presentations in the seat of an airplane.

In this chapter, you learn to

- Use the PRESENTS 6 tools

- Quickly get started creating a presentation

- Peek into animation, mapping, and charting utilities

- Add special effects to type and graphics

- Discover how PRESENTS works with sound and video

- Create audience handouts and speaker notes

- Use PRESENTS' Runtime Player

This chapter provides an overview for using Corel PRESENTS. For more information, refer to PRESENTS' online help.

Using PRESENTS 6 Views and Tools

To enable you to easily work on one aspect of your presentation at a time, PRESENTS has eight ways of looking at your presentation in progress. To format or otherwise compose a specific aspect of your presentation, you must first be in one of these specific views:

- *Slide view*. This view shows all the backgrounds, text, objects, and their placement on the slide. Slide view is where you do specific slide assembly.

- *Slide Sorter view*. This view is extremely useful at any point in the preparation of your presentation. Slide Sorter view enables you to jostle and reorganize your slides into various orders. You may drag slides to new positions in the sequence, or add or delete slides.

- *Outline view*. Outline view is where you may want to be when you begin typing the first words of your presentation. Outline is the perfect tool for enabling you to focus on the content of your presentation and how it communicates to your audience. You're not bogged down worrying about fonts, color, graphics embellishments, animation, video, or sound.

- *Master view*. There are four Master views for controlling the layout of Title Slides, Slide Master, Speaker Notes, and Handouts. By setting the master layout in each of these views, your format is set automatically for each slide.

- *Background view*. You use this view to select, compose, or assemble your slide backgrounds. You can use text, vector graphics, and bitmaps in the creation of backgrounds. After you exit this view, your background objects remain intact and secure.

- *Speaker Notes view*. The Speaker Notes view is where you can formulate presenters' text or a structure for verbal delivery. You may enter separate personal notes for each slide.

- *Handout view*. This view enables you to format the text you have entered in your slide for the purpose of handing out hard copies of the presentation to the audience.

- *Animation view*. Use this view for quick or custom animation sequences applied to text or objects.

The tools in PRESENTS are similar to CorelDRAW! tools, only some are not as elaborate. Tool properties are very simple in that what you see is basically what you get. You may not adjust or customize tools beyond the selections in the tool flyouts. Double-clicking the Pick tool still selects all objects in Slide view, and double-clicking the Shape tool still displays the Node Edit roll-up.

You should become familiar with seven tool flyouts and six toolbars before getting too far into PRESENTS. Tool flyouts include Zoom, Freehand Drawing, two Basic Shape tools, Text, Outline, and Fill; toolbars are Toolbox, Standard, Text, Outline View, Slide Sorter, and Animation Controls. You open flyouts by holding down the right mouse button on the Toolbox tool button. You display toolbars by choosing View, Toolbars. The flyouts and toolbars are described in the following list:

- *Zoom flyout.* Contains the Zoom toolset identical to DRAW minus DRAW's Panning tool.

- *Freehand Drawing flyout.* Contains only two tools enabling you to draw bezier curved or straight line objects onto your slides.

- *Basic Shape flyout.* PRESENTS has two flyouts named Basic Shape, but they are easy to tell apart by the number of tool buttons they hold. This first tool flyout has three buttons for creating rectangles, ellipses, or polygons.

- *AutoShapes flyout.* Contains a collection of 24 2D and 3D arrows, stars, starbursts, and symbols to use as quick graphics embellishments for your slides.

- *Text flyout.* Contains only two tool buttons for creating Artistic and Paragraph text objects.

- *Outline flyout.* Similar to CorelDRAW's Outline flyout, this flyout contains all the access buttons to outline attributes.

- *Fill flyout.* Similar to CorelDRAW's Fill flyout, this flyout contains all the access buttons to object fill attributes including fountain, texture, uniform, 2-color, full-color, and vector bitmap fills.

- *Toolbox toolbar.* Similar to the CorelDRAW Toolbox toolbar except for the two Shape tool buttons, one containing quick arrow and symbol shapes and the other containing Rectangle, Ellipses, and Polygon tools.

- *Standard toolbar.* Contains the usual file and clipboard buttons, plus quick access to specific views, background libraries, and utility applications.

- *Slide Sorter toolbar.* Contains three buttons for applying transitions, showing or hiding slides, or showing or hiding the slide "jacket" (also called a slide mount). This toolbar is available only in Slide Sorter view, where it appears by default.

Note

If you're new to presentation programs, refer to the section "Using Special Effects" for more information on working in Slide Sorter view and applying transitions.

- *Text toolbar.* Includes the usual shortcut buttons to instant text formatting for Artistic and Paragraph text, style, alignment, and a color flyout for quick text-fill color.

- *Outline view toolbar.* Very useful and available only when in Outline view. Toolbar includes promote, demote, move up, and move down buttons for controlling the level of text importance in your outline. It also includes quick access to Zoom controls.

- *Animation toolbar.* Contains shortcut buttons to all controls in the Animation menu.

Creating Presentations

Designed to produce presentations, PRESENTS lets you bring together text, graphics, charts, animation and sound. Whether you are creating overhead transparencies, 35mm slides, or a multimedia extravaganza with video and music, in PRESENTS, you'll find a variety of impressive, timesaving, and practical tools for designing professional presentations.

Getting Started Using Wizards

PRESENTS 6 incorporates wizards, which are ready-made templates for quickly formatting large, complex presentations or individual slides. If you are in a hurry, wizards are an excellent way to get started on your text—which is usually the first place you want to start. Wizards offer preformatted PRESENTS presentations in categories such as Financial, General, New Products, Sales, Status Report, and Training (see fig. 18.1). All backgrounds, text formatting, and framework content are already entered for you. You may use the wizard format exactly as it appears, replacing only the text, or you may want to use the wizard as a starting point for your own presentation, adding your own personal tastes. Either way, wizards are a great time-saver.

Click the Presentation Wizard button displayed when you first launch PRE-
SENTS or select File, New, From Wizard to begin a presentation. To build a
new presentation from scratch, click the Start a Blank Presentation button or
select File, New, Document. You can add slides and backgrounds as you build
the presentation.

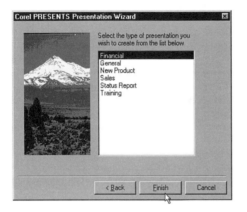

Fig. 18.1
You can start
developing your
presentation
format using a
wizard template.

Typing Text into Outline View

Entering text is one of the first things to do after creating the presentation
file. The Outline view provides a "text only" view enabling you to focus on
the content. The tools, color controls, and window features are nearly identical to those found in the rest of the CorelDRAW! 6 suite.

In Outline view, PRESENTS enables you to concentrate on the words of your
presentation without being distracted by later concerns such as backgrounds,
color, or animation (see fig. 18.2). Outline view also has shortcut features
such as clicking the slide icon in the left margin for selecting all text in a
slide.

When you enter Outline view, the Text toolbars are automatically opened
and waiting. The Outline view toolbar contains controls for organizing your
text importance. By clicking a line of text, you are able to promote or demote
the text level of importance according to your master format. You also can
Move Up or Move Down the text's position on the slide or layout. The Show
Formatting button enables you to see the text with or without formatting,
and the Zoom tool enables you to navigate your view.

Fig. 18.2
Composing text in
Outline view is
much easier when
working from a
wizard template.

Slide Icons

Promote

Move Down

Move Up

Demote   Zoom

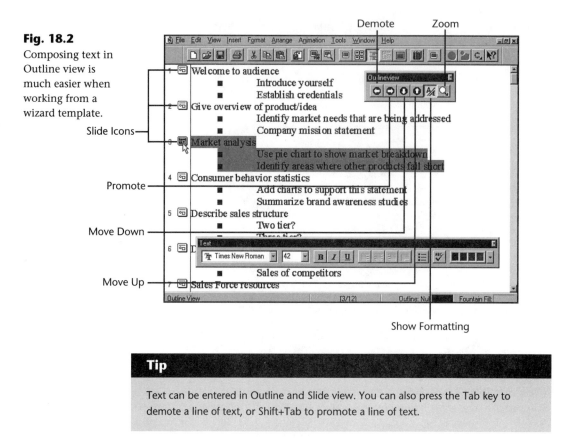

Show Formatting

> ### Tip
>
> Text can be entered in Outline and Slide view. You can also press the Tab key to
> demote a line of text, or Shift+Tab to promote a line of text.

Setting the Scene in Background View

Adding a background to any slide presentation is an important step. Backgrounds tend to form an audience mood or subject setting for a presentation;
when used wisely, backgrounds can be extremely effective.

In Background view, you may choose your background from a preset collection, or compose your own with the Edit Background command (see fig.
18.3). Click the Libraries button to select a pre-designed background or
choose View, Background Library (see fig. 18.4). To choose a background,
click the arrow by the drop-down list. The backgrounds are divided into
groups. Once the group is displayed, select a background and click OK.

Clicking the Libraries button also allows you to set the layout type of your
slide presentation.(see fig. 18.5). Click the Pre-set library option to display
layouts for all kinds of slides.

IV

Beyond CorelDRAW!

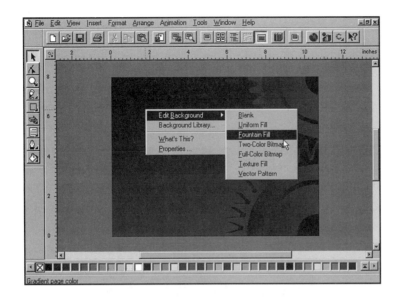

Fig. 18.3
Background view
allows you to
create and edit the
background for the
slides in your
presentation.

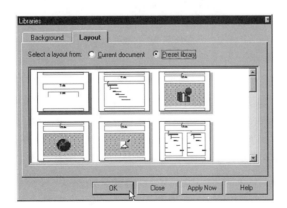

Fig. 18.4
Choose a
preformatted
background from
the Background
library.

Fig. 18.5
Choose a
preformatted
layout from the
Layout library.

Adding a Chart or Map to Your Slide

PRESENTS 6 features a built-in chart maker that enables you to create bar, line, area, and pie charts of various types. This feature is appealing to any presenter of statistical information.

PRESENTS' charting utility is an idea based on an older version of Corel-CHART. To launch CorelCHART, choose Insert, Chart. The cursor will change. Click and drag a rectangle where you want the chart to appear and then select a chart type from the Chart Type dialog box (see fig. 18.6). After you select a chart type, choose OK to begin the charting program, which runs as a program within PRESENTS (see fig. 18.7).

Fig. 18.6
Select a chart type from the Chart Type dialog box.

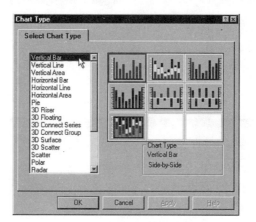

Fig. 18.7
PRESENTS accesses the tools of CorelCHART to build and format charts.

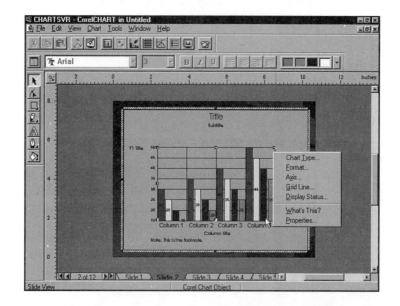

Common bar and line charts include vertical bar or line, vertical area, horizontal bar and line, and horizontal line and area. Pie chart formats include 3D, 3D riser, 3D floating, 3D connect series, 3D connect group, 3D surface, and 3D scatter. Other, more obscure formats available include scatter, polar, radar, bubble, high-low-open-close, spectrally-mapped, gantt, histogram, and table. Check out some books on charting and statistical data for more information on selecting the chart type that best represents your data.

CorelCHART is a program rich in features. It is well worth spending some time exploring the program and developing your own statistical presentation skills.

Tip

When formatting charts, double-clicking a chart object, such as a title or pie slice, displays a dialog box with formatting options.

The CorelMAP utility enables you to create demographic and statistical information in a geographical map format. Options are available for you to set legend, color, layout, and format types, which you may select quickly in the CorelMAP Wizard (see fig. 18.8). To add a map to your presentation, click the Insert a Map button. The cursor will change. Click and drag a rectangle where you want the map to appear. The map wizard will open after you select a mapping layout, CorelMAP is launched (see fig. 18.9).

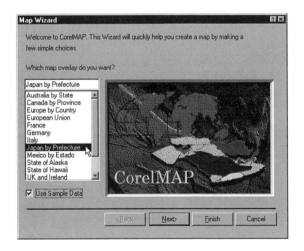

Fig. 18.8
New to version 6, the CorelMAP Wizard helps you add geographical maps to the slides in your presentation.

Fig. 18.9
Right-click
to access the
formatting tools
of CorelMAP.

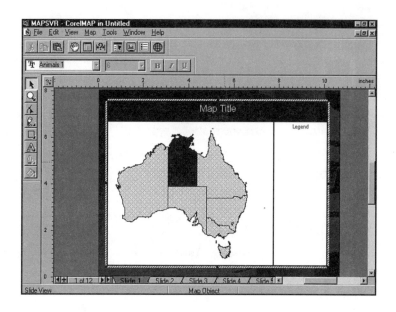

Working with Animation Tools

In Animation view, PRESENTS offers tools to enable you to animate text and
graphics objects. You can add transitions and paths to objects. Transitions
allow you to control how the image fades in and out of your audience's view.
The title might "wipe on" in 5 steps across the screen. Paths let you move
objects. You could assign a path to a ball that makes it bounce across the
slide. Select View, Animation to move to Animation view. The Animation
toolbar includes tools for playing, advancing, reversing, and stopping animation effects during proofing. After selecting the text or object to be animated,
select Transitions from the Animation menu. In the Objects Settings dialog
box you can add opening and closing Transitions, animation Paths, and object Attributes, such as fills and outlines (see fig. 18.10).

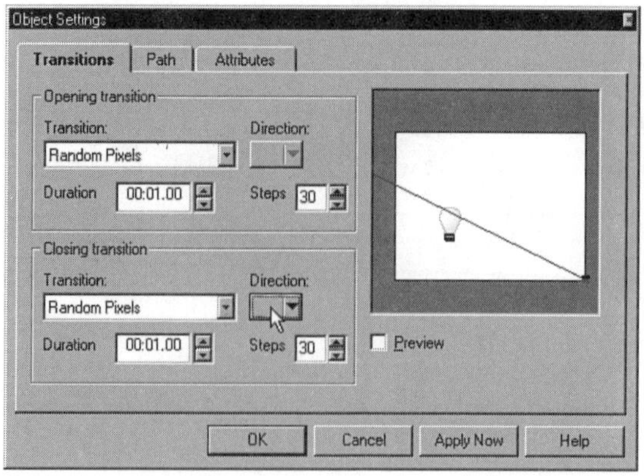

Fig. 18.10
Once in Anima-
tion view, use the
Object Settings
dialog box to set
transitions and
animation paths
to objects in the
presentation.

Using Audience Handouts and Speaker Notes

PRESENTS 6 offers tools for formatting not just your presentation design, but all the other paraphernalia you need to make a presentation successful. In fact, while you are busy composing what you're going to say during your show, PRESENTS is already forming the basis for the other things you may need, including audience handouts and speaker notes. You need only switch to those views to see that as you formulate your presentation, your handouts and speaker notes are taking shape simultaneously.

To see the PRESENTS 6 Handouts format, choose View, Handouts (see fig. 18.11). The Handouts format you see is the default (the automatic format for the wizard you are working with). You can change this format by choosing View, Master Layout, Handouts, then selecting the Layout library (see fig. 18.12). Make the formatting changes on the handout master. Use the Page Setup command to add custom headers and footers on the page to identify you, your company, or your product.

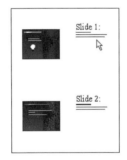

Fig. 18.11
As you build the presentation, handouts are automatically created. Switch to Handout view to see the handouts.

Fig. 18.12
Change the Handouts format using the Master Layout, Layout library dialog box.

If you rely on speaker notes to follow during your presentation, PRESENTS has a view for creating those, too. Choose <u>V</u>iew, Speaker <u>N</u>otes to view the current format (see fig. 18.13). To change the format, choose <u>V</u>iew, <u>M</u>aster Layout, Speaker <u>N</u>otes.

Fig. 18.13
Move to the Master Layout of the Speaker Notes to make any formatting changes.

Organizing Your Presentation in Slide Sorter

In Slide Sorter view (see fig. 18.14), you can quickly arrange the order of your slides by dragging the slides with your mouse. Choose View, Slide Sorter to add, delete, or rearrange your presentation as you see fit. Use the Slide Sorter view in combination with the Slide Sorter toolbar, which features shortcuts for setting Transitions and Slide Properties, hiding slides from the presentation, and displaying slides without the slide jacket. Changing the order of your slides in this view changes the order in all other views including your Outline, Handouts, and Speaker Notes.

Fig. 18.14
Slide Sorter view enables you to add, delete, rearrange, or temporarily hide slides in your presentation.

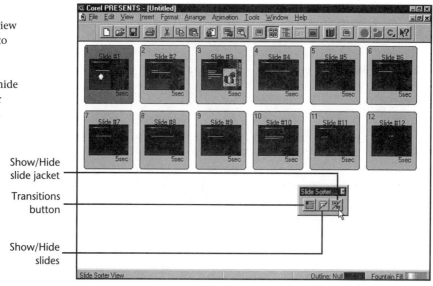

Show/Hide slide jacket

Transitions button

Show/Hide slides

IV

> **Tip**
>
> You can double-click a slide in Slide Sorter view to quickly display that slide in Slide view.

Adding Sound and Video

If you are using a multimedia-equipped system, you may need to add sound to your presentation at some point by importing or recording. You may insert both digital sound and video into your PRESENTS 6 file using the Insert, Sound and Insert, Video commands. Choosing Insert, Video links a video file to your presentation, and choosing Insert, Sound launches the Wave Editor utility (see fig. 18.15). The Wave Editor is a basic digital audio recorder and player that enables you to record directly into PRESENTS. It involves using buttons for record, playback, stop, and rewind, and includes some very basic audio effects such as reverse, echo, amplify, fade in, and fade out.

PRESENTS 6 can take files from any other OLE 2 compatible software by way of the Clipboard, or by dragging and dropping. You also can import from a broad range of software including the following formats: Corel PHOTO-PAINT, CorelSHOW, Corel Presentation Exchange, Video for Windows, WAV audio format, Macintosh SND and AIF, Autodesk FLIC, Adobe PhotoShop, Micrografx, AutoCAD, Kodak PhotoCD, Macintosh Paint and PICT, WordPerfect, and Amiga, to name a few.

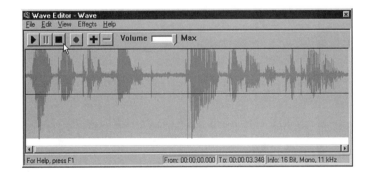

Fig. 18.15
The Wave Editor records directly into PRESENTS.

Using Special Effects

Special effects in PRESENTS boil down to slide transitions, object transitions, and path animation. Transitions enable you to further set mood and atmosphere in your presentations by controlling how images fade in and out of your audience's view. A bright image bursting onto the screen may startle some of your audience, and dark, subtle images slowly fading into view may put others to sleep. Transitions are best used very carefully and very sparingly for a number of reasons, the most important of which is that transitions slow down your system's performance and may cause other undesirable effects such as sloppy screen redraw and sound interruption.

You assign all slide and object transitions in Slide view, which you enter by choosing View, Slide. To assign a slide opening and/or closing transition, move to the slide where you want to apply the transition and right-click the background of the slide. Choose Transitions to open the Object Properties dialog box. Select the Transitions tab (see fig. 18.16). Choose an opening and closing transition by clicking the down arrow by the drop-down list. To apply a text transition, right-click the text where you want to apply the transition, and select Transitions again to display the Object Properties dialog box. Select the Text Effects tab to select your opening and/or closing transition (see fig. 18.17).

Tip

Click the Preview Slide button to display a full-screen preview of a slide and its transitions.

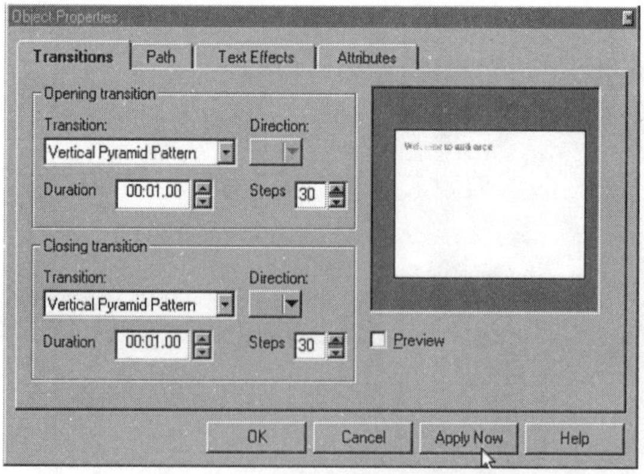

Fig. 18.16

To specify a slide opening or closing transition, use the Transitions tab of the Object Properties dialog box.

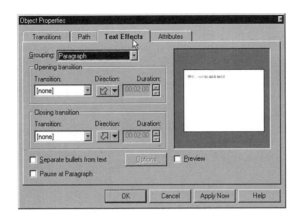

Fig. 18.17
To specify a text
transition, use the
Text Effects tab
of the Object
Properties dialog
box.

Running the Presentation

When the presentation will be presented on a computer screen or output to
video display, PRESENTS includes several options for enhancing the performance. You can set the slide and object timings, work with the Runtime
player and use the Annotation feature.

Controlling Time

After you have your presentation composed for the most part, choose View,
Timelines to display the timing controls for all slides (see fig. 18.18). Double-
click the slide name to display the objects in the slide. If you have included
such things as text, animation, video, or sound in your slide, they display in
the Timelines dialog box, where you have the option of setting the timing for
each. For example, a sound or animation file attached to a slide may be set to
begin and end at a point within the duration of the slide (see fig. 18.19). To
resume viewing the main timing controls for all slides, click the yellow button in the upper-left corner of the dialog box.

> **Tip**
>
> Timing is crucial to a presentation, so take time to practice the show again and again.

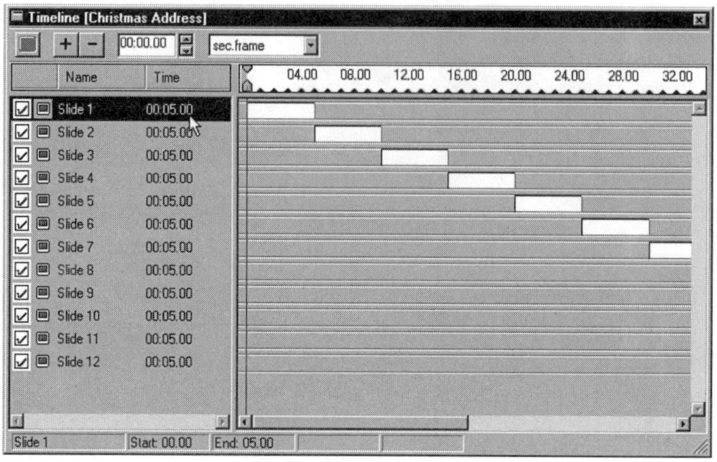

Fig. 18.18

Drag the white bars in the Timeline to adjust the timing of your presentation.

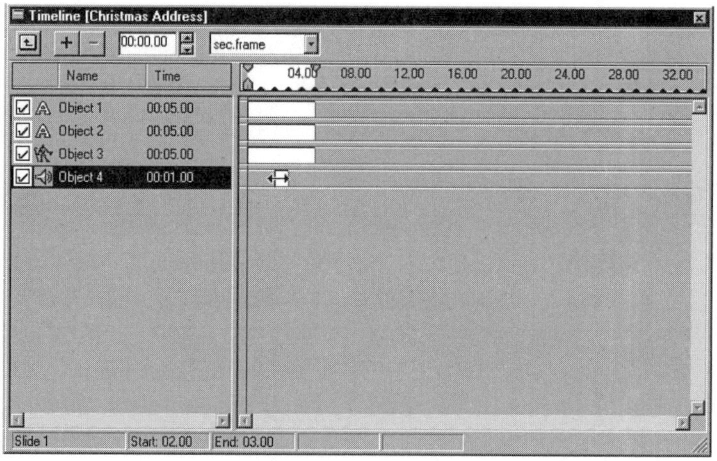

Fig. 18.19

The arrow is used to drag the white bars adjusting the timelines for individual objects on the slide.

Using the PRESENTS 6 Runtime Player

After you complete your presentation, you should perform a dry run to determine precisely how much time you need for each slide. You can transform a completed PRESENTS 6 show into a self-running or portable screen show. The Runtime Player program is included in the Corel 6 package for the purposes of playback only, incorporating all the settings and effects you chose for your presentation. Click the Runtime Player icon in the COREL60 folder to launch the program.

> **Note**
>
> The Runtime Player program is considered shareware, and you can distribute it freely for this purpose.

You can save your presentation for use with the Runtime Player, or as a stand-alone, self-running presentation. Choose File, Save As and select the appropriate format from the Save As Type drop-down list (see fig. 18.20). You must save a Runtime Player file with a CPR file extension, and a self-running file must have the EXE extension.

> **Note**
>
> For a self-running presentation to work properly, you must select the Run Continuously option found in the Presentation tab under Tools, Options.

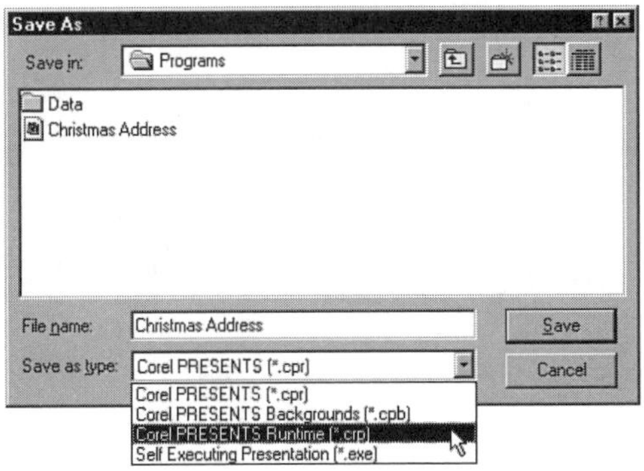

Fig. 18.20
You can save your presentation for use with the Runtime Player or as a self-executing screen show.

Using the Annotation Feature

Both Corel PRESENTS 6 and its Runtime Player feature on-screen annotation. Annotation works much the same way as a marker or pointer used to draw attention or make notes directly on your slide during a presentation. The annotation features are available after your presentation is running. To preview the presentation, choose File, Run Presentation, or press F5. While your presentation is running, access the annotation controls by clicking the mouse. A pencil icon appears in the bottom-right corner of your screen. Click the pencil icon to access the Pen Width or Color controls (see fig. 18.21). Once selected, your cursor works as a digital magic marker, enabling you to draw directly on-screen.

> **Note**
>
> When you use the annotation feature, any marks you make to slides are erased forever when the slide advances. You cannot save the marks you make on-screen using this tool.

Fig. 18.21
While your presentation is running, you may use the annotation controls to access a digital magic marker feature.

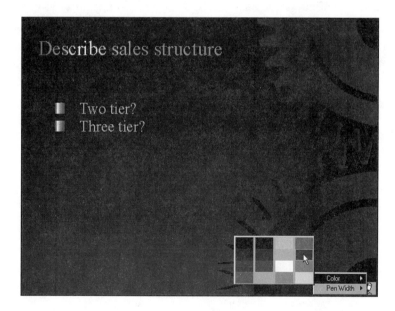

From Here...

With the inclusion of PRESENTS, Corel now has a major contender in the presentation application category. This chapter provided an overview of creating and formatting slides in a presentation by adding text, graphics, charts, and audio and video. As discussed, PRESENTS also includes powerful tools for enhancing the display of the presentation. You can add transitions, control slide timings, and on-screen annotation.

The collision of artists with high-technology tools will change the way we experience slide shows. With the introduction of Corel PRESENTS 6, Corel is playing a major role in dropping those tools right into your hands.

IV

Beyond CorelDRAW!

Chapter 19

Creating 3D Illustrations in CorelDREAM 3D

CorelDREAM 3D is a program that the electronic desktop artist has been waiting for since the onslaught of desktop publishing programs a dozen years ago.
CorelDREAM is based on a program produced by California software devel-
oper Ray Dream called Designer 3D. Corel's program has been updated with
an easier-to-use interface and tailored to work under Microsoft's new Windows 95 32-bit environment. CorelDREAM 3D enables users to create 3D
illustrations using 1,000 prepared 3D artwork and wireframes and more than
300 mapping surfaces. CorelDREAM 3D uses sophisticated ray-tracing technology to create realistic-looking, three-dimensional effects.

To say that CorelDREAM is feature-rich is a gross understatement. Although
an entire manual easily could (and likely will) be dedicated to learning and
using only CorelDREAM 3D, this chapter gives merely an overview of the
program's capabilities. DREAM is filled with features, tools, and options that
one day may even rival those of CorelDRAW! 6, although the technology
and drawing concepts are far different from that of DRAW!. CorelDRAW!
experts should have little trouble immersing themselves in the world of
three-dimensional object creating; however, the beginning user may become
disoriented with the DREAM concepts and terminology. Taking the DREAM
tutorial provided with the CorelDRAW! 6 documentation is a wise step and
likely the fastest way to obtain some hands-on experience using the program.

This chapter focuses on these topics:

- Becoming familiar with DREAM 3D's working windows and tools used
  for creating and manipulating three-dimensional objects

- Becoming familiar with DREAM's importing and exporting features

- Overview of DREAM's ray-trace rendering process

Understanding DREAM's Three-Dimensional Concept

Making the leap from two-dimensional drawing to three-dimensional modeling may take some degree of patience and concentration on your part. But DREAM's 3D concept is straightforward, and after you have become familiar with the processes you must take your projects through, the rest should be easy. The process is exciting, rewarding, and will undoubtedly stimulate your imagination.

DREAM's basic processes involve five ordered steps:

1. Create three-dimensional objects from scratch or by selecting a preformed object from the Objects Browser library.

2. Apply color and texture maps to the objects using your own custom texture mapping or by selecting a preset texture map from the Shaders Browser library to complete the object creation.

3. Create a scene and compile your creations into the scene.

4. Add lighting to create photo realism and three-dimensional effects, and add camera views to view the objects in your scene.

5. Render your scene using the ray-tracing technology to produce a file that may be printed directly or imported into other image-editing applications.

To this same end, the creation of a complex three-dimensional scene may be broken down into basic elements, characteristics, and processes. For example, to create a three-dimensional object, which may at first seem nearly impossible to draw with a two-dimensional graphics program, first imagine all the basic shapes that compose that object. One way or another, you can break down all objects into a collection of basic shapes such as blocks, spheres, tubes, and cones.

Imagine for a moment a human figure dissected into a series of basic shapes such as a sphere for the head and tubes for the torso, arms, and legs. With refinement and shape editing, you can make these basic shapes more closely resemble an actual person. To become more detailed, you could make a hand into a series of shapes such as blocks for the main hand section, tubes for the fingers, flat cones for the knuckles, and half spheres for the finger tips.

After the individual parts of the object are completed, you may group them so they become a unit. Then you subsequently assemble the parts with other finished parts to make up the whole object.

Then you must apply surface color, texture, and reflective characteristics to the objects to enable them to react properly when lighting is applied. You may assign each part of a group of objects different surface characteristics. For example, the human figure may have black, shiny hair, and the skin texture is likely pink or brown with a dull finish. The eyes may be shiny and reflective, while still featuring color characteristics. Together, the surface color and textures help define the object groups and subgroups.

To add realism to your assembly, you may decide to place your human figure in a room that features fluorescent lighting or a dark room lit by low-intensity lamps placed around the figure. Lighting has its own set of characteristics including color, intensity, and direction. How you light your three-dimensional objects makes them come to life and adds a sense of reality and depth to them.

How you view your objects adds even more information to the scene. For example, a very low viewpoint using a wide-angle camera lens may simulate a worms-eye view, and viewing your objects from eye level may simulate the view from another person. An aerial camera view may imply other characteristics to your scene and certainly provide a different set of visual information to the viewer of your image.

You may control all characteristics of shape, surface, color, lighting, and viewpoint within DREAM 3D. Having the ability to create an object or series of objects and place them into a scene must likely stir the imagination of any electronic artist previously restricted to a mere two dimensions. Just the ability to create an object one time and quickly produce multiple views of the object without having to start from scratch is appealing, even in cases of the simplest objects.

Using DREAM's Windows and Tools

To begin understanding the control you have in DREAM over shape, surface, color, lighting, and viewpoint, you first want to become extremely familiar with DREAM's windows and tools. On your journey through the program, you should find that much of the interface controls are common to those used in other CorelDRAW! 6 applications.

Working with Windows in DREAM 3D

The interface windows you first see on launching DREAM include the Perspective, Hierarchy, Objects Browser, and Shaders Browser windows, each with its own set of controls and options (see fig. 19.1).

Fig. 19.1
When first
opened, DREAM
3D has four
interface windows.

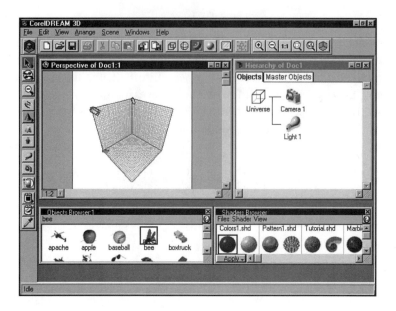

The windows are described in this list:

- *The Perspective window.* The Perspective window is the main working window. It displays a triple-planed environment aimed at simulating three dimensions. Objects that exist in this view reflect those dimensions. The view you see through the Perspective window is like looking through a camera. This camera may be positioned anywhere in the scene and may be set to various types of lenses. You may also add more camera views to your scene or open another Perspective window to view your objects from a different angle. The Perspective window also changes to the *modeler window* whenever you double-click any of the objects. In the modeler window, a different toolset is available specific to creating and editing three-dimensional shapes (see fig. 19.2). Press Enter to exit the modeler.

- *The Hierarchy window.* The Hierarchy window works like a visual object manager and is synchronized to the Perspective window. Whatever is placed in the Perspective window becomes an object in the Hierarchy window. Everything viewed in the Hierarchy window such as objects and object groups, cameras, and light sources exist in the Perspective window and in your scene. However, the Hierarchy window provides additional information about how the entire scene exists. For example, viewing an object in the Perspective window does not provide information about whether the object is grouped or made up of multiple sub-groups of objects. The Hierarchy window enables you to break objects apart to inventory their individual parts.

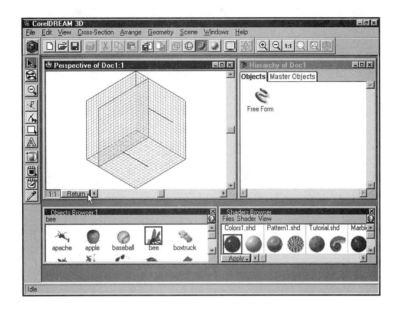

Fig. 19.2
The Perspective window also doubles as the object modeler window when you edit the shape of an object.

■ *The Objects Browser window*. The Objects Browser window works like a library or visual inventory of all objects available to you as clip art. In many cases, editing an existing group of objects is easier than beginning a creation from scratch. The Objects Browser enables you to view, select, and drag out any object that appears useful to your project and position it in the Perspective window or edit its shapes in the modeler window. The Objects Browser may contain simple or complex objects featuring color and textures already applied and saved to the object. You may double-click objects in this window for editing or drag them directly into your Perspective window (see fig. 19.3).

■ *The Shaders Browser window*. The Shaders Browser window contains a collection of color and texture characteristics, which when dragged onto an object in the Perspective window, are immediately applied. Shaders contain texture characteristic information including color, transparency, highlights, reflection, refraction, and shininess. The Shaders Browser makes available all the different color and texture characteristics currently loaded, enabling you to quickly apply a Shader surface to an object or edit and apply an existing surface. You may also save your own Shader surfaces to the collection. You may edit Shaders by double-clicking them to reveal the Shader Editor controls (see fig. 19.4).

Fig. 19.3
To edit an object in the Objects Browser window, double-click the object and a new Perspective window opens.

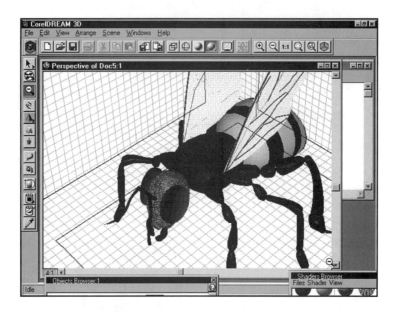

Fig. 19.4
You may edit items in the Shaders Browser by double-clicking them and using the Shader Editor.

Using the Perspective Toolbox

The Perspective Toolbox contains

- *Selection tools.* Two types of selection tools, including the Pick tool, are available for selecting objects in the Perspective, Hierarchy, and Objects Browser windows. The Paint Shape selection tool is used for selecting three-dimensional paint shapes applied to object surfaces.

- *Rotation tools.* Two rotation tools are available in this flyout including the Virtual Trackball and One Axis Rotation tools, the latter being a distant relative of the first. The Virtual Trackball tool enables you to rotate objects freely in three dimensions while in the Perspective window. The One Axis Rotation does the same thing only it is restricted—but offers more control—on two dimensions.

- *Zoom/Pan tools*. Tools accessed through the Zoom/Pan tool flyout include the Zoom In, Zoom Out, and Hand tools. The Zoom In and Out tools enable you to obtain a closer or farther view to a selected area in the Perspective window. These two tools toggle if you press the Alt key while zooming. The Hand tool enables you to grab and pan a selected view.

- *Free Form tool*. The Free Form tool enables you to access the Free Form modeler window, which is used to create or edit three-dimensional objects.

- *3D Shape tools*. The Shape tools enable you to begin creating your 3D object starting with an existing shape rather than from scratch. Among the shape tools provided are the Cone, Cube, Cylinder, Icosahedra, and Sphere Shape tools. You may not modify basic shapes in the Free Form modeler.

- *3D Text tool*. The 3D Text tool is used for creating and editing three-dimensional text in the Perspective window. You may set text to any size, font, or style and may also set beveled edges using the text controls available (see fig. 19.5).

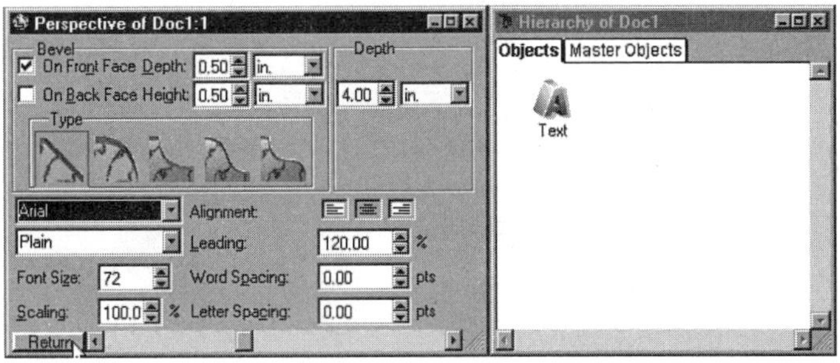

Fig. 19.5
The text options available using the 3D Text tool.

- *Modeling Wizard tool*. The Wizard Shape tool is perhaps the ultimate tool in choosing shapes to create in your Perspective window. The Modeling Wizard opens as a sub-divided catalog of shapes, enabling you to navigate through and narrow down your search for the perfect shapes (see fig. 19.6).

Fig. 19.6

The Modeling Wizard is a truly amazing feature worth exploring. It enables you to select basic shapes and further redefine your selection with additional choices in a rich database of preformed modeling shapes.

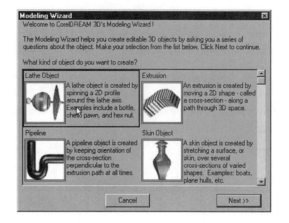

 ■ *Create Lighting tool.* The Create Lighting tool enables you to add various types of light sources anywhere in the Perspective window. You can access the Lighting Parameters dialog box (shown in fig. 19.7) by clicking the Create Lighting tool or by double-clicking the light source in the Perspective window.

Fig. 19.7

The Lighting Parameters dialog box features interactive sliding controls to adjust brightness, angle, intensity, and range values for various types of light sources.

 ■ *Create Camera tool.* The Create Camera tool enables you to add different cameras to various positions in your Perspective window. Each camera may have a different position, viewing angle, or lens type (see fig. 19.8).

Fig. 19.8
The Camera
Settings dialog box
enables you to set
parameters of each
camera and set the
position and view
using interactive
tools.

- *Render Area tool.* You can use the Render Area tool to preview the shaders applied to objects in a specific area. You see maximum detail without having to wait for the entire scene to be rendered.

- *3D Paint Shape tool.* You use the tools in this flyout for creating shapes to which you can later apply painted designs or textures using the 3D Paint Brush tool. This flyout features basic shapes including rectangular, polygonal, and oval Paint Shape tools.

- *3D Paint Brush tool.* You use the 3D Brush tool for digitally painting designs onto a Free Form object. Clicking this tool opens the Brushes dialog box, which contains all controls and options available (see fig. 19.9).

Fig. 19.9
The Brushes dialog
box displays when
you select the 3D
Paint Brush tool.

- *Shader Eyedropper tool.* Use this tool to quickly sample shaders from objects for the purpose of applying them to new objects.

Using the Free Form Modeler Toolbox

When you launch the Free Form modeler, a portion of the main toolbox changes to reveal several tools specific to the Free Form modeler including Bezier, Vertex Editing, 2D Primitive shapes, and 2D Primitive text:

- *The Bezier tool.* You operate the Bezier tool the same way you do in CorelDRAW!, drawing straight and curved lines separated and controlled by line nodes. Nodes set the slope, angle, and curve of lines they separate. Bezier lines drawn in DREAM represent the edge of surfaces in a three-dimensional object.

- *Vertex Editing tool.* The Vertex Editing tool (also known as the Convert Point tool) is grouped with the Add Point and Delete Point tools specially designed for working in the Free Form modeler window. The Vertex Editing tool enables you to change the curve and slope characteristics of shapes by manipulating the nodes that describe them.

- *2D Primitive tools.* These tools enable you to create regular and rounded-corner rectangles, polygons, and ovals in the Free Form modeler.

- *2D Primitive Text tool.* For greater effect and control than you have when using the 3D Text tool, use the 2D Primitive Text tool. You create text in the Free Form modeler window and then add depth by controlling the extrude effect.

Using DREAM's 3D Clip Art

CorelDREAM 3D comes with over 750 three-dimensional models you can use to experiment and learn or to build new objects. However, how to access and select models from the collection may not be obvious.

First, you need to have access to Disc 3 of the CD-ROM version of CorelDRAW! 6. It contains all the 3D clip art models that come with the program. Corel's color clip art guide gives samples of all 3D models included; you can find the samples in the very back of the book at the end of the table of contents indicating section N. On Disc 3 in a folder named 3DModels, the artwork is divided into 18 named categories corresponding to the printed samples in the clip art manual.

To browse one of these folders from within DREAM, follow these steps:

1. Place Disc 3 in your CD-ROM drive and choose File, Browse 3D Clipart (or press Alt+F1). Select the Aircraft folder within the 3DModels folder and choose the Select button. A new Objects Browser window opens in DREAM. If you have a slow CD-ROM drive, be prepared to wait a few minutes while the thumbnails for each of the images are read and built for your screen.

2. After your CD-ROM drive completely reads the folder, you see small representations of the models contained in the folder (see fig. 19.10).

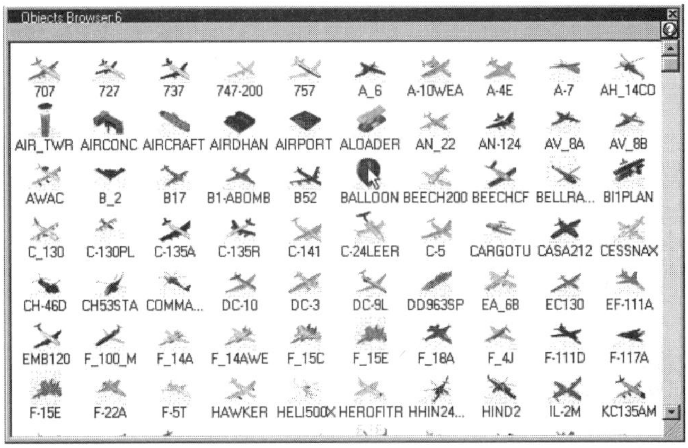

Fig. 19.10
You can browse
the 3D models
on Disc 3 of the
CorelDRAW! 6 clip
art collection.

Tip

To position a new object in the exact center of your Perspective working area, drag the object into the Hierarchy window.

3. Drag any one of these models out of the folder and into the Perspective window.

4. Your object is available for editing.

Using the printed clip art manual is perhaps the fastest way to see thumbnail drawings of the models on the CD, unless you have an extremely fast CD-ROM drive such as a six-speed. Read times for some of the directories can sometimes take a few minutes. The folders containing the most material are the Aircraft, Transportation, and Weapons folders. Perhaps the most interesting models are in the Food-Drinks folder where common, everyday items are modeled in interesting ways.

Take some time to explore the 3D model clip art included on your CorelDRAW! 6 discs. Browsing, sampling, and taking apart other works is an excellent way to learn more about the medium.

Understanding Rendering

The creation of images through the rendering process is achieved by a method of rendering called ray tracing. *Ray tracing* involves mathematical calculations to produce simulations of how objects will look when certain lighting is applied to them. Ray tracing will render many of the effects seen in actual life situations such as transparency, highlights, shadows, and reflections.

After you have created your first three-dimensional object complete with a scene and you are ready to render, you need to set your Render Setup. For the expert CorelDRAW! user, rendering comes as no strange feat because essentially it is an export process by which the three-dimensional objects you have created in DREAM are translated into two-dimensional bitmap image formats such as TIF, BMP, or PCX. The objects also are translated directly to a format that is readable by Adobe PhotoShop 2.5, PHOTO-PAINT 6, or even a Macintosh TIF format.

Rendering can be extremely taxing on your computer system, and for the most part you probably should perform your rendering tasks during a time when your computer isn't busy (like overnight) or on a completely dedicated computer system. The higher the detail you request of your final rendered image, the more complex the rendering calculations are and the longer it takes to render.

You access the Rendering Setup options for final rendered images by choosing Scene, Render Setup, Final. The options are divided into three different areas including Image Size, File Format, and Options.

Setting Size Options

The Size option enables you to set the physical size of the image DREAM can render (see fig. 19.11). Choose from High (300 DPI), Medium (150 DPI), or Other Resolution. The Other option enables you to set a specific resolution dependent on rendering time, file size, and resolution requirements. Resolution may be set to a maximum of 2,400 DPI, and an Estimate Time button option exists to have DREAM calculate the time required to render given the current settings.

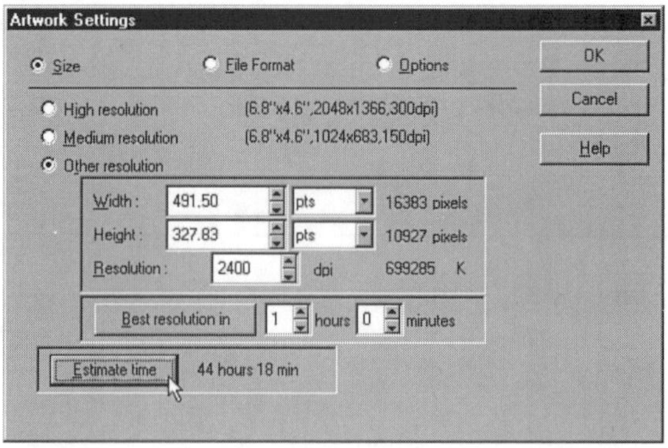

Fig. 19.11

Setting the Size and Other Resolution options before rendering involves setting a number of options including a custom resolution setting.

Troubleshooting

I have just created a simple object in a simple environment, but CorelDREAM is taking hours to render an image. Why?

Even a simple object rendering may take many hours to render when set at a very high resolution. If rendering time is excessive, try reducing the amount of resolution in your Artwork Settings dialog box by choosing Scene, Render Setup, Final. You may also consider using the Best Resolution In option if rendering time is a determining factor.

Setting File Format Options

The File Format options are critical when preparing a rendered image for use in another program (see fig. 19.12). These options determine how the rendered file is prepared, possibly restricting the types of applications that will be able to read your rendered image file format.

Fig. 19.12
The File Format options of the Artwork Settings dialog box enable you to set which format your final render will be created in.

The rendered image may take a number of formats including Windows BMP, Paintbrush PCX, Targa TGA, TIF (including Macintosh format options), PHOTO-PAINT CPT, and PhotoShop 2.5 PSD formats. Further options are available for Targa formats to save the rendered image as a 16-, 24-, or 32-bit image.

A set of special CorelDREAM 3D G-Buffer options exist, enabling you to include special information in specific data channels including Pixel Color, Mask, Distance, Object Index, Normal Vector, 3D Position, and Surface Coordinates.

Setting Options

◀ See "Using PHOTO-PAINT's Tools and Controls," p. 558

The render Options available include Renderers, and a series of options enabling surface characteristics including Reflection, Transparency, Refraction, Shadows, Lighting through transparent objects, and Bump (see fig. 19.13). Options also exist to render the image using an Adaptive Oversampling method of anti-aliasing in combination with a silhouette quality option set to a value between 1 and 200 percent. You also may set the Rendering Camera used to perform the rendering.

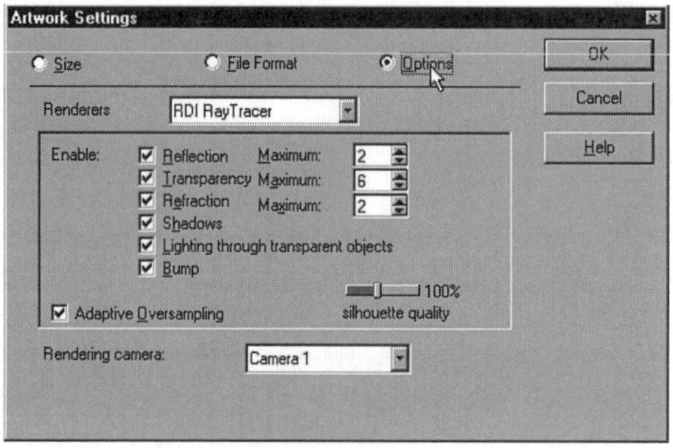

Fig. 19.13
Setting the render Options includes specific rendering controls such as which camera is used and which rendering features are enabled.

It is also important to note that although rendering operations are time consuming, you may set them to perform in batches, perhaps overnight, when the most computer time is available. By choosing Scene, Render Queue, you can display information about the rendering in progress, and set options including Adding, Deleting, and Clearing files to be rendered. You also may set different render settings for each file in the Queue by using the Settings options that give access to the Final Render options.

Importing into DREAM 3D

The mastering of successful importing and exporting operations in any program opens doors of opportunity. For this simple reason alone, it is worth researching and exploring the file exchange-filter capabilities in DREAM.

CorelDREAM is capable of importing a number of different file formats on two different levels, including many vector-format files. In the main Perspective view, imported files are limited to 3D model-type file formats including Ray DREAM Designer 3D files and prepared DXF files from most popular CAD-type software applications. In the Free Form modeler window, you may use the import function also to import vector-format files including GEM,

Computer Graphics Metafile (CGM), AutoCAD (DXF), Macintosh PICT (PCT), IBM PIF, WordPerfect Graphic (WPG), Corel Metafile (CMF), HPGL Plotter File (PLT), Enhanced Windows Metafile (EMF), Lotus PIC, Micrografx (DRW), MET Metafile, NAP Metafile, CorelDRAW! (CDR), Corel Presentation 5.0 & 6.0 (CMX), Windows Metafile (WMF), PostScript Interpreted (PS), Adobe Illustrator (AI, EPS), CorelTRACE (AI, EPS), CorelCHART (CCH), Corel CPX Compressed, and CrelDRAW Compressed (CDX).

Although most object types in graphics programs are supported through the import filters in DREAM, some of the more advanced features may not be supported and are ignored during the import operation. While importing files from 2D drawing programs, DREAM is capable of recognizing all the basic elements contained in objects such as open and closed paths, lines, and basic shapes such as rectangles and ellipses. You also may import grouped objects while their grouping is retained.

CorelDREAM 3D is compatible with most Adobe PhotoShop-compatible plug-ins, which means you can set your system up so you are scanning paint images as surface paint mapping textures directly onto objects.

To import a file into DREAM's Perspective window, follow these steps:

1. Bring the Perspective window to the forefront by selecting it. Choose File, Import.

2. From the Import dialog box, choose the Files of Type drop-down list and select the file format that matches the file you are importing (see fig. 19.14).

3. Select a file to import and choose the Open button.

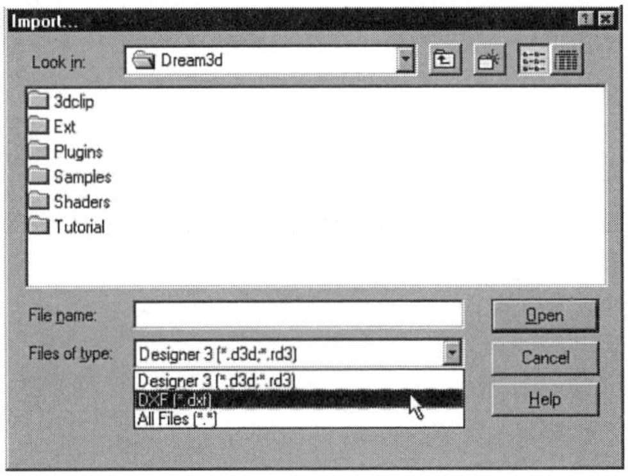

Fig. 19.14
Use the Import dialog box to import a file into DREAM's Perspective window.

To import a file into DREAM's Free Form modeling window, follow these steps:

1. Bring the Perspective window to the forefront by selecting it.

2. Open the Free Form modeling window by selecting the Free Form drawing tool and clicking anywhere in the Perspective window. DREAM asks you to name the free form object. Enter a name for your object in the Name text box and click the OK button.

3. Choose File, Import to display the Import dialog box (see fig. 19.15). Choose the Files of Type drop-down list and select the file format that matches the file you are importing.

4. Select the file and click the Open button. The two-dimensional file is imported into the Free Form modeling window and is ready for applying the third dimension.

Fig. 19.15
Use the Import dialog box to import a file into DREAM's Free Form modeling window.

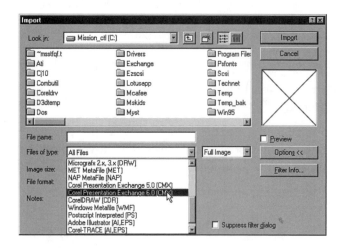

From Here...

CorelDREAM 3D is a powerful three-dimensional modeling program that has great potential for the traditional 2D artist to gain full control over image creation. Although this chapter explains only the very basic concepts, tools, and capabilities required to use the program, you have learned enough to get started. You can explore the rest on your own. If you haven't already done so, consider familiarizing yourself with the following topics:

- See Chapter 15, "Importing and Exporting Files," to learn all about importing and exporting, including export filters.

- See Chapter 17, "Creating and Editing Images with PHOTO-PAINT," to learn about PHOTO-PAINT's tools and controls.

Chapter 20

Using CorelDRAW! 6 Utilities

In this chapter, you will learn the benefits of using a full suite of applications. If you're in the business of preparing layouts, designs, or illustrations, you may not even give these applications a second look. But, if you do have the time, many of the applications included in the CorelDRAW! 6 suite are worth investigating—if even to broaden your professional horizons. While this book deals mainly with the working operations of CorelDRAW! 6, the applications that surround and support it have been looked at, briefly.

This chapter will present overviews of

- Corel MOTION 3D
- Corel Multimedia Manager
- Corel Capture

Using Corel MOTION 3D

Among Corel's latest forays into programs that do more than just graphic illustration is Corel MOTION 3D for creating moving, three-dimensional objects. This borderline animation program will enable you to take simple objects—such as text or imported files—and turn them into short, animated media clips for use with multimedia, presentation, or electronic publications. Motion 3D is an easy-to-use program that will amaze the beginning animation artist with its speed and simplistic controls.

MOTION 3D's Animation Concept

MOTION 3D enables you to create simulated, three-dimensional worlds by extruding simple objects to three dimensions, adding a bit of perspective, and adding stationary backdrops. The object characteristics may be controlled in terms of surface type, object uniform depth, and size; the worlds they exist in may be controlled in terms of lighting and scenery. Motion can occur by moving viewpoints called cameras, while the detail of the views is taken care of by shaders or ray-tracing commands.

Working with MOTION 3D Tools and Windows

◀ See "Under-
standing
Rendering,"
p. 609

Upon opening MOTION 3D, you may notice that it looks everything like a CAD application and nothing like a graphics program. Even the crude inter-face characteristics and the four views appearing as Camera, Top, Right, and Front will seem quite primitive to the seasoned CorelDRAW! user (see fig. 20.1).

Fig. 20.1
The Motion 3D
workspace features
three position
views and a
camera view.

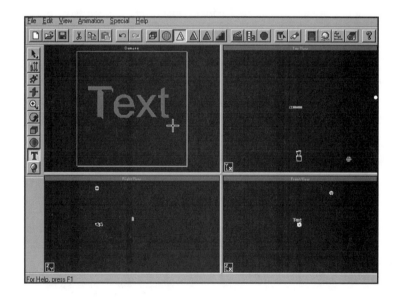

The main view, which handles most of the viewing and previewing, is the Camera window. This is the window through which you will preview your object effects, lighting, backdrops, and other graphic embellishments. The Top, Right, and Front views mainly function to provide you with quick infor-mation about the other elements in MOTION 3D's world, while most of the object manipulation is done in the Camera view. The main Toolbox is posted to the upper-left of the Camera window, and includes the following:

■ *Toolbox.* As in all CorelDRAW! 6 applications, the main Toolbox contains all MOTION 3D tools and tool flyouts.

■ *Edit Object tool*. This tool has a dual role by serving as an object while in the main Corel MOTION 3D view and serving as a quick access to the Extrude and Lathe Object Editor utilities. These are two utilities that enable you to shape objects created using the Extrude and Lathe Object tools.

■ *Squash & Stretch tool*. The Squash & Stretch tool enables you to scale objects along one dimension at a time while in Camera view.

■ *Extrude Object tool*. Enables you to create an extruded cube by default, which may then be edited using the Extrude Editor utility. This is accessed by clicking the Extrude Object and clicking the Editor tool.

■ *Lathe Object tool*. Enables you to create a sphere by default, which may then be further shaped using the Lathe Editor utility. This is accessed by clicking the Lathe Object and clicking the Editor tool.

■ *3D Text tool*. Enables you to create 3D text while in Camera view. Text may be set to a certain font, size, and style.

■ *Light tool*. Using the Light tool while in Camera view, you may add additional lights to the MOTION 3D world.

■ *Arrow flyout*. Contains the Pick tool used for selecting objects and the Horizontal Move tool used for moving objects in the Camera view left, right, closer, or further away.

■ *View flyout*. Contains Pan, Move In, Zoom In, and Zoom Out tools similar to the tools used in other CorelDRAW! 6 applications. Holding down the mouse button while using any of these tools exaggerates the specific function. For example, to zoom in, click the Zoom In tool; click and hold the mouse button down while MOTION 3D draws an outline of the object. You can release the mouse button once the object is at your desired size.

■ *Rotation toolbar*. The rotation tools include Vertical, Horizontal, and Tilt rotate tools representing changes to the X, Y, and Z three-dimensional axis.

■ *Standard toolbar*. The Standard toolbar contains all file, clipboard, and preview shortcuts as well as shortcuts to specific roll-ups including Stagehands, Environment, Timelines, and Surface roll-ups.

■ *Editor toolbar*. The Editor toolbar becomes active only in the Extrude and Lathe Editor functions and includes Pick, Shape, Pan, Zoom, Line, and Rotate tools (see fig. 20.2).

■ *Zoom toolbar*. The Zoom toolbar may only be accessed by selecting View, Toolbars and choosing the Zoom toolbar to display.

■ *Outline toolbar.* The Outline toolbar only becomes available while in the Extrude or Lathe Editor and includes the Line, Pencil, Rectangle, Ellipse, Open Polygon, and Closed Polygon tools.

■ *Viewing Pane Rotation toolbar.* The Viewing Pane Rotation toolbar contains the three rotate tools available in the Camera view or in either the Extrude or Lathe Editors, and includes Vertical, Horizontal, and Tilt Rotate tools.

■ *Preview options.* There are five previewing options including Bounding Box, Wireframe, Shade Faster, Shade Better, and Ray-Trace, along with an Anti-Aliasing option. Each of the previewing options offers a different degree of detail. Selecting a higher degree of detail requires more time for the preview image to be created.

■ *Movie options.* Once all of your 3D effects have been achieved and you have set your Motion options, you can render your MOTION 3D file into an AVI file. Choosing Animation, Make Movie enables you to render to AVI format which may be played back on any Windows media player.

■ *Lathe Editor.* The Lathe Editor enables you to edit Lathe Objects by clicking the Lathe Object and clicking the Editor button in the main Toolbox. The Lathe Editor (see fig. 20.2) contains its own set of tools and menu bars, most of which are accessed through the Editor Toolbox. Using basic CorelDRAW! node-editing conventions, lathe shapes may be edited to varying forms.

Fig. 20.2
The Lathe Editor utility illustrated here features a primitive outline view for shaping objects and the Editor toolbox.

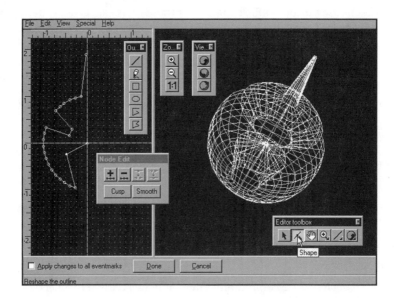

■ *Extrude Editor.* Very similar in operation to Lathe Editor, the Extrude Editor enables you to edit Extrude Objects by selecting the Extrude Object and clicking the Editor button in the main Toolbox. The Extrude Editor (see fig. 20.3) contains its own set of tools and menu bars, most of which are accessed through the Editor Toolbox. Using basic Corel-DRAW! node-editing conventions, extrude shapes may be edited to varying forms.

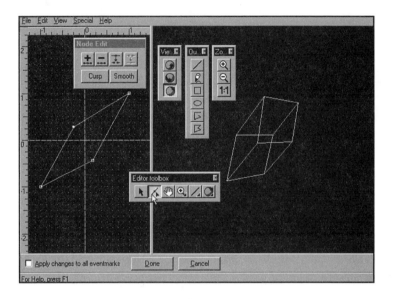

Fig. 20.3
The Extrude Editor utility enables you to customize three-dimensional extrusions.

Creating a Flying Object Movie

While the purpose of this section is to simply give a quick overview of MOTION 3D, the best way for you to gain an understanding of the applications function is to follow some examples.

One of the most intriguing uses of MOTION 3D is its capability to import objects and quickly apply effects to them, including backdrops and special lighting.

To create the effect of a flying logo, follow these steps:

1. Choose File, Import DXF, choose the SAMPLE.DXF file included in your Corel60/Win95/Tutorial folder, and select the Import button.

A dialog box will appear with a number of options for importing the file, including Smoothing and Object options (see fig. 20.4).

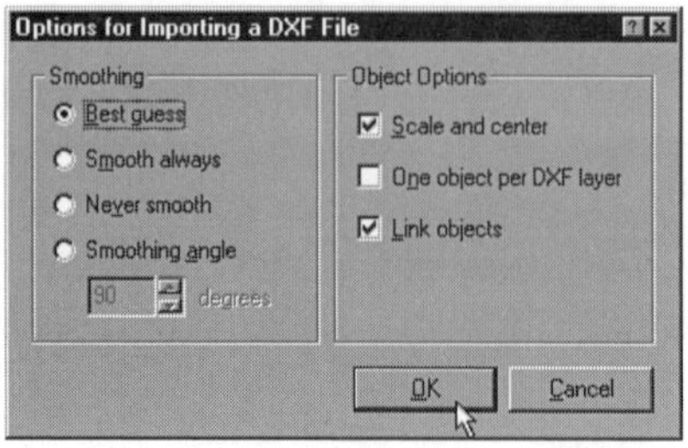

Fig. 20.4

The Extrude Editor utility allows you to import DXF files directly into the editor so that you may begin shaping your new three-dimensional object.

2. A yellow Star shape will appear in your Camera view. Notice that it will also appear as a wireframe object in the other three views of Front, Right, and Top.

3. Select Edit, Properties to display the Object Properties dialog box. Select the Surface tab (see fig. 20.5). Click the selection called Blue Steel. To adjust the surface characteristics, select the Edit button. If not, select OK.

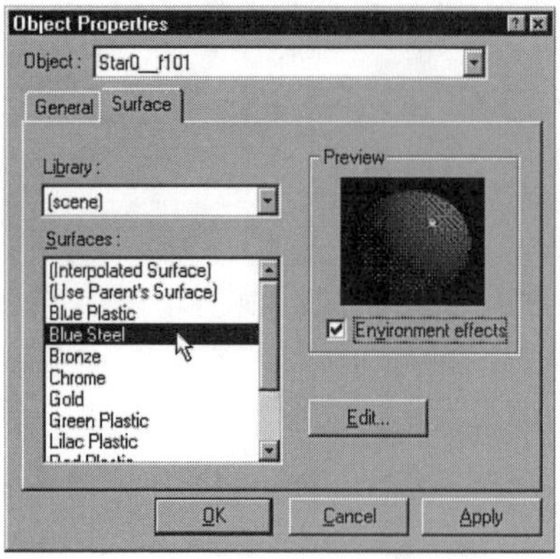

Fig. 20.5

The Object Properties dialog box contains tools for setting General and Surface attributes for your objects.

4. Select the Horizontal Rotate tool from the main Toolbox, and turn your star shape slightly to the right by clicking and dragging (see fig. 20.6).

5. Click the Top View window. Grab the Camera marker in the lower center of the window and move it parallel to the right side of your object (see fig. 20.7).

6. Right-click the camera, choose Point At from the pop-up menu, and select the object named Star0_f101 in the Point At dialog box.

7. Select View, Timelines—Timelines (Ctrl+L). Select the Camera and select Animation, Set Keyframe to set a starting point for the Animation, which will generate your fly-by camera move. Notice that the marker moves ahead half of a second.

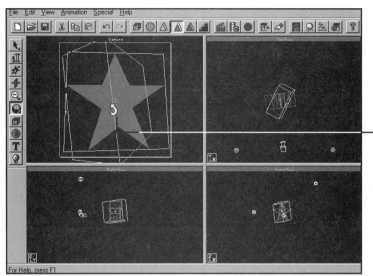

Fig. 20.6
You may rotate
your object in one
direction only
using the Horizon-
tal Rotate tool.

Horizontal
Rotate tool

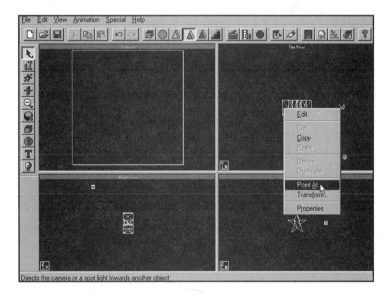

Fig. 20.7
Moving your
camera over time
enables you to set
up a camera fly-by.

8. In the Top View, select the camera again and move it to the lower
left of the window. Notice that the timelines sequencer adds an event
marker indicating a change in the animation movement of the camera.

9. Using the right mouse button, select the camera and choose Point At;
choose the same object Star0_f101 from the Point At dialog box.

10. Click the Camera View window and choose <u>A</u>nimation, Previe<u>w</u> to see the result of the animation. The animation you see will occur in wireframe format. If you wish, save your MOTION 3D file by selecting File, Save and naming your file.

Creating a MOTION 3D Using Stagehands

In MOTION 3D, Stagehands are essentially embellishments to the stage your objects exist in. Stagehands include camera and lighting effects and props. These are added to your MOTION 3D stage to create a sense of realism and interest.

To create an animation using Stagehands, follow these steps:

1. Using a new document, create a simple text object by choosing the Text tool from the main Toolbox, clicking in the Camera View, and typing a single word or title. Choose any font or style you wish (see fig. 20.8).

Fig. 20.8
Text object may be created quickly using the 3D Text tool.

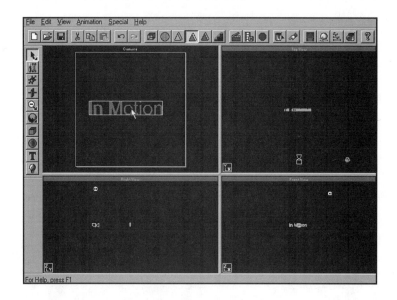

2. Right-click the text object in the Camera View and choose P<u>r</u>operties to display the Object Properties dialog box (see fig. 20.9). Select the Surface tab and click a surface style from the <u>S</u>urfaces library and select the Bevel tab.

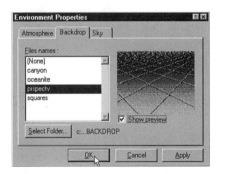

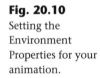

Fig. 20.9
The Object Properties dialog box contains four tabbed areas that enable you to change General, Text, Surface, and Bevel properties of text.

3. Select Straight from the Type pull-down menu and choose OK.

4. Right-click the background area of the Camera View and choose Properties to display the Environment Properties dialog box (see fig. 20.10); select the Backdrop tab. Choose the backdrop style named Perspective and choose OK. The Perspective backdrop appears in the background of your Camera View.

Fig. 20.10
Setting the Environment Properties for your animation.

5. Choose Special, Stagehands (Alt+F11) to display the Stagehands dialog box (see fig. 20.11), and select the Camera tab. Choose the Panaround style from the File Names library. If you wish, choose the Show preview option and select the play button to preview the effect. Choose Load to set up the effect.

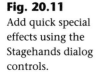

Fig. 20.11
Add quick special effects using the Stagehands dialog controls.

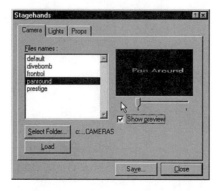

6. Select the Lights tab (see fig. 20.12) and choose the style named Spotlight from the Files Names library. Choose Show Preview to see a quick preview of the effect. Choose Load to set up the effect.

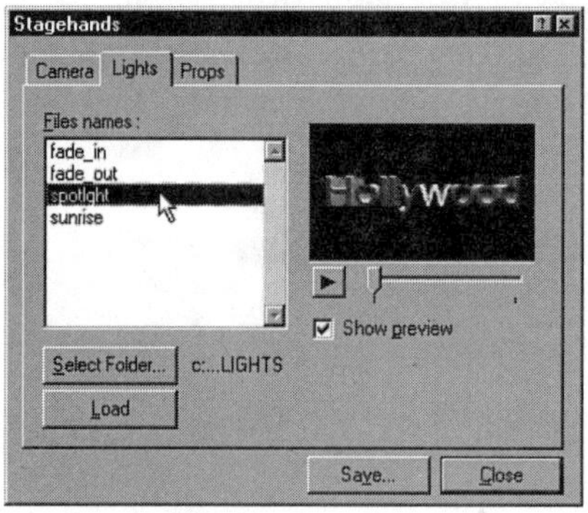

Fig. 20.12
Quick lighting effects may be set using the Stagehands Lights effect.

7. Select the Props tab (see fig. 20.13). Select the style named Stars from the Files Names library and preview again if you wish to see the effect. Choose Load to set up the effect. Once completed, select the Close button to set the Stagehands you have selected.

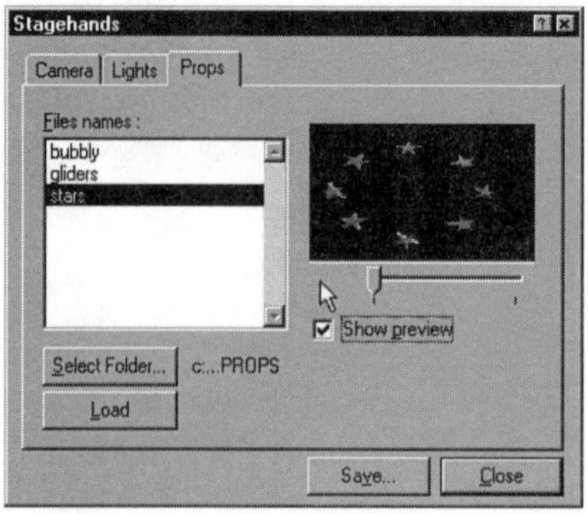

Fig. 20.13
Stagehand Props include animated backdrops to add interest to your motion.

8. Click the Camera view to bring it to the forefront and choose <u>A</u>nimation, <u>M</u>ake Movie (Ctrl + R). Name and save your movie using the Make Movie dialog box that appears. These effects may take a few minutes to render into a movie.

9. To play back your movie, choose <u>A</u>nimation, <u>P</u>lay Movie and locate your movie.

By using the prepared effects available in MOTION 3D, you can create simple but impressive animations of text and/or objects. In these examples, you learned to import DXF files and animate text and objects adding special effects that took only moments to select. You also discovered that you can create AVI movies of your animations.

Using Multimedia Manager

With all the programs and file formats that today's electronic artist has to contend with, losing track of files and forgetting names of directories is not surprising. After all, we're only human. So, it's no wonder that Corel has developed a software tool to let you use the power of your computer to assist you.

Multimedia Manager 6 is an effective tool for cataloging, tracking, and archiving many different types of files used in today's rapidly expanding graphics industry. Previously named CorelMOSAIC in earlier versions (Corel 3, 4, and 5), and named Corel Gallery and Corel Gallery 2 in later releases, this utility is now part of the CorelDRAW! 6 suite.

Multimedia manager is capable of many different tasks—not just file management—and in this chapter, you will explore ways of increasing your productivity by developing a broader understanding of how files can be categorized, grouped, and organized so they can be easily tracked and cataloged.

What Is Multimedia?

Multimedia is already one of the most overly used terms you'll hear in the publishing and communications industry. Some still think of multimedia shows as corporate presentations in which photographic images are married with sound recordings to produce elaborate slide shows projected onto a presentation screen. Others think of it as sound and video images playing on a computer screen. But multimedia involves much more than just integrating sound and video. As users of programs such as DRAW, PAINT, PRESENTS, and DREAM 3D, you might have some idea of the full potential of what is referred to as "digital media."

Multimedia, as far as your computer is concerned, encompasses any digital data type available in a format that software can interpret. A few of the most popular formats you might come in contact with are: several video formats, including audio-video interleaved (AVI) and QuickTime for Windows (MOV); digital audio in both WAV and MIDI (MID) formats; various bitmap formats of which there are a multitude of different types; animation formats from various applications; vector graphics of all types; and textual formats too numerous to list. Multimedia Manager gives you the tools you need to manage not only graphical file types represented as thumbnails, but also non-graphical files represented as icons.

Multimedia Manager's Hierarchy Concept

The hierarchy of Multimedia Manager may seem tricky at first, but if you have a large family or belong to a large clan and like to save pictures, you'll pick this software up very quickly. Multimedia Manager is set up the same way you might set up your own personal scrapbook. You know, the place where you save your first lock of hair, pictures of your siblings, a happy-snap of the family dog long since passed away, and that precious studio shot of cousin May's newly born daughter, what's-her-name.

You've decided your new item is important enough to warrant saving in a safe place. Now, whenever you're going to either store something new (or look up something already packed away) you begin by looking for the correct "bookshelf" where you stored it. Once you remember the right "bookshelf," you need to find the right "album." But, the albums you create may be so complex and organized that you need to subdivide. Now, let's say you find the correct album and flip to exactly the right sub-album. You probably want to open everything up somewhere like on a desk, on the floor, on your bed— wherever. In this case, let's just call it your "workspace."

Multimedia Manager's user-friendly interface includes features to make the concept of file management closely resemble real life. Directory tree structures, album icons, and customizable thumbnail representations of your actual files make it easier to imagine the items you are managing and organizing. The interface also features split-second animations of files opening and closing to give a better idea of the action that is taking place.

Using Corel CAPTURE 6

Corel CAPTURE 6 is a relatively uncomplicated screen-capturing utility that enables you to quickly take a snapshot of the contents of your computer screen, and save that image to a bitmap file format. CAPTURE also enables you to automatically capture screens using a number of different capture procedures and save your images to eight different bitmap file formats using standard or optional compression.

Corel CAPTURE 6 will be of great interest to individuals preparing materials for training, presentations, technical manuals, magazines, and other computer-related communications material. CAPTURE can be used in companion with PHOTO-PAINT 6, Multimedia Manager's bitmap editor, or even the MSPaint utility that comes with your Windows software for editing of your captured images.

If you have ever been in the situation of needing a record of your computer screen and have unfortunately had to resort to the screen capture controls that come with your Windows 3.1 or Windows 95 software, you'll quickly learn to appreciate the control and flexibility you have with a professionally designed screen capture utility such as CAPTURE. There are plenty of instances when Microsoft's window capture method (ALT+PRINT SCREEN) or full-screen capture method (PRINT SCREEN) just don't cut the mustard. CAPTURE allows you to work in any application with CAPTURE waiting in the background. At a moment when you have decided to record the contents of your screen, you press a certain keyboard combination and CAPTURE does the rest of the work for you, without ever interrupting your work momentum.

With CAPTURE, you can set the exact size, color, shape, and moment of your capture as well as whether the image is recorded in a specific file format and location of your choice, launched immediately into a specific application, or printed to a specific printer. CAPTURE can be set to be triggered by certain keyboard combinations and will also automatically name and number consecutive captures in background-style operation for near hands-free capturing.

To use this feature, follow these steps:

1. Set your screen up with the image that you would like to capture.

2. Choose Corel CAPTURE from the Corel Applications menu of the Windows 95 Start button. The Capture dialog box opens. You may also launch Corel CAPTURE using the Application Launcher from any of the CorelDRAW! 6 programs.

3. Set up the Corel Capture options via the six tabs (see explanations in the following figure).

4. In the Activation tab, choose No Selection Capture; then click the Capture button. A message will appear giving you instructions.

5. Click and hold down the right mouse button x and marquee-select the desired area to be captured using the left mouse button.

6. When the left and right mouse buttons are released, CAPTURE displays the message The capture has been completed.

When the <u>N</u>o Selection Capture feature is selected, you'll notice the Timing area becomes grayed out and unavailable. In other words, the capture will take place at the moment CAPTURE senses that both mouse buttons have been depressed and the left mouse button has subsequently been released. There will be no delay and no repetition of the capture, but CAPTURE will notify you once the capture is complete.

Along with this capture that uses the Two Mouse Buttons feature is a caution no selection under cursor, which refers to a Preferences option discussed later in this chapter. It deals with mouse-button actions already being performed with the mouse, such as depressing an application button, menu, or flyout while attempting to use the capture with Two Mouse Buttons feature discussed here.

Activation

Activation controls in CAPTURE 6 are intended to enable you to trigger screen captures to occur how and when you choose. When set up properly, the Activation controls can make capturing much quicker and without having to access menu bars and capture selection buttons.

Capturing is a multistep procedure with Corel CAPTURE 6. First, you need to set all of your capture settings. Then, with your target application opened and ready, you click the Capture button and CAPTURE minimizes itself and, if selected to, begins a delay countdown. After the delay has expired, the capture takes place either automatically, or as defined by the user.

■ *Hot Key.* The first of Corel CAPTURE's Activation controls (see fig. 20.14) begins with setting a keyboard trigger. Having a keyboard trigger of your own choosing enables you to Mi<u>n</u>imize CAPTURE and continue working in your application until you are ready to capture. Then, by selecting the <u>H</u>ot Key, you are able to trigger your screen capture sequence to begin, without having to Ma<u>x</u>imize CAPTURE once again and manually press any more buttons.

Fig. 20.14
The Activation tab features Hot key and Timing settings.

Your Hot Key may be selected from the pull-down menu list. By default, it is set at F7, but also includes choices for selecting F2 through F10 inclusive, and a User defined setting. This User defined setting may incorporate any keyboard combination of either Shift, Ctrl, or Alt keys combined with any of the F2 through F10 keys or A to Z keys.

Tip

While Corel CAPTURE 6 offers a preset selection of hot keys for triggering captures, be sure not to select a hot key that has been used in the application you are working in. Using a hot key already assigned in your application may cause your system to hang or cause an unrecoverable error to occur.

■ *Setting timing controls.* CAPTURE timing settings offer two on/off controls to allow for a delay between the moment the hot key is pressed to the moment of capture. This delay may be necessary in some cases (depending on which application you are using) to allow sufficient time for you to set up for the capture—such as pulling down menus or flyouts, positioning your cursor, highlighting objects on the screen or simply to allow the screen to redraw all of its contents as in the case with complex drawings or bitmap images. Without this control it would be impossible to capture a complex CorelDRAW! drawing or elaborate, high-resolution PHOTO-PAINT images, for example. In situations where you are capturing from a program such as CorelDREAM, it may even be wise to first time how long it takes for the entire screen to completely redraw before setting the time delay.

When activated, the Initial <u>D</u>elay Before First Capture setting may be set in the range of 1–60 seconds. Timing controls may also be set to capture repeatedly between 2–999 times by activating the <u>R</u>epeat Captures control and entering the number of captures to take place. Once the Repeat Captures feature has been activated, a further setting is enabled, allowing you to select a time <u>I</u>nterval Between Repetitions, once again between 1–60 seconds.

Caution

Before deciding on the number of <u>R</u>epeat Captures to take place during your capture, be sure that the device you have set your captures to be saved to (see "Destination" later in this chapter) performs a quick check to determine whether the drive or printer can handle the number of captures and the Interval Between Captures settings you have selected. For example, if you are capturing to a device that is characteristically slow (for instance, a network printer, a bubble-jet printer, or a floppy drive) be sure to perform a test to ensure that your captures are carried out smoothly.

If you have set the Destination as a local or network drive, be sure that the drive has enough space to collect the number of captures you have decided on. To do this, try a single capture only, make a note of its memory size, and multiply that figure by your required number of captures. Allow for a 10 percent "safe" zone of empty space to be left on the drive. If the total works out to more memory than your drive can safely accept, you may have to reduce the number of repetitive captures. The last thing you want is to exceed the capacity of your hardware!

- *Mouse-trigger options.* Activating the function <u>N</u>o Selection Capture allows you to capture anything you choose that is displayed on your screen.

Source

The Source controls (see fig. 20.15) in CAPTURE let you specify exactly which part of the contents of your screen you want to record and includes six capture types: <u>C</u>urrent Window, C<u>l</u>ient Window, <u>F</u>ull Screen, <u>R</u>ectangular Area, <u>E</u>lliptical Area, and Free-<u>H</u>and Area. The terminology used to describe the first two options may be a bit confusing for some. It helps to understand the difference between the terms current window and client window before selecting them.

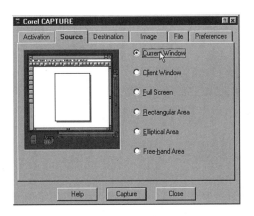

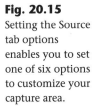

Fig. 20.15
Setting the Source tab options enables you to set one of six options to customize your capture area.

Beyond CorelDRAW!

IV

- *Current Window*. When the capture source is set to Current Window, the area that is recorded will be only the contents of the application window (including all open dialog boxes and cursors).

- *Client Window*. The Client Window option sets CAPTURE to record only the window currently on the very top of your screen, such as an application dialog box, caution message, or anything else that happens to be on the top surface of your application.

- *Full Screen*. Full Screen CAPTURE will record your entire screen contents including (if displayed) the current application, other applications, the desktop area, and the Windows Taskbar.

The last three capture sources available in Sources are relatively new features as far as screen capturing utilities go. They involve a two-step capture process: first you trigger your capture to take place, and then you define the capture area.

- *Rectangular Area*. After triggering your capture to take place with the Rectangular Area option selected, Capture will first change your cursor to an icon resembling the Corel CAPTURE icon (a Corel balloon with a butterfly net around it). CAPTURE then waits for you to define an area by marquee-selecting the area using the cursor.

Tip

When selecting to capture from a particularly shaped area using either the Rectangle, Ellipse, or Free-Hand Area feature, it is worth knowing ahead of time exactly which portion you are targeting. Take a moment to visualize what you are trying to illustrate with your capture. Note also that the reference point of

(continues)

> (continued)
>
> the balloon cursor is the upper left of the image (the broken part of the butterfly net handle), and that rectangular and ellipse areas are drawn from the corners as opposed to from the center; holding down the Ctrl key while defining a rectangle or ellipse constrains to a perfectly square or circular shape.

- *Elliptical Area.* As with the Rectangular Area control, the Elliptical Area option allows you to capture a circular or elliptical area.

- *Freehand Area.* Capturing a free-hand area is perhaps the trickiest of the six options. Once the capture has been triggered and the time delay has elapsed, the balloon cursor is displayed and CAPTURE awaits the reference points of your freehand defined area. Begin defining the area by clicking with the mouse button using the far-left corner of the cursor as the cursor point. Select a starting point, any number of intermediate points, and complete the defined area by re-selecting the first point again. Once your capture is completed, CAPTURE will display the message `The capture has been completed`.

Destination

The Destination tab (see fig. 20.16) of CAPTURE contains controls for setting where the captured information will be sent. Capture information can be sent to File, meaning it can be sent to be written to a specific file format with a specific name and to a specific directory on a local or network drive. The captured information may also be collected to the Clipboard or set to a Printer and is accompanied by a Select Printer button that enables you to choose a destination printer.

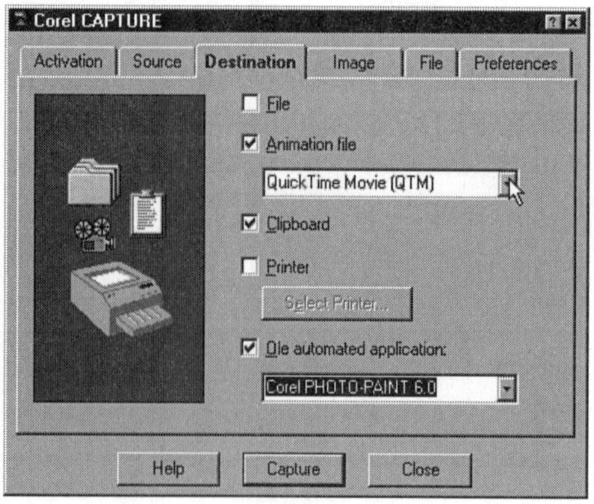

Fig. 20.16
The Destination tab options determine where the information you have captured will end up including Clipboard, File, Printer, and OLE options.

■ *Capturing to File.* Activating the option File sets CAPTURE to direct all screen capture data to a specific file format set by the user (see "File" further on in this chapter) and stored on a local or network drive of your choosing.

■ *Capturing to Clipboard.* Activating Clipboard will send all screen capture data to your Windows 95 clipboard from where you can either paste it as a figure, or diagram directly into another application, or into an image manipulation program such as Corel PHOTO-PAINT.

■ *Capturing to Animation File (AVI).* The Capture to Animation File option enables you to select an animation file format, which includes Quick Time Movie (QTM), AutoDesk FLIC (FLI), MPEG Animation (FLC), PICS Animation (PCS), or Video for Windows (AVI).

> **Tip**
>
> When selecting the destination, it may be wise to choose to collect your captured information—at least to a saved file format—so that you may at least have the opportunity to reproduce the information later.

> **Caution**
>
> If you choose to set your capture destination to your clipboard, you will only be able to save—and subsequently paste—one image at a time, until the next image is captured. Therefore, this destination would be impossible to select if you plan repeated timed captures. Capturing to the clipboard is only recommended for single one-time captures that will be immediately pasted somewhere else. Also, beware of sending large screen capture images to your clipboard if you have limited random-access memory (RAM) available and/or have multiple applications opened at once.

■ *Capturing to Printer.* Selecting the Capture to Printer option sends the image you have just captured directly to the printer you have designated. If you haven't designated a printer, click the Select Printer button to gain access to controls that enable you to do this.

■ *OLE Automation.* Choosing the OLE Automation option will allow CAPTURE to immediately open the application you choose from the pulldown menu and place the capture into a new, untitled document.

Image

Image controls (see fig. 20.17) enable you to control the resolution, size, and color of your captured images. Depending on how your captures will be used and to which device they will be sent, your screen display colors, screen resolution, and screen size will affect how your captures will look. These controls enable you to customize the final appearance of your captures.

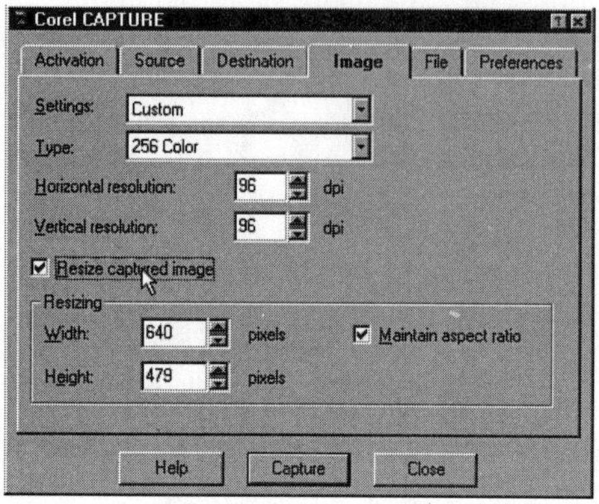

Fig. 20.17

Image options enable you to determine how your image will be captured and saved, including color, resolution, and size options pictured here.

- *Screen Settings.* There are three image Settings to choose from the pull-down menu. The first two, Screen and Printer, offer predetermined settings from your current Windows screen settings and your default printer. When you select the Screen option, you'll notice that all other options become unavailable and CAPTURE will take its data directly from your screen.

- *Printer Settings.* When the Settings option Printer is selected, the color options that become available are settings for Black and White, 16 Color, Grayscale, 256 Color, and 24-bit color. When the Printer option is selected, CAPTURE will automatically set the colors according to information provided by the Windows default printer. Otherwise, the option is available for you to set them yourself.

- *Custom Resolution Settings.* With the Settings option Custom selected, all of the options in this dialog box become available including measures for Horizontal and Vertical Resolution, a Resize Captured Image option, and Resizing controls for Width and Height, and an option for Maintain Aspect Ratio. The Horizontal and Vertical measures control the actual number of dots per inch of your capture, whereas the Width and Height measure in pixels will set the physical size of the screen area to be captured.

■ *Resizing Captured Images.* Before setting the <u>W</u>idth and H<u>e</u>ight measure fixed as pixels, determine what your current Windows display settings are. A display setting of 640 by 480 (always measured as first width and then height) will mean that if your capture settings are set to the same measure, you will capture everything on your screen. And, if your display settings are set to 1024 by 768 and your Width and Height measure is set to anything less, you won't get the whole screen. This concept may be confusing to some, but with the aid of a few test captures (highly recommended) you'll immediately understand how changing these settings will affect your captured images.

Selecting <u>M</u>aintain Aspect ratio (likely the setting you will use for most of your captures) will lock out the width and height measure fields to ensure your captures are not vertically or horizontally distorted in relation to your Windows display settings.

Note

Screen size and display-color settings can easily be scaled downward (for example, from 256 colors to 16 colors) but cannot be scaled upward to exceed your current monitor settings (see the Windows 95 Control Panel Display settings under the Settings tab). If you require a higher number of colors for your captures, you will first have to increase the Windows 95 main settings. See your Windows manual for the exact procedures.

When choosing the color and resolution settings, note that a higher number of colors, a higher <u>H</u>orizontal and <u>V</u>ertical resolution measure, and a larger <u>W</u>idth and H<u>e</u>ight measure will all contribute to increasing your capture file size, and in some cases (as when a higher number of colors are selected), the increase in file size will be dramatic!

File

The File tab (see fig. 20.18) of Corel CAPTURE offers controls for establishing your own file-naming system, the bitmap file format to be used, a compression type for saving disk space, a path location for CAPTURE to write the files to, and an automatic sequential naming function complete with a numbering option.

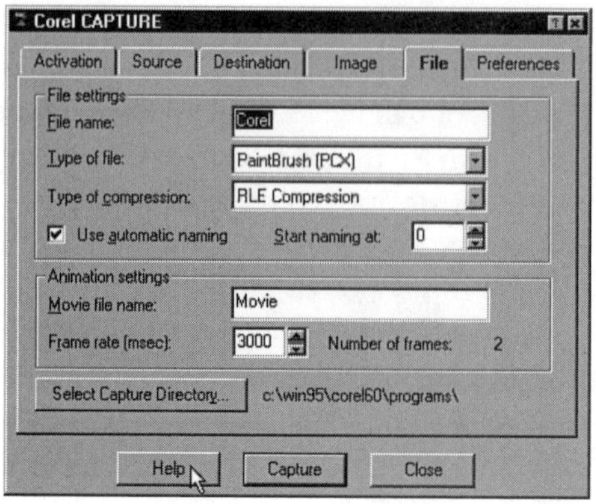

Fig. 20.18

Setting File options include determining the type of file and the file's name.

These controls will be especially useful for users who wish to perform multiple, consecutive captures without having to laboriously provide a name, file type, and path for the captured files.

- *File Name.* If you choose not to enter your own File Name in this field, CAPTURE will use the default name "Corel" as the prefix for each consecutive capture. Customizing the naming function is definitely a recommended habit to form since final captures are much easier to track if they are named according to the subject matter. For example, if you were preparing exhibits for a training manual or product documentation, you may want to precede each capture with the section number, page number, or subject name. In cases like this, you may decide to name your file beginning with Part-1, Part-2, and so on. That way, when you viewed the files on disk, they would automatically fall into the order that they appeared in your documentation. Windows 95 supports long file names and so the options are nearly limitless.

- *Type of File.* CAPTURE offers seven bitmap file formats to save to, including Windows bitmap (BMP), OS/2 bitmap (BMP), Paintbrush (PCX), Targa (TGA), JPEG Bitmaps (JPG), GEM Paint File (IMG), TIFF bitmap (TIF), and Corel PHOTO-PAINT Image (CPT). Before deciding which one to use, be sure to investigate and determine exactly which file format works best for your destination application. The most useful and universal format for capturing to the PC platform may be the Paintbrush (PCX) format, or if you are planning to take your file to a platform, such as the Macintosh, you might consider a TIFF bitmap (TIF) format.

- *Type of Compression.* The compression option within the Image tab offers a somewhat advanced control for file saving. Compression types offered include: Uncompressed, RLE, LZW, and Packbits. Selections vary depending on the file type chosen.

> **Caution**
>
> Compression is an excellent feature to have the option of using, especially when file size or disk space is a priority. However, if you choose to use a compression and you'll eventually be importing your files into another application, be sure the new application supports the compression type you choose or you may end up having to recapture all of your files. If you aren't sure which compression works, don't use any. It is much easier to resave your captures with new compression using another image manipulation program—such as PHOTO-PAINT—than it is to capture them over again.

- *Setting the Destination Directory.* The destination directory for your files can be set by clicking the Select Capture Directory, and using the Browse button to define a path.

- *Automatic Naming.* Perhaps the most valuable feature in CAPTURE is its capability to name files automatically and according to your own custom-designed naming convention. By selecting Use Automatic Naming, you allow CAPTURE to sequentially organize your files using a three-digit number suffix. CAPTURE then checks the directory you have selected, and determines where to begin naming. For instance, if you had selected to name your captures beginning with "Corel" and you had already captured files Corel001 through Corel023, CAPTURE would automatically name the next file Corel024.

  You may also tell CAPTURE to begin numbering at a certain point by entering the first number of your capture. This essentially tells CAPTURE to begin at a certain number, and ignore checking the directory for the number of the most recent capture in the directory it is writing to.

> **Caution**
>
> When using the auto-naming feature, be sure to double-check the path of your files before beginning your capture process. For example, let's say you are continuing a capture session that you began the previous day, but have mistakenly let CAPTURE continue writing the files to the same directory when what you really intended was to begin the numbering over again. Human error will make you renumber your files manually.

- *Animation Settings.* The Animation Settings area allows you to name your movie file the default which is "movie," and the capture Frame Rate, the default which is 3,000 msec.

Preferences

The Preferences tab (see fig. 20.19), the last of CAPTURE's control tabs, offers options for your captured images, including settings for cursor controls and optional borders of various weight and color for your captures.

Fig. 20.19

The Preferences tab controls contains a potpourri of controls, including icon and cursor controls, capture notification, and border options.

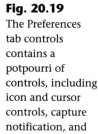

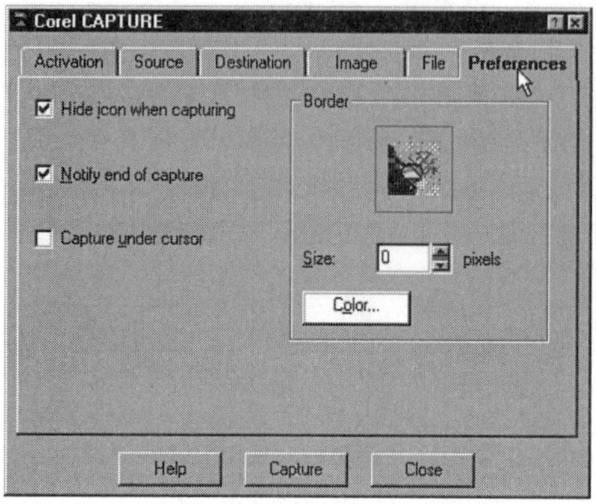

- *Cursor and more capture options.* There are three cursor controls available when capturing your screen images. The first, Hide Icon When Capture, will make your cursor invisible no matter if it lies within the live capture area. If it is off, this control will allow the cursor to show up, which will allow you to point to a relevant item in your capture.

  The Notify End of Capture option enables CAPTURE to display an on-screen message once your capture is complete. This seems most useful during tricky capture procedures, for instance, when capturing with Two Mouse Buttons.

  The Capture Under Cursor option is meant to allow further control when capturing active windows. In some applications, a window is considered either the main program window, a dialog box, a caution message, or notification window. However, in other applications, a window may be considered a tool flyout, a menu bar, or a pop-up menu. With the Capture Under Cursor option enabled, CAPTURE will capture the "parent" window as well as the smaller window element.

- *Border settings.* You may want to include an automatic border on your captured images. If you do, CAPTURE offers a border width option from 0 (no border) to 10 pixels in Size. A Color function (see fig. 20.20) also allows you to further customize the color of your border. A basic selection of 24 various Red, Green, and Blue (RGB) color values is available. You may also choose to define your own color by numerically entering RGB or Hue, Luminosity, and Saturation (HLS) color values. The color controls also allow you to visually select colors using a color picker and save favorite colors in a custom color palette in much the same way the color palettes in DRAW, PAINT, PRESENTS, and DREAM work.

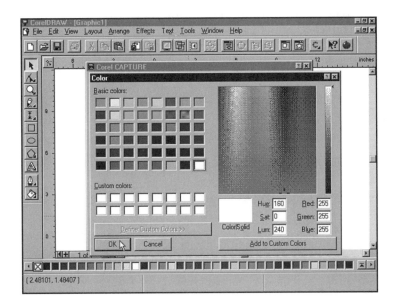

Fig. 20.20
Setting the optional border colors of your capture frame.

Corel CAPTURE 6 incorporates vast improvements over previous Corel CAPTURE versions. It will also make an effective capture tool not only for use with Corel products, but also with any other Windows 95-compatible applications. CAPTURE's controls and customization tools help to earn credit for being among the best screen capture tools currently available.

From Here...

The resources and utilities included with CorelDRAW! 6 are powerful accessories to the suite of applications. Corel's strategy is to include as many value-adding tools as possible, making the Corel suite an irresistible combination. While just a few years ago some of these utilities may have been packaged and sold as stand-alone applications, now they are being placed in the hands of the electronic artist as a way of enticing you to use its other products. With the inclusion of applications such as MOTION 3D, Multimedia Manager, and Corel CAPTURE as companion programs to CorelDRAW! 6, the user benefits greatly.

For more information on some of the subject matter this chapter touches on:

- See Chapter 3, "Making CorelDRAW! 6 Easy to Use," to learn more advanced customization techniques.

- See Chapter 15, "Importing and Exporting Files," to learn how to use Corel's import tools as well as how to master DRAW!'s export filters.

- See Chapter 19, "Creating 3D Illustrations in CorelDREAM 3D," to understand rendering.

Part V

Appendixes

A   Glossary of Terms

B   Keyboard Shortcuts

C   What's on the *Special Edition Using CorelDRAW! 6 for Windows 95* CD

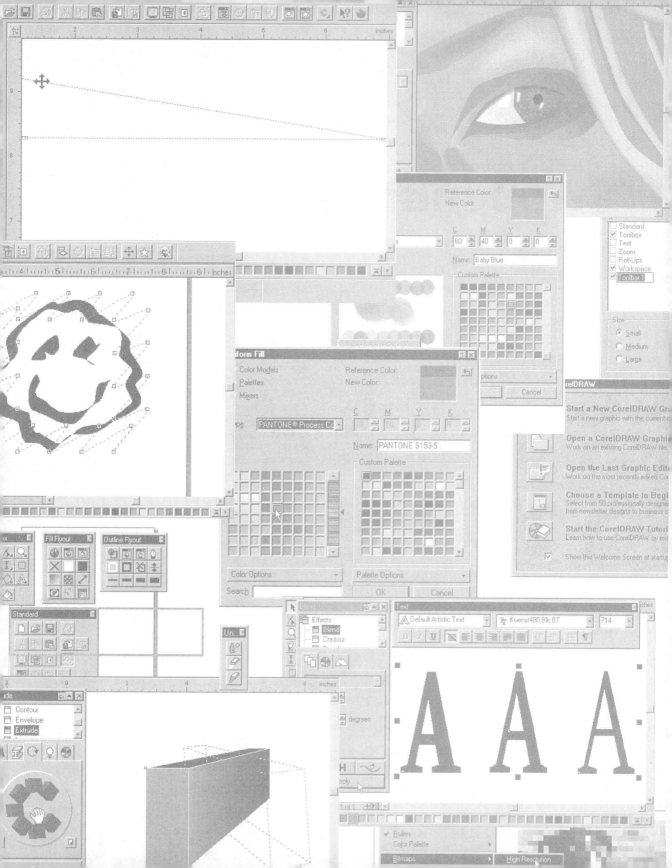

Appendix A

Glossary of Terms

A

All Fonts Resident   When printing, the All Fonts Resident option causes the application to omit any font information from being transferred to the printers memory.

ascender   This is the part of a character that extends above the x-height.

aspect ratio   A value measured as a ratio that represents the relationship between height and width of an object.

attributes   Color, size, pen, and fill characteristics assigned to an object, specific to the type of object (for example, text objects, shape objects, and so on).

auto-trace   Utility built into the Pencil and Bezier tools for tracing imported bitmap images to produce vector shapes.

B

baseline   The imaginary line on which characters rest, aligning in approximation with the bottom of the x-height of characters.

BBS   Stands for Bulletin Board Service. A type of online service offered by vendors usually capable of both uploading and downloading data.

bezier curve   Bezier curves are curves that may be created in CorelDRAW! and contain nodes that are used to shape the slope and angle of connecting lines.

bezier tool   A tool that allows you to draw editable curved lines controllable through curve handles.

bitmap File format containing dot patterns measured in resolution values. Bitmaps may be 1-bit, 2-bit, 8-bit, 24-bit, or 32-bit and contain black and white, grayscale, or color information.

bleed The portion of an object that overlaps the assigned page border or trim area of a file.

blend A dynamically linked and layered arrangement of objects containing two control objects linked together by a blend group. The internal elements adapt their shape, color, and size to form the illusion of one control object becoming the shape of the other control object. The term blend also may be used to describe a fountain fill.

C

calligraphic The simulation of a hand-drawn line that has been created using a traditional-style calligraphy pen. The thickness of the line changes with the angle and slope.

child object An object contained within a collection of objects that have been grouped using the Group command in CorelDRAW!

cicero A European measure of font sizes. One cicero is equivalent to 4.55 millimeters.

clone A dynamically linked object created using the Clone command, located in the Effects menu. Changes to the master clone are reflected in the cloned object.

CMYK Stands for cyan, magenta, yellow, and black and represents the color model used in traditional-style printing for re-creating full-color images. Also known as process color.

color model The method in which color is represented including CMYK, RGB, HSB, HLS, and so on.

color palette A collection of colors within a color model. Also refers to the on-screen collection of colors displayed within the CorelDRAW! window.

columns The vertical division of text within a paragraph text frame.

composite The result from printing all document layers and color together to produce a single printout.

compression A mathematical process used to reduce the amount of memory space used to fully describe a collection of data. A compression package is the software program that uses this process.

constrain   Restriction of movement of an object or objects to either horizontal or vertical movement, or set increments of rotation.

continuous tone   The illusion created by an ultra-high collection of colors and shades used to describe an image such as in traditional-style photographic prints.

contour   A collection of dynamically linked objects that are concentrically formed around or within an object's center of origin.

control point   The manipulation handle used to change the slope and curve of a curved line.

crop marks   The lines added to the black layer of a printout that indicate where the corners are without touching the page borders, enabling things such as accurate page trimming after printing.

cross hair   The state of a cursor created from a single vertical and single horizontal line intersection.

CT Scan   Stands for continuous tone scanned image, which is an image scanned at such a high resolution that it appears to have no digital dot pattern.

cusp   Describes a type of node on a line in CorelDRAW!. The line on either side of the node may take its own direction.

cyan   One of four ink colors used in process color reproduction represented by CMYK, which stands for cyan, magenta, yellow, black.

D

default   The typical setting of a variable, value, or feature option. Default settings are nearly always updatable.

density   Relative opaqueness value of a traditionally developed film negative.

descender   This is the part of a character that extends below the x-height of a font.

deselect   To unselect or change an object's state from selected to not selected.

didot   A unit of measure equivalent to 1.07 times a U.S. point. 67.567 didots equals one inch.

digital halftone   A printed digital image composed of various-sized dots of resolution and arranged in rows to simulate a continuous-tone, photographic or graphic image. A digital halftone is usually produced from scanning hardware, or from a digital-image manipulation software program.

digital image   An image that is described by way of data, or ones and zeros. More specifically, a digital image is a term that usually refers to a photographic-type image.

directory   A DOS term referring to a named partitioned area where files may be stored.

dot gain   This term refers to the reaction that occurs when printer ink soaks into the paper the image is being printed on. In cases of absorbent paper, the area in which dots are close together may result in black, or where dots were intended to be medium-sized become large-sized, making the overall image darker and less detailed. In most cases, dot gain may be compensated for by reducing the size of the dot to begin with.

double-click   The act of quickly clicking twice on the left mouse button, or the right mouse button if it is specified.

download   To transmit a file from a larger main computer to a remote computer, or from a server to a workstation.

DPI   Stands for dots per inch and refers to a measure of resolution.

driver   A software routine enabling hardware to communicate with software. May also be referred to as a hardware device driver.

dropout   Also referred to as a reverse. A dropout is one object overlapping another object so that the resulting image is a white object on top of a black or colored object.

drum scanner   A scanner that translates images into digital information by spinning them on a drum-type cylinder read by a laser.

DTP   In the publishing industry this stands for desktop publishing. In the computer software industry in general this can also refer to data processing.

E

emulsion   The light-sensitive, silver-coated side of traditional-type film. It can be recognized by its dull finish in comparison to the shiney, uncoated side of the film.

EPS Stands for encapsulated PostScript. A file format that contains code that is written in PostScript format and contains all the necessary information required to print the image on a PostScript or PostScript-compatible printer.

extension The three-letter suffix contained in a DOS-type file, which, in most cases, designates its file format or the proprietary program that it belongs to.

F

facsimile The product of either a manually or mechanically reproduced document or item. The long term for the generally accepted term, "fax," which has been accepted as the transmission of a hard copy or digital copy document by a dedicated fax machine or computer system software and modem.

field The open areas of a program interface that may accept either keyboarded or selected information.

fill The texture, color, shade, or pattern applied to a closed object.

flatbed scanner A device capable of digitally recording an image by way of placing the original document face-down on a stationary document glass while a reflection-sensitive light bar records data based on the reflected image.

flatness This is a value given to the degree of detail that describes a printed curve. Setting various flatness levels will affect the appearance of printed curves only and will not affect the image on your screen.

flush A term given to text or objects that align along a given edge or side.

flyout A term given to part of the CorelDRAW! interface, which is given to a menu or toolbar item that, when selected, expands further to reveal more options.

FOCOLTONE A European-based company that has designed a 750-color palette geared toward reducing the need for color trapping by standardizing CMYK screen percentages to five percent increments. The thrust of this standardization is to increase the likelihood of common color screen percentages by reducing the variety of screens used. The Focoltone palette has been arranged in such a way so that a full spectrum of colors is displayed on the palette at any given point.

folder   The new Windows 95 name given to a Windows 3.*x* directory.

font   A comprehensive set of characters that make up a typestyle adapted for the digital-imaging industry. Individual fonts may also be part of a larger font family and be designed to emulate a font style within a family such as plain, italic, bold, or bold-italic font styles. The name font has been carried over from the early days when typesetting systems used large metal or nylon discs with images of letters cut out of them to represent typefaces.

font conflict   Largely a problem with systems which use older font identification standards, a font conflict is indicated on printouts where the font specified in your source file is different from the printed font.

FTP Site   A site on the Internet that uses FTP (File Transfer Protocol) to make drivers, patches, and updates available. Becoming a very popular way of disseminating information. See also *x-ref BBS*.

G

GCR   Stands for gray component replacement. The process during color separations whereby the amount of cyan, magenta, yellow, and black color is reduced and replaced with various percentages of black.

grayscale   An available option in your Print Options dialog box that allows you to add an object to your digital output when separations are selected. In the early days of process camera work and hand-developing, a grayscale was a small printed strip of continuous-tone grayscale colors graduated in dark to light shades of black and placed in with the original artwork being shot on a graphic arts camera. The purpose of the grayscale was to ensure a consistent exposure time and film developing process by measuring the amount of film density in each of the shades of black after developing.

H

hairline   A term given to the thinnest line weight possible for an output device, or the equivalent to a line having approximately 0.125 points in thickness.

halftone   A printed image composed of various-sized dots arranged in rows to simulate a continuous-tone, photographic, or graphic image. A halftone is traditionally produced by photographing a continuous-tone original onto graphic arts negative film contacted with a halftone screen.

handle   In a software program, it's the term given to any part or extension of an object that may be manipulated to change the size, slope or angle, or characteristics of lines or curves in an object or the object itself.

header   A low-resolution image that visually represents the information contained in an electronic file. Header information is usually contained in the preceeding part of the data that describes a file.

high-res   Short for high-resolution, this is a term given to an image where the dot composition cannot be recognized with the naked eye or without a magnifier.

HQS   Stands for high-quality screening. This is a name given to a software screening procedure used in conjunction with Linotronic high-resolution imagesetters. HQS screening may be selected from the Advanced options of the Print Options dialog box in CorelDRAW!

I

image recorder   The name given to a device that translates information from a computer onto photo-sensitive diapositive film with the purpose of making presentation slides. Image recorders are usually capable of resolutions much higher than imagesetters, but tend to be restricted to 35-millimeter to four-inch by five-inch film formats.

Imagesetter   A hardware device that physically transfers an image onto photo-sensitive material using a laser-type imaging process. Taken literally though, an imagesetter may be considered any hardware device that prints an image onto any type of material.

imaging   The process of electronically transferring a collection of images to film by way of ink, toner, or laser printing process onto receiver material such as paper, film, or polyester.

interface   Visual and interactive elements that make up a user environment and applications that run under that environment.

intersection   An effect found under the Arrange menu in CorelDRAW! whereby new objects may be created from the areas where other objects overlap.

V

Appendixes

J

justified   The term given to columns of multiple lines of text that align with each other on both the left and right sides. In more sophisticated layout software, columns of text may also be justified vertically.

K

kerning   Often wrongly confused with letterspacing or wordspacing, this is the process of adjusting the space between specific letter combinations that fit together. For example, an uppercase T and a lowercase o may appear more smoothly integrated if they are moved close together, whereas two uppercase TT characters may appear better if moved farther apart.

L

laminate   Pronounced *la-men-it*, this is a multi-color proofing method that produces a printout comprised of layers of micro-thin colored transparent film. When the various film layers are laminated together onto a paper backing the result is a closely-matched facsimile of the final printed product.

landscape   A document orientation style whereby the page setup is horizontally aligned. References a common landscape-style painting canvas orientation.

leading   Pronouced *ledding*, this refers to the vertical spacing of baselines. Increasing the leading of type increases the vertical space it occupies.

lens   An arrange effect applied to objects in CorelDRAW! whereby objects seen through the lens effect have an altered appearance.

line art   An older term that refers to an original document comprised of only black and white, without any gray or color shades.

line screen   A measure of the frequency of resolution of a screen tint or halftone screen. Digital output must be set to image to a line screen specific to the reproduction process that it will be used for.

linen tester   Term given to a self-supporting optical magnifier that is used in graphic arts to closely examine film or output. Traditionally, these magnifiers were used to examine material or fabric quality.

lino output   Nickname given to a machine called a Linotronic, which is made by a company called Linotype. Has also been adapted to cover all film output generated by high-resolution printers.

linotronic   Name of a brand-name, high-resolution imagesetter made by a company named Linotype. Current popular models include the 330, 630, and 830.

loop   An old printing term, this is a magnifier used in closely examining film printout or printed matter.

LPI   Stands for lines per inch and measures the screen frequency of print output.

M

magenta   One of four ink colors used in process color reproduction represented by CMYK, which stands for cyan, magenta, yellow, black.

mixing area   An area in the CorelDRAW! 6 Uniform Fill dialog box that enables you to create new color combinations by blending together existing colors using a Brush tool.

moires   A pattern produced when one dot pattern is applied over another—digital or otherwise—resulting in an undesirable checkerboard pattern. Also caused during the printing of film separations when one or more overlapping process-color screens has been printed at an incorrect angle.

N

nested files   This is a problem that occurs when several stages of importing and exporting commands have been performed on a file. For example, file A is imported into file B, while file A already contains previously imported file C. File C is considered nested because it has undergone more than one import-export process.

nested fonts   This is a problem that occurs as above, with nested files. The problem begins when a file containing text is exported using the All Fonts Resident option, and subsequently imported into another file. If the imagesetter printing the file cannot find the font it needs to print the nested fonts it will substitute Courier as the default and there will be no way to correctly identify the fonts required.

node   A controlling point on a line that may be assigned attributes to designate curve slope and/or angle. A node may contain control handles that determine the relationship of the lines on either side of it as cusp, smooth, or symmetrical.

O

OLE Stands for object-linking and embedding, a method whereby the image or data belonging to one application may reside in another application so long as both native programs reside on the system.

OPI Stands for open prepress interface and is a little-known method whereby PostScript print files may have embedded code that actually calls out to other files at printing time.

overprint The procedure of printing one ink color overtop of another, usually with the purpose of hiding misregistration flaws in printing.

P

PANTONE Maker of the largest and most comprehensive color matching system, and one of the first internationally-recognized color systems to dominate the printing industry. PANTONE has spot and process color systems sampled by ink swatches printed on uncoated and coated paper. Their process color palette contains over 3,000 colors, designed for optimal printing. Colors are composed of screen percentages ranging from 0 to 100 percent in 5 percent increments, including a 3 percent step between 0 and 5 percent.

parameters The measure or amount of a variable.

pica Printer's measure of column width and line length. One inch is equal to approximately 6 picas in the traditional measure. One pica is also equal to 12 points.

pixel A measure of monitor resolution.

PKZip The name of a shareware compression program produced by a company called PKWARE in Brown Deer, Wisconsin. PKZip is widely used for compressing PC files.

plate The traditional term given to individual color separations. Carried over from the manual process of stripping film that would eventually be used to burn a metal plate. The metal plates then install onto the printing press rollers and provide the actual image for the printed product.

PMS Stands for Pantone Matching System and is widely used for specifying colors in the printing industry.

point A division of measure associated with graphic arts and the printing industry. One inch equals 72 points.

point size A measure of the size of a character.

portrait   A document orientation style whereby the page setup is vertically aligned. References a common practice of portraiture photography or painting.

PostScript   A machine language developed by Adobe Systems of Mountain View, California that has been widely adapted by the software industry as the unofficial standard for printing program files.

PowerClip   A CorelDRAW! effect that allows objects to be contained within other objects.

powerline   A CorelDRAW! effect that allows curves or lines to take on an editable, dynamically linked shape.

print file   A file usually consisting of machine-language commands that contains all the information necessary for printing to a specific printer. Print files can usually be identified by a PRN file extension.

process color   A printing process whereby full-color images may be reproduced on a printing press using screen combinations of only the four colors of ink: cyan, magenta, yellow, and black.

processing   Refers to the developing, fixing, washing, and sometimes drying of printer film. May also refer to the calculations of data.

processor   A machine used by service bureaus to develop the unexposed, light-sensitive material used in imagesetters.

properties   A widely used feature of CorelDRAW! 6, which refers to any collection of data associated with an object within the program. Properties may be created, measured, counted, interrogated, or altered.

pull-down menu   A small selection list built into the user interface of a software program usually found to the right of an entry field, which allows the user to quickly make a choice from a predetermined list of variables.

R

ragged   A condition of the uneven side of a text column. Text may sometimes be described as flush left, ragged right, specifying rhetorically that while the text aligns flush on the left side, it is not aligning flush on the right. Also sometimes referred to as rag right.

raster graphic   A term that describes bitmapped images such as TIF, BMP, PCX, and so on.

registration   A term describing the procedures related to lining up various multiple-color film separations using a visual alignment system printed directly on the separations.

resident scans   These are usually scanned images that are used consistently and repeatedly over time that are kept at the service bureau permanently in an effort to save time. The scanned images are then re-linked by the service bureau operator.

resolution   A measure of detail recorded by a digital scanner, or the measure of detail recorded onto film by a digital imagesetter.

RGB   Stands for red, green, blue and is the method in which all color is rendered by your color monitor.

RIP   Stands for raster-image processor and is the front-end number cruncher of a high-resolution imagesetter that digests and translates the PostScript printer information language into a machine language that the imagesetter can accept.

roll-up   An interface element that can be temporarily displayed, minimized, or maximized, giving the user access to a collection of specific controls. Termed roll-up, because of the animated action of the display rolling up or down as it minimizes or maximizes.

RRED   Stands for right read emulsion down, and describes a condition of film negative whereby the image reads properly while the emulsion side of the film is held facing away from you. This is usually the condition that film should be in for offset printing.

RREU   Stands for right read emulsion up, and describes a condition of film negative whereby the image reads properly while the emulsion side of the film is held facing away from you. This is usually the condition that film should be for silkscreen printing.

S

sans serif   An attribute used to describe type that does not have tiny leading or trailing tail features integrated into the characters. For example, Helvetica is a common sans serif typeface, while Times New Roman is a serif typeface because it has the tails.

screen frequency   The lines per inch (LPI) measure of rows of dots in imagesetter or printer output.

script   Term used to describe text containing a series of program commands. Also used to describe text that appears as if it was created using a traditional-style calligraphic ink pen.

SelectSet   The model name of a series of imagesetters developed and distributed by AGFA, Inc.

separations   The various layers of film that, when combined in registration, form a composite of the image.

serif   The tiny tails on the characters of type such as Times New Roman, or Century Schoolbook.

service bureau   A relative newcomer to the printing industry trade, a service bureau is a vendor providing the services of some or all of imagesetter output, scanning, color proofing, software sales, technical support, and/or traditional pre-press services.

set solid   A term used to refer to leading—or baseline-to-baseline spacing—of text where the point spacing between lines is the same as the point size of the text. For example, 12-point type with a line spacing of 12 points. For body text this isn't always desirable; however, for headlines—especially headlines that use all uppercase letters—solid leading or even negative leading may make the text more readable or at least save valuable space.

solid color   Referring to either spot or CMYK colors, a spot color is one that contains no screen percentages. Also referred to as 100 percent solid, or simply 100 percent of ink.

source file   The name given to a native file format owned by a specific program.

spooler   A software program that manages the flow of printed documents to a printer or imagesetter.

spot color   A color that is assigned to a specific color model, not including any of the process color models. The more commonly used spot color model is the PANTONE spot color model.

spreads and chokes   A procedure mainly used in trapping that either exaggerates or degrades the shape of an object with the aim of having it uniformly fit into an adjacent color or area.

stripping   The function of manually assembling film in an arrangement for printing. In the print and graphic arts industry someone who does this function is known as a film stripper.

subscript   A placement of type in which the text is set smaller and below the natural baseline of text.

superscript   A placement of type in which the text is set smaller and above the natural baseline of text.

system profile   The term given to the color capabilities of either or all of your color monitor, color printer, and/or color scanner.

T

texture fill   A term given by Corel to a bitmap-based fill pattern that may be seemingly random in creation composed of any number of spot or process colors and resembling or simulating certain named textures.

thumbnail   A small-sized, visual representation of an image or graphic. The term thumbnail is adopted from the graphic design industry where concepts were first produced in thumbnail sketches or roughs before being fully developed into final designs.

tracking   An algorithm that, when applied to text, uniformly reduces the overall letterspacing and wordspacing of text.

transparency   One of the lens effects found in the CorelDRAW! Lens roll-up. Objects may be set to be see-through by a percentage ranging from 0 (not transparent) to 100 (fully transparent).

trap   An overlap or overprinting outline and/or fill of an object done with the aim of reducing the chance of press misregistration or misalignment of inks.

trapping   The process of overlapping ink colors in an effort to reduce the chances of poor press registration.

trim   An effect found under the Arrange menu in CorelDRAW! whereby new objects may be created by removing portions of objects where two or more objects overlap.

TrueType   Originally developed as the answer to eliminating the monopoly enjoyed by Adobe with their type 1 standard, the TrueType font format was developed as a joint effort by Apple and Microsoft.

TruMatch TruMatch is a color system vendor based in the U.S. The Trumatch Color process color palette is composed of over 2,000 achievable colors. Trumatch has specifically customized their color matching system to suit the digital color industry using the Computer Electronic Prepress System (CEPS). The palette is comprised of 40 tints and shades of each hue while black is varied in 6 percent increments.

U

upload To transmit a file from a smaller remote computer to a larger computer system, or from a workstation to a main network server.

V

vector A format by which straight or curved paths are formed by joining vector points assembled in relationship to each other so that they may be resized or transformed while still retaining part or all of their original relationship.

W

weld An effect found under the Arrange menu in CorelDRAW! whereby new objects may be created by combining two or more other objects.

V

Appendixes

Appendix B

Keyboard Shortcuts

This appendix provides you with all of the known shortcuts in CorelDRAW! 6 with one proviso—any keyboard assignments (also referred to as Accelerator Keys or Hotkeys) may be changed by the current user, using the Tools, Customize commands.

General Keyboard Conventions

The following is a list of keyboard shortcuts that will help make using CorelDRAW! 6 that much easier. Shortcuts separated with a + mean you should hold down the first key while pressing the second.

◀ See "Cutomizing Corel-DRAW! 6," p. 459

To access Help, press F1

To access Context Help, press Shift+F1

Shift key with Pick tool to multiple select

Shift key with drawing tool draws from center origin

Ctrl key with a drawing tool constrains the shape to circle or square

Ctrl key while dragging constrains object(s) vertically or horizontally

Ctrl+Shift with a drawing tool draws a perfect square or circle from the center origin

Alt key while marquee-selecting selects all objects that come in contact with the marquee

Tab key cascades between selection windows in dialog boxes

Tab key cycles through object selection in the order that the objects were created

Shift+Tab cycles backward through object selection in the reverse order that the objects were created

Shift+click with Pick tool multiple-selects/deselects objects

CorelDRAW! 6 Keyboard Shortcuts

File Functions	
Command/Function	**Shortcut**
Open file	Ctrl+O
New file	Ctrl+N
Save file	Ctrl+S
Close file	Ctrl+F4
Print	Ctrl+P

Edit Commands	
Command/Function	**Shortcut**
Undo last command	Ctrl+Z
Redo last command	Alt+Return key
Repeat last function	Ctrl+R
Cut	Ctrl+X
Copy (Windows command)	Shift+Delete
Copy	Ctrl+C
Copy (Windows command)	Ctrl+Insert
Paste	Ctrl+V
Paste (Windows command)	Shift+Insert
Delete	Delete key
Duplicate	Ctrl+D

View Commands

Command/Function	Shortcut
Wireframe toggle on/off	Shift+F9
Full Screen Preview toggle on/off	F9

Layout Commands

Command/Function	Shortcut
Layers Manager	Ctrl+F3
Styles Manager	Ctrl+F5
Snap to Grid	Ctrl+Y

Arrange Commands

Command/Function	Shortcut
Group objects	Ctrl+G
Ungroup objects	Ctrl+U
Combine objects	Ctrl+L
Break apart objects	Ctrl+K
Convert to curves	Ctrl+Q

Text Commands

Command/Function	Shortcut
Character Attributes	Ctrl+T
Fit text to path	Ctrl+F
Align text to baseline	Alt+F10
Edit text	Ctrl+Shift+T

V

Appendixes

Text Editing Keyboard Shortcuts	
Command/Function	**Shortcut**
Left, right, up, down arrow	Moves the text entry point in direction of arrow
Home	Moves the text entry point to start of current line
Ctrl+Home	Moves the text entry point to the beginning of the document
End	Moves the text entry point to the end of the current line
Ctrl+End	Moves the text entry point to the end of the document
PgUp or PgDn	Scrolls the Text Editing window in the Text dialog box up or down
Shift+left or right arrow	To select one character at a time in the Text dialog box
Shift+Home	To select all text from the left of the text entry point to the start of the line
Shift+End	To select all the text from the right of the text entry point to the end of the line
Backspace	To delete the selected text or individual characters before the text entry point
Delete	To delete the selected text or individual characters following the text entry point
Enter	To begin a new paragraph
Shift+Enter	To begin a new line without beginning a new paragraph
Ctrl+C	To Copy selected text to the clipboard
Ctrl+X	To Cut selected text to the clipboard
Ctrl+V	To Paste text from the clipboard
Ctrl+left arrow	To move the text entry point from the beginning of a word to the left of the text entry point
Ctrl+right arrow	To move the insertion point from the beginning of the word to the right of the text entry point
Ctrl+up arrow	To move the text entry point to the previous paragraph

Command/Function	Shortcut
Ctrl+down arrow	To move the text entry point to the next paragraph
Ctrl+Home	To move the text entry point to the top of the paragraph text frame
Ctrl+End	To move the text entry point to the end of the paragraph text frame
Shift+left arrow	To select the character to the left of the text entry point
Shift+right arrow	To select the character to the right of the text entry point
Ctrl+shift+left arrow	To select the word to the left of the text entry point
Ctrl+shift+right arrow	To select the word to the right of the text entry point
Shift+up arrow	To select one line up from the text entry point
Shift+down arrow	To select one line down from the text entry point
Ctrl+shift+up arrow	To select the text from the left of the text entry point to the previous paragraph
Ctrl+shift+down arrow	To select the text from the right of the text entry point to the end of frame
Ctrl+Shift+Home	To select the text from the left of the text entry point to the start of frame
Ctrl+Shift+End	To select the text from the right of the text entry point to the end of frame
Ctrl+Shift+PgUp	To select the text from the left of the text entry point to the start of the text block
Ctrl+Shift+PgDown	To select the text from the right of the text entry point to the end of the text block
Ctrl+Backspace	To delete a word to the left of the text entry point
Ctrl+Del	To delete a word to the right of the text entry point
Ctrl+numeral key	To apply a paragraph style pre-defined by a numeral key

V

Appendixes

Tools Commands

Command/Function	Shortcut
Options	Ctrl+J
Multimedia Manager	Alt+F1
Symbols	Alt+F11
Presets	Alt+F5
Duplicate	Ctrl+F12

Window Commands

Command/Function	Shortcut
Refresh window	Ctrl+W

Menu Access

Menu	Shortcut
File	Alt+F
Edit	Alt+E
View	Alt+V
Layout	Alt+L
Arrange	Alt+A
Effects	Alt+C
Text	Alt+X
Tools	Alt+T
Windows	Alt+W
Help	Alt+H

Tools

Feature	Shortcut
Zoom in	F2
Zoom out	F3
Zoom to fit all objects in window	F4
Previous zoomed view	Shift+F4
Zoom into selected object	Shift+F2
Pencil tool	F5
Rectangle tool	F6
Ellipse tool	F7
Artistic text tool	F8
Shape tool	F10
Uniform Fill dialog box	Shift+F11
Fountain Fill	F11
Outline Pen dialog box	F12
Outline color dialog box	Shift+F12
Nudge object up	Up arrow
Nudge object down	Down arrow
Nudge object left	Left arrow
Nudge object right	Right arrow

Roll-Ups

Feature	Shortcut
Layers roll-up	Ctrl+F3
Align & Distribute roll-up	Ctrl+A
Position roll-up	Alt+F7
Rotation roll-up	Alt+F8

(continues)

V

Appendixes

Roll-Ups	
Feature	**Shortcut**
Scale & Mirror roll-up	Alt+F9
Size roll-up	Alt+F11
Skew roll-up	Alt+F12
Envelope roll-up	Ctrl+F7
Blend roll-up	Ctrl+B
Extrude roll-up	Ctrl+E
Contour roll-up	Ctrl+F9
Powerline roll-up	Ctrl+F8
Lens roll-up	Alt+F3
Pen roll-up	Shift+F7
Fill roll-up	Shift+F6
Dimension roll-up	Alt+F2
Styles roll-up	Ctrl+F5
Object Data roll-up	Ctrl+F12
Symbols Roll-up	Ctrl+F11
Node Edit roll-up	Ctrl+F10
Fit Text to Path roll-up	Ctrl+F

Hidden Interface Controls

Double-clicking a page border opens the Page Setup dialog box

Double-clicking a toolbar tears it away from a window border, or re-installs it back into a window border

Click-dragging a status bar tears it away from its current position and moves it to either the top, bottom, left, or right side of the screen

Dragging a toolbar causes the toolbar to slide around in the window interface, while dragging it onto the screen tears it away from the window interface

Numeric Keyboard Functions	
Command/Function	**Shortcut**
Bring object to front	Shift+Page up
Send object to back	Shift+Page down
Bring object forward one layer	Ctrl+Page up
Send object back one layer	Ctrl+Page down
Plus sign with Shape tool	Add Node
Minus sign with Shape tool	Delete node

Right-clicking a bitmap enables pop-up menu to bitmap properties

Right-clicking an ellipse enables pop-up menu to ellipse properties

Right-clicking a rectangle enables pop-up menu to rectangle properties

Right-clicking a group enables pop-up menu to Ungroup command

Right-clicking an effect enables pop-up menu to specific effect Properties

Right-clicking a text enables pop-up menu to edit Text or Character properties

Right-clicking a Blend enables pop-up menu to Separate command

V

Appendixes

What's on the *Special Edition Using CorelDRAW! 6 for Windows 95* CD

Using the Royalty-Free Images

Both CorelDRAW! 6 and PHOTO-PAINT 6 are equipped with filters to interpret Kodak's PhotoCD image format, which is how these digital images are stored. To import a PhotoCD image into a CorelDRAW! 6 document, select File, Import (Ctrl+I). In the Import dialog box, change the Files of Type drop-down menu to PhotoCD (PCD). Locate the file you wish to import on the Special Edition, Using CorelDRAW! 6 CD and select Import. To open a PhotoCD image in PHOTO-PAINT 6 select File, Open. In the Open File dialog box change Files of Type drop-down menu to PhotoCD (PCD). Locate the image you wish to open into PHOTO-PAINT 6 and select Open.

Fifty royalty-free photographs are in photoCD format, including:

IMAGE1001	Tidal sand
IMAGE1002	Cherry blossoms, holly hedge
IMAGE1003	Lichen on rock
IMAGE1004	Solidified sand bags
IMAGE1005	Stone wall
IMAGE1006	Volcanic rock wall

IMAGE1007	Tidal markings
IMAGE1008	Wave reflections
IMAGE1009	Ocean reflections
IMAGE1010	Macadamia nut shells
IMAGE1011	Great Pine
IMAGE1012	Tidal moss
IMAGE1013	Volcanic rubble
IMAGE1014	Stone wall
IMAGE1015	Tidal pool
IMAGE1016	Ventilation grate
IMAGE1017	Tidal pools
IMAGE1018	Rusted conduit tubing
IMAGE1019	Harvest rock
IMAGE1020	Naturally faulted rock
IMAGE1021	Sydney Harbour Bridge at night
IMAGE1022	Green leaf veins
IMAGE1023	Petrified log
IMAGE1024	Beach sand marks
IMAGE1025	Shallow stream
IMAGE1026	1957 Jaguar front grill
IMAGE1027	Hang glider
IMAGE1028	Hang glider launch
IMAGE1029	Outdoor market
IMAGE1030	Zoo chimps
IMAGE1031	Catamaran
IMAGE1032	Mountains and sugar cane fields
IMAGE1033	Pidgeon Park
IMAGE1034	Plaid bird
IMAGE1035	Cactus and cow

IMAGE1036	Mountain orchid
IMAGE1037	Cumulous cloud
IMAGE1038	Bridge at night
IMAGE1039	Japanese goldfish
IMAGE1040	Pines and mountain
IMAGE1041	Tulips
IMAGE1042	Winter mountaintop
IMAGE1043	Ferns and moss
IMAGE1044	Black comb rock formation
IMAGE1045	Summer glacier
IMAGE1046	Forest waterfall
IMAGE1047	Dew drops
IMAGE1048	Red tulips
IMAGE1049	Bird of Paradise
IMAGE1050	Towering cumulous

Corel Magazine Sampler

The *Corel Magazine* sampler contains sixteen recent articles from the monthly magazine dedicated to CorelDRAW! users worldwide. These articles are a great resource providing information on design, type, paint, and draw. See the ad in the back of this book for the CorelDRAW! 6 *Special Edition* subscription form.

To view the *Corel Magazine* articles choose Start, Run, and Browse. In the Look in drop-down list choose Corelcd (D:) where D: is the name of your CD-ROM drive. Open the Corelmag folder and choose Setup and OK. The installation will begin; simply follow the prompts on the screen. If a particular font already exists on your system, you will get a message which states that a font cannot be installed. Click OK and the installation will continue. Once the installation is complete *Corel Magazine* will be available on your Start, Programs menu.

V

Appendixes

Ray Dream Gallery

See what's possible with DREAM 3D by viewing the interactive product demonstration of Ray Dream Designer 3D, predecessor to Corel DREAM 3D. This technology was purchased by Corel as an addition to the CorelDRAW! 6 suite of applications. To view the demonstration choose Start, Run, Browse. From the Look in drop-down list choose Corelcd (D:) where D: is the name of your CD-ROM drive. Open Raydream, Windows and choose Gallery. Choose OK in the Run dialog box.

CorelDRAW! 6 Working Model

Direct from Corel Corporation, a working version of CorelDRAW! 6 for you to try. It has most of the functionality of the retail version, except for certain commands in the File and Edit menus: Save, Print, Cut, Copy, and Paste. In addition, the OLE Automation feature has been disabled. However, you can work freely with all the special effects, styles, technical drawing features and more.

To install the Working Model choose Start, Run, and Browse. From the Look in drop-down list select Corelcd (D:) where D: is your CD-ROM drive. Open Corl_mdl, and Draw6wm. Choose Setup and OK. Follow the prompts on the screen. By default the working model will be stored in C:\Draw6wm. The installation adds the CorelDRAW! 6 Working Model to your Start, Programs menu with options for opening or uninstalling the model.

Index

Symbols

* (asterisk) wildcard, 51
256-color dithering, 68
2D
    effects; PHOTO-PAINT 6, 569
    Primitive Text tool (DREAM 3D; Free Form Model, 608
3D
    effects; PHOTO-PAINT 6, 570
    Paint Brush tool (DREAM 3D; Perspective Toolboxr, 607
    Paint Shape tool (DREAM 3D; Perspective Toolboxr, 607
    Shape tools (DREAM 3D; Perspective Toolbox), 605
    Text tool (DREAM 3D; Perspective Toolbox), 605
    Text tool (MOTION 3D toolbox), 617
    Wells for Color Palettes, 71

A

About CorelDRAW! command (Help menu), 204
accelerator keys, *see* keyboard shortcuts
accessing menus, 664

activation controls, CAPTURE 6, 628-630
    hot keys, 628
    mouse-trigger options, 630
    timing controls, 629-630
Add Colors button (Uniform Fill dialog box), 237
Add line button (Node Edit roll-up), 192
Add nodes button (Node Edit roll-up), 192
Add Page Border button, 61
Add Page Frame option (Page Setting dialog box), 61
Add Perspective command (Effects menu), 167, 315
Add Presets button (Envelope roll-up), 212
Add to Selection button (Search by Properties roll-up), 196
adjust filter (PHOTO-PAINT 6), 570
Adobe Illustrator, exporting, 497
Advanced options, 71-72
    command (Options menu), 149
    File Backup options, 71-72
    Pop-up menus, 72
    proofreading utilities, 152-153

Save and Restore feature, 72
Advanced Separations Settings dialog box, 531-532
Align & Distribute roll-up, 108, 204, 322
    Snap to Grid option, 326
Align button (Node Edit roll-up), 192
Align command (Arrange menu), 324
aligning
    justified, 650
    objects, 322-326
    text, 166
Alignment preferences menu, 322
Alignment tabs, 112
Always Provide a Spelling Alternative option (proofreading option), 152
Ami Professional, exporting, 497
animation
    files, capturing, 633
    settings, CAPTURE 6, 637
    toolbar (PRESENTS 6), 582
    view, 580
        tools, 588
annotations, 596
Application Launcher button, 116

applications
Corel CAPTURE 6, 626-628
Corel Multimedia Manager, 625-626
MOTION 3D, 615-625
PHOTO-PAINT 6, 555
Arrange menu commands, 107-108
Align, 324
Break Apart, 205
Capture, 627
Combine, 208
Convert to Curves, 205
Group, 21, 204
Intersection, 343
keyboard shortcuts, 661
Separate, 162, 321, 367
Transform, 401
Transform Roll-up, 35
Trim, 341
Ungroup, 21, 204, 368
Weld, 338
arrow controls, 266-267
Arrow flyout (MOTION 3D toolbox), 617
arrow tab, paragraph text, 133
Arrowhead Editor, 267
arrowheads, editing, 267
artistic text, 125-130
converting to paragraph text, 158
creating, 126-127
curves, breaking, 205
editing, 127-131
character attributes, 127
keyboard shortcuts (table 5.1), 140-142
effects (PHOTO-PAINT 6), 571
envelopes applying to, 164-166
finding, 157
formatting
Artistic Text tool, 137
Shape tool, 138-139
size, 137

perspective applying to, 166-168
resizing handles, 131
setting default, 133
skewing handles, 131
Artistic Text tool, 13, 125
creating artistic text, 126-127
editing artistic text, 127-131
formatting artistic text, 137
Arts & Letters, exporting, 497
Artwork Settings dialog box, 611
ascenders, 643
aspect ratio, 643
asterisk (*) wildcard, 51
attributes, 643
character attributes, editing artistic text, 127
text, setting, 128
auto increase flatness, printing, 515
auto trapping, 531
Auto-Backup feature, 71
Auto-Blend button (Uniform Fill dialog box), 236
Auto-Join feature, 75, 404
Auto-Panning feature, 69
Auto-Reduce feature (Powerline Node Edit roll-up), 76, 373
nodes button (Node Edit roll-up), 192
auto-spreading, 531
auto-trace, objects, 643
Autobackup function, customizing, 474
AutoCAD
exporting, 497, 501-502
filters
DXF filter, 482
exporting files, 491-492
importing files, 491-492
troubleshooting, 491-492
Automatch option (Color Wizard), 429
automatic naming (CAPTURE 6), 637
Automatically Center New Powerclip feature, 67-68

autoshapes flyout (PRESENTS 6), 581
AutoTrace Feature, 403-404
AutoTrace Tracking feature, 75, 404

B

Back Parallel option (extrusion), 218
Back Up function, customizing, 474
Background Library (View menu; PRESENTS 6), 584
background view (PRESENTS 6), 580
scenes, 584
backspace key, 53
backups, 71
baselines, 643
leading, 650
basic shape flyout (PRESENTS 6), 581
BBS (Bulletin Board Service), 545, 643
Behind Fill option (Outline Pen dialog box), 267
bezier curves, 643
Bezier tool (DREAM 3D; Free Form Modeler Toolbox), 95, 607
closed objects, creating, 179
options, 74-76
tools, 643
Big Back option (extrusion), 217
Big Front option (extrusion), 218
Bitmap Color Mask Roll-up, 110
Bitmap command (View menu), 395
Bitmap (BMP) format, 388
bitmaps, 388-396, 644
AutoTrace feature, 403-404
bitmapping
raster graphics, 653
texture fills, 656

color, 392
  applying, 402-403
cropping, 397-400
files, 494
  exporting, 498-499
  importing images, 394, 407-408, 455-456
fills, 403
  lighting controls, 313
formats, 388-389
  Bitmap (BMP) format, 388
  Compatible Bitmap Formats (table 11.1), 388-389
  Tagged Image Format (TIF), 388
headers, 393-395
images
  cropping, 408
  editing, 397-407
  importing, 394, 407-408, 455-456
  loading, 240, 241
  loading into mixing area, 241
  resampling, 408
objects, 22
PNTAREA.BMP, 454
print jobs, 536
printing, 539
  font limits, 534
  font size threshold, 535
properties, 404-405
resolution, 392-393
rotating, 400-402
sampling colors from images, 454-456
size, 389-391
  pixel grids, 389
  pixels, 389
skewing, 400-402
Text-Wrapping option (General tab), 406-407
two-color pattern fills, 242-247
  assigning patterns, 244-245

creating patterns, 245-247
editing patterns, 246-247
importing images into, 247
resolution, 247
viewing, 395-397
  high resolution, 396
  Visible Bitmap Display command, 396
bleeding, 545, 644
Blend Color tab (Blend roll-up), 273
Blend command, assigning a path, 283-285
Blend Object tab (Blend roll-up), 273
Blend Path menu
  commands
    Detach From Path, 284
    Full Path, 284
    New Path, 284
    Rotate All, 285
    Show Path, 284
Blend roll-up, 272
  blend color tab, 273
  blend object tab, 273
  editing object blend, 287
  mapping options tab, 273-274
blending
  applying Powerline effects, 300-301
  blends, 644
    fountain fills, 644
    mixing area, 651
    see also contours
  cloning, 289-290
    troubleshooting, 290
  colors, 235, 452-456
    Add Colors button (Uniform Fill dialog box), 237
    Auto-Blend button, 236
    color wheel, 254
    creating mixed colors, 238
    fountain fills, 250-258

    Mixing Area color picker, 237
    Paint Brush tool, 237
    saving mixed colors, 238
    saving mixing area, 240
    selecting mixed colors, 238
  compound blend, 292-294
  controls, 274-275
  copying, 289
  defined, 271-272
  font styles, 295-296
  highlighting, 296-299
  objects, 276
    looping, 282
    nodes, 279
    similar, 282-283
    troubleshooting, 283
  preparing to create, 275-279
  reverse highlighting, 299
  rotating, 280
  scales, 276-279
  spacing, 276-279
  splitting, 274, 290-291
  Start/End Path buttons, 286
blurring filters (PHOTO-PAINT 6), 572
books, imposition, 64
borders (CAPTURE 6), setting, 638
bounding boxes (bitmaps)
  cropping adjustments, 399
  see also envelopes
Break Apart button (Node Edit roll-up), 192
Break Apart command (Arrange menu), 205
Break node button (Node Edit roll-up), 192
breaking
  curves, 205-208
  object types, 206-207
  roll-ups, 470
brighten lens, 377
Browse 3D Clipart command (File menu), 608

Brush tool, 453
    mixing area, 651
bullet style (Powerline
roll-up), 357
Bulletin Board Service (BBS),
see BBS (Bulletin Board
Service)
bullets, 112
    paragraph text, 147
bureaus service, printing,
543-544

C

calibrating
    monitors, 426-427, 432
    printers, 433
    scanners, 431-432
calligraphic, 644
Calligraphic text option
(Clipboard), 170
calligraphy controls, 265-266
caps, lines, 265
capstan imagesetters, 549
Capture 6, 626-628
    activation controls, 628-630
        hot keys, 628
        mouse-trigger
            options, 630
        timing controls, 629-630
    destination controls,
    632-633
        capturing to clip-
            board, 633
        capturing to file, 633
        capturing to printer, 633
        OLE automation, 633
    file controls, 635-637
        animation settings, 637
        automatic naming, 637
        setting destination
            directory, 637
    image controls, 634-635
        custom resolution
            settings, 634
        printer settings, 634
        resizing captured
            images, 635

screen settings, 634
        selecting maintain aspect
            ratio, 635
    preferences controls, 638
        border settings, 638
        cursors, 638
    source controls, 630-632
        client window, 631
        current window, 631
        elliptical area, 632
        freehand area, 632
        full screen, 631
        rectangular area, 631
    starting, 627-628
Capture command
(Applications menu), 627
Capture dialog box, 627
CD-ROM
    clip art, 608-609
    CorelDRAW! 6, 608-609
CDs, CorelDRAW! 6, 669-672
centering objects, 67
Change Case command
(Text menu), 158
Channels roll-up (PHOTO-
PAINT 6 roll-ups), 565
character attributes, editing
artistic text, 127
Character Attributes dialog
box, 112, 127
Character command
(Text menu), 127, 133
characters, fonts, 648
Chart command (Insert menu;
PRESENTS 6), 586
Chart Type dialog box, 586
charts
    CorelCHART, 587
    slides, adding with
        PRESENTS 6, 586-587
child objects, 644
chokes, 655
chromaticity, defined, 429
Clear All button
    Guidelines Setup dialog
        box, 333
    Search by Properties
        roll-up, 196

Clear button (Guidelines
Setup dialog box), 333
Clear Contour command
(Effects menu), 321
Clear Envelope command
(Effects menu), 217
Clear Perspective command
(Effects menu), 317
clearing
    contours from objects, 321
    envelope effects, 217
    perspective from objects, 317
clip art, CD-ROM, 608-609
Clipboard option
(Text tab), 170
clipboards
    capturing to, 633
    OLE, 508-509
Clockwise color blend option
(Contour Color tab), 321
Clone command
    Edit menu, 66, 197
    Effects menu, 321, 644
Clone control,
customizing, 475
Clone tool (PHOTO-PAINT 6
Toolbox), 565
cloned objects, 22
cloning, 644
    blends, 289-290
    contours, 321
    extrusions, 315
    objects, 197-198
        reverting
            transformations, 198
        troubleshooting, 198
closing files, 56
CMY color model, 437-457
CMYK (cyan, magenta,
yellow, black)
    255-color model, 438-457
    colors, cyan, 645
    model, 438-457, 644
color add lens, 379
Color Blend mixer, 453-454
Color Blend tools, 235-239
Color Fill tab (Extrude
roll-up), 313-327

color gamut
  defined, 429
  mapping, 429
color limit lens, 379
Color Manager
  color system profiles, 427-428
  command (Tools menu), 428, 435
  system color profile, 549
Color Mask roll-up (PHOTO-PAINT 6 roll-ups), 565
color models, *see* models (color)
Color Options menu commands, Load Bitmap, 241
Color options tab (Extrude roll-up), 221-222
color palette, *see* palettes (color)
Color Palette command (View menu), 235, 240, 444
Color Picker tool, 452
color space, defined, 429
color wheel, 254
Color Wizard
  assigning color system profiles, 435-436
  creating color system profiles, 428-434
  creating printer profiles, 434
  creating scanner profiles, 430-431
  system color profile, 549
  troubleshooting color system profiles, 436
colorimeter, 429
colors
  3D Wells for Color Palettes, 71
  adjust filters, 572
  bitmaps, 392
    applying, 402-403
    grayscale images, 392
    sampling colors from, 454-456
  calibration issues, 426-427
    monitor calibration, 426-427
  chromaticity, 429

colorimeter, 429
composites, 644
continuous tones, 645
contour color options, 320-322
custom colors, 235-239
cyan, 645
dynamic range, 429
fills
  bitmaps, 403
  default, 229-230
  extrusion, 313-327
  fountain fills, 250-258
  full-color pattern fills, 249
  postscript fills, 250
  selecting, 37-41
  Special Fill roll-up, 260-262
  texture fills, 258-260
  troubleshooting, 234
  two-color bitmap pattern, 242-247
  uniform fills, 231-232
  vector pattern fills, 247-248
gamut, 429
  mapping, 429
K-curve, 429
mixers, 452-456
  Color Blend mixer, 453-454
  Mixing Area mixer, 452-453
  troubleshooting, 454
mixing, 235
  Add Colors button (Uniform Fill dialog box), 237
  Auto-Blend button, 236
  color wheel, 254
  creating mixed colors, 238
  fountain fills, 250-258
  mixing area, 651
  Mixing Area color picker, 237
  Paint Brush tool, 237
  saving, 238

saving mixing area, 240
selecting mixed colors, 238
models, 232-234, 436-443
  assigning to objects, 233
  CMY, 437-457
  CMYK, 438-457, 644
  CMYK255, 438-457
  defined, 443
  Grayscale, 233, 442
  HLS, 440-457
  HSB, 439
  L*A*B, 441-457
  Registration, 233
  RGB, 438-457
  selecting, 233
  YIQ, 441
objects
  extrusion, 221-222
  as search parameters, 195
outlines, 268-269
palettes, 443-451, 644
  commands, 235
  creating custom palettes, 449-451
  custom palettes, 239-244
  customizing, 239, 471-472
  defined, 443
  Focoltone palette, 234, 647
  prioritizing colors, 451
  process color palettes, 443
  saving, 238, 450
  selecting, 235, 445
  spot palettes, 443
  third-party color matching systems, 444
  Trumatch palette, 234
Pantone, 652
paper, selecting, 61
Preset roll-ups, 415
printers, troubleshooting management system, 430
process, 644, 653
process color palettes
  Focoltone, 447
  Pantone, 445-447

SpectraMaster, 449
Trumatch, 447-448
profiles, 427-428
assigning, 435-436
creating with Color
Wizard, 428-434
target original, 428
troubleshooting, 436
registration, 442
RGB (red, green, blue), 654
saturation mapping, 429
separations, 548, 655
plates, 652
solid, 655
space, 429
spectrophotometer, 429
spot palettes
Focoltone, 447
Pantone, 445-447
SpectraMaster, 449
Trumatch, 447-448
swatches, 234
system profiles, 656
TAC (total area
coverage), 429
transform filters (PHOTO-
PAINT 6), 573
trapping, 445
TruMatch, 657
UCR (unser color
removal), 429
white point, 429
columns, 644
paragraph text, 134-135
Columns command
(Text menu), 134
Columns dialog box, 134
Columns tab, 112
Combine command
(Arrange menu), 208
combining
curves, 208-211
extrusions, 227
objects, 211
Command Recorder roll-up
(PHOTO-PAINT 6 roll-up),
566

commands
Applications menu,
Capture, 627
Arrange menu
Align, 324
Break Apart, 205
Combine, 208
Convert to Curves, 205
Group, 21, 204
Intersection, 343
Separate, 162, 274,
321, 367
Transform, 401
Transform roll-up, 35
Trim, 341
Ungroup, 21, 204, 368
Weld, 338
assigning keyboard
shortcuts to, 464
Blend Path menu
Full Path, 284
New Path, 284
Rotate All, 285
Show Path, 284
Color Options menu,
Load Bitmap, 241
color palettes, 235
Detach From Path
(Blend Path menu), 284
Edit menu
Clone, 66, 197
Copy, 101
Copy Properties
From, 101
Cut, 101
Duplicate, 66
Insert New Object, 506
Link, 507
Paste, 101
Paste Special, 101, 508
Redo, 100
Select All, 21, 56
Select by Properties, 87,
101, 196
Undo, 100, 367
Effects menu
Add Perspective, 167, 315
Clear Contour, 321

Clear Envelope, 217
Clear Perspective, 317
Clone, 321, 644
Contours, 418
Envelope, 135
Envelopes, 164
Place Inside Con-
tainer, 67
Powerclip, 347
Powerline, 362
Remove Extrusion, 306
File menu
Browse 3D Clipart, 608
Export, 171, 495
Import, 347, 407,
482, 614
New, 12, 44, 100, 462
Open, 44, 462
Print, 476, 517
Print Merge, 543
Save, 49
Save All, 57, 86, 100, 463
Save As, 49
Send, 100
Help menu
About CorelDRAW!, 204
Help Topics, 16
Tutor Notes, 17
Tutorial, 17
What's This?, 17
Insert menu (PRESENTS 6)
Chart, 586
Sound, 591
Video, 591
Layout menu
Grid and Ruler Setup, 335
Grid Setup, 327
Guidelines Setup, 23, 330
Layers Manager, 336
Page Layout, 59
Snap to Guidelines, 333
Snap to None, 107
Styles, 105, 144
Nudge, 67
Object menu
Curve Properties, 118
Ellipse Properties, 119

Polygon Properties, 120
Rectangle Properties, 119
Text Properties, 120
Options menu
Advanced Options, 149
Create New
Dictionary, 150
Explain Error, 149
Formality Level, 150
Personal Dictionary, 150
Rule Manager, 149
Undo Edit, 149
Polygon menu, Star, 187
presets, 411-412
applying, 414
functions, 412-413
removing, 423-424
program, scripts, 655
Special menu,
Stagehands, 623
Start menu, Run, 672
Text menu
Change Case, 158
Character, 127, 133
Columns, 134
Convert to Artistic
Text, 158
Convert to Paragraph
Text, 158
Edit, 132
Find, 157
Fit Text to Path, 159
Paragraph, 144
Replace, 157
Straighten Text, 162
Text Options, 168
Thesaurus, 155
Tools menu
Color Manager, 428, 435
Create, 173
Customize, 461
Options, 47
Presets, 414
Task Progress, 473
Tools menu (PHOTO-PAINT
6), Customize, 568

View menu
Bitmap, 395
Color Palette, 235,
240, 444
Editable Wireframe, 362
Properties, 76, 147, 187,
195, 476
Ruler, 139
Screen Redraw, 102
Status Bar, 80
Styles, 147
Toolbars, 28, 78, 460, 568
Visible Bitmap
Display, 396
View menu (MOTION 3D),
Timelines, 620
View menu (PRESENTS 6)
Background Library, 584
Slide, 592
Timelines, 593
see also functions
**communications, faxing
facsimile, 647**
**Compatible Bitmap Formats
(table 11.1), 388-389**
composites, 545, 644
separations, 548
compressions, 637, 644
packages, 545
programs
PKZip, 547, 652
**computers, downloading
files, 646**
conical fountain fills, 252
Connector tool, 95
Constrain Angle feature, 67
constrains, 645
context-sensitive help, 17
continuous tones, 545, 645
**Contour Color Options tab,
320-322**
Contour controls, 319
**Contour Properties Tab
(Contours roll-up), 319-320**
contours, 645
applying to objects, 318-319
copying/cloning, 321
editing, 321

objects
converting, 321
removing, 321
**Contours command
(Effects menu), 418**
Contours roll-up, 319-320
control objects, blends, 644
control points, 645
controls
arrow controls, 266-267
calligraphy controls, 265-266
CAPTURE 6
activation controls,
628-630
destination controls,
632-633
file controls, 635-637
image controls, 634-635
preferences controls, 638
source controls, 630-632
timing controls, 629-630
Contour controls, 319
corner controls, 264
cropping (Import dialog
box), 408
Customize dialog box, 461
customizing, 475
Envelope roll-up feature, 164
Extrude controls, 217-227
First Tile Offset controls, 243
hidden interface, 666
layout controls, labels, 63
line cap controls, 265
paper control (Page Settings
dialog box), 60
paragraph text,
columns, 134
pen controls, 262-269
perspective controls,
315-318
presets controls (Fountain
Fill dialog box), 258
resampling (Import dialog
box), 408
Text tab, 169-170
see also tabs
**Convert to Artistic Text
command (Text menu), 158**

Convert to Curves command (Arrange menu), 205

Convert to Paragraph Text command (Text menu), 158

converting

contours, 321

fonts into curves, 516

objects into curves, 205

paragraph text into curves, 516

text, 158

into curves, 516

Copy command (Edit menu), 101

Copy Properties From command (Edit menu), 101

copying contours, 321

Corel CAPTURE 6, *see* **CAPTURE 6**

Corel Magazine sampler, 671

Corel MOTION 3D, *see* **MOTION 3D**

Corel Multimedia Manager, *see* **Multimedia Manager**

Corel PHOTO-PAINT 6, *see* **PHOTO-PAINT 6**

Corel PRESENTS 6, *see* **PRESENTS 6**

Corel Ventura, exporting, 497

CorelCHART, 587

CorelDRAW! 6

CD-ROM version, 608-609

CDs, 669-672

customizing

color palettes, 471-472

customizing features, 474-477

keyboard shortcuts, 462-465

menus, 465-467

roll-ups, 468-471

Task Progress feature, 472-474

toolbars, 460-462

help system, 16-17

context-sensitive help, 17

help topics, 16

printing help topics, 16

tutor notes, 17

tutorial, 17

installing, 672

keyboard shortcuts, 659-660

Arrange commands, 661

Edit commands, 660

File functions, 660

Layout commands, 661

Text commands, 661

tools, 665

Tools commands, 664

View commands, 661

Window commands, 664

Magazine sampler, 671

menus, 99-116

new features, 85-88

customization of toolbars and menus, 116

object properties, 117-120

new tools, 88-98

options, *see also* options, 65-77

PHOTO-PAINT 6, 555

status bars, customizing, 80-83

toolbars, customizing, 78-80

welcome screen, 46-47

CORELFLT.INI file, 485

CorelMAP, 587

CORELPRN file, 539-540

CorelTRACE EPS filter, 493

corner controls, 264

Corner Threshold feature, 75, 404

corners

Corner Threshold, 75

rectangles

editing, 184

resizing rectangles, 185

Counter-clockwise color blend (Contour Color Options tab), 321

crashes, 71

Create Camara tool (DREAM 3D; Perspective Toolbox), 606

Create command (Tools menu), 173

Create From button (Envelope roll-up), 212

Create Lighting tool (DREAM 3D; Perspective Toolbox), 606

Create New Dictionary command (Options menu), 150

crop marks, 545, 645

Crop tool (PHOTO-PAINT 6 Toolbox), 560

cropping

bitmaps, 397-400, 408

PHOTO-PAINT 6 crop tool, 560

printing crop marks, 526

Cropping dialog box, 408

Crosshair Cursor option, 74

crosshairs, 545

CT scan (continuous tones), 545, 645

cursor, 74

Curve, Bezier Tool Properties dialog box, 95

Curve Properties (objects), 118

Curve Properties command (Object menu), 118

Curve Properties dialog box, 118

curves

bezier curves, 643

bezier tool, 643

combining, 208-211

multiple curves, 209-211

two curves, 208-209

control points, 645

converting

fonts into, 516

objects into, 205

paragraph text into, 516

text into, 516

corner controls, 264

cusped curves (Powerline Node Edit roll-up), 373

editing, 181, 193

Node Edit roll-up, 191-193

flatness, 546, 647

line cap controls, 265

manipulating, 193
nodes, 651
    Node Edit Buttons
        and their Functions
        (table 6.1), 192
normal curves (Powerline
    Node Edit roll-up), 373
objects, 205-211
    breaking, 205-208
    combining, 208-211
    combining multiple
        curves, 209-211
    combining two curves,
        208-209
powerlines, 653
resolution, exporting
    files, 492
sine curve (Powerline Node
    Edit roll-up), 373
smoothed curve (Powerline
    Node Edit roll-up), 373
**Cusp node button (Node Edit
roll-up), 192**
cusps, 645
Custom Color Map lens, 110
custom colors, 235-239
    adding to Color blend
        display, 239
    creating, 238
    heat map, 382
custom fountains, 254
**Custom Label preview
window, 63**
custom menus, 116
custom palettes
    creating, 239-244, 449-451
    prioritizing colors, 451
    sampling colors from bitmap
        images, 454-456
    saving, 450
custom toolbars, 116
    creating, 460-461
    removing, 462
**Customize command
(Tools menu), 461, 568**
Customize dialog box, 461
**Customize Label button (Page
Settings dialog box), 62**

**Customize Label dialog
box, 62**
Customize tab, 471-472
customizing
    color palettes, 471-472
    controls, 475
    CorelDRAW!
        color palettes, 239,
            471-472
        customizing features,
            474-477
        keyboard shortcuts,
            462-465
        menus, 465-467
        roll-ups, 468-471
        Task Progress feature,
            472-474
        toolbars, 460-462
    fountain fills, 476
    functions
        Save, Backup and
            Autobackup, 474
        start up functions, 474
    keyboard shortcuts, 462-465
    labels, 62-64
    menus, 465-467
    objects, 476
    pop-up menus, 474
    roll-ups, 468-471
        breaking, 470
        grouping, 469
        Left-Align, 468
        naming, 471
        Right-Align, 468
    screen resolution, 476
    status bars, 80-83
    Task Progress feature,
        472-474
    toolbars, 78-80, 460-462
    tools, 475
        Panning tool, 476
        Zooming tool, 476
**Cut command (Edit
menu), 101**
cyan, 645

D

data processing, 548, 646
defaults, 545, 645
    fills, 229
        changing, 230
        texture fills, 260
    greek text, 170
    Outline Pen, changing, 179
    setting
        artistic text, 133
        Auto-Reduce feature, 76
        CorelDRAW!, 76
        paragraph text, 133
deleting
    contours from objects, 321
    envelope effects, 217
    extrusions, 306
    guidelines, 333
    labels, 64
    page frames, 61
    perspective from objects, 317
    toolbars, custom
        toolbars, 462
**Delrina Perform,
exporting, 497**
density, 545, 645
depth of objects, *see* **extrusion**
**Depth tab (extrusions),
308-309**
descenders, 645
deselecting, 645
    High Resolution Display
        option (bitmaps), 396
    objects, 21, 179
**desktop publishing (DTP),
545, 646**
**destination controls
(CAPTURE 6), 632-633**
    capturing to animation
        file, 633
    capturing to clipboard, 633
    capturing to file, 633
    capturing to printer, 633
    OLE automation, 633
**destination directory
(CAPTURE 6), setting, 637**

Detach From Path command (Blend Path menu), 284
Detail properties (objects), 117
Detail Properties dialog box, 117
Details function, 46
device driver, 646
device options, 521
devices, output, 648
dialog boxes
    Advanced Separations Settings, 531-532
    Artwork Settings, 611
    Capture, 627
    Character Attributes, 112, 127
    Chart Type, 586
    Columns, 134
    Cropping, 408
    Curve, Bezier Tool Properties, 95
    Curve Properties, 118
    Customize, 461
    Customize Label, 62
    Detail Properties, 117
    Edit Layout Style, 528
    Edit Positioning, 529
    Edit Preset, 418
    Edit Text, 127, 132
    Ellipse Properties, 119
    Emboss, 558
    Environment Properties, 623
    Fill Color, 417
    Fill Properties, 118
    Fill roll-up, 39
    Filter Effects, 569
    Fountain Fill, 251
    Grid & Ruler Setup, 327
    Grid Box Tool Properties, 188
    Guidelines Setup, 23, 330
    Import, 482-483
    Make Movie, 625
    Node Edit Tool Properties, 76
    Object Properties, 183, 195, 592, 622

Open Drawing, 45-46, 50, 52-53
Outline Color, 269, 449, 452
Outline Pen, 179, 262, 262-269
Page Settings, 59-65
Page Setup, 104
Paragraph, 144
Paste Special, 509
Point At, 620
Polygon properties, 120
Polygon Tool Properties, 187
PostScript pattern, 250
PostScript Preferences, 538-539
Preferences, 56-57, 76
Print, 517-519
Print Options, 521
Properties, 519-520
Rectangle Object Properties, 96
roll-ups tab, 468
Ruler and Grid, 327
Save Drawing, 54
Save Extrude Preset, 307
shortcuts, 36
Spelling, 149-150
Spiral Tool Properties, 188
Stagehands, 623
Task Progress, 473
Text Columns, 112
Text Options, 169-170
Text Properties, 120
Texture Fill, 259, 260
Tool Properties, 88, 91
Toolbar, 79
Toolbars, 460
True Type Export, 172
Two-Color Bitmap Pattern, 242, 247
Two-color bitmap pattern Editor, 245
Type Assist, 156
Uniform Fill, 39, 230-240, 436, 444, 449, 452
Vector Pattern, 247
Welcome, 99

didots, 645
digital
    halftones, 646
        defined, 393
    images, *see also* images, 646
Digital Brush tool, 452
Dimension toolbar, 94
Dimensioning tools, 94-95
dimensions
    bitmaps, 389-391
    entities, exporting files, 492
    pages, editing, 61
directories, 646
    destination, setting, 637
    names, 53
Display Chapters During Manual Kerning option (Text tab), 170
Display name function (status bar), 83
Display options, 68-71
Display Pop-Up Menu option (Customize tab), 472
Display Rows option (Customize tab), 472
displaying
    bitmaps, 395-397
        high resolution, 396
        Visible Bitmap Display command, 396
    fonts, 169
    keyboard shortcuts, 463
    Object Properties dialog box, 96
    rulers, 139
    text, paragraph text, 133
    toolbars, 78-79, 461
    View Manager roll-up, 93
Distribute preferences menu, 322
dithering, 68
dockable toolbars, 102
documents
    flatbed scanner, 647
    landscapes, 650
    line art, 650
    opening, 11-12

orientations, portraits, 653
printing options, 532-533
see also files
DOS (disk operating system),
directory, 646
dot
gains, 545, 646
patterns
bitmaps, 644
halftones, 648
high resolution
(high res), 649
moires, 651
dots per inch (DPI), 392,
545, 646
Double-arc button
(Envelope roll-up), 212
double-clicking (mouse), 646
downloading files, 545, 646
DPI (dots per inch), 392,
545, 646
drag and drop
font substitution, 51
moving files, 50
objects, 30
OLE, 510-511
opening files, 49-51
DRAW! Objects When
Moving option, 73
drawing
calligraphic, 644
color, *see* colors
creating, 370
curves
bezier curves, 643
bezier tool, 643
control points, 645
editing, 181, 193
manipulating, 193
ellipses
creating, 180
editing, 185-186
grids, 188, 335
editing, 190
ungrouping, 190
guidelines, *see* guidelines

layers, 336-338
creating, 337
settings, 337-338
lines, 178-179
editing, 181
nodes, cusps, 645
objects
creating, 15
finding number of, 204
shaping, 306-321
see also objects
rectangles, 180
editing, 183-185
in grids, 190
using rulers, *see* rulers
screen drawing,
fountain fills, 255
searching drawings
by properties, 196-197
colors, 195
fill types, 195
object type
parameters, 195
outlines, 195
Select by Properties
roll-up, 195-199
special effects, 195
spirals, 188
editing, 190
stars, 187-188
reshpaing, 189-190
text, 13-14
DREAM 3D
exporting, 612-614
file format options, 611
Free Form Modeler Toolbox,
607-608
importing, 612-614
Perspective Toolbox,
604-607
setting options, 612-614
sizing, 610-611
windows
Hierarchy window, 602
Objects Browser
window, 603
Perspective window, 602
Shaders Browser
window, 603

drivers, 545, 646
dropouts, 646
drum model imagesetter, 549
drum scanners, 545, 646
DTP (desktop publishing),
545, 646
Duplicate command
(Edit menu), 66
Duplicate control,
customizing, 475
dynamic range, defined, 429

E

Edge Pad options (fountain
fills), 257
Edit command (Text
menu), 132
Edit Layout Style dialog
box, 528
Edit menu, 100-101
Edit menu commands
Clone, 66, 197
Copy, 101
Copy Properties From, 101
Cut, 101
Duplicate, 66
Insert New Object, 506
keyboard shortcuts, 660
Link, 507
Paste, 101
Paste Special, 101, 508
Redo, 100
Select All, 21, 56
Select by Properties, 87,
101, 196
Undo, 100, 367
Edit Object tool (MOTION 3D
toolbox), 617
Edit Positioning dialog
box, 529
Edit Preset dialog box, 418
Edit Resolution option, 77
Edit Text dialog box, 127, 132
Edit Text on Screen option
(Text tab), 169
Editable Preview view, 25

Editable Wireframe command (View menu), 362

editing
arrowheads, 267
artistic text
keyboard shortcuts (table 5.1), 140-142
bitmaps, 397-407
contours, 321
curves, 181, 193
Node Edit roll-up, 191-193
ellipses, 185-186
lines, 181
objects
manipulating handles, 318
properties, 195
pages, dimensions, 61
paragraph text
keyboard shortcuts (table 5.1), 140-142
PHOTO-PAINT 6, 556-558
Powerlines, 370-374
preset roll-ups, 416
preset scripts, 421-422
rectangles, 183-185
spirals, 190
text
artistic text, 127-131
Edit Text on Screen option (Text tab), 169
keyboard shortcuts, 662-663
paragraph text, 131-132
two-color bitmap patterns, 246
see also transforming

Editor toolbar (MOTION 3D), 617

editors
Memo, 114
MOTION 3D
Lathe Editor, 618
Object Editor, 619
Node Editor, 370-374
PRESENTS 6, Wave Editor, 591

Effect menu commands
Clear Perspective, 317
Powerline, 362

Effect tool (PHOTO-PAINT 6 Toolbox), 564

effects
contours, *see* contours
envelopes, 135
alignment of text, 166
applying to artistic text, 164-166
applying to paragraph text, 168
clearing effects, 217
handles, 213
mapping options, 215
objects, applying, 211-217
Shape tool, 165
extrusions
copying/cloning, 315
creating presets, 306-315
Depth tab, 308-309
lighting controls, 311-313
merging, 227
minimum extrude facet size, 308
objects, *see* extrusions, objects
removing, 306
rotation, 309
saving, 307
vanishing points, 309
lenses, 374-375
brighten lens, 377
color add lens, 379
color limit lens, 379
custom color heat map, 382
fisheye lens, 383
heat map lens, 381
invert lens, 378
magnify lens, 377
removing, 384
tinted grayscale lens, 380
transparency lens, 376
wireframe lens, 383

objects
envelopes, 211-217
extrusion, 217-227
perspective
applying to artistic text, 166-168
see also perspective
Powerclip effects, 346-352
Powerlines, 354-374
applying, 362-366
PRESENTS 6, 591-592

Effects Menu, 109-110

Effects menu commands
Add Perspective, 167, 315
Clear Contour, 321
Clear Envelope, 217
Clone, 321, 644
Contours, 418
Envelope, 135
Envelopes, 164
Place Inside Container, 67
Powerclip, 347
Remove Extrusion, 306

Effects menu roll-ups
Blend, 272
Lens, 375
Powerline, 354

Elastic Mode feature (Node Edit roll-up), 192

electronic files, headers, 649

elements, interfacing, 649

Ellipse properties (objects), 119

Ellipse Properties command (Object menu), 119

Ellipse Properties dialog box, 119

Ellipse tool, 96, 180

ellipses
creating, 180
editing, 185-186
exporting files, AutoCAD filters, 492

embedding, 652

Emboss dialog box, 558

emulsions, 546, 646

Encapsulated PostScript (EPS) filters, exporting, 493, 499-500, 647

End Task button (Task Progress feature), 473

entity files, exporting, 492

Envelope command (Effects menu), 135

Envelope roll-up, 136
  applying envelopes to objects, 211-217
  controls, 164
  Keep Lines option, 164
  mapping options, 164-165, 215-217

envelopes, 135
  alignment of text, 166
  applying to artistic text, 164-166
  applying to paragraph text, 168
  clearing effects, 217
  handles, 213
  objects
    applying, 211-217
    mapping options, 215
  Shape tool, 165

Envelopes command (Effects menu), 164

Environment Properties dialog box, 623

EPS (encapsulated Post-Script), 647
  filters, 493, 499-500

Eraser tool, 89-90, 561

Error Language option (proofreading option), 152

Explain Error command (Options menu), 149

Export command (File menu), 171, 495

export filters, 482, 495-506

export filters, *see* exporting files, filters

exporting files
  AutoCAD, 501-502
  bitmap files, 498-499
  curve resolution, 492
  dimension entities, 492

DREAM 3D, 612-614

ellipses, 492

Encapsulated PostScript (EPS) filters, 499-500

entity files, 492

export filters, 491-492, 495-506

fonts, 505-506

formats, 496-498

HPGL (Hewlett-Packard Graphical Language) filters, 503

Import/Export Formats 489-491

JPEG (Joint Photographers' Expert Group) files, 502-506

lines, 492

Macintosh PICT (PCT) files, 506

MPEG files, 502-506

nested files, 547, 651

nested fonts, 547

SCODL export filter, 500

text anomolies, 492

text justification, 492

three-dimensional images, 492

troubleshooting AutoCAD filters, 491-492

extensions, 546, 647
  handles, 649

Extrude Facet Size. Min. option, 76

Extrude feature, 76

Extrude flyout menu, 227

Extrude Object tool (MOTION 3D toolbox), 617

Extrude roll-up, 109, 221-227
  color fill controls, 313-327
  creating extrusion presets, 306
  lighting controls, 311-313

Extrude Wizard, 226-227

extruding (objects), *see also* extrusions, 306-315

extrusions, 217-227
  copying/cloning, 315
  creating presets, 306-315

Depth tab, 308-309
lighting controls, 311-313
merging, 227
minimum extrude facet size, 308
objects
  color options, 221-222
  Extrude Wizard, 226-227
  light sources, 222-225
  maintaining, 227
  preset extrusions, 226
  rotating, 225
  saving, 227
  types of extrusion, 217-219
  vanishing points, 220-221
removing, 306
rotation, 309
saving, 307
vanishing points, 309

Eyedropper tool, 452
  loading bitmap images, 241
  PHOTO-PAINT 6 Toolbox, 561

F

Facing Pages option (Page Setting dialog box), 61

faxing facsimile, 647

fields, 647

File Backup options, 71-72

file controls
  CAPTURE 6, 635-637
    animation settings, 637
    automatic naming, 637
    setting destination directory, 637

File functions, keyboard shortcuts, 660

File menu, 99-100

File menu commands
  Browse 3D Clipart, 608
  Export, 171, 495
  Import, 347, 407, 482, 614
  New, 12, 44, 100, 462
  Open, 44, 462

Print, 476, 517
Print Merge, 543
Save, 49
Save All, 57, 86, 100, 463
Save As, 49
Send, 100
File Transer Protocol (FTP),
see ftp (File Transer Protocol)
**File Types and Extensions
(table 15.1), 484-485**
files
animation, capturing, 633
bitmap files, 494
exporting, 498-499
see also bitmaps
capturing to, 633
closing, 56
compressing, PKZip,
547, 652
CORELFLT.INI file, 485
CORELPRN file, 539-540
directory, 646
downloading, 545, 646
DREAM 3D
file format options, 611
importing, 613
electronic, headers, 649
export filters, 495-506
exporting
AutoCAD filters, 491-492
curve resolution, 492
dimension entities, 492
ellpises, 492
entity files, 492
Import/Export Formats
489-491
JPEG (Joint Photo-
graphers' Expert Group)
files, 502-506
lines, 492
Macintosh PICT (PCT)
files, exporting, 506
MPEG files, 502-506
text anomalies, 492
text justification, 492
three-dimensional
images, 492

finding, 48
fonts, nested, 651
formats
bitmaps, 644
EPS (encapsulated
PostScript), 647
extensions, 647
headers, 46
importing, 482-491
AutoCAD filters, 491-492
bitmap images, 407-408
EPS filters, 493
File Types and Extensions
(table 15.1), 484-485
Filter Inventory List
(table 15.2), 485-488
filters, 491-495
image headers, 394
Import/Export Formats
489-491
oversampling images, 395
resampling images, 395
selecting filters, 483
troubleshooting, 484
management of, 52-53
merged
preset files, 422-423
printing, 540-543
moving, drag and drop, 50
names, 45
nested, 547, 651
OLE (object linking and
embedding), 506-511
opening
CorelDRAW! versions 3–5,
48
drag and drop, 49-51
existing, 44-53
new, 43-44
Pattern (.PAT), 51
shortcut keys, 47-48
template files, 48-49
wild cards, 51-52
Pattern file (.PAT), 45
postscript, OPI (Open
Prepress Interface), 652
print files, 548, 653
creating, 550-552

saving, 72
earlier versions of
files, 54-55
image headers, 56
Optimize for Speed
option, 57
Optimize for Storage
option, 57
selected files, 55-56
template files, 49
troubleshooting, 55
source files, 549, 655
Template File (.CDT), 45
TrueType Font file, 173
uploading, 657
viewing, 483
see also documents
Fill Color dialog box, 417
fill flyout (PRESENTS 6), 581
Fill properties (objects), 118
Fill Properties dialog box, 118
Fill roll-up dialog box, 39
**Fill tool (PHOTO-PAINT 6
Toolbox), 563**
fills, 647
applying to objects
troubleshooting, 264
Behind Fill option
(Outline Pen dialog
box), 267
bitmaps, 403
lighting controls, 313
color controls for extrusions,
313-327
colors, 37-41
default, 229-230
fountain fills, 250-258
assigning to objects, 256
conical, 252
contouring objects, 321
custom fountains, 254
customizing, 476
Edge Pad options, 257
linear, 251
presets, 258
printing, 255, 476
radical, 252

square, 253
Steps option, 256-257
two-color fountains, 253
full-color pattern fills, 249
mixers, 239
models, *see* models
(color), 234
objects, 195
palettes, *see* palettes (color)
postscript fills, 250
Special Fill roll-up, 260-262
texture fills, 258-260, 656
assigning to objects, 259
default setting, 260
patterns, 258
printing, 260
troubleshooting, 234
two-color bitmap pattern,
242-247
assigning patterns,
244-245
creating patterns,
245-247
editing patterns, 246-247
importing images
into, 247
uniform fills, 231-232
color models, *see* models
(color)
color palettes, *see* palettes
(color)
vector pattern fills, 247-248
film
emulsions, 646
grayscale, 648
image recorder, 649
imaging, 649
output materials, 550
laminating, 546, 650
linen tester, 547, 650
magnifiers, loops, 651
moires, 547, 651
negatives
density, 545, 645
halftones, 648
plates, 652
printer, processing, 653
processing, 548

registrations, sepa-
rations, 655
resolutions, 548
RRED (right read emulsion
down), 548, 654
RREU (right read emulsion
up), 548, 654
separations, 548
registrations, 654
stripping, 655
Filter Effects dialog box, 569
Filter Inventory List
(table 15.2), 485-488
filters, 491-495
AutoCAD filters
exporting files, 491-492
effects (PHOTO-PAINT 6),
569-575
2D effects, 569
3D effects, 570
adjust filter, 570
artistic effects, 571
blurring filters, 572
color adjust filters, 572
color transform
filters, 573
noise filters, 574
rendering filters, 574
sharpening filters, 575
Encapsulated PostScript
(EPS) filters, exporting,
499-500
EPS filters, 493
export filters, 482
File Types and Extensions
(table 15.1), 484-485
Filter Inventory List (table
15.2), 485-488
import filters, 482
AutoCAD DXF filter, 482
AutoCAD filters, 491-492
CorelTRACE EPS
filter, 493
SCODL export filter, 500
selecting, 483-485
Find command (Text
menu), 157
finding

files, 48
text, 157
First Tile Offset controls, 243
Fish Eye lens, 110, 383
Fit Text roll-up, 159-162
Fit Text to Path command
(Text menu), 159
flatbed scanner, 546, 647
flatness, 546, 647
auto increase printing, 515
floating toolbars, 78-79
flush, 647
flyouts (Presents 6)
autoshapes flyouts, 581
basic shape flyouts, 581
fill flyouts, 581
freehand drawing flyout, 581
outline flyouts, 581
text flyouts, 581
zoom flyout, 581
Focoltone, 647
contact information
(home offices), 447
palette, 234, 447
folders, 648
Font Attributes tab, 112
fonts, 546, 648
all fonts resident option,
544, 643
bitmap font
limits, 534
size threshold, 535
conflict, 546, 648
converting to curves, 516
creating, 171-173
Blend command, 295-296
displaying, 169
exporting, 505-506
names, 171
nested, 547, 651
overboards, printing, 514
sizes, Cicero, 644
substitution, 51
symbol fonts, creating,
173-174
TrueType, 656
For Speed option, 72

For Storage option, 72
Formality Level command
(Options menu), 150
formats
  bitmaps, 388-389, 494, 644
    Bitmap (BMP)
      format, 388
    Compatible Bitmap
      Formats (table 11.1),
      388-389
    Tagged Image Format
      (TIF), 388
  exporting, 496-498
  extrusion formats, 226
  files
    EPS (encapsulated
      PostScript), 647
    extensions, 647
  Import/Export Formats
    489-491
  plotters, 494
formatting
  artistic text
    Artistic Text tool, 137
    Shape tool, 138-39
    size, 137
  attributes, 643
  paragraph text, 139-142
    Paragraph text tool, 139
    Shape tool, 140
  text
    bullets, 147
    hyphenation, 145
    leader characters, 146
    saving in styles, 144
Formatting tab (Text Options
  dialog box), 170
Fountain Fill dialog box,
  251, 258
fountain fills, 69, 250-258
  assigning to objects, 256
  blends, 644
  conical, 252
  contouring objects, 321
  custom fountains, 254
  customizing, 476
    troubleshooting, 476

Edge Pad options, 257
linear, 251
presets, 258
  saving, 258
printing, 255, 476
radical, 252
screen drawing, 255
square, 253
Steps option, 256-257
two-color fountains, 253
fractal fills, *see* texture fills
frames
  paragraph text
    reshaping, 135-136
    stretching, 133
  text, columns, 644
Free-Form tool (DREAM 3D;
  Perspective Toolbox), 605
Freehand
  button (Envelope
    roll-up), 212
  drawing flyout
    (PRESENTS 6), 581
  tool, 95
    creating lines, 178-179
  Tracking feature, 75, 404
Front Parallel option
  (extrusion), 219
ftp (File Transer Protocol), 648
Full Path command
  (Blend Path menu), 284
Full-Proofreading feature, 151
Full-screen preview view, 26
functions
  assigning to Status bar, 82
  Break Apart, 108
  Combine function, 108
  customizing
    Save, Backup and
      Autobackup, 474
    startup functions, 474
  Details function, 46
  Missing Right Mouse
    Button, 73
  Split Transform, 107
  Status bar display
    (Table 3.1), 83
  see also commands

G

gallery (PHOTO-PAINT 6)
  filter effects, 569-575
GCR (gray component
  replacement), 429, 546, 648
GEM Artline, exporting, 497
General options, 66-68
General tab
  Text-Wrapping option,
    406-407
  Wrap Paragraph Text option,
    troubleshooting, 407
General properties
  (objects), 117
grabbing objects, 30
graphics
  halftones, 646-648
  points, 652
  printing
    halftoning, 521
    resolutions, 520
    scaling, 521
    special, 521
  raster, 548, 653
  stripping, 655
  thumbnails, 656
gray component replacement
  (GCR), 429
grayscale, 546, 648
  color model, 233, 442
  images, 390-392
greek text, 170
Greek Text Below option
  (Text tab), 169
Grid & Ruler Setup dialog
  box, 327
Grid and Ruler Setup
  command (Layout
  menu), 335
Grid Box Tool Properties
  dialog box, 188
Grid Setup command
  (Layout menu), 327
Grid tools, 97-98, 188
grids, 335
  creating, 188
  editing, 190
  ungrouping, 190

Group command (Arrange menu), 21, 204, 644
grouping
  objects, 204
    selecting, 21
  roll-ups, 469
guidelines, 329-335
  adding, 332
  deleting, 333
  moving, 333
  Snap to Guideline
    option, 333
  selecting, 23
  setup, 106
  Show Snap Locations Marks
    option, 333
  Snap to Objects feature, 334
Guidelines Setup command
  (Layout menu), 23, 330
Guidelines Setup dialog box,
  23, 330
gutter, defined, 63

H

hairlines, 648
halftones, 648
halftoning, 521
handles, 649
  control points, 645
  envelopes, 213
  nodes, 651
  objects, 318
handout view, 580
handouts, presentations,
  589-590
hardware
  digital halftones, 646
  drivers, 545, 646
  imagesetter, 649
headers, 649
  files, 46
  images, 393-395
    importing files, 394
    saving, 56
heat map lens, 381
height, aspect ratio, 643

Height control (Page Settings
  dialog box), 60
help, CorelDRAW!, 16-17
  context-sensitive help, 17
  help topics, 16
  printing help topics, 16
  tutor notes, 17
  tutorial, 17
Help menu commands
  About CorelDRAW!, 204
  Help Topics, 16
  Tutor Notes, 17
  Tutorial, 17
  What's This?, 17
help topics, 16
Help Topics command
  (Help menu), 16
hidden interface controls, 666
hiding welcome screen, 47
Hierarchy window
  (DREAM 3D), 602
high resolution (high-res), 649
High-quality Screening (HQS),
  see HQS
High-to-Low Priority button
  (Task Progress feature), 473
highlighting with Blend
  command, 296-299
HLS color model, 440
home offices
  Focoltone, 447
  Pantone, 446-447
  Trumatch, 448
Horizontal option (Envelope
  roll-up), 216
Horizontal tab, 332
hot keys
  CAPTURE 6, 628
  selecting, 629
hot zones, 146
HPGL (Hewlett-Packard
  Graphical Language) filters,
  exporting, 503
HQS (High-quality Screening),
  546, 649
HSB color model, 439-457
hyphenation, 145

I

images
  auto-trace, 643
  bitmaps, 388-396
    color, 392, 402-403
    cropping, 397-400, 408
    editing, 397-407
    formats, see also formats,
      bitmaps, 388-389
    headers, 393-395
    importing, 407-408
    loading into mixing
      area, 241
    pixel grids, 389
    resampling, 408
    resolution, 392-393
    rotating, 400-402
    size, 389-391
    skewing, 400-402
  continuous tones, 645
  controls
    CAPTURE 6, 634-635
    custom resolution
      settings, 634
    printer settings, 634
    resizing captured
      images, 635
    screen settings, 634
    selecting maintain aspect
      ratio, 635
  digital
    halftones, 646
    images, 646
  dropouts, 646
  drum scanners, 646
  halftones, 648
  headers, 56, 649
  imagesetter, 649
  importing
    oversampling images, 395
    PhotoCD image format,
      669-671
    resampling images, 395
    two-color bitmap
      patterns, 247
  line screen, 650

loading, 240-241
PHOTO-PAINT 6
  creating, 556-558
  editing, 556-558
printing
  EPS (encapsulated
    PostScript), 647
  resolution, 393
recorder, 649
scanned
  ct scan (continuous
    tones), 645
  resident scans, 548, 654
sources, 395
thumbnails, 656
imagesetters, 546, 549, 649
  capstan, 549
  drum model, 549
  linotronic, 651
  processors, 548, 653
    RIP (raster image
      processor), 549
  resolutions, 548, 654
  RIP (raster image processor),
    548, 654
  screen frequency, 548, 654
  SelectSet, 548, 655
  spoolers, 655
imaging, 649
  output materials, 550
**Import command (File menu),
344, 407, 482, 614**
Import dialog box, 482-483
import filters, *see also*
importing files, filters 482
**Import/Export Formats
(table 15.3), 489-491**
importing files, 482-491
  bitmap images, 407-408,
    455-456
    two-color bitmap
      patterns, 247
  DREAM 3D, 612-614
  filters, 491-495
    AutoCad filters, 491-492
    CorelTRACE EPS
      filter, 493
    EPS filters, 493

File Types and Extensions
  (table 15.1), 484-485
Filter Inventory List
  (table 15.2), 485-488
  selecting filters, 483
formats, Import/Export
  Formats, 489-491
images
  headers, 394
  oversampling, 395
  PhotoCD image format,
    669-671
  resampling images, 395
Kodak PhotoCD files, 494
nested, 547, 651
troubleshooting, 484
imposition, defined, 64
indenting, 143-147
ink
  dot gains, 545, 646
  flow (Powerline roll-up), 361
  options tab (Powerline
    roll-up), 361
  spread (Powerline
    roll-up), 361
  tracking colors, 444
**Insert menu commands
(PRESENTS 6)**
  Chart, 586
  Sound, 591
  Video, 591
**Insert New Object command
(Edit menu), 506**
installing
  CorelDRAW! 6, 672
  menus, new, 466-467
**intensity, numeric (Powerline
roll-up), 361**
interface (CorelDRAW!)
  customizing
    Status bar options, 80-83
    Toolbar options, 78-80
interfacing, 649
  fields, 647
  flyouts, 647
  hidden interface
    controls, 666
  roll-ups, 654

Interruptible Refresh, 70
**intersection (objects),
343-346, 649**
  multiple objects, 345
  priorities, 346
**Intersection command
(Arrange menu), 343**
**Intersection/Trim/Weld
roll-up, 108**
invert lens, 378

J

**Join node button (Node Edit
roll-up), 192**
joing curves, 208-211
**JPEG (Joint Photographers'
Expert Group) files,
exporting, 502-506**
justification
  exporting files, 492
  text, 650

K

K-curve, 429
**Keep Lines option (Envelope
roll-up), 164, 217**
kerning, 170, 650
key color (preset roll-ups), 415
keyboard shortcuts, 659-660
  accessing uniform fill
    mixers, 239
  Arrange commands, 661
  assigning to commands, 464
  creating, 462-465
  dialog boxes (table 1.4), 36
  displaying, 463
  Edit commands, 660
  editing text, 662-663
    table 5.1, 140-142
  File functions, 660
  Layout commands, 661
  numeric keyboard
    functions, 667
  opening files, 47-48
  reverting to original, 465

roll-ups, 665
saving, 464
selecting nodes in
objects, 208
selecting objects, 24-25
Text commands, 661
tools, 665
Tools commands, 664
transformation roll-ups, 35
View commands, 661
Window commands, 664
zooming, 28
**Keyboard Shortcuts for
Navigating Dialog Boxes
(table 1.4), 36**
**Keyboard States function
(Status bar), 83**
Keyboard tab, 463
Knife tool, 89-90
**Kodak PhotoCD, importing
files, 494-496**

L

L*A*B color model, 441-457
labels
customizing, 62-64
deleting, 64
gutter, 63
layout controls, 63
margin measurements, 63
saving, 64
size, 62
laminating, 546, 650
**Landscape control (Page
Settings dialog box), 60**
landscapes, 547, 650
**Language option
(proofreading option), 152**
languages
imagesetters, 654
PostScript, 653
**Large Color Swatches function
(Status bar), 83**
Large Status Bar option, 82
**Large Swatches option
(Customize tab), 471**
Lathe Editor (MOTION 3D), 618

**Lathe Object tool (MOTION
3D toolbox), 617**
layers, 336-338
creating, 337
settings, 337-338
**Layers Manager command
(Layout menu), 336**
Layout Menu, 103-107
Layout menu commands
Grid and Ruler Setup, 335
Grid Setup, 327
Guidelines Setup, 23, 330
Layers Manager, 336
Page Layout, 59
Snap to Guidelines, 333
Snap to None, 107
Styles, 105, 144
layouts
controls, labels, 63
printing, 527-529
Special Purpose layouts,
changing, 64-65
leader characters, 146
leading, 650
set-solids, 655
**Leave Original Other
Objects option**
Weld roll-up, 339
Trim roll-up, 342
**Leave Original Target
Objects option**
Weld roll-up, 339
Trim roll-up, 342
**Left-Align roll-ups,
customizing, 468**
Lens Effect roll-up, 110, 375
lenses, 650
brighten lens, 377
color add lens, 379
color limit lens, 379
custom color heat map, 382
effects, 374-375
fisheye lens, 383
heat map lens, 381
invert lens, 378
magnify lens, 377
removing, 384
tinted grayscale lens, 380

transparency lens, 376, 656
wireframe lens, 383
light
controls
extrusions, 311-313
bitmap fills, 313
sources, extrusion of objects,
222-225
adding light sources to
extrusion, 224
setting, 222-223
troubleshooting, 222-224
**Light tool (MOTION 3D
toolbox), 617**
**Lighting tab (Extruse roll-up),
222-225**
line art, 547, 650
line cap controls, 265
**Line tool (PHOTO-PAINT 6
Toolbox), 562**
linear fountain fills, 251
linen tester, 547, 650
lines
calligraphy controls, 265-266
corner controls, 264
creating, 178-179
editing, 181
exporting files, 492
hairlines, 648
line cap controls, 265
Outline Flyout option, 268
pen color, 268
powerlines, 653
screen, 650
styles, applying, 263-264
lines per inch (LPI), *see* **LPI**
**Link command (Edit
menu), 507**
linking, 652
lino output, 650
Linotronic, 547, 650-651
**Load Bitmap command
(Color Options menu), 241**
loading
bitmap images into mixing
area, 241
images, 240-241
vector patterns, 248

looping blended objects, 282
loops, 547, 651
Low-to-High Priority button
 (Task Progress feature), 473
LPI (lines per inch), 393,
 547, 651
  screen frequency, 548, 654

M

Macintosh
  PICT (PCT) files,
   exporting, 506
  vector, exporting, 497
macros, *see* preset commands
magazines, *Corel Magazine*
 sampler, 671
magenta, CMYK (cyan,
 magenta, yellow, black), 651
magnifiers
  linen tester, 650
  loops, 651
magnify lens, 377
Make Movie dialog box, 625
management, files, 52-53
manipulating
  curves, 193
  ruler settings, 328-329
  see also transforming
Manual Refresh, 70
map nodes (Blend
 roll-up), 274
mapping
  objects, 215
  options (Envelope roll-up),
   164, 165
  options tab (Blend roll-up),
   273-274
maps
  CorelMAP, 587
  slides, adding with
   PRESENTS 6, 586-587
margins, labels, 63
markers
  add marker (Powerline Node
   Edit roll-up), 373
  delete marker (Powerline
   Node Edit roll-up), 373

marks
  crop, 545, 645
  printer, 526-527
marquee-selecting, 19-20
masks (PHOTO-PAINT 6),
 575-577
  creating, 575-577
Master view, 580
mathematical functions,
 compressions, 644
maximum width style
 (Powerline roll-up), 358
MDI (Multiple Document
 Interface), 86
measurements
  conventions, 60
  didots, 645
  DPI (dots per inch), 545, 646
  hairlines, 648
  line screen, 650
  LPI (lines per inch), 547, 651
  parameters, 652
  picas, 652
  pixels, 652
  points, 652
  screen frequency, 548, 654
Memo (editor), 114
memory
  function (Status bar), 83
  space, compressions, 644
menus
  access, 664
  adding new menus, 466-467
  Alignment preferences
   menu, 322
  Arrange menu, 107-108
  custom menus, 116
  customizing, 465-467
  Distribute preferences
   menu, 322
  Edit menu, 100-101
  Effects Menu, 109-110
  Extrude flyout menu, 227
  File menu, 99-100
  flyouts, 647
  Layout Menu, 103-107
  names, 466
  new features, 99-110

pop-up menus, 72
pull-down menus, 653
Text Menu, 111-116
View menu, 101-103
merging
  extrusions, 227
  preset files, 422-423
  printing, 540-543
Micrografx Designer,
 exporting, 497
Min. Extrude Facet Size
 feature, 70
Minimum Line Width option
 (Text tab), 169
mirroring objects, 202
Missing Preference options, 72
Missing Right Mouse Button
 Function, 73
Mitre Limit feature, 67
mixers (color), 452-456
  Color Blend mixer, 453-454
  Mixing Area mixer, 452-453
  troubleshooting, 454
  see also mixing
mixing
  area, 651
  colors
    accessing mixers with
     keyboard shortcut, 239
    Add Colors button
     (Uniform Fill dialog
     box), 237
    Auto-Blend button, 236
    color wheel, 254
    creating mixed
     colors, 238
    fountain fills, 250-258
    Mixing Area color
     picker, 237
    Paint Brush tool, 237
    saving, 238
    saving mixing area, 240
    selecting mixed
     colors, 238
Mixing Area color picker, 237
Mixing Area mixer, 452-453
  sampling colors from bitmap
   images, 454-456
  window, 238

models (color), 232-234, 436-443, 644
assigning to objects, 233
CMY, 437-457
CMYK, 438-457, 644
CMYK255, 438-457
defined, 443
grayscale, 233, 442
HLS, 440
HSB, 439-457
L*A*B, 441-457
palettes, *see also* palettes (color), 644
registration, 233, 442
RGB, 438-457
selecting, 233
YIQ, 441
modems, faxing facsimile, 647
moires, 547, 651
monitors
calibrating, 426-427, 432
colorimeter, 429
resolution, pixels, 652
white point, adjusting, 433
MOTION 3D, 615-619
flying objects, creating, 619-621
stagehands, 622-625
toolbars, 617-618
toolbox tools, 616-619
mouse
double-clicking, 646
Mouse Coordinates function (Status bar), 83
Movie Options (MOTION 3D), 618
movie toolbar (PHOTO-PAINT 6), 568-569
moving
files, 50
guidelines, 333
objects, 35, 199-200
constrains, 645
text, paragraph text, 140
see also positioning
MPEG files, exporting, 502-506

Multimedia Manager, 625-626
Multiple Document Interface, *see* MDI

N

names
directories, 53
files, 45
fonts, 171
menus, 466
roll-ups, 471
toolbars, 460
navigating color palette, 38
Navigator roll-up (PHOTO-PAINT 6 roll-ups), 566
nested
files, 547, 651
fonts, 547, 651
nesting Powerclip effects, 351
New button (Advanced options; proofreading), 153
New Color window, 237
New command (File menu), 12, 44, 100, 462
New Path command (Blend Path menu), 284
New Selection button (Select by Properties roll-up), 196
nib
angle, numeric (Powerline roll-up), 361
intensity, slider (Powerline roll-up), 360
ratio, numeric (Powerline roll-up), 361
shape (Powerline roll-up), 360
style (Powerline roll-up), 359
Nibs roll-up (PHOTO-PAINT 6 roll-up), 567
Node Edit Buttons and Their Functions (table 6.1), 192
Node Edit roll-up, 181, 188-190
editing bitmaps, 397
editing curves/nodes, 191-193
see also Shape tool

Node Edit Tool Properties dialog box, 76
Node Editor, 370-374
nodes, 651
Auto-Reduce feature, 76
compared to selection handles, 24
cusps, 645
Node Edit Buttons and Their Functions (table 6.1), 192
objects, blending, 279
overloaded printing, 514
selecting, 24-25
noise filter (PHOTO-PAINT 6), 574
notes, presentations, 589-590
Nudge command, 67
Nudge control, customizing, 475
numbers, numeric keyboard functions, 667

O

Object Details function (Status bar), 83
Object Editor (MOTION 3D), 619
Object Information function (Status bar), 83
Object Linking and Embedding (OLE), *see* OLE
Object menu commands
Curve Properties, 118
Ellipse Properties, 119
Polygon Properties, 120
Rectangle Properties, 119
Text Properties, 120
Object Picker tool (PHOTO-PAINT 6 Toolbox), 559
Object Properties (table 6.2), 194-195
Object Properties dialog box, 183, 195, 592, 622
objects
aligning, 322-326
alignment preference controls, 324
Snap to Grid option, 326

applying Powerlines, 374
aspect ratio, 643
attributes, 643
auto-trace, 643
bitmap
    images *see* bitmaps
    objects, 22
bleeding, 644
blending, 276
    applying Powerline
      effects, 300-301
    cloning, 289-290
    copying, 289
    creating compound
      blend, 292-294
    looping, 282
    nodes, 279
    rotating, 280
    similar, 282-283
    splitting, 290-291
    Start/End Path
      buttons, 286
    troubleshooting, 283
breaking apart object types,
  206-207
centering, automatically, 67
child, 644
cloned objects, 22, 644
cloning, 197-198
    reverting
      transformations, 198
    troubleshooting, 198
closed objects, creating, 179
color models, assigning, 233
combining, 211
constrains, 645
contour, 318-319
contours, 645
    cloning, 321
    color options, 320-322
    Contour Properties tab
      controls, 319-320
    converting, 321
    editing, 321
    removing, 321
control blends, 644
converting to curves, 205

creating, 15
curves, 205-211
    breaking, 205-208
    combining, 208-211
    combining multiple
      curves, 209-211
    combining two curves,
      208-209
    editing, 193
    manipulating, 193
customizing, 476
deselecting, 21, 179, 645
dragging, 30
dropouts, 646
editing
    blends, 287
    manipulating
      handles, 318
effects
    envelopes, 211-217
    extrusion, 217-227
ellipses
    creating, 180
    editing, 185-186
envelopes
    applying, 211-217
    clearing effects, 217
    mapping options, 215
extrusions, 306-315
    3D effect, 306-315
    color fills, 313
    color options, 221-222
    copying/cloning, 315
    creating presets, 306-315
    deleting, 306
    Extrude Wizard, 226-227
    lighting controls, 311-313
    light sources, 222-225
    maintaining, 227
    merging, 227
    minimum extrude facet
      size, 308
    preset extrusions, 226
    rotating, 225, 309
    saving, 227, 307
    types, 217-219
    vanishing points,
      220-221, 309

fills, 647
    colors, 37-41
    fountain fills, 250-258
    full-color pattern
      fills, 249
    PostScript fills, 250
    texture fills, 258-260
    troubleshooting, 264
    see also fills
finding number of in
  drawing, 204
flush, 647
fountain fills, 250-258
    assigning, 256
full-color pattern fills, 249
grabbing, 30
grids
    creating, 188
    editing, 190
    ungrouping, 190
grouping, 204
handles, 649
highlighting, 296-299
intersection, 343-346, 649
    multiple objects, 345
layers
    moving objects on, 337
    settings, 337-338
lenses, *see also* lenses, 650
lines, creating, 178-179
mirroring, 202
MOTION 3D, 619-621
moving, 35, 199-200
outlines, *see also* outlines,
  37-41
overlaps, 644
perspective, 168
    applying, 316-318
    creating three-
      dimensional
      objects, 318
    removing, 317
polygons, stars, 187-188
postscript fills, 250
Powerclip, 653
Powerclip effects, 346-352
    nesting, 351

priorities, 346
  intersection, 346
  trim priorities, 346
  weld priorities, 346
properties, 117-120, 653
  editing, 195
  Object Properties, 194-195
rectangles
  creating, 180
  editing, 183-185
  in grids, 190
reverse highlighting, 299
rotating, 32, 200-202
  around corners, 33
  clockwise/counterclockwise, 201
  viewing origin point, 201
scaling, 29-31, 202
search parameters
  colors, 195
  fill types, 195
  object types, 195
  outlines, 195
  Select by Properties roll-up, 195-199
  special effects, 195
selecting
  grouped, 21, 204
  multiple, 19-22
  Pick tool, 18-19
  shortcuts, 24-25
  single grouped, 204
  Treat All Objects as Filled option, 74
  troubleshooting, 22
shadowing, presets, 417-421
shaping, 306-321
sizing, 203
skewing, 33-34, 203
Special Fill roll-up, 260-262
spirals
  creating, 188
  editing, 190
stars, 189-190
text wrapping, 406-407
texture fills, 258-260
  assigning to objects, 259

trimming, 341-343
two-color bitmap patterns
  assigning, 244-245
  creating, 245-247
  editing, 246-247
  importing images into, 247
ungrouping, 204
vanishing point, 167
vector objects, 22
vector patterns, 247-248
  creating, 248
  loading, 248
welding, 338-341, 657
Objects Browser window (DREAM 3D), 603
Offset option (Contours Properties tab), 320
OLE (Object Linking and Embedding), 506-511, 652
  clipboard, 508-509
  drag-and-drop feature, 510-511
  OLE automation, 633
online services, BBS (Bulletin Board Service), 643
Open command (File menu), 44, 462
Open Drawing dialog box, 45-53
  documents, 11-12
  files
    CorelDRAW! versions 3–5, 48
    drag and drop, 49-51
    existing, 44-53
    new, 43-44
    Pattern (.PAT), 51
    shortcut keys, 47-48
    template files, 48-49
    wild cards, 51-52
  PhotoCD images, 669
  Task Progress, 473
Optimize for Speed option (Preferences dialog box), 57
Optimize for Storage option (Preferences dialog box), 57

Optimized 256-Color Palette option (Display tab), 69
options, 65-77
  Advanced options, 71-72, 152-153
  Bezier Tool options, 74-76
  defaults, 645
  Display options, 68-71
  Edit Resolution, 77
  flyouts, 647
  General options, 66-68
  Missing Preference options, 72
  Pick Tool properties, 73
  text, setting, 168
Options command (Tools menu), 47
Options menu commands
  Advanced Options, 149
  Create New Dictionary, 150
  Explain Error, 149
  Formality Level, 150
  Personal Dictionary, 150
  Rule Manager, 149
  Undo Edit, 149
orientations
  landscapes, 547
  portraits, 547
Original option (Envelope roll-up), 215
Outline Color dialog box, 269, 449, 452
outline flyout (PRESENTS 6), 581
Outline Flyout option (Outline Pen dialog box), 268
Outline Pen, 179
Outline Pen dialog box, 179, 262-269
Outline properties (objects), 118
Outline Roll-up, 269
Outline toolbar (MOTION 3D), 618
Outline view, 580, 583-584
  toolbar (PRESENTS 6), 582
outlines
  Behind Fill option, 267
  color, 268-269

objects
colors, 37-41
as search parameters, 195
text, troubleshooting, 263
output
devices, hairlines, 648
imaging, 550
lino, 650
overboards (font), 514
overlapping objects, 646
overlaps, bleeding, 644
overloaded nodes,
printing, 514
overprinting, 652
oversampling images, 395

P

Page Color option (Page
Settings dialog box), 61
page frames
deleting, 61
troubleshooting, 61
Page Layout command
(Layout menu), 59
page numbers, 526
Page Settings dialog box,
59-65
Add Page Frame option, 61
Facing Pages option, 61
measuring conventions, 60
Page Color option, 61
page size setting options,
60-61
Special Purpose layouts,
64-66
Page Setup dialog box, 104
PageMaker, exporting, 497
pages
setup, portraits, 653
size, 520
Paint Brush tool, 237
Paint tool (PHOTO-PAINT 6
Toolbox), 564
palettes (color), 443-451, 644
commands, 235
creating, 239-244, 449-451

custom palettes
creating, 239-244,
449-451
prioritizing colors, 451
sampling colors from
bitmap images, 454-456
saving, 450
customizing, 239, 471-472
defined, 443
Focoltone palette,
234, 647
prioritizing colors, 451
process color palettes, 443
Focoltone, 447
Pantone, 445-447
SpectraMaster, 449
Trumatch, 447-448
saving, 238
selecting, 235, 445
spot palettes, 443
Focoltone, 447
Pantone, 445-447
SpectraMaster, 449
Trumatch, 447-448
swatches, 234
third-party color matching
systems, 444
Trumatch palette, 234
Pan tool, 92
Pan/Zoom tools (DREAM 3D;
Perspective Toolbox), 605
Panning tool, 28-29, 476
Panose Font Matching Editing
option (Text tab), 170
Pantone, 652
color palette system, 445-447
contact information
(home offices), 446-447
Pantone Matching System
(PMS), see PMS
paper
color, selecting, 61
control (Page Settings
dialog box), 60
imaging output
materials, 550
size, 61, 520
Paragraph command
(Text menu), 144

Paragraph dialog box, 144
paragraph text, 130-136
applying envelopes to, 168
arrow tab, 133
bullets, 147
columns, 134-135
converting to
artistic text, 158
curves, 516
creating, 131
displaying, 133
editing, 131-132
keyboard shortcuts
(table 5.1), 140-142
finding, 157
formatting, 139-142
Paragraph text tool, 139
Shape tool, 140
frames
reshaping, 135-136
stretching, 133
moving, 140
positioning, 133
resizing handles, 131
setting default, 133
skewing handles, 131
Paragraph Text tool, 130-131
creating paragraph text, 131
editing paragraph text,
131-132
formatting paragraph
text, 139
parameters, 652
Paste command (Edit
menu), 101
Paste Special command
(Edit menu), 101, 508
Paste Special dialog box, 509
Path Node Edit tool (PHOTO-
PAINT 6 Toolbox), 560
paths
assigning with Blend
command, 283-285
Fit Text to Path feature, 162
fitting text to, 159-163
separating text from, 162
Pattern (.PAT) files, 45, 51

patterns
  bitmaps, 644
  full-color pattern fills, 249
  texture fills, 258, 656
  two-color bitmap pattern
    fills, 242-247
    assigning, 244-245
    creating, 245-247
    editing, 246-247
    importing images
      into, 247
    resolution, 247
  vector patterns, 247-248
PC Paintbrush, exporting, **497**
pen
  controls, 262-269
  leakiness (Powerline
    roll-up), 361
  options tab (Powerline
    roll-up), 360-361
**Personal Dictionary command
  (Options menu), 150**
perspective
  adding realism to objects,
    315-318
  applying to artistic text,
    166-168
  controls, 315-318
  objects, 168
    applying to, 316-318
    clearing, 317
    creating three-
      dimensional ob-
      jects, 318
  window (Dream 3D), 602
PHOTO-PAINT 6, 555
  controls, 558-569
  filter effects
    2D effects, 569
    3D effects, 570
    adjust filter, 570
    artistic effects, 571
    blurring filters, 572
    color adjust filters, 572
    color transform
      filters, 573
    noise filter, 574

    rendering filters, 574
    sharpening filters, 575
  gallery, 569-575
  mask/object toolbar, 568
  masks, 575-577
  movie toolbar, 568
  roll-ups, 565-567
    toolbar, 569
  standard toolbar, 568
  Toolbox tools, 559-565
PHOTO-PAINT utility, 455
PhotoCD images
  importing, 669
  opening, 669
photography
  continuous tones, 645
  digital
    halftones, 646
    images, 646
  halftones, 648
  image recorder, 649
picas, 652
Pick tool, 19, 88
  compared to Shape tool, 24
  editing grids, 190
  formatting artistic text, 137
  properties, 73
  resizing shapes, 188
  skewing bitmaps, 400
pictures
  continuous tones, 645
  digital
    halftones, 646
    images, 646
  halftones, 648
  image recorder, 649
pixels, 652
  bitmaps, 389
  grayscale images, 390
  grids, 389
  RGB-color images, 391
PKZip, 547, 652
**Place Inside Container
  command (Effects menu), 67**

plates, 547, 652
plotters, format supports, 494
**PMS (Pantone Matching
  System), 652**
PNTAREA.BMP bitmap, 454
Point At dialog box, 620
points, 652
  control, 645
  picas, 652
  size, 652
**Polygon menu commands,
  Star, 187**
**Polygon properties
  (objects), 120**
**Polygon Properties command
  (Object menu), 120**
**Polygon properties dialog
  box, 120**
Polygon tool, 186
**Polygon Tool Properties
  dialog box, 187**
polygons
  Auto-Join, 75
  stars, creating, 187-188
pop-up menus, 72
  customizing, 474
portraits, 547, 653
Position roll-up, 199-200
positioning
  objects, 199-200
  Status bar, 81
  text, paragraph text, 133
  toolbars, 78
  see also moving
PostScript, 653
  dialog boxes
    Pattern dialog box, 250
    Preferences dialog box,
      538-539
  fills, 250
  options, 521
  preferences, 533
PowerClip, 653
  command (Effects
    menu), 347
  effects,, 346-352, 351
Powerline roll-up, 360-361

Powerline command (Effect menu), 362

Powerline Node Edit roll-up, 373

powerlines, 354-374, 653
  applying, 362-366
    objects, 374
    preset styles, 367-370
  custom, saving, 374
  drawings, creating, 370
  editing, 370-374
  in blends, 300-301
  roll-up, 361
  styles, 355-359

preferences controls (CAPTURE 6), 638
  border settings, 638
  cursors, 638

Preferences dialog box, 56-57, 76

presentations
  PRESENTS 6, 593-596
    annotations, 596
    creating, 582
    handouts, 589-590
    Runtime Player, 595
    slide sorter view, 590
    sound, 591
    speaker notes, 589-590
    time, 593
    video, 591
  slides
    charts, 586-587
    maps, 586-587

PRESENTS 6
  animation toolbar, 582
  CorelCHART, 587
  CorelMAP, 587
  flyouts, 581-582
    autoshapes flyouts, 581
    basic shape flyouts, 581
    fill flyouts, 581
    freehand drawing flyout, 581
    outline flyouts, 581
    text flyouts, 581
    zoom flyout, 581

outline view toolbar, 582
presentations, 593-596
  annotations, 596
  creating, 582
  handouts, 589-590
  Runtime Player, 595
  slide sorter view, 590
  slides, 586-587
  sound, 591
  speaker notes, 589-590
  time, 593
  video, 591
side sorter toolbar, 581
slides
  charts, 586-587
  maps, 586-587
special effects, 591-592
standard toolbar, 581
text toolbar, 582
toolbars, 581-582
toolbox toolbar, 581
views, 580
  animation view, 580, 588
  background view, 580, 584
  handout view, 580
  master view, 580
  outline view, 580, 583-584
  slide view, 580
  slide sorter view, 580, 590
  speaker notes view, 580
wizards, 582-583
preset commands
  applying, 414
  color, 415
  defined, 411-412
  editing controls, 416
  files, merging, 422-423
  functions, 412-413
  key color, 415
  preset flyout menu, 416
  recording, 417-421
  removing, 423-424
  roll-ups, 415-416

preset pull-down, 415
preview window, 415
saving, 417-421
scripts, editing, 421-422
shadowing, 417-421
start recording/stop recording, 416
thumbnails, 416
presets
  command (Tools menu), 414
  controls (Fountain Fill dialog box), 258
  flyout menu, 416
  pull-down (preset roll-ups), 415
  styles, applying, 367-370

pressure style (Powerline roll-up), 358

Preview Colors option (Display option), 68

Preview Fountain Steps feature, 69

Preview options (MOTION 3D), 618

Preview Selected Only view, 26

Preview window, 415

previewing print jobs, 523-524

Print command (File menu), 476, 517

Print dialog box, 517-519

print files, creating, 550-552

Print Merge command (File menu), 543

Print Options dialog box, 521, 527-529

printers
  calibrating, 433
  CAPTURE 6 settings, 634
  capturing to, 633
  color management system, troubleshooting, 430
  Linotronic, 547, 650-651
  output, screen frequency, 654
  print files, 653
  printing press, plates, 547
  profiles, creating, 434

resolution, 393
spoolers, 549
printing
all fonts resident option, 544, 643
colors, 653
composites, 545, 644
compression packages, 545
crop marks, 645
crosshairs, 545
curves, flatness, 647
defaults, 545
density, 545
dot gains, 545
dowloaded files, 545
drivers, 545
emulsions, 546
extensions, 546
font conflict, 546
fonts, 546
fountain fills, 255, 476
graphics
halftoning, 521
resolutions, 520
scaling, 521
special, 521
grayscales, 546
halftones, 648
help topics, 16
images
EPS (encapsulated PostScript), 647
resolution, 393
imagesetters, 546, 649
imaging, 649
inks, dot gains, 646
layout options, 527-529
loops, 651
LPI (lines per inch), 547, 651
marks, 526-527
crop marks, 545
merged files, 540-543
options, 521, 532-533
grayscale, 648
proofing options, 533

orientations, 520
landscapes, 547
portraits, 547
overprinting, 652
page
numbers, 526
size, 520
PMS (Pantone Matching System), 652
PostScript, 653
PostScript Preferences dialog box, 538-539
preparing, 513-515
previewing, 523-524
print
files, 548, 653
jobs, information sheet, 533
processing, 548
Properties dialog box, 519-520
screen frequency, 533
separations options, 529-532
service bureaus, 655
preparing output, 543-544
settings, 534-537
spoolers, 549, 655
stripping, 655
styles, 525-526
texture fills, 260
trapping, 517, 656
troubleshooting, 513-515
auto increase flatness, 515
fit to page hazards, 515
font overboards, 514
overloaded nodes, 514
texture fill hazards, 514
priorities, objects, 346
intersection, 346
trim priorities, 346
weld priorities, 346
PRN files (print files), *see* **print files**

process
colors
CMYK (cyan, magenta, yellow, and black), 644
cyan, 645
palettes, 443
Focoltone, 447
Pantone, 445-447
SpectraMaster, 449
Trumatch, 447-448
processors, 548, 653
RIP (raster image processor), 548-549
profiles
color system profiles, 427-428
assigning, 435-436
creating with Color Wizard, 428-434
target original, 428
troubleshooting, 436
printers, creating, 434
scanners, creating, 430-431
system, 549, 656
programs
Kodak PhotoCD, 494-496
Ray Dream Designer 3D, 672
proofreading, 115
advanced options, 152-153
text
Full-Proofreading feature, 151
Quick Proofreading feature, 150-151
properties, 653
bitmap, 404-405
CorelDRAW!, 87-88
objects, 117-120
editing, 195
Object Properties (table 6.2), 194-195
Pick Tool properties, 73
searching drawings, 196-197
text, 147-148
Properties command (View menu), 76, 147, 187, 195, 476

Properties dialog box, 519-520
Portrait control (Page Settings dialog box), 60
pull-down menus, 653
Putty option (Envelope roll-up), 215

Q-R

Quick Proofreading feature, 150-15

radical fountain fills, 252
ragged text, 653
raster graphics, 548, 653
Ray Dream Designer 3D, 672
ray tracing, 609-610
recorder images, 649
recording presets, 417-421
Rectangle Mask tool (PHOTO-PAINT 6 Toolbox), 560
Rectangle Object Properties dialog box, 96
Rectangle properties (objects), 119
Rectangle Properties command (Object menu), 119
Rectangle tool, 15, 96
    creating rectangles, 180
    PHOTO-PAINT 6 Toolbox, 562
rectangles
    adding perspective to, 318
    creating, 180
    editing, 183-185
    in grids, 190
    resizing, 185
Redo command (Edit menu), 100
regions (Status bar)
    assigning functions to, 82
    dividing Status bar into, 81
    sizing, 82
registrations, 548, 654
    color model, 233, 442
    printing mark types, 536
Remove Extrusion command (Effects menu), 306

Remove nodes button (Node Edit roll-up), 192
removing
    contours from objects, 321
    extrusions, 306
    guidelines, 333
    lens effects, 384
    perspective from objects, 317
    preset commands, 423-424
    toolbars, custom toolbars, 462
Render Area tool (DREAM 3D; Perspective Toolbox), 607
rendering
    defined, 609-610
    DREAM 3D
        file format options, 611
        setting options, 612-614
        sizing options, 610
    filters (PHOTO-PAINT 6), 574
    ray tracing, 609-610
Replace command (Text menu), 157
replacing text, 157
reproduction, line screen, 650
resampling
    bitmap images, 408
    images, 395
reshaping frames, paragraph text, 135-136
resident scans, 548, 654
resizing
    rectangles, 185
    handles
        artistic text, 131
        paragraph text, 131
    see also sizing
resolution, 520, 531, 548, 654
    CAPTURE 6, 634
    high (high res), 649
    line screen, 650
    printers, 392-393
    two-color bitmap patterns, 247
restoring toolbars, 462
reverses, 646

reverting
    clone transformations of objects, 198
    keyboard shortcuts, 465
RGB (red, green, blue), 654
    color model, 438-457
    images, pixels, 391
right read emulsion down (RRED), see RRED
right read emulsion up (RREU), see RREU
Right-Align roll-ups, customizing, 468
RIP (raster image processor), 548-549, 654
roll-ups, 654
    Align & Distribute roll-up, 204, 322
    Contours roll-up, 319
    customizing, 468-471
        Left-Align, 468
        Right-Align, 468
    defined, 135
    Effects menu
        Blend, 272
        Lens, 375
        Powerline, 354
    Envelope roll-up, 136, 164-166
        applying envelopes to objects, 211-217
        mapping options, 215-217
    Extrude roll-up, 221-227
        creating extrusion presets, 306-315
        lighting controls, 311-313
        see also extrusions
    Fit Text roll-up, 159-162
    grouping, 469
    keyboard shortcuts, 665
    naming, 471
    Node Edit roll-up, 181, 188-190
        editing bitmaps, 397
        editing curves/nodes, 191-193

Outline roll-up, 269
PHOTO-PAINT 6, 565-567
Position roll-up, 199-200
Powerlines, 354-374
    ink options tab, 361
    pen options tab, 360-361
preset, 415-416
    color, 415
    editing controls, 416
    flyout menu, 416
    key color, 415
    preview window, 415
    pull-down, 415
    start recording/stop
      recording, 416
    thumbnails, 416
Rotation roll-up, 200-202
    rotating bitmaps, 401
Scale & Mirror roll-up, 202
Select by Properties, 195-199
Size roll-up, 203
Skew roll-up, 203
    skewing bitmaps, 401
Special Fill roll-up, 260-262
splitting, 470
Symbols roll-up, 173
toolbar (PHOTO-PAINT 6), 569
    Transform roll-up, 199
    Trim roll-up, 341-343
    Weld roll-up, 338-341
Roll-Ups tab dialog box, 468
**Rotate All command (Blend
Path menu), 285**
**Rotate button (Node Edit
roll-up), 192**
**Rotate tab (Extruse
roll-up), 225**
rotating
    bitmaps, 400-402
    blends, 280
    extrusions, 225, 309
    objects, 32, 200-202
      around corners, 33
      clockwise/
        counterclockwise, 201
      viewing origin point, 201
Rotation roll-up, 200-202
    rotating bitmaps, 401

**Rotation toolbar
(MOTION 3D), 617**
**Rotation tools (DREAM 3D;
Perspective Toolbox), 604**
**RRED (right read emulsion
down), 548, 654**
**RREU (right read emulsion
up), 548, 654**
**Rule Language option
(proofreading option), 152**
Rule Manager
    command (Options
      menu), 149
    rule options, 153-154
**Ruler and Grid dialog
box, 327**
**Ruler command (View
menu), 139**
rulers, 326-329
    displaying, 139
    manipulating settings,
      328-329
    setting scale options,
      327-333
    setting units, 327
**Rulers command
(View menu), 326**
**Run command (Start
menu), 672**
Runtime Player, 595

S

sans serif, 654
saturation mapping, 429
**Save All command (File
menu), 57, 86, 100, 463**
Save and Restore feature, 72
**Save As command
(File menu), 49**
**Save command (File
menu), 49**
Save Drawing dialog box, 54
**Save Extrude Preset dialog
box, 307**
**Save function,
customizing, 474**
saving
    custom palettes, 450
    extrusions, 307

files, 72
    earlier versions of files,
      54-55
    image headers, 56
    Optimize for Speed
      option, 57
    Optimize for Storage
      option, 57
    selected files, 55-56
    template files, 49
    troubleshooting, 55
keyboard shortcuts, 464
labels, 64
mixed colors, 238
mixing areas, 240
palettes (color), 238
Powerlines, custom, 374
presets, 417-421
    fountain fills, 258
text, formatted, 144
Scale & Mirror roll-up, 202
**Scale with Image option
(Outline Pen dialog
box), 267**
scales
    blending, 276-279
    gray, 546
scaling, 521
    objects, 29-31, 202
scanners
    bitmap images
      importing, 455-456
      sampling colors from,
        454-456
    calibrating, 431, 432
    drums, 545, 646
    flatbed, 546, 647
    profiles, creating, 430-431
scans
    continuous tones, 545, 645
    resident scans, 548, 654
scenes, background view, 584
SCODL export filter, 500
**Screen Redraw command
(View menu), 102**
screens
    CAPTURE 6
      display, 635
      settings, 634

Corel CAPTURE 6
full screen, 631
drawing, fountain fills, 255
frequency, 533, 548, 654
HQS (High-quality
Screening), 649
line, 650
resolution, customizing, 476
scripts, 655
presets, editing, 421-422
subscripts, 656
superscripts, 656
searching drawings
by properties, 196-197
colors, 195
fill types, 195
object type parameters, 195
outlines, 195
Select by Properties roll-up,
195-199
special effects, 195
Select All command
(Edit menu), 21, 56
Select by Properties command
(Edit menu), 87, 101, 196
Select by Properties roll-up,
195-199
selecting
colors
fill colors, 37-41
paper, 61
filters, 483-485
guidelines, 23
mixed colors, 238
models (color), 233
nodes, 24-25
in objects, 208
objects
grouped, 21, 204
multiple, 19-22
Pick tool, 18-19
shortcuts, 24-25
single grouped, 204
Treat All Objects as Filled
option, 74
troubleshooting, 22
palettes (color), 235, 445

Selection Shortcuts (table 1.1),
24-25
selection tools (DREAM 3D;
Perspective Toolbox), 604
SelectSet, 548, 655
Send command (File
menu), 100
Separate command (Arrange
menu), 162, 274, 321, 367
separations, 548
printing options, 529-532
registrations, 654
text from paths, 162
serifs, 655
sans, 654
servers, downloading
files, 646
service bureaus, 655
DTP (desktop pub-
lishing), 545
imaging output
materials, 550
preparing output for
printing, 543-544
printing press, plates, 547
resident scans, 654
services, BBS (Bulletin Board
Service), 545, 643
Set Outline Color option
(Customize tab), 472
set-solids, 655
setting
attributes (text), 128
default settings, 645
artistic text, 133
paragraph text, 133
DREAM 3D, 612-614
light sources for extrusion of
objects, 222-223
options, text, 168
tabs, 143-147
Undo Levels, 67
Settings option
(Display option), 68
Shade Fill option (Color
tab), 222
Shade option (Color Fill
tab), 314

Shader Eyedropper tool
(DREAM 3D; Perspective
Tool, 607
Shaders Browser window
(DREAM 3D), 603
shades, continuous tones, 645
shadows, applying as presets,
417-421
Shape tool, 24-25, 89-91
compared to Pick tool, 24
editing
artistic text, 129-131
bitmaps, 397-399
ellipses, 185-186
spirals, 190
envelopes, 165
formatting
artistic text, 138-139
paragraph text, 140
reshaping
frames, paragraph
text, 135
stars, 189-190
see also Node Edit roll-up
shapes
ellipses, see ellipses
grids, see grids
polygons, see polygons
rectangles, see rectangles
spirals, see spirals
stars, see stars
shaping objects, 306-321
sharpening filters (PHOTO-
PAINT 6), 575
shortcuts, keyboard, 659-660
accessing uniform fill
mixers, 239
Arrange commands, 661
assigning to commands, 464
creating, 462-465
dialog boxes (table 1.4), 36
displaying, 463
Edit commands, 660
editing text, 662-663
table 5.1, 140-142
File functions, 660
Layout commands, 661

numeric keyboard functions, 667
opening files, 47-48
reverting to original, 465
rollups, 665
saving, 464
selecting nodes in objects, 208
selecting objects, 24-25
Text commands, 661
tools, 665
Tools commands, 664
transformation roll-ups, 35
View commands, 661
Window commands, 664
zooming, 28
Show Font Sample in Font Drop-down lists option (Text tab), 169
Show 'No Color' Well option (Customize tab), 472
Show non-printing characters option (Text menu), 113
Show Page Border check-box (Page Settings dialog box), 61
Show Path command (Blend Path menu), 284
Show Snap Location Marks feature, 69, 106, 333
Show Tooltips feature, 70
Single arc button (Envelope roll-up), 212
Single line button (Envelope roll-up), 212
size
 artistic text, 137
 bitmaps, 389-391
  pixel grids, 389
  pixels, 389
 extrusions, minimum extrude facet size, 308
 images, bitmaps, *see also* bitmaps, 388
 labels, 62
 paper, maximum, 61
Size roll-up, 203
sizing
 DREAM 3D, 610-611
 objects, 203

point, 652
regions (Status bar), 82
toolbars, 80
Skew roll-up, 203
 skewing bitmaps, 401
skewing
 bitmaps, 400-402
 objects, 33-34, 203
 handles
  artistic text, 131
  paragraph text, 131
Slide command (View menu; PRESENTS 6), 592
Slide Sorter
 toolbar (PRESENTS 6), 581
 view (PRESENTS 6), 590
Slide view, 580
Small Back option (extrusion), 217
Small Color Swatches function (Status bar), 83
Small Front option (extrusion), 217
Smooth node button (Node Edit roll-up), 192
Snap to
 All feature, 107
 Grid option (Align and Distribute), 326
 Guidelines command (Layout menu), 333
 None command (Layout menu), 107
 Objects feature, 107, 334
software
 digital halftones, 646
 drivers, 545, 646
 handles, 649
 HQS (High-quality Screening), 649
 programs, compressions, 644
 spoolers, 549
solid colors, 655
Solid Fill option (Color tab), 222
Sound command (Insert menu; PRESENTS 6), 591
sounds, presentations, 591

source controls (CAPTURE 6), 630-632
 client window, 631
 current window, 631
 elliptical area, 632
 freehand area, 632
 full screen, 631
 rectangular area, 631
source files, 549, 655
sources, images, 395
spaces
 baselines, leading, 650
 kerning, 650
spacing
 blends, 276-279
 set-solids, 655
Spacing tab (Paragraph dialog box), 145
speaker notes, presentations, 589-590
Speaker Notes view, 580
Special Fill roll-up, 260-262
Special menu commands, Stagehands, 623
Special Purpose layouts, 64-66
SpectraMaster, 449
spectrophotometer, 429
speed style (Powerline roll-up), 358
Spelling Check feature, 115, 149-150
Spelling dialog box, 149-150
Spiral tool, 97-98
 creating spirals, 188
Spiral Tool Properties dialog box, 188
spirals
 creating, 188
 editing, 190
Split Transform functions, 107
splits, blending, 274
splitting
 curves, 205-208
 roll-ups, 470
spoolers, 549, 655
spot colors, 655
spot palettes, 443

Focoltone, 447
Pantone, 445-447
SpectraMaster, 449
Trumatch, 447-448
spreading, auto-spreading, 531
spreads, 655
square fountain fills, 253
Squash & Stretch tool (MOTION 3D toolbox), 617
Stagehands
    command (Special menu), 623
    dialog box, 623
    MOTION 3D, 622-625
Standard toolbar
    MOTION 3D, 617
    PHOTO-PAINT 6 , 568
    PRESENTS 6, 581
Star & Polygon tool, 97-98
Star command (Polygon menu), 187
Star tool, creating stars, 187-188
stars
    creating, 187-188
    curves, combining multiple, 209-211
    reshaping, 189-190
Start menu commands, Run, 672
start recording/stop recording (Preset roll-ups), 416
Start/End Path menus (blending), 286-287
starting CAPTURE 6, 627-628
Status bar, 102
    command (View menu), 80
    customizing, 80-83
    display functions (Table 3.1), 83
    Large Status Bar option, 82
    positioning, 81
    regions
        assigning functions to, 82
        dividing into, 81
        sizing, 82
Steps option
    Contour Properties tab, 320
    fountain fills, 256-257

Straight color blend option (Contour Color Options tab), 321
Straight Line Threshold (AutoTrace feature), 75, 404
Straighten Text command (Text menu), 162
Stretch button (Node Edit roll-up), 192
stretching frames, paragraph text, 133
stripping, 655
Style Properties sheet, 148
styles, 355-359
    applying, 148
        to lines, 263-264
        preset styles, 367-370
    printing, 525-526
    saving formatted text, 144
    text, 147-148
Styles command
    Layout menu, 105, 144
    View menu, 147
Styles Flyout, 105
Styles Manager, 104
subscripts, 656
substitution of fonts, 51
superscripts, 656
Suspend/Resume button (Task progress feature), 473
swatches (color), 234
switching views, 25
symbol fonts, creating, 173-174
Symbols roll-up, 173
Symmetrical node button (Node Edit roll-up), 192
system profiles, 549, 656

T

tables
    Compatible Bitmap Formats, 388-389
    File Types and Extensions (table 15.1), 484-485
    Filter Inventory List, 485-488

    Import/Export Formats, 489-491
    Keyboard Shortcuts for Navigating Dialog Boxes, 36
    Node Edit Buttons and their Functions, 192
    Object Properties, 194-195
    Selection Shortcuts, 24-25
    Text-Editing Keyboard Shortcuts, 141-142
    Transformation roll-up Shortcuts, 35
    Zoom shortcuts, 28
tabs
    Color Fill tab (Extrude roll-up), 313-327
    Color options tab (Extrude roll-up), 221-222
    Contour Color Options tab, 320-322
    Contour Properties Tab (contours roll-up), 319-320
    Customize tab, 471-472
    Depth tab (extrusions), 308-309
    Formatting tab (Text Options dialog box), 170
    Keyboard tab, 463
    Lighting tab (Extrude roll-up), 222-225
    Rotate tab (Extrude roll-up), 225
    setting, 143-147
    Tabs tab (Paragraph dialog box), 146
    Text Options tab, 169-170
    see also controls
TAC (total area coverage), 429
Tagged Image Format (TIF), 388
target original, defined, 428
Task Progress
    command (Tools menu), 473
    dialog box, 473
    Task Progress feature customizing, 472-474

limitations, 473-474
opening, 473
troubleshooting, 474
teardrop style (Powerline roll-up), 357
Template File (.CDT), 45
templates
files
opening, 48-49
saving, 49
text
alignment, envelopes, 166
anomalies, exporting files, 492
artistic text, 125-130
applying envelopes to, 164-166
applying perspective to, 166-168
breaking curves, 205
creating, 126-127
editing, 127-131
formatting, 137-139
resizing handles, 131
skewing handles, 131
Change Case command (Text menu), 158
columns, 644
converting, 158
to curves, 516
creating, 13-14
editing
Edit Text on Screen option (Text tab), 169
keyboard shortcuts, 662-663
entering, 583-584
finding, 157
fitting to paths, 159-163
flush, 647
fonts
creating, 171-173
styles, creating, 295-296
symbol fonts, creating, 173-174
formatting
bullets, 147
hyphenation, 145

leader characters, 146
saving in styles, 144
justified, 492, 650
options, setting, 168
outlines, trouble-shooting, 263
paragraph text, 130-136
applying envelopes to, 168
arrow tab, 133
columns, 134, 135
converting to curves, 516
creating, 131
displaying, 133
editing, 131-132
formatting, 139-142
moving, 140
positioning, 133
reshaping frames, 135-136
resizing handles, 131
skewing handles, 131
proofreading
Full-Proofreading feature, 151
Quick Proofreading feature, 150-151
properties, 147-148
ragged, 653
replacing, 157
scripts, 655
separating from path, 162
set-solids, 655
Spelling Check feature, 149-150
styles, 147-148
subscripts, 656
superscripts, 656
Text-Wrapping option (General tab), 406-407
thesaurus, 155-156
tracking, 656
Type Assist feature, 156
Text Columns dialog box, 112
Text flyout (PRESENTS 6), 581
Text Menu, 111-116
commands
Change Case, 158
Character, 127, 133

Columns, 134
Convert to Artistic Text, 158
Convert to Paragraph Text, 158
Edit, 132
Find, 157
Fit Text to Path, 159
keyboard shortcuts, 661
Paragraph, 144
Replace, 157
Straighten Text, 162
Text Options, 168
Thesaurus, 155
Text Options
command (Text menu), 168
dialog box, 169-170
tab, 169-170
Text Properties
command (Object menu), 120
dialog box, 120
feature, 114
objects, 120
Text Statistics feature, 114
Text tool (PHOTO-PAINT 6 Toolbox), 563
Text toolbar, 111-114, 582
Text-Editing Keyboard Shortcuts (table 5.1), 141-142
Text-Wrapping option (General tab), 406-407
Texture Fill dialog box, 259-260
texture fills, 258-260, 656
assigning to objects, 259
default setting, 260
hazards, printing, 514
patterns, 258
printing, 260
Thesaurus, 115, 155-156
Thesaurus command (Text menu), 155
third-party color matching systems, 444
three-dimensional
images, exporting files, 492
objects, creating, 318

thumbnails
  defined, 656
  preset roll-ups, 416
Time and Date function (Status bar), 83
Timeliness command (View menu)
  MOTION 3D, 620
  PRESENTS 6, 593
timing controls (CAPTURE 6), 629-630
tinted grayscale lens, 380
To Center option (Contour Properties tab), 320
To curve button (Node Edit roll-up), 192
To Inside option (Contour Properties tab), 320
To line button (Node Edit roll-up), 192
To Outside option (Contour Properties tab), 320
tones
  continuous, 645
  continuous tones scan, 645
  halftones, 648
Tool Properties dialog box, 88-91
Toolbar dialog box, 79
toolbars, 102
  custom toolbars, 116, 460-461
  customizing, 78-80, 460-462
  Dimension toolbar, 94
  displaying, 78-79, 461
  floating, 78-79
  flyouts, 647
  MOTION 3D, 617-618
  names, 460
  PHOTO-PAINT 6
    mask/object toolbar, 568
    movie toolbar, 568
    roll-ups toolbar, 569
    standard toolbar, 568
  positioning, 78
  PRESENTS 6
    animation toolbar, 582
    outline view toolbar, 582

  slide sorter toolbar, 581
  standard toolbar, 581
  text toolbar, 582
  toolbox toolbar, 581
  restoring, 462
  sizing, 80
  Text toolbar, 111
  Workspace, 103
  Zoom toolbar, 92
Toolbars command (View menu), 28, 78, 460, 568
Toolbars dialog box, 460
Toolbox
  Corel DREAM 3D
    Free Form Modeler Toolbox, 607-608
    Perspective Toolbox elements, 604-607
  Corel MOTION 3D, 616-619
  PHOTO-PAINT 6, 559-565
Toolbox toolbar (PRESENTS 6), 581
tools
  Artistic Text tool, 13, 125-126
    creating artistic text, 126-127
    editing artistic text, 127-131
    formatting artistic text, 137
  auto-trace, 643
  Bezier, 95, 179, 643
  Brush tool, 453
  Color Blend tools, 235-239
  Color Picker tool, 452
  Connector tool, 95
  customizing, 475
    Panning tool, 476
    Zooming tool, 476
  Digital Brush tool, 452
  Dimensioning tools, 94-95
  Ellipse tool, 96
    creating ellipses, 180
  Eraser tool, 89-90
  Eyedropper tool, 452
    loading bitmap images, 241

  Freehand tool, 95
    creating lines, 178-179
  Grid tools, 97-98
    creating grids, 188
  keyboard shortcuts, 665
  Knife tool, 89-90
  lens effects, 374-375
  new to CorelDRAW!, 88-98
  Paint Brush tool, 237
  Pan tool, 92
  Panning tool, 28-29
  Paragraph Text tool, 130-131
    creating paragraph text, 131
    editing paragraph text, 131-132
    formatting paragraph text, 139
  Pick tool, 19, 24, 88
    editing grids, 190
    formatting artistic text, 137
    resizing shapes, 188
    skewing bitmaps, 400
  Polygon tool, 186
  Rectangle tools, 96
    creating rectangles, 180
  Shape tool, 24-25, 89-91
    editing artistic text, 129-131
    editing bitmaps, 397-399
    editing ellipses, 185-186
    editing spirals, 190
    formatting artistic text, 138-139
    formatting paragraph text, 140
    reshaping stars, 189-190
  Spiral tool, 97-98
    creating spirals, 188
  Star & Polygon tool, 97-98
  Star tool, creating stars, 187-188
  text tools (Text menu), 111-114
  Zoom tools, 27-28, 91-93
Tools menu commands
  Color Manager, 428, 435
  Create, 173

Customize, 461, 568
keyboard shortcuts, 664
Options, 47
Presets, 414
Task Progress, 473
Tooltips, 70
total area coverage (TAC), 429
tracking, 656
Autotrace Tracking, 75
Freehand Tracking, 75
ink colors, 444
**Transform command
(Arrange menu), 401**
Transform roll-up, 199
**Transform roll-up command
(Arrange menu), 35**
**Transformation roll-up
Shortcuts (table 1.3), 35**
transforming objects, 199-203
position, 199-200
rotation, 200-202
scaling/mirroring, 202
sizing, 203
skewing, 203
transparency, 656
transparency lens, 376
trapping, 656
auto trapping, 531
defined, 445
print jobs, 517
spreads and chokes, 655
**Treat All Objects As Filled
feature, 74**
**Trim command
(Arrange menu), 341**
Trim roll-up, 341-343
trimming, 656
objects, 341-343
multiple objects, 343
priorities, 346
troubleshooting
blends, 283
cloning objects, 198
color fills, 234
color management system,
printers, 430

files,
exporting, AutoCAD
filters, 491-492
importing, 484
opening, CorelDRAW!
version 3-5, 48
saving, 55
fills, applying to objects, 264
fountain fills
customizing, 476
screen drawing, 255
light sources in extruded
objects, 222-224
mixers, 454
movie toolbar (PHOTO-
PAINT 6), 569
objects, selecting, 22
page frames, deleting, 61
printing, 513-515
auto increase
flatness, 515
fit to page hazards, 515
font overboards, 514
overloaded nodes, 514
texture fill hazards, 514
texture fills, 260
Task Progress feature, 474
text outlines, 263
Wrap Paragraph Text option
(General tab), 407
TrueType, 656
Export dialog box, 172
Font file, 173
TruMatch, 657
color palette system, 234,
447-448
home offices, 448
**trumpet style (Powerline
roll-up), 356**
**turning off Automatically
Center New Powerclip
Contents feature, 68**
tutor notes, 17
**Tutor Notes command
(Help menu), 17**
**Tutorial command
(Help menu), 17**

**Two-Color Bitmap Pattern
dialog box, 242, 247**
**Two-Color Bitmap Pattern
Editor dialog box, 245**
two-color fountains, 253
types
subscripts, 656
superscripts, 656
Type Assist, 116
Type Assist dialog box, 156
typefaces
fonts, 648
sans serifs, 654
serifs, 655
typestyles, fonts, 648

U

**UCR (under color
removal), 429**
**Undo command (Edit menu),
100, 367**
**Undo Edit command
(Options menu), 149**
Undo Levels, 67
**Ungroup command (Arrange
menu), 21, 204, 368**
ungrouping
grids, 190
objects, 204
**Uniform Fill dialog box, 39,
230-240, 436, 444, 449, 452**
uniform fills, 231-232
color models, *see* models
(color)
color palettes, *see* palettes
(color)
units, didots, 645
uploading, 657
**Use 3D Wells (Customize
tab), 471**
Use Object Fill option
Color Fill tab, 313
Color tab, 221
**Use Personal Dictionaries
option (proofreading
option), 152**

Use Solid Fill (Color Fill tab), 314
utilities
PHOTO-PAINT, 455
see also applications

V

values
defaults, 645
density, 645
flatness, 647
vanishing points
extrusions, 220-221, 309
objects, 167
perspective, 316-318
variables
defaults, 645
parameters, 652
vector objects, 22
Vector Pattern dialog box, 247
vectors, 657
patterns, 247-248
creating, 248
loading, 248
Vertex Editing tool (DREAM 3D), 608
Vertical option (Envelope roll-up), 217
Vertical tab, 332
video, presentations, 591
Video command (Insert menu; PRESENTS 6), 591
View flyout (MOTION 3D), 617
View Manager roll-up, 92-93
View menu, 101-103
commands
Bitmap, 395
Color Palette, 235, 240, 444
Editable Wireframe, 362
keyboard shortcuts, 661
Properties, 76, 147, 187, 195, 476
Ruler, 139
Rulers, 326

Screen Redraw, 102
Status Bar, 80
Styles, 147
Toolbars, 28, 78, 460, 568
Visible Bitmap Display, 396
MOTION 3D commands
Timeliness, 620
PRESENTS 6 commands
Background Library, 584
Slide, 592
Timelines, 593
viewing
bitmaps, 395-397
high resolution, 396
Visible Bitmap Display command, 396
files, 483
images, headers, 393
keyboard shortcuts, 463
origin point (rotating objects), 201
Viewing Pane Rotation toolbar (MOTION 3D), 618
views
changing, 25
Editable Preview, 25
Full-screen preview view, 26
PRESENTS 6, 580
Animation view, 580, 588
Background view, 580, 584
Handout view, 580
Master view, 580
Outline view, 580, 583-584
Slide Sorter view, 580, 590
Slide view, 580
Speaker Notes view, 580
Preview Selected Only view, 26
Wireframe, 25
Visible Bitmap Display command (View menu), 396
visual elements, interfacing, 649

W

Wave Editor, 591
wedge style (Powerline roll-up), 355
Welcome dialog box, 99
welcome screen (CorelDRAW!), 46-47
Weld command (Arrange menu), 338
Weld feature, 338-341
Weld roll-up, 338-341
welding, 657
objects, 338-341
multiple, 340
priorities, 346
What's This? command (Help menu), 17
white point
defined, 429
monitors, adjusting, 433
width
aspect ratio, 643
control (Page Settings dialog box), 60
wildcards
asterisk (*), 51
opening files, 51-52
Window menu commands, keyboard shortcuts, 664
windows
Corel CAPTURE 6
client window, 631
current window, 631
Custom Label preview window, 63
dithering, 68
DREAM 3D
Hierarchy window, 602
Objects Browser window, 603
Perspective window, 602
Shaders Browser window, 603
Mixing Area, 238
New Color, 237
Print Preview window, 523-524

Wireframe lens, 110, 383
Wireframe view
    advantage, 26
    compare to Editable
        Preview, 25
wizards
    Color Wizard
        assigning color system
            profiles, 435-436
        creating color system
            profiles, 428-434
        printer profiles, 434
        scanner profiles, 430, 431
        troubleshooting color
            system profiles, 436
    Extrude Wizard, 226-227
    PRESENTS 6, 582-583
woodcut style (Powerline
    roll-up), 356
WordPerfect, exporting, 497
Workspace toolbar, 103
workstations, downloading
    files, 646
Wrap Paragraph Text option
    (General tab), 407

X-Z

x-height
    baselines, 643
    descenders, 645

YIQ color model, 441

Zoom
    flyout (PRESENTS 6), 581
    shortcuts (table 1.2), 28
    tool, 27-28, 91-93, 561
    toolbar, 92, 617
Zoom/Pan tools (DREAM 3D;
    Perspective Toolbox), 605
zooming, 25, 27-28
Zooming tool,
    customizing, 476

Get The Whole Picture For Half Price! We'll Meet You 1/2 Way

We want you to get a FULL ANNUAL SUBSCRIPTION TO *COREL MAGAZINE* FOR 1/2 PRICE! That's right, a full year's worth of the most exciting and dynamic computer graphics magazine for the design professional and business graphics user. today—all for a mere $19.98*U.S.!

This is no half-hearted offer. No indeed. Written by CorelDraw users for CorelDraw users, each colorful issue of *Corel Magazine* helps you get the very most out of your software and hardware.

Read *Corel Magazine*, and if you like it even half as much as we think you will, we'll meet you halfway—take us up on our offer. Just fill out the attached card and fax it back for faster service. We're certain you'll appreciate getting the whole picture at half the price!

(*First time subscribers only!)

Fax To: 512-219-3156

P.O. Box 202380 • Austin, Tx 78720

○ YES! I WANT THE WHOLE PICTURE FOR

1/2 PRICE! Sign me up for my full annual subscription to *Corel Magazine*. By responding to this special one-time offer, I'll pay only $19.98 U.S. and save 50% off the regular subscription rate of $39.95 U.S. (Offer Expires July 31, 1996)

Fax: 512-219-3156

○ PLEASE BILL ME $19.98 U.S.

○ PAYMENT ENCLOSED

(Offer restricted to U.S. only)

Name:

Title:

Company

Address

City   State

Postal Code/ZIP

Country

Signature   Date

Please Circle The Appropriate Answers:

1. Do you use CorelDraw?
   A. Yes   B. No
   If yes, which version do you use?
   A. 5.0   B. 4.0   C. 3.0   D. Other   E. 6.0
   On which platform?
   A. Windows B. OS/2 C. Unix   D. CTOS

   E. Other _____

2. Your primary business:
   A. Advertising, publishing, graphic design, public relations
   B. Computer hardware or software manufacturer/distributor
   C. Engineering–all types   D. Financial services–all types
   E. Educational–all levels   F. Science/research
   G. Public utility, telecommunications, transportation
   H. Government–all levels   I. Retail, restaurant
   J. Medical K. Video or entertainment production

   L. Other _____

3. Do you specify, authorize, or purchase computer graphics
   products or services?
   A. Yes   B. No
   If yes, circle all that apply:
   A. Workstations   B. PCs   C. Monitors/boards
   D. Input devices/scanners   E. Printers/output devices
   F. Hard disks/CD-ROM/tape drives

   G. Other _____

4. Primary use of CorelDraw–circle all that apply:
   A. Multimedia   B. Publishing
   C. Technical Documentation   D. Advertising
   E. Training F. Medical Imaging   G. Packaging
   H. Artistic Design   I. Signs/Silkscreening/Stencilling

   J. Other _____

Q

Complete and Return this Card
for a *FREE* Computer Book Catalog

Thank you for purchasing this book! You have purchased a superior computer book written expressly for your needs. To continue to provide the kind of up-to-date, pertinent coverage you've come to expect from us, we need to hear from you. Please take a minute to complete and return this self-addressed, postage-paid form. In return, we'll send you a free catalog of all our computer books on topics ranging from word processing to programming and the internet.

Mr. ☐   Mrs. ☐   Ms. ☐   Dr. ☐

Name (first) ☐☐☐☐☐☐☐☐☐☐☐☐☐   (M.I.) ☐   (last) ☐☐☐☐☐☐☐☐☐☐☐☐☐☐☐☐☐

Address ☐☐☐☐☐☐☐☐☐☐☐☐☐☐☐☐☐☐☐☐☐☐☐☐☐☐☐☐☐☐☐☐☐☐☐

☐☐☐☐☐☐☐☐☐☐☐☐☐☐☐☐☐☐☐☐☐☐☐☐☐☐☐☐☐☐☐☐☐☐☐☐

City ☐☐☐☐☐☐☐☐☐☐☐☐☐☐☐☐☐   State ☐☐   Zip ☐☐☐☐☐ ☐☐☐☐

Phone ☐☐☐ ☐☐☐ ☐☐☐☐   Fax ☐☐☐ ☐☐☐ ☐☐☐☐

Company Name ☐☐☐☐☐☐☐☐☐☐☐☐☐☐☐☐☐☐☐☐☐☐☐☐☐☐☐☐☐☐

E-mail address ☐☐☐☐☐☐☐☐☐☐☐☐☐☐☐☐☐☐☐☐☐☐☐☐☐☐☐☐☐☐

1. Please check at least (3) influencing factors for purchasing this book.

Front or back cover information on book .... ☐
Special approach to the content .... ☐
Completeness of content .... ☐
Author's reputation .... ☐
Publisher's reputation .... ☐
Book cover design or layout .... ☐
Index or table of contents of book .... ☐
Price of book .... ☐
Special effects, graphics, illustrations .... ☐
Other (Please specify): _____ ☐

2. How did you first learn about this book?

Saw in Macmillan Computer Publishing catalog .... ☐
Recommended by store personnel .... ☐
Saw the book on bookshelf at store .... ☐
Recommended by a friend .... ☐
Received advertisement in the mail .... ☐
Saw an advertisement in: _____ ☐
Read book review in: _____ ☐
Other (Please specify): _____ ☐

3. How many computer books have you purchased in the last six months?

This book only .... ☐   3 to 5 books .... ☐
2 books .... ☐   More than 5 .... ☐

4. Where did you purchase this book?

Bookstore .... ☐
Computer Store .... ☐
Consumer Electronics Store .... ☐
Department Store .... ☐
Office Club .... ☐
Warehouse Club .... ☐
Mail Order .... ☐
Direct from Publisher .... ☐
Internet site .... ☐
Other (Please specify): _____ ☐

5. How long have you been using a computer?

☐ Less than 6 months   ☐ 6 months to a year
☐ 1 to 3 years   ☐ More than 3 years

6. What is your level of experience with personal computers and with the subject of this book?

	With PCs	With subject of book
New	☐	☐
Casual	☐	☐
Accomplished	☐	☐
Expert	☐	☐

Source Code ISBN: 0-7897-0295-9

7. Which of the following best describes your job title?

Administrative Assistant ☐
Coordinator ☐
Manager/Supervisor ☐
Director ☐
Vice President ☐
President/CEO/COO ☐
Lawyer/Doctor/Medical Professional ☐
Teacher/Educator/Trainer ☐
Engineer/Technician ☐
Consultant ☐
Not employed/Student/Retired ☐
Other (Please specify): _____ ☐

8. Which of the following best describes the area of the company your job title falls under?

Accounting ☐
Engineering ☐
Manufacturing ☐
Operations ☐
Marketing ☐
Sales ☐
Other (Please specify): _____ ☐

9. What is your age?

Under 20 ☐
21-29 ☐
30-39 ☐
40-49 ☐
50-59 ☐
60-over ☐

10. Are you:

Male ☐
Female ☐

11. Which computer publications do you read regularly? (Please list)

_____
_____
_____
_____
_____
_____
_____
_____
_____
_____

Comments: _____
_____
_____

Fold here and scotch-tape to mail.

NO POSTAGE
NECESSARY
IF MAILED
IN THE
UNITED STATES

BUSINESS REPLY MAIL
FIRST-CLASS MAIL PERMIT NO. 9918 INDIANAPOLIS IN

POSTAGE WILL BE PAID BY THE ADDRESSEE

ATTN MARKETING
MACMILLAN COMPUTER PUBLISHING
MACMILLAN PUBLISHING USA
201 W 103RD ST
INDIANAPOLIS IN 46209-9042

Licensing Agreement

By opening this package you are agreeing to be bound by the following:

This book has one CD-ROM that contains software described in this book. See Appendix C, "What's on the *Special Edition Using CorelDRAW! 6 for Windows 95* CD?" for a description of the programs and instructions for their use. This appendix also will show you how to access the 50 royalty-free photos, *Corel Magazine* articles from experts in the field, the 3D demonstration, and the CorelDRAW! Working Model.